# STOP THE VIOLENCE
# IN LATIN AMERICA

# STOP THE VIOLENCE IN LATIN AMERICA

## A Look at Prevention from Cradle to Adulthood

Laura Chioda

**WORLD BANK GROUP**

# Latin American Development Forum Series

This series was created in 2003 to promote debate, disseminate information and analysis, and convey the excitement and complexity of the most topical issues in economic and social development in Latin America and the Caribbean. It is sponsored by the Inter-American Development Bank, the United Nations Economic Commission for Latin America and the Caribbean, and the World Bank, and represents the highest quality in each institution's research and activity output. Titles in the series have been selected for their relevance to the academic community, policy makers, researchers, and interested readers, and have been subjected to rigorous anonymous peer review prior to publication.

## Advisory Committee Members

**Alicia Bárcena Ibarra,** Executive Secretary, Economic Commission for Latin America and the Caribbean, United Nations

**Inés Bustillo,** Director, Washington Office, Economic Commission for Latin America and the Caribbean, United Nations

**Carlos Végh,** Chief Economist, Latin America and the Caribbean Region, World Bank

**Daniel Lederman,** Deputy Chief Economist, Latin America and the Caribbean Region, World Bank

**Santiago Levy,** Vice President for Sectors and Knowledge, Inter-American Development Bank

**Roberto Rigobon,** Professor of Applied Economics, Sloan School of Management, Massachusetts Institute of Technology

**José Juan Ruiz,** Chief Economist and Manager of the Research Department, Inter-American Development Bank

**Ernesto Talvi,** Director, Brookings Global-CERES Economic and Social Policy in Latin America Initiative

**Andrés Velasco,** CIEPLAN (Corporación de Estudios para Latinoamérica), Chile

# Titles in the Latin American Development Forum Series

*Innovative Experiences in Access to Finance: Market-Friendly Roles for the Visible Hand?* (2017) by Augusto de la Torre, Juan Carlos Gozzi, and Sergio L. Schmukler.

*Beyond Commodities: The Growth Challenge of Latin America and the Caribbean* (2016) by Jorge Thompson Araujo, Ekaterina Vostroknutova, Markus Brueckner, Mateo Clavijo, and Konstantin M. Wacker.

*Left Behind: Chronic Poverty in Latin America and the Caribbean* (2016) by Renos Vakis, Jamele Rigolini, and Leonardo Lucchetti

*Cashing in on Education: Women, Childcare, and Prosperity in Latin America and the Caribbean* (2016) by Mercedes Mateo Díaz and Lourdes Rodriguez-Chamussy

*Work and Family: Latin American and Caribbean Women in Search of a New Balance* (2016) by Laura Chioda

*Great Teachers: How to Raise Student Learning in Latin America and the Caribbean* (2014) by Barbara Bruns and Javier Luque

*Entrepreneurship in Latin America: A Step Up the Social Ladder?* (2013) by Eduardo Lora and Francesca Castellani, editors

*Emerging Issues in Financial Development: Lessons from Latin America* (2013) by Tatiana Didier and Sergio L. Schmukler, editors

*New Century, Old Disparities: Gaps in Ethnic and Gender Earnings in Latin America and the Caribbean* (2012) by Hugo Ñopo

*Does What You Export Matter? In Search of Empirical Guidance for Industrial Policies* (2012) by Daniel Lederman and William F. Maloney

*From Right to Reality: Incentives, Labor Markets, and the Challenge of Achieving Universal Social Protection in Latin America and the Caribbean* (2012) by Helena Ribe, David Robalino, and Ian Walker

*Breeding Latin American Tigers: Operational Principles for Rehabilitating Industrial Policies* (2011) by Robert Devlin and Graciela Moguillansky

*New Policies for Mandatory Defined Contribution Pensions: Industrial Organization Models and Investment Products* (2010) by Gregorio Impavido, Esperanza Lasagabaster, and Manuel García-Huitrón

*The Quality of Life in Latin American Cities: Markets and Perception* (2010) by Eduardo Lora, Andrew Powell, Bernard M. S. van Praag, and Pablo Sanguinetti, editors

*Discrimination in Latin America: An Economic Perspective* (2010) by Hugo Ñopo, Alberto Chong, and Andrea Moro, editors

*The Promise of Early Childhood Development in Latin America and the Caribbean* (2010) by Emiliana Vegas and Lucrecia Santibáñez

*Job Creation in Latin America and the Caribbean: Trends and Policy Challenges* (2009) by Carmen Pagés, Gaëlle Pierre, and Stefano Scarpetta

*China's and India's Challenge to Latin America: Opportunity or Threat?* (2009) by Daniel Lederman, Marcelo Olarreaga, and Guillermo E. Perry, editors

*Does the Investment Climate Matter? Microeconomic Foundations of Growth in Latin America* (2009) by Pablo Fajnzylber, Jose Luis Guasch, and J. Humberto López, editors

*Measuring Inequality of Opportunities in Latin America and the Caribbean* (2009) by Ricardo de Paes Barros, Francisco H. G. Ferreira, José R. Molinas Vega, and Jaime Saavedra Chanduvi

*The Impact of Private Sector Participation in Infrastructure: Lights, Shadows, and the Road Ahead* (2008) by Luis Andres, Jose Luis Guasch, Thomas Haven, and Vivien Foster

*Remittances and Development: Lessons from Latin America* (2008) by Pablo Fajnzylber and J. Humberto López, editors

*Fiscal Policy, Stabilization, and Growth: Prudence or Abstinence?* (2007) by Guillermo Perry, Luis Servén, and Rodrigo Suescún, editors

*Raising Student Learning in Latin America: Challenges for the 21st Century* (2007) by Emiliana Vegas and Jenny Petrow

*Investor Protection and Corporate Governance: Firm-level Evidence across Latin America* (2007) by Alberto Chong and Florencio López-de-Silanes, editors

*Natural Resources: Neither Curse nor Destiny* (2007) by Daniel Lederman and William F. Maloney, editors

*The State of State Reform in Latin America* (2006) by Eduardo Lora, editor

*Emerging Capital Markets and Globalization: The Latin American Experience* (2006) by Augusto de la Torre and Sergio L. Schmukler

*Beyond Survival: Protecting Households from Health Shocks in Latin America* (2006) by Cristian C. Baeza and Truman G. Packard

*Beyond Reforms: Structural Dynamics and Macroeconomic Vulnerability* (2005) by José Antonio Ocampo, editor

*Privatization in Latin America: Myths and Reality* (2005) by Alberto Chong and Florencio López-de-Silanes, editors

*Keeping the Promise of Social Security in Latin America* (2004) by Indermit S. Gill, Truman G. Packard, and Juan Yermo

*Lessons from NAFTA for Latin America and the Caribbean* (2004) by Daniel Lederman, William F. Maloney, and Luis Servén

*The Limits of Stabilization: Infrastructure, Public Deficits, and Growth in Latin America* (2003) by William Easterly and Luis Servén, editors

*Globalization and Development: A Latin American and Caribbean Perspective* (2003) by José Antonio Ocampo and Juan Martin, editors

*Is Geography Destiny? Lessons from Latin America* (2003) by John Luke Gallup, Alejandro Gaviria, and Eduardo Lora

# Contents

Foreword   xix

Acknowledgments   xxi

Abbreviations   xxiii

Overview   1

   Introduction   1

   Stylized facts: The physiognomy of crime and violence in LAC   7

   Never too early: Stopping the transmission of violence across generations   30

   Adolescence and young adulthood: A critical age for policy intervention   34

   The link between poverty and crime and violence   37

   Does crime respond to features of labor market incentives?   40

   The effect of neighborhood characteristics and social networks on crime and violence   42

   Deterrence: The role of incentives in the justice system   46

   Final thoughts   50

   Notes   52

   References   56

Chapter 1: Organizing Framework of the Study and Structure of the Report   63

   The organizing framework of this study   67

   Structure of the report   74

   Notes   77

   References   78

## Chapter 2: Stylized Facts about Crime and Violence in Latin America and the Caribbean   81

Magnitude and persistence   83

A closer look at the different dimensions of the interplay between economic development and violence   91

Heterogeneity: Spatial features of the distribution of crime   104

Victimization, perceptions, and happiness   130

Notes   149

References   154

## Chapter 3: The Transmission of Violence across Generations and Early Interventions   161

The early peak of physical aggression   162

Family history and vulnerability   164

Early interventions: Nutrition, nurse home visitations, and early childhood   175

The underlying mechanisms: The role of personality traits   187

Notes   193

References   196

## Chapter 4: Youth, Education, and Brain Development   205

Education and crime   207

Personality traits, their malleability, and crime and violence   224

Notes   246

References   249

## Chapter 5: The Nexus between Poverty, Labor Markets, and Crime   257

Income, poverty, and crime: Channels and evidence   258

Labor income: Channels and evidence   274

Notes   296

References   300

## Chapter 6: Neighborhoods and Urban Upgrading   307

Evidence on the effects of neighborhoods and social interactions on outcomes   309

Can urban and in situ upgrading affect antisocial behavior? Evidence from the United States and Latin America and the Caribbean   323

Broken window theory: The evidence   331

Notes   339

References   342

## Chapter 7: General and Specific Deterrence    347

The prison population and general deterrence: Insights and limitations    350
Severity versus certainty and their relationship to general deterrence    351
Certainty and deterrence    361
Specific deterrence and recidivism: Is prison always best to prevent future crime?    371
Notes    382
References    385

## Appendix: World Bank Citizen Security Program in Latin America and the Caribbean    391

Note    397
References    397

## Boxes

1.1    Previous analytical reports by the World Bank on crime and violence in Latin America and the Caribbean    65

2.1    Age distribution of homicide rates in Honduras, 2012–13    124

3.1    The link between exposure to lead in young children and crime    171

3.2    Why would child maltreatment lead to subsequent criminality? Criminological and economic theories    180

3.3    The HighScope Perry Preschool program    185

3.4    Promoting Alternative Thinking Strategies (PATHS)    189

4.1    A promising strategy to address bullying and other unintended consequences of keeping youths from dropping out    217

4.2    Programs that may have detrimental effects and even promote violence but continue to receive support despite a lack of evidence    232

4.3    The Becoming a Man program    238

5.1    Broad categorization of employment-focused crime prevention programs    287

5.2    Evaluation of Job Corps: Lasting results only for older youth    290

6.1    Tackling collective efficacy with urban infrastructure    317

6.2    Social cohesion and public policy: The case of cash transfers in Colombia and Indonesia    319

6.3    Is crime contagious?    321

6.4    Medellín: From one of the world's deadliest cities to a showcase for educational and architectural projects    334

7.1    The efficiency trade-off between severity and certainty, for any given level of expected punishment    352

7.2    Police reform, training, and crime: Experimental evidence from Colombia's Plan Cuadrantes    367

7.3     The Cure Violence (cease-fire) model: A disease control method for reducing violence   369

A.1     EVIDENCE 4 PEACE: The World Bank's DIME Impact Evaluation Program on Fragility, Conflict, and Violence   392

A.2     Honduras Safer Municipalities: The World Bank's first stand-alone citizen security project   394

A.3     RESOL-V, Solutions to Violence network: Connecting knowledge and decision making   396

## Figures

O.1     The homicide rates in Latin America and the Caribbean   4

O.2     A model of the supply of criminal offenses, but also a model of crime and violence prevention   6

O.3     LAC's homicide rate relative to other regions in terms of GDP per capita, 2012   8

O.4     Evolution of poverty, the middle class, economic development, and violence in Latin America, 1995–2012   8

O.5     Employment profiles of male perpetrators and the general male population, Mexico, 2010   11

O.6     Victim reporting on where the last crime occurred, 2010 and 2014   17

O.7     LAC homicide age-crime profile, selected years   19

O.8     Trends in homicide rates in the United States and Mexico, by age and race   21

O.9     Age-crime incidence by income level for property and violent crimes, LAC   23

O.10     Marginal effects on victimization of income, education, age, neighborhood safety, social capital, and trust in institutions, LAC   24

O.11     Marginal effects on victimization of the variable "police asked for bribes"   26

O.12     Trends in homicides, concerns about crime, and victimization, LAC, 1996–2013   27

1.1     A model of the supply of criminal offenses, but also a model of crime and violence prevention   69

2.1     Homicide rates in LAC, by country, 2009–12   84

2.2     Homicide rate in LAC, by subregion   85

2.3     Homicide rates in selected LAC countries, 1999–2012   86

2.4     LAC's homicide rate relative to other regions in terms of GDP per capita, 2012   87

2.5     Evolution of poverty, the middle class, economic development, and violence in Latin America, 1995–2012   88

2.6     LAC and world homicide rates and GDP, various periods, 1990–2012   89

2.7     Year- and subperiod-specific effects of income groups on homicide rates, 1996–2010   93

2.8     Employment rates of perpetrators across all age groups and among youth, Mexico, 1997–2011   97

2.9     Employment profiles of male perpetrators and general male population, Mexico, 2010   98

2.10    Effects of distance from the U.S. border on homicide rates in Mexican municipalities, by quantile, 1990s, early 2000s, and late 2000s   100

2.11    Kernel density of homicide rates across municipalities in Brazil, Colombia, Guatemala, and Mexico, selected years   107

2.12    Cumulative distribution of national homicide rates versus state homicide rates by department, Colombia, Guatemala, and Mexico   108

2.13    Homicide rates by zone, Guatemala City, 2012   112

2.14    Distribution of homicides over the course of the day and by gender, Guatemala City, 2012   112

2.15    Victim reporting on where the last crime occurred, 2010 and 2014   114

2.16    Location of all crimes by country, 2014   115

2.17    Where crimes were committed and where criminals came from, Mexico, 1997–2011   116

2.18    LAC homicide age-crime profile, selected years   119

2.19    Age-homicide profiles for Central and South America   122

2.20    Trends in homicide rates in the United States and Mexico, by age and race   123

B2.1.1  Male homicide rate by age, Honduras, 2012 and 2013   124

B2.1.2  Evolution of male homicide rates by age group, Honduras, 2008–13   125

2.21    Age-crime profiles of perpetrators of property crime, violent crime, and homicides, Mexico   127

2.22    Victimization rates versus homicide rates from different data sources, LAC   131

2.23    Marginal effects on victimization of income, education, age, neighborhood safety, social capital, and trust in institutions, LAC   133

2.24    Age-crime incidence by income level for property and violent crimes, LAC   135

2.25    Marginal effects on victimization of trust in the judicial system, the national police, the community, and municipal social capital   138

2.26    Marginal effects on victimization of the variable "police asked for bribes"   139

2.27    Marginal effects of the variable "is paying bribes justified?" by country   139

2.28    Trust in the police, the justice system, and democracy, LAC, 1996–2013   140

2.29    Trends in homicides, concerns about crime, and victimization, LAC, 1996–2013   142

2.30    Marginal effects on crime as a concern in LAC   143

2.31    Marginal effects of age on crime as a concern in LAC   145

3.1     A model of the supply of criminal offenses, but also a model of crime and violence prevention   163

3.2     Possible channels for the intergenerational transmission of criminal behavior   166

3.3     Life-cycle evolution of conscientiousness   192

4.1    A model of the supply of criminal offenses, but also a model of crime and violence prevention   206

4.2    Education levels of perpetrators versus the general population, Mexico, 1998–2011   209

4.3    Effect of the dropout rate on the quantiles of the homicide rate, Brazilian municipalities, 1998–2012   211

4.4    The adolescent brain: From hot cognition to cold cognition   227

4.5    Evolution of personality traits, age 10–80   229

4.6    A path from hot to cold cognition: Channels that affect youth behavior and brain function   232

4.7    A classification of school-based prevention programs   236

5.1    The relationship between poverty and homicides in the LAC region, 1996–2010   259

5.2    A model of the supply of criminal offenses, but also a model of crime and violence prevention   261

5.3    The theoretical indeterminacy of the effect of income on crime: A summary of plausible channels   263

5.4    Selected theories and channels relating employment and crime   274

5.5    Employment shares by age, perpetrators versus general population in Mexico, 2010   283

5.6    Employment rates of male youth ages 16–18, perpetrators versus the general population, Mexico   284

6.1    Neighborhoods, social interactions, and crime: Theory and channels   316

7.1    A model of the supply of criminal offenses, but also a model of crime and violence prevention   348

## Maps

O.1    World cartogram showing country size proportional to homicide rate   2

O.2    U.S. ports of entry, Mexican highways, and homicide rates for the most violent municipalities in 2012   13

O.3    Homicides rates by municipality in Colombia, Guatemala, El Salvador, and Brazil   14

O.4    U.S. cities and LAC countries with comparable homicide rates circa 2012   30

1.1    World cartogram showing country size proportional to homicide rate   64

2.1    Municipal homicide rates and principal highways, Mexico, 2007 and 2012   101

2.2    U.S. ports of entry, Mexican highways, and homicide rates for the most violent municipalities in Mexico, 2012   102

2.3    Homicide rates by municipality and state, and principal highways, Mexico, 2012   105

2.4    Homicide rates by municipality (per 100,000 inhabitants), Brazil, Colombia, El Salvador, and Guatemala   110

2.5     Heterogeneity at the neighborhood levels: Homicide rates and counts
        for the city of Medellín, 2013    113

2.6     U.S. cities and LAC countries with comparable homicide rates, circa 2012    125

## Tables

2.1     Selected coefficients on macro variables from the saturated model    92

2.2     Homicide rates in Mexico, Guatemala, and Colombia, 1995,
        2000, 2005, and 2012    106

2.3     Persistence coefficients from dynamic panel data models for
        Mexican municipalities    117

3.1     Effects of biological and adoptive parents' conviction on the likelihood of a son
        having a conviction    173

3.2     Home nurse visitation and criminal behavior    179

3.3     Perry program effects on crime, females    186

4.1     Marginal effects of education on homicide rates, selected LAC countries,
        1995–2010    212

5.1     Summer job programs and their employment effects    292

6.1     Residual variation in homicide rates after controlling for municipal
        fixed effects    314

6.2     TECHO beneficiaries and nonbeneficiaries, by country    328

# Foreword

For a long time, the logic seemed unassailable: Crime and violence were historically thought of as symptoms of a country's early stages of development that could be "cured" with economic growth and reductions in poverty, unemployment, and inequality. More recently, however, our understanding has changed. Studies now show that economic progress does not necessarily bring better security to the streets. Developments in Latin America and the Caribbean exemplify this point.

Between 2003 and 2011, average annual regional growth in Latin America and the Caribbean, excluding the global crisis of 2009, reached nearly 5 percent. What's more, the growth rate of the bottom 40 percent of the population eclipsed that of the same group in every other region of the world. During that same decade, the region experienced unprecedented economic and social progress: extreme poverty was cut by more than half to 11.5 percent; income inequality dropped more than 7 percent, according to the Gini index; and, for the first time in history, the region had more people in the middle class than in poverty.

Despite all the progress, the region retained its undesirable distinction as the world's most violent, with 24.7 homicides per 100,000 inhabitants. The rate of homicide actually accelerated during the latter half of the decade. The problem remains staggering and stubbornly persistent.

Every 15 minutes, at least four people are victims of homicide in Latin America and the Caribbean. In 2013, of the top 50 most violent cities in the world, 42 were in the region. And between 2005 and 2012, the annual growth rate of homicides was more than three times higher than population growth. Not surprisingly, the number of Latin Americans who mention crime as their top concern tripled during those years. Violence makes people withdraw, hide behind closed doors, and avoid public spaces, weakening interpersonal and social ties that bind us as a community.

Insecurity is the result of a combination of many factors, from drug trafficking and organized crime, to weak judicial and law enforcement systems that promote impunity, to a lack of opportunities and support for young people who live in deprived communities.

Youth bear a disproportionate share of the risk of committing and falling victim to violence, with important repercussions for their life trajectories and society as a whole.

The complexity of the issue and multiplicity of its causes is one of its defining characteristics and the main reason why there is no magic formula or a single policy that will fix the violence in our region. We will not solve the problem relying only on greater police action or greater incarceration, or through more education or employment. We must do all this and do it in a deliberate and effective way, based on reliable data and proven approaches, while continuously striving to fill existing knowledge and data gaps to improve policy design.

To that end, *Stop the Violence in Latin America: A Look at Prevention from Cradle to Adulthood* is a significant contribution. This report takes a new and comprehensive look at much of the evidence that now exists in preventing crime and violence. It identifies novel approaches—both in Latin America and elsewhere—that have been shown to reduce antisocial behavior at different stages in life. Effective prevention starts even before birth, the report argues, and, contrary to common perceptions, well-designed policies can also be successful later in life, even with at-risk individuals and offenders. The report emphasizes the importance of a comprehensive approach to tackle violence and highlights the benefits and cost-effectiveness of redesigning existing policies through the lens of crime prevention. These efforts will require substantial coordination across ministries, as well as accountable and efficient institutions.

While economic and social development do not necessarily lead to a reduction in crime and violence, high levels of crime and violence do take a toll on development. With that in mind, we at the World Bank are fully aware that in order to succeed in our goals to eradicate extreme poverty and boost shared prosperity, the unrivaled levels of crime and violence in the region need to come to an end.

*Jorge Familiar*
*Vice President*
*Latin America and the Caribbean Region*
*World Bank Group*

# Acknowledgments

This regional study is the product of a broader analytical effort by the World Bank's Latin America and the Caribbean Region that focuses on crime, violence, and security.

This study was developed and prepared by Laura Chioda, under the patient direction and support of Augusto de la Torre. It builds on background papers by economists inside and outside the World Bank. We are very grateful for and acknowledge contributions by Pedro Carneiro, Rafael Di Tella, David Evans, Sebastian Galiani, Paul Gertler, Nancy Guerra, Sebastian Martinez, and Ernesto Schargrodsky.

The report has benefited from the encouragement of and conversations with several colleagues, many of whom are also members of the World Bank Crime and Violence Team. The author is indebted to Markus Kostner and Rodrigo Serrano-Berthet, who have unwaveringly and enthusiastically supported this process. The author is particularly grateful to Wendy Cunningham and Maninder Gill, whose guidance and insights shaped the original stages of the study.

The painstaking data work required approximately a googol of long days and was the cause of numerous headaches. The author is grateful for the countless hours that Karen del Mar Ortiz Becerra, Carlos Castañeda, Joaquin Urrego Garcia, Elisa Jacome, Camila Galindo Pardo, and Juan Pablo Uribe dedicated to this report and for their research assistance. Very special thanks go to Luis Diego Rojas Alvarado, Joaquin Urrego Garcia, and Tanya Maureen Taveras, who provided cheerful, outstanding, and tireless research assistance. In particular, the report would not have been possible without Diego and Joaquin's commitment and help.

The author would also like to thank the peer reviewers, Aline Coudouel, Alexandre Marc, and Andy Morrison, for their early feedback on the concept note and for their patience and willingness to review early drafts. Margaret Grosh and Bill Maloney generously also provided insightful and thoughtful comments. Makhtar Diop's encouragement to pursue this line of research and his constant support for the report are gratefully acknowledged.

The study also benefited from insightful comments by and patient conversations with Valentina Calderon, Óscar Calvo-González, Adriana Camacho, Flavia Carbonari,

Tito Cordella, Rafael de Hoyos, Tatiana Didier, David Evans, Ben Feigenberg, Francisco Ferreira, Paul Gertler, Marcus Holmlund, Ana Maria Ibanez, Felipe Jaramillo, Florence Kondylis, Arianna Legovini, Reema Nayar, Marcela Sanchez-Bender, Sameh Wahba, and several others to whom we apologize for omitting. Members of the AL CAPONE Network (America Latina Crime and Policy Network) have been an invaluable source of knowledge, wit, and encouragement: Joao Manoel de Mello and Rodrigo Soares deserve special thanks. We are grateful to Jeremy Biddle, coordinator for the Central America Regional Security Initiative (CARSI) at the U.S. Agency for International Development (USAID), for his and his team's support for this project and for its dissemination.

Ruth Delgado provided excellent production assistance. We are thankful to Joaquin Urrego for his help in preparing the manuscript. We acknowledge the outstanding support and expert advice of the external communications regional team for the report's launch—with particular thanks to Mauro Azeredo and Alejandra Viveros. Nancy Morrison provided superb editorial services and invaluable comments during the editing of this volume and in the drafting of the overview. We would like to thank Susan Graham, Aziz Gökdemir, Patricia Katayama, and Jewel McFadden for their generous help and patience during the production process. Finally, we would like to acknowledge the generous financial support from the government of Spain, under the Spanish Fund for Latin America and the Caribbean (SFLAC) Trust Fund.

# Abbreviations

| | |
|---|---|
| ADHD | attention deficit-hyperactivity disorder |
| BAM | Becoming a Man |
| CBT | cognitive behavioral therapy |
| CCT | conditional cash transfer |
| CDC | Centers for Disease Control and Prevention (United States) |
| COPS | Community-Oriented Policing Strategy |
| ECD | early childhood development |
| EM | electronic monitoring |
| FAWB | Federal Assault Weapons Ban (United States) |
| FFT | functional family therapy |
| GED | General Educational Development degree (United States) |
| GDP | gross domestic product |
| GNI | gross national income |
| IDB | Inter-American Development Bank |
| IV | instrumental variables |
| JYS | Jamaica Youth Survey |
| LAC | Latin America and the Caribbean |
| LAPOP | Latin America Public Opinion Project |
| LST | LifeSkills Training |
| MST | multisystemic therapy |
| MTO | Moving to Opportunity |
| NFP | Nurse Family Partnership |
| NGO | nongovernmental organization |
| NLSY | National Longitudinal Survey of Youth |
| OAS | Organization of American States |
| OLS | ordinary least squares |
| PAHO | Pan American Health Organization |
| POP | problem-oriented policing |

| RCT | randomized control trial |
| RD | regression discontinuity |
| RESOL-V | Red de Soluciones a la Violencia/Solutions to Violence Network |
| SES | socioeconomic status |
| UNESCO | United Nations Educational, Scientific and Cultural Organization |
| UN-HABITAT | United Nations Human Settlements Program |
| UNODC | United Nations Office on Drugs and Crime |
| USAID | United States Agency for International Development |

*All currency amounts are presented in U.S. dollars unless otherwise indicated.*

# Overview

## Introduction

Crime and violence in the Latin America and Caribbean (LAC) region are pervasive and costly—particularly violent crime. LAC has the undesirable distinction of being the world's most violent region, with 23.9 homicides per 100,000 inhabitants in 2012, compared to 9.7, 4.4, 2.7, and 2.9 for Africa, North America, Asia, and Europe, respectively.

The magnitude of the problem is staggering and stubbornly persistent. LAC accounts for only 8 percent of the world's population, but for 37 percent of the world's homicides (map O.1 illustrates the point dramatically by presenting a world map where country sizes are proportional to their homicide rates). Eight out of the 10 most violent countries in the world are in LAC. In 2013, of the top 50 most violent cities in the world, 42 were in the region, including the top 16. The annual growth rate of homicides (3.7 percent) dramatically outstripped population growth (1.15 percent) from 2005 to 2012. In 2012 alone, 145,759 people in LAC fell victim to homicide, corresponding to 400.44 homicides committed per day and 4.17 homicides every 15 minutes.

Eight countries exceed the level of violence defined by the World Health Organization (WHO) as "conflict" (30 homicides per 100,000), with Honduras and República Bolivariana de Venezuela experiencing the staggering rates of 90 and 54, respectively. These figures are well above the rate of any country in Africa, some of which were engaged in civil wars. In 2012, only Lesotho and Swaziland recorded homicide rates above the conflict threshold (38.0 and 33.8 homicides per 100,000 respectively). Unfortunately, the "endemic" level of violence, defined by WHO as 10 homicides per 100,000, appears to be the norm in the LAC region, with only ten countries below the threshold.[1,2]

This is not a recent phenomenon for the region, which has experienced high and persistent levels of violence for several decades (see figure O.1). Over the last 15 years, the homicide rate has hovered stubbornly around 24 homicides per 100,000. The trend started to decline slightly in the first half of the 2000s, but with the deteriorating situation in Central America, any gain has been reversed.

The region's history of elevated homicide rates and the latest uptick in violence are in stark contrast with the most recent decade of significant social progress. Between 2003 and 2011, Latin America and the Caribbean as a whole has made important

**MAP O.1:** World cartogram showing country size proportional to homicide rate

## a. Homicide rates, circa 2000

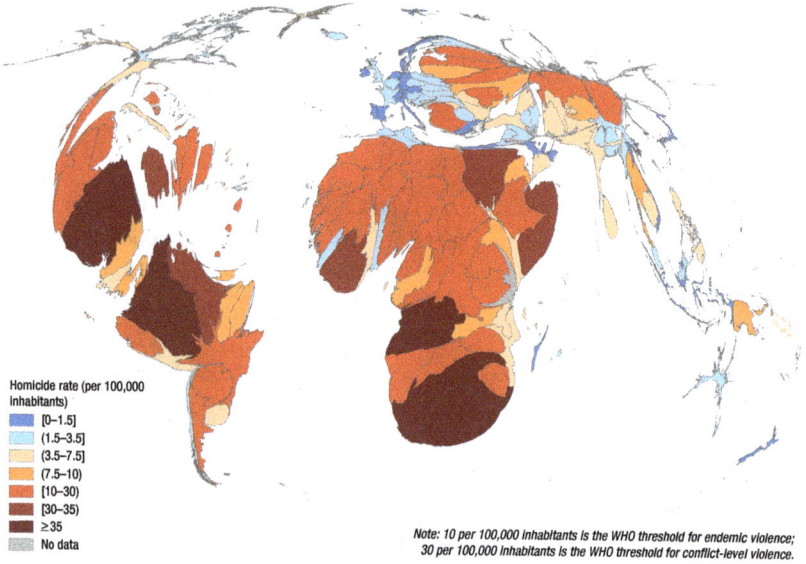

Homicide rate (per 100,000 inhabitants)
- [0–1.5]
- (1.5–3.5]
- (3.5–7.5]
- (7.5–10]
- [10–30)
- [30–35)
- ≥35
- No data

*Note: 10 per 100,000 inhabitants is the WHO threshold for endemic violence; 30 per 100,000 inhabitants is the WHO threshold for conflict-level violence.*

## b. Homicide rates, circa 2012

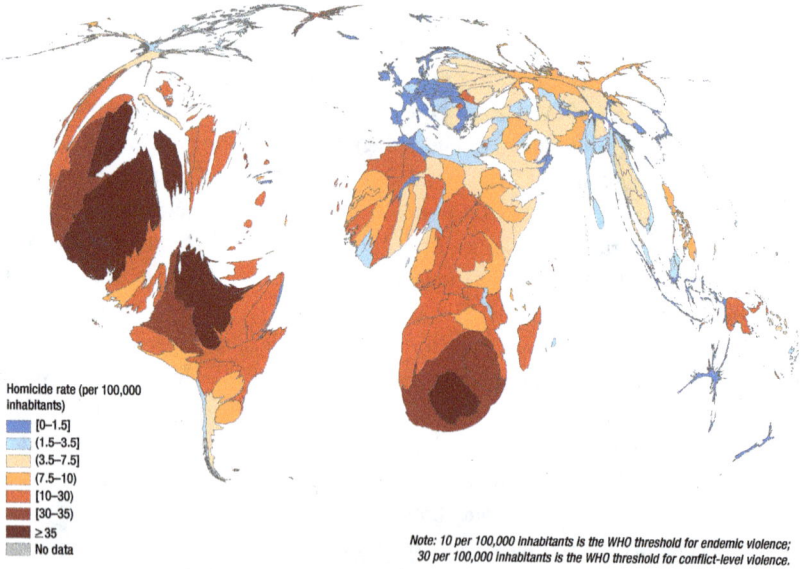

Homicide rate (per 100,000 inhabitants)
- [0–1.5]
- (1.5–3.5]
- (3.5–7.5]
- (7.5–10]
- [10–30)
- [30–35)
- ≥35
- No data

*Note: 10 per 100,000 inhabitants is the WHO threshold for endemic violence; 30 per 100,000 inhabitants is the WHO threshold for conflict-level violence.*

*Source:* World Bank calculations, based on data from UNODC and WHO.

strides toward broader social equity, as reflected by sizable reductions in poverty (from 45 percent to 25 percent) and income inequality, and rising shares of people in the middle class. This contrast—rising violence versus major improvements in social equity—highlights the complexity of the relationship between economic development and crime and violence.

*The focus of this study is the prevention of crime and violence.* In particular, this study seeks to identify novel policies whose impacts have been validated by rigorous empirical evidence. It considers a broad range of policy interventions—both in LAC and elsewhere—that have been shown to reduce antisocial behavior early in life or patterns of criminal offending in youth and adulthood, whether by design or by indirect effect. Further, it highlights the mechanisms underlying the success of such interventions. The study also aims to shed light on the complex landscape of violence in the region by combining several data sources, utilizing econometric techniques, and highlighting a number of background studies that were produced for the report, are centered on the region, and credibly identify causal links between policy and reductions in or prevention of crime and violence. An exhaustive review of all existing literature on crime (criminological, psychological, and economic) would be an overwhelming task and is beyond the scope of this document. Instead, attention is devoted to a selection of recent and innovative studies for which credible evidence exists regarding the links between the interventions in question and outcomes. The emphasis on causality is rooted in policy concerns—policies are best designed where the underlying causal processes are better understood. The delicate nature of the crime and violence problem, the high stakes, and the potential risks from unintended consequences of well-intentioned policies call for this evidence-based approach.

*This study does not address organized crime explicitly, but policies highlighted here remain relevant.* By design, this study does not delve into the causes and dynamics of organized crime in the region (largely drug-related), nor does it explicitly broach the roles of national institutions and international cooperation in determining the level of organized crime and violence. A thoughtful treatment of these topics is beyond the scope of this study. The data requirements and the methodological approach that would be necessary for this exercise would differ greatly—and would, in all likelihood, entail the adoption of an industrial organization perspective in the analysis of drug markets and of interactions among cartels.

Nevertheless, certain aspects of violence, described in this study, overlap with organized crime. In particular, when presenting data on the evolution of violence over time, this study does not attempt to distinguish between interpersonal violence that is unrelated to organized crime and that which is driven by it.[3] The rationale is twofold. First, pursuing that distinction empirically is nearly impossible, given that definitions, methodologies, and data collection systems of drug-related statistics vary enormously across countries, and data are reported too sporadically to create meaningful long-term regional comparisons. Second, conceptually, there are no universally accepted—or

**FIGURE O.1:** The homicide rates in Latin America and the Caribbean[a]

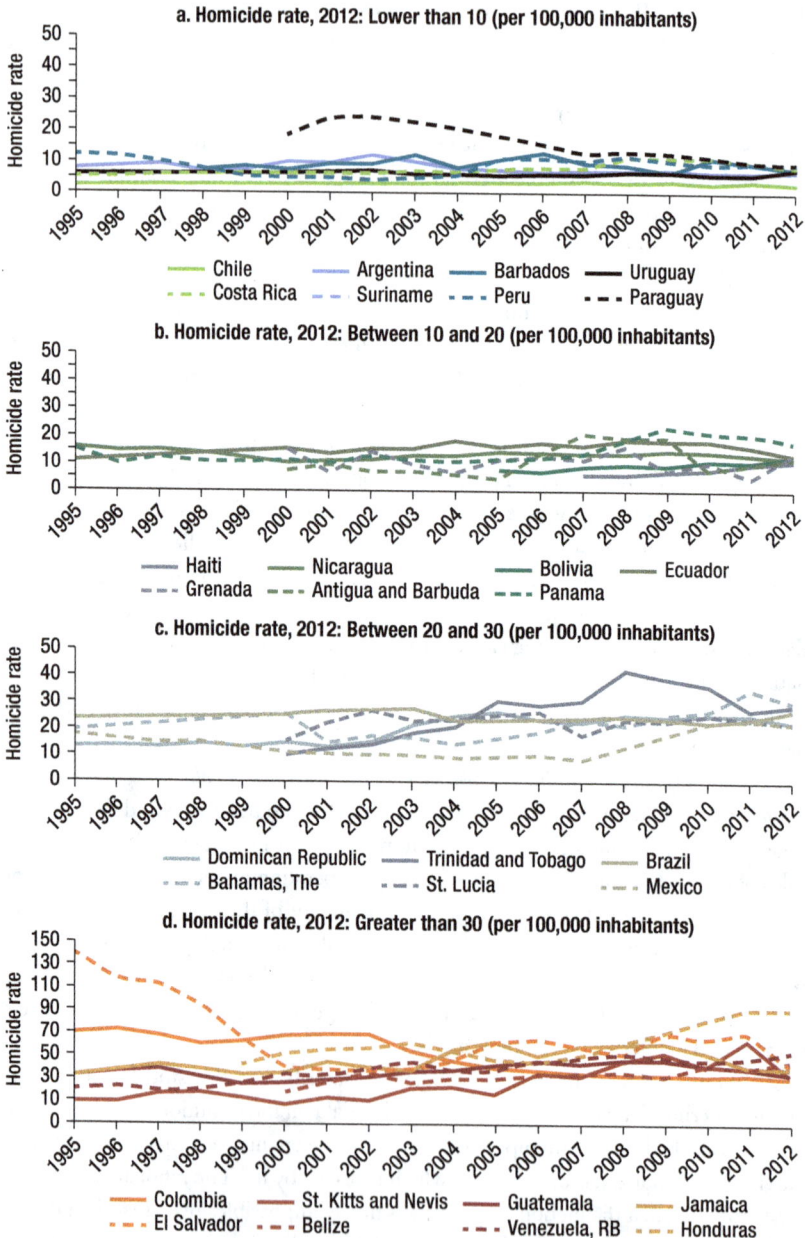

**a. Homicide rate, 2012: Lower than 10 (per 100,000 inhabitants)**

Homicide rate

Legend:
— Chile
— Argentina
— Barbados
— Uruguay
--- Costa Rica
--- Suriname
-·- Peru
--- Paraguay

**b. Homicide rate, 2012: Between 10 and 20 (per 100,000 inhabitants)**

Homicide rate

Legend:
— Haiti
— Nicaragua
— Bolivia
— Ecuador
--- Grenada
--- Antigua and Barbuda
--- Panama

**c. Homicide rate, 2012: Between 20 and 30 (per 100,000 inhabitants)**

Homicide rate

Legend:
— Dominican Republic
— Trinidad and Tobago
— Brazil
-·- Bahamas, The
-·- St. Lucia
--- Mexico

**d. Homicide rate, 2012: Greater than 30 (per 100,000 inhabitants)**

Homicide rate

Legend:
— Colombia
— St. Kitts and Nevis
— Guatemala
— Jamaica
--- El Salvador
-·- Belize
--- Venezuela, RB
--- Honduras

*Source:* World Bank calculations, based on data from UNODC.
a. The thresholds of 10 and 30 homicides per 100,000 inhabitants correspond to the WHO-defined "endemic" and "conflict" levels of violence, respectively.

mutually exclusive—definitions of violence and organized crime. Hence, a unique mapping of crimes into the relevant data categorizations (for example, related or not related to drug-driven organized crime) is extremely difficult and largely unattainable—even abstracting from longstanding debates surrounding the separation of drug-related crimes from other types.

Because the focus is on prevention, the study is only marginally affected by this regrettable data limitation. Much of the evidence on policy interventions and mechanisms discussed in the study has applicability and relevance to many questions surrounding organized crime. Whether in LAC or elsewhere, an intervention that is proven to reduce violence (whether homicides, violent crimes, or property crimes) in neighborhoods where interpersonal violence is intertwined with organized crime (leading to gang affiliation and drug trafficking) will be deemed to have promising preventive effects, regardless of the underlying motives of violence. Notably, policies that prevent youth violence are also frequently effective at reducing gang affiliation.[4] Some of the most promising gang violence prevention programs have been focused on training children, adolescents, and young adults in pro-social behavior and self-control. Of course, the overlap is not always perfect.[5]

*The organizing framework of this study.* The study reviews and assesses the evidence in the context of an organizing framework that encompasses features of three different models of criminal and antisocial behavior, each with origins in different disciplines:

1. Becker's (1968) economic theory of the supply of criminal offenses

2. The ecological framework, whose origins lie in the medical literature

3. The developmental life course theories, building on Bronfenbrenner's (1979) theory of child development and on Loeber and others (1993) and Farrington (2003), who formalize developmental and life cycle insights for the criminological literature

The study's organizing framework builds on the classical Beckerian model, which posits that the number of crimes in any given period is a function of the probability of apprehension and conviction; the severity of punishment; and a residual that captures all other relevant considerations, such as risk aversion, family background, peers, human capital characteristics (for example, education and heath), and wages in the legal labor market (see figure O.2). The residual plays an important role—it is a placeholder for a set of variables that are key determinants in the specific crime and violence problem under consideration.

The ecological elements of the organizing framework are adapted from the medical literature. They organize risk factors (that is, factors that can encourage crime and violence) and protective factors (that is, factors that dissuade or shield individuals from crime and violence) according to the hierarchical levels at which they operate, namely, individual, family, peer, community, or societal levels (WHO 2002).

**FIGURE O.2:** A model of the supply of criminal offenses, but also a model of crime and violence prevention

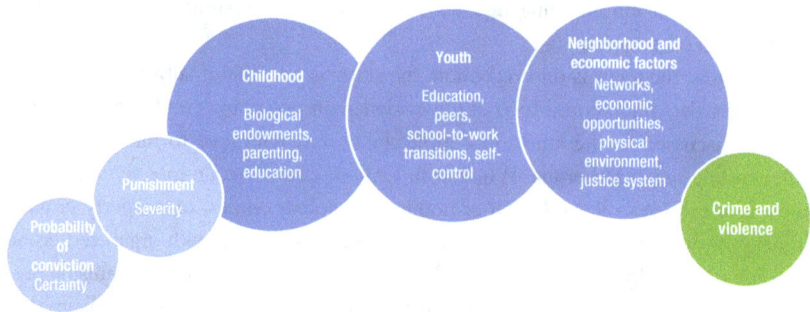

However, the ecological model was originally developed as an organizing descriptive tool and is, as such, static in nature; that is, it is not designed to capture the feedbacks between the various factors. As an individual matures and progresses through adolescence and young adulthood, peers, the quality of schools, and neighborhood characteristics exert increasing influence on his or her behavior, such that different sets of proximal risk and protective factors take greater prominence (Bronfenbrenner 1979 and Plas 1992). In particular, criminal offending is a multifaceted phenomenon with roots in both biological and social causes. The developmental life course theories speak to this complexity, as each stage of one's life is associated with an evolving array of risk factors, including biological endowments; smoking, drug use, or stress during pregnancy; inconsistent and punitive parenting; antisocial peers; poor schooling; disadvantaged or violent neighborhoods; and poor job opportunities. Each of these factors can be accommodated via different formulations for the Beckerian residual.

*Prevention can never start too early or too late, or be too comprehensive.* The organizing framework thus adopts a life cycle perspective and argues that, as individuals progress through stages of their lives (from birth to old age), different sets of risk factors arise, their prominence evolves, and interdependencies among them mutate. These interactions and interdependencies, and the changes in the relative importance of different risk and protective factors, not only shape behavior but also help identify relevant margins for policy action—that is, margins that can be targeted by prevention policies at different stages of the life cycle.[6] Indeed prevention can never start too early, or start too late, or be too comprehensive. Effective prevention starts even before birth and, contrary to common perceptions, well-designed policies can also be successful later in life. At-risk individuals and offenders have been shown to respond to incentives (including those set by labor markets and the criminal justice system) even if their behavior is only boundedly rational (Cook and Ludwig 2011).

Furthermore, better understanding of brain functions and development serves to expand the menu of policy options available for prevention. The success or failure of a violence prevention strategy rests on the ability to implement an integrated set of policies that can exploit these interdependencies; in this way, the ultimate outcome in terms of crime reduction may be larger than the sum of the individual policy outcomes.

*The overview is structured as follows.* The first part of this overview systematically describes a set of key stylized facts that characterize the landscape of crime and violence in the region. These facts are grouped into four broad categories: (a) the nexus between crime and economic development; (b) the geography of crime; (c) the distribution of crime among individuals and over the life cycle; and (d) the determinants of victimization, concerns about crime, and well-being. The second part of the overview focuses on the scope for prevention at different stages of the life cycle (prenatal, early childhood, and youth) and in different contexts (family, school, neighborhoods, labor markets, and criminal sanctions). The discussion in the second part of the overview follows the organizing conceptual framework described above.

## Stylized facts: The physiognomy of crime and violence in LAC

### Crime and violence and economic development

At first glance, the indicators on the extent of crime and violence seem to suggest that Latin America and the Caribbean represents an outlier, with an extraordinary level of violence relative to other regions with comparable levels of economic development, as proxied by GDP per capita (see figure O.3). However, recent research calls into question whether the level of crime and violence in the region has been truly exceptional. During the 1990s, the incidence of crime in the region was found not to be so different from what should be expected given the socioeconomic and policy characteristics of its constituent countries (Soares and Naritomi 2010; Fajnzylber, Lederman, and Loayza 2002a).

This conclusion makes the more recent trends all the more puzzling. The "good" decade of the 2000s witnessed important reductions in poverty (more than 80 million Latin Americans rose above the moderate poverty line between 2003 and 2012[7]) and in income inequality (at least 14 countries in the region experienced a significant decline in their Gini coefficient), and a simultaneous rise in the share of people in the middle classes (from 20 percent in 2003 to 34 percent in 2012, as measured by the proportion of people making more than US$10 a day on a purchasing-power-adjusted basis) (see figure O.4). Yet levels of violence have risen or remained constant in all LAC countries except Argentina, Brazil, Colombia, and Paraguay. The experience of the 2000s—particularly the second half of the decade, when violence appeared to accelerate—suggests that there is no one-to-one mapping between (a) crime and violence and (b) standard indicators of social and economic development and that, instead, the links, if any, are subject to a high degree of complexity.

**FIGURE O.3:** LAC's homicide rate relative to other regions in terms of GDP per capita, 2012

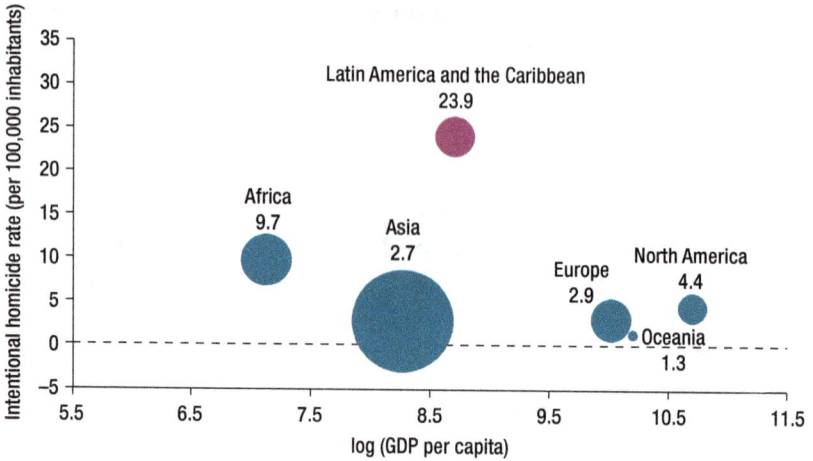

*Source:* World Bank calculations, based on data from UNODC (2012).
*Note:* The size of the spheres is proportional to population.

**FIGURE O.4:** Evolution of poverty, the middle class, economic development, and violence in Latin America, 1995–2012

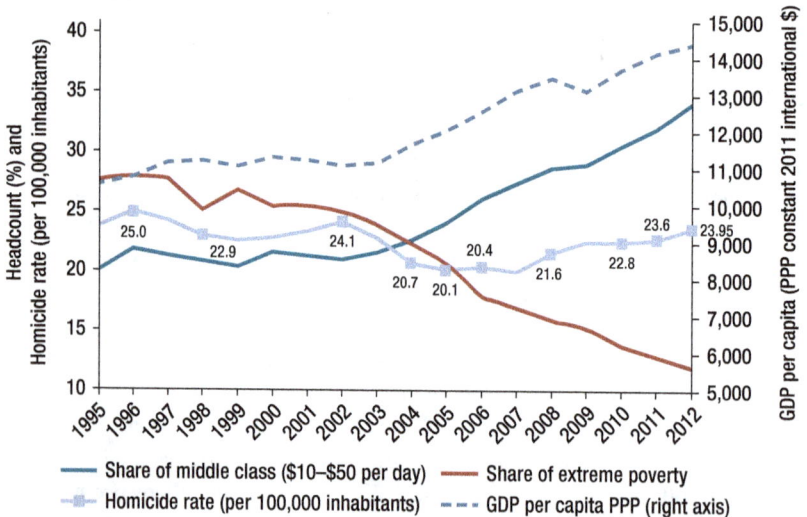

*Source:* Author's calculations. Homicide rates are calculated with data from UNODC, OAS, and official statistics from various countries. Data for poverty and the middle class are from Ferreira et al. (2013) and LAC Equity Lab (2015).
*Note:* PPP = purchasing power parity.

*The relationship between crime and development is highly nonlinear: crime can increase as income rises.*[8] Indeed, the cross-country relationship between homicides and GDP per capita is well approximated by an inverted U shape; homicide rates first increase as per capita income rises and then decline at high levels of per capita income. Empirically, low levels of violence are observed at both low and high levels of economic development. As countries grow from low levels of income, both the opportunities for crime and the returns to criminality increase. At least initially, the probability of crime detection and sanctions declines—as investments in institutions of criminal justice typically lag behind income—lowering the expected costs of criminality ("crime pays").

However, as income continues to grow, the opportunity cost of crime also increases in the form of forgone wages in the legal sector in the event of being apprehended; thus crime declines, as reflected in the downward portion of the curve. It is also possible that, as the level of crime rises, both citizens and the private sector increase their demands for public goods—including security and safety—forcing institutions to devote more resources to controlling crime and thus raising the probability of crime detection and sanctions (being caught and being sentenced to prison). These processes are analogous to Maslow's (1943) "hierarchy of needs," whereby there is a sequence of individual needs and priorities, starting with basic physiological necessities such as food and shelter and moving up to needs for safety. As countries progress through different stages of development, new challenges and needs arise and become more pressing. In this context, as countries become wealthier and their basic physiological needs for survival are met, their concerns and efforts turn to personal safety and a more peaceful society.

*Economic development per se does not seem sufficient to curb violence: development must occur at a fast enough pace and be inclusive.* A closer look at the roles of poverty, of vulnerability (defined as per capita daily income between $4 and $10 per day), and of the middle class (defined as per capita daily income between $10 and $50 per day) delivers more insight into the relationships between income and violence. In the case of LAC, there is a noteworthy break in the early 2000s for certain economic variables as they relate to homicide rates. Before 2003, there is no systematic and statistically significant relation between the size of either the vulnerable class or the upper class (defined as per capita income above $50 per day) and changes in homicide rates. After 2003, the size of the vulnerable class emerges as a risk factor (it rises as the rate of homicides increases), while the size of the upper class emerges as a protective factor (it is associated with a lower homicide rate). In turn, throughout the 15-year period (1996 to 2010), the size of the middle class and the level of poverty are not statistically significant determinants of observed trends in violence. Hence, in the case of LAC, economic development per se does not seem sufficient to halt violence; it must occur at a fast enough pace. Indeed, the data reveal a precise and robust protective effect of real GDP growth on homicide rates: a 1 percentage point increase in the growth rate of GDP is related to roughly 0.24 fewer homicides per 100,000 (all else equal, including income per capita). Growth acts as a protective factor and can help "outstrip" the need for crime. In order for these gains to be sustainable, however, the strength and credibility of institutions (the confidence in the democratic and judicial systems and in law enforcement) also must improve in lockstep with economic development.

The relationship between crime and development is further complicated when alternative measures of development (such as unemployment, demographic structure, and inequality) are considered. Each exerts possibly competing forces on criminality.

*The relationship between crime and inequality is confounded by poverty. If inequality matters for crime, it matters at the local level.* The relationship between crime and the distribution of income has drawn a good deal of scrutiny. Some researchers have estimated significant effects of the Gini coefficient on homicides (Kelly 2000; Fajnzylber, Lederman, and Loayza 2002a, 2002b). More recent studies have found little evidence of a relationship (Brush 2007; Pridemore 2011). The findings in this study—which are based on Latin America data—are consistent with the latter group, with the Gini coefficient appearing not to predict changes in homicides.

How can these two sets of results be reconciled? While differences across countries in the level of the homicide rate are captured by differences in income and income inequality, changes within a particular country over time are poorly predicted by these variables (Brush 2007). Furthermore, a growing body of evidence suggests that the relationship between crime and inequality is confounded by poverty (that is, it vanishes after controlling for poverty), which is the one most consistent predictor of homicide rates in the United States (Pridemore 2011). Qualitatively similar results regarding poverty emerge also for LAC. In particular, proxy measures of extreme poverty, such as the teen pregnancy rate, indicate positive and precisely estimated effects of poverty on national homicide rates: an increase in the contemporaneous teen pregnancy rate is associated with approximately 0.5–0.6 additional homicides per 100,000 (Chioda 2014a).

As discussed in greater detail below, crime is very local in nature. It is therefore not surprising that the degree of inequality measured at the national level is at best a weak predictor of its behavior. What appears to matter is the level of inequality experienced by the individual. Recent research that considers the impact of neighborhood characteristics on behavior suggests that poor boys living in largely well-to-do neighborhoods are the most likely to engage in antisocial behavior (lying, misdemeanors, property crimes, and other problem behaviors), compared to their counterparts in poor areas.

*Not all unemployment is created equal; age and quality of employment opportunities matter.* Economic development is also associated with improvements in labor market conditions: more and better employment opportunities and possibly higher wages. Whether unemployment and crime are related remains an open question, both theoretically and empirically (Bushway 2011).[9] In a panel of LAC countries, the aggregate (lagged) unemployment rate is not related to violence measures (Chioda 2014a). However, when youth and adult unemployment are treated separately, a stable pattern emerges: whereas adult unemployment is unrelated to crime, youth unemployment is consistently and positively related to the homicide rate (a 1 percentage point increase in youth unemployment leads to 0.34 additional homicides per 100,000). Not all forms of unemployment are thus equal; youth unemployment is particularly nocive to citizen security. Since youth are at particularly high risk of engaging in antisocial and criminal behavior (see discussion below), the linkages between the labor market and criminal participation may be particularly important for this group.

*However, employment per se is not sufficient to deter criminality.* Regardless of the type of crime (homicides, robberies, violent or property crimes), perpetrators in Mexico, for instance, are characterized by higher labor market attachment than the general population (see figure O.5).[10] Indeed, crime and work are not perfect substitutes, but instead "imperfect" complements:[11] rather than a dichotomous choice, for many individuals, economic activity appears to lie along a continuum of legal and illegal "work." Micro-level analyses from Brazil and Mexico indicate that the *quality* of employment plays a central role in the relationship between labor markets and criminal offending, rather than employment status per se.

This is especially relevant for youth with low educational attainment (for example, incomplete secondary schooling), who are likely to face (legal) employment prospects that offer limited potential for wage growth, skill acquisition, and job stability, and who may ultimately find employment in the informal sector.

*Development has a dark side. What benefits the formal economy may also benefit illegal markets.* While this regional study does not focus on organized crime and illicit drug markets, it is difficult to avoid acknowledging the spillovers of development into these markets, particularly given LAC's status as a leading producer of illicit drugs and its unique geographical proximity to one of the world's largest

**FIGURE O.5:** Employment profiles of male perpetrators and the general male population, Mexico, 2010

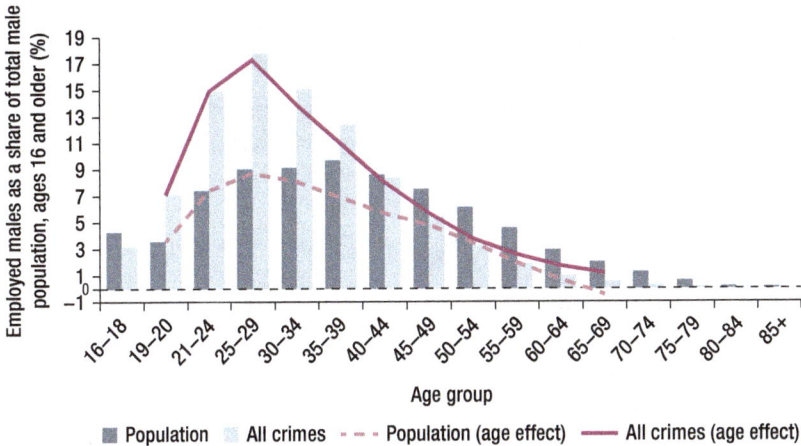

*Source:* Chioda 2014c, based on data from INEGI.

consumer markets (the United States). As countries transition through different stages of economic development, increased tensions can result, with theoretically ambiguous effects of income on violence and illicit opportunities. In particular, while improvements in infrastructure, financial markets, transportation, and income may help economic growth and foster the development of legal markets, they may also increase the economic returns to transactions in illegal markets (lowering both transaction costs and the likelihood of detection by law enforcement[12]). For instance, in LAC, exports—an indirect measure of a country's openness—are positively related to homicides: all else equal, a 1 percentage point increase in exports as a percent of GDP is associated with an increase of 0.2 homicides per 100,000 (Chioda 2014a). One interpretation of this relationship is that increased violence is one of the transitory "costs" of development: Crime and violence are social ills that arise and evolve along with the level of a society's development. In particular, while improvements in infrastructure, financial markets, and rising incomes may foster economic growth and the development of legal markets, they can also increase the economic returns to participating in illegal markets by lowering transaction costs and the likelihood of detection. That is, transaction costs may fall as a result of improved information technology or as transportation costs decline from better roads and infrastructures; the likelihood of detection may similarly decrease if the volume of economic activity from greater trade is not matched by a proportional effort to monitor it.

## Geographically, crime is concentrated, persistent, and contagious

More than 1,560,000 people in LAC fell victim to homicide during the 2000s (UNODC 2013), though this likely represents an underestimate because official statistics are not available for all countries and all years. To put this figure into perspective, it is 2.5 times the population of Washington, DC, and close to half of the population of Panama. Over this ten-year period, homicide victims in LAC far exceeded casualties of the Iraq War (both civilian and military), which have been estimated in the range of 400,000 and 750,000.

*Violence is very local in nature: It is highly heterogeneous across countries, states, and municipalities.* The aggregate levels of violence mask a great deal of heterogeneity. As noted earlier, while LAC as a whole is the most violent region in the world, the variance across countries within LAC is staggering. In 2010, and for most of the decade, Chile—at 3.2 per 100,000—had a lower incidence of homicide than the United States (4.8 per 100,000 in 2010, a historical low). Similarly, in 2008, Uruguay was on par with North America and was only marginally higher in 2010. These optimistic figures are in stark contrast to the gloomy picture painted by the eight LAC countries whose levels of violence exceed the WHO-defined "conflict" threshold of 30 per 100,000.

However, national figures can also paint a misleading picture. For instance, Mexico's homicide rates of 10.34 per 100,000 in 2000 and 21.85 per 100,000 in 2010 were the result of significant variability at the state and municipal levels. Despite the recent dramatic deterioration in security in Mexico, several municipalities experienced declines in violence and homicide (see map O.2). During the 2000s, the state of Chihuahua had the third-highest state-level homicide rate in Mexico (with 19.2 per 100,000), but security deteriorated dramatically, with homicides skyrocketing to 187.6 in 2010.[13,14] Within the state, over the course of one year, the homicide rate in the municipality of Ciudad Juarez soared eightfold, from 14.1 per 100,000 in 2007 to 114.8 in 2008. It increased to 263.2 in 2010, accounting for approximately 60 percent of homicides in the state of Chihuahua and 15 percent of all murders in Mexico, respectively.

One of the distinguishing features of the crime and violence phenomenon is the degree to which it is geographically concentrated, implying that a great deal of heterogeneity underlies aggregate figures, especially at the regional and national levels (see map O.3). Municipality- and state-level data consistently point to handfuls of locations where the majority of homicides occur. For instance, 6 of Guatemala's 22 departments account for 63.7 percent of its homicides; in 2007, the state of Chihuahua alone accounted for one-quarter of the homicides in Mexico, 50 percent of which were accounted for by two of its municipalities. In 2008, not only did violence increase dramatically in Chihuahua, but so did its concentration: two municipalities accounted for 76.8 percent of the state's homicides.

The clustered nature of violence appears at even finer levels of geographical disaggregation, manifesting itself at the neighborhood and even the street levels. Is this feature specific to Latin America and the Caribbean? Here again, the parallel with developed

**MAP O.2:** U.S. ports of entry, Mexican highways, and homicide rates for the most violent municipalities in 2012

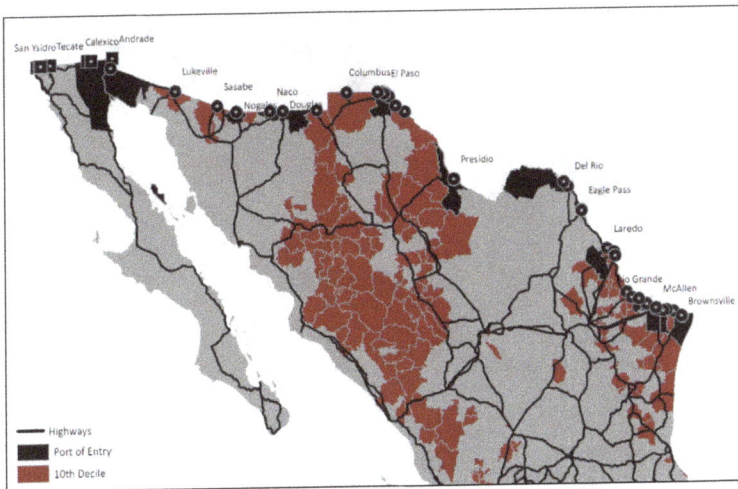

Source: World Bank calculations, based on data from INEGI.
Note: The 10th decile = the 10 percent most violent municipalities.

**MAP O.3:** Homicides rates by municipality in Colombia, Guatemala, El Salvador, and Brazil

**a. Colombia, 2013**

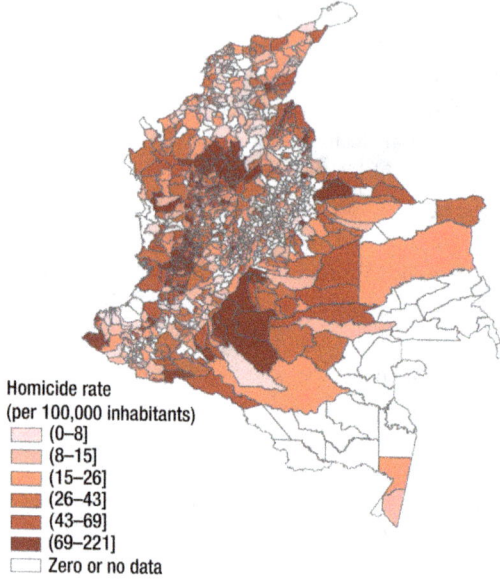

Homicide rate
(per 100,000 inhabitants)
- (0–8]
- (8–15]
- (15–26]
- (26–43]
- (43–69]
- (69–221]
- Zero or no data

**b. Guatemala, 2012**

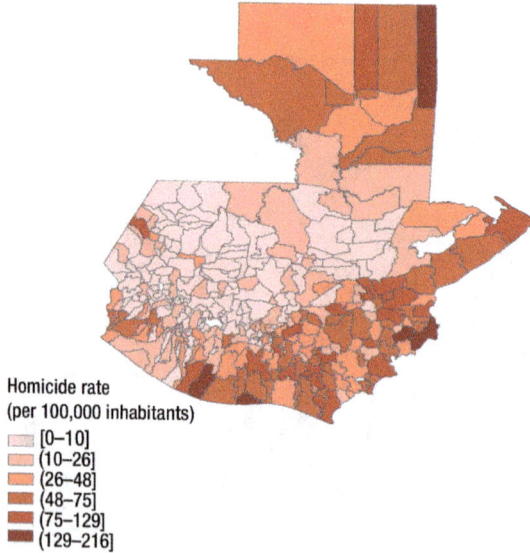

Homicide rate
(per 100,000 inhabitants)
- [0–10]
- (10–26]
- (26–48]
- (48–75]
- (75–129]
- (129–216]

**MAP O.3:** Homicides rates by municipality in Colombia, Guatemala, El Salvador, and Brazil *(continued)*

**c. El Salvador, 2014**

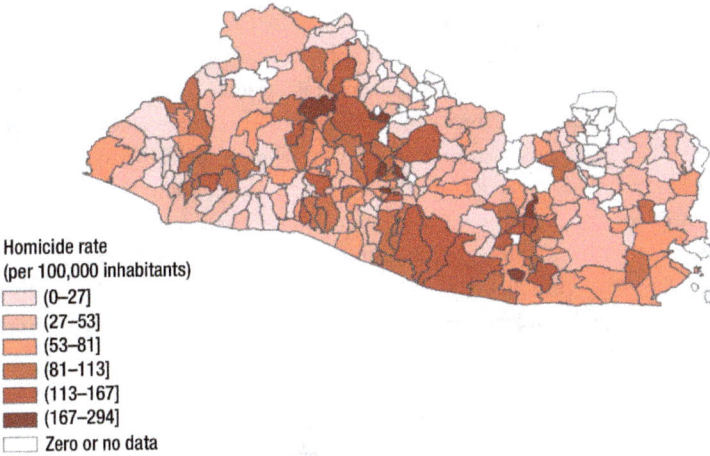

Homicide rate
(per 100,000 inhabitants)
- (0–27]
- (27–53]
- (53–81]
- (81–113]
- (113–167]
- (167–294]
- Zero or no data

**d. Brazil, 2012**

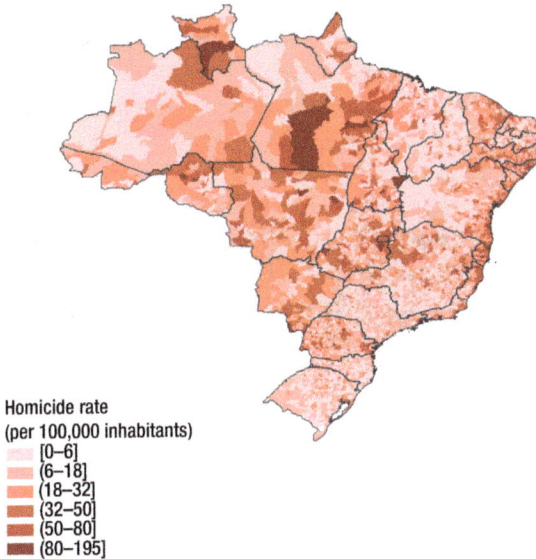

Homicide rate
(per 100,000 inhabitants)
- [0–6]
- (6–18]
- (18–32]
- (32–50]
- (50–80]
- (80–195]

*Sources:* Instituto Colombiano de Medicina Legal, Guatemala's National Police, El Salvador's National Police, and DATASUS.

countries persists: In Seattle, between 4.7 percent and 6.1 percent of street segments accounted for 50 percent of the crimes in 2004; in Minneapolis, Minnesota, 3.5 percent of addresses produced 50 percent of criminal offenders in 1989; and in Tel Aviv, 50 percent of the criminal incidents were concentrated in 5 percent of the street segments in 2010 (Weisburd, Groff, and Yang 2012). LAC is in this sense no different. In Antioquia, Colombia, 18 percent of municipalities accounted for 75 percent of department-wide homicides in 2013. In Medellín, Colombia, approximately 13 and 30 percent of its 317 neighborhoods account for 50 and 75 percent of all the intentional homicides in a given year, respectively, with little change in the degree of concentrations over the last decade.

The marked geographic concentration of violence highlights the importance of understanding local-level determinants and networks in crime. It also stresses the critical need for data that match the nature of the problem, and that draw attention to the limits of analyses with aggregate country-level data. If a few states, a few municipalities, or a few neighborhoods account for a large fraction of the violence, then the implications for policy are clear: effective deployment of resources will likely include geographically targeted interventions.

*Most crime and violence occur close to the homes or neighborhoods of both victims and perpetrators.* Another local aspect of the phenomenon is that crime and violence tend to be extremely proximal to victims; in 2012, 50 percent of victims in the region reported that the last crime occurred at their home or in their neighborhood, and an additional 32 percent fell victim somewhere within their municipality of residence. Only a small fraction fell victim outside their municipality or abroad. Similar patterns hold for both property and violent crimes. The stability of this pattern is noteworthy across countries in the region.

Not only do crimes occur in close proximity to the victims' homes, but at least three-quarters of crimes occur within the same municipality in which the *perpetrators* live. In Mexico, this has been the case for 71 percent of homicides, 76 percent of property crimes, and 85 percent of violent crimes over the last 15 years. Property crimes tend to be more local in nature than violent crimes and homicides (figure O.6).

*Crime is persistent; today's crime rate is a strong predictor of tomorrow's. Crime is also contagious.* What is possibly more worrisome from a policy perspective is that crime in the region is not only concentrated geographically, but also exhibits high degrees of persistence. Research discussed in the study formalizes and quantifies this notion for the region as a whole and for a handful of specific countries. All else constant, on average in Latin America and the Caribbean, an additional homicide in a given year predicts 0.66 additional homicides in the following year. Persistence over time is not only a feature of homicide statistics at the national level, but it is also observed at subnational levels and holds true for different types of crime. Persistence is even higher at the municipal level in Brazil and Mexico, with an additional homicide in one year predicting 0.64 and 0.80 additional homicides the following year, respectively.

The parallel similarity with developed countries continues. The greatest predictor of violence in the streets of U.S. cities is a prior violent incident, which mirrors the behavior typical of epidemic waves (Slutkin 2013). As mentioned, violence in the

**FIGURE O.6:** Victim reporting on where the last crime occurred, 2010 and 2014

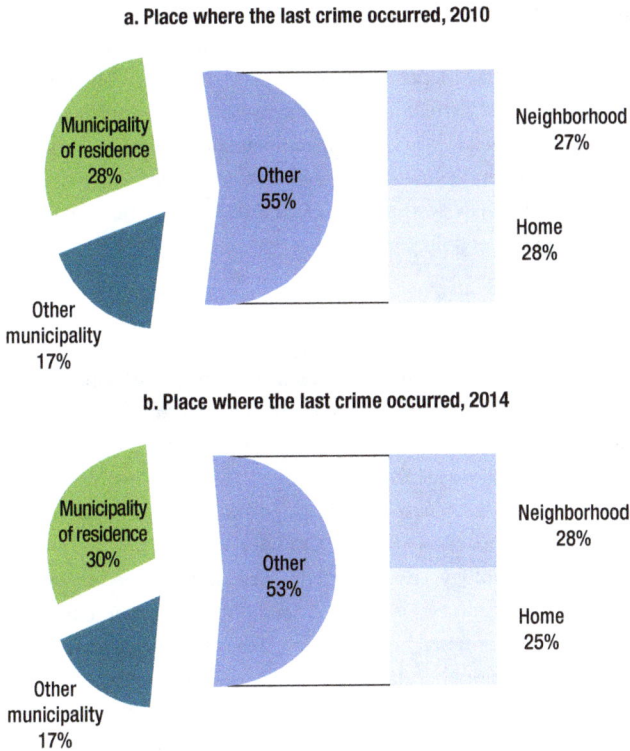

**a. Place where the last crime occurred, 2010**

Municipality of residence 28%

Other 55%

Other municipality 17%

Neighborhood 27%

Home 28%

**b. Place where the last crime occurred, 2014**

Municipality of residence 30%

Other 53%

Other municipality 17%

Neighborhood 28%

Home 25%

*Source:* World Bank calculations, based on 2010 and 2014 data from LAPOP.
*Note:* LAC-weighted averages.

Mexican state of Chihuahua is highly concentrated, with significant clustering during the recent deterioration of security. A closer look reveals that violence first became more acute in locations where its level was already high and then propagated across municipalities outward along the highways, consistent with a model of spatial contagion.

A formal, yet crude measure of contagion (that is, the spreading of crime from one geographic area to another) is whether violence from neighboring municipalities predicts levels of violence in a given locality even after controlling for a number of other predictors, including the municipality's own lagged level of violence. Spillover effects for homicides are sizable and significant; however, their intensity varies across countries. In Mexico, one additional homicide (per 100,000) occurring outside a given municipality, but within the same state, predicts 0.6 additional homicides per 100,000 within that municipality. Smaller magnitudes of contagion are recorded in Brazil and Colombia, where the corresponding measures are 0.14 and 0.20, respectively.[15] Similar patterns of detrimental spillovers also emerge for other types of crimes (violent and property crimes, and robberies), with approximately 0.3 additional crimes (per 100,000) in each crime category predicted by one additional incident in neighboring municipalities.

Geographic and temporal spillovers have important implications and can be exploited in policy design. In particular, the magnitude of declines in violence in a given municipality may depend on the actions of neighboring municipalities; one municipality's crime reduction efforts in one year spill over to future years and to neighbors. Coordinated action by many municipalities may thus yield benefits that exceed the sum of their individual efforts; an additional crime that is prevented yields additional prevented crimes downstream. Hence, the momentum of contagion can be harnessed to the benefit of policy.

### Over the life cycle, crime is concentrated and persistent

Distinguishing features of crime and violence are their degree of concentration, persistence, and proximity to the victim. These features characterize criminal behavior not only across geographic areas (states, municipalities, and even streets) but also across individuals and throughout the life cycle.

*The age-crime profiles of victims and perpetrators are remarkably stable across cohorts, income levels, and types of crime.* One of the oldest and most stable empirical regularities in criminology—documented in several developed countries since the beginning of the 17th century—is referred to as "the age-crime curve" by modern criminologists. That is, criminal behavior increases substantially during adolescence, reaching a peak in early adulthood, and then declines until old age.

Similar patterns emerge in Latin America and the Caribbean. The homicide rate for younger teens ages 10–14 is around 2.8 (per 100,000) and increases more than tenfold (to 31.1 per 100,000 in 2008) for older teens ages 15–19. The risk of homicide victimization peaks at 48.2 per 100,000 for those ages 20–24 (see figure O.7).

Gender differences are stark. Violence is committed by and affects boys at disproportionate rates: at almost all ages, boys are at least 10 times more likely than girls to fall victim to homicide. Homicide rates among young boys (ages 10–14, 15–19, and 20–24) are double those of the general population (4.2, 56.0, and 92.4 per 100,000, for the respective age groups). These numbers further corroborate the parallel with the United States (see figure O. 8). The figures for homicides of African American males, ages 18–24, are remarkably close, reaching a historic low of 91.1 per 100,000 in 2008,[16] after a decade of rates between 105 and 110 per 100,000. This record low is nevertheless still 20 homicides higher than the homicide rate for males, ages 20–24, in Mexico, which peaked at 71.5 in 2010. This consistent trajectory provides a clear picture of how the risk of violence evolves over the life cycle, and how its burden falls disproportionately on adolescents and young adults. While these patterns relate to victims, they are mirrored for perpetrators; the age-crime profiles of perpetrators and of victims are nearly identical and are stable across cohorts and levels of income.

Just as antisocial behavior tends to cluster in very specific geographical areas, life course trajectories of offending suggest that the majority of crimes are perpetrated by a very specific age and demographic group: adolescent and young adult males. The similarity of age profiles for offenders and victims reinforces the notion of their proximity, not only with respect to location, but also with respect to age.

**FIGURE O.7:** LAC homicide age-crime profile, selected years

**a. Total homicide rate, LAC**

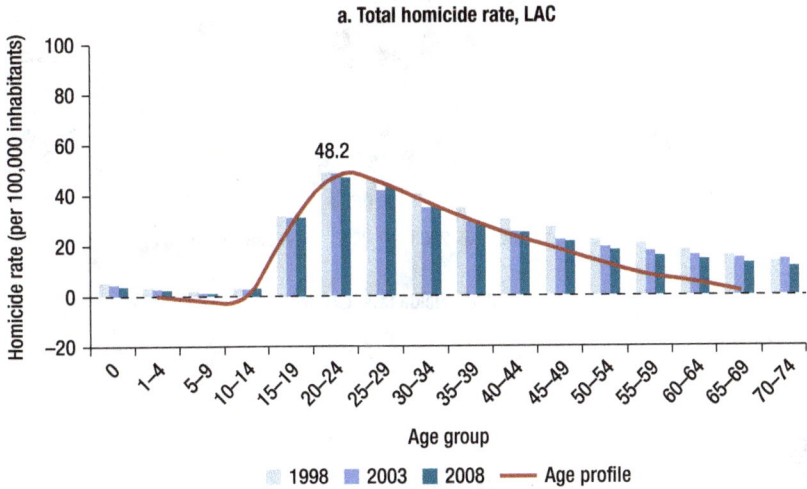

48.2

Legend: 1998 · 2003 · 2008 · Age profile

**b. Total homicide rate, United States**

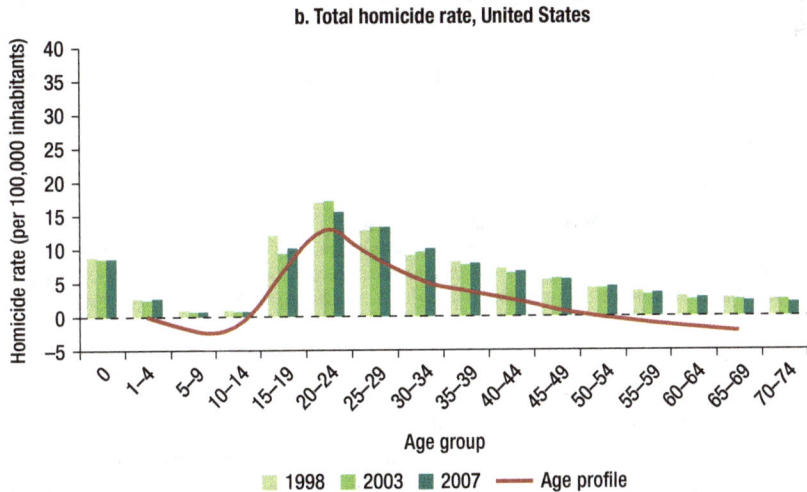

Legend: 1998 · 2003 · 2007 · Age profile

*(continued on next page)*

### c. Homicide rate, LAC males

**1998**  **2003**  **2008** —— Age profile

### d. Homicide rate, LAC females

**1998**  **2003**  **2008** —— Age profile

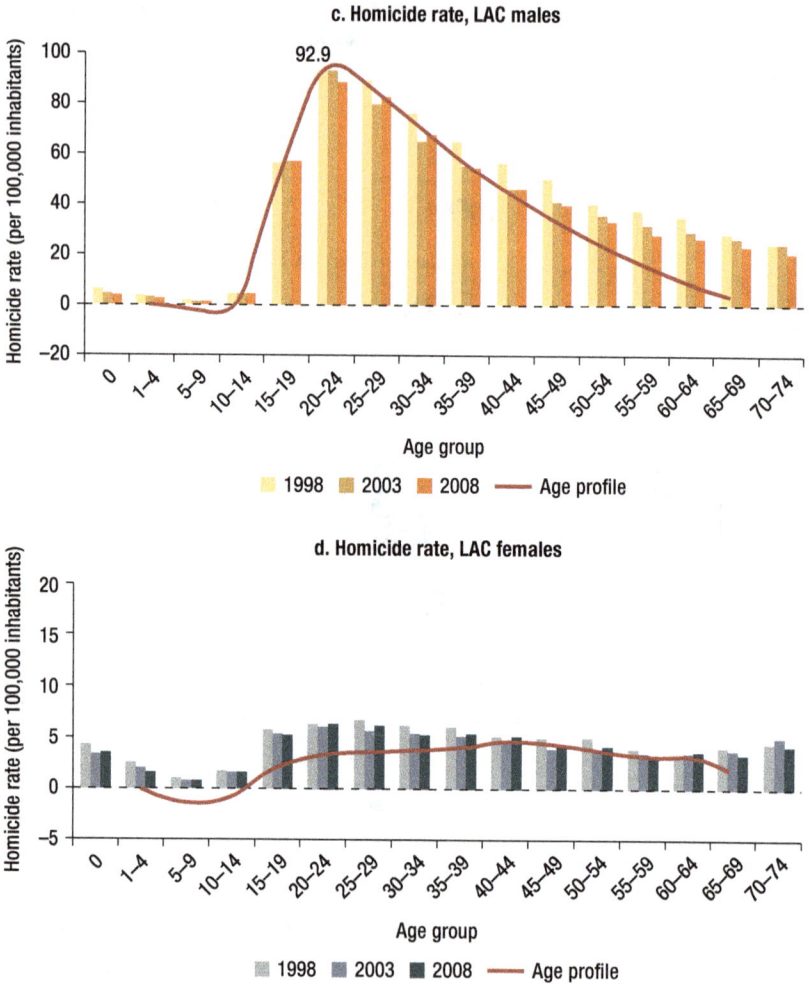

*Source:* Chioda 2014d, based on data from the Global Burden of Injuries.
*Note:* The age profile (solid red line) represents population-weighted estimates of age effects from models estimated across years controlling for year and cohort dummies. In computing the regional average, 2007 data were used for Chile, Colombia, and República Bolivariana de Venezuela, as they were missing for 2008. For Nicaragua, 2006 was used in lieu of 2008.

Evidence on perpetrators supports the conclusion that the adolescent peak reflects a temporary increase in the number of people involved in antisocial behavior, not a temporary acceleration in the offense rates of individuals. Indeed, rates of illegal behavior soar so high during adolescence that participation in delinquency appears to be a normal part of teen life (Elliott and others 1983). This age group is a pivotal target for any policy aimed at violence prevention.

**FIGURE O.8:** Trends in homicide rates in the United States and Mexico, by age and race

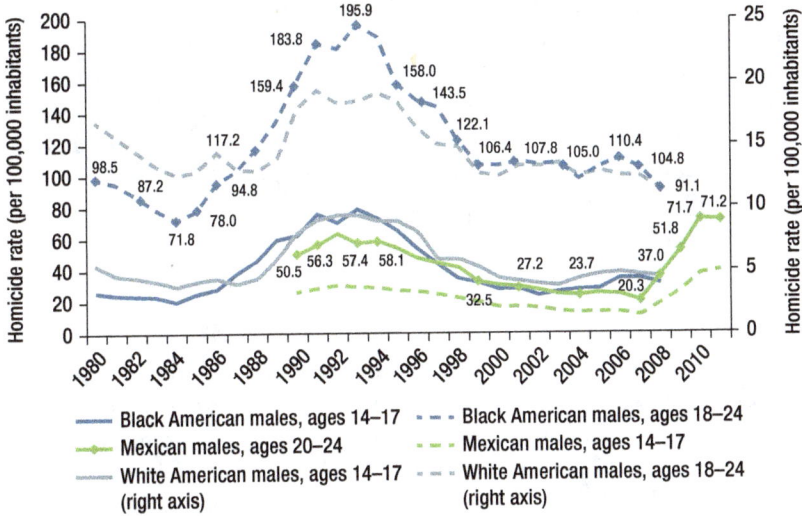

*Source:* World Bank calculations, based on INEGI data for Mexico and CDC data for the U.S. series.

What underlies the age-crime profile? Adolescence and early adulthood are critical stages not only from a socioeconomic point of view because of the transition from child to adult roles, but also because they represent a delicate phase in brain development.[17] As will be discussed later, developmental and biological effects are important factors related to crime and violence. However, their magnitudes are mediated by environmental factors, which may contribute to heightening or lowering the risk for a group of individuals who already exhibit intrinsic vulnerabilities. Is this all bad news? These developmental phases reveal significant plasticity of skills, brain functions, and susceptibility to peers and to environmental factors, which can be harnessed as promising margins for policy to exploit. Hence, there is room for optimism regarding the potential for effective policy.

*Chronic offenders: few individuals are responsible for a large share of crimes.* Studies of the evolution and trajectory of offending identify a specific subgroup of offenders, labeled chronic offenders, as being of particular interest for policy. Not only do their criminal careers exhibit significant longevity, because they do not desist from crimes after the peak years, but they are also responsible for a large fraction of total crimes committed. This fact points to another sense in which concentration appears to be a defining characteristic of crime: a number of studies conclude that, at any given stage in the life cycle (childhood, adolescence, adulthood, old age), a small fraction of the offenders—between 5 percent and 15 percent—is responsible for over 75 percent of crimes committed and of aggressive behaviors (Moffitt 1990; Tracy, Wolfgang, and Figlio 1990; Farrington and West 1993; Garrido and Morales 2007).

The distinction between chronic offenders and those who are transiting through adolescence and young adulthood (developmentally sensitive stages of life) has important implications for theory and research on the causes of crime and on resulting policy responses. For delinquents whose criminal involvement is confined to the adolescent years, the causal factors may be specific to that period of development. Theory must account for this discontinuity in their lives, and policy must target it. In contrast, for persons whose adolescent delinquency is merely one episode in a lifelong antisocial trajectory, a theory of antisocial behavior must identify causal factors beyond the environment and explain personality traits and brain functioning more intensely. Sanctions will also work differently on these two groups, as discussed below.

## Victims of crime and their perceptions

While official crime statistics can be linked to the characteristics of the municipalities in which crimes take place, no such link to information on victims is possible, such as income, age, perceptions about security, and subjective measures of social capital. This void is filled by making use of the two opinion surveys from the region, the Latin American Public Opinion Project (LAPOP) and Latinobarómetro. Each has its strengths and weaknesses, but both record victimization information about their respondents,[18] as well as demographics and opinions. These surveys provide the basis for studying the predictors of victimization, which can then be contrasted with predictors of respondents' concerns about crime in their country. The effects of crime on the health and well-being of its victims are also explored.

### Determinants of victimization

*Income is a risk factor for property crimes, but not for (nonlethal) violent crimes.* As discussed above, the sign of the relationship between income and the risk of falling victim to a crime (victimization) is theoretically ambiguous; wealthier individuals may attract more perpetrators due to their more elevated income (particularly for property crimes, since they represent higher expected payoffs for perpetrators), but their wealth also affords them the possibility of investing in greater protection from crime. The mechanisms at play appear to differ according to the type of crime. For property crimes, a steep income gradient in victimization is observed; individuals in the highest income quartile are one-third more likely to fall victim to property crimes than those in the lowest income quartile. For violent crime, however, there is no evidence of an income gradient. The gradient also appears to hold roughly across all ages (see figure O.9): for every age group, higher income is a risk factor for property crimes but not for violent crimes. Furthermore, the shape of the age-victimization profile for both types of crimes looks very similar across income levels.

*Reflecting the local nature of crime, the most effective crime-avoidance strategy appears to be to live in safer neighborhoods.* Even after controlling for income and education, living in safer neighborhoods lowers the likelihood of victimization by

## a. Incidence of property crimes

**Frequency (% of population)** — y-axis: 0, 2, 4, 6, 8, 10, 12

Age group (x-axis): 18–19, 20–24, 25–29, 30–34, 35–39, 40–44, 45–49, 50–54, 55–59, 60–64, 65–69, 70–74, 75+

- Crime victimization (bottom quartile)
- Crime victimization (top quartile)
- Age group for which the difference between the top and bottom quartiles is statistically insignificant (indistinct)

## b. Incidence of violent crimes

**Frequency (% of population)** — y-axis: 0, 2, 4, 6, 8, 10, 12

Age group (x-axis): 18–19, 20–24, 25–29, 30–34, 35–39, 40–44, 45–49, 50–54, 55–59, 60–64, 65–69, 70–74, 75+

- Crime victimization (bottom quartile)
- Crime victimization (top quartile)
- Age group for which the difference between the top and bottom quartiles is statistically insignificant (indistinct)

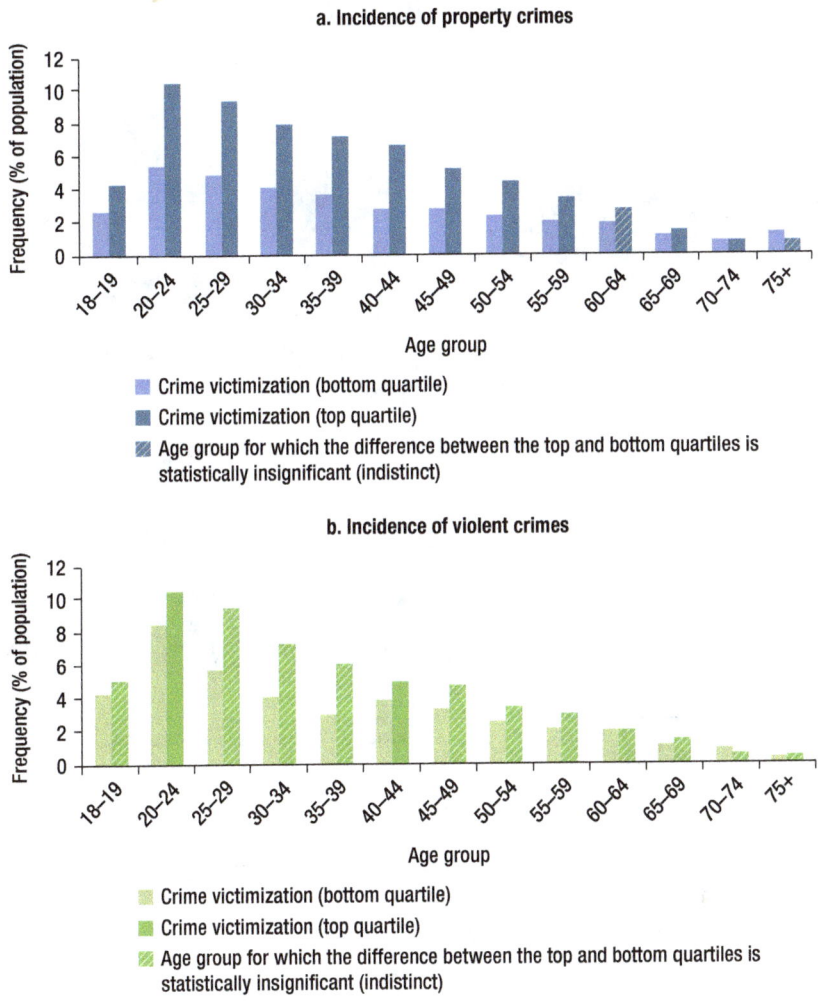

*Source:* Chioda 2014d, based on data from LAPOP 2012.

*Note:* The age 20–24 bars reflect a spike that is common to most Central American countries.

approximately 50 percent, compared to living in a neighborhood deemed "not safe" by the respondent. Of course, this crime avoidance strategy is more readily available to higher-income households. However, meaningful protection from victimization (of approximately 30 percent) can also be achieved by relocating to neighborhoods deemed "somewhat unsafe." These magnitudes provide additional evidence of the local nature of crime (see figure O.10).

**FIGURE O.10:** Marginal effects on victimization of income, education, age, neighborhood safety, social capital, and trust in institutions, LAC

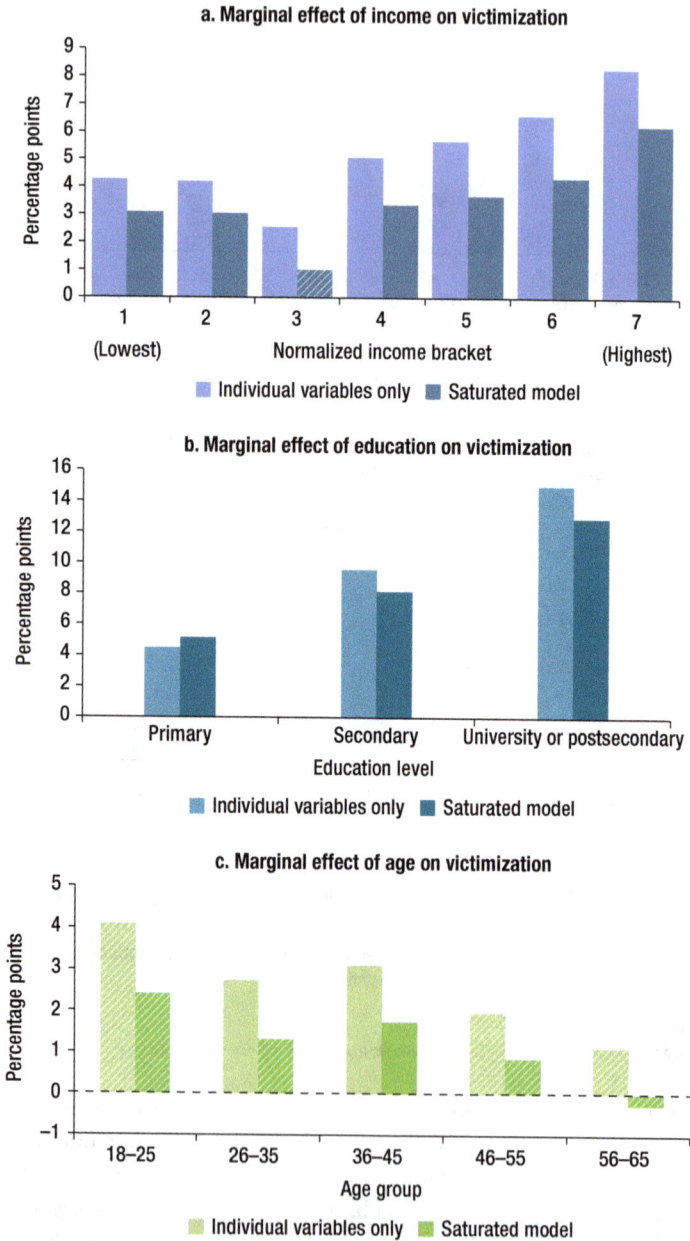

### a. Marginal effect of income on victimization

Legend: Individual variables only ▪ Saturated model

### b. Marginal effect of education on victimization

Legend: Individual variables only ▪ Saturated model

### c. Marginal effect of age on victimization

Legend: Individual variables only ▪ Saturated model

**FIGURE O.10:** Marginal effects on victimization of income, education, age, neighborhood safety, social capital, and trust in institutions, LAC *(continued)*

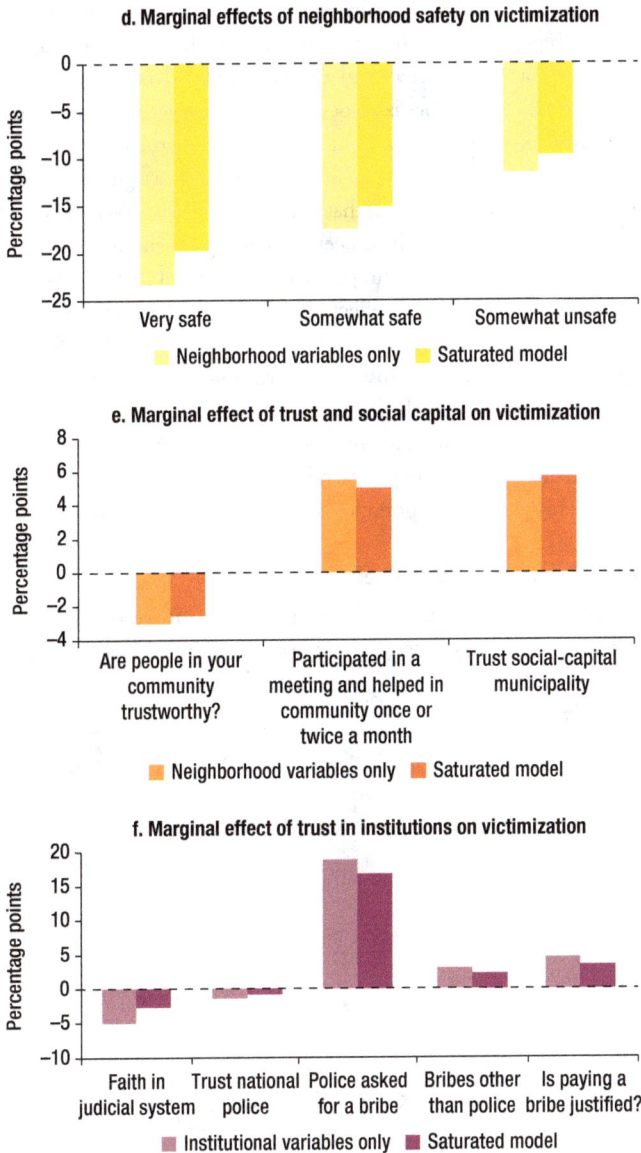

**d. Marginal effects of neighborhood safety on victimization**

**e. Marginal effect of trust and social capital on victimization**

**f. Marginal effect of trust in institutions on victimization**

*Source:* Chioda 2014d, based on LAPOP data.

*Note:* Regressions are weighted by population. Standard errors are clustered at the country level. Income brackets have been normalized for comparability across countries. Income increases by income bracket, with 1 being the lowest and 7 the highest income group. All coefficients are significant at conventional levels, except for the bars that have diagonal lines.

*Institutions matter. Police bribes are very important risk factors and reveal an inherent weakness of institutions in LAC.* The quality of and trust in the police and in the judicial system appear to matter for victimization, though their effects are relatively small in magnitude.[19] The most striking effects among institutional variables relates to respondents' reports about whether police ask for bribes, which directly relate to the police's willingness to detect and apprehend offenders (see figure O.11). All else equal, police soliciting bribes is associated with a staggering 16 percentage point increase (representing nearly a 50 percent increase) in the probability of experiencing some form of crime. The social acceptability of bribes is also a significant risk factor for victimization; respondents who report that paying bribes is justified are between 2 and 8 percentage points more likely to have been victimized, depending on the country. To put these magnitudes of the effect into perspective, the nocive effect of police corruption more than offsets the protective effect of sorting into safer neighborhoods.

Public perceptions of the incidence of public corruption and confidence in government in LAC have improved substantially over the past 15 years. However, measures of trust in the police and in the judicial systems have remained almost flat. As will be discussed in the last section of the overview, the certainty of sanctions (as proxied by the likelihood of apprehension) plays a critical role in deterring crime. The findings discussed above highlight the importance of institutions for crime control.

### Well-being and concern about crime

Having studied the determinants of victimization, it is instructive to consider the factors that underlie the subjective concerns about crime and their relation to victimization.

**FIGURE O.11:** Marginal effects on victimization of the variable "police asked for bribes"

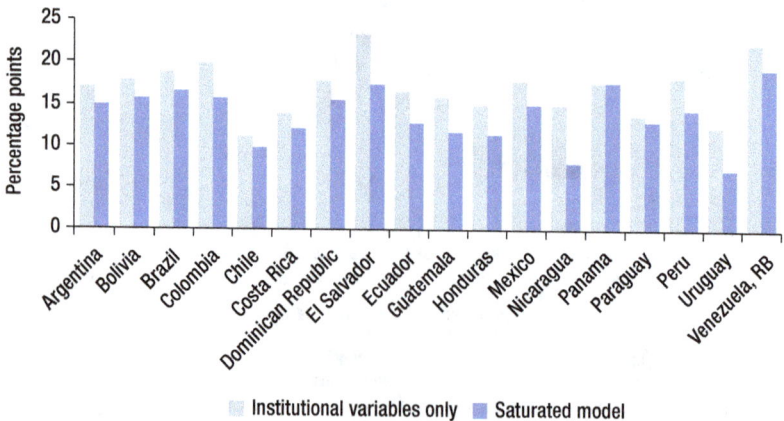

Legend: Institutional variables only ■ Saturated model

*Source:* Chioda 2014d, based on LAPOP 2014.

The psychological burden of crime is not trivial and is an important dimension of well-being. Being a victim of a crime in LAC reduces the likelihood of self-reported happiness (a proxy of well-being) by 3 percentage points, and by twice that amount in Central America.[20] An individual who never falls victim to crime may nevertheless feel a persistent sense of fear, insecurity, and stress in a context of elevated crime rates—a secondary consequence of crime that Bentham (1781) termed the "alarm effect."

*Concern about crime has increased over time, reflecting trends in homicides rather than victimization rates.* In LAC, over the past 15 years, the fraction of people indicating crime as a main concern has tripled to 30 percent. Concerns about crime have risen even as the trend in victimization[21] has declined (see figure O.12). Rather than following personal experience with crime, the rising concern more closely tracks trends in homicides (the most salient and extreme of crimes) over the latter half of the 2000s. A Benthamian "alarm effect" may be at play. A more detailed consideration of the determinants of victimization may thus provide insight into the negative correlation between victimization and concerns about crime.

*Subjective perceptions of insecurity are weakly related to objective determinants of victimization.* Income only marginally predicts concern about crime, whereas it is a strong predictor of (self-reported) victimization. Similarly, holding income constant, the effect of education on concern about crime is negative, whereas it is positively related to victimization: more educated respondents are more likely to fall victim to crime,[22] but are less likely to express concern about it.

**FIGURE O.12:** Trends in homicides, concerns about crime, and victimization, LAC, 1996–2013

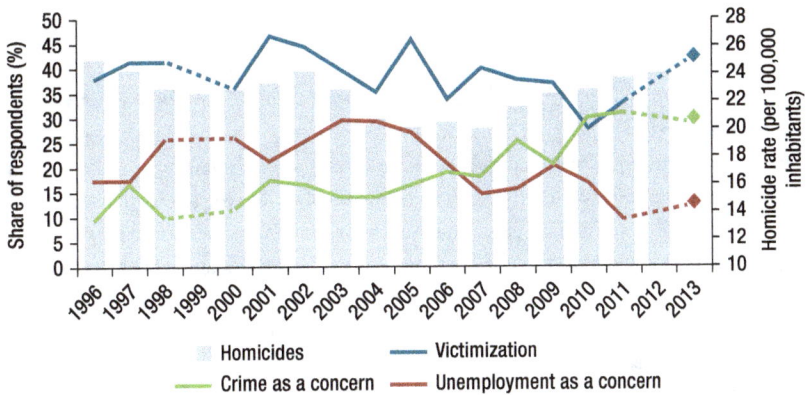

*Source:* World Bank calculations, based on data from Latinobarómetro and UNODC.
*Note:* Homicides, on the right axis, are expressed per 100,000 inhabitants. "Crime as a concern" and "victimization" correspond to the share of people who list crime and delinquency as one of their main concerns and who report being a victim or knowing someone in their family who has been a victim in the last 12 months, respectively.

Demographics are important determinants of concern about crime, though the patterns are also counterintuitive. Men worry less about crime, though they are at higher risk of being victims. Similarly, while the risk of victimization declines with age (overall), concern about crime increases with age, though with a mild gradient. This pattern may reflect the evolution of risk aversion: as individuals age, they typically become more averse to uncertainty and to losses. Likewise, marriage is a mild protective factor for victimization, but it is instead associated with an increased likelihood of expressing concern about crime. Being married may entail more concern about crime because of a lower tolerance for risk, but also because the safety of family members becomes more important: Relationships increase the risk and the concern that someone in one's extended circle will be victimized, thereby raising the psychological costs of crime.

*Neighborhood security strongly predicts both victimization and perceptions of insecurity.* Whereas a number of strong predictors of victimization are weakly related to concerns about crime or exhibit conflicting patterns, neighborhood security strongly predicts both victimization and concerns about security. Sorting into neighborhoods based on safety is a powerful protective strategy for reducing victimization rates and serves to align perceptions about crime and victimization. The safer the neighborhood or residence is, the lower is the psychological burden associated with crime. Living in what respondents perceive to be a "very safe" or "somewhat safe" neighborhood lowers concerns about insecurity by 21 percent and 15.7 percent, respectively, compared to respondents who declare that they live in an "unsafe" neighborhood. This crime avoidance strategy may not be available to resource-constrained households, placing a higher psychological burden of crime on lower-income individuals who care about safety.

*People who live in high-crime areas appear to "adapt" to the elevated criminality.* The weight individuals place on concerns about crime appears to depend more on changes in the incidence of crime than on its level, consistent with the literature on reference points and "adaptation." People who live in consistently high-crime areas appear to "adapt" to the elevated criminality, reporting less impact on their well-being than those living in low-crime areas who experience a sharp rise in violence.

*Worries about crime become more prominent as people perceive that their own or their country's economic circumstances are improving.* As noted earlier, objective measures of economic well-being (income brackets) are only mildly correlated with concerns about crime, while subjective assessments of well-being are highly correlated with concerns about crime, all else equal (including income, education, salary, and job satisfaction). In particular, the concern about crime increases along with the degree of satisfaction with one's economic circumstances, with those who are most satisfied being 30 percent more likely to express concern than those who are least satisfied. Qualitatively similar results are observed for people's perceptions about their country's economic outlook: the more optimistic people's expectations are about the country's economic future, the more they express concerns about crime and violence.

Why might satisfaction with personal or national economic circumstances be positively related to concerns about crime? This pattern is consistent with the hypothesis that security lies higher in the hierarchy of human concerns than economic or physical well-being. As economic circumstances are perceived to improve, material concerns become less important, and attention turns to security. Just as in Maslow's hierarchy of needs, concerns more proximal to an individual's situation (such as one's own economic situation) must be "met" before other concerns become salient. In particular, the significant economic gains experienced by LAC during the past decade may have contributed to the steep rise in the concern about crime over the same period.

## A meaningful parallel: Context matters, but important lessons can be drawn from developed countries

In discussing the evidence, the study frequently refers to and builds on studies from developed countries. The rationale is twofold and follows as a corollary from the stylized facts presented. While rigorous empirical evidence from LAC is developing, it is still in its infancy, and the study refers to it whenever possible. More importantly, the evidence from developed countries is relevant for several reasons. First, the study highlights the importance of biological, intergenerational, cognitive, and developmental stages of the brain and their relationship with antisocial behavior. Many of these mechanisms are invariant to context and are rooted in human nature.

Second, while aggregate levels of violence may be considerably lower in developed countries, certain subgroups of their populations are characterized by levels of violence that resemble those of LAC (see map O.4). New Orleans and Detroit are the 17th and 21st most violent cities in the world, respectively, with homicide rates well above 50 per 100,000, which puts them on par with some of the most violent cities in the region. In 2014, one of the most violent neighborhoods in Chicago, Englewood, was plagued by a homicide rate of 65.5 per 100,000, higher than that of Ciudad Juarez in Mexico (55.9 per 100,000 in 2013) and similar to that of Salvador, Brazil (65.6 per 100,000). Sadly, the murder rate among African Americans in the United States is significantly higher than the U.S. national average. In 2008, the homicide rate for young black men ages 18–24 was 91.1 per 100,000, compared to 37 per 100,000 for young men ages 20–24 in Mexico. Therefore, while the analogy between developed and developing countries appears stretched at the national level, it remains accurate for particular subgroups of the population, and for the at-risk population in particular. Third, certain stylized facts documented in this study—such as the age-crime profile of offending, the degree of geographic concentration of violence, and its persistence—are also common traits of the physiognomy of antisocial behavior in developed countries. Indeed, one of the contributions of the study is to formalize and document the stylized facts for the region and to establish appropriate parallels between LAC and developed countries.

With these parallels in mind, it is not unreasonable to consider prevention approaches with proven effectiveness in reducing crime among disadvantaged and

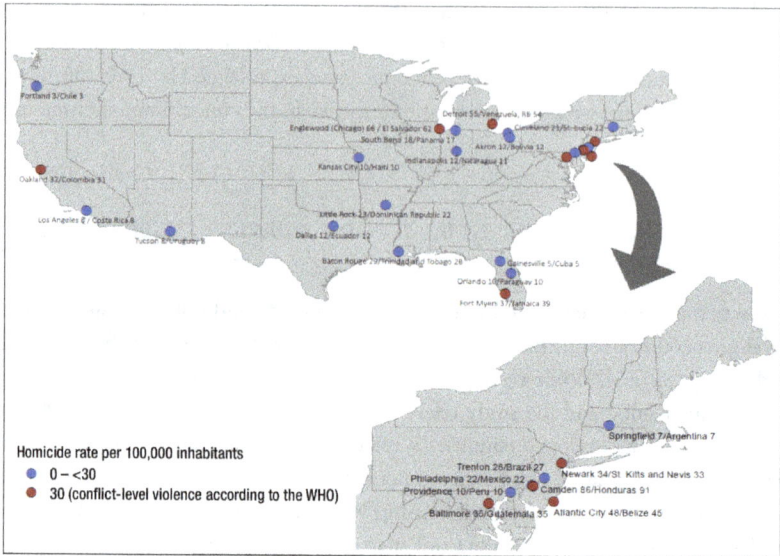

*Source:* World Bank calculations, based on data from UNODC and FBI.

at-risk youth in developed countries as being suggestive for policy in the LAC region. Of course, context and the capacity of institutions matter. For instance, Sherman and others (2005, 39) stress the importance of these factors in conditioning the effectiveness of community-based crime-prevention programs: *"In study after study, evidence emerges that crime-prevention programs are more likely to take root, and more likely to work, in communities that need them the least. Conversely, the evidence shows that communities with the greatest crime problems are also the hardest to reach through innovative program efforts."* This observation does not invalidate optimism about certain promising policy margins and interventions discussed herein. But it serves as a cautionary warning and highlights the role of institutions when implementing these policies.

## Never too early: Stopping the transmission of violence across generations

Research on crime and violence as well as antisocial behavior has traditionally focused on adolescents and adults, motivated in part by the age-crime profile, which identifies youth and young adults as being at particularly high risk. However, some recent studies have provided new insights on the development of physical aggression, taking advantage of longitudinal data that follow children over many years as they become adults. The peak frequency of physical aggression occurs in early childhood (between 24 and 42 months)—suggesting that, as children age, they learn ways to control their behavior and limit or avoid physical aggression. Children who fail to learn how to self-regulate and exhibit high levels of aggression and conduct problems in the primary school years are at higher risk of negative behavior in adolescence and adulthood.

Parents and families can therefore serve as entry points for policies tackling crime and violence, in their roles helping children self-regulate and "unlearn" violence. Moreover, the link between family and crime appears to run much deeper than a mere window of opportunity for parenting during these early stages.

Family history is a powerful predictor of serious criminal offending; it includes both a family's biological and social vulnerability to crime. A large body of evidence highlights how crime is concentrated not only in specific geographic areas, but also across families, and appears to be passed on from generation to generation.[23] "Crime runs in the family" has become a recurring stylized fact in criminology. Family background (in general) and parental criminality (in particular) are among the strongest predictors of an individual's criminality, stronger even than his or her income or employment status.

Indeed, research indicates that crime and violence have a biological basis, which involves both genetic factors and deficiencies in the (autonomic and central) nervous systems. A series of studies indicates that as much as 50 percent of differences in individuals' antisocial behavior can be explained by a combination of biological and prenatal conditions,[24] including genetic make-up, the environment *in utero*, and infant birth weight. Causes of aggression and violent behavior have been traced back to complications at the time of birth, and even to disruptions in fetal brain development during early stages of pregnancy.

The relevance of biological and prenatal factors does not imply that social factors are irrelevant. The latter account for the other 50 percent of the differences in individuals' antisocial behavior. Social mechanisms related to antisocial behavior during early stages of life include behavioral channels (role modeling, parenting styles); psychological channels (childhood traumas and abuse, family conflict); and biological channels occurring well after birth (head injuries, exposure to environmental toxins such as lead). The harmful effects of biological vulnerability related to poor endowments at birth are greatly augmented when they are coupled with social vulnerability, such as maternal rejection and child abuse.

The evidence discussed in the report establishes two key points in this regard. First, chronic disruptive behavior early in life tends to lead to frequent and often serious delinquency during adolescence and adulthood (McCord and others 2001; Piquero and others 2003). Second, family histories (biological factors) and parental behavior can greatly influence adult criminal behavior as early as during gestation. Once these early processes are identified, new pivotal margins for prevention become available. Taking family history and genetic factors as predetermined, one of the first entry points for crime prevention is the family and begins before an individual is conceived.

## Policies that work

*Perinatal home visitation programs.*[25] A combination of prenatal care and home visits by nurses or other trained experts to at-risk pregnant women and to at-risk households with very young children have been demonstrated to improve the behavioral outcomes of children, adolescents, and young adults. Children whose at-risk mothers received home nurse visitations for the two years following birth were less likely to run away from home, to get arrested (53 percent reduction), or be convicted (63 percent reduction), and to violate probation.[26]

It is informative from a policy perspective to consider the mechanism underlying these outcomes. The mediating factors can be classified into two broad categories: mothers' health-related outcomes and parenting styles. In the very short run, the prenatal phase of the program reduced fetal exposure to tobacco, improved the qualities of women's prenatal diets, and improved levels of informal social support, with positive implications for children's health at birth.

*Reducing or eliminating child abuse or neglect.* The program also appears to lower the rate of child injury, child abuse, and child neglect—key risk factors in the early onset of violence—and self-reported arrests (including for mothers). Maltreatment, in particular, is a major determinant of future criminal behavior.[27] These results suggest that, while not everyone who is abused becomes a criminal, maltreatment is a major determinant of future criminal behavior.

Effects of home visitation programs have been strongest among more vulnerable families, in keeping with other preventive interventions that have shown greater effects for children of families at greater social risk (defined by such factors as low socioeconomic status [SES], prenatal habits, family conflict, and low cognitive abilities).[28] This suggests that these kinds of services may have higher returns for families in greater need, highlighting the importance of well-targeted programs.

*Early childhood development programs.* The results linking criminal careers to early stages of life broaden the well-established observation that early childhood is a critical period for cognitive and psychosocial development. From a human capital perspective, investments during this period create the foundations for the evolution of cognitive and psychosocial skills that are central determinants of lifetime outcomes.

Long-term evaluations of early childhood development (ECD) interventions—that improve young children's thinking and reasoning abilities as well as skills such as memory, attention, and self-control and self-regulation—are scant. Even fewer are those that track their impacts on crime and violence for youth and young adults. However, the existing research discussed in this study points to ECD interventions as promising avenues to reduce early aggression as well as criminal behavior later in life.

The returns to well-designed and well-targeted ECD programs can dwarf their costs. For example, a detailed cost-benefit analysis that followed children for 40 years in one such program (the HighScope Perry Preschool Program in the United States, which targeted African-American preschool-age children with low intelligence quotient [IQ] and low SES) concludes that every dollar invested in the program repays taxpayers $12.90—and that the bulk of this return is accounted for by the reductions in male criminality (Belfield and others 2006). Similar results have been documented also in a developing country setting (see Gertler and others' 2014 study in Jamaica). However, it is worth cautioning that not all early interventions deliver declines in offending, suggesting that much more research is needed, particularly on the mechanisms through which different types of early interventions operate.

*Addressing personality traits that lead to crime and violence.* One of the salient (and perhaps surprising) conclusions that emerge from recent research on the mechanisms underlying the success of ECD programs reveals that not only are measures of IQ and academic performance malleable, but so are personality traits. Furthermore, changes in academic achievement and IQ do not necessarily predict longer-term antisocial behaviors; personality traits such as agreeableness and conscientiousness (which in turn regulate externalizing behaviors, a psychological construct that encompasses aggressive, antisocial, and rule-breaking behaviors) do. Biologically, all of these traits are regulated by a very specific area of the brain known as the prefrontal cortex, the locus of self-control and executive functions, which are key determinants of antisocial behavior, aggression, and criminal behavior.

Remarkably, personality traits appear to be amenable to policy interventions outside the typical window of opportunity (in childhood) identified for cognitive ability (Cunha and others 2006). Indeed, different traits might be more responsive to investments at different ages (Heckman, Stixrud, and Urzua 2006). In particular, as discussed later, self-control and executive functions can be influenced by suitable policy interventions in adolescence and young adulthood.

*Cost effectiveness.* A well-designed and well-run home visitation program would likely pay for itself, even using conservative estimates of the costs of crime. For example, the costs to society of crime induced by child maltreatment in the United States range between $6.4 billion (Lochner and Moretti 2004) and $55 billion per year (Cohen 2004). A nurse visitation program costs roughly $4,000 per child per year, implying that the cost for all births in the United States would be about $14 billion per year.[29] However, crime induced by maltreatment is only one of the many social costs of maltreatment. If society assigns some benefit to improving the lives of poor children (beyond the value attached to saving taxpayers money), then the cost-benefit analysis looks even more favorable (Currie and Tekin 2012).

For ECD programs, there are reasons to suspect that benefits may be higher in developing countries, where children typically live in homes where the environment is less stimulating than in developed countries, and where they may therefore enter ECD programs with lower levels of skills.[30]

Lastly, some interventions seem promising and cost-effective, even when for conservative measures of the cost of crime. A critical element for their success is the quality of delivery—specifically, the quality of the human capital of those who deliver the intervention, defined both in terms of specific knowledge and, more importantly, in terms of intangibles: the ability to connect and establish functional relationships with at-risk youth, parents, and children.

## Adolescence and young adulthood: A critical age for policy intervention

Adolescence and young adulthood are delicate phases of human development from a socioeconomic point of view because of the loosening of parental control, the increased pull of peers, and the transition from youth to adult roles, including from school to work. This is an especially difficult period to navigate for youth with low SES, who are at more elevated risk of leaving or dropping out of school.

These life stages are also critical periods in the development of three different regions of the brain, which are responsible for the regulation of automatic or instinctive reactions, risk-taking behavior, self-control, and reflective reasoning. During adolescence and young adulthood, the activity in the brain's reward system is heightened by the mere presence of peers (even in the absence of any interaction with them). Only adolescents and young adults exhibit this pull—precisely when they are spending an increasing amount of time with their peers. Evidence suggests that the pull of peers increases young people's risk-taking by enhancing the brain's sensitivity to the potential rewards of risky decisions. Taken together, these factors generate a perfect storm of vulnerability for this age group.

This set of vulnerabilities is reflected in the shape of the age-crime profile, discussed earlier. The pattern of rapid rise in crime among adolescents and young adults and of decline thereafter is stable across both developed and developing countries, across types of crime, and over time, and it applies to both perpetrators and victims. However, arrest and crime statistics reflect only a small fraction of deviance during these life stages, as made clear by research based on self-reports of antisocial behavior (Hood and Sparks 1970; Klein 1989; Elliott and others 1983). Actual rates of illegal behavior soar so high during teen years that participation in delinquency appears to be a normal part of adolescence.

Is this all bad news? The critical stages of brain development, which accompany young people's social and economic transitions to independence and adulthood, also reveal the plasticity of their skills and personality traits, and their susceptibility to peers and environmental factors—which can present opportunities for policy interventions. Research results challenge the notion that it may be too late to correct antisocial behavior during teen years and young adulthood, and favor optimism regarding the potential for effective policy during this period. Far from being "hardened," adolescents and young adults are a critical age group for policy intervention.

## School-based interventions

Education policies can significantly reduce property crime as well as violent crime. School-based interventions designed to alter behavior, thinking patterns, attitudes, and beliefs appear to be particularly successful.

*Time spent in school.* Research that carefully isolates the short-run effect of changes in school attendance uniformly finds that additional time in school reduces serious juvenile property crime (between 14 percent and 28 percent, depending on the study), confirming that when adolescents are not provided a structured or supervised environment, they are likely to engage in antisocial behavior. However, most studies also indicate that violent offenses among juveniles increase by roughly 28 percent on school days. The amount of interaction among youth plays an important role in determining the level of juvenile violence, highlighting the volatile nature of juvenile interactions.[31]

*Discouraging young people—especially those at high risk—from dropping out of high school.* Policies discouraging dropping out in the final years of secondary education generate the most sizable and persistent reductions in both violent and property crime for several years—and even decades—after school completion. Benefits also transmit to the next generation, thus turning a vicious circle into a virtuous one. Because crime rates are already quite low among high school graduates, policies that encourage young people to attend or complete postsecondary schooling are likely to yield much smaller social benefits in the form of crime reduction.

*Improving access to high-quality schools.* Not all schools are created equal. Evidence is emerging that attending a higher-quality school reduces contemporaneous crime. A promising message emerges from the heterogeneous effects of these two margins (quantity and quality): in both instances, the larger benefits are concentrated among the most at-risk youth, illustrating the malleability of behavior in the target population. Furthermore, the gains appear to be sustained throughout adulthood.

*A proviso: The concentration effect.* While discouraging young people, especially at-risk youth, from dropping out and encouraging them to stay in school for longer periods of time have been shown to reduce crime committed outside schools. These policies, however, can also have unintended consequences. Specifically, they can push criminal activity and delinquency back into schools. Bringing together hundreds of adolescents for the day concentrates opportunities for social interactions, including criminal or violent ones. In the short run, these effects are not trivial and may appear disappointing at first glance. However, these findings offer guidance as to how to design policies to accompany interventions that alter schooling decisions. For instance, academic curricula might be complemented with behavioral features that target self-control and aggression, including programs to curb bullying and violence in school.

Long-run cost-benefit analyses of policies that delay dropping out show that the short-run costs associated with concentration effects are more than compensated by the long-run declines in lifetime involvement in criminal offending. For the United States, the social benefit from the decline in murders caused by a 1 percent increase in the male high school graduation rate is conservatively estimated at $1.1 billion (Lochner and Moretti 2004).

*Behavioral interventions.* Behavioral interventions that focus on personality traits, social skills, and decision making related to "automatic" responses to triggers of perceived aggression can be surprisingly effective at addressing antisocial behavior, including violent crime. Effective interventions focus on improving self-control and decision making.[32] Even small-dose interventions (lasting three to five months) targeting at-risk youth can have large effects, pointing again to the malleability of personality traits during adolescence and young adulthood, and their role in shaping offending.

## Complementary interventions

*Improving nutrition, treating mental health, and promoting mindfulness.* Provocative evidence is emerging about interventions that aim to reduce criminality and aggression by directly altering the brain structures that regulate behavior and impulsiveness.

Three channels—nutrition, mental health treatments, and mindfulness—have delivered surprisingly promising and lasting results. This evidence provides a basis for the case that health policies should be included in the policy maker's toolkit to prevent and "treat" crime, violence, and aggression.

- Among nutrition interventions, enriching diets with essential fatty acids (EFA—typically found in fish oil) has been shown to be effective in attenuating aggression in a number of contexts, ranging from early interventions in developing countries to incarcerated youth (Mann 1999; Hamazaki and Hamazaki 2008; Gesch and others 2002; Buydens-Branchey, Branchey, and Hibbeln 2008). Essential fatty acids help remediate deficiencies in brain chemistry and serotonin, in particular, which is in turn related to impulsive behavior.

- An increasing number of studies points to the effectiveness of drugs in treating aggression across a wide range of psychiatric conditions in childhood and adolescence (Pappadopulos and others 2006). These are not limited to attention deficit hyperactivity disorder (ADHD), but also include bipolar disorder, schizophrenia, and chronic cognitive deficiencies. Surprisingly, certain medications are effective in directly treating children and youth who primarily exhibit antisocial behavior, rather than having been diagnosed with a psychosis and other mental conditions (Lichtenstein and others 2012; Dalsgaard, Nielsen, and Simonsen 2014).

- Evidence is mounting on the efficacy of mindfulness meditation in improving brain functioning. The benefits are not merely psychological (in the form of improved well-being, reduced stress, etc.) but are physical and translate into alterations in the structure of the brain. These changes affect regions of the brain that regulate antisocial behavior and violence. Improvements in behavior, hostility, and other outcomes have been documented in both prison and school settings (Hölzel and others 2011; Himelstein 2011).

### Additional remarks

*Behavioral and educational interventions should be thought of not as substitutes, but as complements.* Most studies of the impact of education on criminal behavior find at best marginal improvements in test scores, suggesting that education policy need not raise academic achievement to reduce crime. This conclusion is consistent with the findings of the early interventions section and further highlights the importance of personality traits and self-control, in particular, in explaining antisocial behavior. The efficacy of behavioral interventions and insights from brain development research directly corroborate this point. Traditional education policy and behavioral interventions should be thought of as complementary, thus expanding the menu of policy options.

*Schools represent a unique targeting opportunity.* As discussed in the section on stylized facts, crime is highly concentrated, with between 5 and 15 percent of individuals being responsible for 75 percent of crime. School-based interventions provide a unique opportunity to reach chronic offenders. After the mandatory schooling requirements are met and students are no longer in school, targeting this group becomes very difficult to reach with demand-side interventions. These typically attract lower-risk individuals. This observation further helps explain the large effects of policies discouraging or delaying interruptions of school careers.

## The link between poverty and crime and violence

One of the unintended costs of poverty can be crime and violence. Many channels link poverty and crime and violence, and can be addressed through various policy approaches. In particular, in light of the costs to taxpayers of incarceration, shifting resources from the penal system to social programs aimed at reducing poverty and disadvantage would represent a more cost-effective (preventative) strategy to controlling crime and violence.

*Complex links.* Income, or the lack of it—and in particular the adequacy of disposable income—influences individual and family behavior, investments in children, and social networks. Lack of income may operate on crime and violence through a direct income effect; robbery, for instance, makes desired goods attainable. Increases in income may also increase consumption of criminogenic goods like alcohol and drugs.

For low-income families, if parents are actively engaged in the labor market, then there may be little time for parental supervision and investments. Conversely, additional income may lead to higher quantities and quality of parental investments in children. More generally, recent evidence supports the notion that poverty, as a condition of scarcity, increases stress and impedes decision making. It forces people into a kind of cognitive tunnel that, on the one hand, makes them less aware of cognitive biases in making economic decisions and, on the other, imposes a significant "cognitive tax"[33] that limits the individuals' ability to perform well. It may deplete the self-control and cognitive ability of the poor and even influence antisocial behavior. Finally, while additional resources render more affordable changes in routines and investments that lower certain types of victimization, they may also entail higher returns to crime and more leisure time spent outside the home, thereby increasing the likelihood of victimization. The relative importance of risk versus protective factors associated with income cannot be established theoretically; the impact of income on crime and violence is ultimately an empirical matter.

The evidence from both developing and developed countries points to a causal relationship between income and crime and violence.[34] In particular, additional income targeting low-income segments of the population has been shown to lead to sizable reductions in

- Criminal activity, the benefits being heavily concentrated among male youth[35]
- The number of adolescent male arrests, including arrests in connection to violent crime[36]

In particular, recent studies have found that conditional cash transfer programs (CCTs) have had the positive yet unintended consequence of reducing crime and violence. In Brazil, CCTs led to important declines in violent and drug-related crimes, in addition to robberies (Chioda, De Mello, and Soares 2015). In Colombia, property crime declined significantly on the days immediately after beneficiaries received their transfer payments (Camacho and Mejia 2013).[37] Blattman, Jamison, and Sheridan (2015) also highlight the importance of income in shaping antisocial behavior. The authors randomized grants in combination with behavioral therapy targeting executive functions to criminally engaged Liberian men. Cash alone and therapy alone dramatically reduced crime and violence, but the effects dissipated within one year. More persistent crime reduction (50 percent after one year) was observed when cash and therapy were combined, speaking to the importance of both the resources and soft skills channels.

### Evidence points to two sets of mediating factors

In influencing crime and violence, two main channels are at work, with particular nuances for LAC:

- *The resource channel.* Additional income may improve the ability of households to devote sufficient resources to children's development in the form of goods and time (improving the quantity of parenting). Pure income effects on crime matter more for developing countries, reflecting the inability of families to achieve the desired degree of consumption smoothing—likely the result of credit constraints. Consistent with this observation, the resource channel has been found to be more prominent in LAC than in developed countries, reflecting higher levels of poverty and the greater prevalence of credit constraints (Fiszbein and Schady 2009; Bobonis 2009; Macours, Schady, and Vakis 2008).

- *The family process channel.* Additional resources can improve the psychological well-being and mental health of parents, resulting in a higher quality of parenting. Across developing and developed countries, the family process channel for parents emerges as a vital mechanism in shaping children's outcomes, particularly behavioral outcomes such as aggression and bullying tendencies (Yeung, Linver, and Brooks-Gunn 2002; Ozer and others 2010, 2011).

The effects operating through the family process channel are frequently much larger than those operating through the resource channel.

*Unintended consequences.* One of the channels through which additional household income affects violent criminal behavior of youth and adolescents is through increased parental supervision—made possible by a reduction in the time that parents (typically the mother) allocate to work outside the household.

Cautionary lessons emerge from research identifying the impacts of additional household resources in the form of welfare programs that are conditional on employment. While additional income is unambiguously welfare-enhancing, all else equal, additional resources that are conditional on work generate a tradeoff between the additional income provided by the transfers and the reduction in the quantity and quality of time parents can devote to parenting and investments in their children. The unintended consequences take the form of adverse effects on children in the household, who exhibit more behavioral problems and criminality. The observed negative effects are especially large for adolescents.

The relationship between income, parental labor force participation, and children's outcomes is of great importance in the design of policies that focus on the transition from welfare to work and out of poverty. These considerations are particularly relevant for single mothers, who are at elevated risk of stress given their status as the sole income earner and parent in the household, and highlight the need to consider policies more comprehensively and to foresee their possible unintended consequences.

## The expanded menu of policies

When considering policies related to income and poverty and their possible effects on crime and violence, the entry point for policy is no longer limited to the family and school, but extends to communities (defined as geographic units or groups of individuals who may be targeted by a social program). Unlike early interventions that target young children and youth who are in or leaving school, the focus is now on individuals who, as earners, expand their "sphere" of interaction to include not only family members and peers but also local labor markets, coworkers, and the welfare system, among others.

## Does crime respond to features of labor market incentives?

Legal labor income is ascribed an important theoretical role in its relationship with antisocial behavior. Participation in the labor force generates "incapacitation" (that is, it crowds out the time that could otherwise be used in criminal activities) and traditional income (the latter is discussed in the previous section) among those employed. In addition, labor force participation builds social networks, strengthens social identity, and forges bonds with the community that act as protective factors against offending. However, there may also be crime and violence costs associated with labor force participation. For parents, these include important tradeoffs between employment and the quantity and quality of parental supervision; for youth, especially those at risk, employment may interfere with investments in education.

The multiplicity of theoretical links between employment and antisocial behavior has generated a rich body of economic and criminological research. Various studies have found that individuals at the margin of offending, particularly those with low skills, are responsive to certain incentives in the labor market, notably unemployment, quality of employment opportunities (including formal jobs), and wages. Thus crime prevention can include well-targeted labor market policies.

*Employment and unemployment.* Crime and violence are largely unrelated to the overall unemployment rate for the entire workforce. Aggregate unemployment is arguably too coarse a measure of labor market conditions since it aggregates across individuals with heterogeneous skills and different likelihoods of criminal offending. Instead, crime and violence are responsive to the unemployment rate of the segments of the population at higher risk of offending: youth and low-skilled workers. Hence, *focusing solely on unemployment misses the important point that crime and work may coexist.* Large proportions of offenders in the United States are employed at the time of the crime (Grogger 1998; Fagan and Freeman 1999). Similarly, in Mexico, perpetrators are employed at significantly higher rates than the general population, irrespective of their age and the type of crime they have committed.

Criminals do not appear to make "all-or-nothing" decisions to perpetrate. They remain attached to the labor market as they engage in criminal acts, challenging the view that any form of employment is a protective factor against crime and violence. The interaction between legal and illegal work is fluid and complex.

Why? In the face of low wages, individuals may choose to reduce their work efforts to devote more time or effort, or both, to crime, especially in contexts where the returns to illegal labor may be significant. This type of response to labor market incentives will not be captured by movements in labor force participation.

*Wages.* Thus, studying how the relevant wages of those at risk of offending related to illegal behavior may be a more appropriate avenue to reconcile how offending and employment coexist, and it offers two important insights.

First, market wages in the low-skilled segment of the labor market are powerful determinants of criminal behavior, including violent crimes. They can tip work choices toward legal or illegal activities—especially in contexts where the expected returns in the illegal markets may be high. Indeed, the elasticity of offending with respect to wages in low-skill jobs exceeds that with respect to the rate of unemployment of low-skilled workers.

Second, this line of research provides strong support for the hypothesis that work and illegal activities should not be thought of as mutually exclusive; rather, individuals "double up" by combining legal and illegal work in an overall strategy to earn higher incomes (see Grogger 1998; Fagan and Freeman 1999).

*Not all employment is created equal in terms of its "protective" benefits.* Studies in both the United States and LAC have found that the quality of employment opportunities matters for crime and is particularly relevant for male youth.[38] Higher-quality employment opportunities for young adults that ensure stability, formality, wage growth, and opportunities for advancement and skill formation have strong protective properties against crime and violence, especially in a context in which young adults may be tempted to or actually supplement legal employment with criminal activity.

*By contrast, early and low-quality employment can be a risk factor.* Adolescents and young adults who start their work lives early—working long hours at low-skill, low-paying informal jobs alongside "bad" peers (who may have low education and skill sets, and are potentially already involved in illegal activities)—are at particularly high risk of dropping out of school permanently, or of moving into crime, or both. Early intensive attachment to the labor market may thus have counterproductive consequences because the opportunities available to adolescents tend to be of low quality.

## Can policy improve the labor market opportunities of individuals at the margin of offending?

One implication of these observations is that policy could attempt to address criminality that results from the low-skill/limited prospects employment equilibrium with well-targeted training programs that build human capital, improve skills, and raise stakes in the labor force.

Various studies offer insights as to where to focus such training. Demand-side programs alone that stimulate demand for the labor of at-risk individuals have often been shown to be ineffective (Bushway and Reuter 2002).[39] This conclusion is consistent with the results discussed above. In particular, demand-side programs stimulate demand for at-risk individuals' preexisting sets of skills, rather than improving soft and vocational skills that can lead to higher-quality employment opportunities.

Supply-side interventions that develop participants' skills fare better. But there are some limitations.

- Transitional employment programs for ex-offenders are frequently found to be unproductive in terms of reducing recidivism (that is, reducing the risk that the ex-offender would relapse into criminal behavior), although there is some evidence as to their effectiveness among older and higher IQ ex-offenders, who are on average at lower risk of re-offending and, perhaps, more motivated to reintegrate into legal life and employment (Bushway and Reuter 2002; Bloom, Gardenhire-Crooks, and Mandsager 2009; Raphael 2010).

- Intensive skill training programs, directed at high-risk youth, show more consistent promise, particularly if the investment in participants' human capital is substantial (Schochet, Burghardt, and McConnell 2008; Raphael, 2010; Attanasio, Kugler and Meghir 2011; Card and others 2011). These programs, which typically last six to eight months, include an array of components, including technical and life skills/behavioral training, academic skills, and placement assistance, among others. However, larger and longer-term effects tend to be concentrated among older individuals who are at relatively lower risk.

- Encouraging results also emerge from short-term interventions that target at-risk youth in school and complement summer job opportunities with approaches, such as cognitive behavioral therapy, that effectively help them control behaviors that can lead to crime and violence.

In sum, while well-targeted training programs that build human capital, improve skills, and raise stakes in the labor force show promise, further research is needed on how to effectively design supply-side interventions that develop the skills that will have a a long-lasting impacts on at-risk (out-of-school) individuals. Complementing training with job opportunities could enhance the potential benefits of supply-side programs. However, the potential displacement of existing workers—who could also be at the margin of offending—remains an unresolved issue.

## The effect of neighborhood characteristics and social networks on crime and violence

Crime and violence are localized and persistent, as the introduction discussed. Thus it is important to understand how certain features of localities may encourage or deter crime. Two dimensions, in particular, have drawn the attention of researchers and policy makers:

- The social context, including such aspects as community pride, social cohesion, and sense of control. The social context (frequently determined by geographic proximity), networks of relationships, and community norms can influence behaviors that are social in nature, such as crime.

- Physical characteristics, including the quality (or lack of quality) of housing, infrastructure such as street lighting, and the presence/absence and condition of neighborhood amenities such as parks.

*Observational studies,* which relate individual behavior to neighborhood characteristics, attribute an important role to the social and physical aspects of neighborhoods, especially in explaining antisocial behavior, including crime, and risky behaviors, such as drug use, alcohol consumption, and truancy. However, interpreting changes in crime and violence as the result of changes in the social and physical characteristics of a neighborhood is inherently difficult because such changes could also be consistent with a variety of other explanations, including, for example, changes in the individual characteristics of the inhabitants of the neighborhood (Manski 1993).

*Experimental and quasi-experimental studies* deliver findings that may at first glance seem somewhat disappointing. Neither "better" neighborhoods alone (which have lower levels of poverty and higher degrees of social cohesion and control) nor improved physical characteristics alone (better housing, better lighting, less graffiti, and so on) may be sufficient to yield better outcomes in terms of preventing or reducing criminal and violent behavior. However, underlying these seemingly disappointing conclusions are some important lessons about the actual mechanisms at work in neighborhoods and social networks as they relate to crime and violence, with implications for improving policy; these lessons include:

- Relocating people to better neighborhoods (that is, neighborhoods with higher social cohesion and social control, and lower poverty) may yield important benefits—but mostly for adults and girls. Paradoxically, disadvantaged at-risk boys seem to fare better in poorer neighborhoods, where they commit fewer crimes and score better in emotional well-being.

- Physical characteristics of localities alone do not appear to be sufficient to deter crime. The reality is more complex. The state of the physical environment acts as a marker for a set of intangible community characteristics, including social cohesion and a higher likelihood of reporting crime, that in turn serve to deter crime and violence.

These insights are important for policy since interventions at the neighborhood and community levels, including many popular ones, do not always work as expected. Better understanding of these aspects, and their interrelationships, will lead to better policy interventions.

## Neighborhood effects

Some of the most rigorous evidence is provided by a series of studies on the Moving to Opportunity (MTO) for Fair Housing Demonstration in the United States in the 1990s.[40] MTO randomly relocated groups of low-income families into neighborhoods with very different characteristics, such as higher levels of social cohesion and control, police responsiveness, and lower poverty.

*Short-term effects were encouraging.* Delinquency among youth declined. Violent crime arrests fell for young males and females, and female arrest rates were lower also for other types of crimes (Kling, Ludwig, and Katz 2005). However, benefits disappeared several years after the program was implemented, when most children in beneficiary households were adolescents. In particular, the effects for male and female youth diverged; while the protective effects persisted for females, the incidence of arrests for property crime increased among males.[41] Female youths also reported engaging in fewer risky behaviors such as consuming alcohol or marijuana, as well as a higher likelihood of being enrolled in school. In contrast, not only did males engage in more criminal acts, but they also adopted more risky behaviors.

The striking gender differences in youth outcomes appear to be explained by differences in behavior and daily routines,[42] but also in the way in which boys and girls were viewed and treated in their new neighborhoods (Kling, Ludwig, and Katz 2005; Clampet-Lundquist and others 2011; and Kessler and others 2014). Girls had better baseline interpersonal skills and could more readily acclimate to the new neighborhood, where they were also viewed more favorably. As Kessler summed it up, "When the boys came into the new neighborhood, they were coded as these juvenile delinquents. Whereas the girls [were] embraced by the community—'You poor little disadvantaged thing, let me help you'" (Sloat 2014).

These findings may seem disappointing at first glance. However, the improvements in neighborhood characteristics had important effects on the mental health and well-being of residents, though these benefits were not universally shared. Adults and girls significantly benefited from improved neighborhoods. The magnitude of the improvement in girls' mental health was roughly equal in size to that of the depression that results from sexual assault among young women, only of opposite sign. By contrast, the well-being of boys declined; the incidence of post-traumatic stress disorder (PTSD) increased among boys who were relocated from low-quality neighborhoods to levels comparable to those found among veterans of war. The paradox of disadvantaged boys faring worse in terms of criminal involvement and mental health has also been documented in other contexts. It highlights the roles of alienation, neighborhood segmentation, and local inequality, more generally, in shaping problem behaviors.

### Broken windows, disorder, and cues from the environment

In an influential article in the *Atlantic Monthly*, Wilson and Kelling (1982) posited that addressing minor disorders could help reduce more serious crime. They argued that potential criminals take cues from their environment and adjust their behavior based on what they observe; thus broken windows or other forms of neighborhood disorder are symbols of unaccountability and signal that transgressions will not be punished.

In spite of its popularity, there is very limited evidence supporting this theory (see the next section on deterrence for a discussion of "broken-windows policing").

*Small stakes experiments.* Experiments in which the orderliness of public spaces is manipulated (through changes in relatively small features, such as graffiti or illegal parking) are at best suggestive of a link between the physical environment and antisocial behavior. Keizer, Lindenberg, and Steg (2008) show that if people see one norm or rule being violated (such as graffiti or a vehicle parked illegally), they are more likely to violate other minor norms, such as littering or stealing an unattended 5-euro bill left outside a graffiti-covered mailbox. However, because the experiments' stakes are relatively small (both their returns and the costs of being caught are low), it is difficult to generalize to higher-stakes environments; that is, it is difficult to determine whether misconduct would spread to higher-payoff crimes for which the consequences in terms of penalties are more severe.

*Larger-scale interventions.* Some support for the broken-windows hypothesis is found in certain observational studies of larger-scale interventions. For example, an urban upgrading project in poor neighborhoods of Kingston, Jamaica, added street lighting and removed fencing, with some reductions in crime (Guerra and others 2012). Nonetheless, the observed reduction in crime could be also explained by factors unrelated to urban upgrading—for instance, increased traffic on the street during the cleanup phase and employment of at-risk youth to remove the fences. Rigorous research on the causal impacts of physical disorder and of urban upgrading on crime has yet to replicate these tentative results of the Jamaica project, although this field is still in its infancy.[43]

*In situ upgrading (on-site improvements).* Compared to advanced economies, where large-scale interventions such as MTO have been undertaken, in situ interventions are more common in LAC. Rather than displace individuals and families, these interventions provide improved housing and neighborhood amenities for recipient households or neighborhoods, or both. Examples include urban upgrading schemes, which enhance or alter the attributes of existing neighborhoods. One of the first rigorous studies of the causal impact of *housing upgrading* on crime and the well-being of extremely poor households in LAC yields conclusions similar to those that emerge from the long-term evaluations of MTO (Galiani and others 2013). First, neither appears to reduce the incidence of crime and violence. Second, although both interventions had the objective of reducing the concentration of poverty or achieving other economic goals such as self-sufficiency, they were more successful in changing cognitive and physical elements of individuals' well-being (such as adult physical and mental health and subjective well-being). To quote Sampson (2012), these interventions "impacted what the residents cared most about, rather than what policy makers deemed most important."

*Street lightning.* Quasi-experimental studies in the United States and the United Kingdom deliver promising evidence on the deterrent effect of improved street lighting; crime fell between 7 and 20 percent (Welsh and Farrington 2008). Interestingly, the decline occurred during both the day and the night. None of the evaluations found that nighttime crime fell more than daytime crime. Deterrence does not appear to operate through greater visibility, which in turn might lead to higher detectability. Instead, the evidence is consistent with the theory that improved lighting boosts community pride and social cohesion and, to a certain extent, increases social control over what happens within the community. Improved lighting might be effective in deterring crime only under certain circumstances, although the exact confluence of circumstances remains unresolved and should be the subject of future research that must overcome methodological difficulties.

*Additional remarks.* At least in the short run, it is difficult to engineer a sense of community pride and social cohesion in support of lawful institutions simply by externally altering a low-income neighborhood's appearance and makeup. Community pride and social cohesion can be malleable and can be responsive to policy—as suggested by Medellín's urban, social, and educational transformation engineered during the latter half of the 2000s. Nonetheless the causal relations and interdependencies are complex, remain elusive, and require more study.

Policy makers should be cautious about the unintended consequences of certain relocation experiments. Recent studies show that, while they may have meaningful benefits for parents and girls, they can also lead to fragmented neighborhoods or segmentation of subgroups of the population, especially among disadvantaged boys (Kling, Ludwig, and Katz 2005). These results represent something of a conundrum for policy makers: How does one trade off the substantial welfare gains for girls and adults against the harm that results for boys? Are relocation efforts that aim to break up clusters of poverty ultimately detrimental? Answers may lie in future research that endeavors to understand the interactions between the individual, family, and neighborhood so as to guide policy regarding public housing, neighborhood upgrading, and relocation experiments. Regarding the latter, in all likelihood, thoughtful strategies are required to prepare young boys in the transition following relocation (such as providing case worker assistance or a mentor in the receiving community), and some preparation may be necessary in the receiving communities as well.

## Deterrence: The role of incentives in the justice system

What can the criminal justice and penal systems do to deter crime and violence more effectively? To what extent do criminals and potential criminals take into account the probability of being caught and the harshness of prison sentences before they commit criminal and violent acts? Can the criminal justice system be made more efficient in its ability to maximize deterrence by finding the optimal combination of two key policy parameters: the certainty of sanctions and the severity of sanctions? The available body of research offers provisional answers to these questions.

*Severity of sanctions: The length of prison sentences exhibits diminishing returns and may have unintended consequences*

Overall, the severity of sanctions has only a weak deterrent effect on criminal offending. Moreover, as sentences lengthen, the additional deterrence declines, and there are diminishing returns to longer sentences. In particular, when sentences are not commensurate with the gravity of the crime, the severity of offenses may escalate. Prominent examples include so-called "three strikes" laws that impose a zero marginal cost of gravity of crime after the second offense—the punishment for the third offense does not depend on its gravity. Such types of sanctions can lead criminals to commit more serious crimes—a form of moral hazard (Iyengar 2010).

Longer sentences and harsher prison conditions may have sizable unintended consequences, increasing the likelihood that ex-offenders will commit more crimes after they are released from jail. For prisons to deter reoffending, it is paramount to ensure that time served is productive in the sense that it improves offenders' education, pro-social and decision-making skills, self-control, and employability.

Further evidence on the potential unintended consequences of imprisonment on recidivism emerges from research that considers alternatives to status quo prison sentencing. Rigorous evidence on electronic monitoring (EM), for instance, is provided by the experiences of England and Wales (Marie 2013) and of Argentina (Di Tella and Schargrodsky 2013), with remarkably similar positive conclusions. Electronic monitoring[44] is more effective than incarceration in reducing recidivism, with an approximately 50 percent decline in recidivism in Argentina. This alternative sentencing strategy also generates large short-term savings to society: $18,460 per offender relative to imprisonment, or 2.4 times Argentina's average GDP per capita in 2009.

*Prison may do more harm than good for young offenders.* Adolescents and youth are not particularly responsive to the length of sanctions—including when facing much harsher penalties imposed at majority and by the legal definition of adulthood—either because young people are myopic or they underestimate sentence lengths (Hjalmarrson 2009; Lee and McCrary 2009; Guarín, Medina, and Tamayo 2013). Moreover, young offenders tend to build more criminal capital and expand their criminal networks in prison more than older offenders. These crime-inducing (crimogenic) effects are large, and have led some researchers to provocatively conclude that a better strategy would be to let youth "age out" of crime and do nothing to arrest or jail them.

*Certainty of sanctions (the likelihood of being caught): Some forms of policing work better than others*

*The size of the police force.* The second central policy parameter that affects the expected value of punishment is the probability (or the perception of the certainty) of punishment. This notion is intrinsically related to the probability of detection and, thus, to policing.

The certainty of sanctions has been found to have a larger deterrent effect than the severity of sentences. The likelihood of being caught depends on the size of the police force and the effectiveness of policing.

Most of the evidence on the effects on crime of the *size of the police force* comes from natural experiments and quasi-experimental studies. While results vary considerably, one consistent pattern does emerge: violent crime is systematically more responsive to the size of the police force than property crime.

Regarding the *effectiveness of policing*, the key message of rigorous studies is that some police deployment strategies work better than others. Some seem completely ineffective, such as rapid-response and broken-windows policing (see below). Others deliver sizable effects, such as hot-spots policing and problem-oriented policing. The latter strategies share a key element: the shift from reactive, incident-driven policing to a more proactive and preventive policing stance.

## Policing methods that work

*Hot-spots policing* builds on the observation that crime is highly concentrated—a few states, municipalities, and even street segments account for the majority of crimes. These are known as "hot spots." The appeal of focusing limited resources on a small number of high-crime areas is straightforward. If crime can be prevented in these hot spots, then sizable declines in crime can occur overall. Hot-spots policing has delivered noteworthy declines in crime and disorder (Braga 2008; Weisburd and others 2006). One of the main concerns regarding this strategy relates to possible displacement effects, whereby crime shifts to another area that is less heavily policed.

Whether crime is displaced depends on the nature of the crime and the extent to which the profitability of the particular crime is tied to specific geographic locales. For instance, drug markets and prostitution tend to be less mobile and harder to relocate. However, the channel through which hot-spots policing operates has not been formally established; it remains unclear as to whether it is incapacitation (due to arrest or imprisonment) of frequent offenders at hot spots or deterrence (through prevention).

*Problem-oriented policing* (POP) uses iterative approaches to identify, analyze, respond to, and evaluate the determinants of crime and disorder, and uses a wide array of (often nonstandard) approaches to reduce crime. POP is preventive in nature. It devises strategies to increase the likelihood of apprehension (which is a powerful deterrent) and to reduce criminal opportunities in ways that are tailored to the specific crime-related problems of a particular location or that involve a specific type of activity (such as altercations in schools). POP often engages various public agencies as well as the community and the private sector. POP has been shown to be effective against a wide array of crimes (Weisburd and Eck 2004; Braga and others 2001).

*Incapacitation vs. deterrence.* The preventive nature of both hot-spots policing and POP suggests the plausibility of the deterrence channel, rather than incapacitation. Indeed, reductions in crime do not appear to be achieved by increases in arrests and convictions.[45]

### Policing strategies that do not work

*Rapid-response policing*, whereby police are rapidly deployed to scenes after crimes have been committed, does not reduce crime (Nagin 2013). By design, it operates only through an incapacitation effect rather than deterrence.

*Broken-windows policing* strategies have been adopted in some form by many cities in the United Kingdom, Indonesia, the Netherlands, South Africa, and the United States since Wilson and Kelling published their influential article in 1982. In particular, laws related to minor misdemeanors have been aggressively enforced, and policing has been stepped up even for victimless crimes, such as panhandling. Surprisingly little consensus has emerged about the effectiveness of such policing strategies. The most methodologically careful studies provide little support for the hypotheses that underpin broken-windows policing.[46] Most importantly, the evidence suggests that alternative forms of law enforcement, such as those discussed above, are more cost-effective.

### Closing remarks

Overall, research suggests that potential offenders respond to incentives set by the criminal justice system (in the form of sentence lengths and certainty of sanctions). However, certain combinations of incentives may yield bigger reductions in crime, while others may even be counterproductive. For a given level of expected punishment, shorter-but-certain sentences appear to have the largest deterrent effect.

The evidence suggests that efforts to increase police resources as a crime-prevention strategy are incomplete without details as to how the resources will be employed. Furthermore, establishing whether these policing strategies operate through deterrence or incapacitation is critical for designing policies and understanding their social costs. If law enforcement is able to deter potential criminals, then the social cost of police-induced crime reductions is relatively low. If, instead, the effect of a heightened police presence is simply to increase the number of arrests and subsequent incarcerations, then it could be more efficient to allocate resources to a strategy that prevents crime (Owens 2013).

While there is cause for optimism regarding hot-spots and problem-oriented policing deployment strategies, their efficacy is likely to depend on the context. In particular, the evidence comes largely from developed countries. The crime-reducing effects of police plausibly depend heavily on the quality of and trust in local institutions, such as law enforcement and the criminal justice system, especially in contexts where trust in police may be compromised. As discussed in the section on stylized facts, victimization rates in LAC are significantly related to the degree of corruption and corruptibility of law enforcement.

## Final thoughts

*An expanded menu of policies.* The interventions discussed above and the mechanisms underlying their effectiveness provide reason for cautious optimism. They also highlight the complexity of the crime and violence phenomenon. Complexity notwithstanding, the available evidence makes it fairly clear that it is never too early nor too late for prevention policies. While long-term approaches to prevention may begin before birth, with successful results in adolescence and adulthood, effective policy interventions with shorter-term horizons are also available. Importantly and contrary to the popular belief that it is "impossible to fix a crooked tree," a wide range of crime-preventing interventions applied later in life have shown to be effective. This in part reflects the now better-understood fact that there is substantial plasticity in humans at older ages—including with respect to brain functioning critical to regulating risky behaviors, especially during adolescence and young adulthood—that allows greater margins for affecting behavior away from crime and violence through suitable interventions. At-risk individuals and offenders are responsive to incentives, including those set by labor markets and the criminal justice system. Policy designs that carefully identify and take into account incentive effects can therefore be exploited to discourage criminal acts. Furthermore, an improved understanding of brain function and physical and socioemotional development serves to expand the menu of available policy options, as evidence is mounting on the effectiveness of behavioral, nutritional, and even mindfulness interventions, all of which are known to affect the brain's structures and its chemistry as well as habits and self-control.

Equally important, recent research also sheds light on popular yet less promising avenues for prevention. "Get tough" approaches—which expose offenders and at-risk individuals, particularly adolescents and young adults, to strict discipline (for example, boot camps and youth transfer laws that allow juveniles to be tried and punished as adults in the courts of law) and attempt to shock them out of future crime—tend to command political and popular support, in part because they cater to the public's taste for law and order and discipline. Yet rigorous studies indicate that these interventions are largely ineffective and can even backfire (for instance, jail time for youth can intensify their incentives and wherewithal to engage in criminal behavior after jail),[47] indicating that merely imposing harsh discipline on young offenders or frightening them is unlikely to help them refrain from problem behavior. Better ways of turning around at-risk youth involve teaching them how to engage in positive behaviors by correcting maladaptive thinking patterns and behaviors rather than by punishing them for negative ones.

*Harnessing interdependencies.* As discussed, crime and violence exhibit substantial spillovers across time, space, individuals, and generations. The success of crime-prevention strategies thus may rest on their ability to exploit these temporal and spatial dependencies. More importantly, the deployment of policies that harness these interdependencies may lead to greater crime prevention than the sum of the individual policies would predict.[48] Developing a comprehensive response to violence then poses a practical challenge for governments, as it requires substantial coordination across ministries.

*Redesigning existing policies through the lens of crime prevention can be cost effective.* Comprehensive short- and long-run prevention strategies involve a wide array of interventions that target the different stages of the life cycle and the individual's different spheres of influence (for example, families, schools, neighborhoods), all of which requires high degrees of political will and coordination. This may seem a daunting task, particularly in the face of binding budget constraints. Where to begin? Does crime prevention imply abandoning existing policies? The evidence presented offers cause for some optimism.

First, certain findings highlight how a number of policies and interventions not specifically designed to prevent criminality have substantial crime-prevention benefits, such as early childhood development, mandatory education, and poverty-reduction programs. In other words, important crime-prevention features may already be embedded in existing social and educational programs; hence, important gains could be achieved by identifying, redesigning as needed, and suitably harnessing existing policies with a more deliberate crime- and violence-prevention purpose. For instance, vocational training could be directed specifically to at-risk youth and augmented to include socioemotional skills components targeting executive functions; the conditionality of CCTs could be extended to require completion of secondary school; and laws governing the minimum dropout age could be enforced more strictly, and urban upgrades and improvements to infrastructure could be implemented to foster social cohesion in communities and minimize marginalization of at-risk individuals.

Furthermore, most of the interventions discussed in the study are relatively inexpensive in absolute terms (that is, on a cost-per-participant basis), including intensive ones and those whose treatment programs are highly customized, such as multisystemic therapy. Perhaps more important, on the basis of crime prevention *alone*, their cost-effectiveness is extremely elevated, even for conservative estimates of the cost of crime. The obstacles to implementation of many of these interventions may lie in the human capital required to deliver them. This involves both specific knowledge and, possibly more important, intangibles such as the ability to connect and establish functional relationships with at-risk youth, parents, and children, so as to earn their trust and the de facto increase the take-up rate. For many of these programs, this may require that benefits accrue not only to program participants but to their children as well, such that the programs bear returns across generations.

*Beyond targeting: take-up is a key feature to ensure efficiency and effectiveness.* One of the most distinctive features of crime is its concentrated nature. Crime clusters geographically (in a few municipalities and street segments), over the life cycle (during adolescence and young adulthood), and across individuals (with chronic offenders accounting for a disproportionate share of crimes). Considerable reduction in crime cannot be achieved without targeting hot spots, youth, and chronic offenders. However, ensuring that those segments of the population in which crime "concentrates" benefit from promising interventions may not be as simple as it appears. With high-quality data, policy makers will know critical age groups and where at-risk individuals and offenders concentrate. Yet, most of the programs in question—vocational and behavioral training, early education, and even certain forms of urban upgrading—tend to be on-demand. That is, individuals voluntarily select into these programs by signing up for them. However, selection into the pool of beneficiaries is often inversely related to the likelihood of being at-risk; that is, participants tend to be more motivated, have relatively higher abilities, and have more concerned parents, and the like.

The inability to reach those at elevated risk of involvement in crime and antisocial behavior may severely weaken the crime-prevention potential of the interventions. As such, the take-up rate among the at-risk population should be viewed as an important intermediate policy outcome, which could determine both efficacy and efficiency of the crime- and violence-prevention strategy. Indeed, in the context of policies and programs for which the scope for self-selection is minimized, such as laws defining the minimum dropout age or efforts to increase school quality, the greatest benefits are typically concentrated among those most at risk.

*The role of institutions.* Finally, by design, this study does not focus on institutions. However, in a number of analyses specific to the region, indicators of the quality of institutions and of police corruption in particular emerged as powerful predictors of victimization rates. Furthermore, the effectiveness of school- and community-targeted policies relies heavily on the institutional capacity to deploy them, with the outcomes of community-based programs being particularly sensitive. As noted in Sherman's (1998) report to the U.S. Congress, the community context of crime prevention requires a critical mass of institutional support to deter criminal behavior informally. Without that critical mass, neither families, nor schools, nor labor markets, nor police, nor prisons can succeed at preventing crime. These observations highlight the central role played by institutions, law enforcement, and the justice system in building trust and social capital.

## Notes

[1] The safest country in Latin America and the Caribbean is Chile, with just 2.74 murders per 100,000 people in 2013. Only 10 countries in the region have homicide rates below 10. These are Chile, Cuba, Argentina, Suriname, Peru, Barbados, Uruguay, Dominica, Costa Rica, and Paraguay.

[2] Since 2000, the number of homicides in El Salvador per year has been above 30 per 100,000—five times the world average. It peaked at over 60 homicides per 100,000 before a truce was declared between *maras* (gangs) in March 2012. The truce has since unraveled, and homicides escalated again in 2014. Experts forecast that the country may surpass Honduras as the most violent country in the world.

[3] Drug-related crimes have gradually but persistently increased over the past decade, according to crime reports compiled by the United Nations Office on Drugs and Crime.

[4] A study by the U.S. Centers for Disease Control and Prevention (CDC), "Gang Homicides—Five U.S. Cities, 2003–2008," concludes that 90 percent of gang-related homicide incidents in the United States involve firearms, and that perpetrators are mostly young (CDC 2012).

[5] For instance, the study does not discuss secondary prevention programs that intervene when youths have been injured by gang violence, such as hospital emergency department interventions that might interrupt the retaliatory nature of gang violence and encourage youths to exit gangs.

[6] Throughout the study, "policy margins" or simply "margins" refer to opportunities for policy intervention.

[7] The World Bank sets the "moderate" poverty line at 4 purchasing-power-adjusted U.S. dollars per person per day.

[8] This relationship is studied with the help of a detailed dynamic panel data analysis based on a sample of 19 LAC countries over the past 15 years, focusing on predictors of year-to-year changes in homicide rates within a country (Chioda 2014a).

[9] In a rational Beckerian model of crime (Becker 1968), unemployment would lead to more crime by lowering its opportunity cost and increasing the attractiveness of illegal income. On the other hand, routine theory suggests that unemployment would, in the very short run, increase more home-based activities, so that the impact of unemployment on crime might be indeterminate in the short run.

[10] Perpetrators of all ages are employed at much higher rates (above 85 percent) than their counterparts in the general population (around 60 percent employed) and in the adult population (Chioda 2014c).

[11] This idea originates from evidence emerging from developed countries (see Grogger 1998; Fagan and Freeman 1999).

[12] For instance, trade agreements or improved infrastructure significantly increase the number of cross-border transactions, which mechanically lower the risk of detection if the proportion of inspected transactions does not remain constant.

[13] The state of Chihuahua occupies a strategically and logistically unique position in terms of U.S. ports of entry, and has experienced dramatic deteriorations in security.

[14] In contrast, over the same period, the state of Yucatan experienced a decline in homicides from 2.7 per 100,000 in 2000 to 1.8 in 2010. Variance across municipalities is likewise substantial. In Mexico, the closest 25 percent of municipalities to the U.S. border accounted for 58.6 percent of total homicides in 2010, while the furthest 25 percent accounted for only 8.4 percent.

[15] The lower magnitudes may in part be due to the much larger sizes of Brazilian states and the more geographically targeted nature of violence in Colombia.

[16] The most recent year available for which the U.S. Department of Justice reported figures disaggregated by age and race is 2008.

[17] In particular, this is a critical phase of development of the frontal cortex—the locus of executive functions—which regulates impulsivity, risk-taking behavior, delayed gratification, and self-control (Raine 2013).

[18] In this section victimization refers to both violent and property crimes. It is worth acknowledging that, among violent crimes, homicides remain rare events.

[19] Their effects all tend to be of the expected sign, with trust in the police and in the judicial system associated with 0.8 and 2.6 percentage points lower likelihood of victimization, respectively.

[20] These findings are consistent with the conclusions of Di Tella, MacCulloch, and Ñopo (2009).

[21] Victimization measured by LAPOP and LatinoBarometro refers to property and violent crimes.

[22] In the longitudinal analysis it is not possible to distinguish between violent and property crimes, the latter representing the larger share of crimes. In practice, higher-income individuals are more often targets of property crime.

[23] Studies from London and Pittsburgh have shown that over 60 percent of crimes were committed by members of fewer than 10 percent of families (Farrington and others 1996, 2001). In their study of Boston, Glueck and Glueck (1950) document that 66 percent of delinquent boys in Boston had a criminal father, compared to 32 percent of nondelinquents. A New Zealand cohort study documents that a family history of disorderly conduct, antisocial personality, and alcohol and drug abuse assessed in cohort members' parents and grandparents was a strong marker of antisocial behavior early in life and of persistent offending in adulthood (Moffitt 1990).

[24] More than 100 heritability studies of antisocial behavior indicate a range of heritability in antisocial behavior between 0 to 80 percent, with a modal value of 50 percent (Raine 2013), meaning that in the largest share of studies, 50 percent of the variation in antisocial and aggressive behavior is explained by genetic factors. Furthermore, large sample twin studies (Arsenault and others 2003; Moffit 2005; Viding and McCrory 2012) have shown that genetic influences are particularly strong for criminal careers that start at an early age and persist over the life cycle.

[25] The results detailed in the subsection pertain to the Elmira project (recently renamed Nurse Family Partnership, NFP). The results of its evaluation (Olds and others 1997, 1999) are particularly noteworthy and have been replicated in several contexts. NFP was awarded the rating of "model program" by the University of Colorado, Boulder's *Blueprints for Healthy Youth Development*. The *Blueprints* model programs are the highest-quality U.S. youth prevention interventions focusing on violence, delinquency, and drug prevention that have demonstrated effectiveness.

[26] Children of women in the group that received home visitations during pregnancy only also experienced declines in arrests, though these were less dramatic than those of the more comprehensive program.

[27] Currie and Tekin's (2012) estimates indicate that the effects of maltreatment are large relative to other factors that have been studied in the economics literature, such as unemployment (Corman and Mocan 2005), education (Jacob and Lefgren 2003), gun ownership (Mocan and Tekin 2006; Duggan 2001), the introduction of crack cocaine (Grogger and Willis 2000), the legalization of abortion (Donohue and Levitt 2001), and exposure to lead through paint or gasoline (Reyes 2007; Nevin 2007).

[28] This report documents a number of other interventions for which effect sizes are larger among more vulnerable participants. See the effects of the Brazilian conditional cash transfer (Chioda and others 2015) and of dwelling upgrades in Mexico and El Savador (Galiani and others 2013).

[29] Rather than weight the costs against some measure of the cost of crime, Raine (2013) considers *only* the benefits to society from the reductions in lifetime receipt of food stamps induced by the home visit program. With a total cost per birth of around $11,511 in 2006, the food stamps savings *alone* amount to roughly $12,300 per person.

[30] This conjecture finds support in the first study of the long-term effects of an ECD intervention in a low-income country setting, in Kingston, Jamaica (Gertler and others 2014).

[31] Jacob and Lefgren (2003) and Luallen (2006) observe daily changes in crime, such that their estimates are of contemporaneous effects of days in school. In contrast, Berthelon and Kruger (2011) can only measure crime at the annual level for the municipalities in their study, implying that their estimates are more medium-term in nature and, therefore, less comparable to those of Jacob and Lefgren (2003) and Luallen (2006).

[32] Effective behavioral interventions include cognitive behavioral therapy, functional family therapy, and life skills training.

[33] See Mullainathan and Shafir (2013) and, for a review, the *World Development Report 2015* (World Bank 2015).

[34] These findings are consistent with those discussed in the section on the physiognomy of crime and violence in LAC. In particular, proxies of poverty, such as the (contemporaneous) incidence of teen pregnancy and low educational attainment, are highly predictive of the level of violence, whereas GDP per capita appears to be unrelated, all else equal. Reconciling these results requires recalling that the relationship between GDP per capita and violence is highly nonlinear (such that the sign of the relationship depends on the level of per capita income). Furthermore, while GDP per capita measures the mean level of income, it fails to captures the degree of poverty. In turn, the above proxies express the same margin of poverty that is affected by exogenous changes in income studied in this section.

[35] See, for instance, Jacob and Ludwig (2010) and citations therein.

[36] In the United States, Akee and others (2010) and Jacob and Ludwig (2010) document 20 percent declines.

[37] Borraz and Munyo (2014) provide evidence from Uruguay that the criminal response to welfare payments may be sensitive to the method with which funds are delivered to CCT recipients. They show that the incidence of property crime increases when welfare payments take the form of cash (as opposed to a credit in a bank account, say).

[38] See Wadsworth (2006) for evidence in developed countries. In Mexico, Chioda (2014b) shows that the number of workers employed in the formal sector consistently predicts declines in the homicide rate. In Brazil, Chioda and Rojas-Alvarado (2014) show that not all employment is relevant to violence; only formal jobs for young men that have been created or destroyed are robustly related to homicides, while those for adults and women have no predictive power. Dix-Carneiro, Soares, and Ulyssea (2016) find that labor market conditions have a strong effect on homicide rates in Brazil. Exploiting the 1990s trade liberalization as a natural experiment, they document how regions facing more negative shocks experience larger relative increases in crime rates in the medium term.

[39] Demand-side programs aim to reduce the costs of employment borne by the employer through either wage supplements or subsidized bonds (insuring the employer against theft by the employee, who is an ex-offender or at-high risk of antisocial behavior). Among demand-side interventions are also community development programs, which lower costs for businesses locating in particularly needy communities.

[40] A subset of 4,600 low-income families with children living in high-poverty public housing projects were randomly offered housing vouchers to relocate into low-poverty areas.

[41] Interestingly, the effect on the total number of lifetime arrests was much larger than the effect on ever being arrested; offering vouchers yields much larger effects along the intensive margin of criminality (number of arrests) than along the extensive margin (any arrests at all).

[42] Clampet-Lundquist and others (2011) conclude that six factors likely contributed to the divergent experiences of young males and females: daily routines, fitting in with neighborhood norms, neighborhood-navigation strategies, interactions with neighborhood peers, delinquency among friends, and involvement with father figures. Females were significantly more likely to spend time in the neighborhoods of school and workplaces, and were typically indoors with friends or family, whereas boys more frequently spent their time outside or on the street. In particular, boys in the treatment arm were half as likely as control group males to describe a meaningful relationship with a close, caring male other than a biological father or to report that they had such a presence in their lives.

[43] For additional correlational evidence from the United States, see Sampson and Raudenbush (1999).

[44] U.S. electronic monitoring involves fitting offenders with electronic devices on the ankle or wrist that can be monitored remotely by correctional facilities that can verify whether the individual is violating a set of pre-established conditions.

[45] Nor does incidence of reported robberies and violent crimes decline in treatment areas.

[46] Indeed, Wilson conceded in a 2004 interview in the *New York Times* that the theory lacked substantive scientific evidence that it worked, adding: "I still to this day do not know if improving order will or will not reduce crime. People have not understood that this was a speculation" (Hurley 2004).

[47] Youth with conduct disorders are often angry and alienated, harboring feelings of resentment toward authority. "Get-tough" programs may fuel these emotions, boosting youth's propensity to rebel and to adopt nonconforming behavior. Some programs may inadvertently provide adolescents with role models for bad behavior.

[48] For instance, crime prevention in one municipality will induce declines in crime in the neighboring municipality, such that adopting a global strategy in both municipalities will yield greater prevention than the individual strategies in isolation. Similarly, as a result of intertemporal linkages and the persistence of crime over time, crimes averted in one year yield declines in offenses in subsequent years. Similarly, given the intergenerational linkages in criminality, preventing one individual from embarking on a criminal career tends to do the same for his/her offspring.

## References

Akee, Randall K. Q., William E. Copeland, Gordon Keeler, Adrian Angold, and E. Jane Costello. 2010. "Parent's Incomes and Children's Outcomes: A Quasi-Experiment with Casinos on American Indian Reservations." *American Economics Journal: Applied Economics* 2 (1): 86–115.

Arsenault, Louise, Terrie E. Moffitt, Avshalom Caspi, Alan Taylor, Fruhling V. Rijsdijk, Sara R. Jaffee, Jennifer C. Ablow, and Jeffrey R. Measelle. 2003. "Strong Genetic Effects on Cross-Situational Antisocial Behavior among Children according to Mothers, Teachers, Examiner-Observers, and Twins' Self-Reports." *Journal of Child Psychology and Psychiatry* 44 (6): 832–48.

Attanasio, Orazio, Adriana Kugler, and Costas Meghir. 2011. "Subsidizing Vocational Training for Disadvantaged Youth in Colombia: Evidence from a Randomized Trial." *American Economic Journal: Applied Economics* 3 (3): 188–220.

Becker, Gary S. 1968. "Crime and Punishment: An Economic Approach." *Journal of Political Economy* 76 (2): 169–217.

Belfield, Clive R., Milagros Nores, Steve Barnett, and Lawrence Schweinhart. 2006. "The High/Scope Perry Preschool Program: Cost-Benefit Analysis Using Data from the Age-40 Followup." *Journal of Human Resources* 41 (1): 162–90.

Bentham, Jeremy. 1781. *An Introduction to the Principles of Morals and Legislation.*

Berthelon, Matias, and Diana Kruger. 2011. "Risky Behavior among Youth: Incapacitation Effects of School on Adolescent Motherhood and Crime in Chile." *Journal of Public Economics* 95 (1–2): 41–53.

Blattman, Christopher, Julian C. Jamison, and Margaret Sheridan. 2015. "Reducing Crime and Violence: Experimental Evidence on Adult Noncognitive Investments in Liberia." NBER Working Paper 21204, National Bureau of Economic Research, Cambridge, MA.

Bloom, Dan, Alissa Gardenhire-Crooks, and Conrad Mandsager. 2009. "Reengaging High School Dropouts: Early Results of the National Guard Youth Challenge Program Evaluation." MDRC, New York.

Bobonis, Gustavo J. 2009. "Is the Allocation of Resources within the Household Efficient? New Evidence from a Randomized Experiment." *Journal of Political Economy* (University of Chicago Press) 117 (3): 453–503.

Borraz, F., and I. Munyo. 2014. "Conditional Cash Transfers and Crime: Higher Income but also Better Loot." Working Paper, Centro de Economia, Sociedad y Empresa, Montevideo University Business School.

Braga, Anthony A. 2008. "Police Enforcement Strategies to Prevent Crime in Hot Spot Areas." Crime Prevention Research Review 2, Office of Community Oriented Policing Services, U.S. Department of Justice, Washington, DC.

Braga, Anthony A., David M. Kennedy, Elin J. Waring, and Anne Morrison Piehl. 2001. "Problem-Oriented Policing, Deterrence, and Youth Violence: An Evaluation of Boston's Operation Ceasefire." *Journal of Research in Crime and Delinquency* 38 (3): 195–225.

Bronfenbrenner, Urie. 1979. *The Ecology of Human Development: Experiments by Nature and Design*. Cambridge, MA: Harvard University Press.

Brush, Jesse. 2007. "Does Income Inequality Lead to More Crime? A Comparison of Cross-Sectional and Time-Series Analyses of United States Counties." *Economics Letters* 96 (2): 264–68.

Bushway, Shawn. 2011. "Labor Markets and Crime." In *Crime and Public Policy*, edited by Joan Petersilia and James Q. Wilson. New York: Oxford University Press.

Bushway, Shawn, and Peter Reuter. 2002. "Labor Markets and Crime." In *Crime: Public Policies for Crime Control*, edited by James Wilson and Joan Petersilia, 191–224. San Francisco: ICS Press.

Buydens-Branchey, Laure, Marc Branchey, and Joseph R. Hibbeln. 2008. "Associations between Increases in Plasma N-3 Polyunsaturated Fatty Acids following Supplementation and Decreases in Anger and Anxiety in Substance Abusers." *Progress in Neuropsychopharmacology and Biological Psychiatry* 32 (2): 568–75.

Camacho, Adriana, and Daniel Mejía. 2013. "The Externalities of Conditional Cash Transfer Programs on Crime: The Case of Familias en Acción in Bogota." Working Paper, Universidad de los Andes.

Card, David, Pablo Ibarraran, Ferdinando Regalia, David Rosas, and Yuri Soares. 2011. "The Labor Market Impacts of Youth Training in the Dominican Republic: Evidence from a Randomized Evaluation." *Journal of Labor Economics* 29 (2): 267–300.

CDC (Centers for Disease Control and Prevention). 2012. "Gang Homicides: Five U.S. Cities, 2003–2008." *Morbidity and Mortality Weekly Report* 61 (3): 46–51.

Chioda, Laura. 2014a. "Violence in Latin America: Dynamic Panel Data Analysis." Working paper.

———. 2014b. "The Determinants of Violent vs. Property Crime in Mexico: A Dynamic Panel Data Approach." Working paper.

———. 2014c. "Offending and Labor Force Participation over the Life Cycle in Mexico." Working paper.

———. 2014d. "Victimization, Crime, and Safety Perceptions in LAC." Working paper.

Chioda, Laura, João M. P. De Mello, and Rodrigo R. Soares. 2015. "Spillovers from Conditional Cash Transfer Programs: Bolsa Família and Crime in Urban Brazil." *Economics of Education Review* 54 (October): 306–20.

Chioda, Laura, and L.D. Rojas-Alvarado. 2014. "Brazil Violence across Municipalities." Working paper.

Clampet-Lundquist, Susan, Kathryn Edin, Jeffrey R. Kling, and Greg J. Duncan. 2011. "Moving Teenagers Out of High-Risk Neighborhoods: How Girls Fare Better Than Boys." *American Journal of Sociology* 116 (4): 1154–89.

Cook, Philip, and Jens Ludwig. 2011. "Economical Crime Control." In *Controlling Crime: Strategies and Tradeoffs*, edited by Philip Cook, Jens Ludwig, and Justin McCrary, 1–39. Chicago: University of Chicago Press.

Corman, Hope, and Naci Mocan. 2005. "Carrots, Sticks, and Broken Windows." *Journal of Law and Economics* 48 (April): 235–66.

Cunha, Flavio, James J. Heckman, Lance J. Lochner, and Dimitriy V. Masterov. 2006. "Interpreting the Evidence on Life Cycle Skill Formation." In *Handbook of the Economics of Education*, vol. 1, edited by Eric A. Hanushek and Finis Welch, 697–812. Amsterdam: North-Holland.

Currie, Janet, and Erdal Tekin. 2012. "Understanding the Cycle: Childhood Maltreatment and Future Crime." *Journal of Human Resources* 47 (2): 509–49.

Dalsgaard, Søren, Helena Skyt Nielsen, and Marianne Simonsen. 2014. "Consequences of ADHD Medication Use for Children's Outcomes." Discussion Paper 8208, IZA.

Di Tella, Rafael, Robert MacCulloch, and Hugo Ñopo. 2009. "Happiness and Beliefs in Criminal Environments." Research Department Publication 4605, Inter-American Development Bank, Washington, DC.

Di Tella, Rafael, and Ernesto Schargrodsky. 2013. "Criminal Recidivism after Prison and Electronic Monitoring." *Journal of Political Economy* 121 (1): 28–73.

Dix-Carneiro, Rafael, Rodrigo R. Soares, and Gabriel Ulyssea. 2016. "Local Labor Market Conditions and Crime: Evidence from the Brazilian Trade Liberalization." Working paper.

Donohue, John J., and Steven D. Levitt. 2001. "The Impact of Legalized Abortion on Crime." *Quarterly Journal of Economics* 116 (2): 379–420.

Duggan, Mark. 2001. "More Guns, More Crime." *Journal of Political Economy* 109 (5).

Elliott, Delbert S., Suzanne S. Ageton, David Huizinga, Brian A. Knowles, and Rachelle J. Canter. 1983. *The Prevalence and Incidence of Delinquent Behavior: 1976–1980*. Boulder, CO: Behavioral Research Institute.

Fagan, Jeffrey, and Richard B. Freeman. 1999. "Crime and Work." *Crime and Justice* 25: 225–90.

Fajnzylber, Pablo, Daniel Lederman, and Norman Loayza. 2002a. "What Causes Violent Crime?" *European Economic Review* 46 (7): 1323–57.

———. 2002b. "Inequality and Violent Crime." *Journal of Law and Economics* 45 (1): 1–40.

Farrington, David P. 2003. "Developmental and Life-Course Criminology: Key Theoretical and Empirical Issues—The 2002 Sutherland Award Address." *Criminology* 41 (2): 221–56.

Farrington, D.P., R. Loeber, M. Stouthamer- Loeber, W. B. Van Kammen, and L. Schmidt. 1996. "Self-Reported Delinquency and a Combined Delinquency Scale Based on Boys, Mothers, and Teachers: Concurrent and Predictive Validity for African Americans and Caucasians." *Criminology* 34: 493–517.

Farrington, David P., Darrick Jolliffe, Rolf Loeber, Magda Stouthamer-Loeber, and Larry M. Kalb. 2001. "The Concentration of Offenders in Families, and Family Criminality in the Prediction of Boys' Delinquency." *Journal of Adolescence* 24 (5): 579–96.

Farrington, David P., and Donald J. West. 1993. "Criminal, Penal and Life Histories of Chronic Offenders: Risk and Protective Factors and Early Identification." *Criminal Behavior and Mental Health* 3 (4): 492–523.

Ferreira, Francisco H. G., Julian Messina, Jamele Rigolini, Luis-Felipe López-Calva, Maria Ana Lugo, and Renos Vakis. 2013. *Economic Mobility and the Rise of the Latin American Middle Class*. Washington, DC: World Bank.

Fiszbein, Ariel, and Norbert Schady. 2009. *Conditional Cash Transfers: Reducing Present and Future Poverty*. Washington, DC: World Bank.

Galiani, Sebastian, Paul Gertler, Ryan Cooper, Sebastian Martinez, Adam Ross, and Raimundo Undurraga. 2013. "Shelter from the Storm: Upgrading Housing Infrastructure in Latin American Slums." NBER Working Paper 19322, National Bureau of Economic Research, Cambridge, MA.

Garrido, Vincente, and Luz Anyela Morales. 2007. "Serious (Violent or Chronic) Juvenile Offenders: A Systematic Review of Treatment Effectiveness in Secure Corrections." *Campbell Systematic Review* 7, Campbell Collaboration Library.

Gertler, Paul, James Heckman, Rodrigo Pinto, Arianna Zanolini, Christel Vermeersch, Susan Walker, Susan M. Chang, and Sally Grantham-McGregor. 2014. "Labor Market Returns to an Early Childhood Stimulation Intervention in Jamaica." *Science* 344 (6187): 998–1001.

Gesch, C. Bernard, Sean M. Hammond, Sarah E. Hampson, Anita Eves, Martin J. Crowder. 2002. "Influence of Supplementary Vitamins, Minerals, and Essential Fatty Acids on the Antisocial Behaviour of Young Adult Prisoners: Randomised, Placebo-Controlled Trial." *British Journal of Psychiatry* 181 (July): 22–28.

Glueck, Sheldon, and Eleanor Glueck. 1950. *Unraveling Juvenile Delinquency*. New York: Commonwealth Fund.

Grogger, Jeffrey. 1998. "Market Wages and Youth Crime." *Journal of Labor Economics* 16 (4): 756–91.

Grogger, Jeffrey, and Michael Willis. 2000. "The Emergence of Crack Cocaine and the Rise in Urban Crime Rates." *Review of Economics and Statistics* 82 (4): 519–29.

Guarín, Arlen, Carlos Medina, and Jorge Tamayo. 2013. "The Effects of Punishment of Crime in Colombia on Deterrence, Incapacitation, and Human Capital Formation." Working Paper Series IDB-WP 420, Inter-American Development Bank.

Guerra, Nancy, Kirk R. Williams, Ian Walker, and Julie Meeks-Gardner. 2012. "Building an Ecology of Peace in Jamaica: New Approaches to Understanding Youth Crime and Violence and Evaluating Prevention Strategies." Background paper for this study.

Hamazaki, Tomohito, and Kei Hamazaki. 2008. "Fish Oils and Aggression or Hostility." *Progress in Lipid Research* 47 (4): 221–32.

Heckman, James J., Jora Stixrud, and Sergio Urzua. 2006. "The Effects of Cognitive and Noncognitive Abilities on Labor Market Outcomes and Social Behavior." *Journal of Labor Economics* 24 (3): 411–82.

Himelstein, Samuel. 2011. "Meditation Research: The State of the Art in Correctional Settings." *International Journal of Offender Therapy and Comparative Criminology* 55 (4): 646–61.

Hjalmarsson, Randi. 2009. "Juvenile Jails: A Path to the Straight and Narrow or Hardened Criminality?" *Journal of Law and Economics* 52 (4): 779–809.

Hölzel, Britta K., Sara W. Lazar, Tim Gard, Zev Schuman-Olivier, David R. Vago, and Ulrich Ott. 2011. "How Does Mindfulness Meditation Work? Proposing Mechanisms of Action from a Conceptual and Neural Perspective." *Perspectives on Psychological Science* 6 (6): 537–59.

Hood, Roger G., and Richard F. Sparks. 1970. *Key Issues in Criminology*. New York: McGraw-Hill.

Hurley, Dan. 2004. "Scientist at Work—Felton Earls; On Crime as Science (A Neighbor at a Time)." *New York Times*, January 6.

Iyengar, Radha. 2010. "I'd Rather Be Hanged for a Sheep Than a Lamb: The Unintended Consequences of 'Three-Strikes' Laws." CEP Discussion Paper 1017, Centre for Economic Performance, London.

Jacob, Brian A., and Lars Lefgren. 2003. "Are Idle Hands the Devil's Workshop? Incapacitation, Concentration, and Juvenile Crime." *American Economic Review* 93 (5): 1560–77.

Jacob, Brian A., and Jens Ludwig. 2010. "The Effects of Housing Vouchers on Children's Outcomes." Working Paper, University of Michigan, Ann Arbor.

Keizer, Kees, Siegwart Lindenberg, and Linda Steg. 2008. "The Spreading of Disorder." *Science* 322 (5908): 1681–85.

Kelly, Morgan. 2000. "Inequality and Crime." *Review of Economics and Statistics* 82 (4): 530–39.

Kessler, Ronald C., Greg J. Duncan, Lisa A. Gennetian, Lawrence F. Katz, Jeffrey R. Kling, Nancy A. Sampson, Lisa Sanbonmatsu, Alan M. Zaslavsky, and Jens Ludwig. 2014. "Associations of Housing Mobility Interventions for Children in High-Poverty Neighborhoods with Subsequent Mental Disorders during Adolescence." *Journal of the American Medical Association* 311 (9): 937–947.

Klein, Malcolm W. 1989. "Watch Out for That Last Variable." In *The Causes of Crime: New Biological Approaches*, edited by Sarnoff A. Mednick, Terrie E. Moffitt, and Susan A. Stack, 25–41. Cambridge, U.K.: Cambridge University Press.

Kling, Jeffrey R., Jens Ludwig, and Lawrence F. Katz. 2005. "Neighborhood Effects on Crime for Female and Male Youth: Evidence from a Randomized Housing Voucher Experiment." *Quarterly Journal of Economics* 120 (1): 87–130.

Lee, D. S., and J. McCrary. 2009. "The Deterrence Effect of Prison: Dynamic Theory and Evidence." Working paper, UC Berkeley.

Lichtenstein, P., L. Halldner, J. Zetterqvist, A. Sjölander, E. Serlachius, S. Fazel, N. Långström, and H. Larsson. 2012. "Attention Deficit Hyperactivity Disorder Medication and Criminality." *New England Journal of Medicine* 367: 2006–14.

Lochner, Lance, and Enrico Moretti. 2004. "The Effect of Education on Crime Evidence from Prison Inmates, Arrests, and Self Reports." *American Economic Review* 94 (1): 155–89.

Loeber, Rolf, Phen Wung, Kate Keenan, Bruce Giroux, Magda Stouthamer-Loeber, Welmoet B. Van Kammen, and Barbara Maughan. 1993. "Developmental Pathways in Disruptive Child Behavior." *Development and Psychopathology* 5: 101–32.

Luallen, Jeremy. 2006. "School's Out … Forever: A Study of Juvenile Crime, At-Risk Youths, and Teacher Strikes." *Journal of Urban Economics* 59 (1): 75–103.

Macours Karen, Norbert Schady, Renos Vakis. 2008. "Cash Transfers, Behavioral Changes, and Cognitive Development in Early Childhood: Evidence from a Randomized Experiment." Policy Research Working Paper 4759, World Bank, Washington, DC.

Mann, J. John. 1999. "Role of the Serotonergic System in the Pathogenesis of Major Depression and Suicidal Behavior." *Neuropsychopharmacology* 21 (supp. 1): S99–105.

Manski, Charles F. 1993. "Identification of Endogenous Social Effects: The Reflection Problem." *Review of Economic Studies* 60 (3): 531–42.

Marie, Olivier. 2013. "Early Release from Prison on Electronic Monitoring and Recidivism: A Tale of Two Discontinuities." Maastricht University, Maastricht, the Netherlands.

Maslow, Abraham H. 1943. "A Theory of Human Motivation." *Psychological Review* 50 (4): 370–96.

McCord, J., C. S. Widom, and N. A. Crowell, eds. 2001. *Juvenile Crime, Juvenile Justice.* Washington, DC: National Academies Press.

Moffitt, Terrie E. 1990. "The Neuropsychology of Delinquency: A Critical Review of Theory and Research." *Crime and Justice* 12: 99–169.

———. 2005. "The New Look of Behavioral Genetics in Developmental Psychopathology: Gene–Environment Interplay in Antisocial Behaviors." *Psychological Bulletin* 131 (4): 533–54.

Mullainathan, Sendhil, and Eldar Shafir. 2013. *Scarcity: Why Having Too Little Means So Much.* New York: Times Books.

Nagin, Daniel S. 2013. "Deterrence: A Review of the Evidence by a Criminologist for Economists." *Annual Review of Economics* 5: 83–105.

Nevin, Rick. 2007. "Understanding International Crime Trends: The Legacy of Preschool Lead Exposure." *Environmental Research* 104 (3): 315–36.

Olds, D. L., J. Eckenrode, C. R. Henderson, Jr., and others. 1997. "Long-Term Effects of Home Visitation on Maternal Life Course and Child Abuse and Neglect: Fifteen-Year Follow-Up of a Randomized Trial." *Journal of the American Medical Association* 278: 637–43.

Olds, D. L., C. R., Henderson, Jr., H. J. Kitzman, J. J. Eckenrode, R. E. Cole, and R. C. Tatelbaum. 1999. "Prenatal and Infancy Home Visitation by Nurses: Recent Findings." *The Future of Children* 9: 44–65.

Owens, Emily G. 2013. "COPS and Cuffs." In *Lessons from the Economics of Crime: What Works in Reducing Offending?*, edited by Philip J. Cook, Stephen Machin, Olivier Marie, and Giovanni Mastrobuoni, 17–44. Cambridge, MA: MIT Press.

Ozer, Emily J., Lia C. H. Fernald, Ann Weber, Emily P. Flynn, and Tyler J. VanderWeele. 2011. "Does Alleviating Poverty Affect Mothers' Depressive Symptoms? A Quasi-Experimental Investigation of Mexico's Oportunidades Programme." *International Journal of Epidemiology* 40 (6): 1565–76.

Pappadopulos, Elizabeth, Sophie Woolston, Alanna Chait, Matthew Perkins, Daniel F. Connor, and Peter S. Jensen. 2006. "Pharmacotherapy of Aggression in Children and Adolescents: Efficacy and Effect Size." *Journal of the Canadian Academy Child and Adolescent Psychiatry* 15 (1): 27–39.

Piquero, A. R., D. P. Farrington, and A. Blumstein. 2003. "The Criminal Career Paradigm." In *Crime and Justice: A Review of Research*, edited by M. Tonry. Chicago, IL: University of Chicago Press.

Plas J. 1992. "The Development of Systems Thinking: An Historical Perspective." In *The Handbook Of Family-School Intervention: A Systems Perspective*, edited by M. Fine and C. Carlson. Boston: Allyn and Bacon.

Pridemore, William A. 2011. "Poverty Matters: A Reassessment of the Inequality–Homicide Relationship in Cross-National Studies." *British Journal of Criminology* 51 (5): 739–72.

Raine, Adrian. 2013. *The Anatomy of Violence: The Biological Roots of Crime.* New York: Pantheon Books.

Raphael, Steven. 2010. "The Causes and Labor Market Consequences of the Steep Increase in U.S. Incarceration Rates." In *Labor in the Era of Globalization*, edited by Clair Brown, Barry Eichengreen, and Michael Reich, 375–413. Cambridge, U.K.: Cambridge University Press.

Reyes, Jessica Wolpaw. 2007. "Environmental Policy as Social Policy? The Impact of Childhood Lead Exposure on Crime." NBER Working Paper 13097, National Bureau of Economic Research, Cambridge, MA.

Sampson, Robert J. 2012. "Moving and the Neighborhood Glass Ceiling." *Science* 337 (6101): 1464–65.

Sampson, Robert J., and Stephen W. Raudenbush. 1999. "Systematic Social Observation of Public Spaces: A New Look at Disorder in Urban Neighborhoods." *American Journal of Sociology* 105 (3): 603–51.

Schochet, Peter Z., John Burghardt, and Sheena McConnell. 2008. "Does Job Corps Work? Impact Findings from the National Job Corps Study." *American Economic Review* 98 (5): 1864–86.

Sherman, Lawrence W., Denise Gottfredson, Doris MacKenzie, John Eck, Peter Reuter, and Shawn Bushway. 1998. "Preventing Crime: What Works, What Doesn't, What's Promising: A Report to the United States Congress." Prepared for the National Institute of Justice.

Sherman, Laqrence W., Denise Gottfredson, Doris L. MacKenzie, John Eck, Peter Reuter, and Shawn D. Bushway. 2005. "Preventing Crime: What Works, What Doesn't, What's Promising." Research in Brief, National Institute of Justice, Washington, DC.

Sloat, Sara. 2014. "For Boys, Moving to a Wealthier Neighborhood Is as Traumatic as Going to War: Leaving Poverty Is More Complicated Than You Think." *New Republic*, March 5. http://www.newrepublic.com/article/116886/boys-report-ptsd-when-they-move-richer-neighborhoods.

Slutkin, G. 2013. "Let's Treat Violence Like a Contagious Disease." *TEDMED*, Oct, 2013.

Soares, Rodrigo, and Joana Naritomi. 2010. "Understanding High Crime Rates in Latin America: The Role of Social and Policy Factors." In *The Economics of Crime: Lessons for and from Latin America*, edited by Rafael Di Tella, Ernesto Schargrodsky, and Sebastian Edwards. Chicago: University of Chicago Press.

Thornberry, Terence P., ed. 1996. *Advances in Criminological Theory: Developmental Theories of Crime and Delinquency.* London: Transactions.

Tracy, Paul E., Marvin E. Wolfgang, and Robert M. Figlio. 1990. "Delinquency Careers in Two Birth Cohorts." *Contemporary Sociology* 20 (6): 920–22.

Viding, Essi, and Eamon J. McCrory. 2012. "Genetic And Neurocognitive Contributions to the Development of Psychopathy." *Development and Psychopathology* 24: 969–83.

Wadsworth, Tim. 2006. "The Meaning of Work: Conceptualizing the Deterrent Effect of Employment on Crime among Young Adults." *Sociological Perspectives* 49 (3): 343–68.

Weisburd, David, and John E. Eck. 2004. "What Can Police Do to Reduce Crime, Disorder, and Fear?" *Annals of the American Academy of Political and Social Science* 593 (1): 42–65.

Weisburd, David, Elizabeth Groff, and Sue-Ming Yang. 2012. *The Criminology of Place: Street Segments and Our Understanding of the Crime Problem.* Oxford, U.K.: Oxford University Press.

Weisburd, David, Laura A. Wyckoff, Justin Ready, John E. Eck, Joshua C. Hinkle, and Frank Gajewski. 2006. "Does Crime Just Move around the Corner? A Controlled Study of Spatial Displacement and Diffusion of Crime Control Benefits." *Criminology* 44 (3): 549–91.

Welsh, Brandon, and David Farrington. 2008. "Effects of Improved Street Lighting on Crime." *Campbell Systematic Review* 13, Campbell Collaboration Library.

WHO (World Health Organization). 2002. *World Report on Violence and Health.* Geneva, Switzerland: WHO.

Wilson, James Q., and George L. Kelling. 1982. "The Police and Neighborhood Safety: Broken Windows." *Atlantic*, March, 29–38.

World Bank. 2015. *World Development Report 2015: Mind, Society, and Behavior.* Washington, DC: World Bank.

Yeung, W. Jean, Miriam Linver, and Jeanne Brooks-Gunn. 2002. "How Money Matters for Young Children's Development: Parental Investment and Family Processes." *Child Development* 73 (6): 1861–79.

# 1

# Organizing Framework of the Study and Structure of the Report

Crime and violence—particularly violent crime—in Latin America and the Caribbean (LAC) are pervasive and costly. LAC has the undesirable distinction of being the world's most violent region, with 23.9 homicides per 100,000 inhabitants in 2012, compared to 9.7, 4.4, 2.7, and 2.9 for Africa, North America, Asia, and Europe, respectively (map 1.1). The magnitude of the problem is staggering and stubbornly persistent. LAC accounts for only 8 percent of the world's population, but for 37 percent of the world's homicides. Eight out of the 10 most violent countries in the world are in LAC. Of the top 50 most violent cities in the world in 2013, 42 were in the region, including the top 16. The annual growth rate of homicides (3.7 percent) dramatically outstripped population growth (1.15 percent) from 2005 to 2012. In 2012 alone, 145,759 people in LAC fell victim to homicide, corresponding to 400.44 homicides committed per day and 4.17 homicides every 15 minutes.

LAC lost more than 1,560,000 people to homicide from 2000 to 2012, according to the United Nations Office on Drugs and Crime (UNODC); this likely represents an underestimate, given that official statistics are not available for all countries and all years. This figure is equivalent to two and a half times the population of Washington, DC; close to 3 times the population of Lisbon: and close to half the population of Panama. Over this twelve-year period, homicide victims in LAC were more than double the casualties of the Iraq war (both civilians and military), which have been estimated in the range of 400,000 to 750,000.

This is not a recent phenomenon for the region, which has experienced high and persistent levels of violence for decades. Its history of elevated homicide rates and the escalation of violence of the late 2000s are in stark contrast with recent decades of improvements and successes in many other important arenas. LAC has made

World cartogram showing country size proportional to homicide rate

## a. Homicide rates, circa 2000

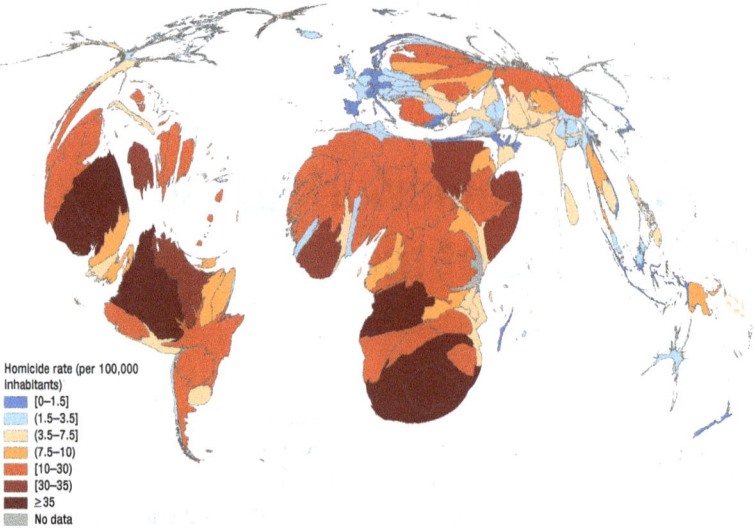

Homicide rate (per 100,000 inhabitants)
- [0–1.5]
- (1.5–3.5]
- (3.5–7.5]
- (7.5–10)
- [10–30)
- [30–35)
- ≥ 35
- No data

## b. Homicide rates, circa 2012

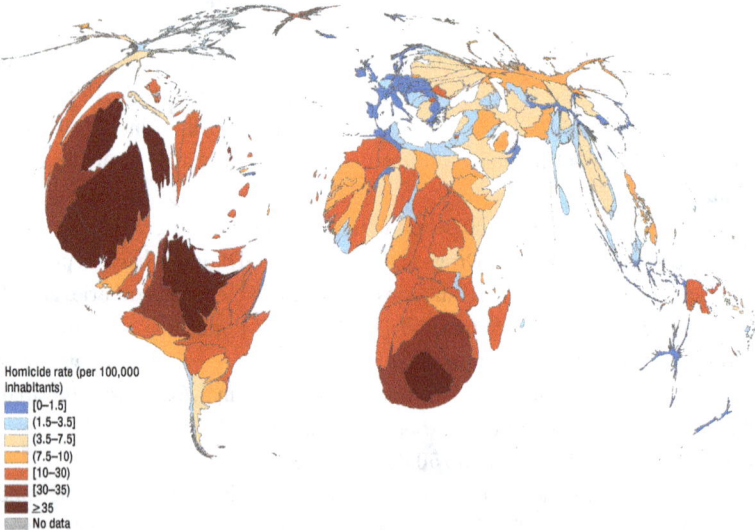

Homicide rate (per 100,000 inhabitants)
- [0–1.5]
- (1.5–3.5]
- (3.5–7.5]
- (7.5–10)
- [10–30)
- [30–35)
- ≥ 35
- No data

*Source:* World Bank calculations, based on data from United Nations Office on Drugs and Crime (UNODC) and World Health Organization (WHO).
*Note:* The size of the country corresponds to the severity of the homicide rate. The WHO threshold for endemic violence is 10 per 100,000 inhabitants. The WHO threshold for conflict level violence is 30 per 100,000 inhabitants.

important strides toward broader social equity, as reflected by significant reductions in poverty and income inequality, and rising shares of people in the middle class. This contradiction—whether apparent or not—highlights the complexity of the relationship between economic development and crime and violence.

The focus of this study is the prevention of crime and violence. The study seeks to identify innovative policy interventions that, whether by design or through their indirect effects,[1] have been shown to affect antisocial behavior early in life and patterns of criminal offending in youth and adults. An exhaustive review of all existing literature on crime (in the fields of criminology, psychology, and economics) and related evidence would be an overwhelming task and is beyond the scope of this document. Previous analytical reports by the World Bank are summarized in box 1.1.

In recent years, the crime and violence analytical and operational agenda has grown rapidly, becoming an integral part of the region's financial, convening, and knowledge services. Appendix A presents an overview of the World Bank's Social, Urban, and Resilience Global Practice operational engagements in the region.

---

**BOX 1.1:** Previous analytical reports by the World Bank on crime and violence in Latin America and the Caribbean

The World Bank has recognized the importance of crime and violence to development, and is committed to understanding it, and thus has commissioned studies from a variety of perspectives. Two sets of regional studies were prepared in the late 1990s to map out the main determinants of the region's crime and violence trends. *Crimen y Violencia en América Latina* (*Crime and Violence in Latin America*) uses the (Beckerian) economic model of crime and violence and finds that key country-level determinants of criminal activity include weak economic growth, income inequality, and low levels of education (Fajnzylber, Lederman, and Loayza 2001). Fajnzylber, Lederman, and Loayza (2002) obtain similar results from micro-level evidence on key risk factors for criminality and victimization across several cities in the region. Lederman, Loayza, and Menéndez (2002) also note a robust negative relationship between a nationally aggregated measure of trust and homicide rates.

A second set of studies on crime and violence was carried out in Brazil, the Caribbean and, most recently, Central America, and provides an overview of the trends in crime and violence and the socioeconomic costs associated with crime; analyzes particular drivers of crime and violence in each subregion (drug trafficking, organized crime, and youth violence, among others); and considers prevention policies (World Bank 2011). All three studies adopt the "ecological risk model" and highlight six trends in policies to address the problem: a shift from a relatively narrow focus on crime control to broader issues of community safety and security as a public good; a developing

*(continued on next page)*

This study, therefore, devotes particular attention to recent and innovative studies that rigorously and credibly establish a causal link between the interventions in question and outcomes. The emphasis on causality is rooted in policy concerns. The delicate nature of the problem, the high stakes, and the scope for potential risks from unintended consequences call for this approach. The evidence is structured according to the organizing framework discussed in the next section. In summary, this study adopts a life-cycle perspective and argues that as individuals progress through different stages of the life cycle, not only do different sets of risk factors arise and take more prominence, but their interactions and interdependencies also shape human behavior. These interactions and the relative importance of different sets of risk factors identify different margins that can effectively be targeted by prevention policies.[2]

Evidence that is specific to LAC is growing,[3] but remains somewhat limited, so it is complemented with evidence from developed countries. One of the critical obstacles in LAC is the paucity of adequate and available data—beyond national statistics—to study this topic. As will be discussed, crime and violence are very local in nature and tend to be concentrated in particular municipalities—even specific streets. Further, they are committed by and affect very specific subgroups of the population at a disproportionate rate. In order to be useful, data must reflect the nature of the problem. Victimization surveys are limited, and their samples are often not representative at the municipal level. In turn, crime data at the municipal or neighborhood level, along with associated socioeconomic and demographic characteristics, remain the exception and, when they do exist, are rarely available publicly.

By design, this study does not consider the causes and nature of organized crime, nor does it explicitly broach the role of national institutions. We recognize that these are extremely important dimensions of the crime and violence problem in the region. A thoughtful treatment of these topics that does them justice is beyond the scope of this study and should be explored in future work. While abstracting from organized crime, much of the evidence and many of the mechanisms discussed here may have applicability and relevance to the questions surrounding organized crime.

## The organizing framework of this study

This study discusses evidence in the context of an organizing framework that blends and encompasses features of three different models of criminal and antisocial behavior, each with origins in different disciplines: Becker's 1968 economic theory of the supply of criminal offenses; the ecological framework, whose origins lie in the medical literature; and the developmental life course theories, which build in part on Bronfenbrenner's 1979 theory of child development and in part on work by Farrington (2003), Thornberry (1996), and Loeber and others (1993), who formalize developmental insights for the criminological literature.

Specifically, to organize thinking about criminal offending, this study builds on Becker's 1968 theory of the supply of criminal offenses. In this framework, the number of crimes in any given period is a function of three elements: the probability of apprehension and conviction, the severity of punishment, and a (theoretical) residual that captures other relevant considerations such as risk aversion, family background, peers, human capital investments, and wages in the legal labor market. While Becker's 1968 model is neoclassical, it is general enough that it can easily accommodate "behavioral" phenomena that have recently been documented by behavioral economists (such as bounded rationality, overconfidence, subjective probabilities, and impatience) and that would suggest that criminal offending is not the result of purely rational thinking. Indeed, allowing for a behavioral model of offending does not imply that crime is unresponsive to incentives (Cook and Ludwig 2011). Even in the behavioral view, crime remains amenable to policy intervention.

The residual variable[4]—the third component in the model—should not be viewed as unimportant. Rather, it plays a pivotal role because it is the element that confers flexibility to the model by virtue of being left unspecified. It can be thought of as a flexible placeholder for a set of variables that should naturally enter the model as key determinants specific to the problem under consideration. For instance, when interested in the impact of biological inputs and parenting strategies on youths' antisocial behavior, the Beckerian residual may include factors such as parents' socioeconomic background, their criminal record, and their parenting styles. When studying whether vocational training can affect antisocial behavior, however, the residual is accordingly modeled to make explicit the role of peer effects and social networks, labor market conditions, impatience, and the like.

The framework proposed in this study thus builds on Becker's insights and assigns a very particular structure to the residual by combining elements from two conceptual models in criminology: the ecological model and developmental theories.

The ecological model adopts (or adapts) the approach from the medical literature to explore the factors underlying violent behavior and victimization. Based on empirical correlates, the model identifies risk and protective factors for violence and aggressive behavior, and organizes them according to hierarchical levels at which they operate (individual, family, peer, community, or societal) (Krug and others 2002). The different hierarchical domains identified by the ecological model are assumed to populate the residual in Becker's (1968) model. That is, the decision as to whether to engage in criminal or violent acts is viewed as being shaped by factors that capture individual characteristics, family background, network of peers, the physical environment, and features of the community and economy such as labor markets. Even the cost of crime (defined as the expected severity of the sentence for a given crime) may be permitted to depend on these same factors.

However, the ecological model was originally developed as an organizing descriptive tool and is, as such, static in nature; that is, it is not designed to capture the feedback among the various factors. As individuals move through different stages of the life cycle, not only may different sets of risk factors become more relevant than others, but their interactions and interdependencies also shape human behavior. For instance, during childhood, biological factors and parenting play "bigger" roles than peers or institutions. However, as an individual matures and progresses through adolescence and young adulthood, peers, the quality of schools, and neighborhood characteristics exert increasing influence on his or her behavior, such that different sets of proximal risk and protective factors take greater prominence. Youth alcohol and drug consumption in the neighborhood may not have an immediate impact on a child's aggression, but may matter later have an impact on a teenager's truancy and dropout decisions. The concept of interdependent spheres of interactions is reminiscent of Bronfenbrenner's (1979) system theory elaborated in the context of child development. In particular, he argues that a child's developmental outcomes cannot be accurately viewed by being examined within a single domain.

Instead, development occurs within several subsystems, wherein the more contiguous systems (such as family, school, and friends) are all interconnected; this view also follows from systems theory (Plas 1992). Clearly, all immediate interactions of a child (family, school, friends) are subsumed within the broader context of the child's environment (culture, government, economy).

This organizing framework permits us to highlight how different policy margins may be more effective and relevant as individuals progress through the life cycle by highlighting the prevention potential of policies that are not traditionally thought of as preventive (such as early childhood development and prenatal, health, and nutrition interventions), thus expanding the menu of policies available to policy makers.

Figure 1.1 provides a simplified graphical representation of the model. The (smaller) light blue circles correspond to the original elements of the Beckerian model, while the three (larger) blue circles represent the expanded and structured residual, according to the previous description.

Models are stylized and partial representations of reality; so is the analytic framework of this study. One potential criticism might be the following. Because of the interdependencies among different domains, it might be argued that the claim that different sets of risk and protective factors change in relevance over the life cycle is something of a white lie. Institutions, poverty levels, and neighborhood characteristics all frame parents' decisions and behaviors at the micro level (such as whether or not to smoke during pregnancy, to engage in criminal acts, to live in a given neighborhood, to adopt a coercive parenting style, or to invest in early childhood education). These in turn influence children's outcomes. Thus one could conclude that any level of the ecological model is equally important at any given stage.

The following two points clarify why the previous argument, while true, may not be a valid criticism of this framework for the purposes and scope of this study.

**FIGURE 1.1:** A model of the supply of criminal offenses, but also a model of crime and violence prevention

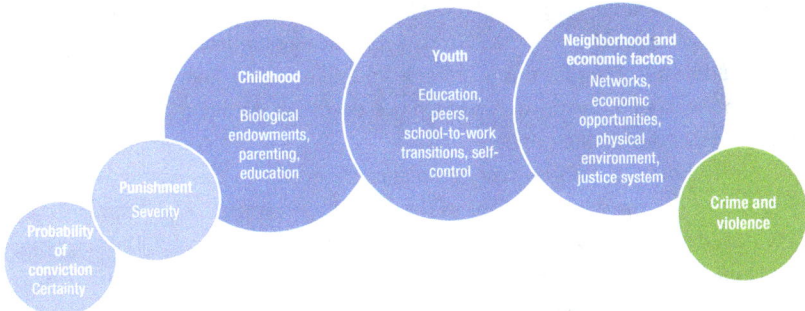

First, the framework is akin to a partial equilibrium model in economics, in which the interdependencies across markets are held constant in the short run. Similarly, the effects of institutions, poverty levels, and neighborhood characteristics can be taken as predetermined in the short run. In addition, they tend to be slower-moving variables than a teen's decision regarding whether to attend school on a given day, for instance.

Second, stating that during some life stages, some characteristics of a given hierarchical domain may be more directly related to behavior than others does not imply that other factors are irrelevant. If we were to analyze the decision by one individual to assault another in the street and how it depends on whether the street is lit, we would still want to control for individual characteristics—ranging from parents' education to their criminal history, and education level, to the labor supply, wages, police presence, efficiency of the criminal justice system, and the like. Thus in discussing prevention strategies and their effectiveness, which are the focus of this study, "all else equal" is a necessity to establish the proper causal link and is hence reflected in the framework.

Figure 1.1 and the organizing framework described in this section serve as a guide for the reader throughout the report and shape the econometric models in certain background papers that are presented. They do not pretend to fully capture the complexity of the motives of antisocial behaviors. Indeed, in the final remarks, emphasis is placed on the idea that the successes and failures of any crime and violence prevention strategy rests on the ability to implement an integrated set of policies that can exploit the synergies across different stages of the life cycle and across hierarchical systems.

## By not focusing on institutions, this study partly omits a discussion of organized crime

In part as a corollary to the choice not to consider the role of institutions in the level of crime and violence,[5] this study does not examine the nature and causes of organized crime; nor does it explicitly broach the role of national institutions and international cooperation in addressing drug trafficking and related criminal activity. We recognize that these are important determinants of the crime and violence problem in the region. However, a thoughtful treatment of these topics is beyond the scope of this study and should be explored in future work. The data requirements and the economic approach that would be necessary for this exercise would differ greatly and would likely entail the adoption of an industrial organization perspective in the analysis of drug markets and of interactions among cartels.

Nevertheless, certain aspects of violence described in the section on stylized facts and in the analysis are bound to overlap with organized crime, particularly in LAC. According to crime reports compiled by the United Nations Office on Drugs and Crime (UNODC), there has been a gradual but persistent upward trend in drug-related crimes over the past decade.

When presenting figures on the evolution of violence over time, the study does not attempt to distinguish between interpersonal violence that is unrelated to organized crime from that which is driven by it. First, definitions, methodology, and the collection of drug-related statistics vary greatly across countries, and reports are provided too sporadically to create meaningful long-term regional comparisons. Second, in the literature and among practitioners, there are no universally accepted—or mutually exclusive—definitions of violence and organized crime.[6] These two factors render a unique mapping of crimes into the relevant data categorizations extremely difficult—even abstracting from long-standing debates distinguishing drug-related crimes from other types of crime.

Because the focus of this study is on prevention, this regrettable limitation of data affects it only marginally. Indeed, much of the evidence and many of the mechanisms discussed may have relevance to questions surrounding organized crime.

This claim is consistent with the main findings of the 2012 report by the U.S. Centers for Disease Control and Prevention (CDC), "Gang Homicides—Five U.S. Cities, 2003–2008," which concludes that 90 percent of gang-related homicide incidents involve firearms, and that perpetrators are concentrated among youth. The CDC study adds that while rigorous evaluations of gang violence prevention programs are limited, interventions targeting child and youth training in pro-social behavior and self-control have shown promising reductions in gang affiliation. Interventions that operate through these mechanisms are covered in this regional report.

However, by design, the study does not report on policies specifically targeting mechanisms linked to affiliations with gangs or organized crime. For instance, secondary prevention programs that intervene when youth have been injured by gang violence—such as hospital emergency department interventions that might interrupt the retaliatory nature of gang violence and encourage youths to exit gangs—are not discussed.

In sum, whether in LAC or in the United States, an intervention that is proven to reduce violence in neighborhoods where interpersonal violence is intertwined with organized crime, gang affiliation, and drugs is deemed to have a preventive effect and therefore as relevant with respect to policy dialogue on the prevention of crime and violence, regardless of the underlying motives of violence. As discussed later, policies that prevent youth violence are also often effective in reducing gang affiliation.

## *Why evidence from developed countries is relevant*

In discussing the relevant evidence, this study refers to and builds on studies from developed countries. While rigorous empirical evidence for LAC is developing, it is still in its infancy. This study refers to it whenever possible and pertinent to the narrative of the various chapters.

However, after a cursory glimpse at certain aggregate statistics, one may question the extent to which the parallel between the two contexts can be drawn.

For instance, the homicide rate in the United States in 2011 was roughly 4.7 per 100,000, while the average for the LAC region was five times as large, at 23.9 per 100,000. The "endemic" level of violence, defined by the World Health Organization (WHO) as 10 homicides per 100,000, appears to be the norm in the region, with only 10 countries below the threshold. In 2012, eight countries in the region were above the WHO-defined "conflict" level of violence of 30 homicides per 100,000.

Are the differences in the levels of violence between developed and developing countries so dramatic as to invalidate any meaningful comparisons and render the evidence from developed countries only marginally relevant? This study puts forward at least three arguments to validate the parallel.

First, as is discussed in chapter 2, central tendencies from aggregate/national data can be misleading, and hide a marked degree of underlying heterogeneity. This is especially true of crime and violence. While developed countries have enjoyed considerably lower levels of violence, certain subsets of their populations and selected neighborhoods/cities are characterized by levels of violence that are not dissimilar to those of LAC. New Orleans and Detroit are the seventeenth and twenty-first most violent cities in the world, respectively, with homicide rates well above 50 per 100,000, putting them on par with some of the most violent cities in the region. One of the most violent neighborhoods in Chicago, Englewood, is plagued by murder rates of 65.5 homicides per 100,000, higher than that of Ciudad Juarez in Mexico (55.9 per 100,000, in 2013) and similar to that of Salvador, Brazil (65.6 per 100,000). The parallel does not only hold for certain U.S. cities, but also for specific subgroups of the U.S. population. The murder rate among African-Americans in the United States is significantly higher than the national average. Throughout the 2000s, black males ages 18–24 were plagued by homicide rates hovering between 105 and 110 per 100,000. In 2008, the homicide rate for this group was 91.1 per 100,000, compared to 36.98 per 100,000 for young men age 20–24 in Mexico. These figures confirm that while the analogy between developed and developing countries may feel stretched at the national level, the national averages mask substantial heterogeneity, such that it remains rather accurate for particular subgroups of the population, and for the at-risk population in particular.

Second, by design, the study considers the roles of biological, intergenerational, and cognitive mechanisms, as well as of stages of brain development and their relationships with antisocial behavior. Many of these channels are invariant to context and are rooted in biology. Indeed, key insights (which are consistent across contexts) about life course trajectories and patterns of criminal behavior, including desistence, emerge from longitudinal studies that follow relatively large cohorts of individuals as early as infancy and through their life cycles. These types of data are unavailable in developing countries, but the evidence presented in this study is remarkably consistent with the findings that derive from them, highlighting the stability of the age-crime profile, for instance, and possibly of the underlying mechanisms that give rise to it. It is indeed the report's emphasis on brain development and functions that yields the provocative conclusion that brain plasticity and the malleability of skills that matter for antisocial behavior reach their peaks during adolescence (that is, well past early childhood). These results emerge from recent medical research that makes use of functional magnetic resonance imaging (fMRI), among other recent medical developments. This emphasis in turn yields important policy implications, whose relevance is not limited to the contexts of the specific studies. This study:

- Underscores the importance of policies that directly target executive function and personality traits beyond the traditional human capital and labor market interventions.

- Highlights the importance of policies that alter the structure and chemistry of brain functioning (pertaining to such areas as meditation, nutrition, and lead poisoning).

- Provides a justification for the unsatisfactory or negative outcomes of "get tough" approaches in terms of their effects on prevention and recidivism (this point is discussed further later).

- Disproves the commonly held belief that prevention may be ineffective at later ages, during adolescence and early adulthood.

Third, certain stylized facts documented in this study—such as the age-crime profile of offending, the degree of geographic concentration of violence, and its persistence—are also common traits of the physiognomy of antisocial behavior in developed countries. Indeed, one of the contributions of the study is to formalize and document the stylized facts for the region to establish appropriate parallels between the experience of LAC countries and that of developed countries. That there is a meaningful parallel between the level of violence in LAC and in the United States, and that violence is characterized by common distinctive features across the two contexts that are interesting in their own right. However, this set of stylized facts bears an important implication for this study.

A prevention program from the United States with proven effectiveness in reducing crime among disadvantaged youth—in neighborhoods where violence, drugs, and gang problems are pervasive—may at the very least be thought of as suggestive for policy in LAC. The obvious but critical caveat is that context and the capacity of institutions matter. For instance, Sherman and others (2005) stress the importance of these factors in conditioning the effectiveness of community-based crime prevention programs: "In study after study, evidence emerges that crime prevention programs are more likely to take root, and more likely to work, in communities that need them the least. Conversely, the evidence shows that communities with the greatest crime problems are also the hardest to reach through innovative program efforts" (Sherman and others 2005, 39).[7]

This observation does not invalidate optimism regarding certain promising policy margins established in developed countries, but serves as a cautionary warning and highlights the role of institutions when putting these policies into operation. As mentioned, this regional study does not broach the role of institutions, which are at the outermost sphere of the ecological model, though the study acknowledges that their role in interacting with programs is crucial.

## Structure of the report

The rest of the study is organized as follows. Chapter 2 presents salient features of the crime and violence phenomenon in the LAC region. The first group of empirical regularities relates to the relationship between economic development and crime. Particular attention is devoted to the last decade, when the security situation deteriorated dramatically while important strides were made toward broader social equity, as reflected by significant reductions in poverty. The focus of the second set of stylized facts is the spatial distribution of crime. Aggregate statistics for crime and violence can conceal a great deal of heterogeneity: crime is highly geographically concentrated; it exhibits acute geographical clustering and high degrees of persistence; and it spills over across neighboring municipalities. The third set of stylized facts highlights how heterogeneity manifests itself not only along the geographical dimension but, equally strikingly, over the life cycle, giving rise to one of the most consistent patterns about crime: the age-crime profile, which this study documents for both perpetrators and victims of various crimes. The age-crime curve in part emerges as a consequence of the interplay between two sets of factors: those linked to socioeconomic transitions from youth to adult roles, and those related to a distinctive phase of brain development and plasticity. The last set of stylized facts focus on the determinants of victimization and the cost of victimization in terms of two makers of emotional well-being: perception of insecurity and self-reported happiness.

Following the framework outlined in this section, chapter 3 focuses on the early stages of life. This chapter first discusses the sources of intergenerational linkages in crime and violence and the importance of biological factors. Family history is a powerful predictor of serious offending and comprises both biological and social vulnerabilities to crimes. The set of results presented speaks to the malleability and responsiveness of "biological" factors vis-à-vis the environment, but similarly highlight the relevance of "initial" endowments that are not a product of socialization. In particular, several pre-birth factors (prenatal conditions and perinatal factors) are amenable to policy intervention and could have important consequences for aggression in children and youth, as well as adult criminal outcomes. The responsiveness of children's criminal behavior to the environment (as proxied in these studies by adopted parents) and the interactions of biological predispositions with parents' education are equally suggestive of a window of opportunity to alter antisocial behavior through early and family-focused interventions. The second section of chapter 3 reviews certain policies targeting early stages of children's lives and how these interventions relate to crime and violence later in life.

Chapter 4 focuses on youth. It presents the evidence that establishes a causal relationship between the quantity and quality of education and criminality. In the short term, there is a trade-off between reductions in violence outside of school and increases in violence within the school, as a result of the increased concentration of youths in one location and the conflict that ensues. However, the long-term effects of additional education point to sizable social benefits, including in the form of reductions in future offending, which likely far outweigh the substantial social costs of crime and corrections. Taken together with the life-cycle trajectory of offending, the studies reviewed here identify education investments in late adolescence as particularly beneficial in terms of crime reduction. The chapter then explores recent advances in the understanding of the evolution of brain function, its structure, and personality traits relevant to offending behavior. A critical period during adolescence and early adulthood is identified for executive function, which is akin to the critical window for cognitive development in childhood. These findings provide insight into the mechanisms underlying age-crime trajectories, and evidence from education studies that show that improvements in academic achievement are not necessary to observe ameliorations in aggression and subsequent offending. They also provide insight for policy: the malleability of personality traits among youth makes them a valuable focus for policy interventions. The final section of this chapter reviews the effectiveness of a number of programs that target psychological factors other than cognitive ability.

Given the robust tendency of victimization and perpetrators to be concentrated among the poor, chapter 5 reviews evidence on the relationship of family income and criminal offending. This focus is also motivated by the theoretically ambiguous sign of the relationship between income and crime. The evidence reviewed in the first section of this chapter often relies on quasi-experimental changes in household income that are generated by poverty reduction programs. This chapter tackles these questions by first considering the impact of income transfer programs on antisocial behavior, while the second section discusses the nexus between labor market outcomes and crime and violence. A pure income effect on crime resulting from economic necessity seems to matter more for developing countries. Furthermore, income transfers are associated with improvements in the outcomes of children and youth, even in terms of crime and violence. Increased quality (lower psychological burden associated with poverty) and quantity (via a substitution effect away from labor) of parental investments appear to play a critical role in both developed and developing countries. As an income gradient would predict, these benefits are higher in developing countries. Almost uniformly across contexts, income effects, mediated by better emotional well-being and consequent improvements in the quality of parenting, emerge as pivotal in shaping children's outcomes, particularly behavioral outcomes.

The second half of the chapter takes a closer look at the role of labor market outcomes in determining antisocial behavior. Labor market outcomes seem to matter for at-risk individuals (potential marginal offenders). Unskilled workers and unskilled youth with low educational attainment are particularly vulnerable. However, rather than clear choice, economic activity for those employed in low-quality jobs seems to vary over a continuum of legal and illegal "work." The chapter concludes that not all jobs are created equal in terms of their protective properties, with early intensive attachment to labor force, especially to low-quality employment, having counterproductive consequences.

Chapter 6 discusses the evidence on interventions that target the geographic unit surrounding the individual, rather than individual himself or herself. As individuals progress through childhood and adolescence, the sphere of social interactions expands from their immediate family to neighbors, to the surrounding community, and, ultimately, to society at large. Through these interactions, which take on increasing importance as individuals age, social ties are formed and peer groups are defined. Peers, social context, and neighborhoods shape individuals' social norms, drawing lines between what is and is not acceptable, and influencing behaviors that are social in nature, such as crime. The chapter provides a general review of the evidence on the influence of neighborhoods on the life course of their residents and then focuses more narrowly on the relationship between neighborhood characteristics and crime. The theoretical constructs and the evidence linking neighborhood characteristics and interactions to antisocial behavior are discussed. Recent evidence is examined regarding interventions that aim to improve housing conditions via relocation or *in situ* upgrading, as well as interventions that alter the appearance of streets and neighborhoods.

As mentioned, the focus of the study is on prevention. The discussion would not be complete without a treatment of deterrence, which is the focus of chapter 7. One of the key parameters that governs the supply of crime is the expected punishment, which, by definition, is a function of the severity of sanctions and of the likelihood of detection (or the certainty). Do offenders respond to these incentives? Can crime be deterred by changes either in the severity or certainty of sentencing? The first part of chapter 7 tackles these questions and reviews the existing evidence. In fact, irrespective of the nature of the criminal justice system's regime—whether strict (*mano dura*)[8] or lenient—for any given amount of expected punishment, different combinations of severity and certainty will give rise to different levels of efficiency of the criminal justice system (Durlauf and Nagin 2011). The second part of the chapter focuses on the role of specific deterrence—that is, the deterrence related to the experience of punishment, and how it affects recidivism. Theory predicts a reduction in recidivism from the desire to avoid the negative experience of punishment, but it could also increase outside options through several channels, such as distance from one's criminal network, or investments in human capital (through training programs or health programs). However, the experience of conviction may also entail significant costs and unintended consequences: stigma, severing the ties with families and the labor market, exposing offenders to possibilities of acquiring new "criminal" capital, and depreciation of their productive human capital, rendering reinsertion more difficult.

## Notes

[1] Examples of interventions with secondary impacts on offending are nutritional supplements, conditional cash transfers, and prenatal interventions.

[2] By "margins" or "policy margins," this report means opportunities for policy intervention.

[3] Several original background papers were commissioned for the study, in addition to background papers by Chioda, which have not been published but are available from the authors. Carniero and Evans (2013) study the impact of ECDs on executive functions in Brazil. Di Tella and Schargrodsky (2013) consider the effects on recidivism of electronic monitoring devices rather than imprisonment. Galiani and others (2013) study the impact of housing upgrades in three countries on crime and perceptions of safety. Guerra and others (2013) are concerned with the prevention of youth violence in Jamaica.

[4] It is a residual not in an econometric sense but in a theoretical one.

[5] A 2015 report on safety by the Corporacion Andina de Fomento (CAF) entitled *Towards a Safer Latin America: A New Perspective to Prevent and Control Crime* focuses on the role of society and institutions. The study highlights the importance of democratic forms of coexistence and political and institutional participation to promote trust between citizens and between authorities. The report identifies the design and implementation of public policies that promote the comprehensive development of families and communities as a key regional challenge. The publication includes six chapters that examine subjects such as citizen security and well-being; why some people commit crimes and others do not; the location of crime; drug trafficking and violence; the criminal justice system and electoral incentives; and the capacity and legitimacy of the State.

[6] *The World Report on Violence and Health* by the World Health Organization (WHO) (Krug and others 2002) defines violence as "the intentional use of physical force or power, threatened or actual, against oneself, another person, or against a group or community that either results in or has a high likelihood of resulting in injury, death, psychological harm, mal-development or deprivation." WHO distinguishes types of violence according to the victim-perpetrator relationship. It defines interpersonal violence as violence between individuals (or small groups such as a youth gangs), and subdivides it into family, intimate partner, and community violence. WHO's Organized Crime Convention deliberately avoids a unique definition of organized crime. This choice was intended to allow for a broader applicability of the Organized Crime Convention to new types of crimes that constantly emerge as global, regional, and local conditions change over time. The convention does contain a definition for "organized criminal groups": a group of three or more persons that was not randomly formed; that exists for a period of time; acts in concert with the aim of committing at least one crime punishable by at least four years' incarceration; in order to obtain, directly or indirectly, a financial or other material benefit. Since most "groups" of any sort contain three or more people working in concert and most exist for a period of time, the true defining characteristics of organized criminal groups under the convention are their profit-seeking nature and the seriousness of the offences they commit.

[7] The quality of service delivery in developing economies is an issue whether in the context of early childhood development (ECD), education, or any other intervention. Sherman and others (2005) stress this issue by highlighting the importance of the quality of the human capital of those individuals delivering the programs, by drawing attention to the selection of these service providers,

and by suggesting that specific training is required. However, there is also cause for optimism. For instance, the human capital required to ensure quality of service delivery is also an issue for ECD programs, and yet larger effects are systematically observed in developing countries than in developed ones (see Gertler and others 2014, 998). The literature about incentives for pro-social behavior to encourage volunteering and service providers as well as to improve performance and accountability may hold key insights for implementation. A discussion of this literature is beyond the scope of this study.

[8] *Mano dura* ("firm hand" or "iron fist") is a term used to describe a set of tough-on-crime policies. The defining features of *mano dura* policies are the expansion of police discretion and reduction of civil liberties in pursuit of security.

# References

Becker, Gary S. 1968. "Crime and Punishment: An Economic Approach." *Journal of Political Economy* 76 (2): 169–217.

Bronfenbrenner, Urie. 1979. *The Ecology of Human Development: Experiments by Nature and Design.* Cambridge, MA: Harvard University Press.

CAF (Corporación Andina de Fomento). 2014. *Towards a Safer Latin America: A New Perspective to Prevent and Control Crime.* Caracas, Venezuela: CAF Development Bank of Latin America.

Carneiro, Pedro, and David Evans. 2013. "The Impact of Formal Child Care Attendance in Rio de Janeiro on Child Development and Maternal Outcomes." Working paper.

CDC (Centers for Disease Control and Prevention). 2012. "Gang Homicides—Five U.S. Cities, 2003–2008." *Morbidity and Mortality Weekly Report* 61 (03): 46–51.

Cook, Philip, and Jens Ludwig. 2011. "Economical Crime Control." In *Controlling Crime: Strategies and Tradeoffs,* edited by P. J. Cook, J. Ludwig, and J. McCrary. Cambridge, MA: National Bureau of Economic Research.

Cunningham, Wendy, Linda McGinnis, Rodrigo García Verdú, Cornelia Tesliuc, and Dorte Verner, 2008. *Youth at Risk in Latin America and the Caribbean: Understanding the Causes, Realizing the Potential.* Washington, DC: World Bank.

Di Tella, Rafael, and Ernesto Schargrodsky. 2013. "Criminal Recidivism after Prison and Electronic Monitoring." *Journal of Political Economy* 121 (1): 28–73.

Durlauf, Steven N., and Daniel S. Nagin. 2011. "Imprisonment and Crime." *Criminology & Public Policy* 10: 13–54.

Fajnzylber, Pablo, Daniel Lederman, and Norman Loayza. 2001. *Crimen y Violencia en America Latina.* Washington, DC: World Bank.

———. 2002. "What Causes Violent Crime?" *European Economic Review* 46: 1323–57.

Farrington, David P. 2003. "Developmental and Life-Course Criminology: Key Theoretical and Empirical Issues—The 2002 Sutherland Award Address." *Criminology* 41: 221–56.

Galiani, Sebastian, Paul Gertler, Ryan Cooper, Sebastian Martinez, Adam Ross, and Raimundo Undurraga. 2013. "Shelter from the Storm: Upgrading Housing Infrastructure in Latin American Slums." Working Paper 19322, National Bureau of Economic Research, Cambridge, MA.

Gertler, Paul, James Heckman, Rodrigo Pinto, Arianna Zanolini, Christel Vermeersch, Susan Walker, Susan M. Chang, and Sally Grantham-McGregor. 2014. "Labor Market Returns to an Early Childhood Stimulation Intervention in Jamaica." *Science* 344 (6187): 998–1001.

Guerra, Nancy, Kirk R. Williams, Ian Walker, and Julie Meeks-Gardner. 2013. "Building an Ecology of Peace in Jamaica: New Approaches to Understanding Youth Crime and Violence and Evaluating Prevention Strategies." Background paper for this study.

Krug, Etienne G., Linda L. Dahlberg, James A. Mercy, Anthony B. Zwi, and Rafael Lozano, eds. 2002. *World Report on Violence and Health.* Geneva: World Health Organization.

Lederman, Daniel, Norman Loayza, and Ana Maria Menendez. 2002. "Violent Crime: Does Social Capital Matter?" *Economic Development and Cultural Change* 50 (3): 509–39.

Loeber, R. P. Wung, K. Keenan, B. Giroux, M. Stouthamer-Loeber, W. B. Van Kammen, and B. Maughan. 1993. "Developmental Pathways in Disruptive Child Behavior." *Development and Psychopathology* 5: 101–32.

Plas, J. 1992. "The Development of Systems Thinking: An Historical Perspective." In *The Handbook Of Family-School Intervention: A Systems Perspective*, edited by M. Fine and C. Carlson. Boston: Allyn and Bacon.

Sherman, L. W., D. Gottfredson, D. MacKenzie, J. Eck, P. Reuter, and S. Bushway. 2005. *Preventing Crime: What Works, What Doesn't, What's Promising*. Washington, DC: National Institute of Justice.

Thornberry, T. P., ed. 1996. *Advances in Criminological Theory: Developmental Theories of Crime and Delinquency*. London: Transactions.

World Bank. 2011. *Crime and Violence in Central America: A Development Challenge*. Washington, DC: World Bank.

———. 2013. *Making Brazilians Safer: Analyzing the Dynamics of Violent Crime*. Washington, DC: World Bank.

# 2

# Stylized Facts about Crime and Violence in Latin America and the Caribbean

This chapter provides a view into the defining characteristics and dynamics of crime and violence in Latin America and the Caribbean (LAC). Acknowledging the complexity and scope of the topic and the limited space, this review is by no means exhaustive. The stylized facts discussed in this chapter merely provide some insight into the dynamics of crime and violence in the region over the past 15 years; they motivate the rest of the report and serve as building blocks.

Before delving into the statistics, a disclaimer concerning data is warranted. Concerns regarding the comparability and reliability of crime statistics across countries are legitimate and well documented. These concerns arise not only because the likelihood that a crime will be reported depends on a country's level of economic and institutional development (and thus data on crime are subject to nonclassical forms of measurement error), but also because the legal definitions of crimes vary across countries, which hinders attempts to aggregate data and complicates efforts to analyze them. Further, country-level crime data other than homicide rates remain rare and are plagued by inconsistencies and gaps. Notwithstanding these caveats, some efforts have been made in recent years to harmonize certain statistics.[1] However, these initiatives are in their infancy and data are available only for recent years. Most of the cross-country comparisons and analyses in this chapter are carried out making use of homicide statistics, the reliability of which has been verified across several data sources (national and international). Homicide statistics are less subject to variations in legal definition. However, this study makes a conscious effort to rely as much as possible on crime data at the municipal level. This choice is motivated by the fact that data disaggregated at the most refined geographical level tend to be more appropriate for capturing the local nature of violence, as emerges from the discussion in this chapter. This study went to great lengths to compile and compare several different sources and to ensure that the evidence presented here is robust.

The chapter is organized as follows. It first provides trends over time, documenting the evolution of the incidence of crime and violence in LAC, relying mainly on homicide data. The popular press often cites violence as one of the defining characteristics of the region. Indeed, the magnitude of the problem is worrisome and has been stubbornly persistent over the past 15 to 20 years. High homicide rates have become the norm for the region, despite the significant gains in economic growth and poverty reduction. The stark juxtaposition of security concerns and improvements in economic conditions motivates the second section of the chapter, which attempts to shed light on the complex and nonlinear relationship between crime and economic development.

The third section goes beyond the national statistics. Regional or even subregional averages, by definition, mask the heterogeneity of geographical units over which they average, since they measure only central tendencies. To take an extreme example, the average height across two individuals may be 6 feet, but it will miss the fact that one is 7 feet tall and the other is 5 feet tall. The average is simply not designed to capture these differences, but rather the central tendency between the two. This problem is particularly acute in the case of crime and violence. This third section of the chapter considers specific forms of heterogeneity: across geography and over the life cycle. Antisocial behavior tends to be clustered in very specific geographical units—not only at state or municipal levels, but also at neighborhood and street levels. Furthermore, this concentration is strikingly persistent and stable over time.

Concentration is a feature of crime that is not limited to geography. One the one hand, it is disproportionately perpetrated by adolescent and young adult males. On the other hand, roughly 10 percent to 15 percent of offenders are responsible for approximately 70 percent to 80 percent of crimes.[2] Thus crime also appears to be concentrated over the life cycle and across individuals.

The last section of this chapter focuses on understanding the risks and protective factors of victimization, and explores how victimization and the incidence of crime affect perceptions of security and happiness. The chapter thus documents the personal costs of crime for both victims and nonvictims, whose sense of security can be compromised even they have not been victimized themselves. Interestingly, the patterns that emerge in this section corroborate certain results from the preceding section on the relationship between crime and development: citizens' concerns about crime become much more acute only after the citizenry has achieved a certain level of material well-being. That is, crime and security can be seen as elements in a sequence of features of development and life satisfaction; as countries progress through various stages of development, new challenges arise and different needs become more important and more relevant to the public's well-being.

## Magnitude and persistence

The magnitude of the violence problem in the region is alarming. In 2012 alone, 145,759 people in LAC fell victim to homicide, representing 400 homicides per day and 4.17 homicides every 15 minutes. According to the latest figures for the region, eight countries are above the "conflict" level of violence, as defined by the World Health Organization (WHO), of 30 homicides per 100,000 (see figure 2.1).[3] Honduras and El Salvador have staggering rates of 90 and 54, respectively.

These figures are well above the rate of any country in Africa, some of which have been engaged in civil wars. In 2012, only Lesotho and Swaziland recorded homicide rates above the conflict threshold (38 and 33.8 homicides per 100,000, respectively). Unfortunately, the "endemic" level of violence, defined by WHO as 10 homicides per 100,000, appears to be the norm in the region, with only 10 countries below the threshold.

Sadly, these high homicide rates are not a recent phenomenon for the region, which has experienced high and persistent levels of violence for several decades. According to the UNODC, LAC lost more than 1,560,000 people to homicide from 2000 to 2012; this likely represents an underestimate, given that official statistics are not available for all countries and all years. This figure is equivalent to two and a half times the population of Washington, DC; close to three times the population of Lisbon; and close to a half the population of Panama. Over this 12-year period, homicide victims in LAC were more than double the casualties of the Iraq war (both civilians and military), which have been estimated in the range of 400,000 to 750,000.

Figure 2.2 presents the evolution of the homicide rate for the LAC region as a whole and for its subregions. Strikingly, for the past 15 years, homicides rates have hovered stubbornly around 24 homicides per 100,000, with rates of 23.78 and 23.95 (per 100,000) in 1995 and 2012, respectively. A mild downtrend started to emerge in the first half of the 2000s, but with the deteriorating situation in Central America, any gain has been reversed. Since 2000, homicides due to firearms have increased. While gaps in data availability limit the confidence in such statistics, they indicate that between 60 percent and 73 percent of the homicides in 2010 were committed with firearms. This tendency is largely driven by Central America and the Caribbean. At the beginning of the 2000s, firearm homicides accounted for 40.8 percent and 49.7 percent of homicides in Central America and the Caribbean, respectively; in 2011 the corresponding figures were approximately 59.7 percent and 65.1 percent, respectively.

There was a marked kink in the trend for Central America in 2007. This was in part driven by Mexico's spike in violence, but also by accelerations in violence in Honduras in 2007 and in El Salvador in 2008. Substantial heterogeneity underlies these aggregate statistics, as seen in differences across subregions (a point that is discussed in depth in the next section). South America made important progress in

**FIGURE 2.1:** Homicide rates in LAC, by country, 2009–12

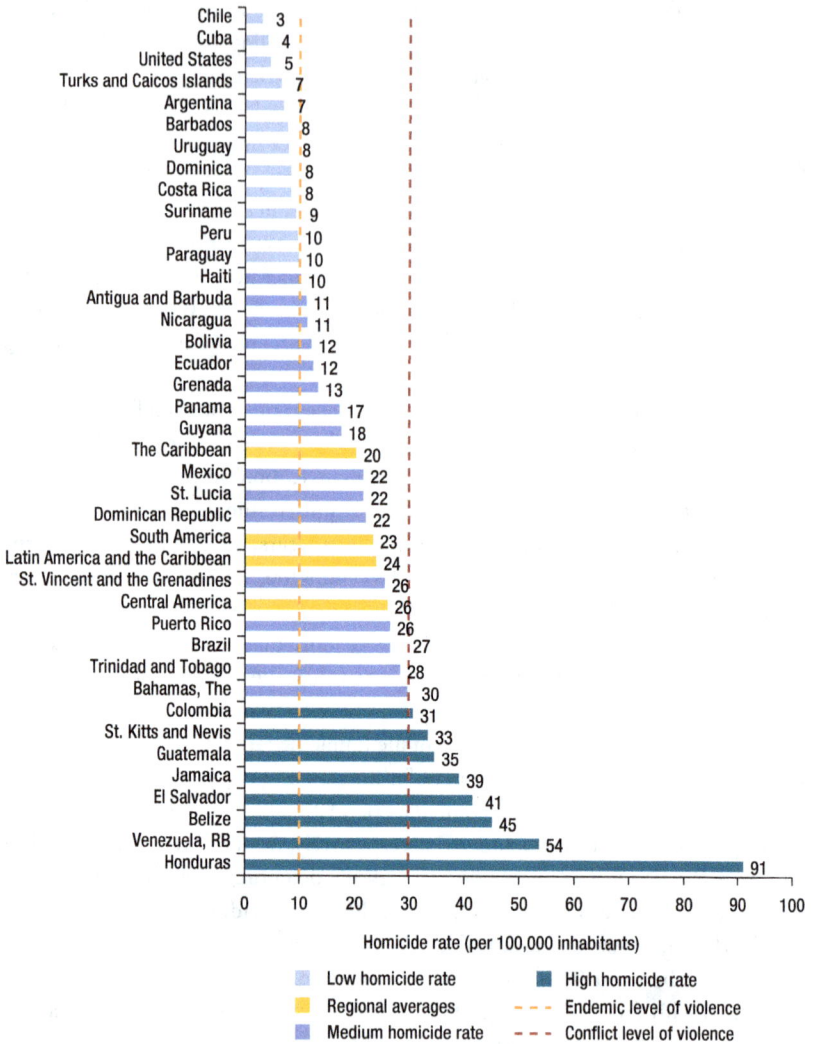

| Country | Rate |
|---|---|
| Chile | 3 |
| Cuba | 4 |
| United States | 5 |
| Turks and Caicos Islands | 7 |
| Argentina | 7 |
| Barbados | 8 |
| Uruguay | 8 |
| Dominica | 8 |
| Costa Rica | 8 |
| Suriname | 9 |
| Peru | 10 |
| Paraguay | 10 |
| Haiti | 10 |
| Antigua and Barbuda | 11 |
| Nicaragua | 11 |
| Bolivia | 12 |
| Ecuador | 12 |
| Grenada | 13 |
| Panama | 17 |
| Guyana | 18 |
| The Caribbean | 20 |
| Mexico | 22 |
| St. Lucia | 22 |
| Dominican Republic | 22 |
| South America | 23 |
| Latin America and the Caribbean | 24 |
| St. Vincent and the Grenadines | 26 |
| Central America | 26 |
| Puerto Rico | 26 |
| Brazil | 27 |
| Trinidad and Tobago | 28 |
| Bahamas, The | 30 |
| Colombia | 31 |
| St. Kitts and Nevis | 33 |
| Guatemala | 35 |
| Jamaica | 39 |
| El Salvador | 41 |
| Belize | 45 |
| Venezuela, RB | 54 |
| Honduras | 91 |

Homicide rate (per 100,000 inhabitants)

- Low homicide rate
- Regional averages
- Medium homicide rate
- High homicide rate
- Endemic level of violence
- Conflict level of violence

*Source:* World Bank, based on United Nations Office of Drugs and Crime (UNODC) data.
*Note:* UNDOC data are for the latest year available (2009–12). Decimals have been suppressed. The dashed lines at 10 and 30 homicides per 100,000 inhabitants represent the endemic and conflict level of violence (according to the WHO).

**FIGURE 2.2:** Homicide rate in LAC, by subregion

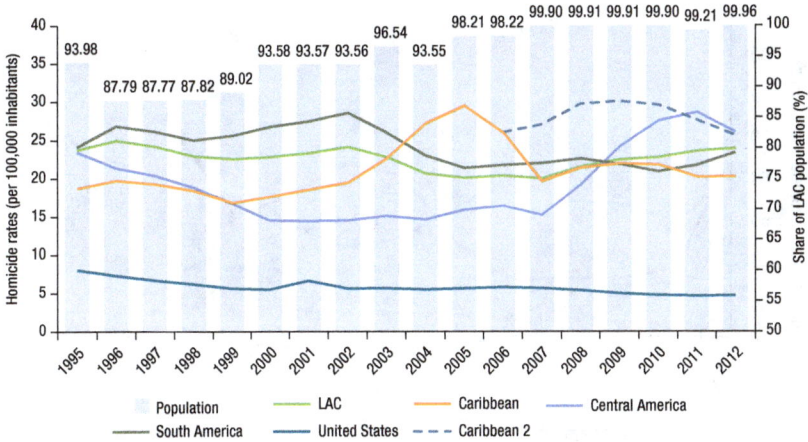

Source: World Bank, based on UNODC data.
Note: The homicide rate per 100,000 is weighted by population. The bars provide a measure of representativeness of the sample of countries used to construct the LAC homicide rate and indicate the fraction of LAC's population with respect to which LAC homicide rates were computed. The dashed line (Caribbean 2) represents the Caribbean, excluding Turks and Caicos and Haiti, whose series start in 2007. The orange line for the Caribbean includes them. Because their homicide rates are lower than those of other Caribbean nations included in the early part of the sample period, their inclusion in the subregional average after 2007 results in a misleading drop in the subregional average.

reducing homicides in the latter half of the decade, mainly thanks to the declining homicides in Colombia and Brazil, whose rates fell from 68.6 to 31.4, and 26.1 to 21.0 from 2001 to 2010, respectively.[4] In contrast, the homicide rate in República Bolivariana de Venezuela rose almost without interruption until 2012, more than doubling from 20.3 in 1995 to 53.6 in 2012. At the other end of the spectrum is Chile (3.1 in 2012), with rates lower than those of the United States in 2012.

El Salvador, Guatemala, and Honduras—a group of countries known as the Northern Triangle—had homicide rates more than double the regional average in 2012 (see figure 2.3). Northern Triangle homicide rates rose steadily from 39.5 in 1999 to 51.3 in 2012, representing a worrisome 30 percent growth rate over the period, equivalent to an annual growth rate of 2 percent. The bulk of the statistics reported here predate the truces between rival gangs that took place in Belize (April 2011) and in El Salvador (February 2012). Both events led to sizable reductions in violence, at least in the short run. In Belize, any truce-related gains were quickly eroded in March 2012, as government funds dedicated to employment opportunities for gang members dried out. El Salvador's homicide rate more than halved during the truce, from 70 in 2011 to 42 per 100,000 in 2012; however, the pact has been fragile. In 2013, homicides per day increased to 16 in July, compared

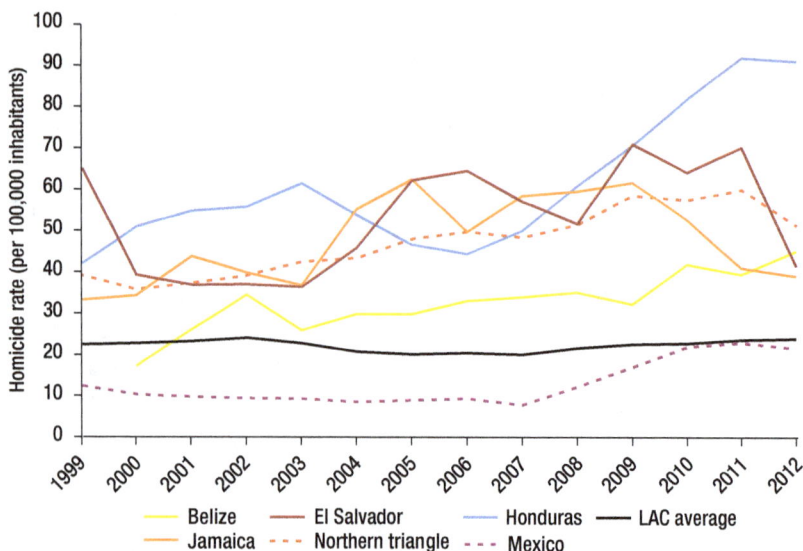

**FIGURE 2.3:** Homicide rates in selected LAC countries, 1999–2012

Source: World Bank, based on UNODC data.

Note: Homicide rates are per 100,000 inhabitants. As a reference point, the figure includes both the regional average, as well as that of the Northern Triangle, comprising El Salvador, Guatemala, and Honduras.

to 5 per day following the agreement and 12 before it (Rodriguez 2013). In 2014, the truce collapsed and homicides spiked. In May 2015, El Salvador broke a grisly record, registering 635 homicides, believed to be the most killings in a single month since its civil war ended in 1992.

Among the most violent countries in the region are Jamaica, Belize, Saint Kitts and Nevis, and Trinidad and Tobago, all with homicide rates exceeding the WHO's "conflict" threshold. Jamaica's rate is particularly volatile, a pattern confirmed by various data sources—WHO, the national police, UNODC, and SES.

## The nexus between crime and development

LAC represents a prima facie outlier compared to other regions, with its extraordinarily high level of violence relative to other regions with comparable levels of economic development—as proxied by gross domestic product (GDP) per capita. This observation becomes clear when illustrated graphically, by mapping regional GDP per capita against levels of violence. In figure 2.4, the size of the spheres is proportional to

**FIGURE 2.4:** LAC's homicide rate relative to other regions in terms of GDP per capita, 2012

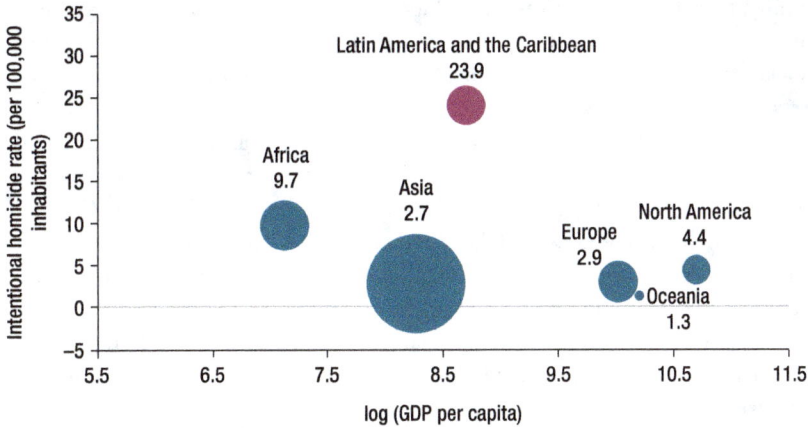

*Source:* World Bank, based on data from UNODC (2012).
*Note:* The size of the spheres is proportional to population.

each region's population. LAC's level of development roughly matches that of Asia, but its homicide rate in 2012 (23.9 homicides per 100,000) is nearly nine times that of Asia, and 46 percent higher than that of Africa.

However, recent research using crime data from the 1990s questions whether the level of crime and violence in LAC is in fact that exceptional. Soares and Naritomi (2010) argue that the incidence of crime in the region is not so different from what should be expected based on socioeconomic and public policy characteristics of its constituent countries. According to the authors, most of the region's seemingly excessive violence can be explained by three factors: high income inequality, low incarceration rates, and small police forces.

As pointed out by Gaviria (2010), a similar conclusion may be drawn from the results of Fajnzylber, Lederman, and Loayza (2002a). In their study of the cross-country determinants of the national homicide rate over the 1970–94 period, the authors estimate dynamic panel data for a sample of countries, and show that, after controlling for average per capita income, the growth rate of real GDP, the educational attainment of the adult population, the level of inequality, and the arrest rate for LAC do not significantly predict the homicide rate. This suggests that mean levels of violence in LAC countries do not differ from what should be expected, given the region's economic, social, and law-enforcement characteristics.[5] This conclusion, however, makes recent trends even more puzzling.

The region's history of elevated homicide rates is in stark contrast with the recent decade's experience of improvements and successes in many important socioeconomic arenas. LAC has made important strides toward broader social equity, as reflected by significant reductions in poverty,[6] in income inequality,[7] and a simultaneous rise in the share of people in the middle classes.[8] Yet these social gains have been accompanied by a deterioration of the security in the region.

What happened in the second half of the 2000s? During this period, an apparent decoupling between GDP per capita and violence took place. This observation is illustrated in figure 2.5, which traces the evolution of poverty, GDP per capita, and homicide rates for LAC. Remarkably, the reduction in violence in the late 1990s and beginning of the 2000s tracked the decline in poverty, with the two variables following similar declining patterns. However, in the second half of the 2000s, poverty and homicide rates began to diverge. Starting in 2005, a positive correlation began to emerge between the homicide rate and GDP per capita (and the size of the middle class).

This contradiction (whether apparent or not) highlights the complexity of the interplay between economic development and crime and violence. Figure 2.6 further

**FIGURE 2.5:** Evolution of poverty, the middle class, economic development, and violence in Latin America, 1995–2012

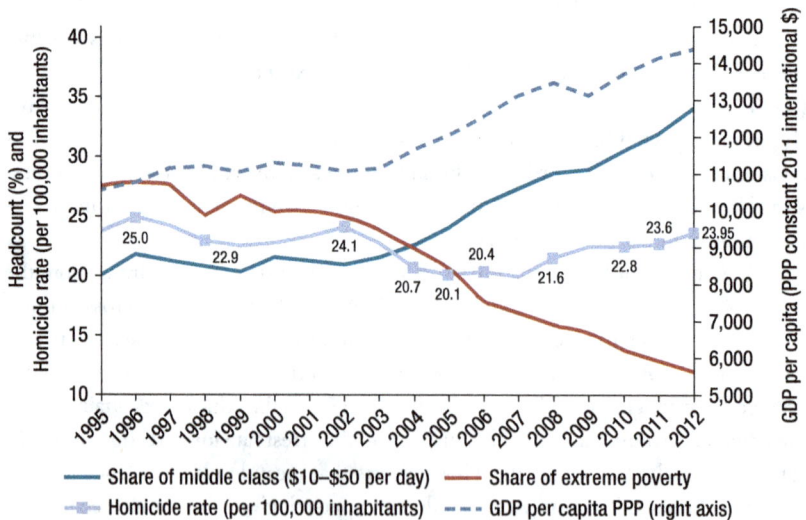

Sources: World Bank. Homicide rates are calculated with data from UNODC, the Organization of American States (OAS), and official statistics from various countries. Data for poverty and the middle class are from Ferreira and others (2013) and LAC Equity Lab data set (2015).
Note: PPP = purchasing power parity.

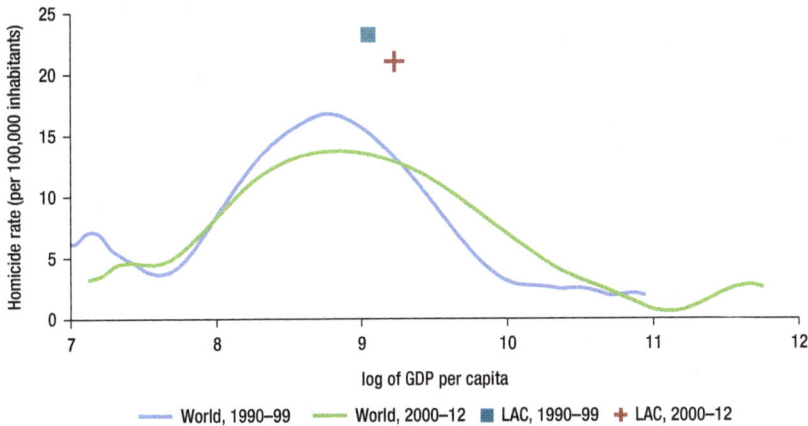

*Sources:* World Bank, based on UNODC data for homicides; World Bank, World Development Indicators (WDI) for GDP per capita.
*Note:* The figure presents nonparametric (kernel-weighted local polynomial regression) estimates of the relationship between economic development and homicides.

illustrates this complexity by flexibly (nonparametrically) estimating the relationship between economic development, as proxied by log GDP per capita, and homicide rates across all countries.[9]

Each dot in figure 2.6 represents LAC's position in a given time period, with the log of per capita income measured on the horizontal axis and the homicide rate along the vertical axis. Each curve corresponds to a separate decade's predicted relationship between log per capita income and the homicide rate, estimated from the cross-section of all countries in the world.

The cross-country relationship between homicides and log GDP per capita is well approximated by an inverted U shape, which flattens out at high levels of per capita income.[10] Empirically, low levels of violence are associated with both low and high levels of development. What generates this inverse U-shape? How does economic development alter the payoffs and (opportunity) cost of crime, as laid out by Becker (1968)?

As countries grow from low levels of income, both the opportunities for crime and the returns to criminality increase—as income rises, wealthier individuals are more attractive criminal targets; this would be akin to an income effect from the perspective of the offender. Since investments in institutions of criminal justice typically lag behind income growth, the likelihood of detection and sanction declines (at least in the short run), implying lower expected costs of crime. These two forces would explain the initial, upward-sloping portion of the relationship. However, as income continues to grow, the opportunity cost of crime likewise increases (in the form of forgone wages in the legal sector in the event of apprehension), thereby reducing the time allocated to "crime" (substitution effect). The higher opportunity cost of crime emerges from the fact that not only do later stages of economic development raise employment prospects, but they could also lead to higher wages (assuming a downward-sloping demand for labor). The interplay between income and substitution effects would be enough to explain the downward portion of the curve. However, it is also possible that as the level of crime rises, both citizens and the private sector increase their demands for public goods—including security and safety—forcing institutions to devote more resources to crime control.

This would correspond to an increased probability of detection and sanction; that is, a higher expected cost of crime, which further contributes to explaining the downward-sloping portion of the relationship. These processes are consistent with Maslow's (1943) "hierarchy of needs," whereby there is a sequence of individual needs and priorities, starting with physiological necessities, and then needs for safety. As countries progress through different stages of development, new challenges and needs arise and become more pressing. In this context, as countries become wealthier, and their physiological needs for survival are met, their concerns and efforts turn to personal safety and a more peaceful society.

In each of the last two decades, LAC's homicide rate has exceeded its expected value, as illustrated by the inverted U-shape and the fact that the two dots for LAC in figure 2.6 are above their respective curves. Encouragingly, comparing the 1990s—a decade characterized by a number of civil conflicts—to the 2000s, the LAC region moved downward toward improving homicide rates, in accordance with the fact that its level of income exceeded the threshold income level at which each curve peaks. However, when the same exercise is replicated over five-year intervals, a decline in homicides is observed for all subperiods other than 2005–10. In the span of five years (2005–10), any prior gains were eroded, yielding an incidence of violence in 2010 that exceeded that of 1995, as also illustrated in figure 2.5. This suggests further complexity in the crime-development relationship. Indeed, the interplay between the factors described above could generate highly nonlinear relationships between the level of crime and violence and various economic variables, each of which is a marker of economic development (such as income, unemployment, demographic structure, and inequality). Depending on the relative magnitudes of the forces at play, these could give rise to multiple local maxima and/or saddle points, such that a subset of the world sample might not deterministically follow the curves in figure 2.6—and yet the relationship would be preserved for the entire sample.

The next section takes a closer look at the evolution of the relationship between some key variables and homicides in LAC.

## A closer look at the different dimensions of the interplay between economic development and violence

The previous discussion presented a reduced-form analysis of the relationship between violence and development. This section explores the relationship in greater detail.

Chioda (2014a) assembles a rich, annual dataset[11] on 19 LAC countries for the latest 15 years in order to conduct a cross-country dynamic panel data analysis.[12] Her analysis formalizes the correlations and trends documented so far in this chapter. It is carried out in stages by sequentially controlling for broader sets of country characteristics to reproduce a hierarchical model. The first set of variables used to explain variation in homicides in LAC includes information about the macro environment, such as degree of country openness and measures of the income distribution (per capita income, Gini coefficient, and GDP growth).[13] The teen pregnancy rate is also included as a proxy for extreme poverty (as in Grogger 1998).[14] The next group of variables reflects features of the population and of the labor market: unemployment, demographic structure, urban population, labor force participation and its gender composition, and education. Chioda's analysis experiments with different markers of education to tease out the relevant gradients. The last group of variables relates to measures of social capital; trust in institutions, democracy, government and the police; measures of corruption; and the amount of drugs seized by country of origin/production.[15]

The choice of variables and the structure of the hierarchical model are aimed at mimicking the spirit of the ecological model of crime (as closely as the data permit), in which risk and protective factors are organized according to three different spheres of influence: family, community, and society. Table 2.1 provides estimated coefficients associated with certain macro variables in one of the most saturated models, which controls for education, police, perceptions of institutions (trust), labor market outcomes, urbanization, drug production, female labor force participation, and demographic structure of the population, among other factors. All specifications include time and country fixed effects.[16]

Prior research on the relationship between crime and measures of the income and income inequality has been equivocal. Some authors have estimated significant effects (Kelly 2000; Fajnzylber, Lederman, and Loayza 2002a, 2002b), while others have found little evidence of a relationship (Brush 2007; Pridemore 2011). The results reported in table 2.1 are consistent with the latter group, with the Gini coefficient and per capital income appearing not to predict changes in homicides. Brush (2007) provides an explanation for the inconsistencies in the literature: while differences across countries in the level of the homicide rate may be well explained by differences in income and income inequality, within-country changes over time are poorly explained by these variables.[17]

**TABLE 2.1:** Selected coefficients on macro variables from the saturated model

| Regressors | Drugs + corruption + adolescent fertility | | Drugs + corruption + adolescent fertility + trust in police, judiciary, and interpersonal | |
| --- | --- | --- | --- | --- |
| | Excluding log pop | Including log pop | Excluding log pop | Including log pop |
| Lag of homicide rate | 0.662*** | 0.661*** | 0.692*** | 0.682*** |
| | (0.0848) | (0.0945) | (0.0916) | (0.100) |
| GDP, growth | −0.240** | −0.240** | −0.159 | −0.163 |
| | (0.0859) | (0.0889) | (0.129) | (0.131) |
| log of GNI per capita | 5.434 | 5.450 | 4.246 | 4.576 |
| | (3.401) | (3.445) | (5.276) | (5.474) |
| Exports of goods & services (% of GDP) | 0.199** | 0.200** | 0.192* | 0.203* |
| | (0.0839) | (0.0795) | (0.0973) | (0.0967) |
| Gini coefficient | −0.325 | −0.324 | −0.257 | −0.242 |
| | (0.313) | (0.320) | (0.442) | (0.452) |
| Unemployment, adult (% of total labor force age 25–64)–lagged | 0.229 | 0.226 | 0.137 | 0.103 |
| | (0.283) | (0.249) | (0.269) | (0.228) |
| Unemployment, youth (% of total labor force age 15–24)–lagged | 0.338** | 0.338** | 0.347** | 0.350** |
| | (0.131) | (0.133) | (0.158) | (0.158) |

*Source:* Chioda 2014a.
*Note:* All specifications include country and year fixed effects. Standard errors are clustered at the country level. The adult unemployment rate is net of the youth employments rate. log pop = log of population.
Significance level: * = 10 percent, ** = 5 percent, *** = 1 percent.

The relationship between crime and inequality, in particular, has been scrutinized and has been found weaker than previously suggested. Pridemore (2011) argues that the majority of studies that document a positive relationship between crime and inequality fail to control for poverty. Poverty is not only the most consistent predictor of homicide rates in the United States, but also a main confounder of the inequality-homicide association.[18] Consistent with this argument, Chioda's (2014a) measures of extreme poverty, such as the teen pregnancy rate,[19] have positive and precisely estimated effects on homicides, which imply that an increase in contemporaneous teen pregnancy (proxied by the number of births per 1,000 women age 15–19) is associated to approximately 0.5-0.6 additional homicides per 100,000. To be clear, these results highlight only that inequality may be a weak predictor of crime when both are measured at the national level. Chioda's estimates cannot yield information about the roles of local-level inequality and social segregation in predicting crime, as discussed in greater detail in the subsequent chapters on poverty and crime, and on the relevance of neighborhoods.

A closer look at the role of poverty (defined as per capita income below $4 per day), of vulnerability (per capita income between $4 and $10 per day), and of the middle class (per capita income between $10 and $50 per day) delivers more insight into the relationships between the income distribution and violence. This analysis is carried out by means of a more parsimonious model[20] that includes only macro-economic variables, whose relationships with homicides rate were permitted to vary flexibly over time.[21]

### Income distribution: Poverty, vulnerability, and the middle class

When the relationships between economic variables and homicides rates are allowed to change from year to year (for a graphic representation of selected estimates, see figure 2.7), the data highlight a curious break in the early 2000s for certain variables. This warrants some discussion.

First, the sizes of the vulnerable class and the upper class (per capita income greater than $50 per day) are systematically (and statistically) related to changes in the homicide rate only after 2003.[22] Whereas these variables have little statistical

**FIGURE 2.7:** Year- and subperiod-specific effects of income groups on homicide rates, 1996–2010

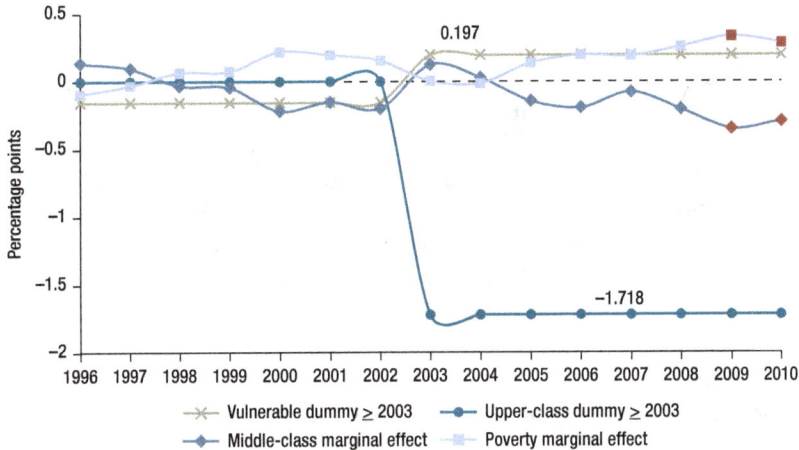

Source: Chioda 2014a.

Note: The figure plots the year- and subperiod-specific effects on the homicide rate of poverty (per capita daily income below $4 per day); of the size of the vulnerable class (per capita daily income between $4 and $10 per day); of the size of the middle class (per capita daily income between $10 and $50 per day); and of the size of upper class. All specifications rely on dynamic panel data models, including time and country fixed effects.

relation to changes in homicides before 2003, after this date, the size of the vulnerable class emerges as a risk factor (that is, it increases the growth rate of homicides), while the size of the upper class is a protective factor (that is, it lowers its growth rate). In turn, throughout the 15-year period, the size of the middle class and the level of poverty have the expected sign in most years, but are not statistically significant determinants of observed trends in violence. However, there is a slight trend toward larger magnitudes of these effects in the latter part of the 2000s, such that income and poverty become significant predictors by the end of the sample: being poor and being middle class become an important risk and protective factor, respectively, at the end of the decade.

Second, taken together, these results suggest that if improvements in the income distribution stem from transitions from poverty to vulnerability, the resulting benefit may not be sufficient to act as an immediate protective factor. It may even lead to higher local inequality (and resulting tensions) if local neighborhood characteristics do not keep up with the changes in income (such as the income of other residents in the neighborhood, and human capital accumulation), which typically follow income with a lag. Consistent with this conjecture is the yearly evolution of the vulnerable and middle-class marginal effects; according to the estimation, being in the vulnerable class in 2003 and 2004 represents a transitory risk factor. A similar "stickiness" characterizes transitions from the vulnerable to the middle class, such that yearly coefficient for the middle class becomes statistically significant only toward the end of the sample, perhaps suggesting that a critical mass in the middle class needs to occur before it becomes a protective factor.

Finally, these findings point to an asymmetry and nonlinearity in the relationship between income and homicides, as the strength of the effects are heterogeneous at different points in the distribution of individuals across income classes. After 2003, hypothetical deteriorations in the economic circumstances of the middle class (which would lead to an increase in the size of the vulnerable class) would be associated with greater violence (with a 1 percent increase in the proportion of the vulnerable population associated with 0.2 additional homicides per 100,000). Instead, improvements in economic conditions that lead to expansions of the middle class do not appear sufficient to mitigate violence. Only substantial economic gains that lead to a broader upper class are meaningfully related with lower homicides rates, with a 1 percent increase in the share of the population in the upper class leading to a decline of 1.7 homicides per 100,000 (all else equal).

In closing, it is important to note that the relationship between income[23] and crime is theoretically ambiguous since, from the perspective of potential criminals, more income implies more opportunities for economically motivated crimes, higher consumption of criminogenic goods, but also greater investment in security among potential victims, diminished economic need for crime among potential offenders, and higher opportunity cost of offending. Indeed, the theoretical uncertainty surrounding the effect of income on criminality is dealt with extensively in chapter 5.

## GDP growth and unemployment

The preceding discussion suggests that economic development per se is not sufficient to induce declines in crime: development that generates a shift in the income distribution whereby the expansion of the upper class delivers the greatest crime-reducing benefits. Consistent with this proposition, Chioda's (2014a) models estimate a precise and robust protective effect of real GDP growth on homicides (see second row of table 2.1). The estimates imply that a 1 percentage point increase in the growth rate of GDP is associated with between 0.215 and 0.290 fewer homicides per 100,000, an effect that is consistently distinguishable from zero at the 1 percent level. Growth, therefore, acts as a protective factor and can help "outstrip" the need for crime—if, for instance, periods of high growth are more inclusive, in the sense that broader swaths of society are invested in the growth. Interestingly, the magnitude and significance of the coefficient on GDP growth are weakened when measures of social capital are included in the estimation (third and fourth columns of table 2.1), although the coefficients on these measures are never themselves statistically significant and their magnitudes tend to be small. One interpretation of this pattern is that society's institutions catch up to crime more rapidly during periods of growth, and measures of trust (particularly in the judiciary and in law enforcement) capture these institutional improvements.

Economic development is also associated with ameliorations in labor markets conditions: better employment opportunities (and possibly higher wages). However, as discussed, it is also associated with increased opportunities and returns to crime. Whether unemployment and crime are related remains an open question (Bushway 2011). In a rational, Beckerian model of crime, unemployment would lead to more crime by lowering the opportunity cost of crime and increasing the attractiveness of illegal income. However, Routine Theory suggests that in the short term, unemployment would lead to more home-based activities (Cantor and Land 1985, 1991), thereby reducing crime.[24] Whereas the short-term impact of unemployment on crime may be indeterminate, its medium-term effect should be less ambiguously positive, making a case for including the lag of unemployment in the model (in addition to the obvious advantage of being predetermined relative to current homicide rate). Empirically, the (lagged) aggregate unemployment rate is unrelated to violence in any of the models considered. However, when distinguishing between youth and adult unemployment and controlling for them separately in the model, a stable pattern emerges. In all specifications, the coefficient associated with adult unemployment remains insignificant, whereas youth unemployment is always positively related to the homicide rate and the coefficient estimate exhibits surprising stability. In both the most parsimonious and the most saturated specifications, the coefficient of youth unemployment is roughly 0.3. This estimate is not only statistically significant, but also economically significant, implying that a 3 percentage point increases in youth unemployment would be associated with 1 additional homicide per 100,000.[25]

However, Chioda's (2014c)[26] analysis of the labor force participation of perpetrators in Mexico is in apparent contradiction to the result that youth unemployment is related to crime (see figure 2.8).

Regardless of the type of crime (homicides, robberies, violent, or property crimes), suspects and perpetrators alike are characterized by higher labor market attachment than the general population. In particular, young perpetrators are employed at much higher rates (between 85 percent and 90 percent are employed) than their counterparts in the general population (between 58 percent and 68 percent are employed) and in the adult population. This wedge might be explained by the observation that many youths between the ages of 16 and 24 are still in school and accumulating human capital. However, the gap between the labor force participation rates of perpetrators and of the general population persists even after controlling for the level of education; for a given level of schooling, offenders are more frequently employed than their counterparts who are not perpetrators.

The result holds not only in the cross-section but is also supported by a (synthetic) cohort analysis, in which repeated cross-sectional samples of individuals are grouped together according to their year of birth, defining cohorts that are then tracked over time. Figure 2.9 shows that, up until age 40, perpetrators are typically employed at much higher rates than the general population. In particular, the age distribution of employment is substantially younger among perpetrators than in the general population. As will be discussed in chapter 5, Chioda (2014c) also shows that, within every age category, offenders are employed at high rates (with employment rates uniformly above 75 percent). These observations challenge the commonly held belief that crime is committed largely by "idle hands."

How might the fact that youth unemployment appears as a risk factor in Chioda's (2014c) macro-level regressions be reconciled with the high rate of employment among perpetrators? The two sets of results may be reconciled if crime and work are not thought of as (mutually exclusive) perfect substitutes, but instead as "imperfect" complements. This idea originates from evidence emerging from developed countries (see Grogger 1998; Fagan and Freeman 1999). Rather than a dichotomous choice, for some individuals, economic activity appears to lie along a continuum of legal and illegal "work." This proposition may be particularly relevant for youth with low educational attainment (such as incomplete secondary schooling), who are likely to face (legal) employment prospects that offer limited potential for wage growth, skill acquisition, and job stability, and who may ultimately find employment in the informal sector.

As will be discussed in chapter 5, the quality of employment, rather than employment status per se, plays a central role in the relationship between labor

**FIGURE 2.8:** Employment rates of perpetrators across all age groups and among youth, Mexico, 1997–2011

*(percentage of perpetrators and of the general population employed)*

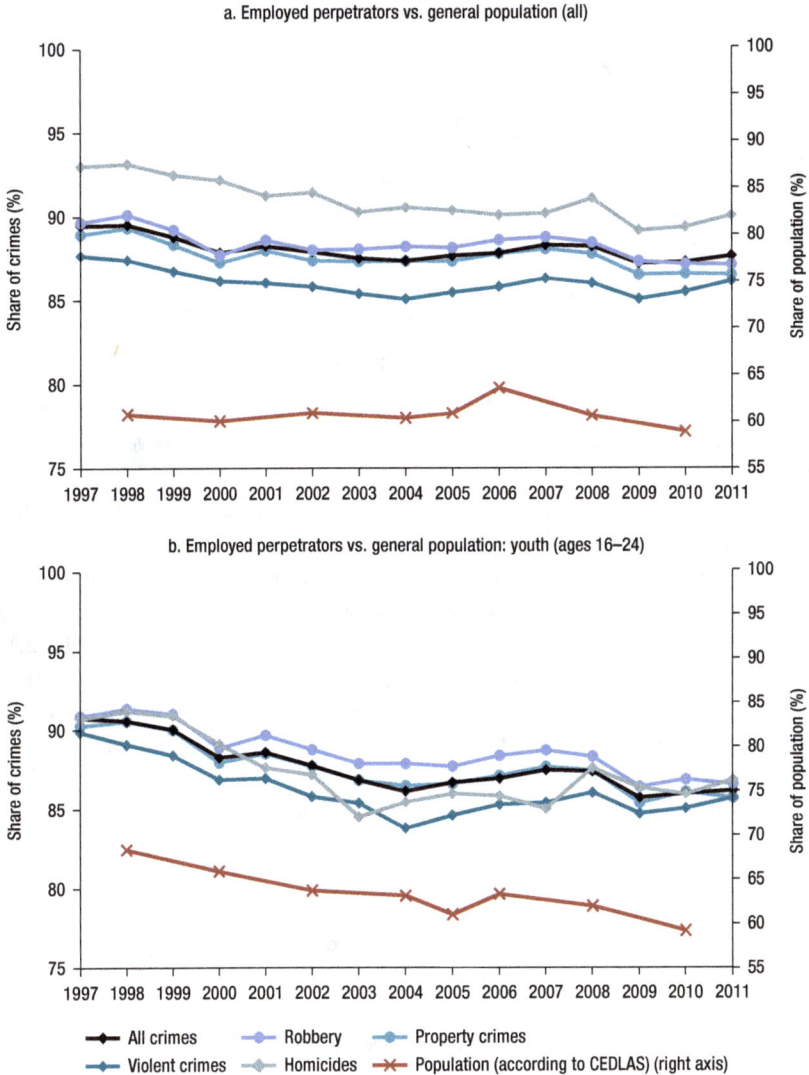

a. Employed perpetrators vs. general population (all)

b. Employed perpetrators vs. general population: youth (ages 16–24)

- All crimes
- Robbery
- Property crimes
- Violent crimes
- Homicides
- Population (according to CEDLAS) (right axis)

*Source:* Chioda 2014c, using data from Instituto Nacional de Estadística y Geografía (INEGI) and Centro de Estudios Distributivos, Laborales y Sociales (CEDLAS).

**FIGURE 2.9:** Employment profiles of male perpetrators and general male population, Mexico, 2010

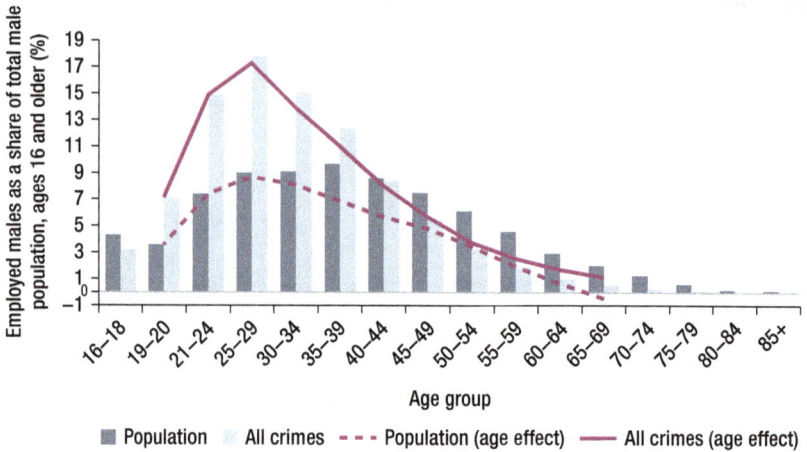

*Source:* Chioda 2014c, based on confidential data from Instituto Nacional de Estadística y Geografía (INEGI).

market outcomes and criminal offending. This finding is also consistent with the results discussed at the beginning of this section and summarized in table 2.1. In that context, youth unemployment refers to employment status in the formal labor market, whereas in figure 2.8 and figure 2.9, its definition includes both formal and informal occupations. As such, youth unemployment of the variety that is reflected in table 2.1 is a measure of the degree of scarcity of higher-quality (formal) employment opportunities. The fact that it is highly positively correlated with violence and that perpetrators are employed (in either the formal or informal sectors) at much higher rates than the general population suggests that criminal offending is sensitive to the availability of high-quality employment opportunities, rather than merely employment status.

## Trade, location, and the "darker" side of development

This section considers how international commerce, as proxied by exports and other indirect measures of a country's openness, relates to the evolution of homicides over the last 15 years (see table 2.1).

Here again, theory is equivocal as to the sign and magnitude of the relationship between a country's openness to trade and crime; it is ultimately an empirical question. Interestingly, table 2.1 reports that exports—an indirect measure of a country's openness—are robustly and positively related to homicides. A 1 percentage point increase in exports as a percent of GDP is consistently associated with 0.2 additional homicides per 100,000 across specifications, highlighting once more that the relationship between crime and development is nonlinear and complex.

Research confirms that increasing violence can be viewed as one of the costs of economic development. As countries transition through different stages of economic development, increased crime may result, given the previously discussed ambiguous impact of income on violence and illicit opportunities. In particular, while improvements in infrastructure and in financial markets and rising income may help economic growth and foster the development of legal markets, they may also increase the economic returns to transactions in illegal markets by lowering the transaction costs, as well as the likelihood of detection. Indeed, violence is known to respond to economic incentives and rents. For instance, Angrist and Kugler (2008) document that exogenous increases in coca prices intensify violence in rural districts in Colombia as combatant groups fight over the elevated economic rents. Dell (2014) studies the escalation of violence in Mexico since 2007 and presents evidence that drug cartels employ violence in response to changes in economic rents. She argues that government crackdowns reduce rents from criminal activity at the time of the government action; but by weakening the incumbent cartel (the target of the crackdown), they also reduce the costs associated with taking control of a municipality where the incumbent previously operated. Controlling territory offers cartels substantial rents from trafficking and a variety of other criminal activities once the crackdown subsides.

While this regional study does not focus on organized crime and drug markets, it is difficult to avoid acknowledging the spillovers of development into these illegal markets, particularly given LAC's unique geographical position as a producer of illicit drugs (such as coca) and also its proximity to one of the world's largest consumer markets (the United States). The drug market is not only a multi-billion-dollar market,[27] but it is also a complex one that imposes a number of constraints on the supply chain. Coca is a fragile plant that grows only at certain latitudes, implying that a business model that brings the drug to market requires decentralized, international production, but with adequate quality control to ensure survival of the consumer base—and furthermore requires delivery in a timely fashion (Canales 2013). A successful intermediate supplier or vertically integrated producer in this market must guarantee that the product will be reliably delivered to the final market. Achieving this requires securing absolute control over the geographic corridors through which drugs are transported so there are minimal interruptions in supply from the authorities and others. How important are these considerations in explaining patterns of violence in LAC?

The next section formalizes the arguments made here and attempts to quantify the importance of geography and trade corridors as determinants of violence. Because of data limitations, the discussion is limited to the Mexican case; however, certain conclusions are likely to be generalizable to other LAC countries.

## Geography, trade corridors, and violence

Does distance from the United States—the main consumer market—matter for the geographic distribution of violence? Does transportation infrastructure matter? Because the data requirements for testing such hypotheses are onerous, this study cannot provide evidence that addresses these questions for the entire region. However, an analysis of Mexican data suggests that both distance and competition for control over major roadways to the U.S. market play important roles in shaping the geography of violence.

Figure 2.10 indicates that a municipality's distance from the U.S. border matters, and its importance has grown over time.[28] The figure provides snapshots of the effect of distance from the U.S. border on the quantiles of the distribution of municipal-level homicide rates at three moments in time: the 1990s, the early 2000s, and the late 2000s. The estimates are obtained from three separate quantile regressions of municipal-level homicide rates on the distance from the border; along the horizontal axis are the 10 deciles of the homicide distribution for which a separate estimate was obtained. For instance, q1 corresponds to the 10 percent of municipalities within a given distance from the U.S. border with the lowest levels of homicides. Each point along a line represents the effect of distance (measured in kilometers) on that decile.[29] The change in patterns from 2007 to 2012 is shown in maps 2.1 and 2.2.

**FIGURE 2.10:** Effects of distance from the U.S. border on homicide rates in Mexican municipalities, by quantile, 1990s, early 2000s, and late 2000s

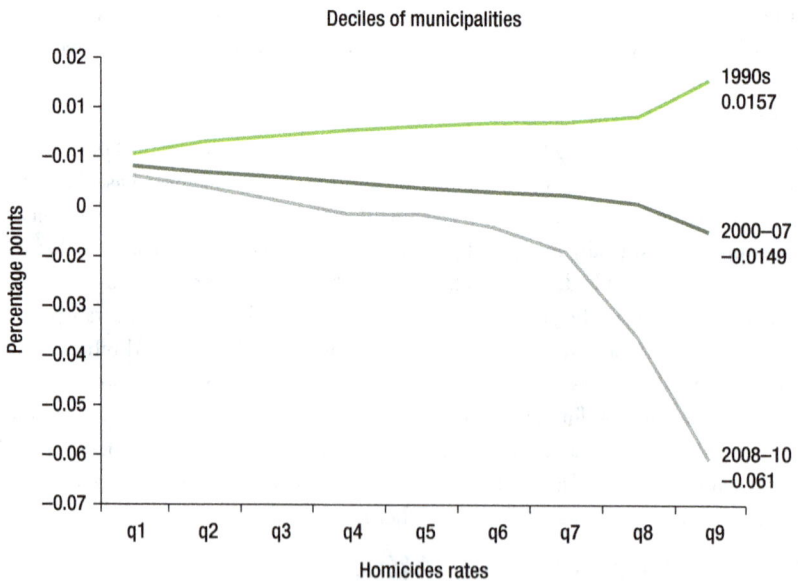

*Source:* Chioda 2014b, based on confidential data from Instituto Nacional de Estadística y Geografía (INEGI).
*Note:* Quantiles are the distribution of municipal-level homicide rates. Distances are in kilometers. Plotted effects along the distribution of homicides are all significant at the 1 percent level, with the exception of the first decile (q1) in the 1990s, which is significant at the 10 percent level.

**MAP 2.1:** Municipal homicide rates and principal highways, Mexico, 2007 and 2012

a. Homicides rate by deciles, 2007

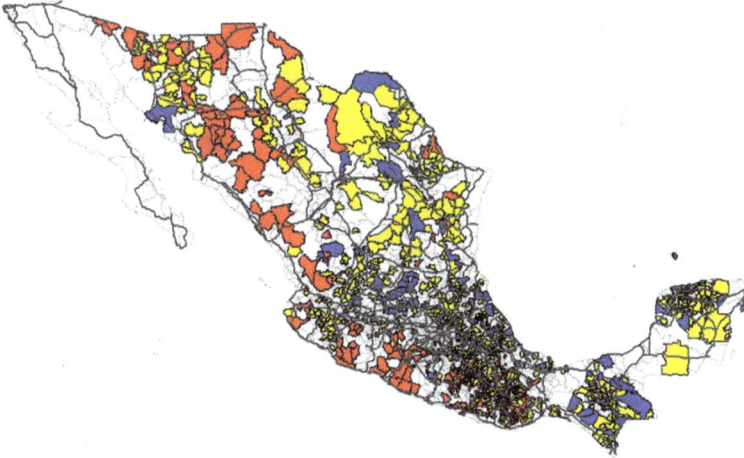

b. Homicides rate by deciles, 2012

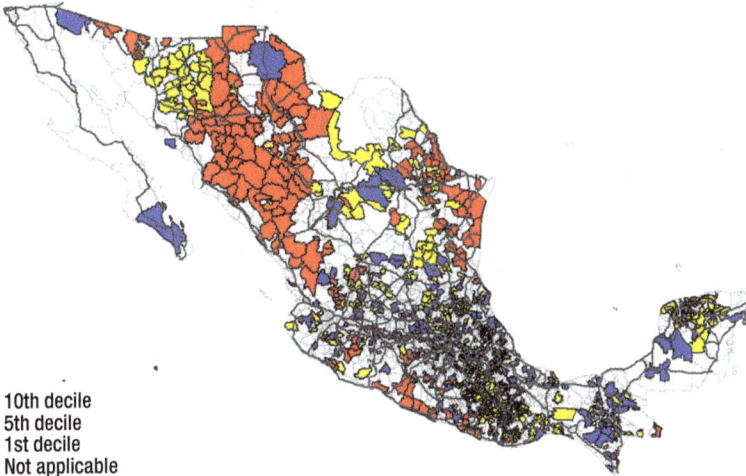

- 10th decile
- 5th decile
- 1st decile
- Not applicable

*Source:* Chioda 2014b, based on data from Instituto Nacional de Estadística y Geografía (INEGI).
*Note:* Yellow, blue, and red shading correspond to municipalities in the 1st, 5th (median), and 10th deciles of homicide rate distribution, respectively. Black lines indicate main highways.

**MAP 2.2:** U.S. ports of entry, Mexican highways, and homicide rates for the most violent municipalities in Mexico, 2012

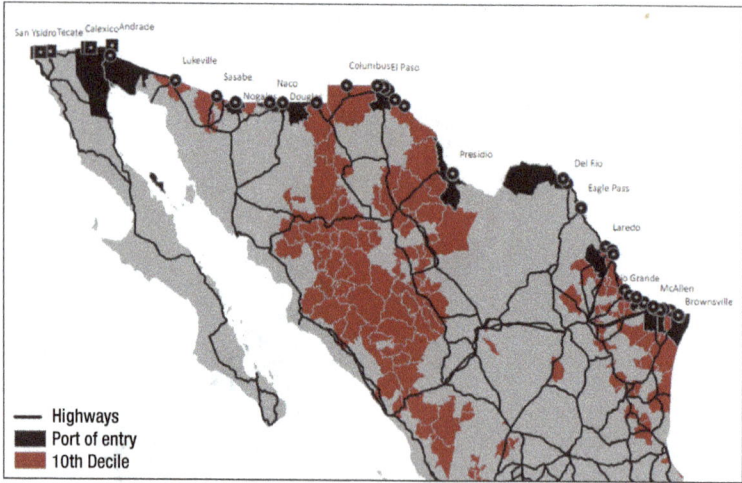

*Source:* World Bank calculations, based on data from Instituto Nacional de Estadística y Geografía (INEGI).
*Note:* The 10th decile = the 10 percent most violent municipalities.

The light green line summarizes the effects of distance in the 1990s. Given that it lies entirely above 0, it indicates that distance to the U.S. border was uniformly a risk factor for homicide in the 1990s; conversely, proximity to the United States was a protective factor. Distance to the United States had a positive impact on every decile of the homicide distribution; municipalities furthest away from the United States were at greatest risk of violence, and this risk increased the more violent was the municipality. An additional 100 kilometers from the U.S. border raised the municipality homicide rate by 1.57 homicides per 100,000 among those most violent municipalities (that is, among the 90th percentile of homicides among municipalities of similar distance from the United States) in the 1990s.

Over the course of the early 2000s, however, proximity to the United States became a risk factor. The effect of distance at each quantile is very similar in magnitude to that of the 1990s, but has the opposite sign. This deterioration continued through the 2000s with a sharper deterioration after 2007; by the late 2000s, for the most violent municipalities, 100 kilometers closer to the U.S. border would have the dramatic effect of raising homicide rates by 6 per 100,000 inhabitants among the most violent municipalities.

**Weapons, U.S. gun laws, and spillovers**

What might explain the change in sign of the relationship between proximity to the U.S. border and violence in the 2000s? One explanation is that violence intensified in municipalities where weapons became more accessible. That is, the market for firearms experienced a supply shock in the 2000s, which differentially affected security in municipalities closer to the U.S. border. This hypothesis is explored by Dube, Dube, and García-Ponce (2013), who study the spillover effects generated by the 2004 expiration of the U.S. Federal Assault Weapons Ban (FAWB) on violence in Mexican municipalities close to the U.S. border. The FAWB had been in place throughout the United States since 1994, and banned a group of firearms with the capacity to fire multiple shots rapidly, including a number of semiautomatic firearms classified as "assault weapons."

Not all (border) states were uniformly affected by the FAWB's expiration; whereas the sunset provision in the law meant that such weapons became available in Arizona, New Mexico, and Texas, California retained its own state-level ban, and was therefore unaffected by the 2004 expiration of the federal law. Dube, Dube, and García-Ponce (2013) argue that the lifting of the federal ban relaxed access to assault weapons in Mexican locations closer to ports of entry into Arizona, New Mexico, and Texas, with little or no (spillover) effect on access in localities bordering California, thereby providing geographic variation in resultant arms flows (see map 2.2).[30] Their baseline estimates suggest that municipalities neighboring ports of entry into Arizona, New Mexico, and Texas experienced a 60 percent increase in homicides as compared to municipalities 100 miles away, which implies an additional 238 homicides (annually) in the area within 100 miles of the border ports. To put this effect into perspective, the additional homicides resulting from the FAWB's expiration represent 30 percent of all gun-related deaths in bordering municipalities after 2004. In this instance, the supply of weapons has a large effect on violence.

As discussed in the context of figure 2.10, the increasing violence in Mexico since 2007 has rendered proximity to the United States a risk factor. The (relative) ease of access to semi-automatic weapons may have contributed to this deterioration, but what is the root cause of conflict that this access has made more severe? The pattern of outbreaks of violence seems consistent with the theory of more intense competition for control over territories, resulting from the growing fragmentation and proliferation of cartels, which expanded from 6 in 2006 to 16 by mid-2011 (Guerrero-Gutiérrez 2011).

Dell (2014) formalizes this argument by exploiting variation in the intensity of efforts by local policies to combat and disable drug cartels generated by close mayoral elections in which the winner belongs to the more conservative and hardline Partido Acción Nacional (PAN). She documents substantial increases in drug-related violence following close PAN victories, due initially to crackdowns on local cartels. However, crackdowns have two additional effects. First, as incumbent cartels are weakened by government crackdowns, competition for control of the territory lost by the incumbent intensifies among rival cartels. In this sense, the violence of crackdowns begets more violence.

Second, violence spills over into other territories; when the authorities wrest control from incumbent cartels, the drug traffic that would otherwise have run through its territory is diverted elsewhere, along other routes to the U.S. market. Violence, therefore, increases along these alternate routes, as a result of the networked nature of the drug trade: if one route to the end market is foreclosed, another will bear the burden of its traffic (and its violence).

However, where drug trafficking is concerned, not all routes are created equal. Those leading to U. S. ports of entry are particularly affected by violence, consistent with cartels competing for strategic routes and pathways to the consumer market (see maps 2.1, 2.2, and 2.4).

For instance, Chihuahua occupies a strategic and logistically unique position as a port of entry to the United States. Although it was among the most violent states in the early 2000s, over the course of the decade, it experienced a particularly rapid deterioration in security, with violence spreading across its municipalities along the highways that fan out from its U.S. ports of entry in accordance with a model of contagion: its homicide rates rose from 15.6 homicides per 100,000 in 2007 to 187.6 in 2010, representing 25 percent of all homicides in Mexico in that year.

In closing, this first set of stylized facts highlights the complexity of the relationship between crime and development. In particular, theories of criminal behavior ascribe unambiguous effects to many standard indicators of economic activity. However, because such relationships can be nonlinear and nonmonotonic—as in the case of the relationship between violence and GDP per capita—even the signs of certain correlations may be difficult to predict. These may ultimately depend on the stage of development: in certain instances, increasing violence may simply be a manifestation of the development process itself.

## Heterogeneity: Spatial features of the distribution of crime

The previous sections examined how location and geography emerged as important determinants of the incidence of violence in Mexico and of its recent escalation. In general, crime and violence exhibit very distinctive spatial patterns. This feature is not limited to LAC, but is also observed in developed countries. Marked spatial heterogeneity, high degrees of geographic concentration and clustering, and spatial and intertemporal spillovers in crime are the features discussed in this section.

### Spatial heterogeneity

Maps 2.1 to 2.4 portray a heterogeneous landscape that is masked by regional and subregional aggregate levels of violence. Throughout LAC, many areas stand in stark contrast to the gloomy picture painted by the eight countries in the region whose levels of violence exceed the WHO-defined "conflict" threshold of 30 per 100,000. For instance, in 2012, and for most of the decade, Chile enjoyed a lower incidence of homicide (3.1 homicides per 100,000) than the United States (4.7 per 100,000, in

### a. Homicide rate by municipality, 2012

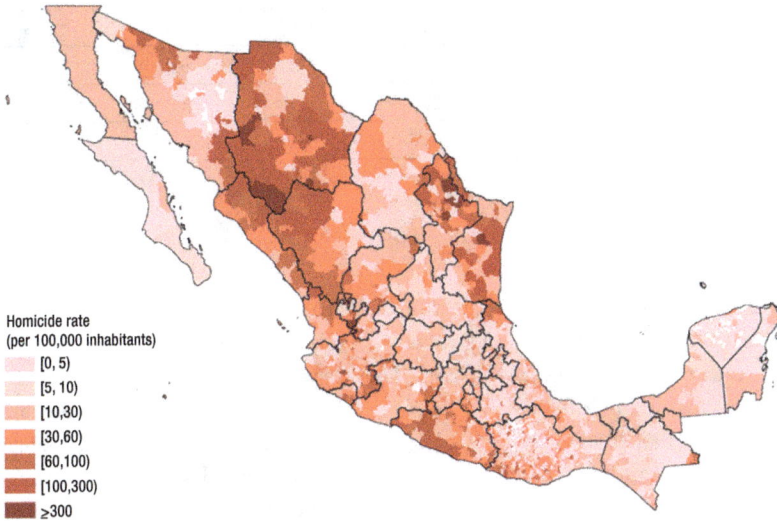

Homicide rate
(per 100,000 inhabitants)

- [0, 5)
- [5, 10)
- [10,30)
- [30,60)
- [60,100)
- [100,300)
- ≥300

### b. Homicide rate by state, 2012

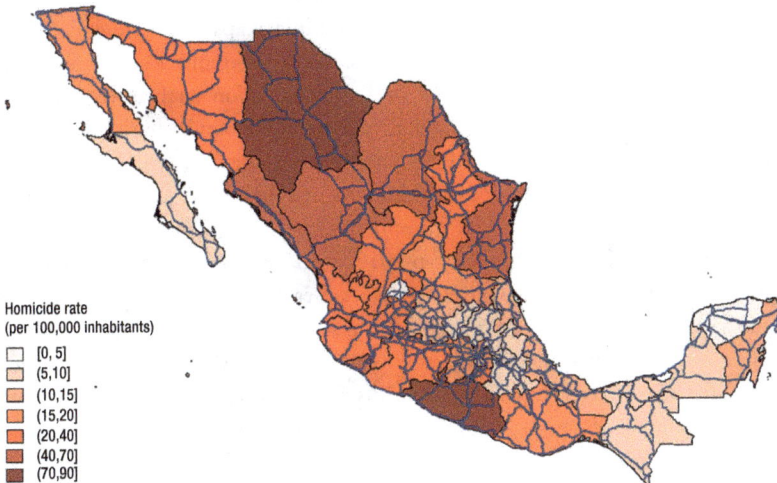

Homicide rate
(per 100,000 inhabitants)

- [0, 5]
- (5,10]
- (10,15]
- (15,20]
- (20,40]
- (40,70]
- (70,90]

*Source:* Chioda 2014b, based on data from Instituto Nacional de Estadística y Geografía (INEGI).

**TABLE 2.2:** Homicide rates in Mexico, Guatemala, and Colombia, 1995, 2000, 2005, and 2012

| Country | Homicide rate (per 100,000), selected years | | | |
|---|---|---|---|---|
| | 1995 | 2000 | 2005 | 2012 |
| Mexico | 16.9 | 10.3 | 9.0 | 21.5 |
| Guatemala | 32.5 | 25.9 | 42.1 | 34.6 |
| Colombia | 69.7 | 66.5 | 39.6 | 30.7 |

*Source:* UNODC data set, 2015.

2012—a historical low). Similarly, in 2007, Uruguay's homicide rate matched that of Canada and the United States, and was only slightly higher in 2012.

Even national figures can mislead. This is evident in a simple comparison of table 2.2, which reports national homicide rates for Colombia, Guatemala, and Mexico, in 1995, 2000, 2005, and 2012 (see also figure 2.11). By definition, averages provide measures of the central tendency of data and are not designed to summarize heterogeneity, or variation in the underlying data. Thus it is no surprise that the data underlying them can exhibit a great deal of dispersion. In the case of violence, dispersion across geographic units is particularly acute.

Figure 2.11 illustrates the distribution of municipality-level homicide rates in four countries, for multiple years, providing multiple snapshots of how dispersed violence is in each country. In some instances, the distributions are "multimodal," in the sense of having multiple "peaks" in their distribution, such as Mexico in all years, and Colombia in 2008. Each country's aggregate homicide rate will therefore tend not to be representative of any particular municipality or department and will miss the shapes and evolutions of these irregular distributions. They thus have limited value in terms of describing a country's experience with violence.

Mexico's homicide rates of 21.9 in 2010 and 22.8 in 2011 are the product of significant state- and municipal-level variability. Despite the recent deterioration in security, some municipalities experienced declines in violence and homicides. Indeed, between 2007 and 2010, municipalities between the 40th and the 60th percentiles and those in the 75th percentile of the distance distribution from the U.S. border experienced substantial declines of 9 and 7 homicides per 100,000, respectively, whereas municipalities in the north (in the 25th percentile, in terms of distance from the United States) saw their rates increase by 26.5 per 100,000.

Figure 2.12 presents state/departmental homicide rates in Colombia, Guatemala, and Mexico (ordered from largest to smallest) and their "contributions" to the total number of homicides, illustrating how concentrated violence is geographically. In Guatemala, the top six departments account for 64 percent

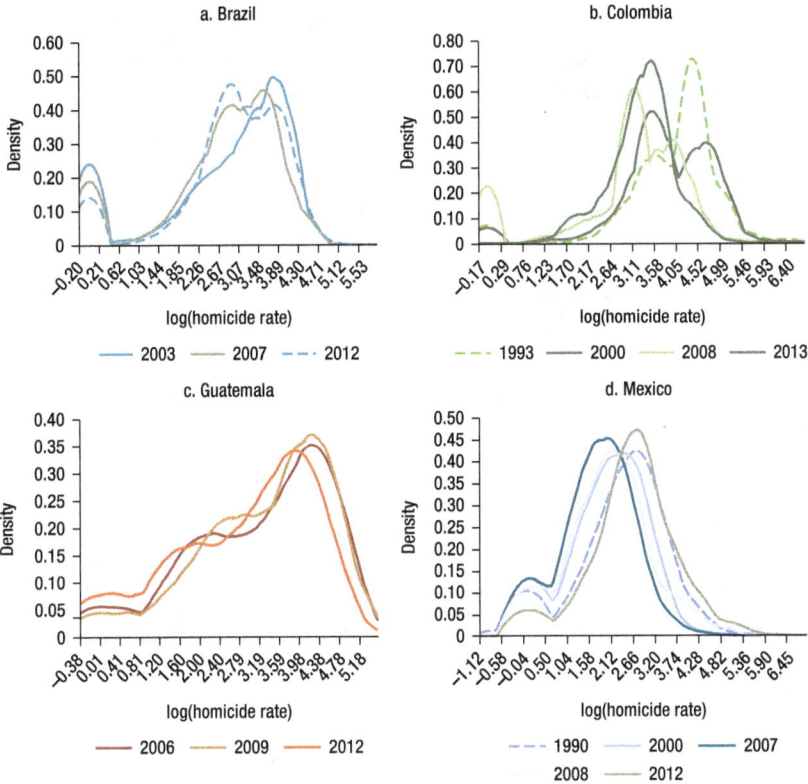

**FIGURE 2.11:** Kernel density of homicide rates across municipalities in Brazil, Colombia, Guatemala, and Mexico, selected years

*Source:* Chioda 2014a.

of the national total. In Colombia, the 10 most violent departments account for 54 percent of the country's homicides. In Mexico, the 9 most violent states represent 50 percent of all homicides. Moreover, in 2010 the state of Chihuahua alone accounted for one-quarter of the homicides in Mexico; one of its municipalities accounted for 59 percent of murders in the state (and five municipalities, for 82 percent).

In sum, crime and violence tend to be highly concentrated geographically. A great deal of dispersion underlies both subregional and national aggregates. Municipality-level and state-level data consistently suggest that handfuls of locations, even neighborhoods, drive aggregate levels of violence, highlighting the importance of local-level determinants and networks in understanding and preventing crime.

## Acute geographical clustering

Map 2.1 categorizes the violence in Mexican municipalities into high, median, and low levels of violence in 2007 and 2012. While they provide an alternate view of the high degree of heterogeneity in violence across the country, they also draw attention to a particular "form" of heterogeneity. In 2008, not only did violence increase dramatically, but so did its concentration. For instance, in the state of Chihuahua, two municipalities

**FIGURE 2.12:** Cumulative distribution of national homicide rates versus state homicide rates by department, Colombia, Guatemala, and Mexico

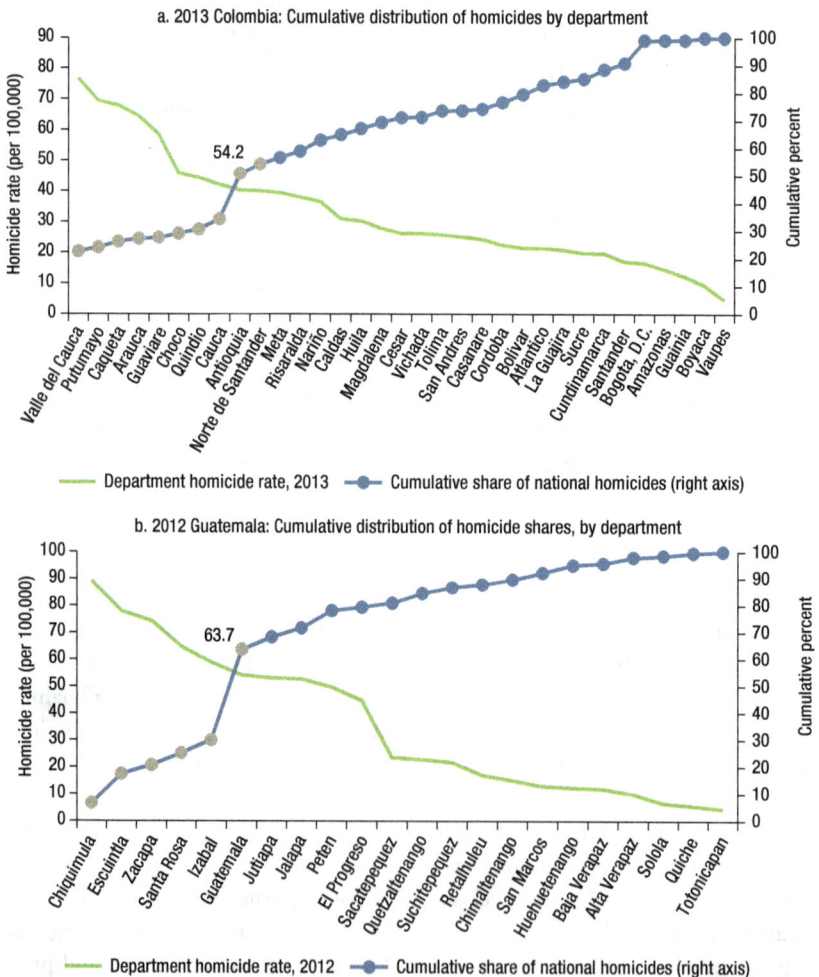

a. 2013 Colombia: Cumulative distribution of homicides by department

— Department homicide rate, 2013 —●— Cumulative share of national homicides (right axis)

b. 2012 Guatemala: Cumulative distribution of homicide shares, by department

— Department homicide rate, 2012 —●— Cumulative share of national homicides (right axis)

*(continued on next page)*

**FIGURE 2.12:** Cumulative distribution of national homicide rates versus state homicide rates by department, Colombia, Guatemala, and Mexico *(continued)*

c. 2012 Mexico: Cumulative distribution of homicide shares, by department

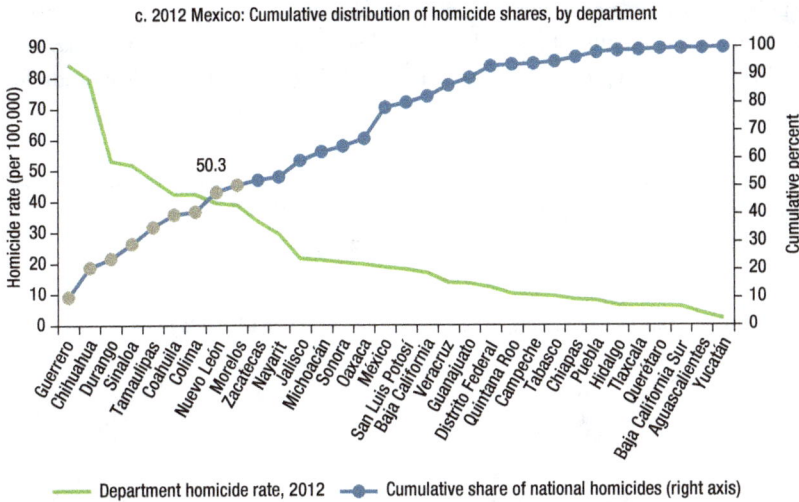

—— Department homicide rate, 2012  ——•—— Cumulative share of national homicides (right axis)

*Source:* World Bank.

accounted for 76.8 percent of the state's homicides (and six municipalities accounted for 84 percent). Ciudad Juarez experienced a staggering eightfold increase in its homicide rate, from 14.1 in 2007 to 114.8 per 100,000 in 2008 and 263.2 in 2010, accounting for approximately 60 percent of homicides in the state of Chihuahua, and 15 percent of the murders in Mexico. The geography of violence in Mexico has thus become more concentrated over time.

Comparable department- or municipal-level maps of Colombia, Guatemala, El Salvador, and Brazil (map 2.4) similarly point to handfuls of locations where the majority of homicides occur. As in the case of Mexico, violence appears to be located geographically in very particular locations and along very particular routes. In sum, violence exhibits a high degree of geographical clustering. Where the level of violence is high, it tends to spill over into nearby geographical areas, highlighting the importance of local-level determinants.

However, the degree of concentration illustrated in these maps does not tell the full story. The clustering of crime that is observed at the national level also occurs at finer levels of disaggregation, and is present at the neighborhood and even street levels. This observation has led to the hypothesis that violence is "contagious" at the neighborhood level, in the sense that "violence begets violence." Figure 2.13 reports the numbers of homicides and homicide rates by zone in Guatemala City and suggests that zones 1, 2, and 24 account for the lion's share of violence in the city; many other zones are much less violent.

In turn, figure 2.14 reports the distribution of homicides by time of day and gender in Guatemala City. Perhaps surprising, more than half the homicides occur during the day, between 8 am and 6 pm. In Honduras, homicides systematically spike every Sunday, decreasing monotonically until midweek, only to rise again over the weekend. In the last three months of 2013, 1,350 homicides were committed on Sunday and 1,036 on Monday, representing 20 percent and 15.5 percent of total violent deaths for

**MAP 2.4:** Homicide rates by municipality (per 100,000 inhabitants), Brazil, Colombia, El Salvador, and Guatemala

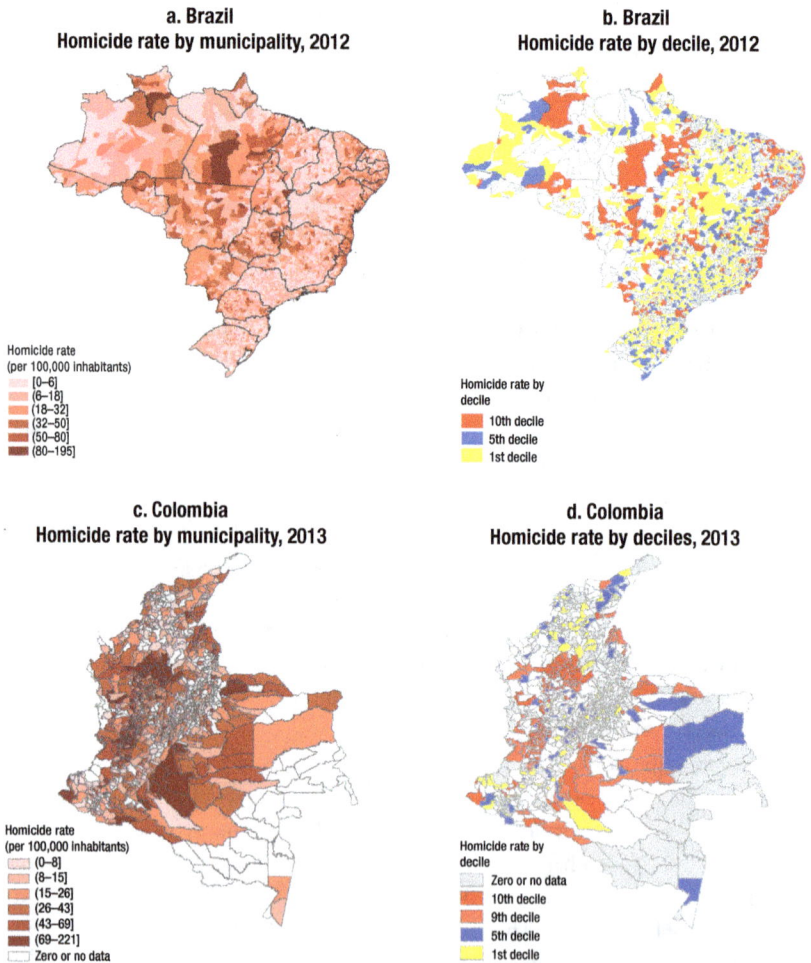

**a. Brazil**
**Homicide rate by municipality, 2012**

Homicide rate
(per 100,000 inhabitants)
[0–6]
(6–18]
(18–32]
(32–50]
(50–80]
(80–195]

**b. Brazil**
**Homicide rate by decile, 2012**

Homicide rate by
decile
10th decile
5th decile
1st decile

**c. Colombia**
**Homicide rate by municipality, 2013**

Homicide rate
(per 100,000 inhabitants)
(0–8]
(8–15]
(15–26]
(26–43]
(43–69]
(69–221]
Zero or no data

**d. Colombia**
**Homicide rate by deciles, 2013**

Homicide rate by
decile
Zero or no data
10th decile
9th decile
5th decile
1st decile

*(continued on next page)*

**e. El Salvador**
**Homicide rate by municipality, 2014**

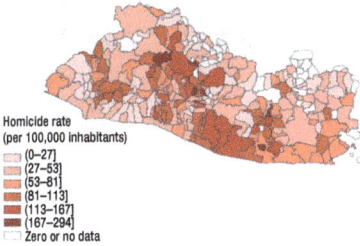

Homicide rate
(per 100,000 inhabitants)
- [0–27]
- (27–53]
- (53–81]
- (81–113]
- (113–167]
- (167–294]
- Zero or no data

**f. El Salvador**
**Homicide rate by deciles, 2014**

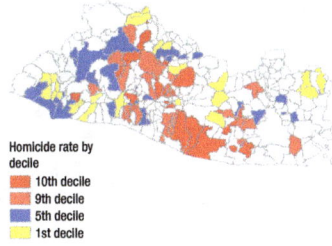

Homicide rate by
decile
- 10th decile
- 9th decile
- 5th decile
- 1st decile

**g. Guatemala**
**Homicide rate by municipality, 2012**

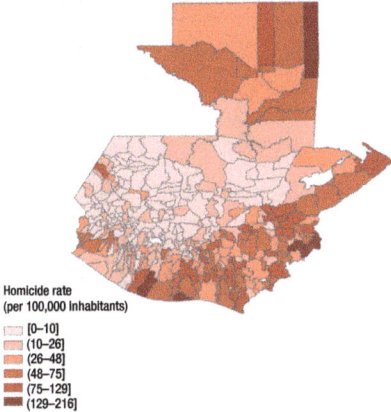

Homicide rate
(per 100,000 inhabitants)
- [0–10]
- (10–26]
- (26–48]
- (48–75]
- (75–129]
- (129–216]

**h. Guatemala**
**Homicide rate by deciles, 2012**

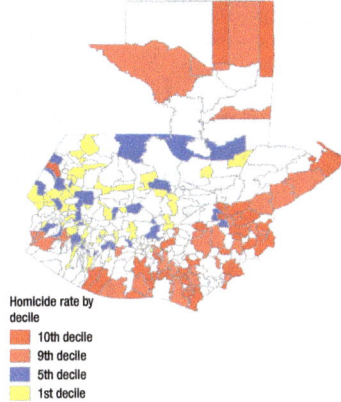

Homicide rate by
decile
- 10th decile
- 9th decile
- 5th decile
- 1st decile

*Sources:* Instituto Colombiano de Medicina Legal, Guatemala's National Police, El Salvador's National Police, and Department of Informatics for the Sistema Único de Saúde (DATASUS).
*Note:* Red, pink, blue, and yellow correspond to municipalities in the 10th, 9th, 5th, and 1st deciles of homicides rates.

the entire period, respectively. In other words, more than one-third of all homicides occurred on two days (Sunday and Monday) during the last quarter of 2013.[31]

It is worth stressing that heterogeneity and clustering are not features of violence that are limited to Latin America. They are also observed in developed countries. Violence exhibits this same pattern across contexts. In Seattle, between 4.7 percent and 6.1 percent of street segments account for 50 percent of the crimes. In Minnesota, 3.5 percent of addresses produce 50 percent of criminal offenders. In Tel Aviv, 50 percent of criminal incidents were concentrated in 5 percent of the street segments in 2010 (Weisburd, Groff, and Yang 2012).[32] In Medellín, 13 and 30 percent of the 317 neighborhoods account for approximately 50 and 75 percent, respectively,

**FIGURE 2.13:** Homicide rates by zone, Guatemala City, 2012

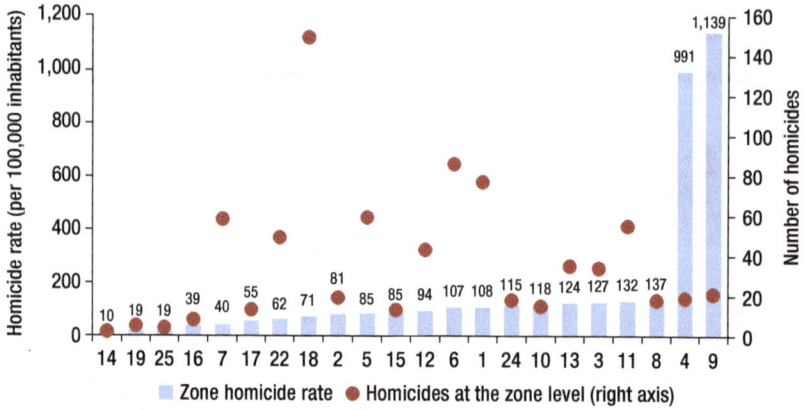

**FIGURE 2.14:** Distribution of homicides over the course of the day and by gender, Guatemala City, 2012

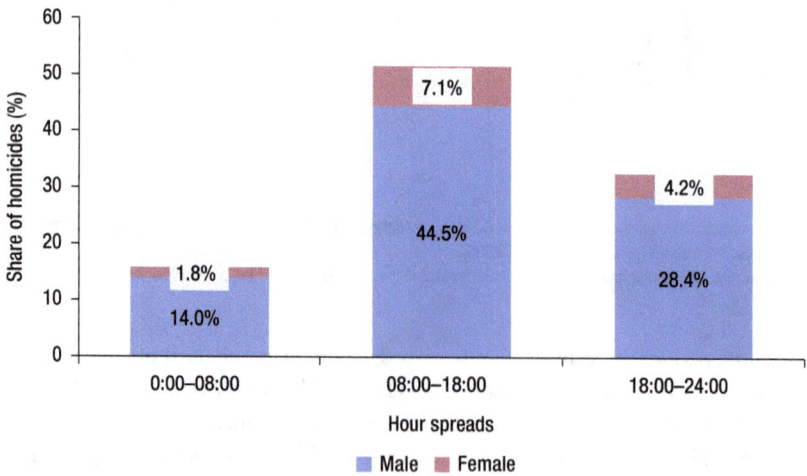

of all the intentional homicides in a given year. These measures of concentration were remarkably stable over the period 2003–2013 (see also map 2.5).

**Proximity to the victim: Where do crimes occur, and where do offenders come from?**

Another dimension of the local nature of crime and violence is that they tend to be extremely proximate to victims. In 2014, 53 percent of victims in the region reported that the last crime occurred at their home (25 percent) or in their neighborhood (28 percent), and an additional 30 percent fell victim somewhere within their municipality of residence, implying that only a small fraction of crime (17 percent) took place outside of victims' municipality of residence or abroad (see figure 2.15.).

This is not a simple artifact of the way crime statistics are constructed, since one major source of data—the Latin American Public Opinion Project (LAPOP)—for instance, deliberately excludes domestic violence, which is by definition proximate to victims. The distributions of crimes across locations of occurrence are remarkably stable across the LAC countries. In only two countries—El Salvador and Peru—do approximately 40 percent of crime take place outside the victims' municipality (see figure 2.16).

In terms of the breakdown between property crime and violent crime in the region, over 60 percent of property crimes occurred in the victim's home or neighborhood,

---

**MAP 2.5:** Heterogeneity at the neighborhood levels: Homicide rates and counts for the city of Medellín, 2013

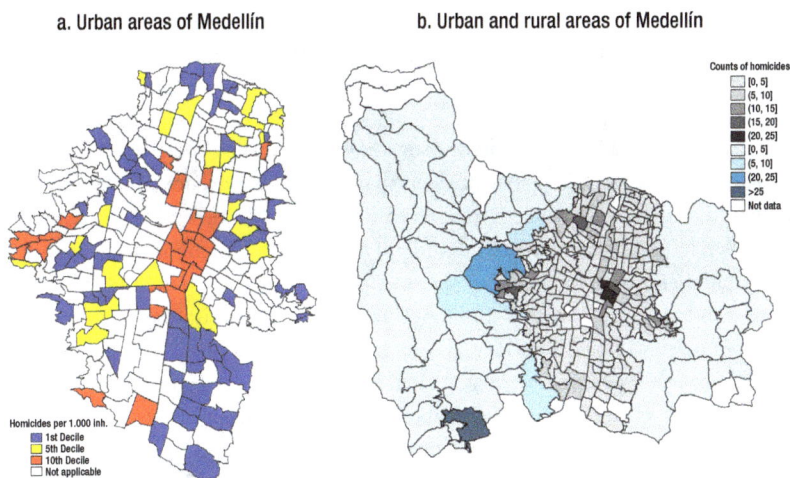

a. Urban areas of Medellín

b. Urban and rural areas of Medellín

*Source:* World Bank, based on Sistema de Información para la Seguridad y Convivencia (SISC) for Medellín (2014).
*Note:* In panel b, the urban areas are shaded in gray, while the rural areas are in blue.

**FIGURE 2.15:** Victim reporting on where the last crime occurred, 2010 and 2014

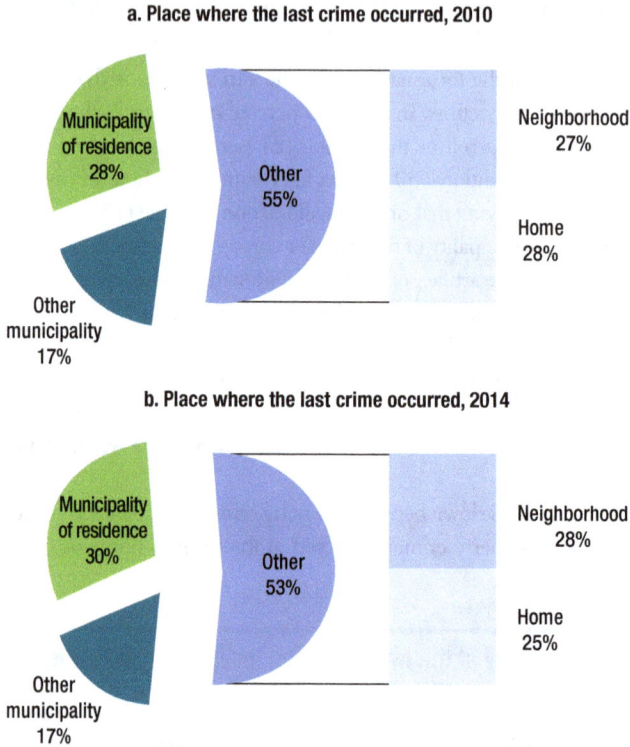

**a. Place where the last crime occurred, 2010**

Municipality of residence 28%

Other municipality 17%

Other 55%

Neighborhood 27%

Home 28%

**b. Place where the last crime occurred, 2014**

Municipality of residence 30%

Other municipality 17%

Other 53%

Neighborhood 28%

Home 25%

*Source:* World Bank, based on 2010 and 2014 data from the Latin American Public Opinion Project (LAPOP).
*Note:* LAC weighted averages.

and an additional 23 percent within their same municipality. Even for violent crime (which excludes domestic violence), a large share of incidents occurred in "close" proximity to the victim's residence (10 percent at home, and 35 percent in the neighborhood), while 36 percent occurred outside of their victims' neighborhood, but within the boundaries of their municipality of residence. Here again, the pattern is noteworthy for its stability across countries in the region. These characteristics of crime point to choice of neighborhood of residence as an important crime prevention strategy from the perspective of potential victims. As will be discussed in chapter 6, the safety and socioeconomic characteristics of neighborhoods are key determinants of individuals' mental health and well-being in contexts characterized by high levels of violence.

Knowing the locations of victims is one side of the coin. Where are offenders located? In Mexico,[33] not only do crimes occurred in close proximity to the victims' residences, but the analogous relationship also holds for perpetrators (figure 2.17). At least

**FIGURE 2.16:** Location of all crimes by country, 2014

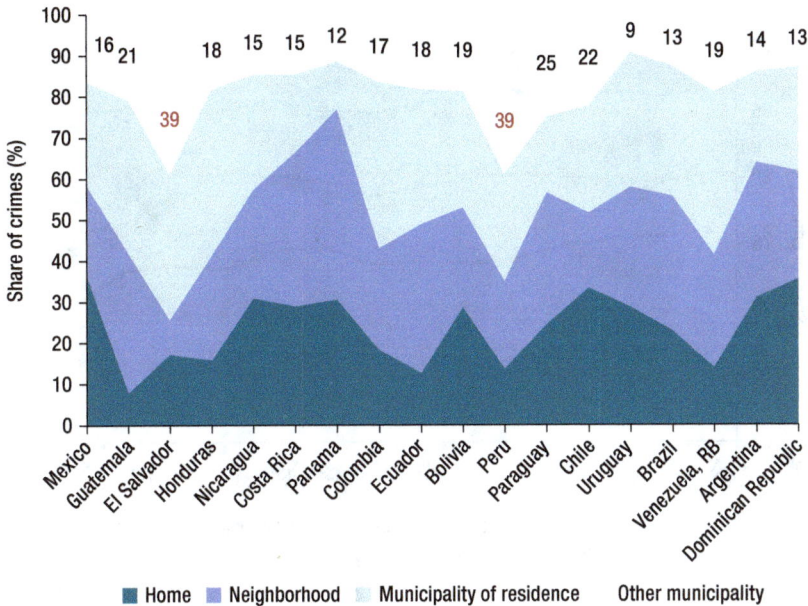

Source: World Bank, based on 2014 LAPOP data.

three-quarters of crimes in 2011 occur within the same municipality in which the perpetrators lived. Violent crimes (whether net of domestic violence or not) are most likely to be committed within the offender's municipality of residence (85 percent), followed by property crimes (76 percent), and homicides (71 percent).

In recent years, however, as violence has escalated in Mexico, there has been a greater degree of discordance between the municipality of occurrence and that of the residence of perpetrators, consistent with violence spilling over from one municipality to the next, as if evolving according to a contagion model. The next section discusses these two features in more detail and attempts to quantify their magnitude.

### Temporal and geographical spillovers, persistence, and proximity

Crime is not only concentrated geographically, it exhibits high degrees of persistence: the greatest predictor of violence today is prior violence, which also mirrors the behavior of epidemics. For instance, in the country-level panel data regressions of table 2.1, the coefficient associated with the lagged homicide rate is around 0.66, implying that each additional homicide in one period is associated with 0.66 additional homicides in the following period.[34] Both statistically and economically, these temporal spillovers are very significant.

**FIGURE 2.17:** Where crimes were committed and where criminals came from, Mexico, 1997–2011

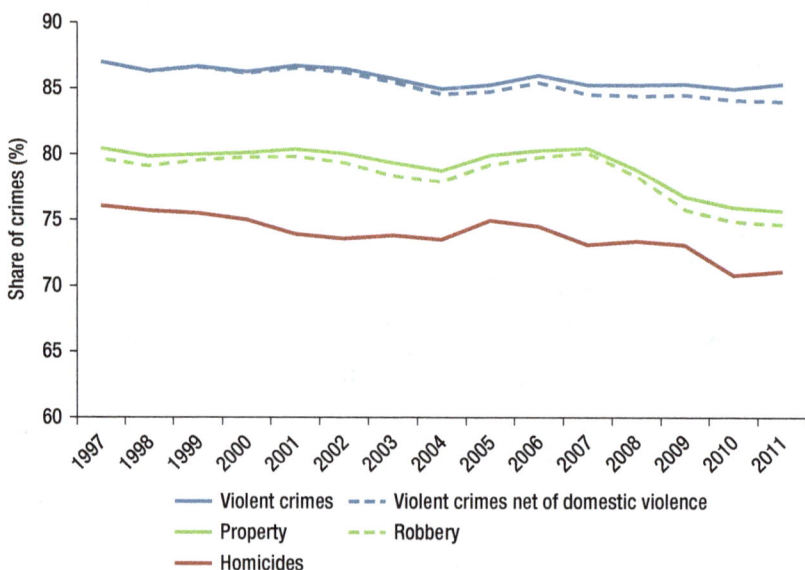

*Source:* Chioda 2014c, based on data from Instituto Nacional de Estadística y Geografía (INEGI).

This degree of persistence is not exclusive to national statistics or to the case of homicide. It is also observed at subnational levels and for different types of crime. Slightly higher or comparable degrees of persistence are estimated from Mexican and Brazilian data at the municipal level, with an additional homicide in one year predicting 0.81 and 0.64 per 100,000 additional homicides the following year, respectively. In Colombia, the degree of persistence of homicides is considerably lower. In parsimonious models that control for few municipal-level characteristics, the baseline degree of persistence is 0.5; however, in more saturated models that control for labor market conditions, education, drug production, and public expenditures, the degree of inertia is roughly halved.[35,36]

Here again, the analogy with developed countries persists. Maps of gun violence in Chicago exhibit similar patterns of geographical and temporal clustering, which also emerge in maps of the progression of infectious diseases. Furthermore, the strongest predictor of violence in the streets of U.S. cities is a prior violent incident, which mirrors the behavior typical of epidemic waves (Slutkin 2013).[37] Along similar lines, the discussion earlier noted the concentrated nature of violence in the Mexican state of Chihuahua, and its acute clustering during the recent deterioration of security in Mexico. A closer look reveals that violence first became more acute where its level was already high, and then propagated across municipalities outward along the highways, consistent with a model of contagion.

**Measures of spillovers and contagion**

As an illustration of geographical spillovers, table 2.3 reports estimates from dynamic panel data models based on municipal-level crime reports in Mexico, for different categories of crime. The models differ in a number of respects from the cross-country regressions reported earlier in table 2.1 since different sets of variables are available as controls (for details, see Chioda 2014b). Aside from being estimated on municipal-level data, one interesting dimension along which they differ from the country-level panel is that, in addition to the lagged crime rate (the homicide rate), they permit state-level measures of crime to be constructed; the lag is included in the models. For instance, to the homicide rate in the municipality of Morelia in 2008, the model associates Morelia's 2007 homicide rate, as well as Michoacán state's homicide rate in 2007 (net of Morelia's 2007 homicides). A formal, albeit crude, measure of contagion is the extent that violence from neighboring municipalities within the same state predicts levels of violence in a given locality. Conceptually, this permits Chioda (2014b) to compare models with and without controlling for the state-level crime rate and to draw conclusions about the source of persistence in the crime rate, and whether there are spillovers from the state to the municipality.

For instance, as table 2.3 indicates, a model of homicides excluding the state-level homicide rate implies that an additional homicide in the municipality in the previous period is associated with 0.806 additional homicides per 100,000 in the current period—a degree of persistence almost 33 percent larger than in the cross-country regressions. In turn, inclusion of the lagged state-level homicide rate suggests that the actual persistence is more in line with that of the cross-country regressions (0.649, second column). Furthermore, the coefficient on the state-level rate is of equal magnitude

**TABLE 2.3: Persistence coefficients from dynamic panel data models for Mexican municipalities**

|  | All homicides registered | | Perpetrators of violent crimes | | Perpetrators of property crimes | | Perpetrators of robberies | |
|---|---|---|---|---|---|---|---|---|
| **Occurrence** | | | | | | | | |
| Lag dependent variable | 0.806*** | 0.649*** | 0.429*** | 0.362*** | 0.427*** | 0.401*** | 0.379*** | 0.349*** |
|  | (0.202) | (0.194) | (0.0239) | (0.0246) | (0.0263) | (0.0296) | (0.0300) | (0.0303) |
| Lag state rate - Net of Muni (Spillover Effects) |  | 0.664*** |  | 0.377*** |  | 0.223*** |  | 0.259*** |
|  |  | (0.139) |  | (0.0469) |  | (0.0568) |  | (0.0583) |

*Source:* Chioda 2014a. Data on perpetrators from Instituto Nacional de Estadística y Geografía (INEGI), 1997–2010.
*Note:* Only temporal and geographical spillover effects are reported. Estimates are from a saturated model, which includes year and municipal fixed effects. For each crime category, the first column reports the coefficient on lagged dependent variable in models that exclude lagged measures of state-level crime; the second column includes them. Significance level: * = 10 percent, ** = 5 percent, *** = 1 percent.

(0.664), meaning that even after controlling for the municipality's past level of violence, state-level homicides that occur outside of the municipality in question raise the locality's homicide rate.

Although still significant, lesser degrees of contagion in homicides are recorded in Brazil and Colombia, where the corresponding measures are 0.15 and 0.20, respectively. However, these lower magnitudes may in part be due to the much larger sizes of Brazilian states and the more geographically targeted nature of violence in Colombia, after controlling for the presence of paramilitary groups.[38]

The phenomena of contagion and persistence are not exclusive to homicides. They also emerge in the analysis of different crime categories. Table 2.3 also reports measures of both geographical and temporal spillovers in Mexico for violent crimes, property crimes, and robberies. Qualitatively, each of these also exhibits temporal and geographic spillovers, albeit spillovers that are smaller in magnitude. One additional violent crime, property crime, and robbery in a given year in a municipality's state (but outside its own borders) is associated with 0.377, 0.223, and 0.259 additional violent crimes, property crimes, and robberies (per 100,000) in the subsequent year, respectively. Interestingly, not only does homicide exhibit the larger spillover effects, but it is also more frequently committed outside the perpetrator's municipality of residence (see figure 2.17). The preservation of the ranking is not trivial.[39] Discrepancies between the municipality of occurrence of the crime and the municipality of residence of the offender do not imply spillovers, although such spillovers could be one of the underlying mechanisms, as long as there is some degree of correlation between criminal behavior in the municipality of residence and the municipality where a crime is committed.

The evidence presented in this section is consistent with the contagious nature of crime and violence, and of homicides, in particular. Spillovers are sizable, whether the temporal (persistence) or geographical dimension (contagion) is taken into consideration. In the case of homicides in Mexico, the magnitudes of both forms of spillovers are approximately equal. That is, 1 additional murder in the previous year yields an additional 0.65 murders the following year, whether the initial additional homicide occurred within the municipality or outside it (but within the state). Violence reduction strategies that rely on the efforts of a single municipality are bound to be less effective than if they take advantage of the externalities that characterize violence. The coordinated action of many subnational entities (or in coordination with the state/region) may yield benefits that amount to more than the sum of the individual efforts. That is, the vicious circle of contagion could be turned into a virtuous circle of prevention.

### Heterogeneity across the life cycle: The age-crime profile

Heterogeneity does not manifest itself only along the geographical dimension, but—equally striking—over the life cycle, giving rise to one of the most consistent facts about crime: the age-crime profile. Criminologists have long documented and studied this pattern. At the beginning of the seventeenth century, a Belgian astronomer-statistician, Adolphe Quetelet, decided to quantify the physical and cognitive development of humans. Based on French crime statistics, he showed that criminal offending increases dramatically during adolescence, peaking in early adulthood, and then declines until old age. This pattern, labeled "the age-crime curve" by modern criminologists, has since been replicated numerous times in the context of developed countries (Blumstein, Cohen, and Farrington 1988).[40]

Before providing details on the pattern, it is important to point out that because data on perpetrators for the entire region are not available, the analysis must rely on data on victims. The implicit assumption is the perpetrators' age-crime and victims' age-victimization profiles are related. This assumption finds support in data from developed countries, but is also corroborated by the Mexican data on perpetrators.

Quetelet's original description of the relationship between age and criminality—whereby the incidence of criminality rises sharply in adolescence and early adulthood, and then declines progressively thereafter—has since been replicated by numerous others[41] and applies to homicides in LAC (see figure 2.18). That the traditional age-crime profile holds for homicides in LAC is noteworthy because it has to do with the most violent of crimes, whereas most U.S. studies focus on less severe categories of crime.

For younger teens ages 10–14, the risk of being a victim of homicides is around 2.8 (per 100,000) and increases more than tenfold (31.1 per 100,000 in 2008) for older teens, ages 15–19. The risk of being a victim of homicides then peaks for those ages 20–24 at 48.2 per 100,000, identifying a critical age group for any policy aimed

FIGURE 2.18: LAC homicide age-crime profile, selected years

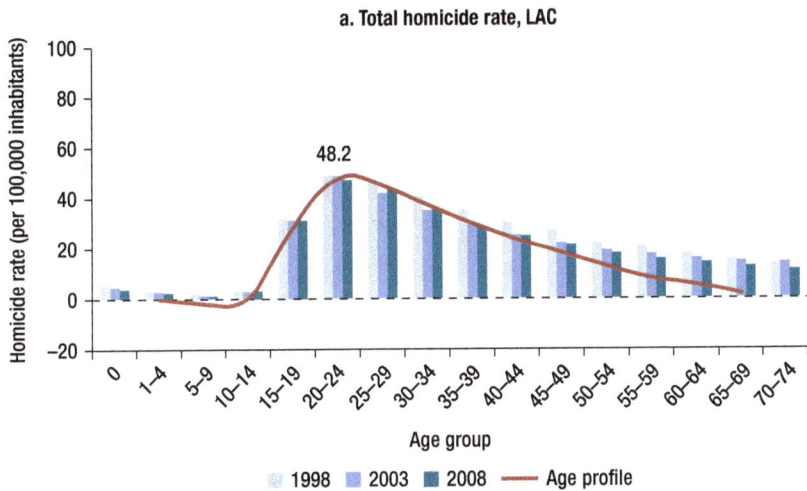

a. Total homicide rate, LAC

1998    2003    2008    —— Age profile

(continued on next page)

**FIGURE 2.18:** LAC homicide age-crime profile, selected years *(continued)*

### b. Total homicide rate, United States

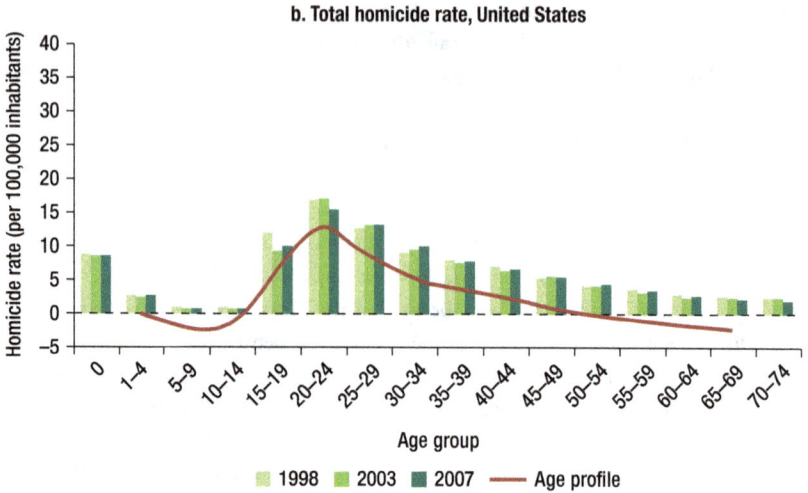

Homicide rate (per 100,000 inhabitants) vs. Age group

■ 1998  ■ 2003  ■ 2007  —— Age profile

### c. Homicide rate, LAC males

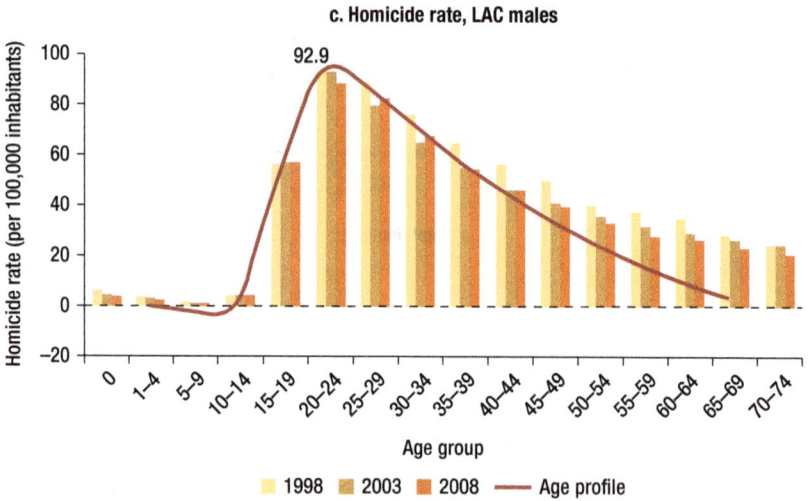

92.9

Homicide rate (per 100,000 inhabitants) vs. Age group

■ 1998  ■ 2003  ■ 2008  —— Age profile

*(continued on next page)*

**FIGURE 2.18:** LAC homicide age-crime profile, selected years *(continued)*

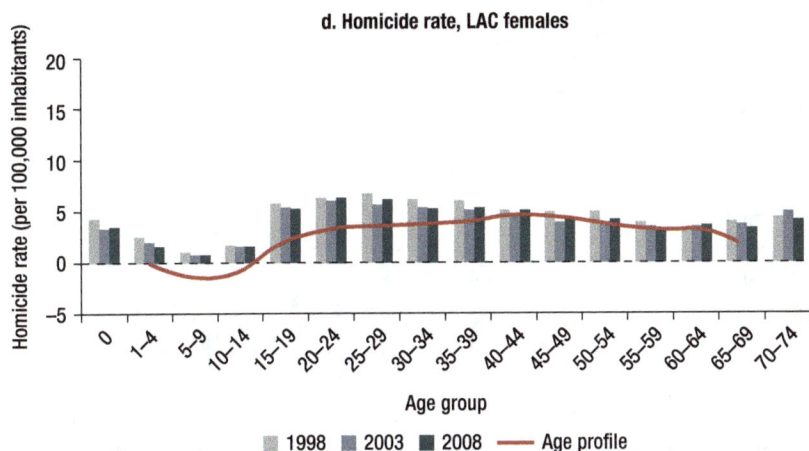

d. Homicide rate, LAC females

Age group

◻ 1998  ▨ 2003  ▪ 2008  —— Age profile

*Source:* Chioda 2014a, based on data from Global Burden of Injuries.
*Note:* The age profile (solid red line) represents population-weighted estimates of age effects from models estimated across years, controlling for year and cohort dummies. In computing the regional average, 2007 data were used for Chile, Colombia, and Venezuela because data were missing for 2008. For Nicaragua, 2006 was used in lieu of 2008.

at violence prevention. The gender differences in victimization differ markedly, with homicide rates for boys twice as high as those for the general population (4.2, 56.0, and 92.4 for boys ages 10–14, 15–19, and 20–24, respectively).

The female age-crime profile is much more attenuated and less steep. The greatest rise in the risk of being a victim of homicide still occurs at age 15–19, but never exceeds 6.5 per 100,000 throughout the life cycle. Violence is committed by and affects boys at a disproportionate rate; at almost all ages, boys are at least 10 times more likely to fall victim to homicide.

The age-crime profile based on cross-sectional data may not properly reflect the evolution of violence through the life cycle, especially if different cohorts have different propensities to offend. The age-crime curve in any given year is essentially a cross-sectional phenomenon, with individuals of each age being compared to individuals of other ages. However, the profiles delivered by the cross-section (the bars in figure 2.18.) survive a more rigorous cohort analysis (as indicated by the red line in figure 2.18, which corresponds to the age-crime profile pooled across all years and controlling for cohort differences).[42] The estimated age profile that holds the cohort constant is very similar to the cross-sectional profile, consistent with very stable age-crime profiles across different cohorts. This is less true for the United States, where the cohort effects for those who were adolescents and young adults in the 1990s—when violence was much more pronounced than at other times—are substantial.

Figure 2.19 presents the age-crime profiles separately for Central and South America. Important differences emerge. The profile for South America rises more

**FIGURE 2.19:** Age-homicide profiles for Central and South America

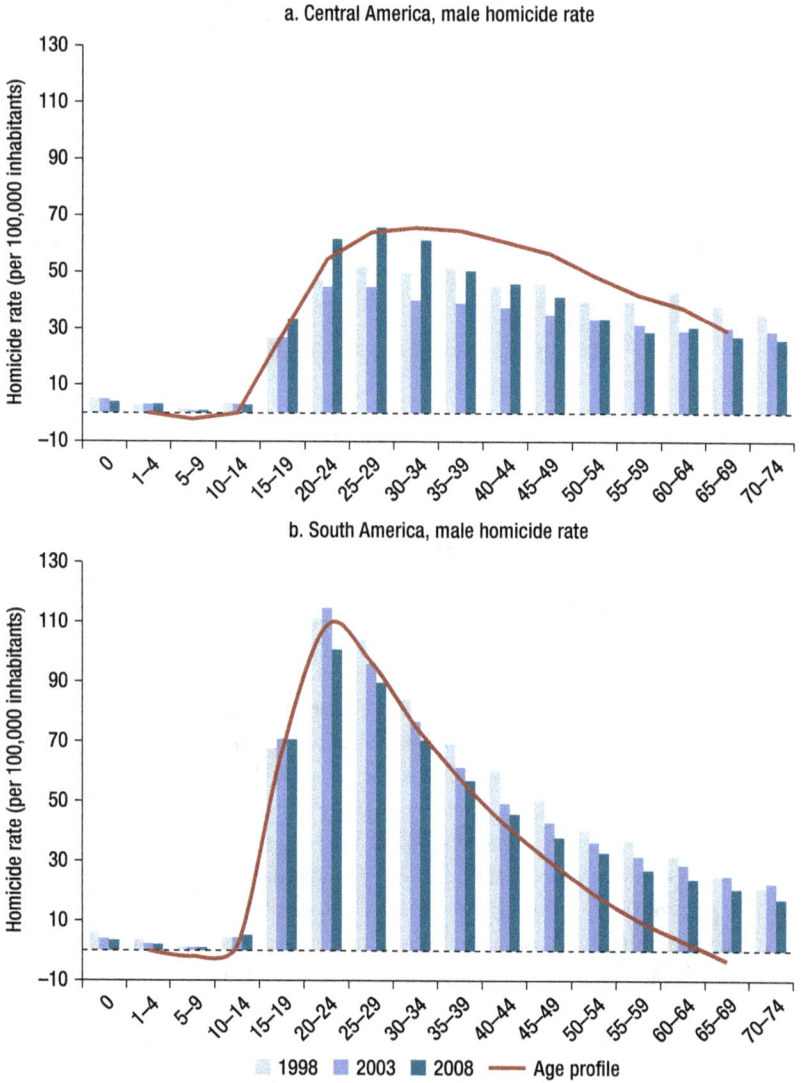

a. Central America, male homicide rate

b. South America, male homicide rate

1998     2003     2008     —— Age profile

*Source:* Chioda 2014a, based on data from Global Burden of Injuries.
*Note:* Central America includes Belize, Costa Rica, El Salvador, Guatemala, Mexico, Nicaragua, and Panama, representing 95 percent of the Central American population. South America includes Argentina, Brazil, Chile, Colombia, Ecuador, and Paraguay, representing 89 percent of the Southern American population.

steeply at younger ages and peaks at a much higher level (between 100 and 111 per 100,000 for ages 20–24), but also declines at a rapid rate. For Central America, homicide rates are much lower across the life cycle, but exhibit much higher persistence into later ages: the homicide rate appears to stabilize around 20 homicides per 100,000. However, in recent years, the Central American distribution has become more concentrated around the traditional at-risk age group, whereas it was more uniform in age in the late 1990s.

This section closes with an important observation: abstracting from their absolute levels, it is noteworthy that the shapes of the age-crime profiles for LAC and the United States are remarkably similar (figure 2.20). That is, the distribution of homicide risk across different age groups is stable across the two contexts; in this respect, the analogy between LAC and the developed countries holds. However, are the differences in their levels of violence so dramatic as to invalidate any meaningful comparison?

The answer lies in the misleading nature of averages (box 2.1). While developed countries may enjoy considerably lower (overall) levels of violence, certain subsets of their populations and selected neighborhoods/cities are characterized by levels of violence that are similar to those of LAC. For instance, Detroit and New Orleans are the 21st and 17th most violent cities in the world (Engel, Sterbenz, and Lubin 2013), respectively, with homicide rates well above 50 per 100,000, making them comparable

**FIGURE 2.20:** Trends in homicide rates in the United States and Mexico, by age and race

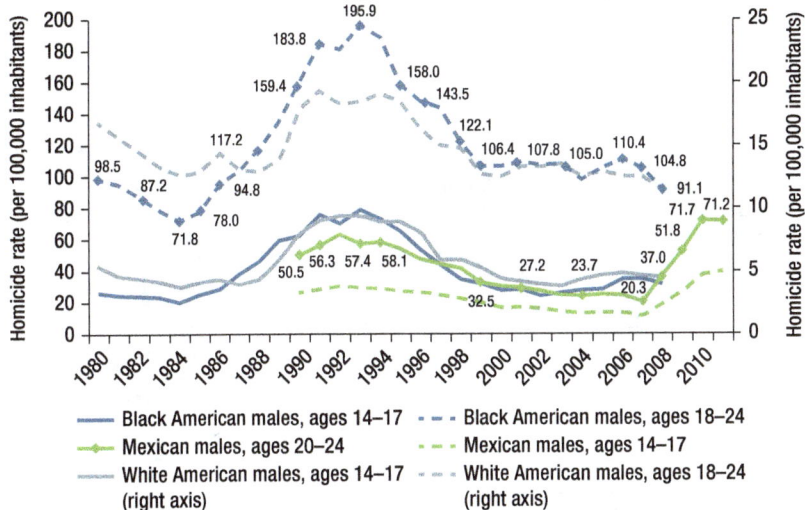

Source: World Bank, based on INEGI data for Mexico, and data from the U.S. Centers for Disease Control and Prevention (CDC) for the U.S. series.

to the most violent cities in the region. One of the most violent neighborhoods in Chicago, Englewood, is plagued by murder rates of 65.5 per 100,000, higher than that of Ciudad Juarez in Mexico (55.9 per 100,000 in 2013) and similar to that of Salvador, Brazil (65.6 per 100,000, in 2013).

In the spirit of Matheson (2013), map 2.6 further supports the analogy, making explicit that a number of cities in the United States experience rates of violence that closely resemble those of the most violent countries in Latin America.

---

**BOX 2.1:** Age distribution of homicide rates in Honduras, 2012–13

Pronounced heterogeneity is one of the defining features of violence. The misleading nature of averages in crime statistics is illustrated for Honduras, one of the most violent countries in the world. At 91 homicides per 100,000 in 2012, its national average is three times higher than the "conflict" level of violence defined by the World Health Organization (WHO). While staggering, these figures pale in comparison to the age-specific rate of violence for men in Honduras. Homicide rates for boys ages 15–19 are approximately 150 per 100,000, and more than double that level for youth ages 20–24 (328 in 2012 and 318 in 2013) (figure B2.1.1).

Since 2008 (the earliest date for which data are available), rates of fatal violence have soared, peaking in 2011 (figure B2.1.1.2). However, since 2011, the country has experienced a slight downward trend, with much of the improvement recorded in 2013. Nevertheless, these improvements are marginal compared to the initial levels.

**FIGURE B2.1.1:** Male homicide rate by age, Honduras, 2012 and 2013

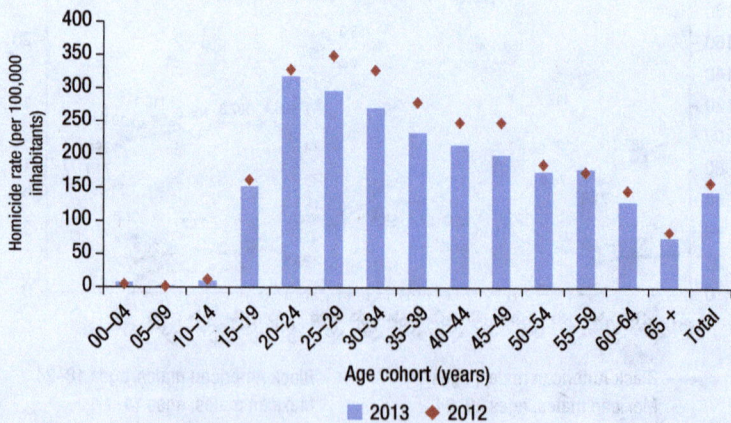

Source: Observatory on Violence, Honduras.

*(continued on next page)*

## BOX 2.1: Age distribution of homicide rates in Honduras, 2012–13

*(continued)*

### FIGURE B2.1.2: Evolution of male homicide rates by age group, Honduras, 2008–13

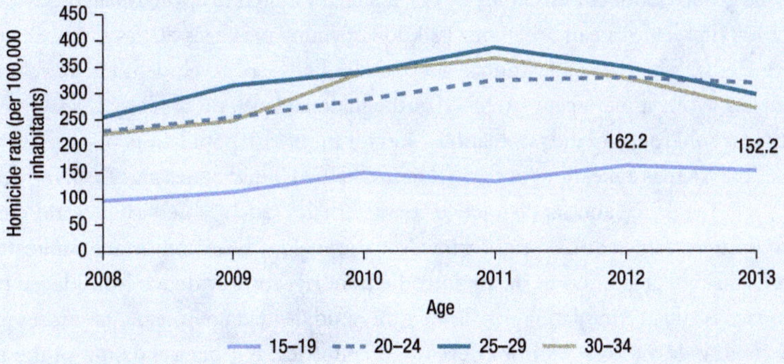


*Source: Observatory on Violence,* Honduras.

## MAP 2.6: U.S. cities and LAC countries with comparable homicide rates, circa 2012

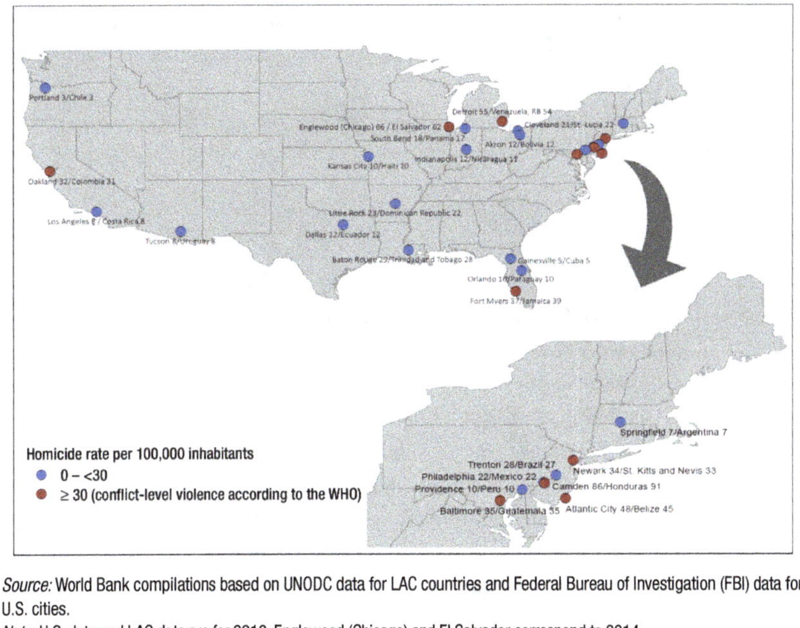


*Source:* World Bank compilations based on UNODC data for LAC countries and Federal Bureau of Investigation (FBI) data for U.S. cities.

*Note:* U.S. data and LAC data are for 2012. Englewood (Chicago) and El Salvador correspond to 2014.

The parallel is not limited to certain U.S. cities, but also holds for specific subgroups of the U.S. population. In the United States, the murder rate for African-Americans is significantly higher than the national average of 4.7 per 100,000 as of 2011. Throughout the 2000s, young black males ages 18–24 were plagued by homicide rates between 105 and 110 per 100,000. The rate for this subpopulation declined to 91.1 per 100, 000 in 2008. While this represented a low not seen since the late 1980s among this demographic group (Cooper and Smith 2011), it still amounted to approximately 2.5 times the 2008 homicide rate of 36.98 per 100,000 of young men ages 20–24 in Mexico (see figure 2.20). These rates legitimize the parallel between developed and developing countries; while it may seem stretched at the national level, the analogy is accurate for particular subgroups of the populations, and for the at-risk population, in particular.

That there is a meaningful parallel between the United States and LAC regarding the level of violence and its distinctive characteristics (such as persistence and contagion) is interesting in its own right. However, the analogy bears important implications for this study. As alluded to in the introduction, rigorous evidence from developing countries is still accumulating—including this study— that complements studies from LAC with data and results from developed countries. Further validation of the parallel comes from the fact that part of the behavior that is documented in this report arises from certain biological and developmental mechanisms that are invariant across individuals. Thus, while the context obviously differs, prevention programs with proven effectiveness in reducing crime among disadvantaged youth in the United States may be suggestive of fruitful interventions in LAC, where neighborhood violence, drugs, and gang problems are similarly pervasive. Of course, the analogy is not perfect; this study makes efforts to be cognizant of the fact that context and the institutional capacity among local authorities matter in the implementation and, ultimately, effectiveness of interventions.

The section that follows provides evidence that the age-crime profile for perpetrators bears a striking resemblance to that of victims and discusses the policy implications.

## Age-crime profiles of Mexican perpetrators

The age-crime profiles of homicide victims provide a clear picture of how the risk of fatal victimization evolves over the life cycle, and indicates that the burden falls disproportionately on adolescents and young adults. However, as mentioned, one limitation of these profiles is that they may not reflect criminal careers if perpetrators commit crimes across very different age groups, such that the ages of victims are not informative of the ages of perpetrators. The question this section asks is whether the age-crime profile of offenders can be inferred from the age-crime profile of homicide victims.

Mexico's unique data set on perpetrators enables one to test the conjecture that victims' and perpetrators' profiles are meaningfully related and investigate whether the shape of the former can proxy for patterns of life-course offending (Chioda 2014c).

Figure 2.21 provides the age-crime profiles of perpetrators of property crimes, violent crimes (excluding homicides), and homicides, based on data recording their age at the time of arrest and the date on which the offense occurred. Our interest is in providing a description of criminal behavior over the life cycle; thus figure 2.21 plots the distribution of ages at which crimes were committed.[43]

Remarkably, the shapes of these profiles closely resemble the distributions of victims' age. Equally surprising is that the age profiles do not differ very much across the

---

**FIGURE 2.21:** Age-crime profiles of perpetrators of property crime, violent crime, and homicides, Mexico

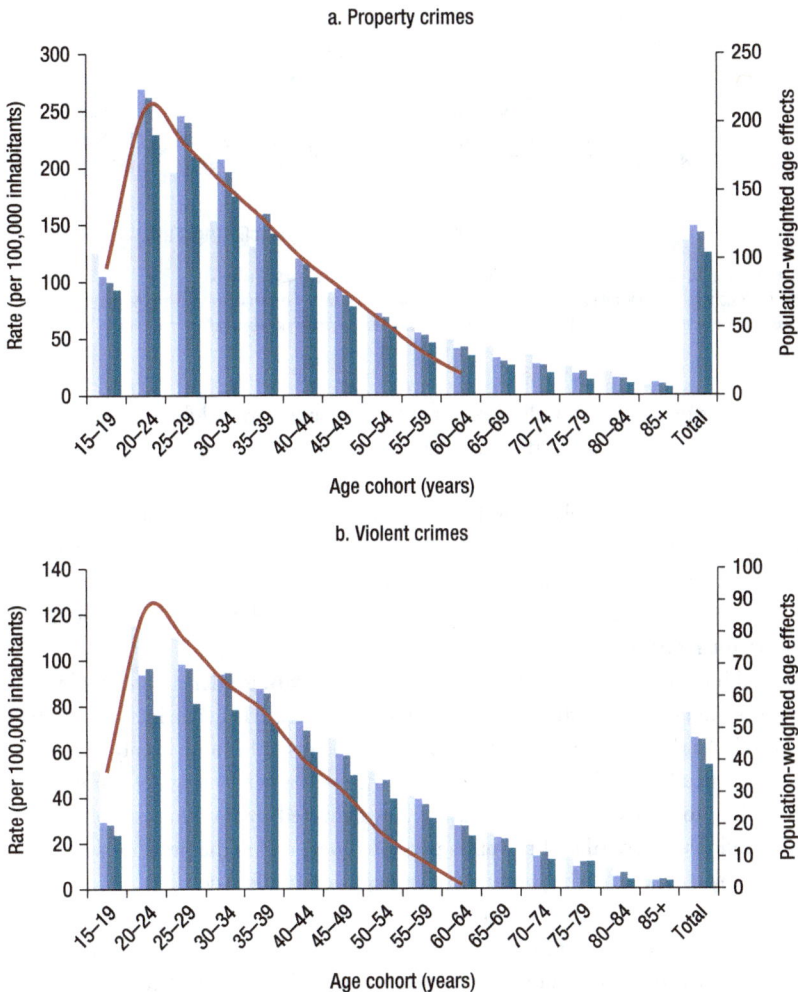

a. Property crimes

b. Violent crimes

Age cohort (years)

*(continued on next page)*

**FIGURE 2.21:** Age-crime profiles of perpetrators of property crime, violent crime, and homicides, Mexico *(continued)*

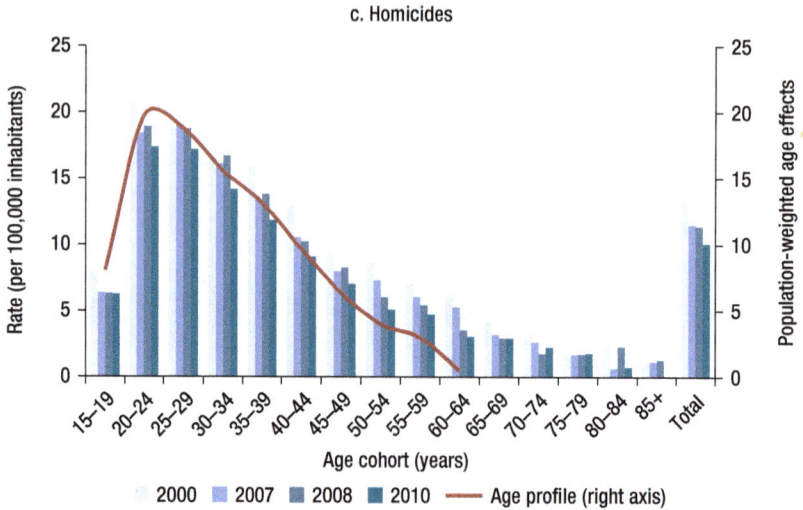

c. Homicides

*Source:* Chioda 2014c, based on data from Instituto Nacional de Estadística y Geografía (INEGI).
*Note:* Bars correspond to the rate of offending per 100,000 individuals in each age group. The solid red line corresponds to population-weighted age effects from models estimated across years, controlling for year and cohort dummies.

three types of crimes: they all peak in adolescence and early adulthood, and steadily decline thereafter. It is worth remarking that these curves likely represent upper bounds on the age of onset of offending because individuals may have committed previous crimes before escalating to homicide, say, and because some of their previous crimes (especially petty property crime) may not have been reported or, if they were reported, no one was caught.[44] However, with these curves as upper bounds in mind, it is striking that there are no differences in the age at which offending is most likely— that is, the modes of their distributions.

Although not presented here for the sake of brevity, gender differences in these profiles mimic those for the region as a whole (see figure 2.18). The incidence of each type of offending is much lower for women, and tends to be more evenly distributed throughout adulthood. Furthermore, as was the case earlier, netting out cohort effects does little to alter the shapes of the profiles delivered by the cross-section. These observations confirm that the profiles presented here and in the previous section are reasonable measures of the pattern of offending over the life cycle.

Across crime categories, two types of heterogeneity emerge. One relates to the severity (and incidence) of crime: homicides are less frequent than violent crimes, which are in turn less common than property crimes. The second relates to the decline in offending following the peaks among 20- to 24-year-olds. The reduction in rates of offending after age 24 can cautiously be interpreted as desistence, or rates at which perpetrators exit their criminal lives (for a discussion of caveats, see Farrington 1986). The drop after age 24 appears to be steeper for property crime. This is consistent with the notion that the least severe criminal careers are much easier to leave behind and that some forms of externalizing behavior are transitory with age. In her study of the age-crime profile based on longitudinal records, Moffitt (1993) concludes that the majority of criminal offenders are teenagers; that by the early 20s, the number of active offenders decreases by more than 50 percent; and that by age 28, almost 85 percent of former delinquents had desisted offending.

Whether the adolescent peak represents a change in the prevalence or a change in incidence has been a matter of debate among researchers: Does adolescence bring an increase in the number of people who are willing to offend, or do a small and constant number of offenders simply generate more criminal acts while in adolescence? Empirical evaluations point to the former explanation. Based on data from the United Kingdom and the United States, Farrington (1983) and Tracy, Wolfgang, and Figlio (1991) show that the adolescent peak reflects a temporary increase in the number of people involved in antisocial behavior, rather than a temporary acceleration in the offense rates of a handful of individuals.

What lies behind this average curve? What kinds of offenders generate it? There does not appear to be a single trajectory of offending that starts in early adolescence and characterizes all offenders. Sampson and Laub (2003) identify five typical profiles. High chronic offenders and low chronic offenders are individuals who start offending early in life, who persist past the typical peak age, and whose decline is slow and starts to emerge only around age 40. The labeling high versus low indicates the intensity of offenses: that is, the number of crimes committed, with high chronic offenders reaching the greatest intensity of their offending at age 30–35, and low chronic offenders characterized by a steady, low offending trajectory. At the other end of the spectrum, moderate desisters and classic desisters are among the largest groups in the population (roughly 26 percent and 20 percent, respectively). These two sets of individuals tend to have short criminal careers that typically start during mid-adolescence and peak between the ages of 17 and 19. The last trajectory is that of moderate offenders; it also starts in mid-adolescence, like the desisters, but peaks at age 24. The desisters and moderate offenders account for between 65 percent and 80 percent of samples in different studies. They ultimately drive the central tendencies of the distribution, and therefore end up shaping the age-crime trajectory.

This level of granularity cannot be achieved with the data from LAC. However, some important general insights can be gleaned from these studies, which can have important implications for policy. Trajectory studies tend to document adolescent peak patterns and chronic offender patterns. As will be discussed in chapter 3, while early onset (in childhood) is a strong predictor of adult violence and of chronic persistence of criminality (Tremblay 2000), trajectory methodologies have also identified a "late-onset" chronic group. This class of offenders begins offending in the middle of adolescence and continues offending at a steady rate into adulthood. Chronic offenders (whether early or late onset) are of particular interest for policy because their criminal careers not only exhibit significant longevity, but they are also responsible for a large fraction of total crimes committed. However, the different timing of onset may suggest that policies that may be effective for the early offenders may not be as effective for "late bloomers," highlighting the importance of understanding which factors drive antisocial behavior at different stages in life.[45]

The specific shapes of these age-crime profiles—whether they refer to victims or to perpetrators—reveal an important margin for policy. The ability to reduce the propensity for antisocial behavior for critical age segments of the population can have significant social returns in terms of mitigating crime. De Mello and Schneider (2010) illustrate the relevance of this age group. In São Paulo state in Brazil, the homicide rate in large cities has dropped sharply following historic highs in the 1990s. Whereas some attribute the decline to changes in such policies as those related to policing, the adoption of dry laws restricting the sale and consumption of liquor, and increasing incarceration rates, De Mello and Schneider (2010) show that it resulted in great part from demographic change, with large cohorts of young men "aging out" of their peak period of criminality. Evidence of the sensitivity of crime to the behavior of young adults is also provided by Chioda, De Mello, and Soares (2016), who show that the expansion of Brazil's national conditional cash transfer to cover 16- to 17-year-olds— who are at a particularly high risk of offending—had the unintended effect of significantly reducing crime in the city of São Paulo.

In conclusion, the remarkable stability of the age-crime profiles across income levels, countries, and types of crimes de facto identifies demographic groups with an especially elevated risk of offending (as well as of being victims): namely, adolescents and young adults. As later chapters discuss, these ages are critical stages not only from a socioeconomic point of view because of the transition from youth to adult roles, but also because they also encompass a critical phase in brain development.[46] It is nevertheless important to note that while developmental effects may be important, the magnitude of their effects on criminal offending and violence are mediated by environmental factors, which may contribute to increasing or lowering the risk for a group of individuals who already exhibit intrinsic vulnerabilities.

## Victimization, perceptions, and happiness

This chapter has so far considered official (national or subnational) statistics. But in order for a crime to be registered in official records, it must first be reported. As mentioned, the probability of reporting a crime is related to institutional and economic characteristics of the country, which can significantly mask the behavior that is of interest to this report. While official statistics can be linked to characteristics of the municipalities in which crimes take place, no such link it possible to information on victims, such as income, age, perceptions about security, and subjective measures of social capital.

This section makes use of the two opinion surveys from the region, the Latin American Public Opinion Project (LAPOP)[47] and Latinobarómetro.[48] Each survey has its strengths and weaknesses. The most obvious one relates to the richness of information provided for analyzing security-related issues and the length of the available panel. LAPOP victimization and security surveys are more detailed, but are available on average for only three time periods, limiting the precision of estimates that rely on within-country variation. The Latinobarómetro panel has been available since 1995, but its security module is less detailed. To assess the sensitivity of results to the data source, Chioda (2014d) conducts an analysis on the two surveys, attempting to match the set of outcomes and controls as closely as possible across the two sources. The analyses that follow are mindful of potential inconsistencies in conclusions across data sources, if any, and point them out (see figure 2.22).[49]

This section first documents the predictors of victimization in LAC. It then contrasts these to reports by survey respondents that crime is the main concern in their country. It finds that the main determinants of victimization are puzzlingly weak predictors of concerns about crime, and discusses why this might be so. It also documents the effects that crime has on the health and well-being of its victims.

**FIGURE 2.22:** Victimization rates versus homicide rates from different data sources, LAC

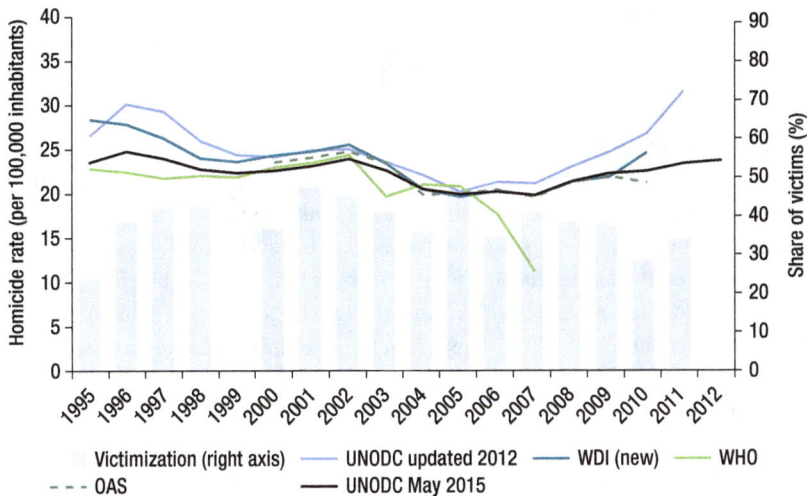

*Source:* World Bank, based on data from the Organization of American States (OAS), World Development Indicators (WDI), World Health Organization (WHO), United Nations Office on Drugs and Crime (UNODC), and revised UNODC. UNODC statistics are revised periodically, not only to be updated, figures from previous years are also revised.
*Note:* Light blue bars indicate victimization rates computed with Latinobarómetro data (2014). Homicide data from the Regional System Standardized Indicators for Citizen Security and Violence Prevention (SES) are omitted and coincide with the UNODC updated series for the last three years.

## Victimization

To gain insight into the determinants of victimization, Chioda (2014d) groups explanatory variables into three sets of variables:

- Individual-level variables (including education, income, age, marital status, and labor force participation) that are directly relevant to the organizing framework and to the ecological model

- Neighborhood-level variables, ranging from perceptions of neighborhood safety, to objective and self-reported measures of community engagement and trust

- Institutional-level variables, such as trust in police and in the judicial system, but also measures of corruption, such as whether the police make requests for bribes.

These three groupings attempt to capture and disentangle the relative effects of the three spheres identified by the ecological model of crime.[50]

A priori, the relationship between income and victimization rates is not clear. While high-income individuals may be valuable targets for criminals, they may also have at their disposal more resources to avoid exposure to crime. Consistent with the latter theory, Levitt (1999) documents that, during the worsening crime epidemic of the 1980s and 1990s in the United States, property crime became more concentrated among the poor. Similarly, Di Tella, Galiani and Schargrodsky (2010) find that higher-income people invest significant resources in avoiding crime. However, the value of income in determining such investments has differential effects according to the location of victimization. Indeed, the authors find that investments in protective devices reduce victimization at home, but not in the streets, where crime avoidance strategies are relatively similar across individuals of different levels of income. In other words, income does not buy a great deal of avoidance of victimization in the street, and optimal behavioral responses to reduce risks, such as not wearing jewelry and avoiding dangerous spaces, are available to all income groups. The net effect of whether income is related to victimization is therefore a priori undetermined. Figure 2.23 provides estimates from regressions of self-reported victimization on controls from the three hierarchical groupings.[51] It reports two set of coefficients for each variable: one corresponding to a model with individual-level controls only, and one that corresponds to a fully saturated model, which controls for factors from all three hierarchical groups.

Panel a of figure 2.23 indicates that there is a marked income gradient in victimization. Belonging to higher income groups raises the likelihood of victimization. Individuals in the highest income bracket are twice as likely to be a victim than those in the (second to) lowest income group. Equivalently, being in the highest income bracket raises the likelihood of being a victim by 8 percentage points, while being in the second lowest income brackets raises the probability of victimization by 4 percentage points,

**FIGURE 2.23:** Marginal effects on victimization of income, education, age, neighborhood safety, social capital, and trust in institutions, LAC

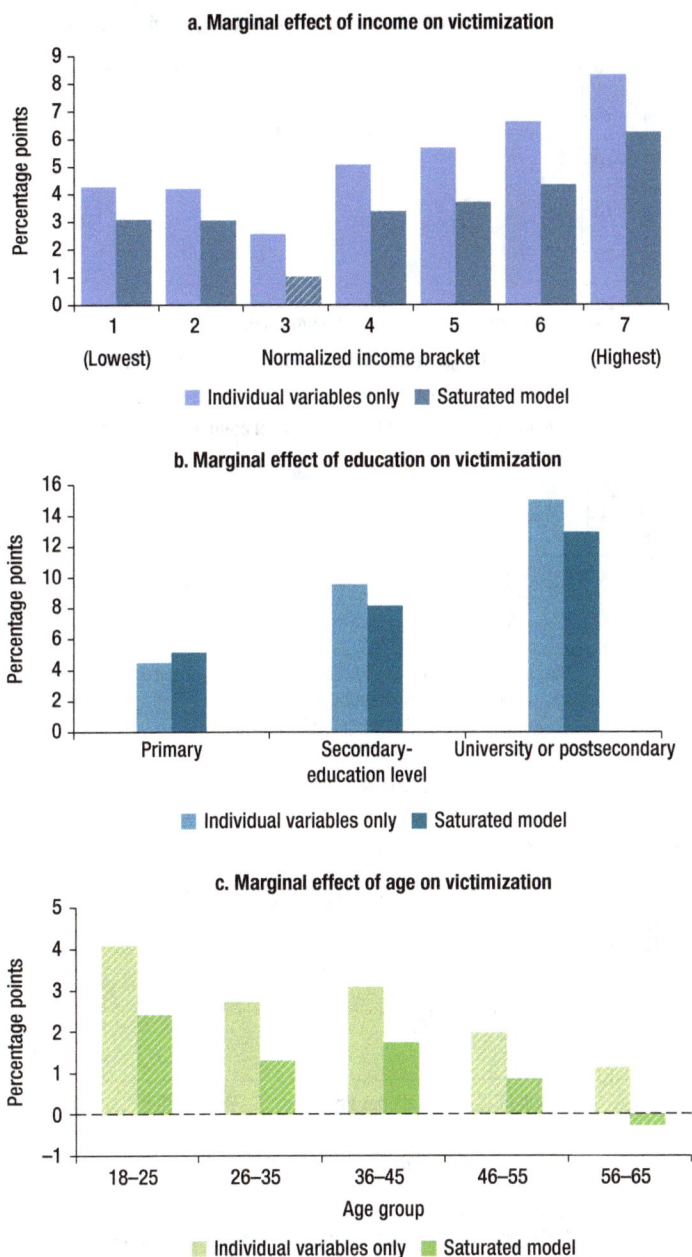

**a. Marginal effect of income on victimization**

Percentage points

Normalized income bracket

1 (Lowest) 2 3 4 5 6 7 (Highest)

Individual variables only  Saturated model

**b. Marginal effect of education on victimization**

Percentage points

Primary  Secondary-education level  University or postsecondary

Individual variables only  Saturated model

**c. Marginal effect of age on victimization**

Percentage points

Age group

18–25  26–35  36–45  46–55  56–65

Individual variables only  Saturated model

*(continued on next page)*

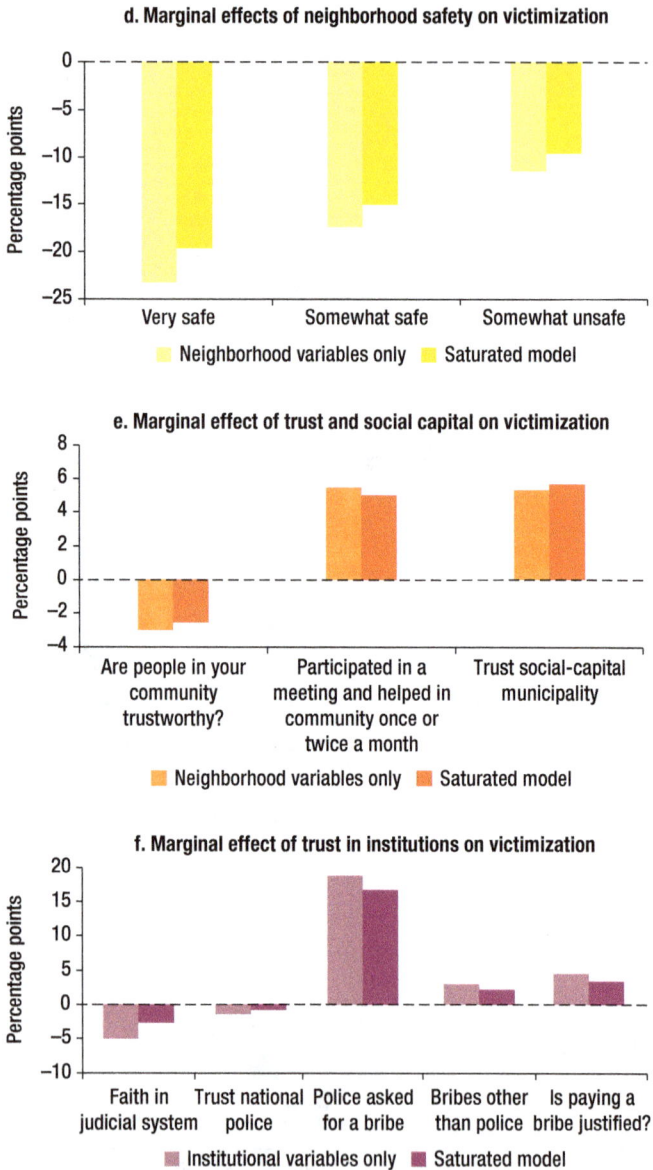

**FIGURE 2.23:** Marginal effects on victimization of income, education, age, neighborhood safety, social capital, and trust in institutions, LAC *(continued)*

**d. Marginal effects of neighborhood safety on victimization**

Neighborhood variables only ■ Saturated model

**e. Marginal effect of trust and social capital on victimization**

Neighborhood variables only ■ Saturated model

**f. Marginal effect of trust in institutions on victimization**

Institutional variables only ■ Saturated model

*Source:* Chioda 2014d, based on LAPOP data.

*Note:* Regressions are weighted by population. Standard errors are clustered at the country level. Income brackets have been normalized for comparability across countries. Income increases by income bracket, with 1 the lowest and 7 the highest income group. All coefficients are significant at conventional levels, except for the bars with diagonal lines.

relative to the lowest income group, which is the omitted category. The inclusion of neighborhood and institutional factors reduces the magnitude of the overall effects of income but not the significance or direction of the relationship.

A more nuanced view of the relationship between victimization and income is provided in figure 2.24, which reports the age distribution of victimization for the

**FIGURE 2.24:** Age-crime incidence by income level for property and violent crimes, LAC

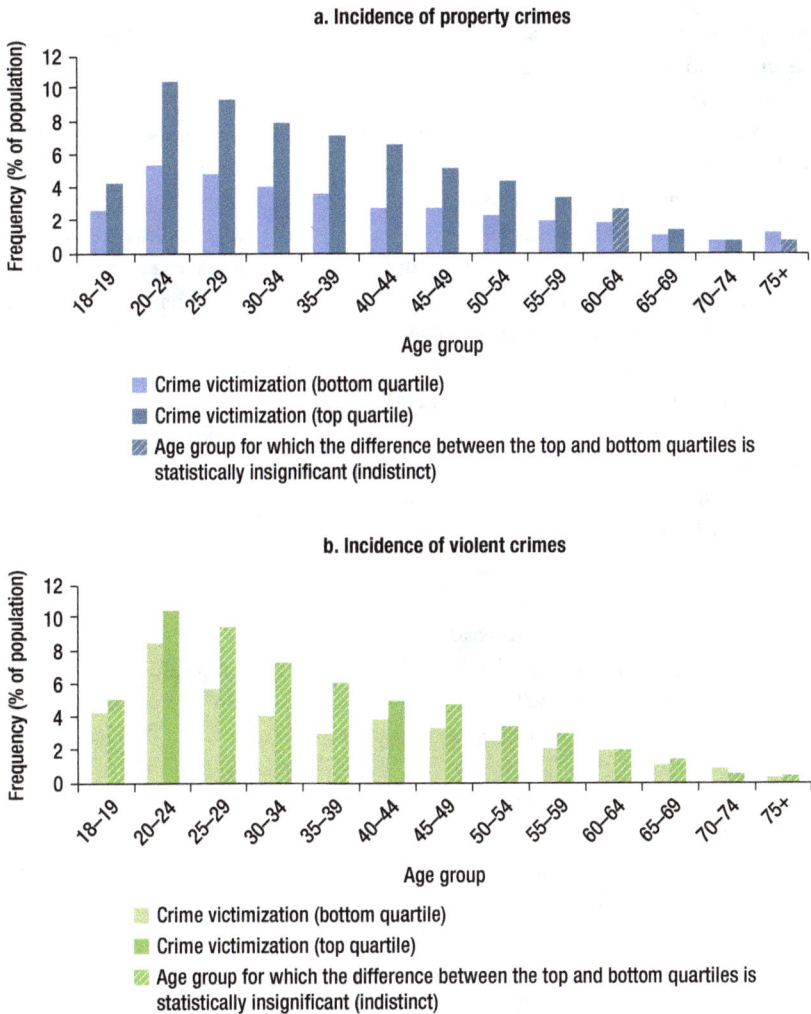

**a. Incidence of property crimes**

Crime victimization (bottom quartile)

Crime victimization (top quartile)

Age group for which the difference between the top and bottom quartiles is statistically insignificant (indistinct)

**b. Incidence of violent crimes**

Crime victimization (bottom quartile)

Crime victimization (top quartile)

Age group for which the difference between the top and bottom quartiles is statistically insignificant (indistinct)

*Source:* Chioda 2014d, based on data from LAPOP 2012.
*Note:* The age 20–24 figure for violent crimes (solid green) reflects a spike that is common to most Central American countries.

top and bottom income quartiles, first for property crime (panel a), then for violent crime (panel b). The profile for property crime has the familiar age-crime shape, initially increasing through the teens, and then declining throughout the rest of the life cycle. Surprisingly, the shapes of the two distributions are remarkably similar for both income quartiles, suggesting that within an income group, variation in risk across different age groups is preserved. Relative to the usual age-crime profile, the incidence of victimization for property crimes peaks slightly later in life (in the 25–29 age group), possibly reflecting higher opportunity for property crime for slightly older young adults. However, individuals in the highest income quartile are at uniformly greater risk of victimization up until their 60s, when the differences between the two categories become indistinguishable. Among the 25–29 age category, for instance, individuals in the top quartile are roughly 3 percentage points (50 percent) more likely to be victims of property crime than those in the bottom quartile. For property crime, therefore, there is a clear income gradient in victimization, which conforms to intuition, as high-income individuals represent better crime opportunities in terms of payoff.

For violent crime, however, there is much less evidence that wealthier individuals are targeted at higher rates, suggesting that violent crimes are much less "economic" in nature. In particular, at younger ages, differences in the incidence across the two income groups are negligible (at ages 18–19 and 20–24, the differences are 0.1 and 0.5 percentage point, respectively).[52] These results conform with evidence from the United Kingdom that violent crime, especially early in life, is driven less by income and more by peer associations (Bellis and others 2012).

Panel b of figure 2.23 indicates a gradient in education similar to that in income. Education and income (brackets) are both included in the models. Among individuals within the same income bracket, the more highly educated are more likely to be victimized.[53] Even in the saturated model, the magnitudes of the education effects are sizable and double those for income. Primary, secondary, and tertiary education are associated with 5, 8, and, 13 additional percentage points in the likelihood of victimization relative to individuals who had not completed primary education. This gradient may appear puzzling, given that it results from models that condition on income. However, the explanation likely lies in the construction of the income variable, which is defined in terms of brackets, rather than absolute levels of income. Thus, the results imply that within a given income bracket, greater education is related to a higher likelihood of victimization. In all likelihood, education levels are capturing variation in income within income brackets, within which there remains residual variation in income that plausibly is positively correlated with education level. That is, more highly educated people within a given income bracket may simply have higher earnings, or have better jobs that are geographically concentrated in locations that can be targeted by criminals, for instance.

An interesting pattern also emerges in the relationship between victimization and age. Age is monotonically related to crime; younger (age 18–25) individuals are at higher risk of victimization (4 percentage points) than individuals older than 65 years old (who are the omitted category), and risk declines throughout the life cycle. The pattern of coefficients from both models coincides with the typical age-victimization profile previously discussed.[54] The magnitudes of the coefficient are not negligible and are comparable to those of income. However, the significance of these effects is sensitive to the model, and vanishes in the saturated model. In particular, the significance disappears after adding neighborhood-level variables to the model that include only individual characteristics, suggesting that different age groups sort into neighborhoods with differential levels of crime. There is evidence that people in young adulthood value different neighborhood amenities and characteristics as they age and form families (such as favoring school quality and safety). The characteristics of neighborhoods will therefore carry information about the age of residents who populate them.

Indeed, the results are consistent with the conjecture that sorting into neighborhoods that are perceived to be safe is an effective crime avoidance strategy. Living in a "somewhat unsafe," "somewhat safe," or "very safe" neighborhood lowers the probability of victimization by 10, 15, and 20 percentage points, respectively, compared to living in a neighborhood deemed "not safe." This result speaks to the importance of neighborhood factors even after controlling for income, education, and labor force participation. Furthermore, it highlights the local nature of crime, alluded to earlier in this chapter. It is worth noting that the magnitude of the effect of one's perception of neighborhood safety dominates any other effect associated with trust or measures of social capital at the neighborhood level (as measured by participation in religious, political, and self-organized community meetings) (see panel d of figure 2.23 and figure 2.25).

While subjective assessments of neighborhood trustworthiness are marginally protective with respect to victimization, the correlations with participation in community meetings and measures of social capital are positive. From a theoretical perspective, the sign of the effect of social capital on victimization is undetermined. First, cohesion in a neighborhood can emerge in response to changes in criminal episodes. For instance, people may meet more often or may coalesce to show support, reversing the direction of causality. Second, cohesion per se does not necessarily entail adherence to common law. Neighborhoods with high concentrations of offenders who identify criminal activity as a way of life may also measure high in terms of social cohesion and even efficacy (see panel e of figure 2.23).

The magnitudes of the effects of institutional variables on victimization are relatively small (see figure 2.23 and figure 2.25). They all tend to be of the expected sign, with trust in the police and in the judicial system associated with a lower likelihood of victimization of 0.8 and 2.6 percentage points, respectively.

The most striking effect among the institutional variables relates to respondents' assessments as to whether police ask for bribes. These responses provide a marker of the quality of institutions and are directly related to the probability of detecting and apprehending offenders. From the perspective of potential offenders, this is a key parameter in their decision to offend, as it determines (expected) criminal payoffs.

**FIGURE 2.25:** Marginal effects on victimization of trust in the judicial system, the national police, the community, and municipal social capital

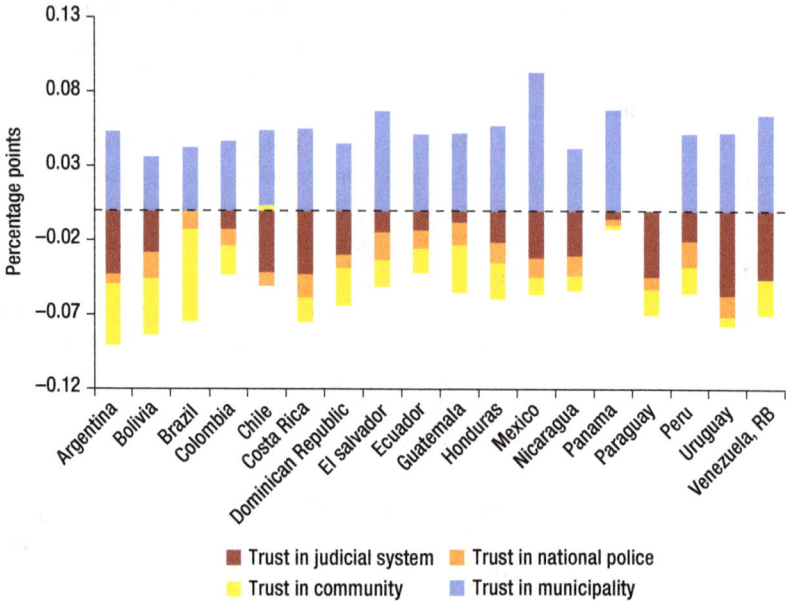

Source: Chioda 2014d, based on data from LAPOP 2014.
Note: Analysis is weighted by population. Standard errors are clustered at the country level. Marginal effects are estimated including the neighborhood and institutional or community coefficient only, to be interpreted as upper bounds on the significance and magnitude of these effects. For Paraguay, there are no data on "Trust in municipality."

As discussed in chapter 7, it greatly affects criminal behavior in practice, consistent with the organizing framework. Police asking for bribes is associated with a 17 percentage point increase in the probability of experiencing some form of crime. More remarkable than the magnitude of its effect are its stability and significance in country-specific analyses (see figure 2.26).[55] To put the magnitude of the effect into perspective, the harmful effect of police corruption more than offsets the protective effect of sorting into safe neighborhoods and trustworthiness of neighbors. The social acceptance of bribes, which reflects the extent to which the general population is aware of and justifies the practice (as captured by the question "Do you believe that bribes are justified?"), is therefore also a significant risk factor, with effects ranging between 2 and 7 percentage points across countries (see figure 2. 27).

In the earlier sections, the arguments regarding the relationship between stages of development and crime and violence have frequently emphasized the mediating role of institutions, which the preceding results confirm. LAC counties have made important improvements to their institutions, and measures of confidence in government rose 13 percentage points between 2002 and 2013 (see figure 2.28). Similarly, the

**FIGURE 2.26:** Marginal effects on victimization of the variable "police asked for bribes"

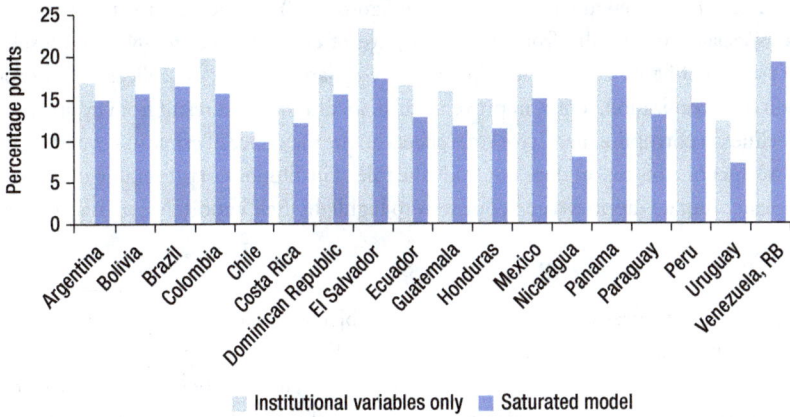

Source: Chioda 2014d, based on LAPOP 2014.

**FIGURE 2.27:** Marginal effects of the variable "is paying bribes justified?" by country

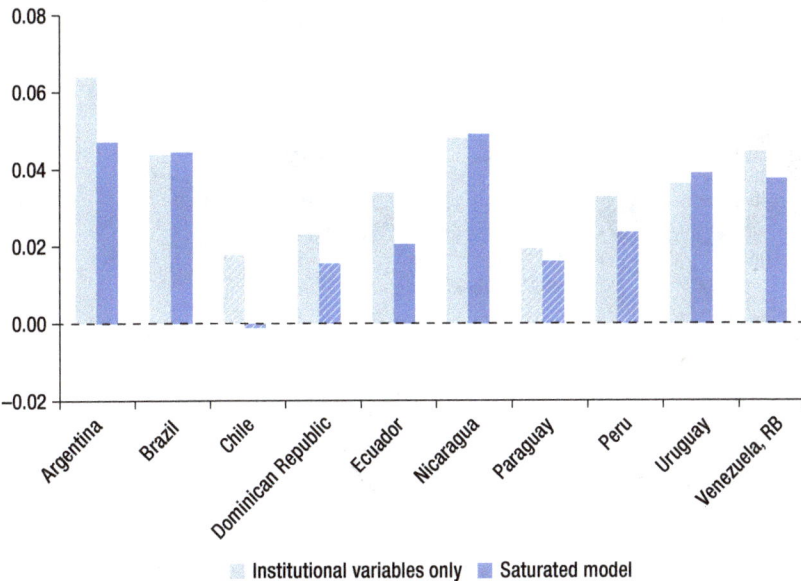

Source: Chioda 2014d, based on LAPOP data.

incidence of corruption steadily declined between 1996 and 2010, and the decline accelerated in the latter half of the last decade, falling 12 percentage points since 2007. While improvements have also occurred in trust in the police and in the judiciary system, they have risen at a slower pace (see figure 2.28).[56] The decline in corruption is especially noteworthy from the perspective of crime reduction, given the results of panel e of figure 2.23, which documents very large and positive effects of corruption on victimization. Thus, improvements in institutions that result from even minor declines in corruption may have large effects on the incidence of crime. As stated in the introduction, this report does not study the role of institutions in preventing crime and violence, but it is appropriate in our view to highlight their importance in this chapter.

## Concern about crime and happiness

This section focuses on two dimensions of subjective well-being: respondents' feelings of insecurity (a marker of stress), and self-assessed happiness and personal satisfaction. Why are these relevant? How crime rates and personal victimization relate to an individual's well-being is central to the welfare costs of crime, which exceed the simple effects of victimization. An individual who never falls victim to crime may nevertheless feel a persistent sense of fear, insecurity, and stress in a context of elevated crime rates. The costs are not only psychological but also physical, in the form of compromised health.

**FIGURE 2.28:** Trust in the police, the justice system, and democracy, LAC, 1996–2013

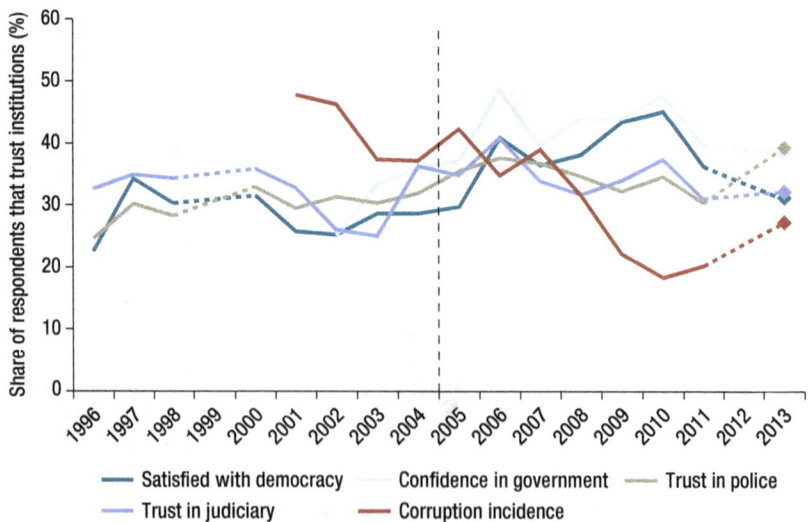

*Source:* World Bank, based on data from Latinobarómetro, 1996–2013. No data are available for 1999 and 2012.

The link between criminal victimization and well-being has been studied by psychologists and sociologists (see Di Tella, MacCulloch, and Ñopo 2008). A common result from the psychology literature is that crime victims have been shown to suffer from a variety of significant and persistent psychological problems, which include depression, anxiety, fear, and post-traumatic stress disorder, as well as feelings of hostility and personal violation.[57] These psychological symptoms commonly found among crime victims, especially fear and anxiety, are negatively associated with individuals' subjectively measured health (Ross 1993) and measures of subjective well-being and overall perceived quality of life (Michalos 1991).

Indeed, Jeremy Bentham (1780) referred to a secondary cost of crime—the "alarm effect"—that follows a criminal incident to describe the resulting sense of insecurity: "a pain of anxiety, a pain based on the fear of suffering mischiefs or inconveniences." Economists have long acknowledged that the costs to crime are substantial.[58] However, the literature on the link between crime and welfare as measured by self-reported happiness/satisfaction is more recent. Di Tella, MacCulloch, and Ñopo (2008) and Graham and Chaparro (2011) rely on data from the Gallup Organization on LAC countries to consider the relationship between insecurity, negative emotions (pain, worry, sadness, boredom, depression, and anger), and well-being (as measured by happiness and health). In the Australian context, Cornaglia, Feldman, and Leigh (2014) provide empirical evidence of "direct" impacts on victims and "indirect" impacts on victims and nonvictims that operate through the crime rate. In particular, they document a decline in the mental well-being of victims after acts of violence, as well as a decline in that of nonvictims, operating through the violent crime rate (which represents the probability of victimization).

This secondary effect may help explain recent trends in reports by LAC citizens that crime is their primary concern (see figure 2.29). While one might expect personal victimization to be most correlated with concerns about crime, figure 2.29 seems to contradict this intuition. In particular, it is puzzling that LAC citizens have increasingly reported crime as being their primary concern since the early 2000s (green line) when the risk of victimization has simultaneously been declining (blue line). Trends in homicides (gray bars), rather than personal experience, appear to be more predictive of the region's sentiment, possibly due to either the higher visibility of the crime or its gravity.[59] It is possible, however, that a Benthamian "alarm effect" is at play, with concerns about crime being more related, for instance, to the risk of homicide (the most salient and extreme of crimes) than to victimization of any other type of crime. However, as discussed later, it may simply reflect an ordering of individual needs and concerns (Maslow 1943), whereby, as people's minimal and economic material needs are met, their attention turns to concerns of personal security and an orderly society.

A more detailed look at the determinants of victimization provides some insight into the negative correlation between victimization and concerns about crime (selected estimated coefficients from an underlying regression model for victimization are reported in figure 2.30).[60]

**FIGURE 2.29:** Trends in homicides, concerns about crime, and victimization, LAC, 1996–2013

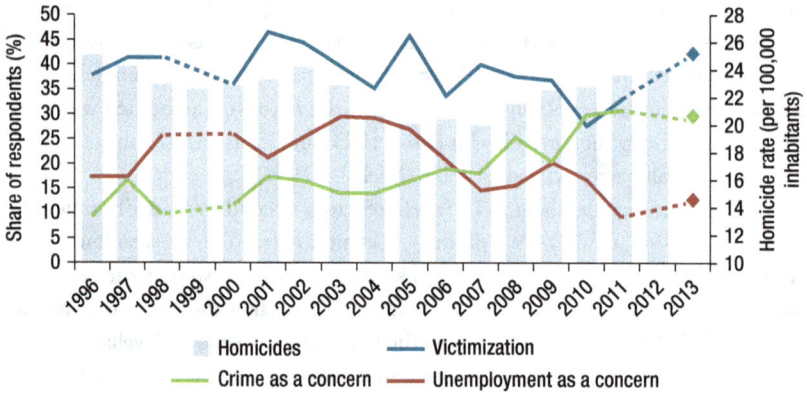

Source: World Bank, based on data from Latinobarómetro and UNODC.
Note: Homicides, on the right axis, are expressed per 100,000 inhabitants. "Crime concerns" and "victimization" corresponds to the share of people who list crime and delinquency as one of their main concerns and who reported being a victim or knowing someone in their family who has been a victim in the last 12 months, respectively.

Possibly the most striking result that emerges from the analysis of the determinants of whether people report crime as being their main concern is the degree to which they are unrelated to the determinants of victimization. Income only marginally predicts concern about crime. This conclusion holds uniformly across specifications and across data sets (with significant effects of around 3 or 4 percentage points, according to Latinobarómetro, but no gradient based on LAPOP data). By contrast, income is a strong predictor of victimization (recall figure 2.23). Intuitively, one would expect effects on concern for crime to reflect the incidence of victimization, with the income groups more affected by violence being more concerned.

Conditional on income, the pattern of education effects on concern for crime implies the opposite gradient of that with victimization: concern declines with level of education, though the magnitude of the gradient is more attenuated; all education levels are positively associated with a higher likelihood of expressing concern about crime. Heads of the household who have completed primary, secondary, and tertiary education are 3.6, 3.5, and 0.1 percentage points more likely to indicate crime as a concern than those who have not completed primary education, though the latter effect is not significant. To put this (and other) results into perspective, in 2014 the share of respondents declaring that crime was the main problem their country faced was approximately 38 percent (unweighted); a 3.6 percentage point effect is equivalent to approximately a 14 percent increase in the probability of expressing concerns about the security in the country.

## The role of demographics

Men worry less about crime, even though they are at higher risk of being victims. Similarly, while marriage is a statistically significant (though small) protective factor for victimization, it is instead associated with an increased likelihood of being concerned about crime. These patterns may reflect an equilibrium in which individuals who are

FIGURE 2.30: Marginal effects on crime as a concern in LAC

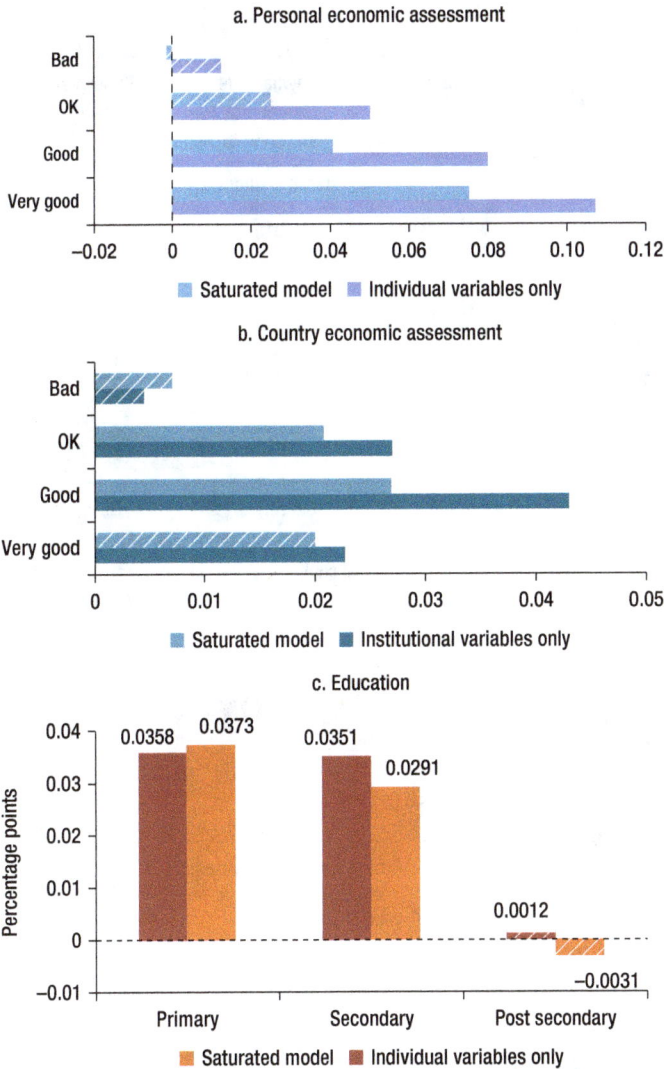

a. Personal economic assessment

Saturated model ■ Individual variables only

b. Country economic assessment

Saturated model ■ Institutional variables only

c. Education

Saturated model ■ Individual variables only

*(continued on next page)*

**FIGURE 2.30:** Marginal effects on crime as a concern in LAC *(continued)*

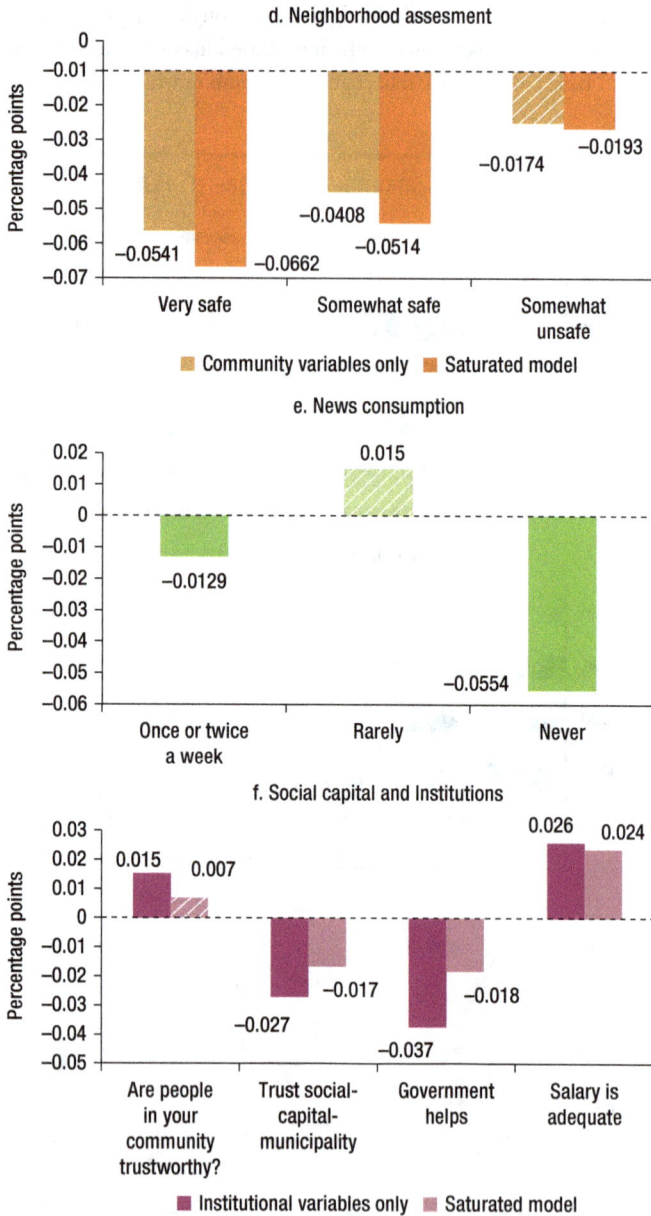

### d. Neighborhood assesment

Community variables only   ■ Saturated model

Bars with labels:
- Very safe: −0.0541, −0.0662
- Somewhat safe: −0.0408, −0.0514
- Somewhat unsafe: −0.0174, −0.0193

### e. News consumption

Bars with labels:
- Once or twice a week: −0.0129
- Rarely: 0.015
- Never: −0.0554

### f. Social capital and Institutions

Institutional variables only   ■ Saturated model

Bars with labels:
- Are people in your community trustworthy?: 0.015, 0.007
- Trust social-capital-municipality: −0.027, −0.017
- Government helps: −0.037, −0.018
- Salary is adequate: 0.026, 0.024

*Source:* Chioda 2014d, based on LAPOP data.
*Note:* Regression weighted by population. Standard errors are clustered at the country level. All coefficients are significant at conventional levels, except those indicated with diagonal lines.

more risk-averse tend to adopt behaviors that avoid the exposure to crime, thereby reducing their likelihood of victimization. In particular, being married may entail more concern about crime because of a lower taste for risk but also because the safety of family members becomes more important: stronger family and friendship ties increasingly expose people to the higher risk that someone in their extended circle will be victimized, thereby raising the costs of crime.

The gradients for concern about crime are stable with age; younger individuals are less concerned than those ages 65 or older (see figure 2.29). However, differences in age are small and imprecisely estimated in LAPOP.[61] The estimates from a similar specification based on Latinobarómetro data exhibit the same pattern and are precisely estimated (see figure 2.31).[62] The positive age gradient may reflect the evolution of risk aversion over the life cycle but, at first glance, contradicts the incidence of violence,

**FIGURE 2.31:** Marginal effects of age on crime as a concern in LAC

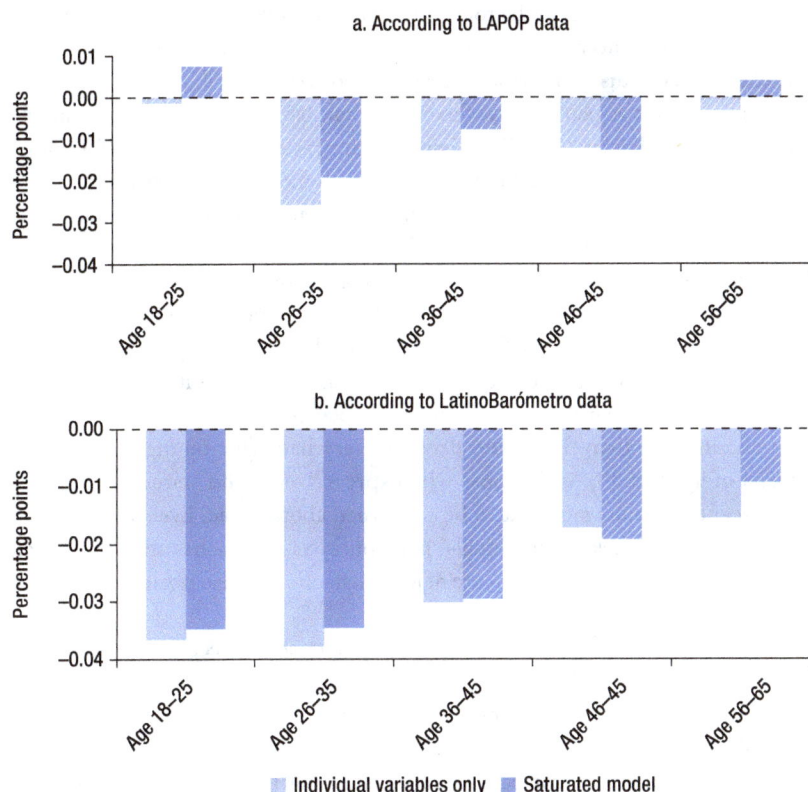

a. According to LAPOP data

b. According to LatinoBarómetro data

Individual variables only ■ Saturated model

*Source:* LAPOP data for panel a; LatinoBarómetro for panel b.
*Note:* Bars with diagonal lines are not significant at the conventional levels.

as seen in the age profile for victimization (figure 2.21). Despite the elevated statistical risk that youth face to be victims or offenders, they tend to exhibit very low risk aversion and are less likely to be concerned about crime, danger, or consequences. Of course, the lower concerns about risk may precisely be the cause for the spike in victimization among youths. However, longitudinal studies from the New Zealand, the United Kingdom, and the United States suggest that the differences in risk aversion are not big enough to justify the discrepancy in victimization rates across age groups. In the U.S. context, Taylor and Hale (1986) also find that the demographic groups at highest risk of victimization (young males) tend not to have the greatest fear of crime.

Chapter 4 discusses explanations for low risk aversion and disregard for consequences among adolescents and young adults. During these periods, the stages of brain development are characterized by heightened rewards from risky behavior, and the brain is wired with a heightened sense of anxiety, fear, and hyperreactivity, but is relatively underdeveloped in terms of calm reasoning.

### The economy, perceptions of economic stability, and satisfaction

The discussion now turns to the role of perceptions about economic well-being and how they relate to concerns about insecurity. As discussed, income—an objective measure of economic status—is not systematically related to concerns about crime. However, individuals' subjective perceptions of their economic circumstances are systematically (positively) related to concerns about crime. That is, even after controlling for household income, the more satisfied individuals are with their economic status, the more concerned they are about crime.[63] This is the case even in country-specific models, in which the effects exhibit remarkable stability across countries. Note that the relationship with one's economic situation persists even after controlling for income; the two variables are both significant, suggesting that they are capturing different information. Indeed, the correlation between them is surprisingly low (for the majority of countries, the raw correlation is no greater than 0.2; and, for LAC as a whole, it is around 0.05).

Those who deem their economic circumstances "bad" have no more concern about crime than those who deem it "very bad" (the omitted category in panel a of figure 2.30), while those who express "very good" circumstances are 7.5 percentage points more like to be concerned about crime. Even after controlling for income bracket, individuals' perception as to whether they receive an adequate salary (an indirect measure of job satisfaction) is also positive correlated with concerns about crime.

Qualitatively similar results emerge with perceptions of economic outlook for the country (panel b of figure 2.30). The more optimistic are people's expectations about the country's future economic performance, the more people express concerns about crime and violence. These results are consistent with the trends from Latinobarómetro presented in figure 2.29. Unemployment and concerns about crime co-move almost in lockstep, but in opposite directions; improvements in the economy are associated with more awareness of and concerns about crime.

The robustness of these results was further tested by including subjective measures of the country's past economic situation. Here again, optimism about one's own or the country's economic situation is positively related to concerns about crime, even after controlling for income, education, neighborhood safety, and social capital.[64]

Why might satisfaction with personal or national economic circumstances be positively correlated with concerns about crime? This pattern is consistent with the hypothesis that security lies further up in the hierarchy of human concerns than economic/physical well-being. As individuals' economic circumstances improve and as their perceptions of the economic outlook improve, concerns about material needs become less important, and their attention turns to security. Just as in Maslow's hierarchy of needs, concerns more proximate to an individual's situation (such as his or her personal economic situation) need to be "met" before others become salient. In other words, the rise in respondents reporting concern about crime may be an indicator of a higher stage of economic development for the individual and for the region. It is also worth noting that, despite the magnitude of the crime and violence problem in LAC, crime is still a "rare" event, while changes in unemployment or in the economy's growth rate are more readily transmitted economy-wide and have a more direct effect on respondents' personal circumstances. If a country experiences a large negative income shock, more people will mechanically be affected at once, whereas increases in homicides may be driven by very localized and clustered episodes, which are likely less to be salient in the midst of a large economic downturn.[65]

It is important to clarify that this study is not comparing the relative importance of mutually exclusive alternatives to the same questions, and therefore detecting mechanical correlations in the survey design. That is, once asked to indicate the most salient concern among a group of alternatives, if respondents select crime, they cannot select unemployment and/or macro stability, by design.

Whereas a number of strong predictors of victimization are weakly related to concerns about crime, or exhibit conflicting patterns, neighborhood security predicts both victimization and concerns about security. The apparently trivial results are somewhat surprising in light of the reported disconnect between the determinants of victimization and worries about crime. However, sorting into neighborhoods based on safety emerges as a powerful protective strategy in reducing victimization rates (thus reducing concerns about safety and security)—and thereby aligning perceptions about crime and victimization rates. Those who are more likely to be concerned about security will engage in more avoidance and invest in ways to reduce the risk of victimization, such as by locating in safe neighborhoods. The safer the neighborhood or residence is, the lower is the psychological burden associated with crime. The effects in panel d of figure 2.30 are precisely estimated and indicate that living in a very safe neighborhood lowers concerns about crime by 25 percent (6.6 percentage points); in a somewhat safe neighborhood by 19.4 percent (5.1 percentage points); and in a somewhat unsafe area by 7.2 percent (1.9 percentage points) relative to those who live in a "criminally unsafe" zone. The significance of these results will be revisited in chapter 6, when the impact of prevention strategies that involve relocation or in situ upgrading is discussed.

This section has documented often-conflicting patterns between the determinants of victimization and determinants expressing concerns about security. An unresolved question is the following: Are people's feelings about security and crime unrelated to victimization? To answer this question, Chioda (2014d) takes advantage of Latinobarómetro's long time series. In addition to the set of controls discussed—demographic characteristics, income, institutional variables, measures of social capital, and perceptions about individuals' economic situation—Chioda includes the contemporaneous and lagged victimization rates in her analysis of concerns about crime. While the contemporaneous victimization rate is unrelated to perceptions of security, the change in victimization is related.[66] In other words, the weight individuals place on concerns about crime depends more on changes in crime than on its level,[67] consistent with the literature on reference points and "adaptation."

The discussion also considered a second marker of mental well-being—self-reported happiness—and its relationship with victimization. Controlling for an array of individual characteristics (including age, income, education, perceptions about one's own and the country's economic situation, labor force participation, and fairness of salary), being a victim reduces the self-reported life satisfaction measure by 2.5 percentage points. This is statistically distinguishable from zero and is consistent with the study by Di Tella, MacCulloch, and Ñopo (2008), which documents a negative and robust correlation between victimization and well-being in Latin America, as measured by feeling pain, boredom, and depression. Remarkably, the magnitude and precision of this estimate is invariant to the source of data (LAPOP or Latinobarómetro), when closely replicating the same set of controls across the two sources. However, the estimated effect of victimization on life satisfaction for Central America is almost double that for the region (4 percentage points).

Consistent with previous results, predictors of individual well-being include income—with the strongest correlation at the top of the income distribution—education, marital status, and gender. Measures of social capital at the neighborhood level are also positively correlated with happiness. Among measures of institutional quality, trust in the police is consistently, positively associated with happiness. Similarly, Graham and Chaparro (2011) find that crime victimization has significant and negative effects on both happiness and health. They also identify similar adaptation mechanisms, as discussed earlier: people who live in high-crime areas appear to "adapt" to the elevated criminality, reporting less impact of crime on happiness than those in low-crime areas, who experience sharp rises in violence. Furthermore, Graham and Chaparro document a detrimental impact of victimization on health.

Together, the analysis of victimization, concerns about security, and the well-being of victims document the burdens that insecurity imposes on society and it citizens.

While the analysis is based on self-reports and presents simple correlations, they are consistent with the more rigorous evidence reviewed in this report. For instance, chapter 6 examines the effects on well-being of large-scale interventions, such as upgrades to existing dwellings and mobility programs that dramatically alter the environment (and exposure to crime) of beneficiaries, who subsequently report large improvements in health and well-being.

## Notes

[1] For instance, 15 countries and two capital cities in LAC have partnered to improve and compare their statistics on crime and violence through the Regional System of Standardized Indicators on Peaceful Coexistence and Citizen Security (SES). This initiative has been promoted and financed by the Inter-American Development Bank under the coordination and execution of the Instiuto de investigación y desarrollo en prevención de violencia y promocion de la convivencia social (CISALVA) at the Universidad del Valle in Cali, Colombia, and in collaboration with the United Nations Office on Drugs and Crime (UNODC), the Organization of American States (OAS/OEA), the Central American Integration System (SICA), and the World Bank. The SES database is still under construction and data are available only for very recent years and for a subset of the indicators. Whenever possible, this study compared national statistics, UNODC data, and World Health Organization (WHO) series with information available from CISALVA.

[2] See Moffitt (1990); Tracy, Wolfgang, and Figlio (1991); Farrington and West (1993); and Garrido and Morales Quintro (2007).

[3] The homicide rate is defined as the number of homicides divided by the total population (expressed in hundreds of thousands) and is equivalent to the weighted average of homicide rates of the individual countries, weighted by their respective populations.

[4] Since 2010, violence has been on the rise in Brazil, where homicides climbed back to 26.5 per 100,000 in 2012.

[5] Both studies use data that cover the 1990s. In addition to homicides, Soares and Naritomi (2010) also consider theft, burglary, and contact crimes, while Fajnzylber, Lederman, and Loayza (2002a) focus exclusively on homicides, given the significant differences in the legal definitions of other crimes across countries.

[6] More than 80 million Latin Americans have risen above moderate poverty since 2003.

[7] Twelve of the 17 countries in the sample experienced a decline in inequality, as measured by the Gini coefficient.

[8] The middle class in LAC expanded from 20 percent to 30 percent of the population, as measured by the proportion of people making more than $10 per day, on a purchasing power parity–adjusted basis.

[9] Figure 2.6 is obtained by kernel-weighted local polynomial regression of cross-sectional homicide rates on log GDP per capita. The flexible estimation has the advantage of not making assumptions about the functional form of the relationship between the expected homicide rate and log GDP per capita, allowing the data instead to "speak for themselves." The methodology is akin to that of Mammen and Paxson (2000).

[10] Buonanno, Ferguson, and Vargas (2014). document the existence of a similar shape in the crime-development relationship for U.S. states since the 1970s: as income levels have risen, crime has followed an inverted-U pattern.

[11] The data were compiled from a number of different data sources to ensure the inclusion of the greatest number of countries and years: UNODC (homicides, drug seizures, and police data); World Development Indicators (macroeconomic variables); LAC household surveys (demographics, labor markets, educational attainment); and opinion surveys, including the World Value Surveys, LatinoBarómetro, and the Latin American Public Opinion Project (LAPOP).

[12] Chioda (2014a) estimates a dynamic panel data model, including time and country fixed effects, in addition to a rich set of controls. The analysis is "dynamic" in the sense that it controls for the lagged value of the dependent variable. As highlighted in the text, the exercise formalizes the correlations with and trends of key risk and protective factors of violence. Dynamic panel data models do not automatically deliver causal estimates of the effects of interest. However, by virtue of controlling for the lagged dependent variable, they rely on very short-term variation in the variables of interest, which is subject to fewer concerns about omitted variables and reverse causality.

[13] The treatment of (per capita) income in the specifications is close to that of Fajnzylber, Lederman, and Loayza (2002a); Gould, Weinberg, and Mustard (2002); Buonanno and Leonida (2009); and Gronqvist (2011).

[14] Teen pregnancy is a particularly good market of poverty in the context of a dynamic panel data model of crime because current teen pregnancy is very likely predetermined relative to changes in violence.

[15] Even at the country level, police data are unfortunately very noisy and are available for only a limited number of countries and years. This variable alone causes Chioda's (2014a) sample size to drop from 160 to 69. While certain results are preserved within this smaller sample, the resulting selectivity of the sample is problematic for the robustness and generalizability of the findings.

[16] Dynamic panel data models can deliver biased estimates in short panels (Nickell 1981), requiring the implementation of more sophisticated methods to address this (Arellano and Bond 1991; Blundell and Bond 1998). However, fixed-effects estimates are not problematic when asymptotics occurs along the time and/or cross-sectional dimensions. Nickell's (1981) formulas imply small biases with $T = 15$ time periods, as is the case in Chioda (2014a). Subsequent Monte Carlo exercises (Flannery and Hankins 2013; Buddelmeyer and others 2008) conclude that the fixed-effects estimator outperforms more sophisticated alternatives for small $N$ (the number of cross-sectional units) and small $T$ for certain parameter values, such as when the degrees of persistence are high. Indeed, fixed-effects models are consistent when $T$ and $N$ are large and, in the context of a fixed but large $T$ and large $N$, the magnitudes of the biases are manageable or negligible. In Chioda's (2014a) setting, the fixed-effects estimator will simply understate the degree of persistence of shocks.

[17] Brush (2007) studies how cross-section versus panel time series estimation techniques affect the coefficient on inequality, finding that the positive and significant coefficient on inequality obtains only in the cross-section.

[18] Pridemore (2011) was able to replicate Fajnzylber, Lederman, and Loayza (2002b) (thanks to the authors' willingness to share their data) and finds that the significance of the positive coefficient on the Gini coefficient disappears when a proxy for poverty is added to their model.

[19] For example, Grogger (2008) also uses maternal age at first birth as a proxy for low socioeconomic status.

[20] All models rely on dynamic panel data specifications (that is, they control for the lagged homicide rate) and include time and country fixed effects.

[21] Because the inclusion of the full set of controls reduces the significance of the macro variables, the parsimonious model represents an upper bound on the magnitude and significance of these variables.

[22] Estimates were obtained by allowing the coefficient of the variable of interest to vary over time, by interacting it with year indicators; see, for instance, the yearly coefficients on poverty in figure 2.7. Based on the yearly coefficients, the relevant subperiod was then selected.

[23] Indeed, in most regression models, income per capita is positively related to crime, although largely insignificant; the magnitude of the coefficient is sensitive to the specification.

[24] According to Routine Activity Theory, crime is relatively unaffected by social causes such as poverty, inequality, and unemployment.

[25] The reduced-form results are consistent with Munyo (2015), who develops a dynamic model of behavior to analyze juvenile crime. Forward-looking youths consistently decide between crime and legal activities depending on their endowment of work and crime-specific human capital, which in turn is shaped by their history of past choices.

[26] Chioda (2014c) has access to confidential data on Mexican alleged and convicted perpetrators from 1990 to 2013, which she uses to construct a synthetic panel and subsequently study the relationship between attachment to the labor market and criminality over the life cycle. In addition to criminal offending, conviction, and labor force participation, the data record the date, type, and location of alleged crimes; demographic information; educational attainment; and sector of employment. When one studies dynamic behavior without having access to longitudinal data that follow the same individuals over time, one can exploit time series of cross-sections and divide the sample into groups that are homogeneous in a well-defined sense, and track the averages of the resulting groups over time rather than the individuals (Attanasio and Davis 1996; Browning, Deaton, and Irish 1985). In contexts involving behavior over the life cycle, individuals are typically grouped by their year of birth, such that a cohort of individuals is observed over time.

[27] The United Nations (UN) estimates that there are 55 million users of illegal drugs in the United States. Under extremely conservative assumptions, this implies a final consumer drug market of anywhere between $30 billion and $150 billion, annually. If one assumes that drug cartels have access only to the wholesale side of the market (which is not known to be true), then yearly revenues could amount to anywhere between $15 billion and $60 billion. To put these numbers into perspective, Microsoft has annual revenues of $60 billion.

[28] Figure 2.10 is based on Chioda (2014b), which assembles annual panel data for upward of 2,000 Mexican municipalities from 1995 to 2013 to study the spatial heterogeneity of property and violent crime and its relationship with economic activity, as well as temporal and geographic spillovers in crime. Chioda's data include detailed information on the educational attainment of local residents; on labor market conditions; on the local infrastructure, such as roadways; on access to running water and electricity; on the number of schools, teachers, and pupils; and on arrests. In the context of dynamic panel data models of property crime / violent crime, this information is used to flexibly control for local socioeconomic conditions. Her models also control for crime in neighboring municipalities, allowing her to assess the degree of geographic spillovers in crime, as well as the extent to which ignoring such spillovers affects estimates of the persistence of crime within a municipality.

[29] All coefficients on all three lines are significantly distinguishable from zero at the 1 percent level, except the q1 effect in the 1990s, which is significant only at the 10 percent level.

[30] That weapons are trafficked from the United States to Mexico is uncontroversial; a 2009 report by the U.S. Government Accountability Office reports that 87 percent of the guns seized by the Mexican authorities between 2004 and 2009 were traced back to the United States.

[31] To be clear, the spikes in violence on Sundays are not limited to the last trimester of 2013, but are a stable feature of homicides in Honduras. See Honduras' *Observatory on Violence Bulletin*, 2014.

[32] It is precisely this clustering of criminality in both time and geographic space that has led researchers and policymakers to advocate the "hot spots" models of policing (discussed in greater detail in chapter 7).

Rather than maintaining a wide presence throughout a city, say, police officers are physically concentrated in particularly troubled locations (the so-called "hot spots") and at particularly troubled times in an effort to deter crime by raising the likelihood of apprehension.

[33] Mexico is the only country for which detailed data on perpetrators are available.

[34] The 0.66 estimate of the coefficient on the lagged homicide rate is obtained from the most saturated model: the one with the largest set of controls. In the context of dynamic panel data models, adding covariates delivers information not only on their direct effects on the dependent variable but also on the degree to which their inclusion changes the coefficient on the lagged dependent variables. That is, they are also informative about whether the persistence of violence can be weakened or broken—whether the strength of the relationship between contemporaneous and lagged values of homicide can be attenuated by other factors, as embodied by the additional covariates. In this instance, because it results from the most saturated specifications, 0.66 is the "weakest" degree of temporal spillovers that Chioda (2014a) was able to obtain.

[35] See Chioda (2014b) and Chioda and Rojas-Alvarado (2014).

[36] Note the implications of high degrees of persistence; strong intertemporal linkages imply that it can be particularly difficult to unwind a cycle of violence once it has begun because every additional incident is associated with 0.75–0.80 more incidents by simple inertia. However, the converse is also true; if efforts to control violent outbreaks are successful, such that one homicide is prevented in the current year, then 0.75–0.80 homicides will be averted the next year, on average.

[37] Gary Slutkin, a physician and epidemiologist who studied the spread of AIDS in Africa, observed that gun violence in Chicago exhibited pronounced clustering, and he drew an analogy to infectious epidemics. This observation ultimately generated the core ideas behind a much-publicized cease-fire program (called Cure Violence) for violence prevention in Chicago. In economics and criminology, a large theoretical literature has developed to explain why the social context may affect an individual's propensity to engage in crime. One theory is that criminal behavior is "contagious." This theory is considered in greater detail in chapter 6, along with the relevant empirical evidence.

[38] In Brazil, the estimated degree of geographical spillovers increases substantially to 0.47 when regions around municipalities are more narrowly defined as the set of neighboring municipalities within 100 km of them.

[39] Mechanically, the estimates in table 2.3 result from a dynamic panel model, which controls for several municipal characteristics, and which defines spillovers as the effect of an incremental crime that occurred within the state, but outside of municipal boundaries. This is a very different measure of spillovers than the number of crimes for which there is discordance between the offender's municipality of residence and the municipality of occurrence.

[40] Studies of developed economies generally benefit from longitudinal data on several cohorts, where each individual is followed over the life cycle. In addition to standard demographic and economic variables, information is also collected on individuals' self-reported criminal activity, which is then combined with police records. Unfortunately, to our knowledge, no such data exist in Latin America. The results presented here rely on both cross-sectional and cohort analyses.

[41] Moffitt, Caspi, Rutter, and Silva (2001); Nagin and Tremblay (2001); Caspi and others (2002); Arseneault and others (2003); Cote and others (2006).

[42] See Browning, Deaton, and Irish (1985) and Attanasio and Davis (1996).

[43] The data are age-censored and include only perpetrators ages 15 and older.

[44] The upper-bound conjecture is confirmed by certain longitudinal studies. With the advent of alternate measurement strategies, most notably self-reports of deviant behavior, researchers have learned that arrest statistics reflect merely the tip of the deviance iceberg (Hood and Sparks 1970; Klein 1989). Actual rates of illicit behavior soar so high during adolescence that participation in delinquency appears to be a normal part of teen life (Elliott and others 1983).

[45] It is worth noting that although the age-crime profiles developed here (and elsewhere) peak in the teen years, a number of authors (including Tremblay 2004; Tremblay and others 2004; Alink and others 2006) have documented that the peak of aggression occurs much earlier in childhood. However, at the young age at which it peaks, the potential for harm from this aggression is minimal. Through socialization, children learn self-control and how not to act on their aggression. These issues are discussed in greater detail in chapter 3.

[46] In particular, this is a critical phase of development of the frontal cortex, the locus of executive functions, which regulates impulsivity, risk-taking behavior, delayed gratification, and self-control (Raine 2013).

[47] LAPOP is the main academic institution carrying out public opinion surveys in the Americas. Every two years, it carries out the Americas Barometer survey, which currently covers 26 nations, including all of North, Central, and South America and the Caribbean.

[48] Latinobarómetro is an annual public opinion survey that involves some 20,000 interviews in 18 Latin American countries, and is representative of more than 600 million individuals.

[49] Chioda (2014d) is interested in the predictors of victimization and those of self-reported concerns about crime, and in the extent of their overlap. To this end, she conducts separate analyses of LAPOP and Latinobarómetro data, assessing the sensitivity of conclusions to the nature and detail of the two surveys. Both data sources carry information specific to the respondent (such as income and educational attainment), as well as the respondents' municipality of residence, allowing her to conduct municipality fixed-effects analyses.

[50] To the extent possible, the controls included in the analyses in this section on victimization, "crime as a concern," and happiness are kept as similar as possible to those that Chioda (2014a) considers in the cross-country exercise presented in the first section of this chapter.

[51] Specifically, figures 2.23 plots the marginal effects of various individual-, neighborhood-, and institutional-level characteristics on the likelihood that someone in the respondent's household has been victimized, and subsequently on the likelihood that they consider crime to be their greatest concern. Estimates from two sets of models are typically reported (both including municipality fixed effects): those that include only the category of predictors of interest (such as individual-only or institutional-only) and those from a saturated model that includes all possible predictors.

[52] The higher rate of violent crime for 30- to 60-year-olds may reflect the income gradient in the incidence of domestic violence.

[53] The converse is true for the income gradient; panel a of figure 2.23 holds education constant, such that higher income within education categories raises the likelihood of victimization.

[54] In the victimization survey, individuals younger than 18 years are not observed, which mechanically censors the age-crime profile. The first age bracket captures the range of increase and the peak in adolescence and young adulthood.

[55] By the 1990s in Mexico, criminal organizations were reportedly spending more than $500 million a year in bribes— double the budget of the Attorney General's Office (Morris 2012).

[56] Relying on Gallup polls, Di Tella, MacCulloch, and Ñopo (2008) report that there seems to be very little confidence in the police in the region. They document that fewer than 50 percent of the population reports trust in the police, well below the levels of trust in other regions.

[57] See, for example, Atkeson and others (1982); Davis and Friedman (1985); Kilpatrick and others (1985); Frieze, Hymer, and Greenberg (1987); Skogan (1987); Burnam and others (1988); Sorenson and Golding (1990); and Norris and Kaniasty (1994).

[58] See Bourguignon (1999); Londoño, Gaviria, and Guerrero (2000); and Soares (2006), among others.

[59] The message conveyed by figure 2.29 is also supported by a regression of an indicator for "crime as a concern" on homicide rates and the incidence of victimization (controlling for country and year fixed effects). The correlation with respect to homicides is positive and significant, at about 0.4, while the correlation with victimization is insignificant (estimated at -0.121).

[60] Chioda (2014d) constructed the variable "Crime as a general concern" as the sum of an array of eight crime-related responses: crime, drug addiction, drug trafficking, gangs, security (lack of), armed conflict, kidnappings, and violence.

[61] The gradient is precisely estimated for Central American countries, while it is imprecise for countries in the Southern Cone.

[62] Recall that the LAPOP panel covers only a short time series; data for most countries cover at most three points in time, which span at most an eight-year period. Within-country variation in the 10-year age brackets over short time spans may not be sufficient to identify the effects of interest precisely. LatinoBarómetro instead provides more statistical power, since it covers a span of 19 years (1995–2013). This explains the remarkable stability of the age gradients across data sets; the discrepancy lies in the precision of estimates from saturated models for "Victimization" and "Crime as a concern."

[63] In the data (LAPOP), actual household income and self-assessed economic well-being are related only weakly. Concern about potential collinearity between the two variables (income and perceptions about economic stability) does not appear to be warranted. As further evidence of this claim, the significance and magnitude of the coefficient on income remain largely unchanged when subjective assessments of economic status are included.

[64] These conclusions are invariant with respect to the data source.

[65] Chioda (2014d) also tests the hypothesis that the increasing concern about violence could be driven by a media-amplification effect. To test this conjecture, she estimates a model that also includes information about the consumption of media and the frequency with which individuals access the news cycle. The coefficients are reported in panel e of figure 2.30 (the omitted category being daily consumption). Relative to the omitted category, less access to news tends to reduce concern about crime.

[66] When only the contemporaneous level of crime is included in the model, its coefficient has the expected sign but is not statistically significant. Only when current and lagged levels of victimization are included is the relationship found to be statistically significant, with the expected sign and magnitude discussed in this chapter.

[67] This is consistent with Maris and Ortega's (2013) results.

## References

Alink, L. R. A., J. Mesman, J. Van Zeijil, M. N. Stolk, F. Juffer, H. M. Koot, M. J. Bakermans-Kranenburg, and M. H. Van Ijzendoorn. 2006. "The Early Childhood Aggression Curve: Development of Physical Aggression in 10-to-50-Month-Old Children." *Child Development* 77 (4): 954–66.

Angrist, Joshua, and Adriana Kugler. 2008. "Rural Windfall or a New Resource Curse? Coca, Income, and Civil Conflict in Colombia." *Review of Economics and Statistics* 90 (2): 191–215.

Arellano, M., and S. Bond. 1991. "Some Tests of Specification for Panel Data: Monte Carlo Evidence and an Application to Employment Equations." *Review of Economic Studies* 58: 277–97.

Arsenault, L., T. E. Moffitt, A. Caspi, A. Taylor, F. V. Rijsdijk, S. R. Jaffee, J. C. Ablow, and J. R. Measelle, 2003. "Strong Genetic Effects on Cross-Situational Antisocial Behaviour among 5-Year-Old Children according to Mothers, Teachers, Examiner-Observers, and Twins' Self-Reports." *Journal of Child Psychology and Psychiatry* 44: 832–48.

Atkeson, B. M., K. S. Calhoun, P. A. Resick, and E. M. Ellis. 1982. "Victims of Rape: Repeated Assessment of Depressive Symptoms." *Journal of Consulting and Clinical Psychology* 50: 96–102.

Attanasio, Orazio, and Steven J. Davis. 1996. "Relative Wage Movements and the Distribution of Consumption." *Journal of Political Economy* 104 (6): 1227–62.

Becker, Gary S. 1968. "Crime and Punishment: An Economic Approach." *Journal of Political Economy* 76 (2): 169–217.

Bellis, Mark A., Helen Lowey, Karen Hughes, Lynn Deacon, Jude Stansfield and Clare Perkins. 2012. "Variations in Risk and Protective Factors for Life Satisfaction and Mental Well-Being with Deprivation: A Cross-Sectional Study." *BMC Public Health* 12: 492. doi: 10.1186/1471-2458-12-492.

Bentham, Jeremy. 1780. *An Introduction to the Principles of Morals and Legislation.* Oxford: Clarendon Press, 1907.

Blumstein, A., J. Cohen, and D. P. Farrington. 1988. "Criminal Career Research: Its Value for Criminology." *Criminology* 26: 1–35

Blundell, R. W., and S. R. Bond. 1998. "Initial Conditions and Moment Restrictions in Dynamic Panel Data Models." *Journal of Econometrics* 87:115–43.

Bourguignon, F. 1999. "Crime as a Social Cost of Poverty and Inequality: A Review Focusing on Developing Countries." *Revista Desarrollo y Sociedad*, Universidad de Los Andes–CEDE. http://economia.uniandes.edu.co/revistadys/44/Articulo44_5.pdf.

Browning, Martin, Angus Deaton, and Margaret Irish. 1985. "A Profitable Approach to Labor Supply and Commodity Demands over the Life-Cycle." *Econometrica* 53 (3): 503–43.

Brush, Jesse. 2007. "Does Income Inequality Lead to More Crime? A Comparison of Cross-Sectional and Time-Series Analyses of United States Counties." *Economics Letters* 96: 264–68.

Buddelmeyer, H., P. H. Jensen, U. Oguzoglu, and E. Webster, E. 2008. "Fixed Effects Bias in Panel Data Estimators." IZA Discussion Paper 3487, Institute of Labor Economics, Bonn.

Buonanno, Paolo, Leopoldo Fergusson, and Juan F. Vargas. 2014. "The Crime Kuznets Curve." Documentos Cede 011012, Universidad De Los Andes–CEDE.

Buonanno, Paolo, and Leone Leonida. 2009. "Non-Market Effects of Education on Crime: Evidence from Italian Regions." *Economics of Education Review* 28: 11–17.

Burnam, M. A., J. A. Stein, J. M. Golding, J. M. Siegel, S. B. Sorenson, A. B. Forsythe, and C. A. Telles. 1988. "Sexual Assault and Mental Disorders in a Community Population." *Journal of Consulting and Clinical Psychology* 56: 843–50.

Bushway, Shawn. 2011. "Labor Markets and Crime." In *Crime and Public Policy*, edited by Joan Petersilia and James Q. Wilson, 183–209. New York: Oxford University Press.

Canales, Rodrigo. 2013. "The Deadly Genius of Drug Cartels." Ted Talk, November, http://www.ted.com/talks/rodrigo_canales_the_deadly_genius_of_drug_cartels.html.

Cantor, D., and K. C. Land. 1985. "Unemployment and Crime Rates in the Post–World War II United States." *American Sociological Review* 50 (3): 317–32.

———. 1991. "Exploring Possible Temporal Relationships of Unemployment and Crime: A Comment on Hale and Sabbagh." *Journal of Research in Crime and Delinquency* 28: 400–17.

Caspi, Avshalom, Joseph McClay, Terrie E. Moffitt, Jonathan Mill, Judy Martin, Ian W. Craig, Alan Taylor, and Richie Poulton. 2002. "Role of Genotype in the Cycle of Violence in Maltreated Children." *Science* 297 (5582): 851–54.

Chioda, Laura. 2014a. "Violence in Latin America: Dynamic Panel Data Analysis." Working paper.

———. 2014b. "The Determinants of Violent v. Property Crimes in Mexico: A Dynamic Panel Data Approach." Working paper.

———. 2014c. "Offending and Labor Force Participation over the Life Cycle in Mexico." Working paper.

———. 2014d. "Victimization, Crime, and Safety Perceptions in LAC." Working paper.

Chioda, Laura, João M. P. De Mello, and Rodrigo R. Soares. 2016. "Spillovers from Conditional Cash Transfer Programs: Bolsa Família and Crime in Urban Brazil." *Economics of Education Review* 54 (2): 306–20.

Chioda, Laura, and L. D. Rojas-Alvarado. 2014. "Violence across Brazilian Municipalities." Working paper.

Cooper, Alexia, and Erica L. Smith. 2011. "Homicide Trends in the United States, 1980–2008." Bureau of Justice Statistics, U.S. Department of Justice, Washington, DC. http://www.bjs.gov /content/pub/pdf/htus8008.pdf.

Cornaglia, Francesca, Naomi E. Feldman, and Andrew Leigh. 2014. "Crime and Mental Well-Being." *Journal of Human Resources* 49 (1): 110–40.

Cote, Sylvana M., Tracy Vaillancourt, John C. LeBlanc, Daniel S. Nagin, and Richard E. Tremblay. 2006. "The Development of Physical Aggression from Toddlerhood to Pre-Adolescence: A Nation-wide Longitudinal Study of Canadian Children." *Journal of Abnormal Child Psychology* 34 (1, February): 71–85.

Davis, R. C., and L. N. Friedman. 1985. "The Emotional Aftermath of Crime and Violence." In *Trauma and Its Wake*, edited by C. R. Figley, 90–112. New York: Brunner/Mazel.

Dell, Melissa. 2014. "Trafficking Networks and the Mexican Drug War." Working Paper, Harvard University.

de Mello, João M. P., and Alexandre Schneider. 2010. "Assessing São Paulo's Large Drop in Homicides: The Role of Demography and Policy Interventions." In *The Economics of Crime: Lessons for and from Latin America*, edited by Rafael Di Tella, Sebastian Edwards, and Ernesto Schargrodsky, 207–35. Chicago: University of Chicago Press for the National Bureau of Economic Research.

Di Tella, Rafael, Sebastian Galiani, and Ernesto Schargrodsky. 2010. "Crime Distribution and Victim Behavior during a Crime Wave." In *The Economics of Crime: Lessons for and from Latin America*, edited by Rafael Di Tella, Sebastian Edwards, and Ernesto Schargrodsky, 175–204. Chicago: University of Chicago Press for the National Bureau of Economic Research.

Di Tella, Rafael, Robert MacCulloch, and Hugo Ñopo. 2008. "Happiness and Beliefs in Criminal Environments." Working Paper 662, Research Department, Inter-American Development Bank, Washington, DC.

Dube, Arindrajit, Oeindrila Dube, and Omar García-Ponce. 2013. "Cross-Border Spillover: U.S. Gun Laws and Violence in Mexico." *American Political Science Review* 107 (3): 397–417.

Elliott, D. S., S. S. Ageton, D. Huizinga, B. A. Knowles, and R. J. Canter. 1983. *The Prevalence and Incidence of Delinquent Behavior: 1976–1980*. National Youth Survey Report No. 26. Boulder, CO: Behavioral Research Institute.

Engel, Pamela, Christina Sterbenz, and Gus Lubin. 2013. "The 50 Most Violent Cities in the World." *Business Insider*, November 27. http://www.businessinsider.com/the-most-violent -cities-in-the-world-2013-11?op=1.

Fagan, Jeffrey, and Richard B. Freeman. 1999. "Crime and Work." In *Crime and Justice: A Review of Research*, Vol. 25, edited by M. Tonry. Chicago: University of Chicago Press.

Fajnzylber, Pablo, Daniel Lederman, and Norman Loayza. 2002a. "What Causes Violent Crime?" *European Economic Review* 46: 1323–57.

———. 2002b. "Inequality and Violent Crime." *Journal of Law and Economics* 45: 1–40.

Farrington, David P. 1983. "Offending from 10 to 25 Years of Age." In *Prospective Studies of Crime and Delinquency*, edited by K. T. van Dusen and S. A. Mednick, 17–37. Boston: Kluwer-Nijhoff.

———. 1986. "Implications of Longitudinal Studies for Social Prevention." *Justice Report* 3 (2): 6–10.

Farrington, D. P., and D. J. West. 1993. "Criminal, Penal and Life Histories of Chronic Offenders: Risk and Protective Factors and Early Identification." *Criminal Behavior and Mental Health* 3: 492–523.

Ferreira, Francisco H. G., Julian Messina, Jamele Rigolini, Luis-Felipe López-Calva, Maria Ana Lugo, and Renos Vakis. 2013. *Economic Mobility and the Rise of the Latin American Middle Class.* Washington, DC: World Bank.

Flannery, Mark J., and Kristine Watson Hankins. 2013. "Estimating Dynamic Panel Models in Corporate Finance." *Journal of Corporate Finance* 19 (C): 1–9.

Frieze, I. H., S. Hymer, and M. S. Greenberg. 1987. "Describing the Crime Victim: Psychological Reactions to Victimization." *Professional Psychology: Research and Practice* 18: 299–315.

Garrido, Vincente, and Luz Anyela Morales Qunitro. 2007. "Serious (Violent or Chronic) Juvenile Offenders: A Systematic Review of Treatment Effectiveness in Secure Corrections." *Campbell Systematic Reviews* 3 (7).

Gaviria, Alejandro. 2010. "Comment on 'Understanding High Crime Rates in Latin America: The Role of Social and Policy Factors.'" In *The Economics of Crime: Lessons for and from Latin America,* edited by Rafael Di Tella, Sebastian Edwards, and Ernesto Schargrodsky, 56–60. Chicago: University of Chicago Press for the National Bureau of Economic Research.

Gould, Eric D., Bruce A. Weinberg, and David B. Mustard. 2002. "Crime Rates and Local Labor Market Opportunities in the United States: 1977–1997." *Review of Economics and Statistics* 84 (1): 45–61.

Graham, Carol, and Juan Camila Chaparro. 2011. *Insecurity, Health, and Well-Being An Initial Exploration Based on Happiness Surveys.* IDB Monograph. Washington, DC: Inter-American Development Bank.

Grogger, Jeffrey. 1998. "Market Wages and Youth Crime." *Journal of Labor Economics* 16 (4): 756–91.

———. 2008. "Consequences of Teen Childbearing for Incarceration among Adult Children." In *Kids Having Kids: Economic Costs and Social Consequences of Teen Pregnancy,* 2nd edition, edited by S. Hoffman and R. Maynard. Washington, DC: Urban Institute Press.

Grönqvist, Hans. 2011. "Youth Unemployment and Crime: New Lessons Exploring Longitudinal Register Data." SOFI Working Paper 7/2011, Stockholm University.

Guerrero-Gutiérrez, Eduardo. 2011. "Security, Drugs, and Violence in Mexico: A Survey." Survey carried out for the 7th North American Forum in Washington, DC. Lantia Consultores, S.C., Mexico City.

Hood, R., and R. Sparks. 1970. *Key Issues in Criminology.* New York: McGraw-Hill.

Kelly, Morgan. 2000. "Inequality and Crime." *Review of Economics and Statistics* 82: 530–39.

Kilpatrick, D. G., C. L. Best, L. J. Veronen, A. E. Amick, L. A. Villeponteaux, and G. A. Ruff. 1985. "Mental Health Correlates of Criminal Victimization: A Random Community Survey." *Journal of Consulting and Clinical Psychology* 53: 866–73.

Klein, M. 1989. "Watch Out for That Last Variable." In *The Causes of Crime: New Biological Approaches,* edited by S. Mednick, T. Moffitt, and S. A. Stack, 25–41. Cambridge: Cambridge University Press.

Levitt, Steven D. 1999. "The Changing Relationship between Income and Crime Victimization." *Federal Reserve Bank of New York Economic Policy Review* 5 (3): 87–98.

Londoño. J. L., A. Gaviria, and R. Guerrero, eds. 2000. *Asalto al desarrollo: Violencia en América Latina* (Spanish edition). Washington, DC: Inter-American Development Bank.

Mammen, Kristin, and Christina Paxson. 2000. "Women's Work and Economic Development." *Journal of Economic Perspectives* 14 (4): 141–64.

Maris, L., and D. Ortega. 2013. "Crime Perceptions and Reality in Latin America." Working Paper. http://cddrl.fsi.stanford.edu/sites/default/files/171.crimeperceptions.pdf.

Maslow, Abraham H. 1943. "A Theory of Human Motivation." *Psychological Review* 50 (4): 370–96.

Matheson, Z. 2013. "Gun Violence in U.S. Cities Compared to the Deadliest Nations in the World." Martin Prosperity Institute, Rotman School of Management, Unversity of Toronto. http://www .vividmaps.com/2016/06/gun-violence-in-us-cities-compared-to.html.

Méndez, Claudia Arriaza, and Carlos Mendoza. 2013. *Siete mitos sobre la violencia homicida en Guatemala. El Periodico*. http://www.elfaro.net/es/201302/internacionales/10873.

Michalos, A. C. 1991. *Global Report on Student Well-Being, Volume 1: Life Satisfaction and Happiness*. New York: Springer-Verlag.

Moffitt, T. E. 1990. "The Neuropsychology of Delinquency: A Critical Review of Theory and Research." In *Crime and Justice*, volume 12, edited by N. Morris and M. Tonry, 99–169. Chicago: University of Chicago Press.

———. 1993. "Adolescence-Limited and Life-Course Persistent Antisocial Behavior: A Developmental Taxonomy." *Psychological Review* 100: 674–701.

Moffitt, T. E., A. Caspi, M. Rutter, and P. A. Silva. 2001. *Sex Differences in Antisocial Behaviour: Conduct Disorder, Delinquency, and Violence in the Dunedin Longitudinal Study*. Cambridge: Cambridge University Press.

Morris, Stephen D. 2012. "Corruption, Drug Trafficking, and Violence in Mexico." *Brown Journal of World Affairs* 18 (2): 29–43.

Munyo, I. 2015. "The Juvenile Crime Dilemma." *Review of Economics Dynamics* 5 (18): 201–11.

Nagin, Daniel S., and Richard E. Tremblay. 2001. "Parental and Early Childhood Predictors of Persistent Physical Aggression in Boys from Kindergarten to High School." *Archives of General Psychiatry* 58 (4): 389–94.

Nickell, Stephen. 1981. "Biases in Dynamic Models with Fixed Effects." *Econometrica* 49: 1417–26.

Norris, F. H., and K. Kaniasty. 1994. "Psychological Distress Following Criminal Victimization in the General Population: Cross-Sectional, Longitudinal, and Prospective Analyses." *Journal of Consulting and Clinical Psychology* 62: 111–23.

*Observatory on Violence* (Honduras). 2014. Bulletin, Edición No. 32, Febrero. Faculty of Social Sciences, University Institute for Democracy, Peace and Security, IUDPAS, Tegucigalpa.

Pridemore, William A. 2011. "Poverty Matters: A Reassessment of the Inequality-Homicide Relationship in Cross-National Studies." *British Journal of Criminology* 51: 739–72.

Raine, Adrian. 2013. *The Anatomy of Violence: The Biological Roots of Crime*. New York: Pantheon Books.

Rodriguez, Ulises. 2013. "El Salvador's Gang Truce." https://widerimage.reuters.com/story /el-salvadors-gang-truce.

Ross, Catherine E. 1993. "Fear of Victimization and Health." *Journal of Quantitative Criminology* 9 (2): 159–175.

Sampson, Robert J., and John H. Laub. 2003. "Life-Course Desisters? Trajectories of Crime among Delinquent Boys Followed to Age 70." *Criminology* 41: 555–92.

Skogan, W. G. 1987. "The Impact of Victimisation on Fear, Crime and Delinquency." 33 (1): 135–54.

Slutkin, G. 2013. "Let's Treat Violence like a Contagious Disease." TEDMED 2013. http://www .ted.com/talks/gary_slutkin_let_s_treat_violence_like_a_contagious_disease?language=en.

Soares, R. 2006. "The Welfare Cost of Violence across Countries." *Journal of Health Economics* 25 (5): 821–46.

Soares, Rodrigo, and Joana Naritomi. 2010. "Understanding High Crime Rates in Latin America: The Role of Social and Policy Factors." Chapter 1 in *The Economics of Crime: Lessons for and from Latin America*, edited by Rafael Di Tella, Ernesto Schargrodsky, and Sebastian Edwards. Chicago: University of Chicago Press for the National Bureau of Economic Research.

Sorenson, Susan B., and Jacqueline M. Golding. 1990. "Depressive Sequelae of Recent Criminal Victimization." *Journal of Traumatic Stress* 3: 337–50.

Taylor, R. B., and M. Hale. 1986. "Testing Alternative Models of Fear of Crime." *Journal of Criminal Law and Criminology* 77: 151–89.

Tracy, Paul E., Marvin E. Wolfgang, and Robert M. Figlio. 1991. "Delinquency Careers in Two Birth Cohorts." *Contemporary Sociology* 20 (6): 920–22.

Tremblay, Richard E. 2000. "The Development of Aggressive Behaviour during Childhood: What Have We Learned in the Past Century?" *International Journal of Behavioral Development* 24 (2): 129–41.

———. 2004. "Decade of Behavior Distinguished Lecture: Development of Physical Aggression during Infancy." *Infant Mental Health Journal* 25: 399–407.

Tremblay, Richard E., Daniel S. Nagin, Jean R. Séguin, Mark Zoccolillo, Philip D. Zelazo, Michel Boivin, Daniel Pérusse, and Christa Japel. 2004. "Physical Aggression during Early Childhood: Trajectories and Predictors." *Pediatrics* 114 (1): e43–e50.

Weisburd, D., E. Groff, and S. Yang. 2012. *The Criminology of Place: Street Segments and Our Understanding of the Crime Problem*. Oxford: Oxford University Press.

# 3

# The Transmission of Violence across Generations and Early Interventions

The organizing framework of this study posits that as individuals progress through the life cycle, they are exposed to ever-broadening and increasingly interdependent environments that mold their behavior and affect their likelihood of criminal offending. This framework views early life stages as an especially critical phase in crime prevention. This chapter endeavors to document this claim and to illustrate how well-designed early interventions can improve the outcomes and lifetime trajectories of individuals who would otherwise be at elevated risk of antisocial behavior and criminal offending in adolescence and adulthood.

The early years have been identified as decisive for cognitive development, and therefore for subsequent behavioral and educational outcomes. Thus during the early stages of life, families play a critical role in shaping children's behavior. But can these early stages shape criminal behavior and/or prevent it?

The evidence presented in this chapter examines this question and leads to the conclusion that early prevention is not only effective, but that prevention can never start too early. The chapter first presents (possibly counterintuitive) evidence that aggression peaks early in childhood, rather than during adolescence or early adulthood, and that the use of aggression is "unlearned" early in life. Furthermore, antisocial behavior among children of primary school age is a strong predictor of adverse long-term outcomes, including adult criminality and aggression, but also unemployment and mental health conditions. This suggests that failure to learn to self-regulate early in childhood may have lasting effects on criminal behavior and long-term welfare. If that is the case, what are the sources of failure to cope with aggressive impulses? Is an inability to self-regulate simply a marker of the environment in which a child is raised, or is there a deeper connection to family history? This chapter next provides somber evidence on the role of families and family history, documenting the intergenerational transmission of violence. It then reviews efforts to disentangle biological/

genetic causes from parental behaviors in this intergenerational link, concluding that parenting and the home environment play important roles. The final section of the chapter presents evidence about the efficacy of early preventive interventions, such as targeted perinatal home visitations and early childhood development programs, and discusses possible mechanisms through which they operate.

## The early peak of physical aggression

Until recently, most research on aggression focused on adolescents and adults. However, a handful of large-scale and long-term longitudinal studies of elementary and primary school–aged children has provided important information about the development of physical aggression, and has led to surprising results.

One unexpected finding is that the vast majority of children reduced the frequency of their physical aggression from the time they began school until the end of high school.[1] For most of the thousands of children who were followed from primary school to adolescence in Canada, New Zealand, and the United States, there was no evidence that they were learning how to become aggressive or how to use physical aggression (Nagin and Tremblay 1999; Broidy and others 2003). That is, they did not start from a low baseline level of aggression and progressively escalate through adolescence and early adulthood. Rather, most children appeared to be at their peak use of physical aggression when they were in kindergarten, and were on a declining trajectory thereafter. These findings not only call into question the age-crime curve hypothesis of human development (documented empirically for Latin America and the Caribbean in chapter 2), but also have led researchers to question when physical aggression actually starts.

To answer this question requires longitudinal information on physical aggression from birth to the time when children enter school. Tremblay (2004) reviews these types of analyses, and finds that the results indicate that physical aggression first manifests itself during the first year of life. Its frequency increases rapidly in the second year of life, reaching a peak between 24 and 48 months, and then decreases steadily. The unexpected picture that is painted by these studies is thus one in which the peak frequency of physical aggression in humans is not during kindergarten, adolescence, or early adulthood, but during *early childhood* (Tremblay 2004; Tremblay and others, 2004; Alink and others 2006). Rather than learning how to employ physical aggression as they age, children are instead learning behavioral mechanisms and developing skills to self-regulate so as *not* to engage in acts of physical aggression—for instance, by interacting with others and being hurt while attempting acts of aggression or being reprimanded by an adult.

Large-scale, longitudinal studies also deliver another important set of conclusions. First, they indicate that those who had aggression problems during adolescence and adulthood had the same problems during childhood.[2] For instance, Huesmann and others (1984) follow a panel of 600 individuals over 22 years and document the persistence of aggression: the more aggressive 8- year-olds were also the more aggressive 30-year-olds. In addition, early aggression was predictive of violent offending such as spousal abuse. Second, high levels of physical aggression during childhood also predict a variety of other problems, such as dropping out of school, drug use, early sexual initiation, accidents, depression, suicide attempts, and unemployment. This suggests that the welfare consequences of not learning to assuage aggressive impulses may be substantial.

These surprising conclusions in turn beg the question: if physical aggression incurs such high costs and manifests itself at such an early age, where does it come from? Is it the result of the environment, or is it inherited from parents, with antecedents in biology? Dionne and others (2003) provide some estimates of the degree of heritability. They follow a large sample of twins from birth and estimate the genetic and environmental contributions to individual differences in the frequency of physical aggression at 19 months of age. Approximately two-thirds of the variation in the frequency of physical aggression is explained by genetic effects, with the rest being attributable to environmental factors that are unique to each individual in the twin pair, rather than common to both of them. This suggests that the differences in use of physical aggression during early childhood are under relatively strong biological control.

As individuals age and transition from childhood to adolescence to adulthood, however, environmental effects become more important (figure 3.1). By adulthood, only about half the variation in antisocial behavior across people can be explained by a combination of biological and prenatal conditions (Moffitt 2005; Moffitt, Ross, and Raine 2010). The fact that biology plays a role does not imply that environmental effects are negligible in the development of physical aggression. In fact, the observation that the vast majority of children starts life with relatively high levels of physical aggression and learn to inhibit it through various strategies as they age suggests

**FIGURE 3.1:** A model of the supply of criminal offenses, but also a model of crime and violence prevention

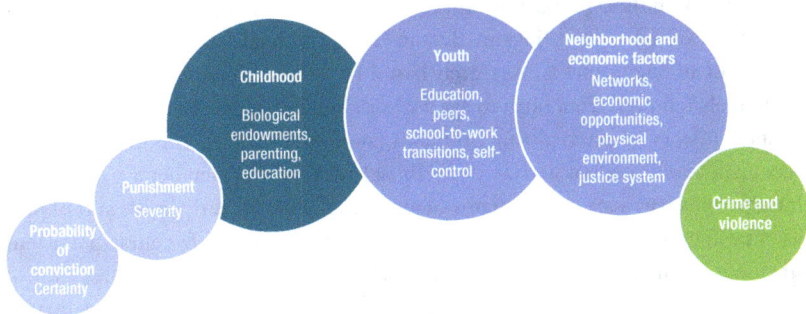

that, over time, there are meaningful environmental effects in the development of self-regulation.

Indeed, there is abundant evidence that the quality of the early environment is an important predictor of life-cycle outcomes and is a powerful tool in preventing the development of serious adjustment problems, including criminal behavior. The latter part of this chapter reviews this evidence and makes a case for early interventions, while discussing the mechanisms through which they might operate. However, the chapter first provides a more detailed review of the role of family history and of the intergenerational transmission of violence as determinants of aggression. The discussion reviews efforts to disentangle aggression that is inherited from aggression that is the result of parental behaviors and the environment in which children grow.

## Family history and vulnerability

Individuals vary markedly in their responses to the social causes of crime, prompting research into the biological vulnerabilities to these causes. Individual- and neighborhood-level vulnerability—as measured by low socioeconomic status, poor infrastructure, or low *social efficacy* (that is, social cohesion and functional social networks)—are not perfect predictors of deviant behavior. Most people from disadvantaged socioeconomic backgrounds never engage in antisocial behavior, while many wealthy and advantaged people commit crimes. This simple observation provides a powerful rationale for research into individual variations in vulnerabilities to the social causes of crime. It is by now uncontroversial that these and other human behaviors are partially under biological influences (Rutter 2007; Plomin and others 2008; Beaver and others 2009) and, by extension, that part of the vulnerability to the social causes of crime is also influenced by the same biological vulnerability.

A surprising feature of criminality is the degree to which it is largely concentrated in families—a fact that a great deal of research has documented. Studies in London and Pittsburgh have shown that over 64 percent of crimes were committed by members of fewer than 10 percent of families (Farrington and others 1996, 2001). In their pioneering work, Glueck and Glueck (1950) document that 66 percent of delinquent boys in Boston had a criminal father, compared to 32 percent of nondelinquents. Research based on a New Zealand cohort of 1,037 individuals followed from birth to age 32 finds similar associations (Moffitt 1990). A family history of externalizing problems (such as disorderly conduct, antisocial personality, and alcohol and/or drug abuse) in a cohort member's parents and grandparents was a strong predictor of antisocial behavior early in life and of persistent offending in adulthood—what Moffitt (1993) calls "life-course-persistent offenders." Somewhat surprisingly, however, family history was not a predictor of antisocial behavior for those individuals with antisocial behaviors that terminated in childhood or adolescence. This finding is consistent with the age-crime profiles documented and discussed in chapter 2, which suggests that youth and young adults "mature out" of criminal offending.

These observations give credence to the notion that "crime runs in the family," which represents a robust and recurring fact in criminology. Despite this, and despite the existence of a rich literature on intergenerational socioeconomic mobility—of which this pattern is a natural extension—only a handful of economic studies have broached the topic of intergenerational linkages in criminality.

One such example is Duncan and others (2005), who report intergenerational correlations in behaviors and attitudes between mothers and their children, measured during adolescence using the 1979 National Longitudinal Survey of Youth (NLSY79). They document that "like begets like" and, with regard to criminality, that daughters whose mothers were convicted were more than five times more likely to have a juvenile crime conviction themselves. However, Duncan and others (2005) are limited in scope, since the NLSY79 does not include information on adult criminality, type of crime, or sentence. Furthermore, the NLSY79 includes data only on maternal criminality, which may be an important limitation, given that men account for the majority of arrests and criminal convictions.[3] Other examples include Case and Katz (1991), who make use of data from the Boston Inner City Youth Survey, and find that children with a family member in jail are 8 percentage points more likely to report committing a crime in the previous year. Based on the 1958 Philadelphia Birth Cohort Study, Williams and Sickles (2002) find that criminals were almost three times as likely as noncriminals to report having a father who was arrested during the respondent's childhood. Smaller-scale studies from the criminology literature similarly document a very strong correlation between an individual's own aggression/criminality and that of his or her parents.

Family background and parental criminality therefore emerge as being among the strongest predictors of an individual's criminality, dominating even an individual's own income and employment status in their predictive power. These conclusions imply that a complete description of the incidence of criminality must find a role for family. Indeed, the nature of the intrafamily correlation and the mechanisms that underlie it have important implications for policy. In the extreme, if the intergenerational correlation in crime is driven by biology—such that criminality is an inherited trait—then the scope for policy is limited. If instead the parent-child association is accounted for by some factor that is common to the environment of both parent and child, such as violent neighborhoods and/or low-quality education, then policies that facilitate mobility and/or improve the quality of instruction may induce declines in crime. If it is instead driven by parental behaviors, whereby children learn from and mimic their parents' criminal paths, then policies that attenuate the draw of criminality in present-day adults may have crime-reducing benefits for the next generation. The discussion that follows reviews possible channels through which intergenerational linkages may operate.

A number of factors before and after birth may combine to explain the intergenerational transmission of crime (figure 3.2). Prebirth factors may be thought of as the sum of genetic influences, prenatal conditions, and perinatal factors, and their interactions. Genetics may play a role if certain genes are associated with a higher incidence of aggression, or if they tend to "express themselves" upon interaction with the environment, through epigenetic effects. A 25-year longitudinal study of a New Zealand birth cohort illustrates this type of interaction between genes and the environment. Boys who were abused during childhood were less at risk of serious antisocial behavior if they had inherited a specific genetic variation (Broidy and others 2003).[4] Similar gene-environment interactions have been observed in experiments with primates.

Prenatal conditions describe the environment *in utero*, including maternal alcohol or tobacco use, and exposure to toxic environments and disease. Each of these

**FIGURE 3.2:** Possible channels for the intergenerational transmission of criminal behavior

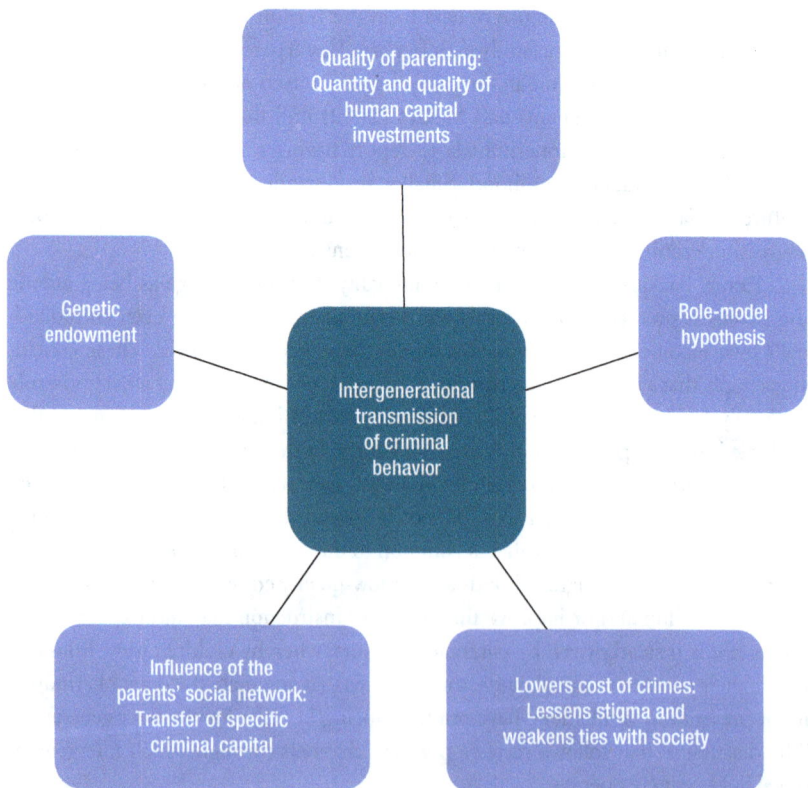

Quality of parenting:
Quantity and quality of human capital investments

Genetic endowment

Role-model hypothesis

Intergenerational transmission of criminal behavior

Influence of the parents' social network: Transfer of specific criminal capital

Lowers cost of crimes: Lessens stigma and weakens ties with society factors affects infant mental health, physical health, and cognitive development, which are themselves known antecedents of antisocial and criminal behavior. Studies have shown that chronic physical aggression is associated with certain social factors, such as mothers' young age at first delivery, low education, low income, and history of behavior problems. Perinatal factors include obstetric complications and health problems that arise during or shortly after birth that can similarly affect child development.

The quality of parenting and the resulting impact on children's human capital is another potential channel that can influence the intergenerational transmission of aggression, crime, and violence. In particular, parents influence their children by making conscious decisions about parenting styles and about their children's investments in education and human capital, more generally.

To the extent that parents' tendency to invest in their children's human capital is related to their own educational attainment, children of more highly educated parents will tend to pursue additional schooling and be exposed to more beneficial cognitive environments. They are thus likely to earn higher wages and select higher-quality peers, thereby raising the opportunity cost of crime, and inducing them to commit fewer crimes. On the other hand, parents may engage in destructive behaviors that amount to disinvestments in human capital. Inadequate parenting, conflict in the house, and poor parental mental health tend to be associated with the development of chronic physical aggression among their children. For instance, child abuse is known to be transmitted across generations and is correlated with criminality,[5] above and beyond the fact that the act is itself criminal.

Whether intentional or not, children also learn from their parents by the power of example, a so-called role-model channel. A father may reprimand his son or daughter for delinquent behavior, but if he himself has a criminal past, those reprimands may carry little weight and be taken as cheap talk.

In addition, having parents with a criminal record may decrease the perceived costs of committing a crime, perhaps through a diminished stigma associated with offending. Similarly, parental criminality may weaken the family's ties to legitimate society—in which case criminal acts are not perceived as "that criminal" within the household.

Finally, while children may learn to engage in crimes through their associations with peers and family members, in households where a parent has a criminal history, there may be a direct transfer of specific criminal capital from parent to child. For instance, children may "learn the trade" from their parents. Alternatively, children may be exposed to parents' criminal networks, possibly facilitating their transition into delinquency. Conversely, parents may provide access to high-quality social and professional networks and positive neighborhood environments (Becker and Tomes 1979), raising the likelihood of attachment to legitimate society.[6]

One of the most compelling studies documenting the intergenerational transmission of criminal behavior is that of Hjalmarsson and Lindquist (2012).[7] The authors draw on data from the Stockholm Birth Cohort Study, which combines administrative criminal records for a cohort of more than 15,000 individuals born in 1953 (and residing in Stockholm in 1963) with those of their fathers.[8] These rich data permit them to disentangle the effects of the intensive margin of fathers' offending (number of convictions and offenses) on children's criminal outcomes from that of the extensive margins (any convictions at all).[9] Importantly, their data are rich enough to allow an investigation of the possible mechanisms underlying the father-child correlation, since they record information on individual, family, and neighborhood characteristics; measures of parental education and behaviors (including parenting styles); as well as metrics of children's cognitive and behavioral characteristics.

Hjalmarsson and Lindquist (2012) begin by documenting a robust relationship between the criminal histories of fathers and those of their children, and note that an economically important portion of this relationship is left unexplained by their numerous controls. In the raw data, boys whose fathers have at least one sentence are 17.2 percentage points more likely to have at least one criminal conviction than their counterparts whose fathers have no convictions. Saturating their model with a full set of controls reduces this figure to 4.3 percentage points, implying that 25 percent of the father-son correlation is unaccounted for by observable characteristics. The corresponding proportion for girls is remarkably similar, at 28.5 percent.

Why is such a high proportion of the father-child association in convictions left unexplained after controlling for observable characteristics? There are several explanations. It is possible that, despite the availability of an unusually large set of controls, the remaining father-child relationship operates through mechanisms for which Hjalmarsson and Lindquist (2012) have no data proxies, such as the direct transference of criminal capital or role-modeling. However, Hjalmarsson and Lindquist (2012) manage to document that the timing of the fathers' convictions (in relation to their son or daughter's date of birth) mattered for the outcomes of the children. Children whose fathers were sentenced only *after* they were born were more likely to have a criminal record than children whose fathers were sentenced only before they were born.

One explanation for this pattern is that fathers serve as role models in crime. The bad example set by the father before the child is born has less relevance than the example he sets after the child's birth, in which case the child can observe the criminal behavior. A competing (though indistinguishable) explanation for the importance of the timing of the father's convictions is that fathers "mature out" of crime as a result of marriage and/or fatherhood, in such a way that they abandon their criminal past and adopt a more proactive, anticrime parenting style.

Related to the direct link between parents' and children's behaviors, Hjalmarsson and Lindquist (2012) document that both sons and daughters who have "unusually good" relationships with their fathers (as reported by their mothers) adopt behavior that is more similar to that of their fathers than those with weaker relationships. Furthermore, sons who are "unusually" close to fathers with criminal convictions are much more likely to be convicted than boys with criminal fathers with whom they do not have as strong a bond. This pattern is also consistent with the role-model hypothesis, since a child is presumably more likely to adopt someone with whom they have an unusually close relationship as a role model. An alternative explanation is that "close" fathers play a larger role in their children's lives, so a father's conviction causes substantial disruption in the household. In that event, their child may act out and have a higher inclination toward crime because of the stressful home environment. As a final alternative (which is similar to the role-modeling hypothesis), it may be that children who are close to their fathers are simply replicating their father's behavior as a result of the values transmitted to them by their fathers.

There are a number of reasons to believe that Hjalmarsson and Lindquist's (2012) results are generalizable to other environments. The sample was relatively large, and the offending rates of the cohort of Swedish men are comparable to rates of samples of men in California, Denmark, London, and Philadelphia. The criminology literature has documented similarities in the development and structure of crime in Sweden, Western Europe, and North America (Westfelt 2001; Killias, Redondo, and Sarnecki 2012). Finally, if one believes that genetics play a role in criminal offending, then this belief should not be limited to Sweden.

## Disentangling biological risks from social risks

The previous section documented a strong correlation between the criminal histories of father and son/daughter, which persists even after controlling for a rich set of possible confounders. Family history is thus a powerful predictor of careers of serious criminal offenses, and encompasses both a family's biological and social vulnerability to crimes. But what is the distribution of these vulnerabilities? How much of the persistence in criminality within families is attributable to social vulnerability? A number of recent studies have endeavored to disentangle biological risks from social risks by analyzing the antisocial behaviors of adoptees, and of twins reared together compared to twins reared apart.

In adoption studies, the correlation between adoptee and biological parent represents a transmission of endowments (genetic or biological), while the correlation between adoptee and adoptive parent reflects the social and environmental contribution to antisocial behavior. In twin studies, genetic influence is captured by comparing differences in antisocial behavior of fraternal (dizygotic) twins to those of identical (monozygotic) twins. In addition to sharing the home environment, monozygotic twins also share the same genes, while fraternal twins are genetically no more similar than any other pair of siblings.

More than 100 heritability studies of antisocial behavior reveal a range of heritability from 0 to 80 percent, with a mode of 50 percent (Moffitt, Ross, and Raine 2010). This means that 50 percent of the variation in antisocial and aggressive behavior is explained by genetic factors. The variability in estimates reflects the intuition that twins (irrespective of their genetic composition) may end up replicating each other's behaviors, thereby underestimating the true effect of heritability, while adoptees deliver upwardly biased estimates by virtue of adoption agencies' policies of positive sorting in screening (that is, agencies, by design, may grant adoptions to parents with better observable characteristics, socioeconomic traits, higher income, and the like). In sum, these two types of studies in conjunction may provide upper and lower bounds on true heritability.[10]

What are the implications of the fact that 50 percent of the variation in antisocial behavior can be explained by biological and prenatal factors? It does not mean that antisocial behavior is resistant to policy interventions. Raine (2013) draws the analogy with height: it has evolved over time because of better nutrition and health care, even though genes have consistently explained a constant amount of the variability in height across individuals. Furthermore, the channel of transmission is a combination of prenatal behavior and biological factors, which are still amenable to policy intervention.

As discussed, factors before, during, and just after birth result from the combination of genetic influences, prenatal conditions, and perinatal factors. Prenatal conditions include intrauterine environmental factors, which depend in part on prenatal maternal behaviors. Perinatal factors include obstetric procedures and health problems arising shortly after birth. Many of these conditions should be seen as important entry points for policy to prevent important risk factors that may predispose children and youth to antisocial behavior. An example of such a program is the nurse home visitations program that is discussed in greater detail later in this chapter.

Maternal behaviors—such as tobacco, alcohol, or drug use, and poor nutrition during pregnancy—are well-known examples of behaviors that cause deteriorations in the intrauterine environment of an unborn child. They are further believed to damage neural development in early pregnancy. Fetal alcohol syndrome, for example, is a cause of mental retardation (Abel and Sokol 1987), and is thought to play a role in the development of serious psychiatric disorders (Famy, Streissguth, and Unis 1998). Maternal smoking is considered to be the single most important preventable cause of low birth weight (Almond and Currie 2011) and is a predictor of the child's likelihood of exhibiting elevated levels of physical aggression by 42 months of age (Tremblay and others 2004). Fetal exposure to environmental toxins such as lead (Hu and others 2006; see box 3.1) and mercury (Murata and others 2004) have harmful effects on the health and cognitive abilities of children.[11]

Prebirth factors also include genetically inherited traits, conditions, and disorders. Unlike most prenatal environmental and perinatal conditions, which are thought to be attributable exclusively to the mother, genetic disorders are also inherited from the biological father. A large number of conditions and mental disorders that are known to correlate with criminal behavior are also believed to be (at least partially) genetically inherited. These include autism, schizophrenia, alcoholism, attention deficit hyperactivity disorder (ADHD), aggression, reading disorders, and low cognitive abilities.

## BOX 3.1: The link between exposure to lead in young children and crime

While lead is an extremely useful metal with numerous valuable applications, it has unfortunately also proven to be a dangerous toxin. Exposure to lead is particularly harmful to young children because they absorb more lead from their environment and are at a sensitive stage of their neurobehavioral development. It was not until after the 1950s that it was widely accepted that the neurological effects of lead persist beyond the stage of acute poisoning and that lead exposure is dangerous even at extremely low levels. Childhood lead exposure increases the likelihood of behavioral and cognitive traits such as impulsivity, aggression, and low IQ, which are strongly related to subsequent criminal behavior as an adult. The association between low-level lead exposure during early development and subsequent deficits in cognition and behavior is widely accepted as being causal. A large literature in epidemiology, psychology, and neuroscience agrees that exposure to lead in early childhood negatively affects cognitive development and behavior in ways that increase the likelihood of aggressive and antisocial acts.

In particular, higher lead levels have been associated with aggressive behavior, impulsivity, hyperactivity, attention impairment, and attention deficit and hyperactivity disorder (ADHD). These effects are present for all lead levels, for exposure from the prenatal period through early childhood, and for cognitive and behavioral performance of all age groups from infants to teenagers. It is generally agreed that early childhood exposure (before age 6) is most harmful to psychological development, and that these effects persist to a great degree. Cellular and animal studies indicate that lead affects neurological function in two ways: it has irreversible effects on the development of the central nervous system, as well as possibly reversible effects on the day-to-day operation of the nervous system. Most importantly, exposure to lead during critical stages of development appears to impair brain development by disrupting the orderly formation of networks of neurons, a process that is important for normal behavior.

The two primary environmental sources of lead exposure for the average child are leaded gasoline and lead-based paint. Reyes (2014) studies the causal impact of lead exposure on crime in the United States, relying on the state-level variation in lead exposure generated by the adoption of the Clean Air Act during the 1970s.

The estimates given by Reyes (2014) indicate that the reduction in lead exposure in the 1970s is responsible for a 56 percent drop in violent crime in the 1990s and will likely produce further declines in the future—up to a 70 percent drop in violent crime by the year 2020. The analysis controls for legalization of abortion (through the U.S. Supreme

*(continued on next page)*

Thus genes may affect the chance of developing one (or more) of these conditions. In turn, these types of conditions and disorders tend to raise one's propensity to engage in antisocial behavior and crime.[12] Similarly, personality disorders and traits— such as risk taking, overconfidence, and the propensity to trust others—are also partly genetically inherited.[13] While it is known that certain personality disorders are related to (and, in some instances, are even defined by) antisocial behavior, it is plausible that more ordinary personality traits—such as generosity, trust, and self-confidence—also play a role in determining an individual's propensity to commit crimes.

In sum, there are a number of in utero environmental factors that are directly related to a child's mental health, physical health, and cognitive abilities and that are ultimately related to antisocial behavior, including crime. In turn, several of these factors can be sourced to prenatal maternal (and, in some cases, paternal) behaviors, and may therefore be thought of as preventable, with an appropriate set of policies.

Of course, the relevance of biological factors does not imply the *irrelevance* of social factors. To the contrary, it is now well accepted that the interaction of biological factors with the environment is a key channel. The social mechanisms related to anti-social behavior during early stages of life include behavioral channels (role modeling, parenting styles); psychological channels (childhood traumas and abuse, an environment of family conflictual environment); biological channels occurring well after birth (head injuries or exposure to environmental toxins, including such as lead) and even socioeconomic status and poverty, as is discussed in chapter 5.

Suggestive evidence that genetic and prenatal environmental factors are casually linked to crime is provided by an adoption study in Denmark by Mednick and others (1984). The authors studied 14,427 adoptions that took place in Denmark between

1927 and 1947. Court conviction information was then linked to biological and adoptive parents, and to adoptees. When neither set of parents had a conviction, the incidence of a conviction among the adoptees was 14 percent. The likelihood of a conviction among adoptees with adoptive parents who had a conviction was 15 percent. If only the biological parent had a conviction, it jumped to 20 percent. However, when both sets of parents had a criminal record, the incidence of a conviction among adoptees reached 25 percent. These figures are suggestive of the fact that the interaction of environmental and biological factors may be even stronger for those individuals carrying some inherited vulnerability. This possibility is formalized and made precise by Hjalmarsson and Lindquist (2013), who combine Swedish adoption data with police registry information to study parent-son associations in crime (table 3.1).

As in the Danish study, for adopted sons born in Sweden, the authors have access to the criminal records of both the adopting and biological parents, allowing the researchers to assess the relative importance of prebirth factors (genes, prenatal environment, and perinatal conditions) and postbirth factors in the parent-son associations in crime. Several features of this study contribute to its generalizability and strength. First, the data include all adopted sons born in Sweden between 1943 and 1967 and span 35 years of crime data. This allows the authors to study later cohorts of adoptees (those born after the 1940s), who have grown up in more recent, higher-crime environments.[14] Further, the sample is not restricted exclusively to adopted children. Thus in addition to a classic adoptees design, parallel experiments using a representative sample of biological parents and their biological children can also be considered.

A number of interesting patterns emerge from the results. Both biological and adoptive mothers and fathers are important in explaining their children's criminal propensities. However, adoptive mothers play a particularly important role.

TABLE 3.1: **Effects of biological and adoptive parents' conviction on the likelihood of a son having a conviction**

| | | Convicted biological father | Convicted biological mother | Convicted adopted father | Convicted adopted mother |
|---|---|---|---|---|---|
| Biological children | Father only | 0.121 | – | – | – |
| | Mother only | – | 0.134 | – | – |
| | Father and mother | 0.113 | 0.115 | – | – |
| Adopted children | Father only | 0.072 | – | 0.089 | – |
| | Mother only | – | 0.108 | – | 0.132 |
| | Father and mother | 0.058 | 0.097 | 0.09 | 0.138 |

*Source:* Hjalmarsson and Lindquist 2013.
*Note:* All coefficients are significant at the 1 percent level.

Consistent with long-standing criminological studies, prebirth and postbirth maternal factors are equally important; prenatal and genetic factors account for roughly 50 percent of the effects. That is, a mother's influence on her son's criminality occurs equally through prebirth and postbirth channels.

Along both the extensive margin (whether an individual has any criminal convictions) and intensive margin (number of convictions), Hjalmarsson and Lindquist (2013) document that factors both before birth (related to biological parents) and after birth (related to adoptive parents) are important determinants of sons' convictions. At the intensive margin, however, postbirth channels appear to be more important than prebirth channels; adoptive mothers are particularly influential.

The conclusions differ slightly based on the extensive margin of specific types of crimes, although the criminal histories of biological parents continue to be strong predictors of their sons' predisposition to commit crimes. This pattern persists across crime categories: violent, property and "other" crimes. For violent crimes, a biological father who has been convicted of a violent crime raises the likelihood that his son will likewise be convicted by 6.9 percentage points, whereas the violent criminal records of adoptive fathers play no significant role. This same pattern also emerges for property crimes: biological fathers matter, while adoptive fathers do not. However, biological mothers also play a significant role in all crime categories. Having a biological mother convicted of a violent, property, or other crime increases the likelihood of a son's conviction by 13.9, 16.0, and 11.5 percentage points, respectively. In contrast to adoptive fathers, adoptive mothers have a large and significant impact on both the son's property crime record (10.4 percentage points) and "other" crime, although there is still no evidence of a postbirth association for violent crimes.

The first takeaway is that biological parents—fathers and mothers—matter. In addition, biological parents matter for sons along both the extensive and intensive margins and in all crime categories. The consistency of the association with the criminal histories of biological parents across categories of offenses and measures of the severity of offenses suggests that Hjalmarsson and Lindquist (2013) are indeed capturing the intergenerational prebirth associations of both minor and serious offenses.

Second, the criminal records of both adoptive mothers and fathers matter, regardless of whether crime is measured along the extensive or intensive margins. Adoptive mothers appear to be particularly influential, possibly due to the gendered roles in childrearing.

Third, at the extensive margin, both mothers' and fathers' influences on their child's criminality occurs approximately equally through prebirth and postbirth channels. However, at the intensive margin, postbirth channels appear to be more important than prebirth channels; adoptive mothers are particularly important.

Fourth, the act of being adopted has a minimal impact on the overall strength of the intergenerational criminal relationship.

Finally, Hjalmarsson and Lindquist (2013) find evidence of a prebirth/postbirth interaction between biological parents' criminality and adoptive parents' education, whereby more highly educated adoptive parents appear to mitigate the impact of the biological parents' criminality. This would be consistent with the theory that education better equips parents to sever the intergenerational linkages that run from biological parent to child, and thus makes them more "productive" in the production of the human capital of their children.

The research reviewed in this section speaks to the responsiveness of behavior to environmental factors, but highlights the relevance of "initial" conditions that do not result from socialization. In particular, several prebirth factors (prenatal conditions and perinatal factors) are amenable to policy intervention and could have important consequences for aggression in children, youth, and adult criminal offending. The responsiveness of children's criminal behavior to environmental conditions (as proxied in these studies by the outcomes of adopted parents) and the interaction of biological predispositions with adoptive parents' education point to the potential for interventions targeted at early childhood and families. The next section reviews interventions that target early stages of children's lives and their effects on offending later in life.

## Early interventions: Nutrition, nurse home visitations, and early childhood

This section does not aim to review all existing early and family-based prevention programs because this is beyond the scope of this regional study. Rather, it aims to highlight interventions that shed light on the channels that have shown promise in reducing antisocial behavior and crime.[15]

As discussed, most children begin deploying physical aggression between 1 and 2 years of age as a response to frustration and as a means to reach a goal. The first aggressive acts displayed with peers are often tugging on another child's toy, followed soon by pushing and hitting. Physical aggression tends to increase in frequency until 30 to 42 months of age, declining thereafter when children develop the ability to regulate their emotions, control their impulses, and use verbal communication to resolve conflicts and express needs. There are important differences between individual children in the early display of aggressive behavior: a majority will act aggressively occasionally, a minority will display little or no aggression, and about 5 percent to 10 percent of children, mostly boys, will frequently use physical aggression. The latter group is at heightened risk of chronic aggression in late childhood, adolescence, and adulthood.

A key observation from longitudinal studies of antisocial behavior, delinquency, and crime is that chronic disruptive behavior that emerges early in life tends to lead to frequent and often serious delinquency and crime during childhood, adolescence, and adulthood (McCord, Widom, and Crowell, 2001; Piquero, Farrington, and Blumstein 2003). It also carries negative repercussions for other, noncrime domains, such as education, employment, and relationship quality (Moffitt 1993). Because of these strong linkages over the life cycle, early prevention has been suggested as an important policy prescription with respect to early childhood problem behavior (Sampson and Laub 1997; Farrington and Welsh 2007). These observations, coupled with the interactions between biological and social risks, have led many criminologists and some economists to conclude that it is never too early to begin prevention.

The rest of the chapter is organized as follows. It first reviews the promising results that emerge from the Nurse Family Partnership, and relates these findings to the understanding of intergenerational transmission of violence and child abuse and perinatal behavior. It then briefly summarizes the impact of the HighScope Perry program on antisocial behavior and crime, and embarks on a discussion of the mechanisms by which it operated. Personality traits (or "soft skills"), as well as several other characteristics, emerge as playing a critical role in explaining the long-term effects of this famous early childhood development (ECD) intervention, as well as in those of 20-year follow-ups of an ECD program in Jamaica by Walker and others (2011) and Gertler and others (2014).

## Home visitation programs

In their review of interventions meeting rigorous standards for impact evaluations, Farrington and Welsh (2007) identify five home visitation programs from which the following key features emerge. All were carried out in the United States, with the exception of Larson's (1980) Montreal experiment. They all targeted at-risk parents and/or children. Treatment varied between 5 months and 2 years, and the length of the follow-up varied from immediate outcomes to 15 years. The main focus of these interventions was parents' education; the Elmira Prenatal / Early Infancy Project (Olds and others 1997, 1999) and its replication in Memphis (Kitzman and others 1997), supplemented parental education with parental support, community support, and family planning. Each of the five home visitation programs produced desirable results for the outcome of interest: lowering the rate of child injury, child abuse, and child neglect—key risks factor for the onset of early violence—and self-reported arrests (for both children as they aged and mothers).

From the perspective of this study, the results of the Elmira project (recently renamed the Nurse Family Partnership, NFP) are particularly noteworthy because they provide powerful and robust evidence on the importance of early life stages (including prenatal environments). As discussed in detail later in this section, this nurse visitation program had large effects on the children and families it targeted in the short run, such as on maternal and infant health. Equally important, however, in its 15-year follow-up, it also showed sizable effects on adolescent and young adult outcomes, such as on criminal records. The rest of this section is devoted to details of the "NFP," which is one of the model programs of the Blueprints for Violence (recently renamed "Blueprints for Healthy Youth Development") initiative of the University of

Colorado, Boulder.[16] The Blueprints model programs are the highest-quality U.S. youth prevention interventions, which focus on violence, delinquency, and drug prevention efforts that have demonstrated effectiveness.

### Effects of the Nurse Family Partnership (NFP) on children's antisocial and criminal behaviors

The NFP started in 1980 and recruited 400 pregnant (mostly white) women from a free prenatal clinic sponsored by the Chemung County, New York, health department and the offices of private obstetricians in Elmira, New York.[17] The women who were recruited had no previous live births, were less than 25 weeks pregnant, were ages 19 years at registration, were unmarried, or were of low socioeconomic status (SES). Women without these sociodemographic risk characteristics were permitted to enroll if they had no previous live births. The program specifically targeted at-risk women: 85 percent were young, unmarried, or from low-SES households. After completing informed consent and baseline interviews, women were stratified by sociodemographic characteristics and randomized into one of four treatment arms. The first group was not provided any services during pregnancy. Women in the second group were provided with transportation vouchers to attend regular prenatal care visits and child visits to physicians. The third treatment arm received the same transportation vouchers, coupled with nurse home visits during pregnancy at an average frequency of once every two weeks. Women in the fourth treatment group benefited from all of the above-noted services, but the home visits continued into the first two years following birth. Because of the absence or low intensity of treatment, the first two groups were considered control groups. The nurses completed an average of 9 visits during pregnancy and 23 visits from birth to the child's second birthday.

### Fifteen-year follow-up and youth outcomes

At the 15-year follow-up of NFP, Olds and others (1998) report strong significant effects on children's criminal and antisocial behavior. Children in the fourth treatment arm (the most intensive treatment) were less likely to run away from home, get arrested or convicted, and violate probation than their counterparts in the control group. The effects are not only statistically significant at the conventional levels, but are also large in magnitude. The incidences of arrest and conviction were 36 percent and 27 percent, respectively, in the control group; and 17 percent and 10 percent for the fourth treatment arm, respectively—implying declines in their incidence of 53 percent and 63 percent, respectively. There were no program effects on less serious forms of antisocial behavior, initiation of sexual intercourse, or use of recreational drugs.

When restricting the sample to low-SES, unmarried women, the sizes of the effects are considerably larger. These results are consistent with the results of other preventive interventions, wherein the largest effects are observed among children in families at greater social risk (in terms of low SES, prenatal habits, conflictual families, low cognitive abilities, and the like).[18] This suggests that these kinds of services may have higher returns for families in greater need, highlighting the importance of a well-targeted program. Table 3.2 reproduces the effects reported by Olds and others (1998) for the entire sample and for the most vulnerable group of mothers.[19] Adolescents from the treatment group (that is, prenatal and infancy home visitations) reported fewer arrests, and convictions and violations of probation. The official PINS records corroborated this pattern.[20] The most vulnerable participants in this group also experienced sizable declines in children's use of alcohol and number of sexual partners, implying a lower overall propensity to engage in risky behavior relative to their comparable counterparts in the control group.

Olds and others (1998) also document that the children of women in the less intensive treatment group (who received prenatal home visitations only; treatment 3) also experienced declines in arrests. Interestingly, even the authors confess that they did not expect prenatal home visitations alone to be as effective as they proved to be in preventing criminal behavior among children born to low-SES, unmarried women. These improvements occurred despite the fact that these children's mothers showed almost none of the postnatal benefits observed among the women who also received visits during pregnancy and infancy (such as reductions in welfare dependence, substance abuse, criminal behavior, and child abuse and neglect).

What explains the large effects on the long-term outcomes of children in nurse home visit treatment arms? The effects of the intervention on shorter-term outcomes may provide some indications. Olds and others (1998) report that the prenatal phase of the program (treatment 3) reduced prenatal maternal smoking, improved the qualities of women's prenatal diets as well as levels of informal social support, and reduced intellectual impairment and irritable behavioral styles associated with fetal exposure to tobacco.[21] Prenatal exposure to tobacco is a risk factor for early poorly modulated behavioral responses, problems with attention, and later crime and delinquency. Moreover, the combination of birth complications (and subsequent neurological impairment) and maternal rejection substantially increases the likelihood of violent offenses by the time children are 18 years old (Raine, Brennan, and Mednick 1994).

For treatment 4, short-term effects indicate that the more intensive intervention resulted in substantial reductions in child abuse and neglect. Thirteen years after completing the program, the mothers in treatment 4 tended to have fewer subsequent births; an average of over two years' longer interval between the birth of their first and second child; fewer maternal behavioral problems due to alcohol and drug abuse; and 30 months less receipt of the federal welfare program now known as Temporary Assistance for Needy Families (TANF) compared to the control group. Differences among treatment and control are statistically significant. Importantly, in their companion study on the effects of the visitation program on child abuse and neglect, Olds and others (1997) document that the mothers in the more intensive treatment arm were

**TABLE 3.2: Home nurse visitation and criminal behavior**

| | Total sample | | | | | Low SES, unmarried sample | | | | |
|---|---|---|---|---|---|---|---|---|---|---|
| | Control (T1+T2) | T3 | T4 | Control vs. T3 | Control vs. T4 | Control (T1+T2) | T3 | T4 | Control vs. T3 | Control vs. T4 |
| Incidence of times ran away | 0.29 | 0.23 | 0.34 | −0.06 | 0.05 | 0.60 | 0.14 | 0.24 | −0.46 | −0.36 |
| Incidence of arrests | 0.36 | 0.16 | 0.17 | −0.20 | −0.19 | 0.45 | 0.15 | 0.20 | −0.30 | −0.25 |
| Incidence of convictions and probation violation | 0.27 | 0.06 | 0.10 | −0.21 | −0.17 | 0.47 | 0.07 | 0.09 | −0.40 | −0.38 |
| Incidence of times sent to youth corrections | 0.05 | 0.05 | 0.04 | 0.00 | −0.01 | 0.06 | 0.03 | 0.02 | −0.03 | −0.04 |
| Incidence of arrests (mother's report) | 0.12 | 0.11 | 0.08 | −0.01 | −0.04 | 0.19 | 0.16 | 0.04 | −0.03 | −0.15 |
| Incidence of PINS records (archived data) | 0.31 | 0.17 | 0.03 | −0.14 | −0.28 | 0.35 | 0.33 | 0.00 | −0.02 | −0.35 |
| Incidence of arrests (archived data) | 0.35 | 0.14 | 0.32 | −0.21 | −0.03 | 0.55 | 0.22 | 0.44 | −0.33 | −0.11 |
| Number of sexual partners | 1.56 | 1.10 | 1.16 | −0.46 | −0.40 | 2.48 | 2.23 | 0.92 | −0.25 | −1.56 |
| Number of cigarettes smoked per day | 1.30 | 0.91 | 1.28 | −0.39 | −0.02 | 2.50 | 1.32 | 1.50 | −1.18 | −1.00 |
| Days drank alcohol | 1.57 | 1.81 | 1.87 | 0.24 | 0.30 | 2.49 | 1.84 | 1.09 | −0.65 | −1.40 |
| Alcohol and drug impairment (as reported by parents) | 0.18 | 0.20 | 0.28 | 0.02 | 0.10 | 0.34 | 0.62 | 0.15 | 0.28 | −0.19 |

*Source:* Olds and others 1998.

*Note:* PINS = Person adjudicated in need of supervision resulting from incorrigible behavior such as recurrent truancy or destroying parents' property; SES = socioeconomic status; T1 = Treatment 1; T2 = Treatment 2; T3 = Treatment 3; T4 = Treatment 4.
Grey shading indicates statistical significance at the 10 percent level.

179

46 percent less likely to be identified as perpetrators of child abuse and neglect than their counterparts in the control group.

In sum, improvements in the outcomes described imply that each margin is a candidate mechanism for achieving reductions in youth violence 15 years after treatment. This study argues that maternal health and well-being and prenatal maternal behaviors, including declines in prenatal tobacco use, are particularly noteworthy because these margins shape parenting style, which, as discussed shortly, carries important consequences for child development and subsequent aggression.

Box 3.2 provides an overview of criminological and economic theories justifying the relationship between coercive parenting styles and subsequent offending. While these theories seem plausible, they lack substantiating empirical evidence to discern between them. Two main obstacles are small, unrepresentative samples and questionable study designs. For obvious reasons, random assignment experiments in the context of parenting are unthinkable.

---

**BOX 3.2: Why would child maltreatment lead to subsequent criminality? Criminological and economic theories**

Psychological explanations for the link between child maltreatment and crime are typically derived from three theories: Social Control Theory, Social Learning Theory, and Social-Psychological Strain Theory

*Social Control Theory* assumes that individuals have a natural tendency toward crime and violence, which is restrained by their social bonds (Hirschi 1969). By disrupting these social bonds, a caregiver's maltreatment makes individuals more likely to offend (see Sampson and Laub 1993; Zingraff and others 1993).

*Social Learning Theory* maintains that victims of maltreatment learn and adopt patterns of violent or delinquent behavior through processes of imitation and modeling. Children observe that these behaviors result in positive outcomes, such as control over others, or the acquisition of material or social benefits (see Widom 1998; Garland and Dougher 1990; Walters and Grusec 1977).

*Social-Psychological Strain Theory (SPST)* focuses on maltreatment as a source of acute stress (Agnew 1985, 1992). Many studies examine the relationships between maltreatment and outcomes such as behavioral problems, developmental delays, and changes in brain functioning (such as elevated cortisol levels) that may permanently alter the way that individuals respond to environmental stimuli (Veltman and Browne 2001; Cicchetti and Rogosch 2001). These studies suggest that maltreatment could predispose a child to risky, self-destructive, or aggressive behaviors. Claussen and Crittenden (1991) and Deblinger and others (1989), for instance, document high rates of post-traumatic

*(continued on next page)*

---

stress syndrome among children who have been abused. Widom (1999) suggests that stress during critical periods may have important effects on the development of aggressive behavior in adolescents.

These psychological theories have their analogues in economic thinking about crime. In the standard Beckerian model (Becker 1968), individuals assess the costs and benefits of committing crime, refraining when the costs exceed the benefits. These costs and benefits depend on the options available to the individual: for example, the wages available to them in the legitimate labor market, their skill at committing crime, and the likelihood of arrest or incarceration. Social Control Theory emphasizes one cost—broken social bonds—but ignores the others.

Social Learning Theory focuses on what an economist would think of as the development of human capital. When a child sees others committing crime, he learns from it and accumulates capital as a criminal, making him both a better criminal and a worse legitimate worker. The human capital perspective also offers insight into Social-Psychological Strain Theory. Economists have begun to explore the effects of events in early childhood on the development of both cognitive and soft skills (Cunha and Heckman 2008; Cunha, Heckman, and Schennach 2010). There is increasing evidence that events early in life have far-reaching consequences for their skills and prospects as adults (Currie 2009; Almond and Currie 2011). Social-Psychological Strain Theory emphasizes one way in which maltreatment impairs the development of critical soft skills in young children.

One of the best-known studies of the long-term effects of child maltreatment is by Widom (1989), who matched a sample of 908 children with substantiated cases of maltreatment to controls who were selected to be similar in age, sex, race, and socioeconomic status. The study distinguished between physical abuse, neglect, and sexual abuse, and also involved long-term follow-ups of the subjects. The author finds substantial effects of both abuse and neglect on arrest both as a juvenile and as an adult. Being abused or neglected as a child increases an individual's risk of arrest as a juvenile by 53 percent, the probability of arrest as an adult by 38 percent, and the probability of an arrest for a violent crime by 38 percent. However, the procedure of matching on a small number of observable traits provides no guarantee that the controls are actually similar to the "treatment" group, in terms of unmeasured characteristics. Widom (1989) also points out the limitation of relying on administrative data from an era in which mandatory reporting of child maltreatment did not exist.

Currie and Tekin (2012) overcome some of these limitations by making use of a large, nationally representative sample of the United States, the National Longitudinal Study of Adolescent Health (Add Health). They use a unified framework to consider the effects of different types of maltreatment on children's subsequent delinquency. The authors adopt a number of different estimation methods, each of which relies on differing assumptions and may have distinct potential limitations, which the authors acknowledge and discuss at length. However, regardless of estimation method, the strength and robustness of the associations between the different forms of child maltreatment and subsequent criminality lead the authors argue that "this uniformity of results provides a strong, if not completely conclusive, argument that we are uncovering a causal effect." Indeed, rather than employing one particular strategy to identify the relationships of interest (as is frequently done in the economics literature), Currie and Tekin's (2012) strategy seems instead to deploy a variety of methods and rely on the surprising consistency of results across them to argue that they are identifying causal relationships.

Currie and Tekin (2012) document large and statistically significant effects of child maltreatment for most indicators of delinquency. Individuals who were subject to any form of maltreatment were 11.1 percentage points more likely to commit some type of nondrug offense in their subsample of siblings. Maltreated children are significantly more likely to commit burglary, assault, and theft, and to damage property. The long-term consequences of maltreatment are quite different, however, and depend on the nature of the maltreatment. Leaving children unsupervised appears to be relatively benign. But having parents who ever failed to meet a child's basic needs (such as keeping the child clean and providing food and clothing) greatly increases the probability of assault and damaging property. Similarly, having a parent who ever struck, hit, or kicked the child increases the probability of criminal offending; the effect tends to increase with the frequency of the abuse. Sexual maltreatment has the largest deleterious effects: respondents who were sexually abused are 24.5 percentage points more likely to have committed a nondrug offense.

Thus, above and beyond its direct effects on the victims of abuse, the large magnitudes of the effects reported by Currie and Tekin (2012) suggest that maltreatment generates large externalities to society in the form of increased crime. One possible explanation for the large effects is that children who experience maltreatment accelerate their initiation in criminal behavior, engaging in crime earlier, and that this criminality is persistent. Indeed, being a victim of maltreatment increases the probability of a juvenile conviction by 2 percentage points—a 143 percent increase relative to the baseline conviction rate of those who were not maltreated.

### Cost-benefit analysis of preventing maltreatment

The results reported above suggest that while not everyone who is abused becomes a criminal, maltreatment is a major determinant of future criminal behavior. Currie and Tekin's (2012) estimates of the effects of maltreatment are large relative to other determinants of criminality that have been studied in the economics literature. These include unemployment (Corman and Mocan 2005); education (Jacob and Lefgren 2003); gun ownership (Mocan and Tekin 2006; Duggan 2001); the introduction of crack cocaine (Grogger and Willis 2000); the legalization of abortion (Donohue and Levitt 2001); and exposure to lead through paint or gasoline (Reyes 2014; Nevin 2007).

In the United States, the costs to society of crime induced by maltreatment are around $6.4 billion per year, Currie and Tekin (201) estimate, based on conservative cost of crime estimates by Lochner and Moretti (2004). A much larger figure of $55 billion per year is obtained when cost of crime estimates by Cohen and others (2004) are used.

How do these figures compare to the costs of the Nurse Family Partnership program? At an annual cost of roughly $4,000 per child (Currie and Tekin 2012), the steady-state cost of an NFP-type intervention for all births in the United States would be about $14 billion per year (with roughly 3.5 million children being born in the United States each year). Given that the crime induced by maltreatment is only one of myriad social costs of maltreatment, these estimates suggest that a home visiting program like the NFP might well pay for itself, even using conservative estimates of the costs of crime. If some benefit is assigned to improving the lives of disadvantaged children (whose welfare the previous calculation ignored), then the benefits of a national version of the NFP likely swamp the costs of implementation. In his estimate of the cost-effectiveness of the NFP, Raine (2013) takes a different perspective. Rather than relying on an estimate of the cost of crime, he instead considers the benefits to society from the reductions in lifetime receipt of food stamps induced by the NFP. With a total cost per birth of around $11,511 in 2006, the food stamps savings alone amount to roughly $12,300.

These calculations are not merely academic. In light of the NFP's impact on youth crime and corresponding expenditures for the juvenile and adult criminal justice systems, the U.S. Department of Justice is now supporting an effort to make this program available to a larger number of high-crime communities. More recently, the benefits of the NFP have attracted attention at the highest levels, with President Obama allocating federal funds for an expanded Nurse Family Partnership program in his 2010 blueprint budget.

As mentioned in the introduction, the evidence emerging from developed countries helps to highlight relevant policy options/margins in Latin America and the Caribbean. In this case, prenatal interventions in the form of home visitations should be considered a promising one. Relatively unintrusive interventions very early on in the life cycle (in this case, during gestation and in the first two years following birth) can reap very large benefits. The obstacles to implementation of many of these interventions may lie in the human capital required to deliver them. This involves both specific knowledge and, possibly more important, intangibles such as the ability to connect and establish functional relationships with at-risk youth, parents, and children, so as to earn their trust and actually increase the take-up rate. However, implementing these policies in low- and middle-income countries may yield larger benefits, even in low-capacity environments. Indeed, high-risk mothers/ families in Latin America and the Caribbean are likely to be at even greater risk than the women targeted by the NFP in the United States.[22]

### Early childhood development interventions

Early childhood is an important period for cognitive and psychosocial skill development because brain plasticity and neurogenesis are very high during this period. Furthermore, as mentioned, the early onset of aggression is highly correlated with persistent criminal behavior in later life.[23] From a human capital perspective, investments during this period create the foundations for the evolution of the cognitive and psychosocial skills that are key determinants of lifetime outcomes (Knudsen and others 2006).

Many early childhood development interventions are based on cognitive tools that deliberately target self-control (examples include Tools of the Mind, Montessori, and PATHS). They aim to regulate behavior and, in particular, to reduce *externalizing behavior* (defined as aggressive, antisocial, and rule-breaking behaviors) because of the impacts of such behavior on academic achievement and on that of peers. Indeed, researchers have also shown that externalizing behavior can predict children's school and adult outcomes (Kokko and Pulkkinen 2000; Segal 2008).

When these observations are combined with those of the criminology literature, which finds that childhood externalizing behaviors have also been linked to adolescent and adult delinquency (Nagin and Tremblay 1999; Broidy and others 2003), one would have high hopes for the impacts on behavior of well-designed and high-quality ECD interventions.

## *HighScope Perry Preschool program*

The HighScope Perry Preschool Program is a noteworthy intervention that has shown a great deal of success, and for which there are numerous evaluations and review articles (see, for example, Shonkoff and Phillips 2000; Karoly, Kilburn, and Cannon 2005; Heckman and others 2010a and 2010b). The program was conducted in the early and mid-1960s and targeted disadvantaged African-American children of low socioeconomic status and low IQs (intelligence quotients) in Ypsilanti, Michigan (see box 3.3). It was designed to improve thinking and reasoning, and extend educational attainment. Of the relatively small sample of 123 children allocated over five cohorts, those in the treatment group attended daily preschool, had weekly home visitations, and their parents had group meetings to involve them and help them in shaping their children's cognitive development. The children were followed from age 3 to age 40 (with surprisingly low attrition). Along a number of socioeconomic dimensions, the Perry program is viewed as a resounding success (table 3.3).

**BOX 3.3:** The HighScope Perry Preschool program

The HighScope Perry program targeted the children of disadvantaged African-American parents (as measured by the level of parental employment, parental education, and housing density) with low IQs (Schweinhart and Weikart 1981). The experiment was conducted in the mid-1960s in the district of the Perry Elementary School in Ypsilanti, Michigan. Children entered the program at age three and were enrolled for two years. Roughly 47 percent of the children in the study did not have fathers present in the household at age 3.

The 123 participants were randomized into treatment and control groups. The Perry sample consists of 51 females (25 treatment and 26 control) and 72 males (33 treatment and 39 control). There was relatively little attrition: only 11 participants left the study by the time of the interview at age 40.

The Perry curriculum is based on the principle of active participatory learning, in which children and adults are treated as equal partners in the learning process. Abilities to plan, execute, and evaluate tasks were fostered, as were social skills, including cooperation and resolution of interpersonal conflicts. The Perry curriculum is viewed as implementing the theories of Vygotsky (1986), teaching self-control and sociability. A program based on these same principles—*Tools of the Mind*—has since been widely implemented and is designed to promote self-control.

The treatment group received the program for one or two academic years. The program was composed of three parts: a center-based program for 2.5 hours per day for each weekday, with a child-teacher ratio of 5:1; home visitations for 1.5 hours per weekday; and group meetings of parents, with the aim of involving them in the socioemotional development of their children. The program thus represented an intensive and structured investment in support of participants' preschool development. The control group had no contact with the Perry program other than through annual testing and assessment (Weikart, Bond, and McNeil 1978).

Numerous measures of socioeconomic outcomes were collected annually from ages 3–15 for treatment and control participants, with three additional follow-ups at ages 19, 27, and 40. The Perry sample was representative of a particularly disadvantaged cohort of the African-American population. About 16 percent of all African-American children in the United States had family and personal attributes similar to those of Perry participants when the Perry program was conducted. The statistically significant treatment effects of the experiment for boys and girls survive rigorous adjustments for multiple hypothesis testing and compromises in the randomization protocol. The program had positive impacts on a number of socioeconomic measures (see main text and table 3.3).

**TABLE 3.3: Perry program effects on crime, females**

| Variable | Treatment effect |
|---|---|
| Number of misdemeanor violent crimes, age 27 | −0.423** |
| Number of felony arrests, age 27 | −0.269** |
| Jobless for more than 1 year, age 27 | −0.292* |
| Ever tried drugs other than alcohol or marijuana, age 27 | −0.227** |
| Number of misdemeanor violent crimes, age 40 | −0.537** |
| Number of felony arrests, age 40 | −0.383** |
| Number of lifetime violent crimes, age 40 | −0.574** |

Source: Heckman, Pinto, and Savelyev (2013).
Note: Significance level: * = 10 percent, ** = 5 percent.

In the economics-of-education literature, it is frequently assumed that cognitive ability is paramount in the production of successful lifetime outcomes (see Hanushek and Woessmann 2008). In this light, however, the success of the Perry program is somewhat puzzling. Although the program initially raised the IQs of participants, the effect soon faded; within a few years of program completion, differences in the IQs of boys between treatments and controls were statistically indistinguishable and were at the margin of statistical significance for girls (Heckman Pinto, and Savelyev 2013). Surprisingly, Heckman and others (2010a) and Conti and others (2013) show that the program significantly improved adult outcomes relative to the control group: education, employment, earnings, marriage, health, and participation in healthy behaviors all improved. The pattern of treatment responses is characterized by strong improvements early on for females, with males catching up later in life (Heckman and others 2010a, 2010b).

With respect to antisocial behaviors, participants in the treatment group committed fewer crimes throughout the life cycle (Barnett 1996). For instance, 48 percent of the control group was ever arrested for a violent crime, compared with 32 percent of the program group; 17 percent of the control group was incarcerated at the time of interview, compared to 6 percent of the program group (Belfield and others 2006). Table 3.3 summarizes the main effects on criminal behavior at ages 27 and 40 for females. For instance, by age 40, females in the treatment group had 0.537 fewer misdemeanor violent crimes than their counterparts who did not receive treatment. Although not reported here, the corresponding effects for males are considerably stronger, perhaps because the incidence of crime is considerably lower among females for many of the criminal outcomes in question; thus there is diminished scope for large effects among females. Interestingly, the pattern of effects by gender is reversed for outcomes that are economic in nature (for instance, academic achievement and labor force participation), with the program having larger effects for females than for males.

Because the Perry program has received a great deal of attention in both the academic and popular press, this section does not devote further discussion to its impacts.[24] It instead focuses on recent research that identifies and describes the mechanisms that might underlie the surprising effects on offending: what are the mechanisms that mediate these outcomes? What ultimately shapes academic performance, and economic and offending outcomes, and how are they affected by ECD interventions such as the Perry program? The section that follows discusses the roles of various personality traits on which the Perry program may have had effect.

## The underlying mechanisms: The role of personality traits

Using data from the National Longitudinal Survey of Youth 1979 (NLSY79), Heckman and Kautz (2012) and Heckman, Pinto, and Savelyev (2013) decompose the variance of a series of socioeconomic and health outcomes (earnings, hourly wages, college degree, jail, welfare dependence, marriage, and depression) into contributions from measures of IQ and achievement test scores. Surprisingly, test scores are systematically more predictive than IQ. However, neither measure is capable of explaining much of the variation in the outcomes under study, leaving considerable room for other determinants.[25] The authors next add personality traits such as measures of self-esteem, and of locus of control (the extent to which an individual feels as though she has control over her life), as well as behavioral variables that are believed to be markers of character, such as the propensity to engage in risky behaviors (Heckman and Kautz 2012). The proportion of variance that is explained by this latter group of variables rivals that explained by measures of cognitive ability—with their relative importance, depending on the outcome in question.[26]

Common sense would suggest that conscientiousness and perseverance should matter for task performance, although economists have only recently started considering their roles. Ironically, one of the earliest advocates of their importance was the creator of the first IQ test. Success in school, Binet and Simon (1916, 254) argue, "admits of other things than intelligence; to succeed in his studies, one must have qualities which depend on attention, will, and character; for example, a certain docility, a regularity of habits, and especially continuity of effort. A child, even if intelligent, will learn little in class if he never listens, if he spends his time in playing tricks, in giggling, in playing truant."[27]

Indeed, Heckman, Pinto, and Savelyev (2013) document that the Perry Preschool Program operated primarily by improving personality traits. Participants recorded better direct measures of personal behavior[28] than their counterparts in the control group. Importantly, participants of both genders improved markedly in their externalizing behavior, a psychological construct that encompasses aggressive, antisocial, and rule-breaking behaviors, and is related to agreeableness and conscientiousness.

Heckman, Pinto, and Savelyev (2013) present evidence that the effects of the intervention on life outcomes operate primarily through the program's enhancement of *externalizing behavior*. Components attributable to changes in externalizing behavior are statistically significant and, in most cases, explain 20–60 percent of the treatment effects on crime for males, and about 40–60 percent for females. In addition to being statistically significant, the mediating effects of externalizing behavior are also economically important. Since externalizing behavior is both malleable at early ages and is strongly predictive of crime, it is no surprise that crime reduction has been found to be a major benefit of the Perry program.[29]

These results formalize the intuition that personality traits likely account for the bulk of the Perry effect. Other studies are broadly consistent with this evidence. Analyses of Project STAR, a program in the United States that randomly assigned kindergartners and teachers to classes of different sizes, yield results similar to the Perry program: Dee and West (2011) find that assignment to a small class is associated with positive changes in personality. In a follow-up analysis, Chetty and others (2011) find that Project STAR students who were placed in higher-quality kindergarten classes— as measured by their peer's average performance on achievement tests—had significantly higher earnings in early adulthood.

Following the lead of interventions such as Perry and Project STAR, programs such as Promoting Alternative Thinking Strategies (PATHS) design their curricula to teach directly to personality traits such as self-control, emotional awareness, and social problem-solving skills. Indeed, as in the case of the Nurse Family Partnership, PATHS is one of the only ten "model" programs deemed "proven effective" according to the Blueprints initiative (see box 3.4). The program is aimed at elementary school children (Bierman and others 2010), and thus qualifies as a "late" childhood program. A random-assignment, longitudinal study demonstrates that the PATHS curriculum reduces teacher and peer ratings of aggression, improves teacher and peer ratings of prosocial behavior, and improves teacher ratings of academic engagement. A recent meta-analysis shows that the program improved grades and achievement test scores by 0.33 and 0.27 standard deviations, respectively (Durlak and others 2011).

In the developing country context, Walker and others (2011) and Gertler and others (2013) study a 20-year follow-up to an early childhood development intervention in Jamaica, where they report results consistent with those of the United States. Enrollment in the Jamaica study was conditioned on stunting because it is an easily and accurately observed indicator of malnutrition that is strongly associated with poor cognitive development (Walker and others 2007). The randomly assigned treatment group received weekly "stimulation" visits for a period of two years from community health workers who actively encouraged mothers to interact and play with their children in ways designed to develop cognitive and psychosocial skills. Unlike many other early childhood interventions whose effects fade over time, the Jamaican stimulation intervention generated large impacts on cognition 20 years later (Walker and others 2011). Furthermore, Gertler and others (2013, 2014) show that assignment

## BOX 3.4: Promoting Alternative Thinking Strategies (PATHS)

PATHS is a late childhood intervention: a comprehensive program to promote emotional and social competencies and reducing aggression and behavior problems in elementary school–aged children (from pre-kindergarten through grade 6), while enhancing the educational process in the classroom.

The Grade Level PATHS Curriculum consists of separate volumes of lessons for each grade level (pre-K–grade 6). Five conceptual domains, integrated in a hierarchical manner, are included in PATHS lessons at each grade level: self-control, emotional understanding, positive self-esteem, relationships, and interpersonal problem-solving skills. A critical focus of PATHS is to facilitate the dynamic relationship between cognitive-affective understanding and real-life situations. PATHS is designed to be taught two to three times per week (or more often if desired, but no less than twice weekly), with daily activities to promote generalization and support ongoing behavior. PATHS lessons follow lesson objectives and provide scripts to facilitate instruction, but teachers have the flexibility to adapt these for their particular classroom needs. Although each unit of PATHS focuses on one or more skill domains (such as emotional recognition, friendship, self-control, and problem solving), aspects of all five major areas are integrated into each unit. Each unit builds hierarchically upon the learning that preceded it. Certain stable outcomes have been recorded in evaluations. Across numerous studies, children who had pursued the PATHS curriculum exhibited the following relative to a control group:

- Lower rate of conduct problems and externalizing behaviors (such as aggression)
- Lower internalizing scores and depression
- Improvements in social problem solving, emotional understanding, and self-control
- Better understanding of cues for recognizing feelings in others
- Higher scores on peer sociability and social school functioning
- Better ability to resolve peer conflicts and identify feelings and problems, and greater empathy for others
- Less anger and attribution bias[a]
- Reduction in ADHD (attention deficit hyperactivity disorder) symptoms
- Better scores on measures of authority acceptance, cognitive concentration, and social competence.

*Source:* Blueprints for Healthy Youth Development.

a. Attribution bias refers to the systematic errors people make when they evaluate or try to find reasons for their own and others' behaviors.

to stimulation increased average earnings by 42 percent 20 years after the intervention. To put the magnitude of this effect on earnings into perspective, it implies that, two decades after intervention, the stunted group's earnings had entirely caught up to those of a nonstunted comparison group that had been identified at baseline.

With regard to antisocial behavior, however, the evidence as to the intervention's effectiveness in mitigating aggression is mixed. The effects based on self-reports are incongruent with those based on police detention and conviction rates (Walker and others 2011). As a result, the early stimulation provided by the Jamaica study had inconclusive effects on adult criminality and aggression.

Nevertheless, in their discussion of the mechanisms through which early stimulation had such sizable effects on labor market outcomes 20 years later, Gertler and others (2013) provide evidence that both cognitive and psychological traits improved in response to the program, and therefore played a role in the outcomes. This is again consistent with the evaluations of the HighScope Perry program and Project STAR.

Taken together, the evaluations of early childhood development programs that are effective in improving the lives of those who benefited from them, in both childhood and adulthood, are converging on a consensus as to how they operate. They appear to operate on personality traits and externalizing behavior. The authors of most studies discussed in this chapter typically point to conscientiousness as a pivotal personality trait that is predictive of positive behavioral effects of ECD interventions. *Conscientiousness* is defined by the *American Psychology Dictionary* as the tendency to be organized, responsible, and hardworking, and is shown to be related to the following traits: grit, perseverance, delayed gratification, impulse control, striving for achievement, ambition, and a work ethic. Biologically, all these traits are regulated by a very specific area of the brain known as the prefrontal cortex, which in turn is the locus of self-control and executive functions, defined as higher-level cognitive skills, including inhibitory control, working memory, and cognitive flexibility. Chapter 4 discusses the linkages between self-control and development of the prefrontal cortex in greater detail.

In their review of interventions targeting executive function, Diamond and Lee (2011) document results not unlike those of the Perry program. A number of random assignment evaluations of Tools of the Mind, a preschool and early primary school curriculum targeting development of self-control, indicate that it improves classroom behavior as well as executive function.[30] Furthermore, these evaluations present evidence that targeted interventions can improve conscientiousness.

With regard to the evidence from Latin America and the Caribbean, Carneiro and Evans (2013) analyze the medium-term impacts of access to formal child care in Rio de Janeiro on child development and maternal and household outcomes. Their research greatly extends the earlier work of Barros and others (2012), which is based on a much earlier sample, by considering several measures of family resources and home environments, and especially, child development. Because the demand for child care far exceeded the supply, the Municipality of Rio de Janeiro relied on a lottery to determine which children in each center's application pool would be offered a spot in that center. Based on medium-term assessments (four to eight months after lottery winners attended child care), the authors find strong impacts of child care attendance on various measures of child assessments, and on certain behavioral problems. In particular, they document rather strong impacts of the program on executive functions, impulsivity, and performance in cognitive assessments, as measured by direct tests administered by psychologists, and by parental reports. Extrapolation from the conclusions of the Perry intervention would suggest that, whether by design or not, public policies whose effect is to improve executive function and externalizing behavior in early childhood, such as the one considered by Carneiro and Evans (2013), may reap large long-term benefits in the form of declines in the incidence of antisocial and criminal behavior.

One of the (perhaps surprising) conclusions that emerge from the evidence presented in this chapter is that cognitive ability and personality traits are malleable. In particular, changes in academic achievements and IQ measures are not necessarily predictive of longer-term impacts on antisocial behaviors.

Furthermore, personality traits appear to be amenable to policy intervention beyond the typical window of opportunity identified for cognitive ability (Cunha and others 2006). For instance, PATHS's curriculum, which explicitly targets emotional and social competencies, has been shown to be effective even for children ages 5 to 11 years old.[31] Thus personality traits are not static constructs; rather, different traits might be more responsive to investments at different ages (Heckman, Stixrud, and Urzua 2006). In addition, the evidence presented here suggests that the evolution of these traits over the life cycle it is not only the result of natural biological (ontogenetic) forces, but they may also be influenced by experiences over the life cycle. Figure 3.3 shows the life-cycle evolution of *conscientiousness* (defined as a tendency to show self-discipline, act dutifully, and aim for achievement against measures or outside expectations; it is related to the way in which people control, regulate, and direct their impulses).[32]

Nevertheless, it is worth clarifying that in spite of the encouraging evidence presented here, not all early interventions exhibit positive impacts on offending. This suggests that much more evidence is needed, along with a deeper understanding of the mechanisms through which early interventions operate. For instance, the Infant Health and Development Program (IHDP) and Abecederian programs are very similar in content to the other programs reviewed here and produce similar gains in test scores in the short term, sometimes with lasting effects, including increased college attendance (Abecedarian only). However, no effects are observed for crime and offending.

High school graduation rates were 70 percent among Abecedarian controls; drop-out rates (as of age 18) were only 10 percent among the IHDP controls. Both compare quite favorably to the control group in the Perry intervention, which had high school completion rates between 30 percent and 50 percent. Yet, neither IHDP nor Abecedarian increased high school graduation rates. While Abecedarian improved college attendance rates, this is empirically not an important margin for crime:

**FIGURE 3.3:** Life-cycle evolution of conscientiousness

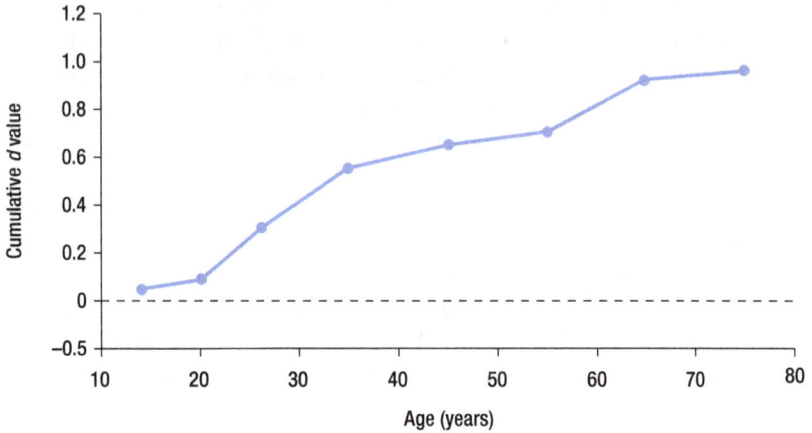

Source: Roberts and Mroczek 2008.
Note: Cumulative *d* value results from adding average amounts of standardized mean-level changes from separate decades of the life course together, under the assumption that changes in personality traits are cumulative.

differences in criminal offending between high school graduates and college graduates are negligible. Given the narrow link between high school dropout rates and crime discussed earlier, it is not surprising that Abecedarian and IHDP did not induce declines in crime, given their negligible effects on high school completion. Yet the Perry program substantially reduced male crime rates without raising the educational attainment of males. Clearly, early interventions may reduce delinquency and criminal behavior without significantly improving final schooling outcomes (Lochner 2010).

What is different about Abecedarian and IHDP such that these programs did not yield the same reductions in crime? It is difficult to point to any particular differences in curriculum—although not all preschools are alike. Abecedarians began preschool education in infancy and continued through kindergarten—the longest of all programs. The program was also full-day and year-round, unlike the Perry program. Like Perry Preschool, it showed sizable gains in academic achievement and IQ, so it is difficult to attribute its lack of effects on crime to the hypothetical inadequacy of the intervention or intensity. The only obvious programmatic difference between Abecedarian and Perry Preschool is a lack of a home visits component. However, IHDP included home visits by nurses from birth through age 3: while it began early, it also ended when Perry Preschool and Chicago Child Parent Center began (age 3). So it is possible that the early home visits, combined with later preschool care, is an important combination of services necessary for long-term impacts on delinquency and crime.

An alternative hypothesis is that the environment, rather than the specifics of the programs, played a role in determining impacts on crime. It does not seem implausible that the same program might have different effects in each city/location. As noted by Barnett and Masse (2007), there may have been little crime to prevent among the Abecedarian sample compared to the Perry group. Ultimately, there is no easy explanation for the different findings across interventions (Lochner 2010). While the results from these studies are encouraging and individually powerful, given their research designs (most are based on random assignment), it may still be premature to draw strong conclusions as to the efficacy of early childhood interventions as a national crime-fighting strategy.[33]

The evidence presented in this chapter suggests that not only is early prevention effective, but also that it can never start too early. The chapter has documented the powerful influence of families and family history in criminality, and the intergenerational transmission of violence. Nevertheless, preventive interventions that are well targeted and begin as early as during pregnancy and early infancy, such as prenatal home visitations and early childhood development programs, can induce sizable improvements in children's life chances and offending behaviors. The evidence provided here points to externalizing behavior as an important mediator.

## Notes

[1] The phenomenon applied equally to girls and boys, although girls systematically showed lower overall levels of physical aggression than boys.

[2] Robbins (1966); Huesmann and others (1984); Farrington (1995); Nagin and Tremblay (1999); Huesmann, Eron, and Dubow (2002).

[3] Most previous studies of intergenerational associations in crime have limitations due to small or unrepresentative samples, and/or self-reported crime data. These data sets tend to lack information concerning adult criminality and focus mainly on boys. On the other hand, the few European studies that have access to large samples using criminal register data lack the information concerning individual, family, and neighborhood characteristics necessary to explore the mechanisms driving familial correlations in criminal behavior. Van de Rakt, Nieuwbeerta, and de Graaf (2008) provide a discussion of the strengths and weaknesses of available data sets.

[4] Specifically, they were less at risk if they had inherited a functional polymorphism in the gene encoding for the neurotransmitter-metabolizing enzyme monoamine oxidase A (MAOA).

[5] See, for instance, Currie and Tekin (2012), which is discussed in greater detail later in this chapter.

[6] Becker and Tomes (1979) stress the importance of the investments that parents make in their children. The quality of such decisions and the efficacy of these investments, however, may depend on "good" parenting practices (Mayer 1997; Duncan and others 2005; Akee and others 2010; Björklund, Lindahl, and Lindquist 2010) or on family culture and norms (Becker and Tomes 1979; Yeung, Duncan, and Hill 2000; Björklund, Lindahl, and Lindquist 2010). Parenting styles and family culture might therefore be included in the list of potential mechanisms that affect the degree of transmission of important characteristics across generations. Chapter 5 discusses the findings of Akee and others (2010), which provides evidence that changes in parenting mediate some of the effects of unearned income on juvenile delinquency.

[7] In their regressions, the authors account for whatever sorting takes place between the biological and adoptive parent because the characteristics of both types of parents are observed.

[8] Ideally, information on the criminal histories of mothers would also figure in the analysis. However, the criminology and economic literatures both find that the correlation between the criminal histories of father and child is much stronger and more stable. One possible explanation is that the mother-child relationship is less precisely estimated because of the much lower incidence of criminality among mothers.

[9] The *intensive margin* refers to the degree (intensity) to which an event occurs; in this case, the number of offenses/arrests. The *extensive margin* is defined as the margin of action or inaction, without regard for the intensity of that action, in this case whether an individual commits or does not commit a crime.

[10] Furthermore, large sample twin studies have recently shown that genetic influences are particularly strong for criminal careers that are characterized by an early onset and are persistent over the life cycle (Arsenault and others 2003; Moffitt 2005; Viding and McCrory 2012).

[11] See Almond (2006) and Almond and Currie (2011) for reviews of the evidence concerning the "fetal origins" hypothesis.

[12] See, for instance, Moffitt and Mednick (1988); Bock and Goode (2008); and Raine (1997).

[13] Cadoret and others (1985); Cadoret, Troughton, and O'Gormon (1987); Loehlin (2005); Cesarini, Dawes, and others (2009); Cesarini, Johannesson, and others (2009); Reuter and others (2011).

[14] The 35-year span of their data also allows the authors to address issues of reporting and measurement error.

[15] For meta-analyses of family-based crime prevention, see Piquero and others (2008); Farrington and Welsh (2007); and Bernazzani and Tremblay (2006).

[16] The Blueprints mission is to identify evidence-based prevention and intervention programs that are effective in reducing antisocial behavior and promoting a healthy course of youth development. The Blueprint has strict criteria for an intervention to be identified as a model program:

- Intervention specificity: The program description clearly identifies the outcome the program is designed to change, the specific risk and/or protective factors targeted to produce this change in outcome, the population for which it is intended, and how the components of the intervention work to produce this change.

- Evaluation quality: The evaluation trials produce valid and reliable findings. This requires a minimum of one high-quality, randomized control trial or two high-quality, quasi-experimental evaluations.

- Intervention impact: The preponderance of evidence from the high-quality evaluations indicates significant positive change in intended outcomes that can be attributed to the program. There is no evidence of harmful effects.

- Positive intervention impact: This is sustained for at least 12 months after the program intervention ends.

- Dissemination readiness: The program is available for dissemination and has the necessary organizational capability, manuals, training, technical assistance, and other support required for implementation with fidelity in communities and public service systems.

[17] The original formulation of this program was based in large part on Urie Bronfenbrenner's (1979) theory of human ecology. Human ecology theory emphasizes the importance of social contexts as

influences on human development. Parents' care of their infants, from this perspective, is influenced by characteristics of their families, social networks, neighborhoods, communities, and cultures, and interrelations among these structures.

[18] This report documents a number of other interventions for which effect sizes are larger among more vulnerable participants. See, for instance, the effects of in situ dwelling upgrades in Mexico and El Salvador (reported by Galiani and others 2013, and discussed in chapter 6), and of the Brazilian conditional cash transfer (reported by Chioda, De Mello, and Soares 2016, and discussed in chapter 5).

[19] Because the assignment of transportation vouchers only (treatment arm 2) had no effect, Olds and others (1998) de facto group the first two arms into one control group, focusing their analyses on comparisons between this "aggregate" control group and treatment arms 3 and 4.

[20] People adjudicated In Need of Supervision (PINS) are records that result from incorrigible behavior, such as recurrent truancy or destroying parents' property.

[21] See Olds and others (1986, 1994, 1997), in addition to the discussion in the previous section.

[22] Of course, the success and effectiveness of such programs hinges on the human capital of those delivering it.

[23] It should be noted that the relationship is not perfect: not all early onsetters mature into persistent offenders.

[24] The Perry program is not alone in having effects on long-term offending. A number of other early interventions have also exhibited long-term reductions in crime. For instance, like Perry, the Chicago Child Parent Center program included a half-day preschool component at ages 3 and 4. By matching treated children in comparison with children based on age of kindergarten entry, eligibility for and participation in government-funded programs, neighborhood characteristics, and family poverty, Reynolds and others (2001) show that arrests by age 18 declined by 32 percent in the program group relative to the matched control group (from 0.25 to 0.17). To evaluate the long-term effects of Head Start, a large-scale early childhood development program in the United States that targets children from low-income families, Garces, Thomas, and Currie (2002) compare the outcomes at age 23–25 of participants to those of siblings who did not participate. They find that Head Start reduces the probability of being charged with a crime by about 12 percentage points among blacks, with no effect on whites (although Deming 2009 finds no effect using the same empirical strategy but a different data set). Carneiro and Ginja (2014) exploit the fact that eligibility for Head Start depends on family income and family structure to adopt a regression discontinuity design in their evaluation. They estimate that participation in Head Start at ages 3–5 significantly reduces the likelihood that a 16- to 17-year-old will be sentenced for a crime (based on self-reports) by 31 percentage points, which is qualitatively consistent with Garces, Thomas, and Currie (2002).

[25] Even allowing for measurement error, it is very unlikely that the residual variation can be entirely explained by it (Heckman and Kautz 2012).

[26] While cognitive ability and personality traits may be correlated, the correlation is not very strong, and each set of traits has independent predictive power in explaining each outcome.

[27] The 1973 edition of the classic 1916 text includes reprints of many of Binet's articles on testing.

[28] Personal behavior is a weighted average of "absences and truancies," "lying and cheating," "stealing," and "swears or uses obscene words," as measured by teachers during the elementary school years.

[29] In their 40-year follow-up, Belfield and others (2006) conduct a detailed cost-benefit analysis of the Perry Preschool Program and conclude that every dollar invested in the program repaid

taxpayers nearly 13-fold ($12.90). The bulk of this return is accounted for by the reductions in male criminality, they found.

[30] Barnett and others (2006); Barnett (2008); Bodrova and Leong (2001, 2007); Lillard and Else-Quest (2006); Diamond and others (2007).

[31] See Uylings (2006) and Rutter (2007) for reviews.

[32] See, for instance, Roberts and Mroczek (2008).

[33] An alternative explanation as to why these interventions do not yield the same crime reduction as the Perry program is that parents (or other family members) in the Abecedarion and IHDP households are already providing the same type of care at home that the programs are meant to deliver. In that event, there is little scope for intervention to improve outcomes, highlighting the importance of identifying and targeting households where such care is less likely to be provided in the absence of an intervention.

# References

Abel, E. L., and R. J. Sokol. 1987. "Incidence of Fetal Alcohol Syndrome and Economic Impact of FAS-Related Anomalies." *Drug and Alcohol Dependence* 19: 51–70.

Agnew, R. 1985. "A Revised Strain Theory of Delinquency." *Social Forces* 64: 151–67.

———. 1992. "Foundation for a General Strain Theory of Crime and Delinquency." *Criminology* 30: 47–87.

Akee, Randall K. Q., William E. Copeland, Gordon Keeler, Adrian Angold, and E. Jane Costello. 2010. "Parent's Incomes and Children's Outcomes: A Quasi-Experiment with Casinos on American Indian Reservations." *American Economics Journal: Applied Economics* 2 (1): 86–115.

Alink, L. R. A., J. Mesman, J. Van Zeijil, M. N. Stolk, F. Juffer, H. M. Koot, M. J. Bakermans-Kranenburg, and M. N. Van IJzendoorn. 2006. "The Early Childhood Aggression Curve: Development of Physical Aggression in 10- to 50-Month-Old Children." *Child Development* 77 (4): 954–66.

Almond, Douglas. 2006. "Is the 1918 Influenza Pandemic Over? Long-Term Effects of *In Utero* Influenza Exposure in the Post-1940 U.S. Population." *Journal of Political Economy* 114 (August): 672–712.

Almond, Douglas, and Janet Currie. 2011. "Human Capital Development before Age 5." Chapter 15 in *Handbook of Labor Economics*, Volume 4B, edited by Orley Ashenfelter and David Card, 1315–1486. Amsterdam: North Holland.

Arsenault, L., T. E. Moffitt, A. Caspi, A. Taylor, F. V. Rijsdijk, S. R. Jaffee, J. C. Ablow, and J. R. Measelle. 2003. "Strong Genetic Effects on Cross-Situational Antisocial Behaviour among 5-Year-Old Children According to Mothers, Teachers, Examiner-Observers, and Twins' Self-Reports." *Journal of Child Psychology and Psychiatry* 44: 832–48.

Barnett, W. S. 1996. *Lives in the Balance: Benefit-Cost Analysis of the Perry Preschool Program through Age 27*. Monographs of the High/Scope Educational Research Foundation. Ypsilanti, MI: High/Scope Press.

———. 2008. *Preschool Education and Its Lasting Effects: Research and Policy Implications*. Boulder, CO and Tempe, AZ: Education and the Public Interest Center and Education Policy Research Unit.

Barnett, W. S., C. Belfield, M. Nores, and L. Schweinhart. 2006. "The High/Scope Perry Preschool Program: Cost-Benefit Analysis Using Data from the Age 40." *Journal of Human Resources* 16 (1): 162–90.

Barnett, W. S., and L. N. Masse. 2007. "Early Childhood Program Design and Economic Returns: Comparative Benefit-Cost Analysis of the Abecedarian Program and Policy Implications." *Economics of Education Review* 26: 113–25.

Barros, R., P. Olinto, N. Schady, M. Carvalho, and S. Franco. 2012. "The Impact of Access to Free Childcare on Women's Labor Market Outcomes: Evidence from a Randomized Trial in Low-income Neighborhoods of Rio de Janeiro." Working paper.

Beaver, Kevin M., Matt DeLisib, Michael G. Vaughnc, and J. C. Barnesa. 2009. "Monoamine Oxidase A Genotype Is Associated with Gang Membership and Weapon Use." *Comprehensive Psychiatry*. http://onlinelibrary.wiley.com/doi/10.1111/j.1469-7610.2010.02327.x/full.

Becker, Gary S. 1968. "Crime and Punishment: An Economic Approach." *Journal of Political Economy* 76 (2): 169–217.

Becker, Gary S., and Nigel Tomes. 1979. "An Equilibrium Theory of the Distribution of Income and Intergenerational Mobility." *Journal of Political Economy* 87 (December): 1153–89.

Belfield, Clive R., Milagros Nores, Steve Barnett, and Lawrence Schweinhart. 2006. "The High /Scope Perry Preschool Program: Cost-Benefit Analysis Using Data from the Age-40 Follow-Up." *Journal of Human Resources* 41 (1): 162–90.

Bernazzani, Odette, and Richard E. Tremblay. 2006. "Early Parent Training." In *Preventing Crime: What Works for Children, Offenders, Victims, and Places*, edited by Brandon C. Welsh and David P. Farrington. Dordrecht: Springer.

Bierman, Karen L., John D. Coie, Kenneth A. Dodge, Mark T. Greenberg, John E. Lochman, Robert J. McMahon, Ellen E. Pinderhughes, and Conduct Problems Prevention Research Group. 2010. "The Effects of a Multiyear Universal Social-Emotional Learning Program: The Role of Student and School Characteristics." *Journal of Consulting and Clinical Psychology* 78 (2): 156–68.

Binet, A., and T. Simon. 1916. *The Development of Intelligence in Children*. Baltimore: Williams & Wilkins. Reprinted 1973; New York: Arno Press.

Björklund, Anders, Lena Lindahl, and Matthew Lindquist. 2010. "What More Than Parental Income, Education and Occupation? An Exploration of What Swedish Siblings Get from Their Parents." *B.E. Journal of Economic Analysis & Policy* 10 (1): Article 102. http://www.umass.edu/preferen/You%20Must%20Read%20This/Bjorklund.pdf.

Bock, Gregory R., and Jamie A. Goode, eds. 2008. *Genetics of Criminal and Antisocial Behavior*. Chichester, "U.K.:" John Wiley & Sons.

Bodrova, E., and D. J. Leong. 2001. *The Tools of the Mind Project: A Case Study of Implementing the Vygotskian Approach in American Early Childhood and Primary Classrooms*. Geneva: International Bureau of Education, UNESCO. http://www.toolsofthemind.org/philosophy /scholarly-publications/.

———. 2007. *Tools of the Mind: The Vygotskian Approach to Early Childhood Education*, 2nd ed. Columbus, OH: Merrill / Prentice Hall.

Broidy, Lisa M., Richard E. Tremblay, Bobby Brame, David Fergusson, John L. Horwood, Robert Laird, Terrie E. Moffitt, Daniel S. Nagin, John E. Bates, Kenneth A. Dodge, Rolf Loeber, Donald R. Lynam, Gregory S. Pettit, and Frank Vitaro. 2003. "Developmental Trajectories of Childhood Disruptive Behaviors and Adolescent Delinquency: A Six-Site, Cross-National Study." *Developmental Psychology* 39 (2): 222–45.

Bronfenbrenner, Urie. 1979. *The Ecology of Human Development: Experiments by Nature and Design*. Cambridge, MA: Harvard University Press.

Cadoret, R. J., T. O'Gorman, E. Troughton, and E. Heywood. 1985. "Alcoholism and Antisocial Personality: Interrelationships, Genetic and Environmental Factors. *Archives of General Psychiatry* 42: 161–67.

Cadoret, R. J., E. Troughton, and T. O'Gorman. 1987. "Genetic and Environmental Factors in Alcohol Abuse and Antisocial Personality." *Journal of Studies on Alcohol* 48:1–8.

Carneiro, Pedro, and David Evans. 2013. "The Impact of Formal Child Care Attendance in Rio de Janeiro on Child Development and Maternal Outcomes." Working paper.

Carneiro, Pedro, and Rita Ginja. 2014. "Long-Term Impacts of Compensatory Preschool on Health and Behavior: Evidence from Head Start." *American Economic Journal: Economic Policy* 6 (4): 135–73.

Case, Anne, and Lawrence Katz. 1991. "The Company You Keep: The Effects of Family and Neighborhood on Disadvantaged Youths." NBER Working Paper 3705, National Bureau of Economic Research, Cambridge, MA.

Cesarini D., C. T. Dawes, M. Johannesson, P. Lichtenstein, and B. Wallace. 2009. "Genetic Variation in Preferences for Giving and Risk-Taking." *Quarterly Journal of Economics* 124: 809–42.

Cesarini D., M. Johannesson, P. Lichtenstein, and B. Wallace. 2009. "Heritability of Overconfidence." *Journal of the European Economic Association* 7 (2–3): 617–27.

Chetty, Raj, John N. Friedman, Emmanuel Saez, Diane Whitmore Schanzenbach, and Danny Yagan. 2011. " How Does Your Kindergarten Classroom Affect Your Earnings? Evidence from Project Star." Working Paper, Harvard Kennedy School.

Chioda, Laura, João De Mello, and Rodrigo Soares. 2016. "Spillovers from Conditional Cash Transfer Programs: Bolsa Família and Crime in Urban Brazil." *Economics of Education* 54 (October): 306–20.

Cicchetti, D., and F. A. Rogosch. 2001. "Diverse Patterns of Neuroendocrine Activity in Maltreated Children." *Development and Psychopathology* 13: 677–94.

Claussen, A. H., and P. M. Crittenden. 1991. "Physical and Psychological Maltreatment: Relations among Types of Maltreatment." *Child Abuse and Neglect* 15: 5–18.

Cohen, Mark A., Roland T. Rust, Sara Steen, and Simon T. Tidd. 2004. "Willingness to Pay for Crime Control Programs." *Criminology* 42 (1): 89–110.

Conti, Gabriella, James Heckman, Seong Moon, and Rodrigo Pinto. 2013. "Long-Term Health Effects of Early Childhood Interventions." Working paper.

Corman, Hope, and Naci Mocan. 2005. "Carrots, Sticks, and Broken Windows." *Journal of Law and Economics* 48 (1, April): 235–66.

Cunha, Flavio, and James J. Heckman. 2008. "Formulating, Identifying and Estimating the Technology of Cognitive and Noncognitive Skill Formation." *Journal of Human Resources* 43 (4): 738–82.

Cunha, Flavio, James J. Heckman, Lance J. Lochner, and Dimitriy V. Masterov. 2006. "Interpreting the Evidence on Life Cycle Skill Formation." Chapter 12 in *Handbook of the Economics of Education*, edited by E. Hanushek and F. Welch, 697–812. Amsterdam: North Holland.

Cunha, Flavio, James J. Heckman, and Susanne M. Schennach. 2010. "Estimating the Technology of Cognitive and Noncognitive Skill Formation." *Econometrica* 78 (3): 883–931.

Currie, Janet. 2009. "Healthy, Wealthy, and Wise: Socioeconomic Status, Poor Health in Childhood, and Human Capital Development." *Journal of Economic Literature* 47 (1, March): 87–122.

Currie, Janet, and Erdal Tekin. 2012. "Understanding the Cycle: Childhood Maltreatment and Future Crime." *Journal of Human Resources* 47 (2): 509–49.

Deblinger, E., S. V. McLeer, M. S. Atkins, D. Ralphe, and E. Foa. 1989. "Post-Traumatic Stress in Sexually Abused, Physically Abused, and Nonabused Children." *Child Abuse & Neglect* 13 (3): 403–08.

Dee, Thomas S., and Martin R. West. 2011. "The Non-Cognitive Returns to Class Size." *Educational Evaluation and Policy Analysis* 33 (1): 23–46.

Deming, David. 2009. "Early Childhood Intervention and Life-Cycle Skill Development: Evidence from Head Start." *American Economic Journal: Applied Economics* 1 (3): 111–34.

Diamond, Adele, W. Steven Barnett, Jessica Thomas, and Sarah Munro. 2007. "Preschool Program Improves Cognitive Control." *Science* 317 (1387, November 30): 1387–88. http://thesciencenetwork.org/docs/BrainsRUs/Education%20Forum_Diamond.pdf.

Diamond, A., and K. Lee. 2011. "Interventions Shown to Aid Executive Function Development in Children 4 to 12 Years Old." *Science* 333 (6045): 959–64.

Dionne, Ginette, Richard Tremblay, Michel Boivin, David Laplante, and Daniel Perusse. 2003. "Physical Aggression and Expressive Vocabulary in 19-Month-Old Twins." *Developmental Psychology* 39 (2): 261–73.

Donohue, John J., and Steven D. Levitt. 2001. "The Impact of Legalized Abortion on Crime." *Quarterly Journal of Economics* 116 (2): 379–420. http://qje.oxfordjournals.org /content/116/2/379.short.

Duggan, Mark. 2001. "More Guns, More Crime." *Journal of Political Economy* 109 (5): 1086–1114.

Duncan, Greg J., Ariel Kalil, Susan E. Mayer, Robin Tepper, and Monique R. Payne. 2005. "The Apple Does Not Fall Far from the Tree." In *Unequal Chances: Family Background and Economic Success*, edited by Samuel Bowles, Herbert Gintis, and Melissa Osborne Groves, 23–79. Princeton, NJ: Princeton University Press.

Durlak, Joseph A., Roger P. Weissberg, Allison B. Dymnicki, Rebecca D. Taylor, and Kriston B. Schellinger. 2011. "The Impact of Enhancing Students' Social and Emotional Learning: A Meta-Analysis of School-Based Universal Interventions." *Child Development Special Issue: Raising Healthy Children* 82 (1): 405–32.

Famy, Chris, Ann P. Streissguth, and Alan S. Unis. 1998. "Mental Illness in Adults with Fetal Alcohol Syndrome or Fetal Alcohol Effects." *American Journal of Psychiatry* 155 (4): 552–4.

Farrington, David P. 1995. "The Development of Offending and Antisocial Behaviour from Childhood: Key Findings from the Cambridge Study in Delinquent Development." *Journal of Child Psychology and Psychiatry* 36 (6): 929–64.

Farrington, David P., Darrick Jolliffe, Rolf Loeber, Magda Stouthamer-Loeber, and Larry M. Kalb. 2001. "The Concentration of Offenders in Families, and Family Criminality in the Prediction of Boys' Delinquency." *Journal of Adolescence* 24: 579–96.

Farrington, D. P., R. Loeber, M. Stouthamer-Loeber, W. B. Van Kammen, and Laura Schmidt. 1996. "Self-Reported Delinquency and a Combined Delinquency Scale Based on Boys, Mothers, and Teachers: Concurrent and Predictive Validity for African Americans and Caucasians." *Criminology* 34 (4): 493–517.

Farrington, David P., and Brandon C. Welsh. 2007. *Saving Children from a Life of Crime: Early Risk Factors and Effective Interventions*. New York: Oxford University Press.

Feigenbaum, James J., and Christopher Muller. 2015. "Lead Exposure and Violent Crime in the Early Twentieth Century." *Explorations in Economic History* 62 (October): 51–86.

Galiani, Sebastian, Paul Gertler, Ryan Cooper, Sebastian Martinez, Adam Ross, and Raimundo Undurraga. 2013. "Shelter from the Storm: Upgrading Housing Infrastructure in Latin American Slums." NBER Working Paper 19322, National Bureau of Economic Research, Cambridge, MA.

Garces, Eliana, Duncan Thomas, and Janet Currie. 2002. "Longer-Term Effects of Head Start." *American Economic Review* 92 (4): 999–1012.

Garland, R. J., and M. J. Dougher. 1990. "The Abused/Abuser Hypothesis of Child Sexual Abuse: A Critical Review of Theory and Research." In *Pedophilia: Biosocial Dimensions*, edited by J. Feierman, 488–509., New York: Springer-Verlag.

Gertler, Paul, James Heckman, Rodrigo Pinto, Arianna Zanolini, Christel Vermeersch, Susan Walker, Susan M. Chang, and Sally Grantham-McGregor. 2013. "Labor Market Returns to Early Childhood Stimulation: A 20-Year Follow-Up to an Experimental Intervention in Jamaica." NBER Working Paper 19185, National Bureau of Economic Research, Cambridge, MA.

———. 2014. "Labor Market Returns to an Early Childhood Stimulation Intervention in Jamaica." *Science* 344 (6187): 998–1001.

Glueck, Sheldon, and Eleanor Glueck. 1950. *Unraveling Juvenile Delinquency*. New York: Commonwealth Fund.

Grogger, Jeff, and M. Willis. 2000. "*The Emergence of Crack Cocaine and the Rise in Urban Crime Rates.*" *Review of Economics and Statistics* 82 (4): 519–29.

Hanushek, Eric, and Ludger Woessmann. 2008. "The Role of Cognitive Skills in Economic Development." *Journal of Economic Literature* 46 (3): 607–68.

Heckman, James J., and Tim Kautz. 2012. "Hard Evidence on Soft Skills." *Labour Economics* 19 (4): 451–64.

Heckman, James J., Seong Hyeok Moon, Rodrigo Pinto, Peter A. Savelyev, and Adam Q. Yavitz. 2010a. "Analyzing Social Experiments as Implemented: A Reexamination of the Evidence from the HighScope Perry Preschool Program." *Quantitative Economics* 1 (1): 1–46.

———. 2010b. "The Rate of Return to the HighScope Perry Preschool Program." *Journal of Public Economics* 94(1–2): 114–28.

Heckman, James, Rodrigo Pinto, and Peter Savelyev. 2013. "Understanding the Mechanisms through Which an Influential Early Childhood Program Boosted Adult Outcomes." *American Economic Review* 103 (6): 2052–86.

Heckman, James J., Jora Stixrud, and Sergio Urzua. 2006. "The Effects of Cognitive and Noncognitive Abilities on Labor Market Outcomes and Social Behavio.," *Journal of Labor Economics* 24 (3): 411–82.

Hirschi, Travis. 1969. *Causes of Delinquency.*, Berkeley: University of California Press.

Hjalmarsson, Randi, and Matthew J. Lindquist. 2012. "Like Godfather, Like Son: Exploring the Intergenerational Nature of Crime." *Journal of Human Resources* 47 (2): 550–82.

———. 2013. "The Origins of Intergenerational Associations in Crime: Lessons from Swedish Ddoption Data." *Labour Economics* 20 (C): 68–81.

Hu, H., M. M. Téllez-Rojo, D. Bellinger, D. Smith, A. S. Ettinger, H. Lamadrid-Figueroa, Joel Schwartz, Lourdes Schnaas, Adriana Mercado-García, and Mauricio Hernández-Avila. 2006. "Fetal Lead Exposure at Each Stage of Pregnancy as a Predictor of Infant Mental Development." *Environmental Health Perspectives* 114 (11): 1730–35.

Huesmann, L. Rowell, Leonard D. Eron, and Eric F. Dubow. 2002. "Childhood Predictors of Adult Criminality: Are All Risk Factors Reflected in Childhood Aggressiveness?" *Criminal Behaviour and Mental Health* 12: 185–208.

Huesmann, L. Rowell, Leonard D. Eron, Monroe M. Lefkowitz, and Leopold O. Walder. 1984. "The Stability of Aggression over Time and Generations." *Developmental Psychology* 20: 1120–34.

Jacob, Brian A., and Lars Lefgren. 2003. "Are Idle Hands the Devil's Workshop? Incapacitation, Concentration, and Juvenile Crime." *American Economic Review* 93 (5): 1560–77.

Karoly, Lynn, M. Rebecca Kilburn, and Jill S. Cannon. 2005. *Early Childhood Intervention: Proven Results, Future Promise.* RAND Monograph Series. Santa Monica, CA: RAND Corp.

Killias, Martin, Santiago Redondo, and Jerzy Sarnecki. 2012. "European Perspectives." In *Persisters and Desisters in Crime from Adolescence into Adulthood: Explanation, Prevention, and Punishment*, edited by Rolf Loeber, Machteld Hoeve, N. Wim Slot, and Peter H. van der Laan. Farnam, U.K.: Ashgate Publishing.

Kitzman, H., D. L. Olds, C. R. Henderson Jr., C. Hanks, R. Cole, R. Tatelbaum, K. M. McConnochie, K. Sidora, D. W. Luckey, D. Shaver, K. Engelhardt, D. James, and K. Barnard. 1997. "Effect of Prenatal and Infancy Home Visitation by Nurses on Pregnancy Outcomes, Childhood Injuries, and Repeated Childbearing. A Randomized Controlled Trial." *JAMA (Journal of the American Medical Association)* 278 (8): 644–52.

Knudsen, Eric I., James J. Heckman, Judy L. Cameron, and Jack P. Shonkoff. 2006. "Economic, Neurobiological, and Behavioral Perspectives on Building America's Future Workforce." NBER Working Paper 12298, National Bureau of Economic Research, Cambridge, MA.

Kokko, K., and L. Pulkkinen. 2000. "Aggression in Childhood and Long-Term Unemployment in Adulthood: A Cycle of Maladaptation and Some Protective Factors." *Developmental Psychology* 36: 463–72.

Larson, C. P. 1980. "Efficacy of Prenatal and Postpartum Home Visits on Child Health and Development." *Pediatrics* 66: 191–97.

Lillard, Angeline, and Nicole Else-Quest. 2006. "The Early Years: Evaluating Montessori Education." *Science* 313 (5795): 1893–97.

Lochner, Lance. 2010. "Education Policy and Crime." NBER Working Paper 15894, National Bureau of Economic Research, Cambridge, MA.

Lochner, Lance, and Enrico Moretti. 2004. "The Effect of Education on Crime: Evidence from Prison Inmates, Arrests, and Self-Reports." *American Economic Review* 94 (1): 155–89.

Loehlin, J. C. 2005. "Resemblance in Personality and Attitudes between Parents and Their Children: Genetic and Environmental Contributions." In *Unequal Chances: Family Background and Economic Success*, edited by S. Bowles and M. Osbourne. New York: Russell Sage Foundation Press.

Mayer, Susan E. 1997. *What Money Can't Buy: Family Income and Children's Life Chances* Cambridge, MA: Harvard University Press.

McCord, J., C. S. Widom, and N. A. Crowell, eds. 2001. *Juvenile Crime, Juvenile Justice: Panel on Juvenile Crime—Prevention, Treatment, and Control.* Washington, DC: National Academy Press.

Mednick, S. A., W. F. Gabrielli Jr., and B. Hutchings. 1984. "Genetic Influences in Criminal Convictions: Evidence from an Adoption Cohort." *Science* 224 (4651): 891–94.

Mocan, Naci, and Erdal Tekin. 2006. "Ugly Criminals." NBER Working Paper 12019, National Bureau of Economic Research, Cambridge, MA.

Moffitt, Terrie E. 1990. "The Neuropsychology of Delinquency: A Critical Review of Theory and Research." In *Crime and Justice* Volume 12, edited by Michael H. Tonry, 99–169. Chicago: University of Chicago Press.

———. 1993, "Adolescence-Limited and Life-Course Persistent Antisocial Behavior: A Developmental Taxonomy." *Psychological Review* 100: 674–701.

———. 2005. "The New Look of Behavioral Genetics in Developmental Psychopathology: Gene-Environment Interplay in Antisocial Behaviors." *Psychological Bulletin* 131 (4): 533–54.

Moffitt, T. E., and S. A. Mednick, eds. 1988. *Biological Contributions to Crime Causation.* Dordrecht: Martinus-Nijhoff Press.

Moffitt, Terrie E., Stephen Ross, and Adrian Raine. 2010. "Crime and Biology." In *Crime and Public Policy*, 2nd edition, edited by J. Q. Wilson and J. Petersilia. Oxford: Oxford University Press.

Murata, K., P. Weihe, E. Budtz-Jorgensen, P. J. Jorgensen, and P. Grandjean. 2004. "Delayed Brainstem Auditory Evoked Potential Latencies in 14-Year-Old Children Exposed to Methylmercury." *Journal of Pediatrics* 144 (2): 177–83.

Nagin, Daniel, and Richard E. Tremblay. 1999. "Trajectories of Boys' Physical Aggression, Opposition, and Hyperactivity on the Path to Physically Violent and Nonviolent Juvenile Delinquency." *Child Development* 70 (5): 1181–96.

Nevin, Rick. 2007. "Understanding International Crime Trends: The Legacy of Preschool Lead Eexposure." *Environmental Research* 104: 315–36.

Olds, D. L., J. Eckenrode, C. R. Henderson Jr., H. Kitzman, J. Powers, R. Cole, Kimberly Sidora, P. Morris; L. M. Pettitt; and D. Luckey. 1997. "Long-Term Effects of Home Visitation on Maternal Life Course and Child Abuse and Neglect: Fifteen-Year Follow-Up of a Randomized Trial." JAMA (*Journal of the American Medical Association*) 278 (81): 637–43.

Olds, D. L., C. R. Henderson Jr., H. J. Kitzman, J. J. Eckenrode, R. E. Cole, and R. C. Tatelbaum. 1999. "Prenatal and Infancy Home Visitation by Nurses: Recent Findings." *Future of Children* 9 (1): 44–65.

Olds, D., C. Henderson, R. Tatelbaum, and R. Chamberlin. 1986. "Improving the Delivery of Prenatal Care and Outcomes of Pregnancy: A Randomized Trial of Nurse Home Visitation." *Pediatrics* 77 (1): 16–28.

———. 1994. "Prevention of Intellectual Impairment in Children of Women Who Smoke Cigarettes during Pregnancy." *Pediatrics* 93 (2): 228–33.

Olds, D, L. M. Pettitt, J. Robinson, C. Henderson Jr., J. Eckenrode, H. Kitzman, R. Cole, and J. Powers. 1998. "Reducing Risks for Antisocial Behavior with a Program of Pre-natal and Early Childhood Home Visitation." *Journal of Community Psycholology* 26 (1): 65–83.

Piquero, A. R., D. P. Farrington, and A. Blumstein. 2003. "The Criminal Career Paradigm." In *Crime and Justice: A Review of Research*, edited by M. Tonry, 359–506. Chicago: University of Chicago Press.

Piquero, Alex R., David P. Farrington, Brandon C. Welsh, Lowell Richard Tremblay, and Wesley G. Jennings. 2008. "Effects of Early Family/Parent Training Programs on Antisocial Behavior & Delinquency." https://www.ncjrs.gov/pdffiles1/nij/grants/224989.pdf?origin=publication _detail.

Plomin, R., J. C. DeFries, G. E. McClearn, and P. McGuffin. 2008. *Behavioral Genetics*, 5th ed. New York: Worth.

Raine, Adrian. 1997. *The Psychopathology of Crime: Criminal Behavior as a Clinical Disorder*. San Diego: Academic Press.

———. 2013. *The Anatomy of Violence: The Biological Roots of Crime*. New York: Pantheon Books.

Raine, A., P. Brennan, and S. A. Mednick. 1994. "Birth Complications Combined with Early Maternal Rejection at Age 1 Year Predispose to Violent Crime at Age 18 Years." *Archives of General Psychiatry* 51: 984–88.

Reuter, Martin, Clemens Frenzel, Nora T. Walter, Sebastian Markett, and Christian Montag. 2011. "Investigating the Genetic Basis of Altruism: The Role of the COMT Val158Met Polymorphism." *Social Cognitive Affective Neuroscience* 6 (5): 662–68.

Reyes, Jessica Wolpaw. 2014. "Lead Exposure and Behavior: Effects on Antisocial and Risky Behavior among Children and Adolescents." NBER Working Paper No. 20366, National Bureau of Economic Research, Cambridge, MA.

Reynolds, Arthur J., Judy A. Temple, Dylan L. Robertson, and Emily A. Mann. 2001. "Long-Term Effects of an Early Childhood Intervention on Education Achievement and Juvenile Arrest: A 15-Year Follow-Up of Low-Income Children in Public Schools." *JAMA (Journal of the American Medical Association)* 285 (18): 2339–46.

Roberts, Brent W., and Daniel Mroczek. 2008. "Personality Trait Change in Adulthood." *Current Directions in Psychological Science* 17 (1): 31–35.

Robbins, T. W. 1996. "Dissociating Executive Functions of the Prefrontal Cortex." *Philosophical Transactions of the Royal Society of London* 351: 1463–70.

Rutter, M. 2007. "Gene-Environment Interdependence." *Developmental Science* 10 (1): 12–18.

Sampson, Robert J., and John H. Laub. 1993. *Crime in the Making: Pathways and Turning Points through Life*. Cambridge, MA: Harvard University Press.

———. 1997. "A Life-Course Theory of Cumulative Disadvantage and the Stability of Delinquency." In *Developmental Theories of Crime and Delinquency*, edited by Terence P. Thornberry. New Brunswick, NJ: Transaction.

Schweinhart, L. J., and D. P. Weikart. 1981. "Perry Preschool Effects Nine Years Later: What Do They Mean?" In *Psychosocial Influences in Retarded Performance, Vol. 2, Strategies for Improving Competence*, edited by M. J. Begab, H. C. Haywood, and H. L. Garber. Baltimore: University Park Press.

Segal, Carmit. 2008. "Classroom Behavior." *Journal of Human Resources* 43 (4): 783–814.

Shonkoff, J., and D. Phillips, eds. 2000. *From Neurons to Neighborhoods: The Science of Early Childhood Development*. Washington, DC: National Academy Press.

Tremblay, Richard E. 2004. "Decade of Behavior Distinguished Lecture: Development of Physical Aggression during Infancy." *Infant Mental Health Journal* 25 (5): 399–407.

Tremblay, Richard E., Daniel S. Nagin, Jean R. Séguin, Mark Zoccolillo, Philip D. Zelazo, Michel Boivin, Daniel Pérusse, and Christa Japel. 2004. "Physical Aggression during Early Childhood: Trajectories and Predictors." *Pediatrics* 114 (1): e43–e50.

Uylings, H. B. M. 2006. "Development of the Human Cortex and the Concept of 'Critical' or 'Sensitive' Periods." *Language Learning* 56 (1): 59–90.

Van de Rakt, Marieke, Paul Nieuwbeerta, and Nan Dirk de Graaf. 2008. "Like Father, Like Son: The Relationship between Conviction Trajectories of Fathers and their Sons and Daughters." *British Journal of Criminology* 48 (2): 538–56.

Veltman, M., and K. Browne. 2001. "Three Decades of Child Maltreatment Research." *Trauma, Violence and Abuse* 2: 215–39.

Viding, Essi, and Eamon J. McCrory. 2012. "Genetic and Neurocognitive Contributions to the Development of Psychopathy." *Development and Psychopathology* 24: 969–83.

Vgotsky, Lev. 1986. *Thought and Language*, translated, revised, and edited by A. Kozulin. Cambridge, MA: MIT Press.

Walker, Susan P., Susan M. Chang, Marcos Vera-Hernández, and Sally Grantham-McGregor. 2011. "Early Childhood Stimulation Benefits Adult Competence and Reduces Violent Behavior." *Pediatrics* 127 (5): 849–57.

Walker, Susan P., Theodore D. Wachs, Julie Meeks Gardner, Betsy Lozoff, Gail A. Wasserman, Ernesto Pollitt, and Julie A. Carter. 2007. "Child Development: Risk Factors for Adverse Outcomes in Developing Countries." *Lancet* 369 (9556): 145–57.

Walters, Gary C., and Joan E. Grusec. 1977. *Punishment.* San Francisco: W. H. Freeman.

Weikart, D. P., J. T. Bond, and J. T. McNeil. 1978. *The Ypsilanti Perry Preschool Project: Preschool Years and Longitudinal Results through Fourth Grade.* Ypsilanti, MI: HighScope Press.

Westfelt, L. 2001. "Crime and Punishment in Sweden and Europe: A Study in Comparative Criminology." PhD thesis, Department of Criminology, University of Stockolm.

Widom, Cathy. 1989. "The Cycle of Violence." *Science* 244 (4901): 160–66.

———. 1998. "Childhood Victimization: Early Adversity and Subsequent Psychopathology." In *Adversity, Stress, and Psychopathology*, edited by B. P. Dohrenwend, 81–95. New York: Oxford University Press.

———. 1999. "Posttraumatic Stress Disorder in Abused and Neglected Children Grown Up." *American Journal of Psychiatry* 156 (8): 1223–29.

Williams, J., and R. C. Sickles. 2002. "An Analysis of Crime as Work Model: Evidence from the 1958 Philadelphia Birth Cohort Study." *Journal of Human Resources* 37 (3): 479–509.

Yeung, W. J., G. L. Duncan, and M. S. Hill. 2000. "Putting Fathers Back in the Picture: Parental Activities and Children's Adult Outcomes." *Marriage and Family Review* 29 (2/3): 97–113.

Zingraff, M. T., J. Leiter, K. A. Myers, and M. C. Johnsen. 1993. "Child Maltreatment and Youthful Problem Behavior." *Criminology* 31 (2): 173–202.

# 4
# Youth, Education, and Brain Development

The age-crime profile documented in chapter 2 suggests that criminal offending peaks around adolescence and early adulthood. However, as discussed in chapter 3, research on childhood conduct disorders documents that aggression and antisocial behavior begin long before the age when it is first encoded by criminal records, peaking around age 4 (Tremblay 2004)—in apparent contradiction to the age-crime profile.

Research on the early onset of aggression enhances our understanding of aggression (Tremblay 2004), but also sheds light on the scope for policy during this phase, including the potential of early interventions presented in the previous chapter. Indeed, life-course studies of criminal behavior are careful to specify that early aggression reflects a combination of environmental and biological factors; while it is an important marker of violence later in life, early aggression does not constitute a deterministic prediction of a life of crime. Most children learn how not to be aggressive as they progress through developmental stages, which can take them into adulthood.

However, during the long transition from early aggression to self-control, the potential for serious consequences (to victims, to society, and to the offender) from acting on aggression and antisocial behavior increases with age (figure 4.1).[1] During this progression, the severity of the effects of youth aggression and antisocial behavior begins to be recorded in police records, victimization surveys, and homicide statistics, thereby building the age-crime profile. The peaks of life-course offending and victimization coincide with adolescence and early adulthood, on average (as seen in chapter 2). With the advent of alternative measurement tools (Moffitt 1993), most notably self-reports of deviant behavior, researchers have learned that arrest statistics reflect only the tip of the iceberg in terms of deviance (Hood and Sparks 1970; Klein 1989). Actual rates of illegal and violent behavior soar so high during this period that participation in delinquency appears to be a normal part of adolescence (Elliott, Huizinga, and Menard 1989; Moffitt 1993).

The elevated statistical risks for youth to offend and be victims may be related to the observation that adolescents tend to exhibit very low risk aversion and are less likely to be concerned about danger or consequences, whether in the present or in the future. From a socioeconomic point of view, adolescence and young adulthood are also delicate stages because of the loosening of parental control, the increased influence of peers, and the transition from youth to adult roles, which can involve navigating transitions from school to work. These transitions can be especially difficult for many individuals with low socioeconomic status (SES), who are at higher risk of school interruption. In conjunction with their growing potential to cause physical harm to others (and themselves), these factors combine to generate a perfect storm of vulnerability for this age group.

It is no coincidence that this transitional period is also critical for brain development, particularly for the prefrontal cortex—the locus of executive function—which regulates impulsivity, risk-taking behavior, delayed gratification, and self-control (Raine 2013). Many of the behaviors that are observed among adolescents can be traced to transitions in the brain, which are discussed in this chapter. Is this all bad news? The critical stages of brain development during youth and early adulthood— phases that are also accompanied by social and economic transition—certainly expose individuals to vulnerability. But they also are characterized by high degrees of malleability of executive functions, as well as susceptibility to peers and environmental factors, which policy interventions can be designed to exploit. Hence there is room for optimism regarding the potential for effective policy during these stages of the life-cycle. In other words, some of the features that expose individuals to higher risk may also define effective policy margins (figure 4.1).

This chapter first reviews the evidence on the causal relationship between the quantity and quality of education on criminality. In the short run, there is a trade-off

**FIGURE 4.1:** A model of the supply of criminal offenses, but also a model of crime and violence prevention

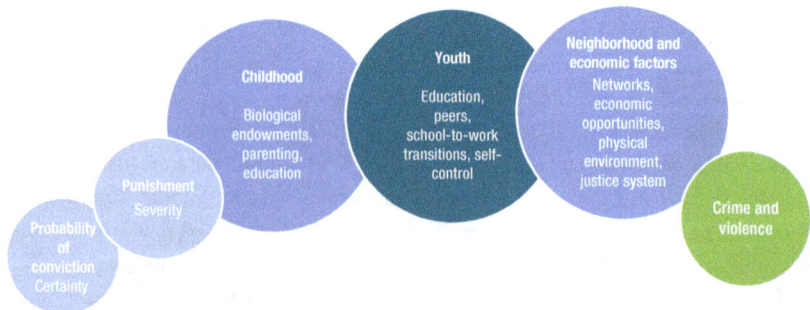

between reductions in violence outside the school and increases in violence within the school because of the increased concentration of youth in one location and the potential conflict that may ensue. However, the long-term effects of additional education point to sizable social benefits, including those from reductions in future offending, which likely far outweigh the immediate (though empirically small) social costs of crime and corrections that result from concentrating youth in school. Taken together with the life-cycle trajectory of offending, the studies reviewed here conclude that educational investments in late adolescence are particularly beneficial and effective in terms of reducing crime. The chapter then explores recent advances in the understanding of the evolution of brain function and structure, and of personality traits that are relevant to offending behavior. A delicate period in the development of executive function is identified, covering adolescence and early adulthood, akin to the critical window of cognitive development in childhood. These findings provide insight into the mechanisms that underlie age-crime trajectories, and into evidence from education studies that improvements in academic achievement are not prerequisites to reductions in aggression and subsequent crime and violence. The findings also provide insight for policy: the malleability of personality traits among youth makes them valuable tools for policy interventions. The third section of this chapter reviews the effectiveness of a number of programs that target psychological factors other than cognitive ability.[2]

## Education and crime

In his study of the interactions between education, attachment to the labor market, and crime, Lochner (2004) emphasizes the role of education as a form of investment in human capital that increases legitimate work opportunities in the future (and thus the opportunity cost of criminality), thereby discouraging participation in crime. If education raises the marginal returns from work above the marginal returns to crime, then human capital investments and schooling should reduce crime. Thus policies that increase schooling (or the efficiency of schooling) should reduce most types of street crime among adults, although certain types of white-collar crime (such as embezzlement and fraud) may increase with education if skills learned in school are sufficiently rewarded.

Education may also teach individuals to be more patient (Becker and Mulligan 1997); patience might discourage crime, since forward-looking individuals place greater weight on any expected future punishment associated with their criminal activities. To the extent that schooling affects time preferences in the hypothesized way, crimes associated with long prison sentences (or other long-term consequences) should decline most. Education may also affect preferences toward risk. If schooling makes individuals more risk averse, it should discourage crimes whose returns and punishment are most uncertain.

Finally, schooling may affect the set of people with whom individuals interact daily in school, at work, or in their neighborhoods. Assuming that peers affect individual behavior and that more educated people interact more with other educated people who are less criminally inclined, then any reductions in crime associated with schooling are likely to be compounded. In most cases, mechanisms related to changes in preferences or to social interactions predict that education is likely to reduce most types of crime among adults.

Empirically, measures of crime are highly negatively correlated with education. Ewert and Wildhagen (2011) report that in 2009, 40 percent of male inmates overall, and 54 percent of those ages 18–24, in the United States had not graduated from high school—a figure that is much higher than in the general population. In saturated models, which account for a rich set of controls, for the United States, Lochner and Moretti (2004) confirm the negative and highly statistically significant effect of schooling on the likelihood of incarceration. This relationship is hardly specific to the United States. Buonanno and Leonida (2009) report that more than 75 percent of convicts in Italy had not completed high school in 2001, while the incarceration rates among male high school dropouts in the United Kingdom was eight times that of males with an education qualification (Machin, Marie, and Vujić 2011).

Carvalho and Soares (2013) use data from a unique survey of drug-selling gangs in Rio de Janeiro's slums (*favelas*) conducted by a Brazilian nongovernmental organization (NGO), Observatório de Favelas, and show that male gang members are on average less educated than men of a similar age also residing in the *favelas*. Gang members are 5 percentage points more likely to be illiterate and 44 percentage points less likely to be attending school. In an interesting symmetry, Carvalho and Soares (2013) document that education is not rewarded with higher earnings within the gang, while experience, displays of bravery, and loyalty are.

As further evidence of the negative correlation between education outcomes and crime, more than 70 percent of the prisoners in the main detention center of Montevideo, Uruguay (ComCar, Complejo Carcelario Santiago Vázquez), which accounts for almost 80 percent of Montevideo's penal population, come from backgrounds characterized by remarkably high social vulnerability, and 92 percent of inmates did not graduate from high school (Munyo and Rossi 2015).

Figure 4.2 contrasts the educational attainment of perpetrators and of the general population in Mexico and indicates a negative correlation between educational attainment and the propensity to offend. Perpetrators tend to have fewer years of schooling than the general population, though most of the difference appears to be accounted for by tertiary education. Surprisingly, perpetrators have kept pace with the level of education of the general population, and, over time, the fraction of offenders who have completed secondary schooling has increased at a slightly faster pace that the general population. Figure 4.2 also indicates that the discrepancy between the general population and perpetrators appears to shrink for more violent crimes. It is important to clarify that the data on Mexican perpetrators do not distinguish between those who have *completed* a given level of education from those who have completed only some schooling within a given level of education. Thus, the data unfortunately classify high school dropouts and graduates in the same way. For instance, the solid blue lines in figure 4.2 refer to the proportion of perpetrators with *some* secondary education, rather than those who have completed secondary education. These are not trivial distinctions; as discussed later in this section, the most sizable reductions in crime appear to be associated with the final year of secondary school: policies that encourage high school completion can be among the most effective in terms of their impacts on crime.

Chioda and Rojas-Alvarado (2014) provide indirect evidence of this proposition for Brazil. Using data on municipal-level homicide rates from 1996 to 2012, they find that a municipality's dropout rate has a large and statistically significant effect on its

**FIGURE 4.2:** Education levels of perpetrators versus the general population, Mexico, 1998–2011

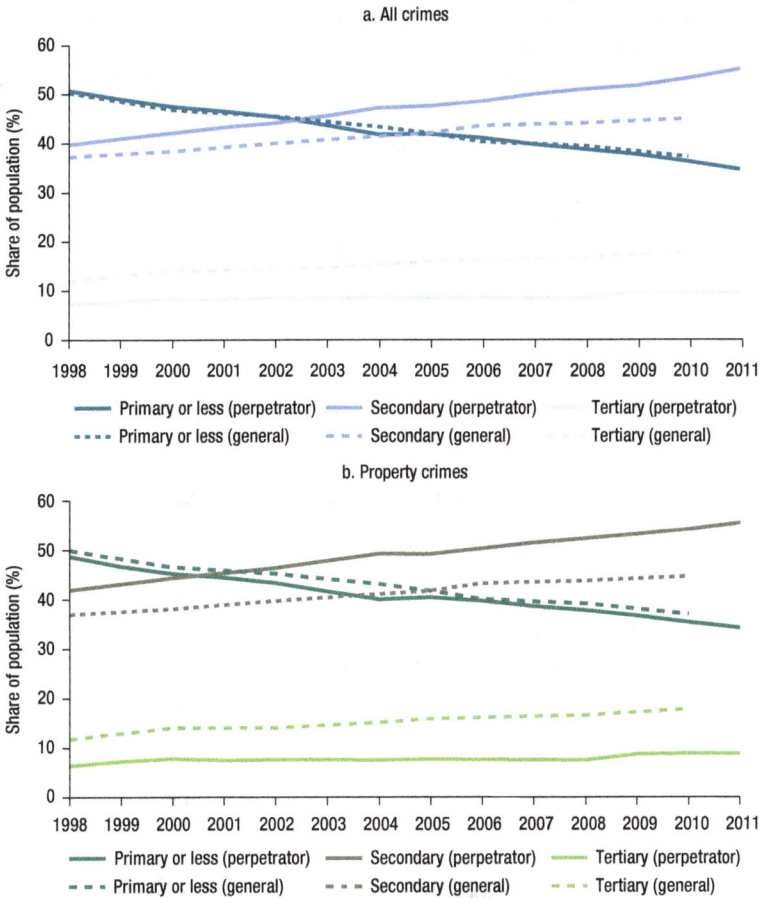

a. All crimes

Primary or less (perpetrator) — Secondary (perpetrator) — Tertiary (perpetrator)
Primary or less (general) - - - Secondary (general) - - - Tertiary (general)

b. Property crimes

Primary or less (perpetrator) — Secondary (perpetrator) — Tertiary (perpetrator)
Primary or less (general) - - - Secondary (general) - - - Tertiary (general)

*(continued on next page)*

**FIGURE 4.2:** Education levels of perpetrators versus the general population, Mexico, 1998–2011 *(continued)*

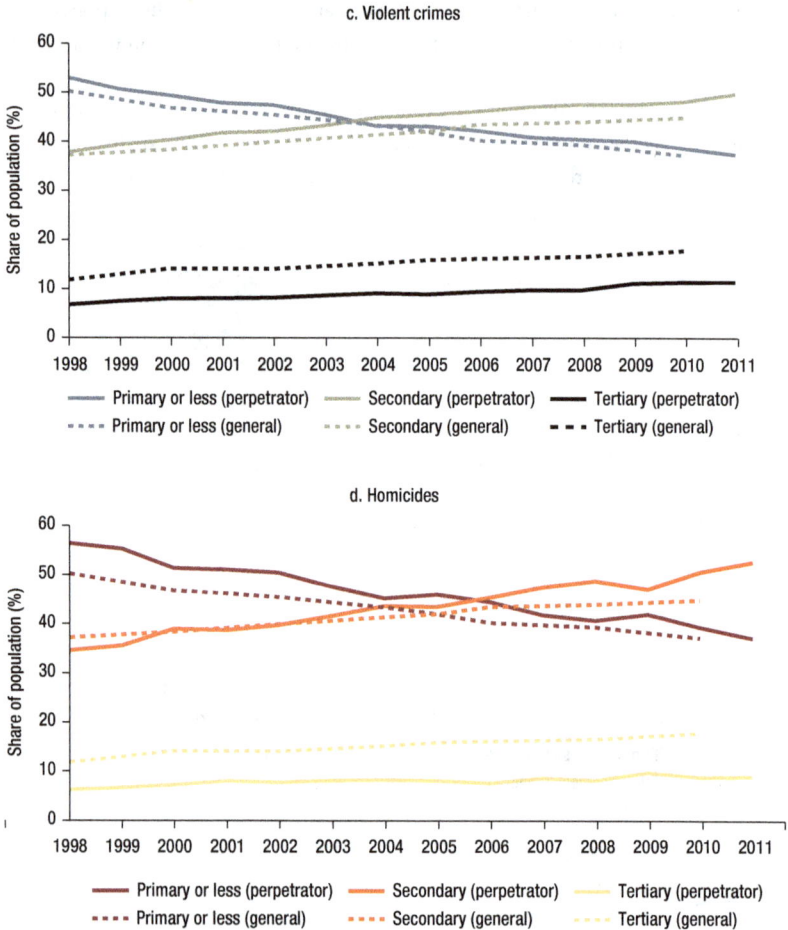

**c. Violent crimes**

Primary or less (perpetrator) — Secondary (perpetrator) — Tertiary (perpetrator)
Primary or less (general) - - - Secondary (general) - - - Tertiary (general)

**d. Homicides**

Primary or less (perpetrator) — Secondary (perpetrator) — Tertiary (perpetrator)
Primary or less (general) - - - Secondary (general) - - - Tertiary (general)

*Source:* Chioda 2014.

homicide rate after controlling for a large number of municipality attributes, such as income, inequality, urbanization, labor market indicators, and demographic structure.[3] The effect is precisely estimated at 0.18; that is, a 1 percentage point increase in the dropout rate is on average associated with 0.18 additional homicides per 100,000 (see red line in figure 4.3). (The average dropout rate is roughly 15 percent across municipalities and years.) Quantile regressions provide some indication as to the composition of the mean effect, and as to which kinds of municipalities are most at risk in terms of dropouts and homicides. For municipalities with similar characteristics, the solid blue line in figure 4.3 maps the effect of dropouts along the percentiles of the homicide rate (the horizontal axis). For municipalities with similar attributes but at comparably low levels of violence, the effect of dropouts is relatively mild. For otherwise comparable municipalities, those below the median level of homicides are subject to an effect of dropouts no greater than 0.05—slightly more than one-quarter of the average effect. However, among comparable municipalities that are otherwise the most violent, a 1 percentage point increase in the dropout rate is associated with 0.35 additional homicides, or close to double the mean effect. Thus among otherwise comparable municipalities, the most violent ones are also at greatest risk of high school students failing to graduate.

Further evidence of the protective benefits of secondary school completion emerges from cross-country, dynamic panel data analyses by Chioda (2014). Dynamic panel data models provide a framework for estimating the correlates of year-to-year changes in the outcome of interest, rather than its level. The data cover 19 countries in Latin America and the Caribbean from 1995 to 2010, recording national homicide rates as well as detailed demographic and socioeconomic characteristics. Unlike Mexico's data set on perpetrators, the education information distinguishes between stages of education that are complete versus incomplete. The estimated coefficients on various measures of education are presented in table 4.1.[4] The second column

**FIGURE 4.3:** Effect of the dropout rate on the quantiles of the homicide rate, Brazilian municipalities, 1998–2012

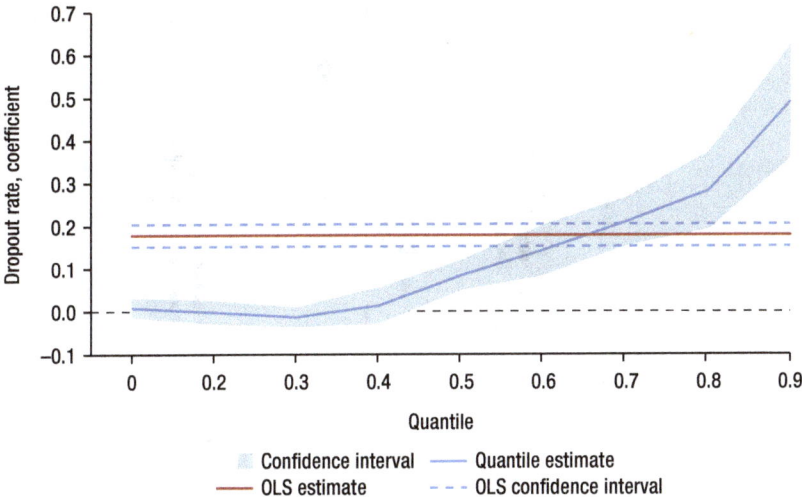

Source: Chioda and Rojas-Alvarado 2014.
Note: The figure presents coefficient estimates from ordinary least squares (OLS) and quantile regressions. Results are weighted by municipality population, and include state, and year fixed effects without clustering.

TABLE 4.1: Marginal effects of education on homicide rates, selected LAC countries, 1995–2010

| | Population education | | | | Only males education | | | |
|---|---|---|---|---|---|---|---|---|
| | Primary and secondary (incomplete) | Primary, secondary and tertiary (incomplete) | Primary and secondary (complete) | Primary, secondary and tertiary (complete) | Primary and secondary (incomplete) | Primary, secondary and tertiary (incomplete) | Primary and secondary (complete) | Primary, secondary and tertiary (complete) |
| Primary education (Population 15-65) | 0.288*** (0.0517) | 0.132 (0.116) | 0.203 (0.341) | 0.0539 (0.437) | 0.301*** (0.0503) | 0.163 (0.109) | 0.0922 (0.303) | 0.0914 (0.305) |
| Secondary education (Population 15-65) | 0.334* (0.158) | -0.0173 (0.233) | -0.553*** (0.162) | -0.499** (0.195) | 0.298* (0.159) | -0.0985 (0.221) | -0.460** (0.185) | -0.457** (0.200) |
| Tertiary education (Population 15-65) | | -1.108* (0.582) | | 0.399 (0.465) | -1.135* (0.551) | | | 0.0270 (0.414) |

Source: Chioda 2014.

Note: The table presents coefficients on education from cross-country, dynamic panel data models. Standard errors are clustered at the country level. The saturated model includes age structure, demographics, urbanization, proxies for quality of institutions, macro environment controls, and others; for more details on the specifications, see chapter 2.

Significance level: * = 10 percent, ** = 5 percent, *** = 1 percent.

reports the results of a specification in which education categories are defined as the proportion of the population with any schooling at all in that category. For instance, "secondary education" measures the fraction of the population with some secondary schooling, whether completed or not. It therefore includes high school graduates as well as dropouts. This specification suggests somewhat surprisingly that having either "some" primary or secondary education carries no protective benefits for the incidence of homicide; only the share of people with "some" tertiary education appears as a protective factor. However, in order to have some tertiary education, one must have completed secondary school. Thus the share of people with "some" tertiary education carries information about the share with completed secondary education; the (large) negative and statistically significant coefficient on tertiary education may reflect the benefits of having a high school credential. The fourth column confirms this intuition. When schooling is defined as the share of the population to have *completed* each level, secondary education emerges as a very protective factor, while the effects of the remaining education measures are imprecisely estimated. Further, the magnitude of the effect is large and indicates that a 2 percentage point increase in the share of high school graduates is associated with 1 fewer homicide per 100,000.

Interestingly, the share of the population that has completed tertiary education does not meaningfully predict homicides, consistent with the hypothesis of diminishing returns to education in reducing violence. Homicide rates are typically quite low among individuals with more than a high school degree, leaving little scope for increases in their ranks to reduce the overall homicide rate. Policies that encourage postsecondary education are thus unlikely to yield much benefit in terms of crime reduction, as also argued by Hjalmarsson and Lochner (2012). When the exercise is repeated controlling only for the educational attainment of males, who are potentially more relevant for predicting homicides given their disproportionate representation among perpetrators and victims (see chapter 2), the magnitudes and significance of the effects are virtually unchanged.

These results—and their interpretation—warrant caution, however, as they do not necessarily prove that high school completion reduces crime, since factors not included in the regression model (that is, unmeasured characteristics) may explain the negative correlation. For instance, unobserved individual characteristics such as risk aversion or the tendency to be forward-looking are likely related to both schooling and criminal decisions. Those who pursue additional education are also unlikely to pursue crime regardless of their education level. Reverse causality could in principle also explain the negative correlation; in high-violence areas, the returns to education may be lower than in low-violence areas, either because of the elevated risk of injury or death or because economic activity slows down because of the violence, thereby depressing wages. However, recent research that exploits reforms in compulsory schooling laws in England, Wales, Sweden, and the United States offers support for a causal interpretation of the association: extensions in the mandatory schooling-leaving age in these countries resulted in an (expected) increase in educational attainment, but also a reduction in lifetime involvement in crime.[5] For instance, in the context of the United Kingdom, Machin, Marie, and Vujić (2011) document that a 1 percentage point decline in the proportion of individuals with no secondary qualifications causes crime to decline by between 0.85 percent and 1 percent.

## Contemporaneous effects of school attendance

This section considers the short-term effects of school attendance that are likely driven by day-to-day changes in the desire and opportunities to commit crime.

In the short term, schooling can affect crime through three principal channels. First, schools may have an *incapacitation effect*; youth cannot simultaneously be at school and commit crimes, given that criminal opportunities are more abundant outside of school. The magnitude of this effect depends in large part on the ease with which youth can commit crimes outside of school hours. The second channel—the *concentration effect*—can potentially have the opposite effect: schools assemble youth in one location for the day and then release them all at the same time. The high concentration of youth in one place for prolonged periods of time could lead to interpersonal conflict, altercations, and more group-based delinquency. The third channel operates through *incentives*: time in school increases human capital, thus improving employment prospects in the legitimate labor market and raising wages, while rendering crime costlier in the event of apprehension (through lost wages). All else equal, this reduces the incentive to engage in crime while attending school.

Jacob and Lefgren (2003) are interested in crime-related policy recommendations, such as lengthening the school day or school year, and providing after-school activities, which implicitly assume a powerful incapacitation effect. However, as the authors point out, such policies frequently assume that there is no temporal displacement of crime—for example, from school days to weekends—in response to lengthening the school day or school year. These policies also ignore (or assume away) the possibility of countervailing concentration effects.

To evaluate these types of policy proposals, Jacob and Lefgren (2003) examine the impacts on juvenile crime and arrests on day-to-day changes in school attendance generated by teacher "in-service" days; these are days that teachers use for professional development or planning purposes and on which students do not attend school. They exploit in-service days, the timing of which the authors argue is extremely unlikely to be correlated with any factors influencing the level of crime, as an exogenous source of variation in attendance days across 29 large U.S. cities from 1995 to 1999. Their strategy is effectively to compare juvenile crime rates on days when school is not in session (but otherwise would be) to those when it is.

If schooling has an effect on criminality that operates through the incapacitation and concentration channels, an increase in school days might be expected to affect the *composition* of crime. The incapacitation effect could induce declines in property crime (since there is no time to commit property crimes outside of school while in school), while the concentration effect predicts increases in interpersonal violence.

Indeed, this is the pattern that they find: an additional day of school reduces serious juvenile *property* crime by 14 percent, but violent offenses among juveniles rise by 28 percent on school days. This analysis confirms that when adolescents are not provided a structured and/or supervised environment, they are likely to engage in antisocial behavior, as manifested by increased property crime. However, it also suggests that the amount of interaction among youth plays an important role in the level of juvenile violence, highlighting the potentially volatile nature of juvenile interactions and the social nature of juvenile violent crime.

Lastly, they find no evidence that crimes were shifted to days immediately preceding or following school closings, suggesting that the changes in crime on days when school is in session are not mere displacements to other days of crimes that would otherwise have occurred.

Luallen (2006) follows a similar logic, but exploits teacher strikes as the exogenous source of changes in days in school; the timing of strikes is unlikely to be related to those days when crime and violence are expected to be particularly high or particularly low. Using data from Washington state covering 1980 to 2001, Luallen estimates that an extra school day reduces arrests for property crimes by about 29 percent, while increasing arrests for violent crimes by about 32 percent in urban areas. While this pattern of changes in crime is consistent with that found in Jacob and Lefgren (2003), Luallen's (2006) estimate of the effect on property crime is roughly double that of Jacob and Lefgren (2003), while the effect on violent crime is quite similar. In rural and suburban areas, Luallen (2003) finds no significant effects on either violent or property crime arrests; the incapacitation and social interaction effects appear to be particularly strong in urban areas and negligible elsewhere. Finally, because the richness of his data permits it, Luallen also provides details on the characteristics of the offenders. He finds that repeat juvenile offenders cause the majority of the increase in violent crime. In contrast, the decline in property crime is due to reductions in incidents committed by individuals for whom the crime would have been their first offense.

Given the nature of the variation in schooling in these two contexts (in-service days and teacher strikes), the most likely mechanisms underlying the effects identified by Jacob and Lefgren (2003) and Luallen (2006) are incapacitation and social interaction. Their results are not merely academic, since both in-service days and teacher strikes affect the entire student body for a given school or school district—just like the typical education reform—such as extending the school year a few days or weeks. In addition to whatever educational benefits they might deliver, such policy proposals must therefore also weigh the benefits of declines in property crime against the costs of increased interpersonal violence.

In the Chilean context, Berthelon and Kruger (2011) consider the effects of lengthening the school day on crime and security. Specifically, the authors study a nationwide school reform, which extended the length of the school day from a half to a full day and its impact on the (contemporaneous) likelihood that youth engage in risky behaviors, such as juvenile crime and teenage pregnancy. To identify causal effects, they take advantage of the gradual implementation of the full-day school reform (FDS), which generates regional and temporal variations that are plausibly uncorrelated with municipal-level crime rates.

They first confirm that the full-day school reform had the desired effect of increasing students' time spent in school: from 32 to 39 hours per week, on average, or a rise of almost 22 percent. They find that the longer school days reduced crime (as well as teen pregnancy) and that the effects are large: an increase of 20 percentage points in FDS coverage in a municipality lowered juvenile crime rates by between 11 percent and 24 percent, depending on the crime category. For total crime, the same increase in coverage reduced the average total crime rate in the municipality by 19 crimes per 100,000. The largest effects are found for property crime, which declines by 24 crimes per 100,000. These results are consistent with those of Jacob and Lefgren (2003) and Luallen (2006). However, contrary to these two studies, Berthelon and Krueger (2011) find that violent crime declines with longer school days over longer periods of time, yielding 2 fewer violent crimes per 100,000—an 11 percent decline. An important distinction between Berthelon and Krueger (2011) and the analyses of Jacob and Lefgren (2003) and Luallen (2006) is the frequency of their data, and the implied interpretation of the resulting effects. Jacob and Lefgren (2003) and Luallen (2006) observe *daily* changes in crime; their estimates are of truly contemporaneous effects of days in school. In contrast, Berthelon and Krueger (2011) observe crime only at the annual level in their municipalities data set. Their estimates are therefore more medium-term in nature, and therefore less comparable to those of Jacob and Lefgren (2003) and Luallen (2006).

Another policy that might affect time spent in school for a specific subgroup of the population is the extension of the minimum dropout age (MDA). The mandatory school-leaving age is the minimum age at which a student is legally permitted to exit secondary education. This section presents evidence on the contemporaneous effects of such a reform, and focuses on its longer-term effects. Anderson (2014) estimates the effect of changes in such laws over the 1980–2006 period on contemporaneous U.S. county-level arrest rates among affected youth, ages 16 to 18.[6] Anderson's estimates for total arrests indicate that raising the compulsory school-leaving age to 17 significantly reduces age 17 arrests by about 8 percent (5.4 arrests per 1,000 youths) compared to a compulsory school leaving age of 16 or less. Similarly, an age 18 compulsory school-leaving age significantly reduces arrests by 9.7 percent to 11.5 percent at ages 16 to 18. Separating arrests by type of offense, he estimates that compulsory schooling laws significantly reduce both property and violent arrests of 16- to 18-year-olds by 9.9 percent and 22.5 percent, respectively.[7] Overall, the estimates generally suggest that forcing youth to spend an extra year or two in high school significantly reduces their arrest rates. A natural question is whether changes in the MDA reduce crime or merely displace it and, if the latter, what is the magnitude of the trade-off?

In follow-up work, Anderson, Hansen, and Walker (2013) consider the potential unintended consequence of keeping youth from dropping out. Specifically, they consider whether changes in MDAs had the effect of displacing criminal activity and delinquency back into schools. This effect would be analogous in spirit to the concentration and social interactions effects documented by Jacob and Lefgren (2003) and Luallen (2006). However, three differences distinguish their estimated effects relative to the margins studied by the latter two studies. First, the number of students affected by changes in the MDA is much smaller than that affected by teacher strikes or teacher in-service days; only a fraction of the total student population would drop out in the absence of changes to the MDA, whereas all students are affected by days lost to strikes or increases in in-service days. However, the affected youth are at much higher risk of offending than the general population (since they are on the margin of dropping out). Finally, Anderson, Hansen, and Walker (2013) define juvenile crime from the perspective of the victims; thus the data reflect incidents that might not be reported as crimes or result in arrests.

Overall, students reported few changes in their victimization because of an increased in the MDA. No effects were statistically significant for violent behavior or for the likelihood of missing school for fear of bullying or in response to threats. However, changes in the MDA appear to raise the incidence of property crime by 4–6 percentage points, consistent with the hypothesis that property crimes are displaced from the streets to schools in response to extensions of the MDA. However, the null effects on violent behavior and missing school mask important heterogeneity, which emerges when considering the effects for subgroups of the student population that are at elevated risk of victimization and bullying: namely, younger and female students (see box 4.1). The authors show that higher MDAs increase the likelihood that females and younger students report missing school out of concern for their safety (the incidence nearly doubles for girls) and younger students are more likely to report

---

**BOX 4.1:** A promising strategy to address bullying and other unintended consequences of keeping youths from dropping out

Extending schools days or delaying dropping out of at-risk youth may yield unintended consequences such as increased bullying and violence in schools (Anderson, Hansen, and Walker 2013; Jacob and Lefgren 2003). These consequences do not invalidate the benefits of the additional schooling, but call for a more nuanced policy design, such as anti-bullying programs.

The *Olweus Bullying Program* (Olweus 1993, 1994, 1995) is viewed as one of the most consistent and effective school-based interventions to reduce aggressive

*(continued on next page)*

behavior in the United States, and has been labeled as one the "promising" programs by the Blueprints Initiative.[a] The program seeks to reduce bullying in schools using a multifaceted approach, with training for students, teachers, and parents. The program has been shown to be effective and offers curricula for several school grades ranging from late childhood (age 5–11) to early adolescence (12–14) and late adolescence (15–18).

The program seeks to address the problem of bullying by first dispelling myths. For example, bullying does not result from larger class sizes, failure in school, or differences in students' appearances. Instead, bullies are marked by their generally aggressive and antisocial dispositions; this observation has implications for interventions.

At the school level, teachers receive training to better diagnose and monitor bullying behavior. They also are taught how to induce better social skills among their students. In class, students engage in role-playing scenarios and cooperative groups to practice better social interactions. When bullying does occur, either in the classroom or on the playground, teachers have serious discussions with both the bully and victim, and report the problems to the students' parents, who also play an important role in discouraging bullying behavior. It is considered paramount that teachers not allow even minor incidents of bullying behavior to persist.

At the family level, parents receive training on how to identify the signs of aggression and bullying at home and are expected to maintain consistent rules and disciplinary practices to deter their children from aggressive behavior. They learn to identify even minor signs of bullying and aggression, such as damaged schoolbooks and cuts or bruises, which can be indicative of victimization, and should be reported to teachers and staff during parent-teacher meetings. In addition, parents should keep track of their child's friends and social activities, which help teachers identify which students are involved.

Olweus (1994) evaluated the effectiveness of the program based on a large sample of students in Norway from grades 4 to 7, following them over 2.5 years. Bullying declined by more than 50 percent, and general antisocial behavior fell markedly, leading to an improved school environment. Teachers reported more positive peer interactions, and better attitudes toward schoolwork. While other reviews have reported smaller effect sizes, the program has consistently recorded reductions in bullying behavior (Limber 2006). Moreover, the program appears to build momentum,

*(continued on next page)*

being threatened or injured with a weapon on school property. The implications of these results are that student exposure to violence and delinquency is associated with increased absenteeism, with possible harmful effects on student performance.[8]

Finally, as reviewed in greater detail in chapter 5, Chioda, De Mello, and Soares (2016) provide evidence on the effects on delinquency of a policy that is akin to an incentivized version of an MDA. They exploit a 2008 reform to the Brazilian conditional cash transfer program Bolsa Família, which expanded youths' eligibility from 15 to 17 years of age, to study the effects of the income on crime. The reform is relevant to the current discussion in that it provided a strong incentive for youth not to drop out of school immediately following their 15th birthday, when they (and their families) would otherwise have lost benefits. The reform therefore operated on a very similar age group as MDA laws, and on youth with similar risks of offending.[9] Based on yearly data, the authors estimate substantial reductions in all crimes in neighborhoods surrounding schools with greater proportions of youth who were induced by the reform to stay in school. Neighborhoods around schools that experienced the average number of additional students covered by Bolsa Família because of the expansion experienced a 7.5 percent decline in all crimes. Although the effects for robberies, drug, and violent crimes are all statistically distinguishable from zero, most of the aggregate effect is attributable to robberies.[10]

Taken together, the evidence presented here points to an important preventive and deterrent effect of time spent in school. Additional time in school yields important short-term declines in crime, and, as will be seen in the next section, in long-term declines, as well. However, the results also caution against the view that increases in time in school only confer benefits, given the potential negative concentration/network effects associated with bringing together for longer periods of time the youths who would have been responsible for crimes outside of school.

Concentration effects are particularly important to consider for any policy that affects at-risk youth, as well as those who have been exposed to previous instances of crime or violence. The unintended spillover effects of "problem" peers should be taken into consideration and factored into any cost-benefit analysis, even for interventions that might otherwise seem "bullet proof."

## Long-term effects of schooling

The previous section provided evidence on the short-term causal link between education and crime, highlighting the potential trade-off between reductions in crime committed outside of school and the higher likelihood of conflict and violence inside, which results from concentrating youth in one place for prolonged periods. However, certain unintended consequences may be worth the cost, as these may be more than offset by the lifetime reductions in crime that result from increased investment in education. This section considers this hypothesis and finds much empirical support for the proposition that education acts as a powerful protective factor against antisocial behavior. Unlike the evidence discussed earlier, the studies reviewed here focus on longer-term effects of changes in human capital investments.

In the context of long-term outcomes, incapacitation effects are unlikely to play a role. The mechanisms at play here are more likely related to the enhancements in human capital acquired in school (whether in the form of knowledge, skills, cognitive ability, patience, or changes in personality traits), as well as any lasting effects of the peer networks developed in school. That is, the longer-term effects on criminality of additional schooling are more likely to operate through subsequent changes in the returns to legitimate work, in the social ties formed in school, or in preferences and personality traits, such as risk aversion, self-control, and the tendency to be forward-looking. The strongest evidence for such effects results from exploiting changes in compulsory schooling laws in Great Britain, Sweden, and the United States; extensions of the mandatory schooling age in these countries resulted both in increases in educational attainment and declines in lifetime involvement in criminal offending (Lochner 2011).

One of the most widely cited studies and one of the first to exploit changes in compulsory schooling laws to establish the causal link with lifetime criminality is that of Lochner and Moretti (2004). They examine state-level arrest rates of men in the United States by criminal offense and age group, based on the Uniform Crime Reports of the U.S. Federal Bureau of Investigation (FBI) for 1960, 1970, 1980, and 1990. Exploiting state-specific compulsory schooling laws, they analyze arrest rates for eight types of crime: murder, rape, assault, robbery, burglary, larceny, auto theft, and arson. They first document that an increase in a state's compulsory schooling age leads to an increase in educational attainment and then show the subsequent reduction in the incidence of crime for the affected cohorts. They find that an additional year in the average state-level education program results in a 0.10 percentage point reduction in the probability of incarceration for whites, and a 0.37 percentage point decline for blacks, corresponding to a 17 percent reduction in state-level arrest rates.[11]

What explains this decline in crime? The authors show that the magnitude of their estimated effects is very similar to that which results from multiplying the increase in wages that results from an additional year of education (the estimated wage returns to education) by the estimate of the effect of higher wage rates on crime in Gould, Weinberg, and Mustard (2002). Thus their estimates are consistent with the hypothesis that much of the effect of schooling on crime operates through increased future wages (through the opportunity cost of offending).

Following the spirit of Lochner and Moretti (2004), Machin, Marie, and Vujić (2011) exploit two national increases in minimum schooling ages in the United Kingdom (taking place in 1947 and 1973) to estimate the effects of schooling on criminal convictions for property crimes from 1984 to 2002 in England and Wales. Among men, they estimate that a one-year increase in average schooling reduced the rate of property crime convictions by about 30 percent, more than twice the effect estimated by Lochner and Moretti (2004) in the United States. The larger effects may be attributable to the fact that the U.K. reforms affected a much larger proportion of the population than those considered by Lochner and Moretti (2004).

Sweden provides another interesting context in which to evaluate the effects of changes in compulsory schooling. Meghir, Palme, and Schnabel (2012) and Hjalmarsson, Holmlund, and Lindquist (2015) use micro data to identify the causal effect of education on crime based on a Swedish education reform. It extended compulsory schooling from seven to nine years, but differed from the U.S. and U.K. reforms discussed in that it had a staggered roll-out and was implemented at different times across municipalities between 1949 and 1962. Thus these Swedish studies compare individuals who were exposed to two different regimes, but who are from the same birth cohort and face the same labor market conditions.

Hjalmarsson, Holmlund, and Lindquist (2015) exploit the reform to carefully study the causal effect of education on the criminality of those affected by it. In the first stage of their analysis, they document that exposure to the reform significantly increased average educational attainment by 0.32 year for males and 0.20 year for females. In their second stage, they find that an additional year of schooling for males decreases their likelihood of incarceration by 16 percent, and the likelihood of conviction by 6.7 percent. However, they find no statistically significant effects for females. They also show that the effects are observed across all crime categories, but are concentrated along the extensive margin of criminality, with little effect on an individual's total number of convictions. Unfortunately, it is difficult to ascertain the mechanisms through which the declines in crime were achieved.

In turn, Meghir, Palme, and Schnabel (2012) are interested in the intergenerational effects of this reform: they focus on the criminal behavior of males directly affected by the reform and on that of the sons of men and women affected by the reform. They also document a negative effect of the reform on the likelihood of conviction but also on the number of convictions among males directly affected by the reform; the number of convictions is concentrated on males from low SES backgrounds. More striking is the finding that sons whose fathers were affected by the school reform were 0.78 percentage point less likely to have a conviction (representing a 3.3 percent decline). In contrast, they find that the reform had no effects on the conviction rates of sons whose mothers were affected by the reform. They argue that these surprising intergenerational effects probably operate through improved parenting and investments in children, which, as discussed in chapter 3, can be powerful in shaping the life courses and outcomes of youth.

While analogous estimates of the effects of compulsory schooling on crime are not available for Latin America and the Caribbean, it is interesting to note that the results of Chioda (2014) (table 4.1) are consistent with the estimates just reviewed for Europe and the United States. In her cross-country, dynamic panel data models, Chioda (2014) finds that *completing* secondary education is the most robust protective factor with respect to criminality. This suggests that completing high school is the margin that is most comparable to spending an additional year in school as a result of compulsory schooling laws.[12]

Although Chioda (2014) does not rely on a natural experiment to estimate the effect of schooling on criminal outcomes, there are reasons to believe that her estimates may be close to causal, since educational investments for the entire population are predetermined relative to *current* homicides. Furthermore, by virtue of being a dynamic model (that is, by including the lagged homicide rate), the author de facto controls for the past history of violence, which contains information about prior investments in human capital. Thus, the education coefficients are based on year-to-year variations in educational attainment that are not already incorporated in the previous period's homicide rate. Furthermore, as Lochner and Moretti (2004) point out, the differences between their ordinary least square (OLS) and instrumental variables (IV) estimates are small. The latter is slightly larger in magnitude than the former, suggesting that OLS might deliver meaningful lower bounds on the causal crime-reducing benefits of education. Taken together, the results discussed provide support for the proposition that adolescence is a critically formative stage of human development and that education has important effects during this period.

## Effects of school quality

The changes in education policy reviewed up to this point operated on the margin of increased attendance or additional years of schooling. Are there any effects from other dimensions of schooling? For instance, do the quality of school infrastructure, peers, and teacher quality have any bearing on criminal offending? If increased quality raises the return to investments in education, forward-looking youths will stay in school longer, earn higher wages as adults, and commit fewer crimes today. Furthermore, if better schools imply better peers while disrupting harmful connections with at-risk youth, then positive spillover effects may reinforce the improved investments in human capital.

Most of the evidence on the effect of school quality on antisocial and criminal behavior emerges from developed countries, particularly from the United States. In many school districts, the allocation of students to oversubscribed schools is resolved with lottery-like mechanisms. This feature of the educational system offers a natural experiment for researchers to exploit to address concerns about self-selection whereby, in the absence of oversubscription, better, more motivated students would otherwise be expected to be matched to higher-quality schools. The lottery mechanism breaks this relationship between school quality and ex ante student quality. Deming (2011) endeavors to identify the effect of school quality on criminal offending in the medium term (four to seven years after intervention). He exploits a lottery-like mechanism used to assign students to oversubscribed (higher-quality) schools within the Charlotte-Mecklenburg school district in North Carolina. The lottery allows him to overcome the selection of better students into better schools and thereby to estimate the causal effect of attending a first-choice (high-quality) school on criminal behavior.

Deming shows that lottery winners experienced large changes in the composition of peers and in teacher quality, equivalent to moving from one of the worst schools in the district to a school of average quality. Across various schools and for both middle and high school students, he finds consistent evidence that attending a first-choice school reduces adult crime. The effect is concentrated among youth who are at highest risk for criminal involvement: across several different measures of crime severity, high-risk youth who win the lottery commit roughly 50 percent less crime than their counterparts who are not able to attend their first-choice school; are more likely to remain enrolled and "on track" in school; and exhibit modest improvements in behavior, as measured by absences and suspensions.

Interestingly, nearly the entire reduction in crime occurs after school completion, four to seven years after random assignment. As discussed, human capital theory would predict that higher-quality schooling would raise the returns to investment in schooling, keep students enrolled in school longer, and raise their opportunity cost of crime as adults (wages). However, Deming (2011) points out that his results are also consistent with a model of social interactions, whereby differential exposure to crime-prone peers exerts lasting influence on behavior, particularly on adult crime. He provides suggestive evidence that the effects of higher quality are attributable to gains in school quality in high school, whereas those in middle school are likely due to peer effects resulting from peers who exert more prosocial influence.

In turn, Cullen, Jacob, and Levitt (2006) study the effects of winning a lottery for admission to oversubscribed "magnet" high schools in Chicago (desirable schools, with specialized curricula that attract enrollment from outside the normal boundaries defined by school boards). They document that winning this lottery significantly improves the characteristics of peers to which the lottery winner is exposed; it raises the graduation rate of peers by 6 percent, and the share of peers who test above national norms by 14 percent. However, lottery winners are placed in lower-performing classes within the better schools and perform no better on traditional measures of academic performance than comparable students who did not win the lottery. Interestingly, the authors show that lottery winners perform no better on a wide range of academic measures, and provide some evidence that they are more likely to drop out of high school, consistent with the hypothesis of mismatch between student ability and school demands. Despite the null effects on academic outcomes, those who won lotteries and were placed into high-achieving public schools reported nearly 60 percent fewer arrests on a ninth-grade student survey. They also reported getting into less trouble at school, and school administrative data show that they had lower incarceration rates during school ages.

It is worth noting that approaches that target the quantity and quality of education should not to be viewed as substitutes, but rather as complements. Indeed, the two operate on distinct margins: additional schooling implies that youth who would otherwise be out of school are kept in school longer (for example, through a mandatory dropout age), while quality is conditional on attending school, and exposes youth to improved educational environments. The synergies between the two may even compensate for truancy laws—which are difficult to enforce (Oreopoulos 2006)—if youth who would drop out of school at the same age regardless of the law are more responsive to quality than to an additional year of schooling at a constant (lower) quality.

The long-term social benefits of increasing educational attainment and school quality can be sizable. Lochner and Moretti (2004) estimate that the net social savings in 1990 from reduced crime resulting from a 1 percentage point increase in the U.S. male high school graduation rates would have amounted to more than $2 billion. This represents more than $3,000 in annual savings per additional male graduate. For Great Britain, Machin, Marie, and Vujić (2011) estimate social savings of over £10,000 per additional high school graduate from reductions in property crime alone. In turn, Deming (2011) estimates that reductions in crime from offering better school quality options to an at-risk youth would lead to at least $16,000 in social savings to victims over the following seven years. Total social savings would be larger still, after factoring in the savings that result from lower expenditures for the criminal justice system.

## Personality traits, their malleability, and crime and violence

The previous section suggests a specific set of conclusions that can be summarized as follows. The most sizable reductions in crime appear to result from policies affecting the final years of secondary school. Those that encourage completion of high school seem especially promising in terms of their impacts on crime. Because crime rates are already quite low among high school graduates, policies that encourage postsecondary attendance or completion are likely to yield much smaller social benefits in the form of crime reduction. These two observations point to a very specific age group that should be targeted by policy—the same group that the age-crime profile draws attention to "for all the wrong reasons": namely, adolescents and young adults.

Encouragingly, the research cited above also suggests that policies designed to encourage schooling among groups that are more prone to crime are likely to yield the greatest benefits in terms of crime reduction. Indeed, many of the highlighted studies indicate that the largest impacts were observed for the most at-risk youth—based on socioeconomic status and family characteristics—suggesting the plasticity of behavior in the target population.[13] Had a deterministic interpretation of life trajectories prevailed, whereby early characteristics of individuals are seen as fatalistic, one might have concluded that the at-risk group would be too "hardened" and at too great a disadvantage to benefit from interventions in the general population, such as those considered here. Instead, as documented, education policies can reduce property crime as well as violent crime (Lochner and Moretti 2004; Anderson 2014; Hjalmarsson, Holmlund, and Lindquist 2011). Even murder appears to be responsive to changes in educational attainment and school quality (Lochner and Moretti 2004).

Finally, most of these studies fail to detect important improvements in test scores or in school achievement (or, at best, find small effects), despite their large effects on crime. This observation echoes the conclusions drawn from the early interventions reviewed in chapter 3 that improved academic performance is not a precondition for observing significant improvements in long-term behavioral outcomes and subsequent crime. Chapter 3 argued instead that personality traits and soft skills play a pivotal role.

If behavior, personality traits, and self-control remain malleable during adolescence, as neuroscience and psychology suggest, then policies that target them directly and explicitly might be considered. Can the encouraging effects of policies directed at the quantity and quality schooling be improved upon by complementing academic curricula with behavioral features? Affirmative answers to this question would not only offer an expanded menu of policy available to policy makers, and potentially increase the effectiveness of traditional education policy, but might also provide insights into the determinants of juvenile antisocial behavior, and its relationship to brain development, in particular.

## Interventions targeting personality traits and behavior

The malleability of personality traits during youth and early adulthood is relevant to policy only to the extent that these traits affect outcomes and there are tools available to policy makers to improve them. Following a review of some important concepts from the literature on personality traits, this section and the next present evidence on both points.

As discussed in chapter 3 on early interventions, personality traits are predictive of a number of significant life outcomes (including divorce, occupational attainment, and mortality), as well as delinquent behaviors (Hirschi 1969; Dodge, Coie, and Lynam 2006). Psychologists have proposed a taxonomy of personality traits with five factors (the Big Five) at the highest level and with progressively narrowly defined traits (or facets) at lower levels. The Big Five traits are openness to experience (also referred to as intellect or culture), conscientiousness, extraversion, agreeableness, and neuroticism (also called emotional stability). The limited evidence on the relationship between personality measures and aggression and crime suggests that conscientiousness and agreeableness are important predictors of criminality (Almlund and others 2011). For instance, in a sample of at-risk youth, boys who had committed severe delinquent behaviors ranked much lower in agreeableness and conscientiousness than boys who had committed minor or no delinquent behaviors up to that age (John and others 1994). Similarly, Miller, Lynam, and Leukefeld (2003) show that personality traits significantly predicted antisocial behaviors such as conduct problems, aggression, and symptoms of antisocial personality disorder in sixth to tenth graders. In particular, low conscientiousness, high neuroticism, and especially low agreeableness were strongly related to the antisocial outcomes.

In criminology, much of the focus is on the effects of self-control on crime, since self-control relates to controlling impulsive behavior and sensation seeking. It is therefore unsurprising that a number of studies confirm the negative correlation between self-control and crime (Horvath and Zuckerman 1993). However, self-control may not tell the full story. Negative emotionality—an inclination toward depression likely related to neuroticism[14]—is also associated with delinquency (Caspi and others 1994; Agnew and others 2002).

Early interventions appear to shape personality traits—including self-control—which ultimately influence criminal behavior. Can they be still affected later in life, or is the uphill battle effectively too steep? Research has documented diminishing returns to efforts to improve the academic skills of disadvantaged youth, and found that efforts to do so are often deemed too difficult and costly. Is the same true of personality traits that explain antisocial behavior? Are they effectively hardened by the time youth reach adolescence and early adulthood?

Key insights into this question come from functional magnetic resonance imaging (fMRI) and recent research on brain development. Until recently, very little was known about brain development during adolescence. The proposition that the brain might continue to develop beyond childhood did not arise until the 1970s, when research on human brains after death revealed that certain areas of the brain continue to develop beyond early childhood, particularly the prefrontal cortex—the region of the brain that governs self-control and executive functions (see chapter 3).[15] Since then, a growing literature has revealed the plasticity of the brain beyond the first years of life (Paus 2005; Casey, Galvan, and Hare 2005), with the development and "wiring" of different regions of the brain extending into the late teens and early twenties. During this period, the prefrontal cortex undergoes changes that entail the creation of new synapses and rewiring of existing connections to improve efficiency (phases of so-called synaptogenesis and synaptic pruning). Adolescence is therefore a period of synaptic reorganization, during which synaptic density in the prefrontal cortex increases (figure 4.4).[16]

During this stage, the brain is more sensitive to experiential input in the realms of executive function and social cognition, where "executive function" describes the capacity to control and coordinate thoughts and behavior (Luria 1980; Shallice 1982) and "social cognition" refers to the ability to gather information related to social interactions and understand the rules and concepts that govern them. Lesion studies[17] and functional imaging experiments[18] suggest that such skills—which also include selective attention, decision making, response inhibition, and working memory—rely heavily on the prefrontal cortex. Each of these executive functions has a role in cognitive control, such as filtering out unimportant information, staying focused to achieve goals, and inhibiting impulses.

The same tools (brain imaging and fMRI technology) that have provided neuroscientists insights into brain structure and composition have led criminologists and psychologists to single out the prefrontal cortex (and its associated functions) as

**FIGURE 4.4:** The adolescent brain: From hot cognition to cold cognition

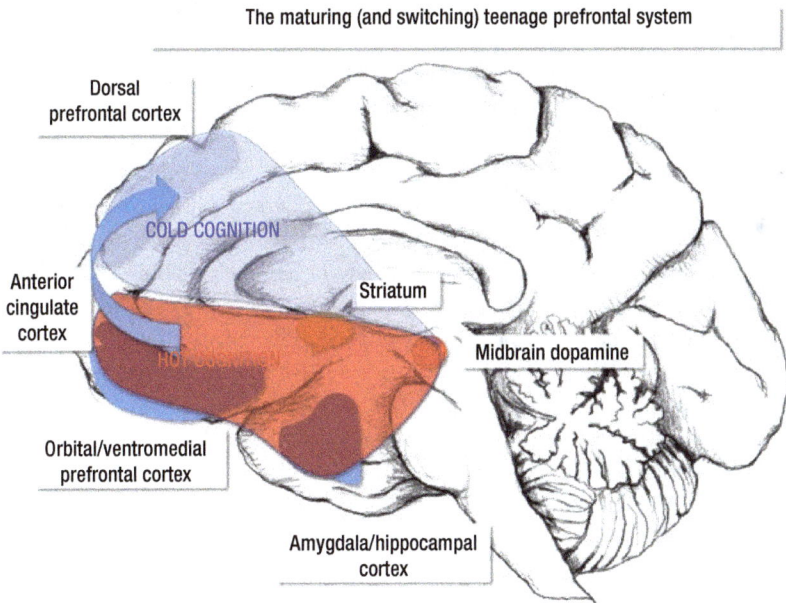

The maturing (and switching) teenage prefrontal system

Dorsal prefrontal cortex

COLD COGNITION

Anterior cingulate cortex

Striatum

HOT COGNITION

Midbrain dopamine

Orbital/ventromedial prefrontal cortex

Amygdala/hippocampal cortex

*Source:* Fallon 2013.

critical to explaining antisocial behavior. Raine (2013) identifies several distinct reasons why the functioning and development of the prefrontal cortex would play essential roles. First, at the emotional level, the prefrontal cortex regulates control over raw emotions like anger. Second, at the behavioral level, its poor functioning results in risk taking, irresponsibility, and rule breaking. Third, the prefrontal cortex plays a central role in defining personality traits like impulsivity and loss of self-control. Fourth, at the cognitive level, its poor functioning results in a loss of intellectual flexibility and poorer problem-solving skills in academic and working environments.

A typical characterization of adolescents and young adults describes them as highly reactive, impulsive risk takers, somewhat irrational, and highly susceptible to peer pressure. This description turns out to have some basis beyond its observational value and is the manifestation of the asyncronicity in three different regions of the brain that are responsible for the regulation of automatic instinctive reaction, risk-taking behavior, self-control, and reflective reasoning.

In a nutshell, the brain circuitry for the amygdala, an essential structure in the brain for decoding emotions and for processing fear—in particular, threatening stimuli—is precocious and develops much earlier than the seat of reasoning and executive function (the prefrontal cortex). Specifically, the frontal cortex—which regulates impulsivity, risk-taking behavior, delayed gratification, and self-control—does not fully mature until age 25 (Raine 2013). This means that adolescents have a brain that is wired with an enhanced capacity for fear and anxiety, but is relatively underdeveloped when it comes to calm reasoning. The notion that adolescents possess a heightened capacity for anxiety seems in apparent contradiction with their propensity to seek novelty and take risks. The puzzle is, in part, resolved by the fact that the brain's reward center, which drives much of teenagers' risky behavior, also matures earlier than the prefrontal cortex.

To add to this delicate complexity, recent studies have found that during adolescence and young adulthood, the activity of the brain's reward center, which drives most risky behavior, is heightened by the presence of peers, suggesting that peers increase adolescent risk taking by increasing sensitivity to the potential reward value of risky decisions. These factors generate a perfect storm of vulnerability for this critical age group (Chein and others 2011).

Additional evidence on the plasticity of personality traits and skills is provided in figure 4.5, which plots the evolution of certain personality traits over the life cycle, as documented by Roberts and Mroczek (2008). The late teens and early adulthood are characterized by relatively low levels of emotional stability, low conscientiousness and agreeableness, and a spike in openness to experience, de facto mimicking the asynchronicity of the brain developments described above. In addition, recent longitudinal and cross-sectional aging research has shown that personality traits continue to change in adulthood, as also suggested in figure 4.5. As people age, they exhibit increased self-confidence, warmth, self-control, and emotional stability—traits that

**FIGURE 4.5:** Evolution of personality traits, age 10–80

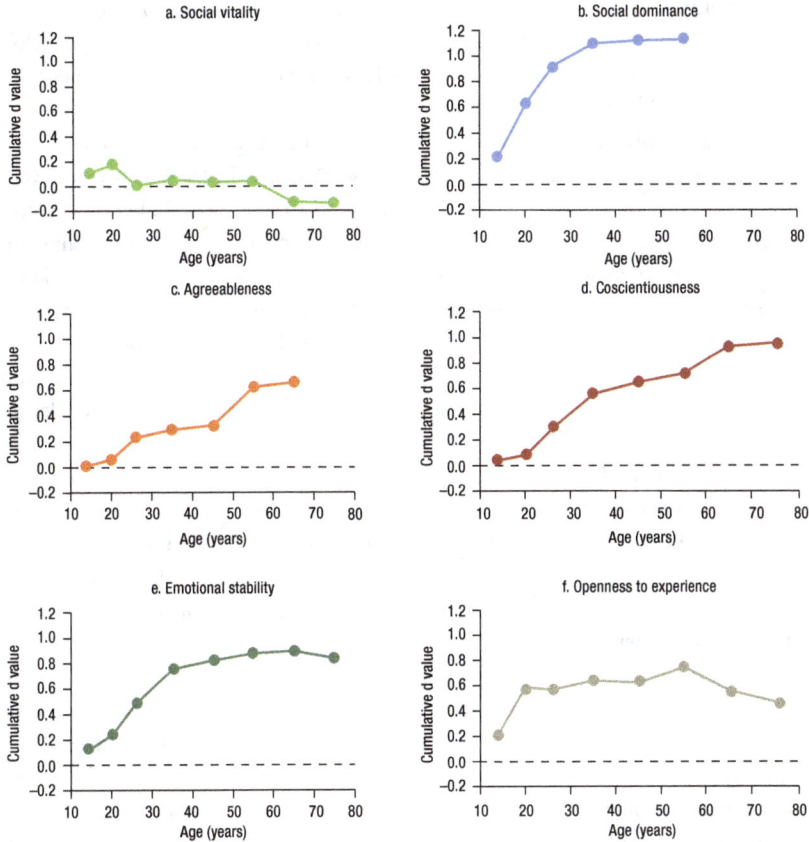

Source: Roberts and Mroczek 2008.

may act as powerful protective factors against risky behaviors, including committing crimes and acts of violence. Rather than being fixed early on, young adulthood (age 20–40) is instead characterized by evolving personality traits, with some traits changing rapidly during late adolescence and early adulthood (as illustrated by the kinks and sudden changes in the slopes of the lines in the figure).

Can a more direct link be established between education interventions for youth and changes in personality traits and executive functions? There is surprisingly little direct evidence on the effect of schooling on cognitive and personality traits. An exception is the analysis of Heckman, Stixrud, and Urzua (2006). The authors show that schooling in the high school years has moderate but positive effects on measures of cognition, consistent with a handful of previous studies.[19] The most dramatic causal effects on cognition arise from college attendance. In contrast, locus of control (one's belief about whether the determinants of one's life events are internal or external) is primarily affected by high school attendance, but not college attendance. On measures of self-esteem, an additional year of high school and college play powerful roles. Locus of control and self-esteem closely relate to emotional stability (neuroticism) in the Big Five personality traits.

Several studies suggest that personality can be remediated in adolescence. Martins (2010) analyzes data from a Portuguese program, EPIS, which was developed to improve the academic achievement of 13- to 15-year-olds. Rather than adopt more standard remedial approaches, which focus on cognitive skills, EPIS aims to improve specific personality traits such as motivation, self-esteem, and study skills. The program consists of one-on-one meetings with a trained staff member (or meetings in small groups). Importantly, remediation is tailored to each participant's individual skill deficit. Martins (2010) reports the program was successful (and cost-effective) in decreasing grade retention (by 10 percentage points), providing indirect evidence of a change in personality.

In turn, Bloom, Gardenhire-Crooks, and Mandsager (2009) analyze data from the National Guard Youth ChalleNGe program, a 17-month intervention for high school dropouts in the United States that stresses aspects of military discipline. After nine months, program participants were 12 percentage points more likely to obtain a high school diploma or an equivalent (GED, general educational development degree); 9 percentage points more likely to be working full time; and almost 6 percentage points less likely to have been arrested, compared to a control group with similar characteristics. Importantly, participants displayed higher levels of self-efficacy (a trait related to emotional stability), suggesting that personality change might have played a role in the improvements. Although these studies show that adolescents' personalities can be improved through intervention, a handful of other studies show less promising results (Rodríguez-Planas 2012; Holmlund and Silva 2014). The evidence for adults corroborates the findings of Cunha, Heckman, and Schennach (2010) for children, suggesting that personality is malleable throughout the life cycle.

The interplay between the amygdala and the frontal cortex is the neurobiological construct underlying what Kahneman (2011) famously labels the "automatic" and "controlled" systems, respectively. System 1 (the automatic system) is fast and intuitive and cannot be switched off. System 2 (the controlled system) is slow, deliberative, and careful. As a result of the asynchronous stages of brain development, young adults essentially possess an imbalance between Systems 1 and 2: they are quick, reactive, anxious, and do not possess a fully developed System 2. In their study of high-risk youth in Chicago, Heller and others (2013) highlight the importance of "biases" that may color System 1 thinking, especially for individuals who have grown up in disadvantaged contexts and where violence (and hence alertness) is embedded in their upbringing.

Consistent with this conjecture, they report that the Chicago police identify roughly 70 percent of homicides as stemming from "altercations," whereas only about 10 percent result from drug-related gang conflicts, which are more systematically planned and do not arise from extemporaneously tense situations. Studies of Chicago also suggest that certain schooling decisions, including dropping out, can be explained by quick and reactive decisions that are often precipitated by a disciplinary action or conflict with a teacher. Heller and others (2013) also note that the literature typically finds that aggressive behavior relates to hypervigilance and reactiveness to threatening cues, as well as the tendency to overattribute malevolent intents to others—so-called hostile attribution bias. However, because of the malleability of automatic thinking and of self-control discussed above, there is hope for well-designed and well-targeted policies to alleviate this source of vulnerability.

### Tackling behavior

The combined evidence from the criminological, medical, and psychological literatures paints a consistent picture about adolescence and personality traits, which informs certain aspects of the life-course trajectories that have been discussed. These findings provide some support for Moffitt's (1997) provocative argument that the incidence of delinquency and antisocial behavior is so elevated during adolescence that they appear to be the norm, rather than the exception. They also provide new insight into the extreme vulnerability of individuals in this specific age range, as well as into the mechanisms underlying the effect of education on crime and violence. Finally, they highlight the error of prior assessments that view criminal trajectories as deterministic, because personality traits that are relevant to antisocial behavior are actually quite malleable. Certain neuroscientists even draw parallels between the critical developmental period of cognitive ability in childhood and the equally critical period of development of executive function, self-control, and emotional stability during adolescence and early adulthood. It is not without irony that the very source of adolescents' vulnerabilities (their as-yet fully developed executive function and its consequent plasticity) could be the key to effective prevention by seeking to achieve a balance between adolescents' reactive (System 1) and controlled/deliberative (System 2) processes.

The sections that follow discuss the effectiveness of policies designed to alter behavior and some of the mechanisms by which they might operate (figure 4.6 and box 4.2). Four sets of policies are considered. In accordance with this study's ecological model, the discussion begins with interventions that target youth through their families as the entry point. It then provides a brief overview of certain successful school-based programs, followed by a discussion of community-level interventions that focus on social networks. The chapter closes with some innovative (if unconventional) interventions that are not typically considered in the context of crime and violence prevention, but that highlight how behavior is affected by the environment, mental health, and even meditation practices.

**FIGURE 4.6:** A path from hot to cold cognition: Channels that affect youth behavior and brain function

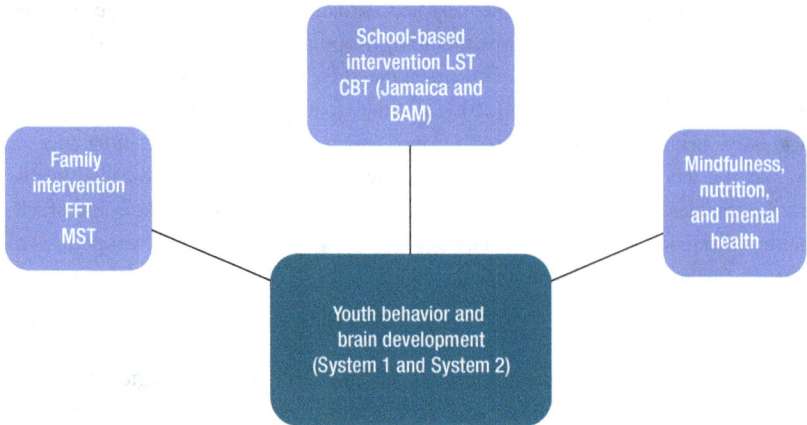

*Note:* BAM = Becoming a Man; CBT = cognitive behavioral therapy; FFT = functional family therapy; LST = LifeSkills Training; and MST = multisystemic therapy.

---

**BOX 4.2:** Programs that may have detrimental effects and even promote violence but continue to receive support despite a lack of evidence

A number of short-term programs are designed to raise awareness of the consequences of delinquency or adopt a "get tough"/disciplinary approach with juveniles, rather than an approach that acknowledges what adolescents are experiencing. Some programs have shown little success or, worse, have been counterproductive, possibly because of their antagonistic approach.

- *Scared Straight*: In these programs, juveniles are confronted with the prison environment (either through prison visits or interactions with prisoners). Petrosino, Turpin-Petrosino, and Buehler (2003) review the literature on these juvenile awareness programs, choosing only those studies that randomly assigned delinquents into no-treatment control or intervention (awareness) groups. They find that delinquents placed in the intervention programs were actually more likely to be incarcerated again than those in control groups.

- *Boot camps*: Based on the assumption that increased discipline and structure will promote self-control and decrease recidivism, the boot camp approach places delinquents in a militaristic environment (Gottfredson and Hirschi 1990;

*(continued on next page)*

*Family-based prevention.* Developmental research on delinquency consistently points to the importance of the family environment, with a number of family indicators being key risk factors for developmental problems, delinquency, and disorderly conduct. These include household structure (such as single-parent households), parent's age at first birth (such as teenage pregnancy), and the stability of the home environment.[20] Family characteristics are important markers of many developmental and behavioral problems, suggesting a role for family-based interventions, such as parental training programs.

Intuition would suggest that these programs would have the greatest effect on parents of young children, as parenting issues are best remediated earlier rather than later. *Functional family therapy* (FFT) is an exception that has shown consistent efficacy with adolescents, however (Alexander and Parsons 1982; Sexton and Alexander 2006). FFT promotes better family interactions and problem solving by working with the entire family unit. Families have 12 sessions on average over the course of 3 months, which has been shown to decrease problem behavior and recidivism (Gordon and others 1988).[21] For example, with respect to misdemeanors and felonies, Gordon, Graves, and Arbuthnot (1995) report a remarkable 79 percent decline in recidivism for FFT participants relative to a comparison group after three years, making it one of the most effective short-term programs with respect to its medium- to long-term effects on recidivism.

*Multisystemic therapy (MST)* targets 12- to 18-year-olds with curricula specific to the age group. It provides intensive family-based and community-based treatments to address the multiple causes of serious antisocial behavior among juvenile offenders. Therapists work with youth and their families to address the known causes of delinquency on an individualized yet comprehensive basis, aiming to improve youths' behavior by altering their surroundings—home, school, and neighborhood—in ways that promote prosocial behavior while decreasing antisocial behavior. They set clear standards for behavior, promote problem-solving skills, and reward prosocial involvement at the peer, school, and community levels. Improving skills for social interaction is at the core of the program's goal.

MST addresses the multiple factors that underlie delinquency across the key "systems" (family, peers, school, and neighborhood) within which youth are embedded by leveraging the strengths of each system to facilitate change. The extent of treatment varies by family according to need, with therapists generally spending more time with families in the initial weeks of the program, and gradually reducing the frequency of therapy over the subsequent three- to five-month course of treatment (to as little as once a week, in some cases).

MST was conceived following the principles of ecological systems theory (Bronfenbrenner 1979), wherein a child's developmental outcomes cannot be accurately addressed by examining only a single domain. It acknowledges that development occurs within several subsystems and that the closer systems (such as family, friends, and school) are all interconnected. Accordingly, MST approaches the adolescent by considering his or her issues within the broader context of these interrelated systems, rather than focusing narrowly on a single area of concern, subscribing to the principle that broad-based interventions are preferable to narrow ones. One of the program's strengths is its flexibility, allowing for individual customization and comprehensiveness, and thus avoiding the pitfall that programs drafted for the population at large may fail to address the individual needs of specific juveniles.

The typical margins of behavior that are targeted during MST include:

- At the individual level: Interventions generally involve using cognitive behavior therapy to modify the adolescent's social perspective-taking skills, belief system, or motivational system, and encouraging the adolescent to deal assertively with negative peer pressure.

- At the family level: MST aims to remove barriers to effective parenting—such as parental substance abuse, parental psychopathology, low social support, high stress, and marital conflict—with an eye toward enhancing parenting competencies, and promoting affection and communication among family members.

- At the peer level: MST interventions are frequently designed to decrease affiliation with and exposure to delinquent and drug-using peers, while increasing affiliation with prosocial peers.

- At the school level: MST may focus on establishing positive lines of communication between parents and teachers, parental monitoring of the adolescent's school performance, and restructuring after-school hours to support academics.

MST programs are widely acknowledged for their efficacy; numerous evaluations have substantiated their effectiveness in reducing behavioral problems. Twenty-five evaluations of MST have been published, 22 of which used randomized designs. The majority were conducted with serious juvenile offenders (such as juveniles who had committed violent, substance abuse, and sex offenses), and suggest that MST generally leads to fewer re-arrests, less drug use, and decreased incarceration in comparison to common juvenile justice services (Henggeler, Melton, and Smith 1992). Among first-time offenders, decreased delinquency and re-offending, and increased school and family functioning, are observed relative to control groups (Sutphen, Thyer, and Kurtz 1995). Importantly, MST's effects are long lived; Henggeler and others (1993) document effects more than two years after intervention. Schaeffer and Borduin (2005) show 50 percent declines in recidivism more than a decade after intervention, relative to controls who received individual therapy. Sawyer and Borduin (2011) document 36 percent and 80 percent declines in the felony recidivism rates and in the frequency of misdemeanor offending, respectively, in their 21.9-year follow-up.

What explains such large effects? Social competence, increased contact with non-aggressive peers, and improved family relationships emerge as the key intermediate outcomes explaining the success of this programs.

Given the consistency and magnitude of MST's effects, researchers have estimated the costs associated with scaling up MST for widespread implementation. Costs per child range between \$4,000 and \$12,000 (Brown and others 1999; Schaeffer and Borduin 2005; Sheidow and others 2004), which are likely swamped by the savings in justice and penal system expenditures that result from the reductions in crime related to MST participants.

### School-based interventions

School-based interventions are delivered in school buildings (even though not necessarily during school hours) or are implemented by school staff or under the auspices of school system. They can be divided into two broad categories: those designed to alter the school or classroom environments; and those that focus on changing behavior, thinking patterns, attitudes, and beliefs (see figure 4.7 for brief descriptions of the types of programs that fall into each group). This classification should not be considered mutually exclusive, however, as the typical school-based program features multiple components.

A detailed review of all the school-based interventions for adolescents and young adult is beyond the scope of this study. Because the emphasis of this section is on behavior and the mechanisms that underlie its modification, this section provides an overview of promising interventions that follow the behavioral change mold and for which there is a credible causal link with outcomes. In particular, the discussion endeavors to highlight key features of the programs that are believed to be important for the intervention's effectiveness. Some discussion is also reserved for programs that have been shown to have counterproductive impacts.

**FIGURE 4.7:** A classification of school-based prevention programs

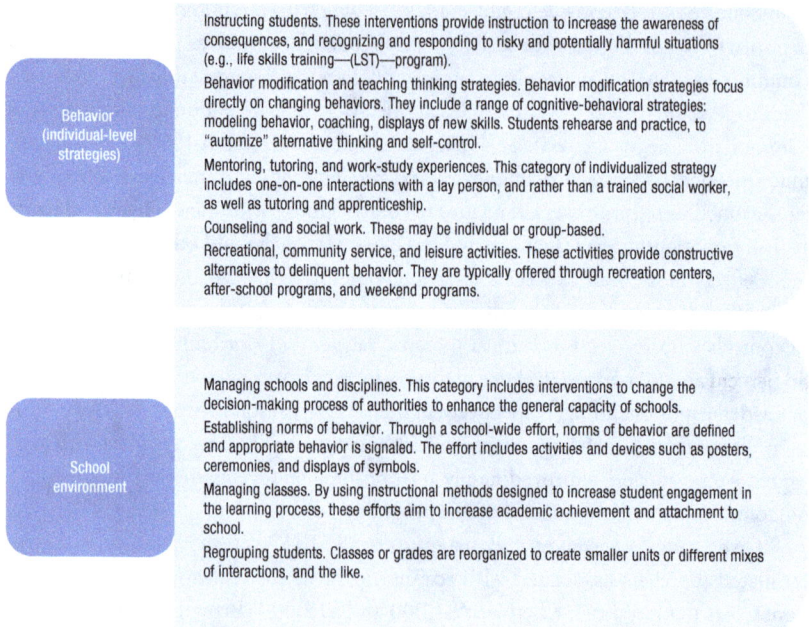

| Behavior (individual-level strategies) | Instructing students. These interventions provide instruction to increase the awareness of consequences, and recognizing and responding to risky and potentially harmful situations (e.g., life skills training—(LST)—program). |
| | Behavior modification and teaching thinking strategies. Behavior modification strategies focus directly on changing behaviors. They include a range of cognitive-behavioral strategies: modeling behavior, coaching, displays of new skills. Students rehearse and practice, to "automize" alternative thinking and self-control. |
| | Mentoring, tutoring, and work-study experiences. This category of individualized strategy includes one-on-one interactions with a lay person, and rather than a trained social worker, as well as tutoring and apprenticeship. |
| | Counseling and social work. These may be individual or group-based. |
| | Recreational, community service, and leisure activities. These activities provide constructive alternatives to delinquent behavior. They are typically offered through recreation centers, after-school programs, and weekend programs. |
| School environment | Managing schools and disciplines. This category includes interventions to change the decision-making process of authorities to enhance the general capacity of schools. |
| | Establishing norms of behavior. Through a school-wide effort, norms of behavior are defined and appropriate behavior is signaled. The effort includes activities and devices such as posters, ceremonies, and displays of symbols. |
| | Managing classes. By using instructional methods designed to increase student engagement in the learning process, these efforts aim to increase academic achievement and attachment to school. |
| | Regrouping students. Classes or grades are reorganized to create smaller units or different mixes of interactions, and the like. |

*Source:* Gottfredson and others 2004.

School-based interventions are among the most commonly adopted. Evaluations provide the fairly consistent conclusion that implementation matters: programs with weak or problematic implementations often exhibit much weaker effects than those implemented rigorously (Garrard and Lipsey 2007).

This issue aside, broadly speaking, Garrard and Lipsey (2007) document that the effects of conflict resolution education on antisocial behavior appear to depend on age: older children tend to benefit more than younger ones. For interventions on aggressive behavior, however, the results are subtler (Wilson and Lipsey 2007); efforts tend to have a greater effect with younger students if they are implemented for classrooms as a whole. Programs targeting at-risk or problem youth typically exhibit the larger effects, without any systematic differences across age groups. This qualitative result is consistent with the narrative of skill formation and brain development previously discussed and runs counter to the frequently held belief that interventions must start in early childhood to be effective (Hill and others 2011).

On the contrary, some interventions are more effective for adolescents, as appears to be the case for after-school programs. A review of programs by Gottfredson and others (2004) that included academic and social skills development as well as recreational services concludes that participation in after-school programs is effective in reducing delinquency among older students (grades 6–8), but not among younger ones (grades 4–5). As to the mechanisms underlying the effects for older students, two of them stand out. First, after-school program participation was positively related to self-reported intentions not to use drugs. Second, these programs may promote positive peer associations. Furthermore, the program effect sizes were greatest for those programs that emphasized social skills and character development (Hill and others 2011).

Taken together, these results suggest that after-school programs are effective not because they emphasize academic skills or participation in constructive activities but because they lower youths' intentions to use drugs and stimulate their social competence.

### Conflict resolution skills

Promoting positive peer relations is an important component of conflict resolution programs in the school. Interventions that include peer mediation frequently exhibit stronger effect sizes than those that exclude them, although such programs are more scarce (Garrard and Lipsey 2007). Broadly speaking, conflict resolution programs tend to be effective in reducing antisocial behavior among youth. Their efficacy is most likely tied to their focus on interpersonal and behavioral skills, which generally reduces problem behavior both in and out of school.

Interventions through ineffective programs may result in increased delinquency, often because they assemble problem adolescents together, rendering participants vulnerable to negative peer influence. However, interpersonal and conflict resolution skills (and thus interventions that foster them) can help mitigate these unintended concentration effects. Lipsey and Wilson (1998) provide evidence that interventions that focus on interpersonal skills are among the most effective for all types of juvenile offenders, whether institutionalized or not.[22] This section provides details of two programs that provide such skill training: Becoming a Man (BAM) and LifeSkills Training (LST).

BAM is a program that has drawn considerable attention from the popular press, as well as from the Obama administration. Its evaluation provides reliable, large-scale evidence that a social-cognitive skill intervention can improve both academic and delinquency outcomes of at-risk youth. In turn, LST is a three-year prevention program for students in middle/junior high school targeting drug use and violence. The program has been extensively evaluated, and has shown positive impacts in both the short and long runs, granting LST the "effective" label program by the Blueprints Initiative. As mentioned in chapter 3, Blueprints is the highest-quality U.S. youth prevention initiative to identify violence, delinquency, and drug prevention programs that have a demonstrated impact.

BAM is designed to address the difficult everyday circumstances facing many low-income, minority male youth in Chicago (box 4.3). Its focus is on the development of skills related to emotional regulation, control of stress response, improved

**BOX 4.3:** The Becoming a Man program

BAM's in-school treatment offers 27 hour-long, weekly group sessions during the school day over the course of the school year. The intervention is delivered in groups to help control costs, with groups kept small, consisting of no more than 15 youth; the average youth-to-adult ratio is 8:1. Students skip an academic class in order to participate in the program, which is one of the draws for many youth to attend. The program follows a manual and can be delivered by college-educated people without specialized training in psychology or social work (although such training is preferred in selecting program providers). Another skill that is essential to success is the ability to keep youths engaged.

The curriculum includes standard elements of cognitive behavior therapy (CBT) (Beck 2011), such as a common structure for most sessions that starts with a self-analysis ("check in") to help identify problematic thoughts or behaviors that need to be addressed. Participants discuss a cognitive model, emphasizing the endogeneity of emotional reactions to events that are often influenced by automatic thoughts. They are taught relaxation techniques to help avoid overly automatic reactions ("out of control" behavior). Stories, movies, and metaphors are used to illustrate unhelpful automatic behaviors and biased beliefs practiced or held by others. Youth are taught to use "behavioral experiments" to empirically test their biased beliefs, both during program sessions and as homework in between sessions, with a special emphasis on common errors in processing social information and problems around perspective-taking, such as catastrophizing (the tendency to view problems as catastrophes) and focusing on overly narrow, short-term goals. Because monitoring automatic thoughts requires effort, CBT helps focus this effort by helping people recognize indicators that some maladaptive automatic thought or biased belief is being triggered. A shift to some aversive emotion is one common cue (Beck 2011). Given the common risks for this population, a key focus is on anger as a cue.

The broader intervention also includes after-school programming delivered designed both to enhance program participation rates and to provide youth with more opportunities to reflect on their automatic responses and decision making. Coaches all receive some training in the BAM program. Sessions last one to two hours each and include nontraditional sports (archery, boxing, wrestling, weightlifting, handball, and martial arts) that require focus, self-control, and proper channeling of aggression. Sessions also provide youth with additional opportunities to reflect on their automatic behavior.

*Source:* Heller and others 2013.

processing of social information, interpersonal problem solving, goal setting/attainment, and personal integrity. The intervention also intended to provide socially responsible role models to youth whose social environments often reward aggression and competition.

The BAM intervention includes both in-school and after-school components that expose youth to prosocial adults, occupies their time after school, and—most innovatively—utilizes cognitive behavioral therapy (CBT). CBT is a short-duration intervention that helps people become aware of and mitigate unhelpful automatic behaviors as well as biased beliefs; in short, to encourage "thinking about thinking." It is also designed to help recognize situations in which automatic, intuitive decision making (System 1 decisions) may result in bad outcomes, and to correct biased beliefs about their experiences (Heller and others 2013).

During the 2009–10 academic year, youth were offered a mix of in-school and after-school BAM programming to develop their social-cognitive skills. The after-school component involved sports activities designed to develop conflict resolution skills. The program was administered by coaches, who had received training on BAM's objectives and on social-emotional learning principles, with encouraging short-term effects (Heller and others 2013).

Participation in the program significantly raised an index of school engagement and performance by 0.14 and 0.19 standard deviation in the program and follow-up years, respectively, leading to a 10–23 percent increase in the graduation rate relative to the control group. The program also induced a 44 percent reduction in violent crime arrests and a 36 percent decline in arrests related to vandalism and weapons crimes.

Impacts on violent crime were no longer statistically distinguishable from zero in the year following the program. However, as pointed out by Heller and others (2013), prior arrest records influence the juvenile justice system's decisions as to whether to detain or release specific youth in response to new arrests. Thus, by reducing arrest rates in the program year, the intervention may reduce youths' likelihood of future detention in a juvenile justice facility.

Are the effects of these programs large or small? One way to answer this question is by way of a cost-benefit analysis. With a cost of $1,100 per participant, the benefit-to-cost ratio is between 3:1 and 31:1 (depending on how the social costs of violent crime are monetized) from the effects on crime in the program year alone. Cost-benefit ratios aside, the simple magnitudes of the program effects merit consideration, as they suggest that even serious youth offending is more elastic to policy intervention than previously thought. This is the case particularly in light of the observation that results are not driven by "incapacitation" of youth after school, because the effects on arrests are at least as large on days when after-school programming is not offered.

While its effects are large, BAM is a relatively "light-touch" and short-lived intervention directed at very specific at-risk youth.[23] In contrast, LST is a three-year prevention program for middle/junior high school students targeting violence as well as the use of gateway substances, such as tobacco, alcohol, and marijuana. The program is designed to provide participants with training in social skills, self-management, and social resistance skills to address a number of cognitive, psychological, attitudinal, and social factors related to risky behaviors (including violence).

LST consists of 15 core sessions in the first year, 10 additional sessions in the second year, and another 5 in the third year. Additional violence prevention sessions are optional each year. Each unit in the curriculum has a specific major goal, measurable student objectives, and classroom activities. During these sessions, students are taught a variety of cognitive-behavioral skills for problem solving and decision making, resisting media influences, managing stress and anxiety, communicating effectively, developing healthy personal relationships, and asserting their individual rights. These skills are taught using a combination of interactive teaching techniques, including group discussion, demonstration, modeling, behavioral rehearsal, feedback and reinforcement, and behavioral "homework" assignments for out-of-class practice.

Numerous evaluations of LST have been carried out and cover a number of outcomes and follow-up periods (for a review, see Griffin, Botvin, and Nichols 2004). Early studies focused on tobacco or drug use, followed by studies focusing on risks related to HIV/AIDS. The effects for violence and delinquency were recently considered in a large-scale randomized study that covered 41 New York City public and parochial schools (Botvin, Griffin, and Nichols 2006). The authors report positive results within the first year of treatment; the LST group exhibited a 36 percent lower likelihood of high-frequency delinquency, a 32 percent lower likelihood of any delinquency, and a 26 percent lower likelihood of fighting with high frequency over the previous year. In addition, across a number of studies, the intervention group has shown significant improvements compared to the control group in knowledge of life skills and substance use, and perceived adult substance use, both in the short and long terms (including 5–6-year and 10-year follow-ups).

Self-control, decision-making skills, prosocial behavior, and relationships are also among the core competencies targeted by a program implemented in Jamaica and evaluated by Guerra and others (2013), one of the background papers for this report. While not providing cognitive behavior therapy, the Jamaican intervention (described in greater detail below) shares some features of BAM, such as social/life skills instruction and behavior management. The study by Guerra and others (2013) represents the first evaluation of this type of intervention in a developing context and provides promising initial evidence about a set of interventions to address aggression and violence in Jamaica.[24]

At 41 homicides per 100,000 in 2009, Jamaica suffers from the fifth-highest homicide rate in Latin America and the Caribbean, and is well above the "conflict" level of violence (of 30 per 100,000). defined by the World Health Organization (WHO). Violence in Jamaica is by no means confined to homicide. Although official statistics recorded 774 rapes island-wide in 2008 (implying that a fraction of a percent of women would have been affected), surveys in Jamaica and the Caribbean report that half of girls and women report having been "forced" or "somewhat forced" into sex (Guerra and others 2013).

With such high rates of violence in Jamaica, it is almost certain that most youth will be exposed to some measure of violence before they reach adulthood (Moser and Holland 1997; Gayle and Levy 2009; Meeks-Gardner, Powell, and Grantham-MacGregor 2007). According to Fernald and Meeks-Gardner (2003), 91 percent of 8- to 10-year-olds in poor urban areas of Kingston acknowledged exposure to some type of violence in their schools and communities. The problem is more acute for inner-city male adolescents, who commit a disproportionate share of the serious violence in Jamaica (consistent with the age-crime profile discussed in chapter 2). As in other high-violence contexts, these young people often struggle to establish their identities in the face of limited legitimate social and economic opportunities and are at heightened risk of engaging in antisocial and criminal acts under the influence of unhelpful peers. In this setting, violence can become part of a strategy for gaining respect and resources.

Guerra and others (2013) first formulate an ecological model of crime. On this basis, they propose an evaluation of a remedial education and training program for very-high-risk adolescents. The Kingston YMCA Youth Development Program (YDP) engages at-risk adolescent boys (ages 14–16) who neither work nor attend school because of academic or social problems, and display aggressive and defiant behavior. It is designed for youth growing up in the most disadvantaged of urban communities in the Kingston metropolitan area, who had already fallen behind academically or were no longer participating in formal schooling. Participants attend the program daily (in lieu of regular school) until they have attained proficiency on the Grade 9 Achievement Test (required for entrance into the equivalent of high school), after which they return to regular schools. The typical length of program participation is four years, although some youth reach the program goals faster, while others continue for a longer time (sometimes briefly cycling out of and then back into the program as a result of personal or economic constraints).

The intervention provides daily supervision (from 8:00 am to 2:00 pm), instruction, and socialization for participants. Remedial education is provided in small classes. Classes average 20 youth per teacher, whereas the typical Jamaican high school has a student-teacher ratio of 30:1 (Gordon 2012). Youth receive comprehensive services—including remedial education, vocational training, instruction in social/life skills, recreation, and positive behavior management—and are provided positive male and female role models; the program shares the latter two characteristics with BAM. Before this study, no empirical evaluations of the program had been conducted.

To evaluate the effects of the YDP, the authors first developed and validated an assessment tool for youth violence prevention mediators, the Jamaica Youth Survey (JYS). It focuses on five core competencies that are empirically related to aggression and violence: a positive sense of self, self-control, decision-making skills, a moral system of belief, and prosocial connectedness (Guerra and others 2013):

- Positive sense of self: This includes self-esteem and self-efficacy—the belief in one's ability to influence the future.

- Self-control: The ability to regulate affect (affective self-control) and behavior (behavioral self-control). It facilitates delaying gratification and conscientiousness, and lowers levels of reactive behaviors such as angry aggression.

- Decision-making skills: Good decision making involves understanding the important facts in any situation, generating alternative solutions, considering positive and negative consequences, and using feedback from actions and their consequences to inform future decisions.

- Moral system of belief: Sensitivity to the impact of one's actions on others and society is also an important feature of prosocial behavior. A moral system of belief includes standards for appropriate behavior that include consideration of the welfare of others and the common good.

- Prosocial connectedness: Healthy development is also facilitated by a sense of embeddedness in a positive social support network that provides role models and guidance. Although this requires certain resources to be available, individuals also must learn to access these resources.

In addition to measuring these competencies, the JYS records demographic characteristics, self-reported gang involvement, and family status, as well as self-reported measures of aggressive behavior and aggressive propensity (intent to behave aggressively).

To conduct their evaluation of the YDP, Guerra and others (2013) base their analysis on data collected in 2007–08. All youth who had participated in the program for at least six months and who were expected to continue were invited to provide data for the survey. To address the concern that the group of respondents is a selected sample (boys who are more motivated may be more likely to fill out the survey, for instance), and are therefore not comparable to the broader population of at-risk youth, the authors compare the outcomes of YDP participants to those of a group of applicants who were wait-listed. The authors provide evidence that the two groups of survey respondents are comparable based on their observable characteristics, which suggests that unobserved confounding between treatment and control may be minimal.

Because treated participants varied in their length of exposure to the program, Guerra and others (2013) construct three categories of "time in program." Program exposure is roughly equivalent to program dosage, and the three categories were apparent: those who started the YDP in 2000–06, 2007, or 2008–09. Although the program was not designed specifically to address the core social-emotional competencies included in the JYS, the authors hypothesized that the structure of the program was such that participation should be expected to improve all areas.

Their preliminary analysis of the YDP suggests that it is a promising approach to preventing aggression. Their results indicate that although the propensity for aggression increased slightly as youth spent more time in the program, participants were less likely to act on that aggression the longer they were enrolled. Although program participants did not differ from their wait-listed counterparts on "triggers" of aggression, as measured on the propensity scale, they did appear to be less willing to *act* on those triggers.

Under conditions of extreme poverty and danger, violence can emerge as a means of self-preservation linked to power, status, resources, and survival. However, through cognitive distortions (whereby trivial incidents are perceived as threats), it can easily translate into a willingness to use aggression with slight provocation. Thus reducing an individual's propensity or willingness to use aggression may be an important outcome to consider, although the authors concede that it is not clear whether this reflected learned self-control (inhibiting aggressive actions) or simply more disciplined behavior in the context of a group setting where aggressive behavior was sanctioned and positive behavior was rewarded. From a developmental perspective, these findings tell the important story that at-risk adolescents are not "lost causes," and that interventions may be designed to operate on their inclinations to act out their aggressions.

## Brain function and nutrition, mental health treatment, and mindfulness

The previous chapter discussed the detrimental effects of lead exposure during the early stages of life, including its connections with patterns of crime in the United States. Lead is just one example of how the physical environment may affect brain development and, in turn, affect patterns of aggression, crime, and violence. Can the link between brain function, violence, and health be more systematically exploited by policy? If so, are the effects sizable enough that this is an effective channel for improving brain development and outcomes later in life? In brief, can we "cure" violence?

Cognitive behavioral therapy and other varieties of interventions that induce "thinking about thinking" and awareness of reflexive reactions as opposed to deliberative ones have proven to be remarkably promising. However, among the more provocative efforts to reduce crime/recidivism are those that target the participants' brain functioning and systems directly through nutrition, mental health treatments, and even medications.

Before the twentieth century, it was frequently assumed that psychological issues resulted from physical or nutritional problems. With the advent of more modern psychological theories, researchers have moved toward new methods for treating mental and behavioral problems. In doing so, however, researchers may have too readily dismissed the impact of physical health on mental health. Indeed, there is mounting evidence that diet can have profound influences on mood and antisocial behavior (Kaplan and others 2011; Benton 2007).

For instance, one strand of research has demonstrated that aggression can be reduced by providing subjects with essential fatty acids, often found in fish oil.[25] In an initial experimental study (Gesch and others 2002), young incarcerated adults were provided vitamin supplements (including essential fatty acids, Omega-3) for approximately 5 weeks. Compared to a placebo group, the treatment group exhibited significant declines in violent prison offenses. Intrigued by these results, the Dutch Ministry of Justice conducted its own analysis: offenders who received Omega-3 for 11 weeks exhibited a 34 percent decline in serious violent incidents within the prison, despite incidents in the placebo rising by 14 percent (Zaalberg and others 2010). Fatty acid supplements have also been shown to decrease aggression in young girls (Itomura and others 2005), as well as anger and anxiety in substance users (Buydens-Branchley and others 2008). One explanation for these effects is that essential fatty acids are known to remediate deficiencies in serotonin, a chemical in the brain, the low levels of which are related to impulsive behavior (Mann 1999; Hamazaki and Hamazaki 2008). Providing individuals with needed fatty acids might help those who are undersupplied with serotonin, and who would otherwise be predisposed to aggressive behavior.

The preceding example illustrates the possibility that changes in nutrition (by way of nutritional supplements) can have profound effects on aggressive behavior by redressing chemical deficiencies in the brain. By extension, it is possible that chemical imbalances can affect behavior; correcting certain kinds of persistent imbalances may help reduce aggression and antisocial behavior. This hypothesis is considered next.

In their study of people diagnosed with a behavioral disorder, Walsh, Glab, and Haakenson (2004) document that a majority of them clearly had chemical imbalances. Of particular interest, a number of earlier studies document that people with attention deficit-hyperactivity disorder (ADHD) are more likely to commit offences than the general population (Barkley and Murphy 2010; Satterfield and others 2007). Estimates suggest that between 7 percent and 40 percent of the prison population may have ADHD and other similar disorders, though in most cases the conditions are not formally diagnosed. With this in mind, Lichtenstein and others (2012) analyzed longitudinal data on more than 25,000 individuals who had been diagnosed with ADHD in Sweden to evaluate whether pharmacologic treatment for the condition could reduce the incidence of criminality among them.

When people were provided medication for ADHD, the authors found that they were 32–41 percent less likely to have a conviction for a crime than when they were off medication for a period of six months or more. The authors posit that medication may operate by reducing the likelihood of making impulsive choices and by enabling people to better organize their lives, so they can maintain employment and preserve relationships.[26] The researchers then considered different crimes, documenting declines in each of them when people took medication. The authors acknowledge that when offered medication, individuals may also get more attention from other support services; this could contribute to the reduction in criminal behavior.[27]

An increasing number of experimental studies provide consistent evidence on the effectiveness of drugs in treating aggression, across a wide range of psychiatric conditions in childhood and adolescence (for a review, see Pappadopulos and others 2006). These conditions are not limited to ADHD, but also include bipolar disorder, schizophrenia, and chronic cognitive deficiencies. Surprisingly, a number of these studies suggest that certain medications are effective in directly treating children and youth who primarily exhibit antisocial behavior, rather than having been diagnosed with a psychosis and other mental conditions. At a minimum, this research corroborates the importance of brain function in explaining violent behavior and shows the responsiveness of the brain (and, by extension, behavior) to chemical imbalances that may be addressed with nutrition or with pharmacological treatment.

Finally, changing the functioning of the brain in the hopes of affecting violence may also be accomplished without pharmaceuticals or changes in nutrition (such as Omega-3). While somewhat esoteric, evidence is mounting on the efficacy of mindfulness meditation in improving brain functioning. The benefits of these practices are not merely psychological (in the form of improved well-being and reduced stress), but are also physical and translate into alterations in the structure of the brain.

As Raine (2013) provocatively put it, "Buddha may help put us on the path of permanent brain change," because these changes affect regions of the brain that regulate antisocial behavior and violence. In a randomized control study, Davinson and others (2003) show that just eight weekly sessions of meditation training altered the structure of regions of the brain involved in empathy and increased the ability to process emotional stimuli. These changes are not merely detected during the moment of meditation but also appear to be long-lived, if not permanent. Hölzel and others (2011) show that only eight weeks of mindfulness practice induced significant increases in the density of cortical gray matter after treatment as well as that of the hippocampus, which is critical for learning, memory, and regulating aggression. Lazar and others (2005) also document increased cortical thickness in the frontal cortex compared to a control group that is not trained in mindfulness practice. In terms of the effects of these changes in the brain on well-being and behavior, scientific reviews conclude that meditation among prisoners reduces anxiety, stress levels, anger, and hostility (see Raine 2013). These conclusions may help explain the results of Himelstein (2011), who provides evidence not just of a reduction in addictive substance use among former convicts after their release, but also of recidivism.

Along similar lines, promising results are emerging from preliminary evaluations of Quiet Time (QT), a stress-reduction program that includes Transcendental Meditation as an optional activity, which has been implemented in several schools in San Francisco. The program consists of two 15-minute periods, one in the morning and the other in the afternoon, when students may choose to sit quietly or meditate. QT was first adopted in the spring of 2007 by a middle school located in a neighborhood where gun violence is very common. Most students knew someone who had been shot or who had done the shooting. Murders are so frequent that the school employs a full-time grief counselor, and the students are understandably under a great deal of stress.

Following the implementation of QT, truancy and externalizing behavior improved markedly. In the first year of the program, the number of suspensions fell by 45 percent. Within four years, the suspension rate was among the lowest in the city, and grade point averages improved markedly. That such a light-touch intervention can be this effective may seem surprising. However, as in the case of cognitive behavioral therapy, meditation affects areas of the brain that control fear (the amygdala / System 1), thereby helping to reduce anxiety in children and increase their ability to reason and concentrate. The success of the QT program in San Francisco has led to the adoption of a similar program in the Oakland school district, where levels of violence are similarly elevated. In the 2011–12 school year, Mindful Schools partnered with the University of California, Davis, to conduct the largest randomized-controlled study to date on mindfulness and its effects on children. It involved 937 children and 47 teachers in three Oakland public elementary schools that serve predominantly at-risk children (71 percent). The intervention had positive and statistically significant effects on social compliance and concern for others. It also resulted in improvements in attention and participation in class, as well as in markers of self-regulation.

It is interesting to note that a number of the interventions mentioned above originated in prisons. With documentation of their effectiveness being disseminated more broadly, they have taken trickled down into the broader society, to the point where some are being implemented in middle schools.

## Notes

[1] Age is more than just a number in this context: it is a proxy for physical strength, access to resources, diminished parental supervision, and increased exposure to different peers, as well as to new role models and identities.

[2] Although employment is a potential protective factor among youth, it is excluded from this review, along with training programs, because they are discussed in detail in chapter 5.

[3] Chioda and Rojas-Alvarado (2014) are interested in the links between labor markets and crime. They argue that the *quality* of labor market opportunities affects the protective properties of employment—a hypothesis that is corroborated by their analysis. They make use of RAIS (*Relação Anual de Informações Sociais, Annual Social Information Report*) data to construct an annual panel covering all municipalities in Brazil, providing detailed municipal-level information on local economic and labor market conditions. For instance, their data record the annual number of jobs created and destroyed by age, gender, and sector, and according to whether the jobs are high- or low-skill. They complement these data with measures of average income, information on government expenditures on public safety, educational attainment, and number of dropouts, as well as markers of poverty such as the number of live births to teenagers and of Bolsa Família beneficiary households in the municipality.

[4] This model controls for a number of macroeconomic variables, population, age structure, demographics, and labor force participation, as well as the quality of institutions and measures of trust, social capital, drug production, and year and country fixed effects.

[5] Lochner and Moretti (2004); Anderson (2008); Hjalmarsson, Holmlund and Lindquist (2015); Machin, Marie and Vujić (2011); Clay, Lingwall, and Stephens (2012).

[6] Specifically, his estimates are identified from changes in state compulsory schooling ages: he considers their effects on county-level arrests of 16–18-year-olds (relative to 13–15-year-olds).

[7] Although estimated effects of school leaving age laws on drug-related crimes are sizable, the effects are typically not statistically significant.

[8] For evidence of the indirect effects of violence on school outcomes in Latin America and the Caribbean, see Severini and Firpo (2010) and Monteiro and Rocha (2013). With evidence of a negative correlation and reverse causality between education and violence, Severini and Firpo (2010) show that, on average, Brazilian students who attended more violent schools also tend to perform worse in national standardized tests, even after controlling for school, class, teacher, and student characteristics. They also document nonlinearities in this relationship; school violence has larger effects for students at the bottom of the proficiency distribution. Monteiro and Rocha (2013) study armed conflicts between drug gangs in Rio de Janeiro's *favelas*. Their within-school estimates indicate that students from schools exposed to violence perform worse on math exams. The effect of violence increases with the intensity, duration, and proximity of conflict to exam dates; and decreases with the distance between the school and the location of conflict. The authors also find that schooling supply is an important mechanism driving the achievement results because armed conflicts are associated with higher teacher absenteeism, principal turnover, and temporary school closings. In the United States, Dake, Price, and Telljohann (2003) and Reid (1990) show that victims of bullying are at increased risk of absenteeism, while Grogger (1997) documents that both minor and moderate levels of school violence lead to lower high school graduation rates and a decreased likelihood of college attendance.

[9] In Brazil, the minimum dropout age is 14, inclusive. Hence the Bolsa Família recipients in the age groups affected by the reform were already older than the MDA.

[10] In the context of this program, which disburses cash to poor families conditional on youths attending school, Chioda, De Mello, and Soares (2016) argue the declines in crime operate through an income effect, rather than through an incapacitation or education channel. They base this conclusion on the observation that most of the aggregate reduction in crime is driven by economically motivated crime (robberies) and that the decline is not concentrated on school days, but is also observed on weekends and holidays.

[11] Interestingly, the estimates delivered by ordinary least squares (which ignore the possible endogeneity of education in the crime equation) are very similar in magnitude to their instrumental variables estimates (which account for endogeneity), suggesting that the relationship is not driven by individuals with (unobservably) high discount rates or tastes for crime, for example, who are more likely both to drop out and to commit at baseline.

[12] Confirming the importance of high school graduation, Lochner and Moretti (2004) had also estimated specifications in which they substituted years of education with high school completion rates as the measure of schooling. Their instrumental variables (IV) estimates suggest that a 10 percentage point increase in high school graduation rates would reduce arrest rates by 9 percent, though the effects vary considerably across categories of crime: an additional year of average schooling reduces murder and assault by almost 20 percent, motor vehicle theft by 12 percent, and arson by 7 percent, while—disturbingly—increasing arrests for rape by 10 percent.

[13] The results cited above are not likely to be a byproduct of mean reversion, given that the definition of "at-risk" includes persistent factors such as SES and neighborhood, as well as family and individual characteristics. Furthermore, if it were driven by mean reversion, the at-risk control group would also have been expected to revert to the mean, and no effect would have been detected.

[14] Neuroticism is defined as a chronic level of emotional instability and proneness to psychological distress.

[15] Studies carried out in the late 1960s, 1970s and 1980s first demonstrated that the prefrontal cortex undergoes significant structural changes during puberty and adolescence (Yakovlev and Lecours 1967; Huttenlocher 1979; Huttenlocher and others 1983).

[16] This process of synaptic reorganization also affects the two main types of cognition. Cold cognition is the use of logical and rational thinking in cognitive processing. Decision making with cold cognition is more likely to involve logic and critical analysis as opposed to hot cognition, which employs emotional influence on decision making. Hot cognition is cognition colored by emotion in which a person is more responsive to environmental factors. As it is automatic, rapid, and led by emotion, hot cognition may consequently cause biased and low-quality decision making. These are also referred to as System 1 and System 2 processes, in Kahneman's (2011) terminology.

[17] See, for instance, Shallice (1982); Goldman-Rakic (1987); and Bourgeois, Goldman-Rakic, and Rakic (1994).

[18] For example, Casey, Getz, and Galvan (2008); Rubia, Taylor, and others (2001); and Rubia, Smith, and others (2005).

[19] See Neal and Johnson (1996); Winship and Korenman (1997); and Hansen, Heckman, and Mullen (2004).

[20] Chapter 3 also discusses evidence on family risk factors.

[21] *Recidivism* is one of the most fundamental concepts in criminal justice. It refers to a person's relapse into criminal behavior, often after the person receives sanctions or undergoes intervention for a previous crime.

[22] A large body of literature documents the effects of peers on delinquency and risky behavior. Chapters 6 and 7 discuss some of the evidence.

[23] It should be noted, however, that the effects estimated by Heller and others (2013) are relatively short term in nature, given that outcomes are measured during the program year and in the year that followed it.

[24] The comparison group was constructed by relying on an oversubscription strategy: excess demand generated by students who spontaneously wanted to participate in the program led to some being waitlisted. These were then matched (based on their observables) to those who received the program.

[25] See, for example, Gesch and others (2002); Hamazaki and Hamazaki (2008); and Buydens-Branchey, Branchey, Hibbeln (2008).

[26] Lichtenstein and others (2012) call attention to the relatively low cost (£100–£300 per month) of providing medication to someone with ADHD. In turn, the costs of unemployment insurance and of the criminal justice system that would be incurred were these individuals not on medication are surely outweighed by the costs of medication.

[27] Recently, Dalsgaard, Nielsen, and Simonsen (2014) have undertaken a careful empirical analysis of childhood ADHD based on data from the Danish Psychiatric Central Register. They rely on the fact that children are exogenously referred to hospitals through specialist physicians who have different tendencies to medicate. They find that children with ADHD who are on the margin of being prescribed pharmacological treatment have fewer interactions with the police if treated.

# References

Agnew, Robert, Timothy Brezina, John Paul Wright, and Francis T. Cullen. 2002. "Strain, Personality Traits, and Delinquency: Extending General Strain Theory." *Criminology* 40 (1): 43–72.

Alexander, J. F., and B. V. Parsons. 1982. *Functional Family Therapy: Principles and Procedures.* Carmel, CA: Brooks/Cole.

Almlund, Mathilde, Angela Lee Duckworth, James J. Heckman, and Tim Kautz. 2011. "Personality Psychology and Economics." In *Handbook of the Economics of Education*, Vol. 4, edited by E. Hanushek, S. Machin, and L. Woessman, 1–181. Amsterdam: Elsevier.

Anderson, D. Mark. 2014. "In School and Out of Trouble? The Minimum Dropout Age and Juvenile Crime." *Review of Economics and Statistics* 96: 318–31.

Anderson, D. Mark, Benjamin Hansen, and Mary Beth Walker. 2013. "The Minimum Dropout Age and Student Victimization." *Economics of Education Review* 35: 66–74.

Anderson, Michael L. 2008. "Multiple Inference and Gender Differences in the Effects of Early Intervention: A Reevaluation of the Abecedarian, Perry Preschool, and Early Training Projects." *Journal of the American Statistical Association* 103 (484): 1481–95.

Barkley, R. A., and K. R. Murphy. 2010. "Deficient Emotional Self-Regulation in Adults with ADHD: The Relative Contributions of Emotional Impulsiveness and ADHD Symptoms to Adaptive Impairments in Major Life Activities." *Journal of ADHD and Related Disorders* 1 (4): 5–28.

Beck, J. S. 2011. *Cognitive Behavior Therapy: Basics and Beyond*, 2nd ed. New York: Guilford.

Becker, Gary S., and Casey B. Mulligan. 1997. "The Endogenous Determination of Time Preference." *Quarterly Journal of Economics* 112 (3): 729–58.

Benton, David. 2007. "The Impact of Diet on Anti-Social, Violent and Criminal Behavior." *Neuroscience & Biobehavioral Reviews* 31 (5): 752–74.

Berthelon, Matias, and Diana Kruger. 2011. "Risky Behavior among Youth: Incapacitation Effects of School on Adolescent Motherhood and Crime in Chile." *Journal of Public Economics* 95: 41–53.

Bloom, Dan, Alissa Gardenhire-Crooks, and Conrad Mandsager. 2009. "Reengaging High School Dropouts: Early Results of the National Guard Youth ChalleNGe Program Evaluation." New York: MDRC.

Botvin, G. J., K. W. Griffin, and T. R. Nichols. 2006. "Preventing Youth Violence and Delinquency through a Universal School-Based Prevention Approach." *Prevention Science* 7: 403–8.

Bourgeois, J. P., P. S. Goldman-Rakic, and P. Rakic. 1994. "Synaptogenesis in the Prefrontal Cortex of Rhesus Monkeys." *Cerebral Cortex* 4: 78–96.

Bronfenbrenner, Urie. 1979. *The Ecology of Human Development: Experiments by Nature and Design.* Cambridge, MA: Harvard University Press.

Brown, T. L., S. W. Henggeler, S. K. Schoenwald, M. J. Brondino, and S. G. Pickrel. 1999. "Multisystemic Treatment of Substance Abusing and Dependent Juvenile Delinquents: Effects on School Attendance at Post-Treatment and 6-Month Follow-Up." *Children's Services: Social Policy, Research and Practice* 2: 81–93.

Buonanno, Paolo, and Leone Leonida. 2009. "Non-Market Effects of Education on Crime: Evidence from Italian Regions." *Economics of Education Review* 28: 11–17.

Buydens-Branchey, L., M. Branchey, and J. R. Hibbeln. 2008. "Associations between Increases in Plasma n-3 Polyunsaturated Fatty Acids following Supplementation and Decreases in Anger and Anxiety in Substance Abusers." *Progress in Neuro-Psychopharmacology Biological Psychiatry* 32 (2): 568—75.

Carvalho, Leandro S., and Rodrigo R. Soares. 2013. "Living on the Edge: Youth Entry, Career and Exit in Drug-Selling Gangs." IZA Discussion Paper 7189, Institute for the Study of Labor (IZA), Bonn.

Casey, B. J., A. Galvan, and T. A. Hare. 2005. "Changes in Cerebral Functional Organization during Cognitive Development." *Current Opinion in Neurobiology* 15: 239–44.

Casey, B. J., Sarah Getz, and Adriana Galvan. 2008. "The Adolescent Brain." *Developmental Review* 28 (1): 62–77.

Caspi, A., T. E. Moffitt, P. A. Silva, M. Stouthamer-Loeber, R. F. Krueger, and P. S. Schmutte. 1994. "Are Some People Crime Prone? Replications of the Personality–Crime Relationship across Countries, Genders, Races, and Methods." *Criminology* 32: 163–95.

Chein, J., D. Albert, L. O'Brien, K. Uckert, and L. Steinberg. 2011. "Peers Increase Adolescent Risk Taking by Enhancing Activity in the Brain's Reward Circuitry." *Developmental Science* 14: F1–F10.

Chioda, Laura. 2014. "Violence in Latin America: Dynamic Panel Data Analysis." Working paper.

Chioda, Laura, João M. P. De Mello, and Rodrigo R. Soares. 2016. "Spillovers from Conditional Cash Transfer Programs: Bolsa Família and Crime in Urban Brazil." *Economics of Education Review* 54 (October): 306–20.

Chioda, Laura, and Luis Diego Rojas-Alvarado. 2014. "Brazil Violence across Municipalities." Working paper.

Clay, Karen, Jeff Lingwall, and Melvin Stephens Jr. 2012. "Do Schooling Laws Matter? Evidence from the Introduction of Compulsory Attendance Laws in the United States." NBER Working Paper 18477, National Bureau of Economic Research, Cambridge, MA.

Cullen, Julie Berry, Brian A Jacob, and Steven Levitt. 2006. "The Effect of School Choice on Participants: Evidence from Randomized Lotteries." *Econometrica* 74 (5): 1191–230.

Cunha, Flavio, James J. Heckman, and Susanne M. Schennach. 2010. "Estimating the Technology of Cognitive and Noncognitive Skill Formation." *Econometrica* 78 (3): 883–931.

Dake, J. A., J. H. Price, and S. K. Telljohann. 2003. "The Nature and Extent of Bullying at School." *Journal of School Health* 73 (5): 173–80.

Dalsgaard, Søren, Helena Skyt Nielsen, and Marianne Simonsen. 2014. "Consequences of ADHD Medication Use for Children's Outcomes." IZA Discussion Paper 8208, Institute for the Study of Labor (IZA), Bonn.

Davidson, R. J., J. Kabat-Zinn, J. Schumacher, M. Rosenkranz, D. Muller, S. F. Santorelli, F. Urbanowski, A. Harrington, K. Bonus, and J. F. Sheridan. 2003. "Alterations in Brain and Immune Function Produced by Mindfulness Meditation." *Psychosomatic Medicine* 65 (4): 564–70.

Deming, David J. 2011. "Better Schools, Less Crime?" *Quarterly Journal of Economics* 126 (4): 2063–115.

Dodge, K. A., J. D. Coie, and D. Lynam. 2006. "Aggression and Antisocial Behavior in Youth." In *Handbook of Child Psychology, Vol. 3, Social, Emotional, and Personality Development*, 6th ed., edited by N. Eisenberg, 719–88. Hoboken, NJ: Wiley.

Elliott, D. S., D. Huizinga, and S. Menard. 1989. *Multiple Problem Youth: Delinquency, Substance Use and Mental Health Problems.* New York: Springer-Verlag.

Empey, LaMar T., Mark C. Stafford, and Carter H. Hay. 1999. *American Delinquency: Its Meaning and Construction.* Belmont, CA: Wadsworth Publishing.

Ewert, Stephanie, and Tara Wildhagen. 2011. "Educational Characteristics of Prisoners: Data from the American Community Survey." SEHSD Working Paper 2011-8, Social, Economic, and Housing Statistics Division (SEHSD), U.S. Census Bureau, Washington, DC.

Fallon, James. 2013. *The Psychopath Inside: A Neuroscientist's Personal Journey into the Dark Side of the Brain.* New York: Penguin Publishing.

Fernald, L. C., and J. Meeks-Gardner. 2003. "Jamaican Children's Reports of Violence at School and Home." *Social and Economic Studies* 52: 121–40.

Garrard, W. M., and M. W. Lipsey. 2007. "Conflict Resolution Education and Antisocial Behavior in U.S. Schools: A Meta-Analysis." *Conflict Resolution Quarterly* 25 (1): 9–38.

Gayle, Herbert, with Horace Levy. 2009. "'Forced Ripe!' How Youth of Three Selected Working-Class Communities Assess Their Identity, Support, and Authority Systems, Including Their Relationship with the Jamaican Police." World Bank, Washington, DC. http://siteresources.worldbank.org/INTEMPOWERMENT/Resources/Jamaica_Forced _Ripe_041209.pdf.

Gesch C. B., S. M. Hammond, S. E. Hampson, A. Eves, and M. J. Crowder. 2002. "Influence of Supplementary Vitamins, Minerals and Essential Fatty Acids on the Antisocial Behaviour of Young Adult Prisoners: Randomised, Placebo-Controlled Trial." *British Journal of Psychiatry* 181: 22–28.

Goldman-Rakic. P. S. 1987. "Development of Cortical Circuitry and Cognitive Function." *Child Development* 58 (3): 601–22.

Gordon, D. A., J. Arbuthnot, K. E. Gustafson, and P. McGreen. 1988. "Home-Based Behavioral-Systems Family Therapy with Disadvantaged Juvenile Delinquents." *American Journal of Family Therapy* 16 (3): 243–55.

Gordon, Peter-John. 2012. "Secondary and Primary Education in Jamaica: Financial Requirements for Quality." Working Paper, Department of Economics, University of the West Indies, Mona, Jamaica.

Gordon, D. A., K. Graves, and J. Arbuthnot. 1995. "The Effect of Functional Family Therapy for Delinquents on Adult Criminal Behavior." *Criminal Justice and Behavior* 22: 60–73.

Gottfredson, D. C., S. A. Gerstenblith, D. A. Soule, S. C. Womer, and S. Lu. 2004. "Do After-School Programs Reduce Delinquency?" *Prevention Science* 5 (4): 253–66.

Gottfredson, G. D., D. C. Gottfredson, E. R. Czeh, D. Cantor, S. Crosse, and I. Hantman. 2000. *A National Study of Delinquency Prevention in Schools.* Ellicott City, MD: Gottfredson Associates.

Gottfredson, M. R., and T. Hirschi. 1990. *A General Theory of Crime.* Stanford, CA: Stanford University Press.

Gould, Eric D., Bruce A. Weinberg, and David B. Mustard. 2002. "Crime Rates and Local Labor Market Opportunities in the United States: 1977–1997." *Review of Economics and Statistics* 84 (1): 45–61.

Griffin, K. W., G. J. Botvin, and T. R. Nichols. 2004. "Long-Term Follow-Up Effects of a School-Based Drug Abuse Prevention Program on Adolescent Risky Driving." *Prevention Science* 5: 207–12.

Grogger, Jeff. 1997. "Local Violence, Educational Attainment, and Teacher Pay." NBER Working Paper 6003, National Bureau of Economic Research, Cambridge, MA.

Guerra, Nancy, Kirk R. Williams, Ian Walker, and Julie Meeks-Gardner. 2013. "Building an Ecology of Peace in Jamaica: New Approaches to Understanding Youth Crime and Violence and Evaluating Prevention Strategies." Background paper for the study.

Hamazaki, Tomohito, and Kei Hamazaki. 2008. "Fish Oils and Aggression or Hostility." *Progress in Lipid Research* 47 (4): 221–32.

Hansen, Karsten T., James J. Heckman, and Kathleen J. Mullen. 2004. "The Effect of Schooling and Ability on Achievement Test Scores." *Journal of Econometrics* 121 (1–2): 39–98.

Heckman, James J., Jora Stixrud, and Sergio Urzua. 2006. "The Effects of Cognitive and Noncognitive Abilities on Labor Market Outcomes and Social Behavior." *Journal of Labor Economics* 24 (3): 411–82.

Heller, Sara, Harold A. Pollack, Roseanna Ander, and Jens Ludwig. 2013. "Preventing Youth Violence and Dropout: A Randomized Field Experiment." NBER Working Paper 19014, National Bureau of Economic Research, Cambridge, MA.

Henggeler, S. W., G. B. Melton, and L. A. Smith. 1992. "Family Preservation Using Multisystemic Therapy: An Effective Alternative to Incarcerating Serious Juvenile Offenders." *Journal of Consulting and Clinical Psychology* 60: 953–61.

Henggeler, S. W., G. B. Melton, L. A. Smith, S. K. Schoenwald, and J. H. Hanley. 1993. "Family Preservation Using Multisystemic Treatment: Long-Term Follow-Up to a Clinical Trial with Serious Juvenile Offenders." *Journal of Child and Family Studies* 2: 283–93.

Hill, Patrick L., Brent W. Roberts, Jeffrey T. Grogger, Jonathan Guryan, and Karen Sixkiller. 2011. "Decreasing Delinquency, Criminal Behavior, and Recidivism by Intervening on Psychological Factors Other Than Cognitive Ability: A Review of the Intervention Literature." In *Controlling Crime: Strategies and Tradeoffs,* edited by Philip Cook, Jens Ludwig, and Justin McCrary, 367–406. Cambridge, MA: National Bureau of Economic Research.

Himelstein, S. 2011. "Meditation Research: The State of the Art in Correctional Settings." *International Journal of Offender Therapy and Comparative Criminology* 55 (4): 646–61.

Hirschi, Travis. 1969. *Causes of Delinquency*. Berkeley: University of California Press.

Hjalmarsson, Randi, Helena Holmlund, and Matthew J. Lindquist. 2015. "The Effect of Education on Criminal Convictions and Incarceration: Causal Evidence from Micro-Data." *Economic Journal* 125 (587): 1290–1326.

Hjalmarsson, Randi, and Lance Lochner. 2012. "The Impact of Education on Crime: International Evidence." CESifo DICE Report 2/2012, Ifo Institute for Economic Research at the University of Munich.

Holmlund, Helena, and Olmo Silva. 2014. "Targeting Non-Cognitive Skill to Improve Cognitive Outcomes: Evidence from a Remedial Education Intervention." *Journal of Human Capital* 8 (2): 126–60.

Hölzel, Britta K., Sara W. Lazar, Tim Gard, Zev Schuman-Olivier, David R. Vago, and Ulrich Ott. 2011. "How Does Mindfulness Meditation Work? Proposing Mechanisms of Action from a Conceptual and Neural Perspective." *Perspectives on Psychological Science* 6: 537–59.

Hood, R., and R. Sparks. 1970. *Key Issues in Criminology*. New York: McGraw-Hill.

Horvath, P., and M. Zuckerman. 1993. "Sensation Seeking, Risk Appraisal, and Risky Behavior." *Personality and Individual Differences* 14: 41–52.

Huttenlocher, P. R. 1979. "Synaptic Density in the Human Frontal Cortex: Developmental Changes and Effects of Aging." *Brain Research* 163 (2): 195–205.

Huttenlocher, P. R., C. De Courten, L. J. Garey, and H. Van Der Loos. 1983. "Synaptic Development in the Human Cerebral Cortex." *International Journal of Neurology* 16–17: 144–54.

Itomura, M., K. Hamazaki, S. Sawazaki, M. Kobayashi, K. Terasawa, S. Watanabe, and T. Hamazaki. 2005. "The Effect of Fish Oil on Physical Aggression in Schoolchildren—A Randomized, Double-Blind, Placebo-Controlled Trial." *Journal of Nutritional Biochemistry* 16 (3): 163–71.

Jacob, B. A., and L. Lefgren, 2003. "Are Idle Hands the Devil's Workshop? Incapacitation, Concentration and Juvenile Crime." *American Economic Review* 93: 1560–77.

John, Oliver P., Avshalom Caspi, Richard W. Robins, and Terrie E. Moffitt. 1994. "The 'Little Five': Exploring the Nomological Network of the Five-Factor Model of Personality in Adolescent Boys." *Child Development* 65 (1): 160–78.

Kahneman, D. 2011. *Thinking, Fast and Slow*. New York: Farrar, Strauss & Giroux.

Kaplan B. J., S. G. Crawford, C. J. Field, and J. S. Simpson. 2011. "Vitamins, Minerals, and Mood." *Psychological Bulletin* 133 (5): 747–60.

Klein, M. 1989. "Watch Out for That Last Variable." In *The Causes of Crime: New Biological Approaches*, edited by S. Mednick, T. Moffitt, and S. A. Stack, 25–41. Cambridge: Cambridge University Press.

Lazar, Sara W., Catherine E. Kerr, Rachel H. Wasserman, Jeremy R. Gray, Douglas N. Greve, Michael T. Treadway, Metta McGarvey, Brian T. Quinn, Jeffery A. Dusek, Herbert Benson, Scott L. Rauch, Christopher I. Moore, and Bruce Fischl. 2005 "Meditation Experience Is Associated with Increased Cortical Thickness." *Neuroreport* 16 (17): 1893–97.

Lichtenstein, P., L. Halldner, J. Zetterqvist, A. Sjölander, E. Serlachius, S. Fazel, N. Långström, and H. Larsson. 2012. "Attention Deficit Hyperactivity Disorder Medication and Criminality." *New England Journal of Medicine* 367: 2006–14.

Limber, S. P. 2006. "The Olweus Bullying Prevention Program: An Overview of Its Implementation and Research Basis." In *Handbook of School Violence and School Safety: From Research to Practice*, edited by Shane R. Jimerson and Michael J. Furlong, 293–307. Mahwah, NJ: Lawrence Erlbaum Associates.

Lipsey, M. W., and D. B. Wilson. 1998. "Effective Intervention for Serious Juvenile Offenders: A Synthesis of Research." In *Serious and Violent Juvenile Offenders: Risk Factors and Successful Interventions*, edited by R. Loeber and D. P. Farrington, 313–45. Thousand Oaks, CA: Sage.

Lochner, Lance. 2004. "Education, Work and Crime: A Human Capital Approach." *International Economic Review* 45 (3): 811–43.

———. 2011. "Education Policy and Crime." In *Controlling Crime: Strategies and Tradeoffs*, edited by Phillip J. Cook, Jens Ludwig, and Justin McCrary. Chicago: University of Chicago.

Lochner, Lance, and Enrico Moretti. 2004. "The Effect of Education on Crime: Evidence from Prison Inmates, Arrests, and Self-Reports." *American Economic Review* 94 (1): 155–89.

Luallen, Jeremy. 2006. "School's Out … Forever: A Study of Juvenile Crime, At-Risk Youths, and Teacher Strikes." *Journal of Urban Economics* 59 (1): 75–103.

Luria, A. R. 1980. *Higher Cortical Functions in Man*, 2nd ed. New York: Basic Books.

Machin, Stephen, Olivier Marie, and Sunčica Vujić. 2011. "The Crime-Reducing Effect of Education." *Economic Journal* 121 (552): 463–84.

MacKenzie, Doris Layton, and Dale G. Parent. 1991. "Shock Incarceration and Prison Crowding in Louisiana." *Journal of Criminal Justice* 19 (3): 225–37.

Mann, J. John. 1999. "Role of the Serotonergic System in the Pathogenesis of Major Depression and Suicidal Behavior." *Neuropsychopharmacology* 21 (supp. 1): S99–S105.

Martins, Pedro S. 2010. "Can Targeted, Non-Cognitive Skills Programs Improve Achievement?" IZA Discussion Paper 5266, Institute for the Study of Labor (IZA), Bonn.

Meeks-Gardner, J. M., C. A. Powell, and S. M. Grantham-McGregor: 2007. "Determinants of Aggressive and Prosocial Behaviour among Jamaican Schoolboys." *West Indian Medical Journal* 56 (1): 34–41.

Meghir, Costas, Mårten Palme, and Marieke Schnabe. 2012. "The Effect of Education Policy on Crime: An Intergenerational Perspective." NBER Working Paper 18145, National Bureau of Economic Research, Cambridge, MA.

Miller, Joshua D., Donald Lynam, and Carl Leukefeld. 2003. "Examining Antisocial Behavior through the Lens of the Five Factor Model of Personality." *Aggressive Behavior* 29 (6): 497–514.

Moffitt, Terrie E. 1993. "Adolescence-Limited and Life-Course Persistent Antisocial Behavior: A Developmental Taxonomy." *Psychological Review* 100: 674–701.

———. 1997. "Neuropsychology, Antisocial Behavior, and Neighborhood Context." In *Violence and Childhood in the Inner City*, edited by J. McCord. New York: Cambridge University Press.

Monteiro, Joana, and Rudi Rocha. 2013. "Drug Battles and School Achievement: Evidence from Rio de Janeiro's Favelas." CAF Working Paper 2013/05, CAF (Development Bank of Latin America), Caracas.

Moser, C., and J. Holland. 1997. *Urban Poverty and Violence in Jamaica*. Washington, DC: World Bank.

Munyo, I. and M. Rossi. 2015. "First-Day Criminal Recidivism." *Journal of Public Economics* 5 (24): 81–90.

Neal, Derek, and William Johnson. 1996. "The Role of Premarket Factors in Black-White Wage Differences." *Journal of Political Economy* 104 (5): 869–95.

Olweus, Dan. 1993. *Bullying at School: What We Know and What We Can Do*. Cambridge, MA: Blackwell.

———. 1994. "Bullying at School: Basic Facts and Effects of a School-Based Intervention Program." *Journal of Child Psychology and Psychiatry* 35 (7): 1171–90.

———. 1995. "Bullying or Peer Abuse at School: Facts and Intervention." *Current Directions in Psychological Science* 4 (6): 196–200.

———. 2005. "A Useful Evaluation Design, and Effects of the Olweus Bullying Prevention Program." *Psychology, Crime, & Law* 11 (4): 389–402.

Oreopoulos, Philip. 2006. "Estimating Average and Local Average Treatment Effects of Education When Compulsory Schooling Laws Really Matter." *American Economic Review* 96 (1): 152–75.

Pappadopulos, Elizabeth, Sophie Woolston, Alanna Chait, Matthew Perkins, Daniel F. Connor, and Peter S. Jensen. 2006. "Pharmacotherapy of Aggression in Children and Adolescents: Efficacy and Effect Size." *Journal of the Canadian Academy of Child and Adolescent Psychiatry* 15 (1): 27–39.

Paus, T. 2005. "Mapping Brain Maturation and Cognitive Development during Adolescence." *Trends in Cognitive Science* 9 (2): 60–68.

Petrosino, Anthony, Carolyn Turpin-Petrosino, and John Buehler. 2003. "Scared Straight and Other Juvenile Awareness Programs for Preventing Juvenile Delinquency: A Systematic Review of the Randomized Experimental Evidence." *Annals of the American Academy of Political and Social Science* 589 (1): 41–62.

Raine, Adrian. 2013. *The Anatomy of Violence: The Biological Roots of Crime*. New York: Pantheon Books.

Reid, K. 1990. "Bullying and Persistent School Absenteeism." In *Bullying in Schools*, edited by D. P. Tattum and D. A. Lane, 89–94. Stoke-on-Trent, U.K.: Trentham Books.

Roberts, Brent W., and Daniel Mroczek. 2008. "Personality Trait Change in Adulthood." *Current Directions in Psychological Science* 17 (1): 31–35.

Rodríguez-Planas, Núria. 2012. "Longer-Term Impacts of Mentoring, Educational Services, and Learning Incentives: Evidence from a Randomized Trial in the United States." *American Economic Journal: Applied Economics* 4 (4): 121–39.

Rubia, K., A. B. Smith, M. J. Brammer, B. Toone, and E. Taylor. 2005. "Abnormal Brain Activation during Inhibition and Error Detection in Medication-Naive Adolescents with ADHD." *American Journal of Psychiatry* 162: 1067–75.

Rubia, K., E. Taylor, A. Smith, H. Oksanen, S. Overmeyer, and S. Newman. 2001. "Neuropsychological Analyses of Impulsiveness in Childhood Hyperactivity." *British Journal of Psychiatry* 79: 138–43.

Sarzosa, Miguel, and Sergio Urzúa. 2015. "Bullying among Adolescents: The Role of Cognitive and Non-Cognitive Skills." NBER Working Paper 21631, National Bureau of Economic Research, Cambridge, MA.

Satterfield J. H., K. J. Faller, F. M. Crinella, A. M. Schell, J. M. Swanson, and L. D. Homer. 2007. "A 30-Year Prospective Follow-Up Study of Hyperactive Boys with Conduct Problems: Adult Criminality." *Journal of the American Academy of Child and Adolescent Psychiatry* 46: 601–10.

Sawyer, Aaron M., and Charles M. Borduin. 2011. "Effects of Multisystemic Therapy through Midlife: A 21.9-Year Follow-Up to a Randomized Clinical Trial with Serious and Violent Juvenile Offenders." *Journal of Consulting and Clinical Psychology* 79 (5): 643–52.

Schaeffer, Cindy M., and Charles M. Borduin. 2005. "Long-Term Follow-Up to a Randomized Clinical Trial of Multisystemic Therapy with Serious and Violent Juvenile Offenders." *Journal of Consulting and Clinical Psychology* 73 (3): 445–53.

Severnini, E. R., and S. Firpo. 2010. "The Relationship between School Violence and Student Proficiency." Texto Para Discussão, Escola de Economia de São Paulo da Fundação Getulio Vargas FGV-EESP, São Paulo.

Sexton, Thomas L., and James F. Alexander. 2006. "Functional Family Therapy for Externalizing Disorders in Adolescents." In *Handbook of Clinical Family Therapy*, edited by J. Lebow, 164–94. New Jersey: John Wiley.

Shallice, T. 1982. Specific Impairments of Planning." *Philosophical Transactions of the Royal Society of London Bulletin* 298: 199–209.

Sheidow, A. J., W. D. Bradford, S. W. Henggeler, M. D. Rowland, C. Halliday-Boykins, S. K. Schoenwald, and D. M. Ward. 2004. "Treatment Costs for Youths in Psychiatric Crisis: Multisystemic Therapy versus Hospitalization." *Psychiatric Services* 55: 548–54.

Sutphen, R. D., B. A. Thyer, and P. D. Kurtz. 1995. "Multisystemic Treatment of High-risk Juvenile Offenders." *International Journal of Offender Therapy and Comparative Criminology* 39: 327–34.

Tremblay, Richard E. 2004. "Decade of Behavior Distinguished Lecture: Development of Physical Aggression during Infancy." *Infant Mental Health Journal* 25: 399–407.

Walsh, W. J., L. B. Glab, and M. L. Haakenson. 2004. "Reduced Violent Behavior Following Biochemical Therapy." *Physiology and Behavior* 82: 835–39.

Wilson, S. J., and M. J. Lipsey. 2007. "Effectiveness of School-Based Intervention Programs on Aggressive Behavior: Update of a Meta-Analysis." *American Journal of Preventive Medicine 33* (Suppl. 2): S130–S143.

Winship C., and S. Korenman. 1997. "Does Staying in School Make You Smarter?" In *Intelligence, Genes and Success: Scientists Respond to the Bell Curve*, edited by B. Devlin, S. E. Fienberg, D. P. Resnick, and K. Roeder. New York: Springer-Verlag.

Yakovlev, P. I., and A.-R. Lecours. 1967. "The Myelogenetic Cycles of Regional Maturation of the Brain." In *Regional Development of the Brain in Early Life*, edited by A. Minkowski, 3–70. Oxford: Blackwell Scientific.

Zaalberg, A., H. Nijman, E. Bulten, L. Stroosma, and C. van der Staak. 2010. "Effects of Nutritional Supplements on Aggression, Rule-Breaking, and Psychopathology among Young Adult Prisoners." *Aggressive Behavior* 36 (2): 117–26.

# 5

# The Nexus between Poverty, Labor Markets, and Crime

Disposable income, whether earned or unearned, influences household behavior, individual behavior, investment in children, and the formation of and attachment to social networks that are linked to crime and violence. In low-income families, if both parents participate actively in the labor market, then the time available to them and their families for both parental supervision and parental investments in children may be limited. These effects may be especially relevant for lower-income families, in or near poverty. Recently, careful research has documented that the added daily stress of poverty in effect forces people into a kind of cognitive tunnel. On the one hand, they are less aware of the cognitive biases in their decision making, and on the other, they experience a significant "tax" on their mental bandwidth that limits their ability to perform well cognitively. These factors deplete people's self-control, erode their cognitive faculties, and even result in antisocial behavior.

Other mechanisms related to income may be at play, as well. As the income of others rises, the opportunities for crime may increase, as well as the returns. However, when an individual's own resources increase, they can afford changes in behavior to avoid crime, such as altering their routines and making investments to lower the likelihood of certain types of victimization. However, the extra resources may also induce more leisure time spent outside the home, where they are at an increased likelihood of becoming victims of crime.

Among various sources of income, labor income has been ascribed an important theoretical role in antisocial behavior, including crime. It operates not only through its traditional income and incapacitation effects, but also because participation in the labor force shapes social networks, social identity, and bonds to a community, any or all of which can have links to crime and violence, as discussed later in this chapter.

Income is received by individuals who have transitioned (or are transitioning) from school to the labor market and from youth to (early) adult roles. Thus the focus in this chapter is on individuals who, as wage earners, expand their "sphere" of interaction beyond family members and peers, to include local labor markets, coworkers, and the welfare system. The entry point for policy is no longer limited to schools and the families, but is broadened to communities (defined either as geographical units or as groups of individuals who may be targeted by social programs).

This chapter explores the evidence from developed and developing countries on the effects of income on criminality. It first discusses evidence that arises from exogenous changes in income received from social protection programs (unearned income) to unearth the mechanisms by which income alone may affect criminal outcomes. It then turns to income earned in the labor market, which reveals different sets of incentives and trade-offs.

## Income, poverty, and crime: Channels and evidence

In both developed and developing economies, criminal offending and victimization are disproportionately concentrated among individuals with low socioeconomic status living in economically disadvantaged areas.[1] Figure 5.1 shows an enlarged version of the poverty and middle-class yearly coefficient trend lines in figure 2.7 (in chapter 2), which confirms the positive correlation between poverty rates and violence. The figure is based on panel data regressions of homicide rates in a sample of Latin American and Caribbean (LAC) countries on a rich set of controls,[2] and plots the year-specific coefficients associated with the shares of the population in poverty and in the middle class. The figure shows that poverty is positively related to violence and the strength of the relationship has risen over time (as indicated by the positive trend in the light blue line). In 2010, for example, the effect of an incremental rise in the poverty rate on homicides was roughly four times that of an equal increase in poverty in 1999.

Although the relationship between homicide and the size of the middle class in LAC is much less precisely estimated, it exhibits a similar pattern, in which the size of the effect increases over the period. However, rather than being a risk factor, the share of people in the middle class appears to have protective properties.[3] The same pattern of effects is observed for the size of the upper class, only it is a much stronger protective factor (as discussed in chapter 2).[4]

The social costs of poverty are therefore likely to exceed their private costs alone; that is, those borne by the impoverished. For instance, relying on existing estimates of the association between children growing up in poverty and their adult earnings, their propensity to commit crime, and the quality of their health later in life, Holzer and others (2008) estimate the aggregate annual costs of child poverty to the U.S. economy. Their estimates suggest that poverty raises the costs of crime by at least $170 billion annually, representing roughly 1.3 percent of current GDP today, although this is likely a lower bound on the true cost of poverty.[5]

Coupled with the costs to taxpayers of incarceration,[6] these elevated costs of poverty have led researchers and policy makers alike to consider whether shifting

**FIGURE 5.1:** The relationship between poverty and homicides in the LAC region, 1996–2010

Marginal coefficient of poverty and the middle class on homicides rates per year

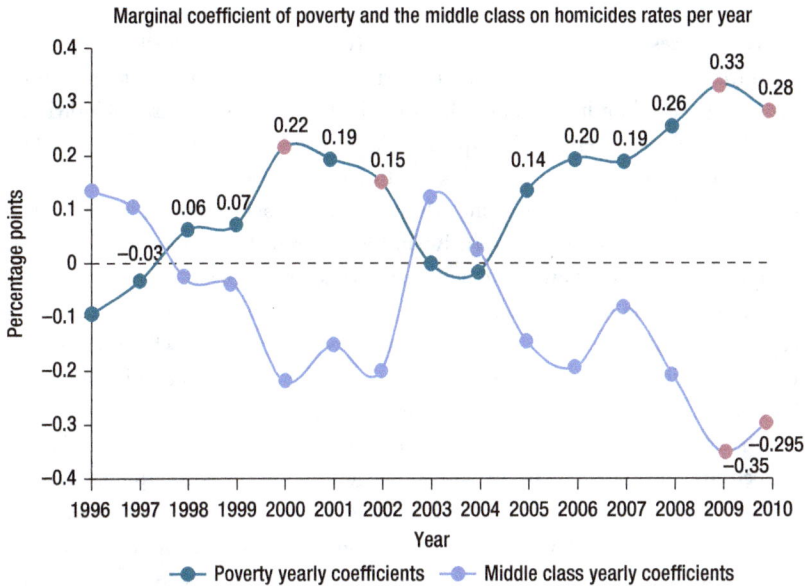

Source: Chioda (2014a).

Note: The sample is of 17 LAC countries, which account for more than 90 percent of the region's population. Each point on a curve represents that year's estimated coefficient of poverty / middle class on the homicide rate, respectively. Data points in pink denote coefficients that are statistically distinct from zero.

resources from the penal system to social programs aimed at reducing poverty and social and economic disadvantage would represent a more cost-effective (prevention) strategy for crime control.[7]

The evidence regarding the prospect of preventing crime through social programs is mixed. For instance, Blau (1999) studies the effects of parents' transitory and permanent incomes on children's cognitive, social, and emotional development in the United States.[8] Using family-fixed effects models and the National Longitudinal Survey of Youth (NLSY), Blau concludes that the effects of permanent family income on test scores are small compared to other family and child characteristics, implying that income transfers per se may be a poor policy lever to improve the outcomes of low-income children.

Chapter 2 cautions against the simplistic view of a monotonic relationship between income and antisocial behavior; the relationship is in fact highly nonlinear. The complex relationship between crime and economic development (as proxied by per capita income) is shaped by the interplay between income and the increased criminal opportunities it attracts—akin to income and substitution effects. In the early stages of development, institutions are often weak and the probability of detecting criminals is low; thus growth in income may be associated with a higher incidence of crime.

Nevertheless, the debate as to whether poverty reduction is an effective strategy to reduce crime and violence has a long history. In the 1930s, the Chicago School of sociology called for interventions that would address the root causes of individual offending such as poverty and inequality. Skeptics questioned the ability of public institutions to manage crime effectively with large-scale government interventions, and expressed concerns about unintended consequences. More recently, in a widely cited article in the *Atlantic Monthly*, Rosin (2008) argued that patterns of crime in Memphis, Tennessee followed public housing voucher recipients to their new locations, raising crime rates in their destination neighborhoods and lowering housing values.[9] While the debate may be fueled by ideology and a priori beliefs about effective crime prevention, ultimately the question as to whether poverty alleviation measures also have crime prevention benefits (or costs) is an empirical one.

As was the case in the discussion on education in chapter 4, the correlations between crime and income/poverty, although suggestive, cannot be interpreted causally. As discussed next, even theory is ambiguous as to the sign (let alone the magnitude) of the relationship between income and crime; the question can be resolved only through a careful empirical analysis. The next section first reviews theories as to how income might affect criminality. It then reviews some empirical evidence on the channels through which income operates to affect criminal offending, particularly among youth in the household. The review is based largely on natural experiments in the United States and in LAC.

## Theories regarding possible channels

Before delving into the evidence, a parsimonious framework is provided for thinking about the relationship between income and crime. The discussion pays special attention to youth, since they are the most frequent offenders and are the group for which there is the most evidence. It then reviews the most convincing research as to income's net effects on their criminality and the likely mechanism(s) through which it operates.

Recall that the organizing framework of this study views individuals as interacting with broader spheres of society as they progress through life stages, first with their parents and immediate kin, then with their neighborhoods and social networks, and then with their community and society at large (figure 5.2). When a household receives income (whether earned or unearned), it may affect its members' interactions within each of these spheres.

As described in chapter 2, the study's framework blends elements of three different models, by complementing Becker's (1968) traditional economic model with features of ecological and developmental theories of crime. In Becker's (1968) theory

**FIGURE 5.2:** A model of the supply of criminal offenses, but also a model of crime and violence prevention

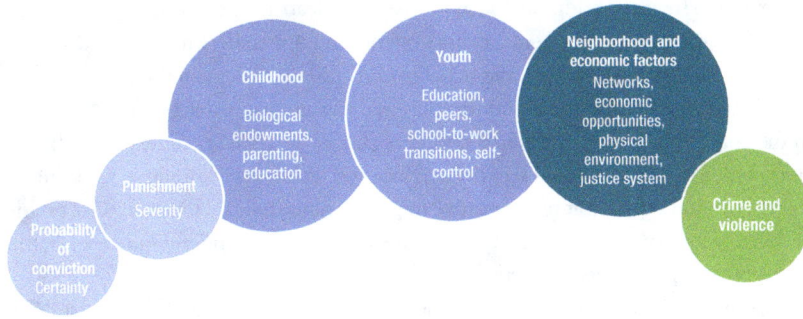

of the supply of criminal offenses, individuals weigh the expected benefits of committing offenses against their expected costs. The number of crimes in any given period is a function of three specified components: the probability of conviction conditional on committing a crime, the expected severity of punishments, and a third variable that is left unspecified and known as Beckerian's residuals.

This variable confers flexibility to the model; it captures other relevant factors such as risk aversion, wages earned in the labor market (which would be forgone should an individual commit a crime and be caught), and peer behavior.[10]

This discussion focuses on the role of poverty / family income in the behavior of youth. Following Heller, Jacob, and Ludwig (2012) and in the spirit of this study's organizing framework, the residual may be thought of as being a function of a number of factors, including:

- Household wealth and socioeconomic status
- Parents' quantity and quality investments in their children (both as inputs to their development and as potential sources of monitoring)
- The human capital of youth
- Income/wealth of other households in the neighborhood
- Local neighborhood characteristics (such as street lighting, cleanliness, and even social capital).

What are some of main mechanisms that can come into play when income changes? The direct effect of income on crime may be the result of economic motivation, resulting from economic necessity through a classical income effect; for example, robbery makes desired goods affordable (that is, it relaxes the budget constraint). On the other hand, additional income could also increase the consumption of criminogenic goods such as alcohol or drugs.

Additional income may also change family routines in such a way that household members reduce their exposure to the likelihood of crime or victimization. For instance, parents may pay for after-school activities for their children to avoid them being idle. However, additional income may also lead to the additional consumption of leisure outside the home, exposing household members to increased risk of victimization. Di Tella, Galiani, and Schargrodsky (2010) document differential avoidance behavior among affluent and poor households in the greater Buenos Aires area in the late 1990s and early 2000s, a period of sharply increasing crime. More affluent households invested in home security services and technology, leading to a decline in their victimization rates at home relative to poorer households. However, their avoidance behavior in public or in the street roughly matched that of poorer households; the two groups fell victim to street crime at roughly equal rates.

Alternatively, more resources may modify parental investments. The mechanisms through which an expansion of family resources may improve children's outcomes can be classified into two channels: the Resource Channel and the Family Process Channel.[11] On the one hand, families may simply use the income to purchase more goods and services (*Resource Channel*), including those goods that maintain basic child welfare (food, physical security), but also goods that enhance child development (clothing, books, and so on). Families may also use additional resources to "purchase" the ability to spend more time with their children, increasing both supervision time and time interacting directly with their children. On the other hand, income transfers may have indirect effects, such as reducing parental and child stress and improving household relations, which may in turn raise the productivity of parenting. These fall under the *Family Process Channel*, which can improve children's ability to function, learn, self-regulate, and ultimately lower the likelihood of engaging in antisocial behaviors.

### The evidence

Following a more in-depth discussion of the Resource and Family Process Channels, this section reviews evidence about the effects of changes in household resources, and the channels through which they likely operate. The second part of the section focuses on the evidence of a casual impact of income on antisocial behavior. Both discussions focus in particular on quasi-experimental evidence from the United States and LAC, in which changes in family resources are exogenous to the behavior and characteristics of the households. It is argued that family processes play an important role in mediating improvements in families' outcomes and criminal behavior.

#### Resource and Family Process Channels in developed and developing countries

The next few sections focus on recent empirical studies that not only establish a credible causal link between income and protective factors such as human capital investments and improvements in the mental well-being of family members, but that are also able to identify the key mediating mechanisms (figure 5.3).[12]

**FIGURE 5.3:** The theoretical indeterminacy of the effect of income on crime: A summary of plausible channels

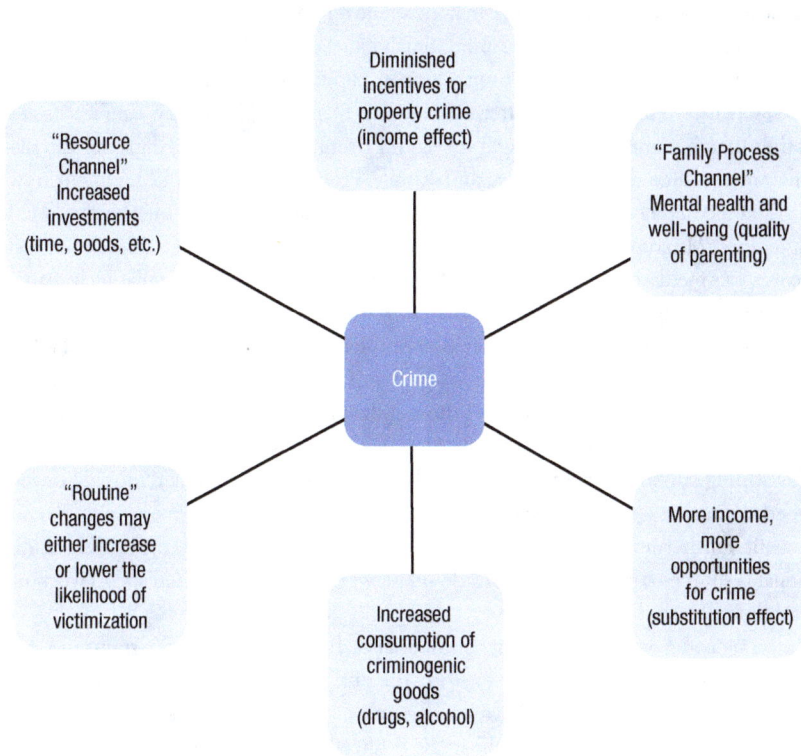

Arguably, if income operates through these channels, then there might be cause for optimism regarding the potential for poverty alleviation programs and policies to reduce crime. However, evidence that household resources affect criminal outcomes must precede any optimism. Are such effects of income detectable? Are they economically significant? Or as Blau (1999) suggested, are they so small as to require implausibly large changes in income to affect outcomes meaningfully, rendering this policy margin impractical?

*Direct purchases of resources useful for child development: The Resource Channel (nutrition and other goods).* In principle, increased resources may have direct effects on investments in children's human capital. However, the magnitude of this effect depends on how much of the additional family income gets devoted to expenditures that enhance human capital. This amount may be small if the household is at a low baseline level of consumption, so that most additional income is spent on more or higher-quality food, for instance.

In the United States, Mayer (1997) documents that when low-income parents receive transfers, they tend to be mainly spent on additional housing expenditures and food consumed away from home. Small effects were also detected for goods or services that are inputs to children's human capital, such as books or stimulating toys/activities. However, the latter effects were mainly explained by families' tastes rather than income levels. Yeung, Linver, and Brooks-Gunn (2002) consider the relative importance of the Resource and Family Process channels, and highlight how distinct mediating mechanisms operate on the association between income and child outcomes. Much of the association between income and children's achievement test scores was mediated by the family's ability to invest in providing a stimulating learning environment. In contrast, as will be discussed in the next few sections, family income was associated with children's behavioral problem, primarily through maternal emotional distress and parenting practices (quality of parenting).

In developing countries such as those in LAC, the potential benefits for children of additional resources are especially large for two reasons. First, poverty levels in developing countries, including those in LAC, are more extreme than those in developed countries; a marginal unit of income if invested in children may yield a larger benefit. Furthermore, child labor is not uncommon in developing countries. The additional resources could resolve the trade-off between time that children spend working and time allocated to school.

The widespread adoption of conditional cash transfer (CCT) programs in LAC represents a unique opportunity to study the link between income and intermediate channels that may ultimately have an impact on crime. While this report does not aim to review all dimensions in which CCTs affect families, this discussion highlights those that are related to the relevance of the Resource Channel.[13] However, because the conditionality of CCTs typically ties receipt of the benefit to school attendance of the young children in the household, caution is required to disentangle the effects of additional income from those of the conditionality.[14]

Does the additional income in LAC translate into additional material investments in children's human capital? Recipients households in Colombia, Ecuador,[15] Mexico, and Nicaragua have been shown to increase the share of total household expenditures spent on food at all levels of income, compared to nonbeneficiary households.[16] Improvements in the quality of food purchases include shifts away from staples (rice, beans, and tortillas) in favor of more nutritious and high-protein food (eggs, dairy, meat, vegetables, and fruit). In Mexico, Bobonis (2009) identifies a substantial positive effect on the share of expenditures on children's clothing—as proxy for children-specific outcomes.[17] Similar findings are found in the case of Atencion a Crisis, a CCT program in rural Nicaragua, where children in the program are more likely to have better diets, books, paper, pencils, medical checkups, and vitamins (Macours, Shady, and Vakis 2012). Both sets of results provide suggestive evidence that CCT resources are ultimately devoted to additional investments in goods that would increase children's human capital.

However, these encouraging results may be offset by the mixed evidence as to whether cash transfers reduce child labor (Fiszbein and Schady 2009). In some instances, there are clear declines in child labor (Oportunidades in Mexico, and Bono de Desarrollo Humano in Ecuador, which, unlike the other programs, are not conditional on children attending school or other child-related investments). In other instances, the evidence is inconclusive (Familias en Acción in Colombia, and Programa de Asignación Familiar in Honduras).

Ultimately, the net effect of income, as mediated by the Resource Channel, on children's human capital will depend on the relative magnitude of its impact on child labor and the relative impact of additional material investments in children. However, even if the net impact of income is positive, it may be too small to represent a meaningful crime reduction strategy if the productivity of the resulting investments in terms of educational and behavioral outcomes is related to the initial level of poverty. That is, deep poverty may attenuate the protective benefits of income; consistent with Blau (1999) and Dooley and Stewart (2004), the magnitudes of transfers typically under consideration in the context of poverty reduction programs are unlikely to induce large enough changes in children's human capital to affect subsequent criminal behavior later in life.

*Quantity of parental supervision: The Resource Channel (time).* Additional income may also induce parents to increase parental investments because of traditional trade-offs between leisure and labor; additional resources are likely to decrease the amount of time dedicated to work (a traditional income effect on leisure, which is a normal good).[18] This channel operates under the assumption that parents spend the extra time engaging their children in developmentally productive activities and/or increase their parental supervision. As discussed in chapter 3, the increased investment in children's human capital could translate into improvements in children's behavioral outcomes in the short term and/or long term. Aizer (2004) examines the consequences of the lack of adult supervision after school on a panel of U.S. school-age children. For these children, adult supervision is related to a decrease in risky and antisocial behaviors—such as skipping school, consuming alcohol or drugs, stealing, or harming others—even after controlling for unobserved family characteristics that may be correlated with both supervision and child behavior, such as the strictness of parents.[19]

Further evidence as to the relative importance of the (time) Resource Channel is provided by a meta-analysis by Gennetian and others (2004) of eight random assignment studies that consider the impact of welfare and work policies targeted at low-income parents. Surprisingly, across the eight studies, the authors document adverse effects on a number of academic outcomes among adolescents ages 12 to 18 years at follow-up. However, a closer examination of the policies reveals that the larger negative impacts on academics were concentrated in programs that required mothers to work or participate in employment-related activities and those that encouraged mothers to work voluntarily. In particular, the most pronounced negative effects on academic outcomes occurred for the group of adolescents who had a younger sibling, possibly because of the increased responsibilities they assumed at home and in sibling care as their mothers increased their "labor supply."

These results are particularly important because they suggest that not all additional resources are created equal. While, all else constant, additional income is unambiguously welfare-enhancing, additional resources that are conditional on work implies that time that would otherwise be spent with children or devoted to parenting is spent at work, leading to a decline in the parenting time, as well as a possible decline in its quality. Instead, income transfers that are not conditioned on work appear to be associated with a substitution away from labor supply, yielding increased time and investments in parenting.

The relationship between income, labor force participation—particularly maternal labor supply—and children's outcomes is therefore chiefly important in the design of policies focusing on the transition from welfare to work, and hence out of poverty. This has specific relevance for single mothers, and highlights the need to consider policies more comprehensively and to foresee the likely unintended consequences of particular interventions, especially those that affect children and adolescents.

*Quality of parental supervision and emotional well-being: The Family Process Channel (time).* A substitution away from labor into child supervision and/or child-enriching activities is not the only channel through which an improvement in parental investments might occur as a result of relaxing budget constraints. Poverty-alleviating income transfers may operate indirectly on children's aggression and outcomes related to the strain and stress that poverty places on adult household members' mental health. Mullainathan and Shafir (2013) carefully document the impact of the effects of scarcity (of time and resources) on behavior and cognitive function. They conclude that scarcity has the power to put people in a kind of cognitive tunnel that, on the one hand, makes them less aware of cognitive biases when handling economic decisions and, on the other hand, can impose a significant "bandwidth tax" limiting the ability of individuals to perform well. It may thus diminish their self-control and cognitive ability. In a related vein, Lund and others (2010), in their review of 115 articles relating to low- and middle-income countries, report that 73 percent of the studies find a positive association between measures of poverty and common mental disorders, including depression, consistent with theories of "strain." To the extent that easing the budget constraint improves parental mental health and faculties, the quality of parents' investments in children may improve, and their time spent with children would de facto become more productive.

To quantify the causal impact of added resources, Milligan and Stabile (2011) exploit changes in the Canada Child Tax Benefit (CCTB), which varied across provinces, time, and family structure exclusively for legislative reasons. In particular, the authors study the impact of the extra resources on outcomes related to improved family relations and the emotional well-being of children and families (family process outcomes). Several indicators of emotional and behavioral well-being indicate improvements in the outcomes of children and their mothers as a result of increased child benefits, with particularly strong effects on children's physical aggression[20] and maternal depression[21] (Milligan and Stabile 2011).

Maternal depression is a matter of concern not only in its own right, but also because of its impact on family dynamics and child development. Women are typically the primary caregivers, so symptoms of depression may compromise mothers' interactions with their children and inhibit nurturing. Indeed, Ozer and others (2009, 2011) and others document that maternal depression is associated with poorer cognitive and physical development of children. It is therefore not surprising that increased child benefits not only improve children's emotional well-being, but are also associated with sizable improvements in academic outcomes, as measured by math scores and the Peabody Test (a standardized test measuring both verbal ability and scholastic aptitude). The average improvement in the math scores is 6.9 percent of a standard deviation per $1,000 of benefits. There are also substantial differences in the effects depending on child gender: child benefits have stronger effects on the educational outcomes and physical health of boys, and on the mental health outcomes of girls. The magnitudes of the effects also tend to be larger for families with lower levels of education, suggesting a gradient in socioeconomic status.

The magnitude of the effect on academic outcomes is comparable to that found by Dahl and Lochner (2012), who make use of the U.S. Earned Income Tax Credit (EITC)—an income maintenance program for low-income families and individuals who have earnings from work—to estimate the (short-term) causal effect of family resources on child academic achievement. To break the confounding effects of other unobserved household characteristics or behaviors in the relationship between family resources and child outcomes, they exploit several expansions of the EITC. Their estimates suggest that current income has a significant effect on a child's math and reading achievement: a $1,000 increase in family income raises math and reading test scores by 6 percent of a standard deviation, on average. The effects are larger for children in more disadvantaged families, for younger children, and for boys.[22]

Both sets of estimates are much larger in magnitude than the estimate in Blau (1999), who found that a $1,000 increase in income would raise test scores by roughly 0.5 percent of a standard deviation. How can the discrepancy between the causal and correlational estimates be reconciled? One possibility is that income matters more for children from the most disadvantaged households, and the EITC-induced variation in income that Dahl and Lochner (2012) examine reflects more the effect of income for these families (in the sense of a local average treatment effect). It is also possible that expectations about future income play an important role in determining child outcomes; that is, "permanent" income may have more of an impact on the effects outcomes than transitory income. Since changes in EITC income imply permanent changes, variation in household income might be expected to have larger impacts.

These effects—and particularly, their income gradient—are consistent with the notion that poverty is particularly taxing in terms of cognitive load, and the resulting stress may manifest itself in diminished faculties, reduced self-control, and worse mental health. These secondary consequences, in turn, may compromise parenting's effectiveness, and ultimately lead to behavioral problems in youth and later in life. These mechanisms can be expected to be more severe in developing countries, where poverty is more acute. The increased adoption of CCTs since the mid-1990s in dozens of low- and middle-income countries provides a valuable opportunity to test this hypothesis rigorously. However, there is a little research that attempts to assess the extent to which poverty alleviation programs improve the mental health of mothers—an outcome that is typically not specifically targeted by the intervention. Available evidence is somewhat mixed. The cash transfer programs in Ecuador and Nicaragua[23] yield no (statistically significant) effect on measures of women's psychological well-being (that is, perceived stress) nor on maternal depression. However, in the context of Mexico's CCT program (Oportunidades), Ozer and others (2011) provide evidence of significantly lower symptoms of depression[24]—a 10 percent decrease—among women who receive the transfer relative to their counterparts in the control group. Furthermore, they also document increases in perceived control over life events, suggesting a pathway though which additional income exerts effects on maternal mental health.

In a companion paper, Ozer and others (2009) demonstrate that children in families participating in the Oportunidades program have lower aggressive and oppositional problems (that is, patterns of angry and irritable behavior and vindictiveness, as well as defiance, disobedience, and argumentative behaviors) after controlling for a range of child characteristics and family-level socioeconomic factors. The strength of the effect was modest, representing a 10 percent decline in problem behavior, even though Oportunidades program components do not explicitly addressing child behavior. Candidate hypotheses for the mechanisms through which the program could act on child behavior include improved child nutrition (through the Resource Channel)[25] or alleviation of severe economic stress on the family—which in turn could promote parental mental health and family relationships (through the Family Process Channel).

How can the differences in results across the three LAC case studies and those from developed economies be reconciled? Differences in the magnitude of the transfer could play a role. The Nicaragua and Ecuador transfers correspond to 15 percent of family income, on average, and measurements of well-being were taken seven to nine months after the onset of the program. Mexico's transfer was larger, amounting to a 25 percent income supplement, and benefits were received for between 3.5 and 5 years, allowing more opportunity for effects on maternal mental health (Ozer and others 2011). These findings are reminiscent of those from previous chapters, which documented a nonlinear relationship between income and well-being. That is, in order to reap the benefits of the additional income, the supplement must move the family beyond a critical income threshold.

Evidence from both developed and developing countries consistently points to the importance of the Resource and Family Process channels. The latter is particularly important, given its sizable effects on mental well-being in developing country contexts. Additional income is productively employed by parents and affords families the opportunity to improve parental investments, in terms of both quantity and quality, yielding improvements in the educational outcomes of children. Why does this matter for crime? This study has already documented the protective benefits of education, but increased parental supervision may also have direct effects on youth delinquency. The next section formalizes and quantifies these conjectures by discussing the impact of income transfers in contexts where criminal outcomes are observed.

### The evidence: Linking crime to exogenous variations in income

The discussion that follows highlights the most compelling empirical research on the value of income as a protective factor with respect to crime and reviews the strengths and weaknesses of the various approaches. In particular, it reviews evidence from studies in which clear exogenous variations in family income arise from a policy or event, and is exploited to estimate effects on crime and violence. Where possible, the discussion highlights research from LAC, which, while limited, is growing.

*The nexus between income and antisocial behavior in the United States.* Jacob and Ludwig (2010) provide some of the most reliable evidence on the effects of income on crime by analyzing a housing voucher program for families in private housing in Chicago. While not a direct transfer of cash per se, the cash equivalent of the voucher is large. Because the program was oversubscribed, the city of Chicago randomly allocated applicants to a waiting list. For program recipients, half the voucher took the form of a housing subsidy that reduced out-of-pocket housing expenses (freeing up resources to spend on other goods); the remaining half was in kind and took the form of improved housing amenities. Empirically, because almost all of the additional resources were devoted to improving the quality of housing rather than changing the characteristics of the neighborhood in which recipients live, the authors can interpret the program as a large resource transfer rather than a mobility and neighborhood intervention. The average subsidy size was $8,265 per year per family, representing approximately a 50 percent increase in family income.

The program had no detectable impact on children's cognitive outcomes, as measured by reading and math scores, but did have beneficial effects on soft skills, such as persistence in school and avoidance of criminal activity. Furthermore, these benefits were heavily concentrated among male youth. The sizable increase in income raised the probability that male youth graduate from high school by 16–24 percent and reduced the number of adolescent male arrests by about 20 percent; impacts on arrests for violent crime were similar. Assuming that the change in arrests is proportional to the reduction in actual crimes committed, the implied income elasticity of crime is roughly −0.4.

The Chicago program is useful from the perspective of studying criminality because it sheds light on the mechanisms underlying the impact on criminal behavior. Three candidate mechanisms emerge as to how the Chicago program had an impact on crime and violence: increased schooling, reduced formal sector work among youth, and increases in parents' time spent with children.

In Jacob and Ludwig's (2010) sample, the average high school graduation rate was approximately 10 percent; the rate rose by 2.5 percentage points among voucher recipients. As with the decline in arrests, this increased graduation rate was almost entirely driven by boys, despite there being no effect on test scores. Given estimates by Lochner and Moretti (2004) that a 1 percentage point increase in high school graduation lowers violent crime by 2 percent, the authors conclude that the 2.5 percentage point increase in high school graduation induced by the voucher alone accounted for one-quarter of the reduction in violent crime among voucher recipients as an indirect (and unintended) consequence of the program. The effects of income that operate through increases in human capital are therefore substantial.

What might account for the remaining 15 percent decline in crime? One candidate explanation is a classical income effect on consumption, whereby feeling wealthier lessens the desire (or need) to steal, or on labor supply. Jacob and Ludwig (2010) find some support for this theory in unemployment insurance records; youth in the voucher program appear to have reduced their labor supply in the formal sector. This is a point to which this chapter returns, after reviewing evidence that being employed and criminally active are not mutually exclusive and that early and intensive attachment to the labor force during youth may in fact have unintended consequences in the form of *more* criminality. This is particularly a concern if available employment opportunities are of poor quality in terms of either skill requirements or work peers.

An alternative channel through which the voucher program might have operated is in the allocation of parental time. Jacob and Ludwig (2010) show that adult labor force participation also responded to the voucher program; the quarterly earnings of recipient mothers declined by 10 percent (presumably through a reduction in hours worked). If less time at work implies increases in time spent at home, this would suggest a protective role for parental supervision with respect to crime and schooling. Indeed, evidence of a tradeoff between maternal labor supply and youth outcomes emerges from a recent review of 13 welfare-to-work experiments run by the Manpower Demonstration Research Corporation (MDRC). In all instances, parental employment rose, between 10 and 30 percent. In some cases, the program was income neutral, with increases in labor income crowding out welfare payments, whereas in others income rose slightly. However, in all cases, the increases in maternal labor supply led to higher rates of academic problems among adolescent children (which is cause for further concern in light of the relationship between education and crime documented in the previous chapter). Of the 13 studies, only 1 recorded delinquent behavior and indicated that the program raised the rate of truancy and alcohol use, but not drug use.[26]

Lastly, Akee and others (2010) exploit a natural experiment whose structure resembles that of a poverty alleviation program.[27] They find that children who reside the longest in households with exogenously increased incomes tend to do better later in life along several dimensions. These children are more likely to have graduated from high school by age 19 than children in untreated households. By age 21, the treated children from the poorest households have an additional year of schooling, implying that, for the poorest families, an average of $4,000 in additional annual household income results in an additional year of education for their child. Additionally, using administrative arrest records, they find that these same children have a statistically significantly lower incidence of criminal behavior for minor offenses. The additional household income reduces the incidence of ever having committed a minor crime by 22 percent at ages 16 and 17 for the children from treated households. These youth also self-report being less likely to have dealt drugs than those from households unaffected by the additional income.

As with other programs, the poorest households in the survey appear to experience the largest gains. Separating the data according to prior poverty status, Akee and others (2010) find that many of their results are driven by the poorer households. Overall, the results indicate that parents in households with additional income make better choices regarding their personal behavior and criminal behavior. They do not appear to make significant changes in their labor force participation efforts. Children report better relationships over time in the households with additional income, and parents report better supervision of their children over time in these same households. While there are many potential causal mechanisms at work here, it is useful to learn that parental time is not responsible for the observed changes in child outcomes. Parental quality and parents' interaction with their children appear to be an important factor for explaining how additional household income translates into better child outcomes (Akee and others 2010).

Qualitatively, these conclusions are consistent with the discussion of resource and process effects of additional income in the previous section, whereby gains in children's educational outcomes resulting from additional income are mediated by increased parental time, as well as (possibly) higher-quality parenting.

In sum, the evidence is that parental time matters for children and is one of the main mechanisms underlying the effects of poverty reduction programs on crime. One could then argue that a more direct and cost-effective way of achieving similar results would be to target either the quantity or quality of time parents spend with their children. Indeed, there is some evidence that changes in parenting through home-based and center-based programs can have desirable effects on children and improve their outcomes.

*Evidence from Latin America and the Caribbean: Conditional cash transfers in Colombia and Brazil.* LAC provides the backdrop for some evidence on the effects of family resources on the antisocial behavior of youth. In particular, two studies consider the effects of CCT programs on criminality and violence, one in Brazil and the other in Colombia.

As mentioned, CCTs have gained considerable traction in the developing world because they are seen as effective tools for poverty reduction (Fiszbein and Schady 2009). They are usually designed to provide beneficiaries a cash transfer, contingent on a number of conditions, such as a minimal number of doctor or nurse visits and a threshold school attendance rate for children and adolescents.

In their evaluation of Brazil's Bolsa Família, Chioda, De Mello, and Soares (2016) were the first to consider the possible links between CCTs and crime. Bolsa Família is one of the earliest and largest CCT programs in the world. It covers over 11 million families and costs almost 0.4 percent of Brazil's GDP. Previous research has documented that Bolsa Família has had the desired effect of substantially raising enrollment rates, improving school progression, and reducing extreme poverty and inequality, though questions remain as to its social rate of return and it effectiveness in urban settings.

The authors combine detailed school characteristics with geo-referenced and time-stamped criminal reports to estimate the contemporaneous impact of the number of children covered by Bolsa Família within a school on crime in the neighborhood surrounding the school (akin to a school district). The empirical problem lies in the fact that the number of children covered by Bolsa Família in an area depends on number of socioeconomic characteristics, including the incidence of poverty and unemployment, that are all likely to confound the effect of receipt of CCTs on crime. As a result, the correlation between Bolsa Família's coverage and crime is unlikely to be causal.

Chioda, De Mello, and Soares (2016) overcome this problem by exploiting a 2008 expansion of the program. Initially, youth could be covered only up to age 15. In 2008, this restriction was expanded to include adolescents up to age 17. They therefore construct an instrument that combines the timing of expansion with the demographic composition of schools before the program was expanded to generate variation in the number of children covered by the CCT that is plausibly unrelated to other contemporaneous and unobserved determinants of receipt of CCTs. This instrument can then be used to estimate the causal effect of Bolsa Família on crime. The authors document robust and significant negative impacts of the number of Bolsa Família beneficiaries on neighborhood crime. They find that the expansion of Bolsa Família to 16- and 17-year-olds caused a 7.6 percent reduction in crime in school neighborhoods, representing 45 fewer crimes per school per year, or 2 fewer crimes per beneficiary student. They find statistically significant effects for violent and drug-related crimes, in addition to robberies.

The authors then endeavor to identify the channel(s) through which the CCT reduces crime. There are at least three possibilities: incapacitation from time spent in school, income effects from the income transfers, and social interactions from changed peer groups. With information on days of the week when crimes are committed, they rule out incapacitation, because there are only minor differences in the magnitudes of effects between school days and nonschool days. Although they cannot rule out the peer group channel, they argue that the effect of Bolsa Família on crime operates mostly through the income channel, because most of its effects are concentrated among low-income schools.

From the perspective of this study, the results of Chioda, De Mello, and Soares (2016) are important because the expansion of Bolsa Família affected an age group that is precisely at highest risk of criminal offending. Indeed, this may in part explain the large magnitude of their effects: the expansion induced a change in behavior among those who were most likely to offend, and perhaps repeatedly offend.

Because the crime data employed by Chioda, De Mello, and Soares (2016) is annual in frequency, the interpretation of their estimated effects are medium term: they represent the effects of the receipt of CCTs on crimes committed over the course of a year. In contrast, Camacho and Mejía (2013) consider the effects of cash receipts from Colombia's CCT program, Familias en Acción, on short-term (daily) changes in crime in Bogotá. Their study differs from Chioda, De Mello, and Soares (2016) in that the frequency of their data allows them to isolate the very-short-term income effects of cash payments. They exploit information on the location of beneficiary households, along with the precise dates on which the transfers are made. This information is then linked to national crime reports. They document significant declines in property crime in the days immediately following the transfers, suggesting a short-term income effect of cash benefits. Specifically, they find that transfers reduce thefts and motor vehicle thefts by 7.2 percent and 1.3 percent, respectively, in the days immediately following cash disbursement.[28] The authors provide a discussion of the main channels underlying their results. First, a pure income effect, associated with the availability of additional resources on payment days, would lower the economic motivation to commit crimes against property. Second, if time allocated to work-related activities responds to short-term variation in income needs, then a positive income shock could lead to a reduction of hours worked (the intensive margin), in favor of increased parental investments in children and increased parental supervision. Both channels, along with the elasticity of crime to short-term (daily) variation in available resources, highlight the importance of credit constraints and limits to consumption smoothing.[29] Blattman, Jamison, and Sheridan (2015) also highlight the importance of income in shaping antisocial behavior. The authors study the impact of randomized grants in combination with behavioral therapy targeting executive functions to men in Liberia engaged in crime. Cash alone and therapy alone dramatically reduced crime and violence, but effects dissipated within a year. More persistent crime reduction (50 percent after one year) was observed when cash and therapy were combined, speaking to the importance of both the resources and soft skills channels.

Note that the effects they identify cannot operate through the increases in human capital that result from the schooling conditionality of Familias en Acción, since the effects relate to day-to-day variations in the timing of receipt of the cash. For education to play a role would require information about the returns to human capital in the labor market to vary drastically from one day to the next, which seems implausible.

Consistent with Camacho and Mejía (2013), Munyo and Rossi (2015) also document very-short-term effects of income on crime for ex-offenders. They use data on prisoners released from custody in Montevideo, Uruguay. They show that on any given day, the number of inmates released from prison significantly affects the number of offenses committed on that day, an effect that they term "first-day recidivism." More relevant for this chapter, however, they also document that an increase in the amount of money provided to prisoners at the time of their release significantly decreases first-day recidivism. They conclude that first-day recidivism is largely driven by liquidity constraints. Known offenders are so cash-strapped and have so few legal sources of income on the day of their release that they are much more inclined to commit another crime the very day that they are released.

## Labor income: Channels and evidence

The previously discussed research on the causal relationship between income and crime often exploits variations in income that are generated by poverty reduction programs.[30] In turn, this section discusses recent evidence regarding the relationship between crime and the labor market, including how crime and violence relate to wages (income that is earned in the labor market in exchange for time). Theory suggests a number of mechanisms through which the labor force participation of either parents or youth may causally relate to crime.

Employment is typically associated with three key factors that may affect criminal activity: a source of income, an incapacitation effect, and a peer group of coworkers. Various schools of thought emphasize the importance of different underlying mechanisms (figure 5.4). Traditional economic models postulate that income from legal employment will reduce the tendency to offend through a standard income effect, but also that forgone future earnings in the event of incarceration represent (potentially large) opportunity costs for committing crimes relative to not being employed, and thereby act as a disincentive for criminality. Conversely, high unemployment implies an

**FIGURE 5.4:** Selected theories and channels relating employment and crime

| Becker model | Strain Theory | Social Control Theory |
|---|---|---|
| • Income effect (–) | • Lack of employment (+) | • Not employment and income but facilitate social bonds |
| • Incapacitation effect (–) | • Perceived fairness and satisfaction of employment (+) (quality of employment) | • Networks if peers are positively selected |
| • Peer effect (+/–), depending on the job | | |
| • Affordability of criminogenic goods (+) | | |
| • Increased interaction (opportunity for crime) (+) | | |
| • Employment may crowd out quantity and quality of parenting, with negative externality on children's outcomes (+) | | |

elevated likelihood of having zero future wages. People living in high-unemployment areas can therefore expect lower wages in the future (lower permanent income). Since wages represent the opportunity cost of crime conditional on being caught, higher unemployment acts to weaken the disincentive to offend.

In addition to the traditional economic theory channels, Strain Theory and Social Control Theory argue that employment has value beyond its monetary compensation, in the form of the psychic and societal rewards of an occupation. In particular, Strain Theory argues that the inability to achieve economic success and the unequal distribution of job opportunities exert negative forces that render criminality more attractive. Other theories do not assign a causal role to employment per se, but identify the social bonds and networks formed in workers' employment as a central mediator for crime. For instance, Hirschi's (1969) Social Control Theory argues that commitment to conventional lines of actions (such as work) generates a "stake in conformity" that renders crimes less attractive. In addition, social interactions at work may act as protective factors if workers tend to be positively selected, in the sense of being more productive than their unemployed counterparts and less inclined to be involved in criminal activities. However, lower-quality peers at work may have the opposite effect; thus employment and wages may have uncertain effects on offending.

However, there could also be costs (in terms of crime) associated with employment. First, as mentioned, additional resources increase the affordability of criminogenic goods and services; this would suggest a countervailing positive relationship with crime, so the net effect on offending is ambiguous. Second, employment may also alter daily routines that either diminish or increase contact with potential victims or offenders. For instance, employment may crowd out time that would otherwise be available for illegal activities; in this case, employment has a mechanical incapacitation effect on offending. Third, households with children could face potential trade-offs between time allocated to the labor market and the quantity and/or quality of parenting and supervision, with unintended negative externalities in terms of crime.

On net, the effects of employment and attachment to the labor force are theoretically ambiguous. Resolving the ambiguity requires reliance on empirical evidence, which is reviewed next.

The remainder of the chapter first reviews the relationship between crime and unemployment. This strand of the literature suggests that, for the general population, the extensive margin of economic activity is too imprecise a measure of labor market attachment. It further finds that other measures of labor market outcomes may be particularly relevant to criminal participation for specific subgroups of the population that are at higher risk of offending. These two insights motivate the section that follows, which focuses on the link between antisocial behavior and more refined indicators of labor outcomes, as captured by the wages of the unskilled and of youth. Low skill, low educational attainment, and low human capital are identified as central factors that lead to the variety of low-quality employment that is associated with more elevated risks of criminality. Thus the last section of the chapter reviews the effectiveness of preventing or reducing criminal behavior through training programs that target at-risk individuals (ex-offenders and youth).

## The evidence: Unemployment

Whatever the sign of the relationship between the labor market and criminal offending, there are clear theoretical links between the two, which have generated a rich body of economic and criminological research. Numerous empirical studies have explored the relationship between fluctuations in aggregate employment and crime, though the conclusions vary across settings, empirical specifications, and populations. The discussion begins with a review of the relationship between offending and unemployment, then transitions to the relationship with more refined measures of labor market conditions, and finally considers specific subgroups of the population, such as youth and unskilled workers.

First-generation studies of the relationship between labor markets and crime often focused on the aggregate comovements of unemployment and crime—though unemployment is only one of multiple measures of how potential criminals might fare in the formal market. In addition, care is needed in interpreting the results of such studies because failure to account for variables that are positively related to both the business cycle and crime may bias estimates downward. For instance, alcohol consumption is procyclical and tends to have independent effects on offending (Ruhm 1995). Thus its exclusion from an analysis might understate the effects of unemployment. The opposite bias may result if criminal involvement renders offenders less employable. Still another concern is that unemployment and crime may be jointly determined; investment, economic activity, and ultimately employment may plausibly stall as a result of elevated levels of crime. Ignoring the possibility of such feedbacks from crime to unemployment will deliver a biased estimate of the costs of unemployment in terms of crime. The large set of inconsistent conclusions led Chiricos (1987) to refer to a "consensus of doubts."[31]

Panel data studies at more refined geographical levels (such as states, metropolitan areas, and census tracts) help alleviate some of these concerns and improve the quality and reliability of estimates. With such data in hand, researchers have come closer to reaching a consensus that unemployment in developed countries does have a positive (albeit small) and significant effect on property crime, but no significant effect on violent crime. This pattern is consistent with the hypothesis that depressed labor market conditions induce economically motivated crimes. This view is further supported by the following three studies, which, in addition to using panel data, exploit three different sources of exogenous variation in unemployment.

Raphael and Winter-Ebmer (2001) undertake a careful analysis of U.S. state-level data, controlling extensively for economic and demographic factors, while allowing for state and year fixed effects, and state-specific time trends. Importantly, they control for the incarceration rate in state prisons in all models, under the hypothesis that it might reduce crime rates via an incapacitation effect (for those criminals who are currently incarcerated), and a deterrence effect (for those currently contemplating crime). They find a robust, positive relationship between state unemployment and property crime (burglary, larceny, auto theft). For violent crimes, their findings are weaker, with little evidence of a consistent relationship with unemployment. These results survive qualitatively, even after accounting for the possible endogeneity of unemployment by instrumenting unemployment with oil costs and federal government defense spending in the state, both of which are plausibly related to economic conditions but unrelated to crime. In models that account for the joint determination of crime and unemployment, violent crime appears unresponsive to rates of state unemployment, while property crime is even more positively related than in ordinary least squares models; a 1 percentage point decline in unemployment decreases property crime by 4 to 5 percent, whereas models that ignore the endogeneity problem deliver closer to a 1.5 percent decline in property crimes. These estimates imply that a substantial portion of the decline in U.S. property crimes during the 1990s is attributable to the decline in the unemployment rate.

Edmark (2005) investigates the nexus between labor market shocks and property crime in Sweden, armed with a panel of county-level data on property crimes from 1988 to 1999. In this context, the author takes advantage of wild swings in unemployment at the county level that resulted from considerable instability in the labor market over the period. In addition to county fixed effects and county-specific trends, Edmark controls for a rich set of social and economic county characteristics to confirm Raphael and Winter-Ebmer's (2001) qualitative result that deteriorations in local labor market conditions are positively related to property crime.

Lin (2008) builds on the concerns about endogeneity and reconsiders the relationship between state-level unemployment and offending in the United States. To instrument for unemployment, Lin employs the real exchange rate, the percentage of state output from various manufacturing sectors, and state union membership. What is the intuition behind this choice of instruments? The demand for manufacturing jobs in the home country is governed by the relative labor cost at home versus that abroad. For instance, if foreign currency depreciates (becomes cheaper), the cost of labor abroad becomes cheaper. In a competitive market, it could become too costly for companies not to respond to a lower cost of labor abroad and thus outsource low-skill manufacturing jobs to foreign countries, de facto raising the unemployment rate at home, particularly among low-skilled workers.

When instrumenting for unemployment with the interaction between changes in the real exchange rate between adjacent years and the percentage of state output (or employment) in the manufacturing sector, the estimated elasticity between unemployment and property crimes is significant and large in magnitude—equal to 4 percent—double the magnitude of the ordinary least squares estimates and those of previous studies.[32]

This larger estimate has significant policy implications because it explains 30 percent of the decline in property crime during the 1990s. More importantly, Lin's (2008) approach is particularly relevant to this report because the variation in unemployment Lin exploits affects those who are most likely at the financial margins of criminal offending. The source of variation exploited by Lin (2008) de facto identifies the impact of unemployment on crime among the subset of the population that is more likely to lose its employment because of global shifts in economic conditions related to the terms of trade and the costs of U.S. labor. That is, the focus is on low-wage and low-education male workers in manufacturing, who are also more likely to be at the margin of offending.

Direct evidence from LAC on the links between the labor market and crime is more scarce. In the spirit of Raphael and Winter-Ebmer (2001), Edmark (2005), Lin (2008), and Chioda (2014a) employ detailed annual data from a panel of LAC countries between 1996 and 2010 to estimate models of the homicide rate on a number of economic and social indicators, such as gross national income (GNI) per capita; measures of inequality, average educational attainment, and institutions; as well as the lagged unemployment rate.[33] Because criminality is typically characterized by a great deal of inertia, Chioda (2014a) also controls for the lagged homicide rate, rendering the model dynamic.

As is frequently the case in dynamic panel data models, little variation in the homicide rate remains after controlling for both country fixed effects and the lagged dependent variable. Despite this, Chioda (2014a) finds that country homicide rates are positively related to unemployment. However, the relationship is statistically significant only for unemployment among youth; conditional on the unemployment rate of youth, adult unemployment appears largely unrelated to homicides. This pattern is consistent with the hypothesis that perpetrators of homicides are more likely to be youth, and that unemployment among this group is particularly costly to society. Importantly, Chioda's estimates are conditional on measures of country demographic structure and education that might otherwise confound the unemployment effects. These variables control (to the extent possible) for the low socioeconomic status and at-risk composition of the population. As such, Chioda's estimates of the youth unemployment effect are not driven by secular declines in education that might be related to unemployment, guaranteeing that her estimates are driven by economic fluctuations.

Finally, Chioda's (2014a) analysis reveals that the costs of unemployment are not merely instantaneous; because the model is dynamic, a change in one independent variable that generates a response in violent crime feeds back into its future realizations through its lag. For example, if youth unemployment rises by 3 percentage points this year, yielding an additional homicide next year (because the *lagged* unemployment is the independent variable), that additional homicide feeds back into the homicide rate two years later through the lagged dependent variable.[34] Thus, a shock today propagates through the system over several periods. In this instance, because of the dynamic specification and because the coefficient on both unemployment and the lagged homicide rate are positive, the long-term costs of unemployment exceed their instantaneous costs.[35]

Dix-Carneiro, Soares, and Ulyssea (2016) find that labor market conditions have a strong effect on homicide rates in Brazil. Exploiting the 1990s trade liberalization as a natural experiment, they document how regions facing more negative shocks experience larger relative increases in crime rates in the medium term. Results show a much stronger link between labor markets and crime than that documented by this literature. This suggests that the criminogenic effects of deteriorations in labor market conditions are likely to be more extreme and relevant for policy in developing countries with poor labor market conditions and high levels of violence.[36]

In sum, there is evidence from the United States and Sweden that property crime is responsive to economic fluctuations that affect the labor market. The evidence from LAC reveals that there is also a relationship between unemployment among the highest-risk individuals (youth) and violent crime. The findings in this section also highlight that labor market attachment may play a central role for more "vulnerable" subgroups (those at higher risk of engaging in antisocial behavior): namely, youth and unskilled workers. In other words, unemployment may be too coarse a measure of the health of the labor market to capture the more relevant margins along which violence and labor market outcomes interact. The next section explores this conjecture.

## Wages, labor markets, unskilled labor, and crime

The previous discussion relied on one specific measure of conditions in the labor market—the unemployment rate—perhaps due to expediency or data availability. However, unemployment is hardly the sole measure of the opportunities in the labor market or of the quality of these opportunities. The average wage rate, for instance, can yield information about the value of formal work. It reflects the returns to participation in the labor market and is a marker of the trade-offs made by individuals. More importantly, focusing solely on unemployment misses the important point that crime and work may coexist. In a low-wage environment, labor supply (or work effort) may decline and more time (and/or effort) may be devoted to crime; this margin of behavior may not manifest itself as a decline in labor force participation.[37] Several studies show a fluid, dynamic, and complex interaction between legal and illegal work (Fagan and Freeman 1999). Among young drug dealers, more than one in four is also employed in the legal sector (Reuter, MacCoun, and Murphy 1990), and legal wages do not necessarily decline as illegal wages increase (Fagan 1992, 1994).

A second important take-away from the previous results is that the nexus between labor market outcomes and antisocial behavior may be more relevant for segments of the market that are more likely to affect subgroups of the population that are at higher risk of engaging in criminal activities. That is, the relationship between labor market opportunities and crime is plausibly better captured by the wages of low-skilled and poorly educated males, who are most likely to be at the margin of offending (Freeman 1996; Mustard 2010). Studies adopting this approach typically provide a sharper definition of the parameter being estimated and of the subpopulations of individuals to which it applies (such as low-skilled workers). Furthermore, whenever it is measured, the relationship also seems to emerge for violent crimes. Empirically, this tends to increase the magnitude of the coefficient estimates, compared to relying merely on the aggregate unemployment rate—which confirms with the intuition that people at the margin of criminality will be more sensitive to changes in labor market conditions.

In this vein, Gould, Weinberg, and Mustard (2002) focus on whether local crime rates are sensitive to the labor market prospects of those most likely to offend (unskilled men), rather than on whether crime rates respond to the general economic conditions of the area.[38] In particular, they control for the state-level average wage and unemployment rate of men who are not college-educated. They also address the endogeneity of labor market conditions in their U.S. county-level analysis by constructing instruments as the interactions between three variables that, they argue, are exogenous to changes in crime within each state and county. Specifically, they interact the initial industrial composition in the state, trends in the national industrial composition of employment in each industry, and a measure of the changes in the demographic composition within each industry at the national level.[39] Their estimates imply that both wages and unemployment are significant (causal) determinants of the crime rate, but that wages play a larger role in the crime trends between 1979 and 1995, explaining more than 50 percent of the increase in both property and violent crime indexes over the sample period.

Noting that the precipitous rise in crime in the United Kingdom from the 1970s through the early 1990s was accompanied by rising wage inequality that reached heights in the early 1990s not seen previously in the twentieth century, Machin and Meghir (2004) study whether the rapidly deteriorating labor market position of less-skilled workers can explain the rise in property crime in England and Wales between 1975 and 1996. In particular, they consider wages at the bottom end of the wage distribution (the wages of those people whose wages are low enough to put them at the margin of committing crime), which they argue are both likely to be an important determinant of crime and a better measure of legal alternatives in the formal sector than the unemployment rate.

They confirm the qualitative conclusions of Gould, Weinberg, and Mustard (2002) that (relative) declines in the wages of low-wage workers lead to increases in crime, and that this relationship is much more important in explaining trends in property crime than the unemployment rate. Furthermore, they document that not only does crime respond to variations in opportunity costs of criminal offending, as measured by lower-end wages, but it also reacts to changes in the rewards to crimes. They provide evidence of this by making innovative use of victimization surveys to construct a measure of the economic returns to criminality; in the British Crime Surveys, victims of property crime are asked to estimate the value of the stolen property.

They show that this variable is positively related to property crimes, without eliminating the relevance of the unemployment rate and the wages of low-skilled workers.[40]

The observation that different subpopulations of potential offenders are sensitive to different characteristics and conditions of the labor market has led researchers to consider the relationship between crime and more refined measures of labor market conditions, which theory suggests have as much bearing on the decision to offend as crude measures of unemployment. These refinements have thus far confirmed that there are robust trade-offs between crime and the labor market. However, rather than a dichotomous choice between committing crimes and being legally employed, criminality varies along a continuum of legal and illegal "work." That is, for potential criminals, employment and participation in crime are not mutually exclusive. Indeed, this observation conforms to the data on perpetrators in Mexico (presented in chapter 2), which indicates that the (legal) employment rate of perpetrators exceeds that of the general population.

The previous chapters argued that youth are at particularly high risk of engaging in antisocial and criminal behavior. This may be especially true in the context of the linkages between the labor market and criminal participation because youth typically have lower skills than the overall population in the labor force, by virtue of their age. Those adolescents who have dropped out of secondary education will face particularly poor job prospects, with limited scope for wage growth, skill acquisition, and job stability. Given these observations, a natural and policy-relevant refinement is the link between the youth labor market and youth crime. Does adolescent criminal behavior respond to economic incentives? Is attachment to the labor market unambiguously a protective factor?

Grogger (1998) was the first to formalize and study the relationship between youth crime and wages and crime. Grogger begins from the observations that crime is widespread among youth, and that criminal acts are often undertaken by individuals who have some form of employment; thus, criminality and employment are not mutually exclusive. In a model in which time can be allocated to legitimate work and crime, such that the two can coexist as income-generating substitutes, the decision to offend (and how much to offend) should be responsive to changes in wages. Grogger (1998) constructs a structural model with individual-level data for the United States from the National Longitudinal Survey of Youth (NLSY) to estimate the relationship between wage offers and the property crimes committed by these young men. The focus on property crime is motivated by the desire to concentrate on crimes that are economically motivated, rather than on acts of interpersonal violence. Grogger finds that young men's criminality is negatively related to their potential wages, and argues that the decline in the real wages of young men during the 1970s and 1980s was a significant contributor to the rise in their criminality.

If offenders and individuals at the margin of offending are responsive to economic incentives, as suggested by the previous findings, could crime be reduced by increasing the floor of the wage distribution (the wages of the lowest-skilled workers, including the young)? The net effects on crime of an increase in the minimum wage are theoretically ambiguous. For workers who remain employed following a rise in the minimum wage, a higher wage implies a higher opportunity cost of crime. However, those low-skilled workers who are displaced or laid off may choose crime as an alternative source of income. In practice, low-skilled workers who are displaced by increases in the minimum wage tend to be youth and workers with weak labor attachment, causing youth in particular to substitute criminality for employment.[41] For instance, Beauchamp and Chan (2014) analyze the relationship between minimum wages and crime in the United States by exploiting changes in state and federal minimum wage laws between 1997 and 2010. They find that workers whose employment was affected by a change in the minimum wage were more likely to work part time and that those who had a criminal past were more likely to lose employment and commit economically motivated crimes, as well as violent crimes—suggesting that the reduced employment effects dominate any wage benefits. The good intentions of raising the minimum wage can thus have unintended consequences, from the perspective of crime and violence, because those who are most affected by its employment effects (in the form of job loss) are low-skill, have lower-quality employment, and weaker a priori attachment to the labor force. They are thus closer to the margin of criminal participation.

Given the high social costs of crime, these unintended consequences are worth averting. It may be possible to complement minimum wage increases with well-targeted training programs that enhance human capital, improve skills, and raise the stakes in the legal labor force of at-risk youth and workers who are most likely to be displaced by rising wage floors, so as to secure their long-term attachment to employment. Some evidence concerning training and skill development is reviewed in the next section, with an eye on their effects both on subsequent labor market outcomes and on offending.

### Insights from the literature

The literature on the wages of at-risk individuals offers two key insights. First, low-skilled workers, who are at higher risk of becoming offenders, are responsive to economic incentives; "market" wages appear to be a robust factor in criminal choices and can tip work choices toward legal/illegal activities. Second, the evidence discussed above provides strong support for the hypothesis that work and illegal activities should not be thought of as mutually exclusive; rather, individuals "double up" by combining legal and illegal work in an overall strategy of earning income (Grogger 1998; Fagan and Freeman 1999).

The notion of a continuum between legal and illegal "work," whereby individuals may engage in both activities simultaneously, is particularly relevant for explaining patterns of employment that emerge from the data on perpetrators from Mexico (see figure 2.8 in chapter 2). The vast majority (roughly 80 percent) of perpetrators in Mexico are employed, irrespective of the type of crime. At all ages, perpetrators consistently report higher employment rates than general population (in figure 5.5, the light-colored bars always exceed the dark-colored bars).

**FIGURE 5.5:** Employment shares by age, perpetrators versus general population in Mexico, 2010

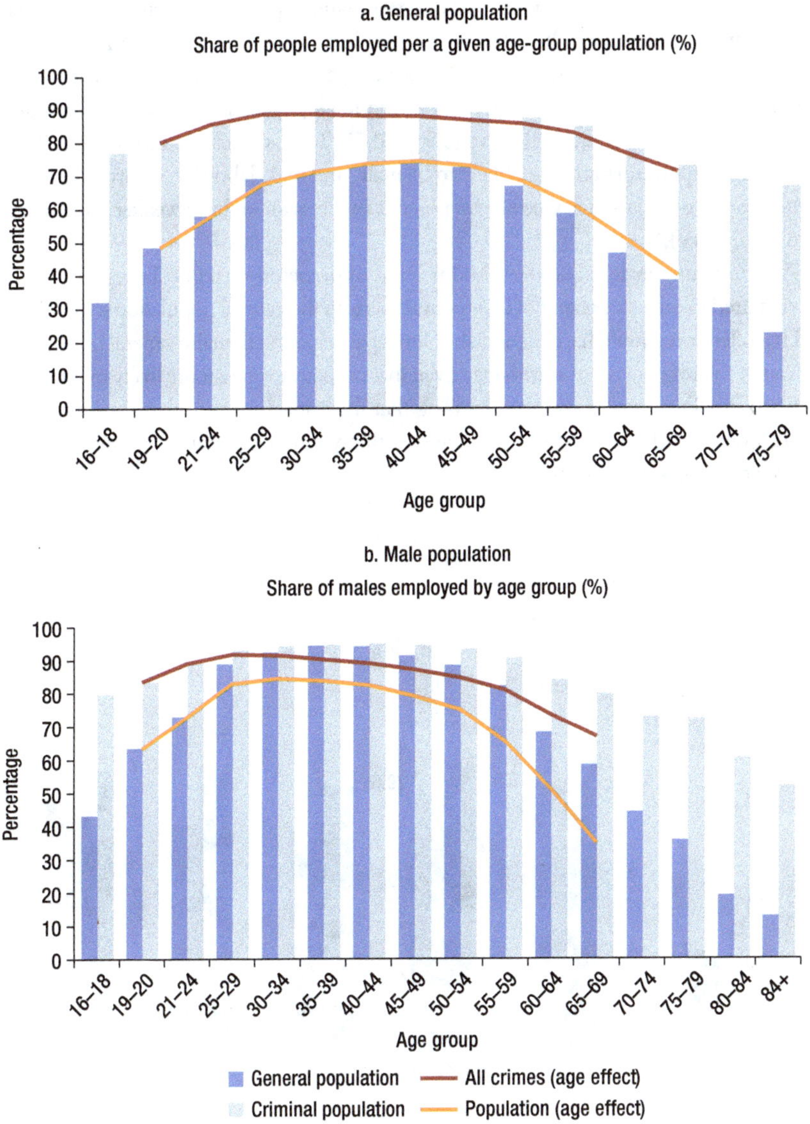
a. General population
Share of people employed per a given age-group population (%)
Percentage
Age group
16–18
19–20
21–24
25–29
30–34
35–39
40–44
45–49
50–54
55–59
60–64
65–69
70–74
75–79
b. Male population
Share of males employed by age group (%)
80–84
84+
General population
Criminal population
All crimes (age effect)
Population (age effect)

*Source:* Chioda (2014c), based on data from Instituto Nacional de Estadística y Geografía (INEGI).
*Note:* Bars refer to 2010 data only, while age profiles are based on the 1997–2010 period.

Perpetrators are not making "all-or-nothing" decisions to be criminals. They remain in the legal market as they engage in criminal acts, thus challenging the hypothesis that employment is a protective factor.

The statement holds in the general population (panel a of figure 5.5) as well as for males only (panel b of figure 5.5): male perpetrators are more likely to be employed that their counterparts of the same age who do not commit crimes. The gap between perpetrators and the rest of the male population is narrower (though still statistically different) between age 30 and 55. This is a direct consequence of the fact that perpetrators are more likely to be male, and male labor force participation in the general population is close to 80 percent (while women have weaker attachment to labor force).[42]

For young males ages 16–18, 80 percent of perpetrators report being employed, compared to only 42 percent of their counterparts in the general population (figure 5.6). That offenders should have higher labor force participation than the general population at such a young age is not surprising, given that perpetrators are more likely to interrupt their schooling. It is, however, surprising that their attachment to the labor market is so elevated, and this contradicts the notion that young perpetrators are idle and not involved in productive activities.

FIGURE 5.6: Employment rates of male youth ages 16–18, perpetrators versus the general population, Mexico

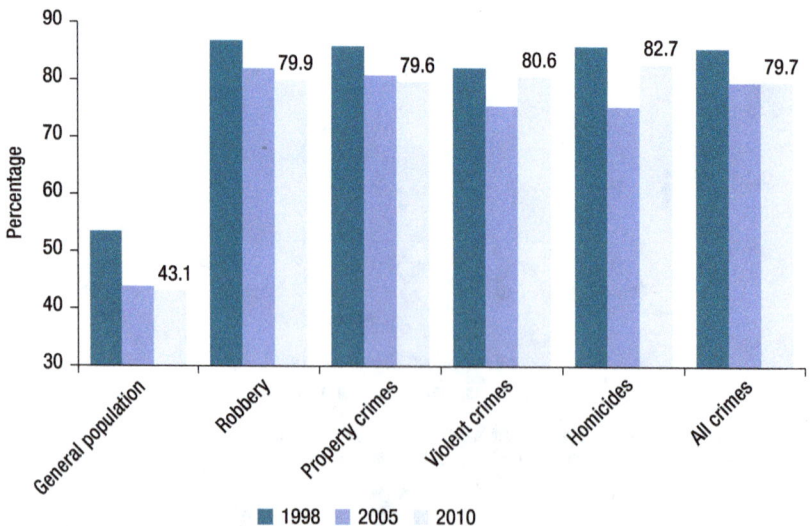

Source: Chioda (2014c), based on data from Instituto Nacional de Estadística y Geografía (INEGI) (1998, 2005, 2010).

While most classic criminological theories suggest that employment may reduce crime, more recent research has shown greater complexity in the relationship among male youth (Liberman 2008). In particular, an intensive adolescent labor supply (full- or close to full-time employment) can result from low educational attainment, but it may also contribute to it if adolescents forgo schooling in favor of employment. Regardless of the direction of causality, the employment opportunities available to adolescents may be of low quality, with limited scope for wage growth, skill acquisition, or job stability—all of which raise the likelihood of offending. Furthermore, in such employment, youth may be exposed to "risky" adult peers, who are themselves low-skilled and poorly educated, and are also likely to be at the margin of offending.

Thus, not all jobs are "created equal"; the *quality* of the employment opportunities available to youth and at-risk individuals plays an important role in deterring crime. The evidence discussed previously corroborates this hypothesis: wages can be thought of as a proxy for job quality and of the opportunity for wage growth and skill acquisition. Wadsworth (2006) formalizes this point, studying the correlations between job characteristics and the likelihood of participation in property and violent crime among young adults. Using data from the NLSY for the United States, he finds that the quality of employment has a stronger influence on the likelihood of criminal behavior than income and educational attainment.

Does the quality of employment matter in Latin America? In a dynamic longitudinal analysis of municipal-level homicides in Mexico, Chioda (2014b) provides indirect evidence that it does. The study shows the importance of formal employment in explaining changes in homicide rates, even after controlling for a rich set of municipal characteristics relating macroeconomic and local conditions that include not only the lagged homicide rate, but also the incidence of drug-related and weapon-related crimes, as well as unemployment, demographic composition, education, poverty, inequality, and housing investment.[43] The number of workers employed in the formal sector consistently predicts a decline in the homicide rate. Estimates by Chioda (2014b) imply that a 1 percent increase in the number of state-level formal workers is associated with 2.1 fewer homicides per 100,000. Chioda also estimates models that allow for spillovers in violence from other municipalities by including the (lagged) homicide rate of all other municipalities in the state. This model implies that a 1 percent increase in formal workers is related to 0.9 fewer homicides per 100,000 in a given municipality. The smaller effect indicates the importance of spillovers and interdependencies across neighboring municipalities.

Estimates from analogous models on Brazilian municipal-level data are consistent with those from Mexico, but reveal further insights because the data record information on the number of formal jobs created and destroyed in each municipality, by gender and age categories. Chioda and Rojas-Alvarado (2014) document that not all formal employment is relevant to violence; only formal job creation and formal job destruction among young men are robustly related to homicides in their most saturated specifications (which control for overall unemployment, among others). Their estimates suggest that a 1 percent increase in formal jobs created and filled by male youths is associated with 0.37 fewer homicides per 100,000, while a 1 percent increase in formal job destruction among male youths is associated with 0.67 additional homicides per 100,000. Thus the quality of jobs matters, and is particularly relevant for male youth. The asymmetry in the effect size is also interesting. The impact of job destruction is almost twice as large as that of job creation, suggesting that adolescent males at the margin of losing their formal sector jobs are at particularly high risk. The unequal effects of job destruction and creation imply that the harm (in terms of violence) from losing a formal job in a given year is not fully offset by re-employment in the formal sector in the same year. The damage from the loss of formal employment is roughly twice as large as the protective benefits of formal job creation.

All told, the evidence from both developed and developing countries indicates an important age-related gradient in the relationship between employment and crime. Early, intensive attachment to the labor force, with employment opportunities that tend to be of low quality, may have counterproductive consequences. By contrast, high-quality employment opportunities for young adults that ensure stability, potential for wage growth, and acquisition and development of skills, have strong protective properties, especially in a context where legal employment and criminal participation are not mutually exclusive.

## Training, skill development, and offending

The previous sections point to low educational attainment, low human capital, and low skills as important factors that lead to low-quality employment prospects, with limited opportunities for wage growth and skill acquisition. In turn, these forms of employment offer limited protective benefits for crime: they do not preclude participation in illicit acts (so that legal and illegal work coexist); and they may even facilitate antisocial behavior and crime as a result of association with (adolescent and adult) peers who may themselves be at elevated risk of criminal behavior.

It follows that a natural policy goal would be to address this low-quality employment equilibrium by introducing *well-targeted* training programs that enhance human capital, improve skills, and raise the at-risk group's stakes in the labor force, in the hopes of securing their long-term attachment to formal employment. These might be directed at youth, low-skilled individuals, and ex-offenders.

These types of interventions fall under the general heading of supply-side programs, according to Bushway and Reuter (2002), who provide a useful survey of crime prevention programs aimed at increasing employment for at-risk individuals. That is, these programs aim to enhance the characteristics of individual job candidates, rendering them more attractive to prospective employers, by increasing their productivity through education or job training (see box 5.1).

**BOX 5.1:** Broad categorization of employment-focused crime prevention programs

Bushway and Reuter (2002) provide a useful survey of crime prevention programs aimed at increasing employment. Their review includes any program intended to increase the employment of individuals or populations at risk of serious criminal involvement through employment and/or to raise employment in high-crime areas. Programs fall into two broad categories.

*Supply-side programs* aim to enhance the characteristics of individual job candidates, rendering them more attractive to employers. These tend to increase the worker's productivity through education or job training. However, some programs in this category also include efforts addressing the fact that many high-risk individuals are at a disadvantage due to their location. These programs improve people's mobility for jobs; for instance, by subsidizing transportation or by providing access to housing in lower-risk communities nearer areas of high employment potential. The latter intervention is expected to have longer-term effects in preventing crime by affording children the opportunity to grow up in communities with better-employed adult role models (though, as will be seen in chapter 6, such programs often produce benefits for young girls, at the expense of generating perverse outcomes for boys).

*Demand-side programs* are designed to reduce the costs of employment for prospective employers, for instance, by enhancing wages or offering subsidized bonds for hiring ex-offenders (which insure the employer against theft by the employee). Alternatively, community development programs lower the costs to businesses of locating in particularly needy communities. The inflow of capital into at-risk communities is expected to generate jobs, thereby reducing crime in the community.

Beyond these broad categorizations, programs often differ in their targeting and delivery. Some are aimed at youth, while others target adults; each has different theoretical justifications and programmatic content. Programs for youth are typically provided by social service agencies, while those for offenders frequently occur in correctional settings. In terms of their impacts, evaluations of criminal justice programs are almost universally interested only in recidivism; they therefore largely ignore employment as an outcome. By contrast, programs aimed at the general population virtually always include employment as an outcome measure, but rarely report crime.

In their review of the research, Bushway and Reuters (2002) are somewhat pessimistic about the potential for demand-side programs to reduce crime. However, certain supply-side programs strike them as more promising, especially those targeted to specific subgroups, such as older males and lower-risk populations. In particular, they find that interventions that offer vocational training aimed at older male ex-offenders are unambiguously effective.

### Transitional employment

Drake, Aos, and Miller (2009) provide a comprehensive review of prisoner reentry and crime abatement programs that deliver services to former inmates or high-risk individuals, including disadvantaged youth. They document that prison vocational services and basic education programs consistently yield benefits in terms of diminished recidivism, although the magnitude of the effect of this type of program varies greatly.[44]

One of the first large-scale experiments involving a training/employment program designed for ex-offenders is the National Supported Work (NSW) intervention in the United States. Its impacts are evaluated by Uggen (2000), among others.[45] The NSW Demonstration Project was designed for criminal offenders, drug users, and youth dropouts with a history of both chronic and recent unemployment. The program targeted four hard-to-employ groups: long-term welfare recipients; ex-offenders (defined as having a conviction and being incarcerated in the last six months); drug addicts (defined as those currently enrolled in a drug treatment program); and high school dropouts, half of whom had a delinquent or criminal record. Participants were deliberately drawn from the ranks of the poor; were referred to the program by the criminal justice system, social services, and job-training agencies; and were randomly assigned to experimental and control groups. From March 1975 to July 1977, more than 3,000 persons from nine U.S. cities were randomly assigned to treatment and control groups after completing a baseline interview. Those in the treatment group were offered minimum wage transitional jobs (mainly in the construction and service industries) in crews of 5 to 10 workers led by a counselor/supervisor, with whom they met regularly to discuss performance. Those in the treatment group were exposed to "graduated stress" in terms of productivity and punctuality requirements as duration in the program increased, and earnings were allowed to increase for satisfactory performance and attendance (LaLonde 1986). Participants were time-limited in terms of how long they could remain employed in the transitional job, with the limits varying across sites from 12 to 18 months. Members of both groups were surveyed for work, crime, and arrests information at 9-month intervals for up to three years.

For former addicts, the program had delayed impacts on employment after the transitional jobs had ended, with substantial increases (10 percentage points) in employment up to two years after program completion and a decline in criminal activity, much of which appeared to coincide with post-transitional employment. For the ex-offender group, however, there was very little evidence of any impact in any domain (Raphael 2010).

Uggen (2000) exploits information on the age of participants to identify "turning points" in the life courses of ex-offenders, with an explicit focus on heterogeneity in program effects by age. Uggen concludes that employment is a turning point in the life courses of criminal offenders over 26 years old, but that it has no discernible effect on the trajectories of younger ex-offenders; offenders over 26 who are provided even marginal employment opportunities are considerably less likely to reoffend than those not provided such opportunities. Thus the age-dependent relationship between crime and employment documented in the previous section re-emerges here. Indeed, the age-dependency of training program effects appears to be a recurrent feature of supply-side interventions (Bushway and Reuter 2002).

The experimental evaluation of another transitional employment initiative, the Center for Employment Opportunity (CEO) in New York City, yielded large employment effects in the first three-quarters of the intervention, but only minor effects on recidivism. Closer inspection reveals another critical dimension of heterogeneity of program effects for ex-offenders: larger effects are observed for those who receive treatment within the first three months of release (Bloom and others 2007; Raphael 2010).[46] Furthermore, indirect support for age-dependent and risk-dependent effects emerges from the literature on the impact of labor market conditions on the likelihood of recidivism. These effects tend to be larger for parolees who are at relatively low risk of re-offending, and are hence positively selected on average in terms on skills (Raphael and Weiman 2007). For the lowest-risk parolees, having a job reduces the likelihood of a parole violation by 6 to 12 percentage points.

In sum, larger and significant effects of transitional employment programs tend to be concentrated among specific subgroups, such as older males and lower-risk individuals (Raphael 2010; Bushway 2011), suggesting that the individuals at the highest risk are the least likely to benefit from this type of intervention. This conclusion may reflect the difficulty of "targeting" programs to attract so-called persistent offenders, who tend to be responsible for a large proportion of crime. The problem is similar to that faced in medical disciplines of identifying people carrying a highly contagious, yet very-low-incidence, virus.

### Skill programs for at-risk youth and marginal offenders

For younger high-risk populations, a number of promising interventions (with experimental evaluations) can be identified, despite the fact that they were not designed or targeted to reduce crime among subpopulations at high risk of offending. Two important examples in the United States are Job Corps, which targets 16- to 24- year-old disadvantaged youth, and JOBSTART, which is modeled after Job Corps and provides academic services to 17- to 21-year-old high school drop-outs. However, unlike Job Corps, JOBSTART is a nonresidential program.[47] Both interventions offer academic services, occupational and vocational training, and a job placement service.

The short-term evaluation of JOBSTART provided cause for optimism, given its large impact on the likelihood of being arrested after the first year (approximately 6 percentage points) concentrated among male participants. However, the four-year follow-up reported no effects for employment, earning, or arrests (Cave and others 1993).

Job Corps is not only the largest training program for disadvantaged youths in the United States, but is also the only such program that has shown short- and long-term benefits (Schochet, Burghardt, and McConnell 2008). Jobs Corps serves youths between the ages of 16 and 24, primarily in a residential setting,[48] lasts eight months, on average, and offers academic education (aimed at completing a high school equivalent degree, the GED), vocational training, and job placement services for one year. In addition, it offers a Life Skill Module, which includes counseling, social skills training, and health education (see box 5.2 for details of the program). The experimental evaluation carried out by Schochet, Burghardt, and McConnell (2008) shows that the program increases educational attainment, reduces criminal offending, and increases earnings for several years following participation.

In particular, it reduced arrest and conviction rates, as well as time spent incarcerated. After 48 months, arrest rates in the treatment group declined 12 percent relative to controls. The largest reductions were observed within the first year of random assignment, and small declines occurred in later years. The decline in arrests was observed for all categories of crimes, but Job Corps had a larger impact on reducing less serious crimes (such as disorderly conduct and trespassing) than on more serious crimes (such as aggravated assault and murder). Interestingly, the program's effects exhibit an age gradient in earnings. Indeed, larger earnings benefits tend to accrue to the older youth (20–24-year-olds), and persist over time.

---

**BOX 5.2:** Evaluation of Job Corps: Lasting results only for older youth

Job Corps is the largest vocational training program for disadvantaged youth in the United States. It serves youths ages 16 to 24, primarily in a residential setting. The program's goal is to help youths become more responsible, employable, and productive citizens. Each year, it serves more than 60,000 new participants, at a cost of about $1.5 billion. To evaluate its effectiveness, the U.S. Department of Labor sponsored the National Job Corps Study, which took place from 1993 to 2006.

The National Job Corps Study is the first nationally representative experimental evaluation of a federal employment and training program for disadvantaged youths, unlike previous evaluations of similar programs that were only conducted in selected sites (LaLonde 1995, 2003). The outcomes of the evaluation and of Job Corps thus have wide generalizability. From late 1994 to early 1996, nearly 81,000 eligible applicants nationwide were randomly assigned to either a program group, whose members were allowed to enroll in Job Corps, or to a control group, whose 6,000 members were not.

The National Job Corps Study found that Job Corps improves outcomes for disadvantaged youth. It provides broad groups of participants—the majority of whom enter the program without a high school diploma—with the instructional equivalent of one additional year in school, and has large effects on the receipt of credentials it emphasizes most: GED and vocational certificates. Four years after graduation from the program,

*(continued on next page)*

participants earned 12 percent more than their counterparts in the control group, which roughly corresponds to what would be expected from an additional year of school (Card 1999). The statistically significant short-term earnings gains experienced by program participants makes Job Corps the only large-scale education and training program that has been shown to increase the earnings of disadvantaged youth.

Job Corps significantly reduced arrest and conviction rates, as well as time spent incarcerated. About 33 percent of those in the control group were arrested during the 48-month follow-up period, compared to 29 percent of treatment recipients (a statistically significant decline). Arrest rate reductions were largest during the first year after random assignment, although Job Corps also led to smaller reductions in later years. Members of the treatment group were less likely to have arrest charges for all categories of crimes, with larger impacts on arrests for less serious crimes (such as disorderly conduct and trespassing) than for more serious crimes (murder). Job Corps also reduced conviction rates by 3 percentage points (from 25 to 22 percent), and incarceration rates for convictions by 2 percentage points (from 18 to 16 percent).

These program benefits appear to be small, however, compared to the program's cost of $16,500 per participant (McConnell and Glazerman 2001; Schochet, McConnell, and Burghardt 2003; Schochet, Burghardt, and McConnell 2006). A cost-benefit analysis found that all measured benefits over four years following graduation from the program—including the benefits of increased earnings, reduced use of other services (education and training programs and public assistance), and reduced crime—were less than $4,000. However, the benefits of Job Corps appear to offset its costs for the oldest youth. The positive initial post-program earnings gains and the finding that the earnings gains appear to persist for older youth suggest that there is promise for the Job Corps model.

*Source:* Schochet, Burghardt, and McConnell (2008).

Raphael (2010) suggests that one of the key reasons for Job Corps' success is its strong effects on educational attainment. Participants added almost a full academic year and earning a GED degree (which is equivalent to a high school diploma). The 12 percent gain in earnings observed in the fourth year is commensurate with what would be expected from an additional year of school. Bushway and Reuter (2002) hypothesize that the success of this program may lie in the structure of the intervention: it resocializes youth by breaking community ties and presenting prosocial role models. Its residential requirement reduces the intensity of contact with antisocial peers and illegal earnings opportunities; and its vocational focus and attachment to the labor force provide academic training in a supportive environment.

Until very recently, there was little optimism surrounding the potential of short-term employment programs (many of them only offering summer jobs) for at-risk youth, typically ages 15 to 21 years (table 5.1). Evaluations of such programs have mostly observed increased employment only during the program period, with no significant effect on earnings, and only a limited effect on human capital and education (Bushway and Reuter 2002).

However, a recent randomized controlled trial conducted by the University of Chicago Crime Lab provides hopeful evidence on the potential of light touch/less intensive employment programs to make an impact on violent crime among high-risk youth (Heller 2014). One Summer Plus is a program that offers youth employment during the summer, so as to minimize the conflict between work and school. It provides 14- to 21-year-olds living in high-crime, high-poverty neighborhoods part-time, minimum wage employment in the nonprofit and government sectors for seven weeks, along with a job mentor—an adult to help youth learn to be successful employees and to navigate barriers to employment (transportation, family responsibilities, conflicts with

TABLE 5.1: **Summer job programs and their employment effects**

| Program | Evaluation method | Effects |
|---|---|---|
| Career Beginnings | Randomized control trial | Services of Career Beginnings include summer jobs, workshops and classes, counseling, and the use of mentors from the junior year of high school through graduation. Treatment group was 9.7 percent more likely to attend college than controls; they therefore worked less and earned less (Cave and Quint 1990). |
| Summer Training and Education Program (STEP) | Randomized control trial | Program lasts 15 months and involved remediation, life skills, summer jobs over two years and school-year support. STEP had little or no impact on youth's educational experiences and did not alter employment patterns for either in-school or out-of-school youth (Grossman and Sipe 1992). |
| Youth Employment and Training Program (YIEPP) | Quasi-experimental matching sites | Guaranteed full-time summer jobs and part-time school year jobs to disadvantaged youth who stayed in school. School-year employment doubled from 20 percent to 40 percent, while summer employment increased from about 35 percent to 45 percent. However, YIEPP was unable to attain its goals of increased school enrollment and success, despite the school enrollment requirement (Farkas and others 1982, 1984). |
| Summer Youth Employment & Training Program (SYETP) | Randomized lotteries | Provides minimum-wage summer jobs and some remedial education for disadvantaged youth. The program appears to have raised the likelihood of employment and average earnings in the year of participation, but lowered earnings slightly in the three subsequent years. It also caused a 10 percent decline in the probability of incarceration and a 20 percent decline in mortality, both driven by decreases among young males (Crane and Ellwood 1984; Gelber, Isen, and Kessler 2014). |

*Sources:* Stanley, Katz, and Krueger (1998); Bushway and Reuter (2002).

supervisors, and so forth). In addition—and perhaps most important—the program also includes a cognitive behavioral training (CBT) component, which, as discussed in chapter 4, effectively teaches youth to reflect on their decision-making process and to think before acting. Contrary to previous summer jobs programs reviewed by Bushway and Reuter (2002),[49] take-up for One Summer Plus was extremely high and attrition was low: 75 percent of youth offered the program participated, and 90 percent of participants completed the full seven weeks. Most striking are the short-term results at the seven-month follow-up for violent crime arrests. Participants experienced 3.7 fewer arrests per 100 youth than their control group counterparts, a decrease of 51 percent. No differences were detected for other types of crime, such as property and drug-related crimes. These results draw an early but optimistic picture about the ability of job programs, coupled with cognitive behavioral therapy techniques, to effectively tackle violence among youth who are at most elevated risk of offending.

In sum, labor market crime prevention programs can be effective for motivated (sometimes older) and/or marginal offenders, but are less effective for younger, lower-skilled criminals, with the exception of high-intensity interventions such as Job Corps. These facts highlight how detachment from the formal labor market is not only a cause of crime but also a marker of substantial structural problems among this group. The labor market is more than a legitimate alternative to income-generating crimes; it provides a normative social context for most of adult life, especially for males.

### Evidence from Latin America and the Caribbean

Evidence from developing countries on the effectiveness of training programs as a crime prevention tool is scant. However, the research from the region discussed earlier in the chapter confirms three key insights that have emerged from the United States. First, antisocial behaviors appear to be responsive to economic incentives, particularly those related to the formal labor market. Second, the effects of employment are age-dependent, with larger effects concentrated among youth (and older youth). Third, participation in the labor market and criminal "work" coexist; labor market attachment rates are higher for offenders than their counterparts in the general population. This observation further corroborates the proposition that the *quality* of (formal) employment plays a central role in reducing crime, rather than whether high-risk individuals are employed at all.

Assuming that there is a relationship between the outcomes in the labor market and criminal behavior, then job training programs directed at disadvantaged youth to improve their skills and employability could in principle deter criminal behavior. While the evidence from the United States on the effectiveness of training is mixed, training programs could represent a solution to the problem of a lack of skills among individuals who have exited formal schooling.

Furthermore, programs that boost skills are likely to have greater benefits in developing countries, where skills are less abundant (Gertler and others 2014), and thus are rewarded well. Consistent with this hypothesis, Psacharopoulos and Patrinos

(2004) show that the returns to schooling are typically higher in developing countries. With less investment in human capital, higher dropout rates, and less stimulating home environments from lower parental investments, there is a good deal of scope for training programs to have beneficial effects. Improving skills could potentially yield large returns. Moreover, specialized skills are more valuable in low- and middle-income countries, where access to high-quality and stable jobs in the formal sector is often limited to more educated workers.

While the returns to training may be high, pervasive levels of crime in developing countries may make it difficult for light-touch interventions, such as training programs, to take hold and have an effect on offending. Breaking the persistence of criminality is a heavy burden for such programs; more intensive interventions may be required. Ultimately, the effectiveness of training programs in high-crime contexts where skills are scarce is an empirical question.

A number of training programs for disadvantaged workers have recently been introduced in several LAC countries in the hopes of increasing skill levels among the poor and helping them gain access to higher-quality employment. Argentina, Brazil, Chile, Colombia, the Dominican Republic, Panama, Peru, and Uruguay have all introduced training programs for disadvantaged youth, with some evidence of positive returns.[50] However, these programs have largely been evaluated using non-experimental techniques, so the robustness of their estimates is still in question. The discussion that follows reviews two rigorous evaluations of recent job training and skill development programs and their effects on criminal behavior and other intermediate outcomes.

Attanasio, Kugler, and Meghir (2011) consider a program in Colombia, Jóvenes en Acción, which was introduced between 2001 and 2005 and provided three months of in-classroom training and three months of on-the-job training to youth between 18 and 25 years of age in the bottom socioeconomic strata of the population. Training centers in the seven largest cities of the country chose the courses to be taught as part of the program and received applications. Each center was asked to accept more individuals than they could accommodate in each of the classes they offered. The program then randomly offered training to applicants to fill the slots in each class. Youths who were not selected for training were then used as the control group. The advantage of this design is that it incorporates the process of trainee selection as it would take place in practice, and makes use of oversubscription to minimize ex ante differences between those who do and do not receive training. This means that estimates focus on the population of individuals who are motivated enough to apply to and get accepted into such a program.

Attanasio, Kugler, and Meghir (2011) report large program effects, especially for women. There were sizable and significant impacts on the likelihood of employment and paid employment, on the number of hours worked, and on wages for women: the probability of paid employment increased by nearly 7 percent; hours per week worked by almost 3 hours; and wages by nearly 20 percent. In contrast, young men were unaffected along of any of these dimensions. However, the program had significant effects on formality for both men and women: male youths were 6 percent more likely to hold a formal contract and 5 percent more likely to have formal employment, while their female counterparts were 8 percent and 7 percent more likely to have a contract and to hold formal employment, respectively. The formal wages of males rose by 23 percent, while the formal wages of women rose by 33 percent.

While the authors do not observe criminal outcomes, their estimates have relevance for the purposes of this study, given the previously discussed importance of job quality for criminal offending. While there are no other measurable benefits for young men, the increased incidence of formality implies greater attachment to higher-quality employment, which, as discussed, can be a protective factor. It is therefore conceivable that the increased formality among young men and, in particular, their higher wages in the formal sector, would represent a sufficient disincentive to refrain from criminal behavior.

In turn, Card and others (2011) report on the outcomes of an early cohort of youth who received training in the Dominican Republic under the auspices of the Juventud y Empleo program, funded by the Inter-American Development Bank. The program targeted less-educated youth—a group that faces substantial barriers to labor market success—with the explicit aims of raising participants' job skills and matching them with suitable employers. As in the U.S. Job Training Partnership Act and Job Corps, these programs combine classroom training with a subsequent internship period of on-the-job work experience.

The Ministry of Labor in the Dominican Republic outsources the provision of training services to private training centers. Courses last 225 hours and are split into two parts: 75 hours of basic or life skills training, and 150 hours of technical or vocational training. Basic skills training is meant to strengthen trainees' self-esteem and work habits, while vocational training is meant to address the technical training needs of local employers. Training is then followed by an internship in a private sector firm, which was previously contacted by the center in order to develop training curricula tailored to the firm's demand for labor.

The authors report that Juventud y Empleo had no significant effect on employment. The impact on earnings per month was modest (10 percent), conditional on employment. However, the authors caution against relying on their estimates too much because, in the implementation of the experiment, some individuals who were initially assigned to training dropped out, and were therefore not included in the follow-up survey after the program ended.

Perhaps because of these implementation problems, a second round of evaluations was commissioned, with appropriate corrections to the earlier iteration. Ibarraran and others (2012) report that the program raised the probability of formal employment among men by roughly 17 percent, and increased monthly earnings among those employed by 7 percent. However, there were no overall effects on employment rates. On other outcomes, the program reduced teenage pregnancy by 5 percentage points (representing a 45 percent decline), which is consistent with an increase in youth's expectations about the future. The program also had positive effects on soft skills, as measured by three different scales. Scores improved between 0.08 and 0.16 standard deviation with the program. In the context of this chapter, the improvements in labor market prospects are promising in terms of lowering the likelihood of turning to crime. However, the improvements in soft skills perhaps bear the most promise for the affected youth because these are most correlated with longer-term outcomes (see chapter 4).

These studies confirm the earlier conjecture of higher returns to training programs in the developing context than in developed countries. However, some caution is warranted. Outcomes in Colombia and the Dominican Republic were measured after shorter follow-up periods than the U.S. evaluations (four years, in the case of Job Corps). One limitation of all training programs (which does not affect the interval validity of evaluation estimates) is that people who enroll tend to be positively self-selected in terms of motivation, skills, previous employment history, and other characteristics relative to the general population. Those individuals also tend to be at lower risk of committing crime. Estimates of the effect of training on their outcomes are therefore difficult to generalize to populations that are more at risk. The results of these evaluations might be considered as upper bounds on the effect that might be expected from higher-risk youth who did not self-select into the program.

The heterogeneity of effects seen in U.S. programs would suggest that harder-to-reach individuals are indeed the higher-risk people. The evidence from LAC also provides some indirect corroboration of this proposition; researchers have systematically found that the larger impacts of interventions tend to be concentrated among women, who are at lower risk of offending or being involved in violence. Finally, positive effects on employment and wages may not necessarily translate into reductions of violence. Vocational training programs in Liberia and Uganda illustrate this; increases in earnings and legal employment that resulted from training did not lead to lower antisocial behavior and violence (Blattman, Fiala, and Martinez 2014; Blattman and Annan 2011). It could be argued that evidence from post-conflict contexts such as Liberia and Uganda is not relevant for LAC. However, as discussed in chapter 2, the endemic level of violence and its persistence in some parts of LAC are comparable to those fragile states, giving some legitimacy to the parallel.

## Notes

[1] See, for instance Shaw and McKay (1942); Sampson and Groves (1989); and Benson and others (2003), who document this relationship even for intimate partner violence.

[2] The model is described in detail in chapter 2.

[3] Holzer and others (2008) show that people living in poverty in the United States are four times more likely to be involved in serious crime than their middle-class counterparts.

[4] In a subsequent dynamic panel data analysis, which exploits only within-country variation in income, Chioda (2014a) shows that the shape of the relationship between homicides and various measures of income changed dramatically in the second half of the 2000s; the size of the upper class became dramatically more protective than in the earlier 2000s.

[5] The $170 billion figure is derived by multiplying an estimate of the cost of crime ($700 billion) by a scaling factor that nets out the proportion of the poverty-earnings relationship that is inherited, so that the remainder results from environmental factors. In turn, $700 billion per year corresponds to the victimization costs of street crime provided by Ludwig (2006), which is based on the best available and most recent data for crime rates in the United States. The scaling factor is taken from Jencks and Tach (2006), who derive it from carefully reviewing studies of siblings, twins, and adoptions (using data mostly from Sweden, but also some data from the United States).

[6] In 2010, for instance, Henrichson and Delaney (2012) estimate the average annual cost to U.S. taxpayers per inmate to be $31,286, with a minimum across states of $14,603 (Kentucky) and a maximum of $60,076 (New York).

[7] This idea is not novel. As early as the nineteenth century, the penal system in France was criticized for failing to address the causes of criminality, drawing particular attention to poverty. See the discussion by Heller, Jacob, and Ludwig (2010).

[8] Blau (1999) exploits the panel data structure of the NLSY, which enables her to control for family fixed effects, so that the variation in income she exploits to estimate the effect of income changes on family outcomes is within family, over time.

[9] The hypothesis was formally tested by Gould Ellen, Lens, and O'Regan (2011), for instance, who found evidence of reverse causality: voucher recipients tended to relocate to higher crime areas.

[10] In the policy arena, the focus is frequently on the first two components: law enforcement—which affects the likelihood of being caught—and the severity of punishment. Indeed, Becker's (1968) original exposition was concerned with the optimal levels of these.

[11] See Mayer (1997) and Yeung, Linver, and Brooks-Gunn (2002) for discussions of these channels.

[12] For a comprehensive and recent review of the effect of income on human capital outcomes, see Almond and Currie (2011).

[13] For recent qualitative review studies of CCT evaluations, see IEG (2011), Fiszbein and Schady (2009), and Rawlings and Rubio (2005). For a meta-analysis of CCTs' effects on enrollment, attendance, and dropout rates from 42 studies of CCT program evaluations in 15 developing countries, see Saavedra and García (2012).

[14] In contrast to evidence from the developed countries, CCTs have not systematically been related to improved academic achievement in developing contexts—only to improved attendance and smaller effects on dropout rates. Estimates of the size of the dropout effect are modest (between negative 3 and 4 percentage points) and statistically different from zero (though only a few CCT studies report dropout effects, so this conclusion should be viewed cautiously) (Saavedra and García 2012). In turn, the effects of CCTs on children's years of schooling are mechanically tied to the conditionality of the program and likely not due to the income transfers. More years of schooling, however, may contribute to reductions in violence through a traditional human capital channel as well as through incapacitation (which is touched upon in the next section).

[15] The Bono de Desarollo Humano in Ecuador is technically a pure cash transfer; there is no conditionality associated to receipt.

[16] For a detailed discussion on the effect of CCT receipt among (poor) families, see Fiszbein and Schady (2009).

[17] Bobonis (2009) endeavors to test the efficiency of household resource allocations among (poor) beneficiary households of Mexico's PROGRESA program (now called Oportunidades).

[18] In economics, normal goods are those for which demand increases as (real) income rises.

[19] The effect of the allocation of parental time on child development and behaviors is an important channel, which is discussed later in the context of the relationship between labor markets and crime. In particular, a number of poverty/welfare programs, in both developed and developing countries, explicitly involve incentives for parents to work. In terms of their children's outcomes, programs with work incentives may have the perverse effect of resulting in greater criminality and problem behavior among beneficiaries' children if the additional time spent at work would otherwise have been spent with children, for whom the interaction improves their human capital development.

[20] The estimated impact of a $1,000 increase in child benefits on physical aggression and social aggression are −0.100 and −0.153, respectively, implying declines of 10 percent and 15.3 percent of a standard deviation. The coefficient estimates reflect the proportion of a standard deviation resulting from a $1,000 change in benefits.

[21] The estimated maternal depression effect resulting from a $1,000 change in benefits in the full sample is −0.101, representing a decline of 10 percent of a standard deviation. Effects are larger for the low education sample; the coefficient rises in magnitude to −0.196, implying a decline of 19.6 percent of a standard deviation.

[22] An alternative approach exploits large (unanticipated) negative shocks to family income. Oreopoulos, Page, and Huff-Stevens (2008) take advantage of firm closures to study the long-term, intergenerational effects of worker displacement using detailed Canadian administrative data. This strategy relies on the assumptions that plant or firm closures are unrelated to the parents' unobserved characteristics. They show that children whose fathers were displaced eventually earn 9 percent less than similar children whose fathers did not experience displacement and that they are more likely to receive unemployment insurance and social assistance. Here again, their estimates are more acute for children whose family income was at the bottom of the income distribution (the most vulnerable families), for whom the displacement was likely most disruptive. However, there are limitations to this approach. In particular, it is unclear whether causality—running from income *alone* to children's outcomes—can be ascribed to the estimated effects. For instance, a job loss from a plant closure represents a very disruptive event for a household. Income surely declines, but stress related to the new circumstances also surely rises, perhaps also leading to dissolution of parents' marriage and other disruptive factors. These other events related to the shock may plausibly have independent effects on children's outcomes above and beyond the effects of income. More important for the purposes of this study, Oreopoulos, Page, and Huff-Stevens (2008) offer no assessment of the effects on crime. Thus impacts must be inferred from external estimates of the effect of education on crime, for example.

[23] For Ecuador, see Paxson and Schady (2007). For Nicaragua, see Macours, Schady, and Vakis (2012).

[24] Ozer and others (2011) frame the results in terms of cut-off scores for clinically significant distress. They found that 19.5 percent of women in the Oportunidades group had scores in the clinical range, compared with 26.6 percent in the control group: the probability of clinically significant scores for depression was 0.74 times lower in the Oportunidades group than in the control group.

[25] For a discussion on the relationship between nutrition and aggression, see chapter 4.

[26] The effect of increased maternal labor supply and income appears to depend on age. Duncan, Morris, and Rodrigues (2011) document positive effects on test scores for 2- to 5-year-olds, and negative effects for 10- to 13-year-olds. The effects were similar in magnitude. Most of the positive effects stemmed from the utilization of childcare services.

[27] In particular, they use data from the Great Smoky Mountains Study of Youth (GSMS). This longitudinal study of child mental health in rural North Carolina sampled both American Indian children and children who were not American Indians. Halfway through the data collection, a casino opened on the Eastern Cherokee reservation. A portion of the profits from this new business operation is distributed every six months on an equalized, per capita basis to all adult tribal members, regardless of employment status, income, or other household characteristics. No choice is involved. Individuals are eligible based on preexisting American Indian status. Therefore, Akee and others (2010) can observe the treatment effect on an entire distribution of household types. Households without American Indians are not eligible for these cash disbursements.

[28] It is interesting to note that the 7.2 percent decline in property crime following cash disbursement is half the size of the incapacitation effect estimated by Jacob and Lefgren (2004) for the same crime category, discussed in chapter 4.

[29] Borraz and Munyo (2014) provide evidence from Uruguay that the criminal response to welfare payments may be sensitive to the method with which funds are delivered to CCT recipients. They show that the incidence of property crime increases when welfare payments take the form of cash (as opposed to a credit in a bank account).

[30] Or, at least, that mimics the structure of poverty reduction policies, as in the case of Akee and others (2010).

[31] Freeman (1983, 1999) reviews this literature.

[32] Lin (2008) confirms the results of Raphael and Winter-Ebmer (2001) that in models that ignore feedbacks from crime to the labor market, a 1 percentage point increase in unemployment is associated with a 1.8 percent increase in property crime.

[33] See chapter 2 for details on the model. The unemployment rate is lagged one period in her specifications out of concern that contemporaneous unemployment may be simultaneously determined with homicides, a process described earlier in the context of the relationship between crime and unemployment. The lagged unemployment rate is thus less likely to suffer from this same form of endogeneity.

[34] In this case, since the coefficient on the lagged homicide rate is 0.66, the additional homicide induced by the higher youth unemployment rate yields 0.66 more homicides in two periods.

[35.] Indeed, with a coefficient on the lagged dependent variable equal to 0.66, the long-term costs exceed short-term costs by a factor of $3 = [1/(1-0.66)]$.]

[36] Consistent with these findings, Munyo (2015) presents evidence that that lower return in legal activities explains more than one-third of the increase in juvenile crime in Uruguay.

[37] The possibility that individuals who are employed may commit crimes was proposed by Fagan and Freeman (1999) and formalized for the first time by Grogger (1998).

[38] Gould, Weinberg, and Mustard (2002) build on Grogger (1998).

[39] Gould, Weinberg, and Mustard (2002) estimate a significant relationship between the labor market conditions of unskilled workers and crime rates, the magnitude of which resembles their OLS coefficient, and conclude that endogeneity of labor market conditions does not result in significant biases in OLS estimates.

[40] It is interesting to note that most studies of the relationship between wages and crime focus almost exclusively on property crime, under the assumption that other classes of crimes are less responsive to this incentive (the exception is Gould, Weinberg, and Mustard 2002). However, Aizer (2010) exploits exogenous changes in the demand for labor in female-dominated industries to document that the incidence of domestic violence declines as the gender wage gap shrinks. Aizer's explanation is based on a model of intrahousehold bargaining between intimate partners, whereby a decline in

the gender wage gap implies that female household members have viable outside options to staying in an abusive relationship.

[41] See Neumark and Wascher (2006) for a review of studies that examine the employment effects of changes in the minimum wage.

[42] Figure 5.5 indicates that perpetrators are more likely to be employed than the general population, not only in the cross-sectional (light and dark blue bars) but also within cohort: the red and orange lines represent nonparametric age effects estimated from a synthetic-cohort analysis.

[43] See Chioda (2014b) and Chioda and Rojas-Alvarado (2014) for an analysis of homicides and crime in Mexico and Brazil, respectively.

[44] Of the more than 500 programs considered in Drake, Aos, and Miller's (2009) meta-analysis, less than 5 percent are randomized controlled studies (RCTs). On average, the effect sizes associated with RCT studies tend to be smaller than the estimates that arise from nonexperimental evaluation. As discussed in Raphael (2010), this difference may be due to failures of nonexperimental approaches to fully address concerns about self-selection; more motivated individuals, with better soft skills and personality traits, are more likely to benefit from the program ex ante and therefore more likely to enroll. Thus individuals in the group are not perfectly comparable to those in the control group. However, the difference could also reflect a fundamental dissimilarity between the populations of individuals who agree to participate in a random assignment trial versus those who independently enroll in a program. If so, program effects for individuals at the margin of program participation will be smaller than those for the inframarginal beneficiaries.

[45] Findings of the evaluation are summarized in several reports and publications. For a concise summary of the program design and results, see MDRC (1983). For a more detailed discussion, see LaLonde (1986) and the references therein.

[46] The likelihood of returning to custody tends to spike within a few months after being released; it then declines rather quickly (Raphael 2010).

[47] The Job Training Partnership Act (JTPA), which targets out-of-school youth, falls into the same category as Job Corps and JOBSTART. It offers on-the-job training, job search assistance, and remedial classroom instruction, but has a shorter duration than Job Corps and JOBSTART. In spite of the large effects on completing a high-school equivalent degree (GED) and employment, the evaluation reported no significant effects on earnings, employment among disadvantaged youth, or arrests (for details on the evaluation, see Bloom and others 1997).

[48] Eighty percent of participants resided at the Jobs Corps centers (Schochet, Burghardt, and McConnell 2008).

[49] The high attrition rates among these programs are plausibly symptomatic of a lack of motivation among participants, perhaps reflecting their perception of weak employment opportunities.

[50] See Attanasio, Kugler, and Meghir (2011) and the citations therein.

# References

Aizer, Anna. 2004. "Home Alone: Supervision after School and Child Behavior." *Journal of Public Economics* 88 (9–10): 1835–48.

———. 2010. "The Gender Wage Gap and Domestic Violence." *American Economic Review* 100 (4): 1847–59.

Akee, Randall K. Q., William E. Copeland, Gordon Keeler, Adrian Angold, and E. Jane Costello. 2010. "Parent's Incomes and Children's Outcomes: A Quasi-Experiment with Casinos on American Indian Reservations." *American Economics Journal: Applied Economics* 2 (1): 86–115.

Almond, Douglas, and Janet Currie. 2011. "Human Capital Development before Age 5." Chapter 15 in *Handbook of Labor Economics*, Volume 4B, edited by Orley Ashenfelter and David Card, 1315–1486. Amsterdam: North Holland.

Attanasio, Orazio, Adriana Kugler, and Costas Meghir. 2011. "Subsidizing Vocational Training for Disadvantaged Youth in Colombia: Evidence from a Randomized Trial." *American Economic Journal: Applied Economics* 3 (3): 188–220.

Beauchamp, Andrew, and Stacey Chan. 2014. "The Minimum Wage and Crime." *B.E. Journal of Economic Analysis & Policy* 14 (3): 1213–35.

Becker, Gary S. 1968. "Crime and Punishment: An Economic Approach." *Journal of Political Economy* 76 (2): 169–217.

Benson, Michael L., Greer L. Fox, Alfred DeMaris, and Judy Van Wyk. 2003. "Neighborhood Disadvantage, Individual Economic Distress and Violence against Women in Intimate Relationships." *Journal of Quantitative Criminology*, 19 (3): 207–35.

Blattman, Christopher, and Jeannie Annan. 2011. "Can Swords Be Turned into Ploughshares? Experimental Effects of an Agricultural Program on Employment, Lawlessness, and Armed Recruitment." Materials used from MIT Open Courseware, JPAL Executive Training: Evaluating Social Programs, http://ocw.mit.edu.

Blattman, Christopher, Nathan Fiala, and Sebastian Martinez. 2014. "Generating Skilled Self-Employment in Developing Countries: Experimental Evidence from Uganda." *Quarterly Journal of Economics* 129 (2): 697–752.

Blattman, Christopher, Julian C. Jamison, and Margaret Sheridan. 2015. "Reducing Crime and Violence: Experimental Evidence on Adult Noncognitive Investments in Liberia." NBER Working Paper 21204, National Bureau of Economic Research, Cambridge, MA.

Blau, D. 1999. "The Effect of Income on Child Development." *Review of Economics and Statistics* 81 (2): 261–76.

Bloom, Dan, Cindy Redcross, Janine Zweig, and Gilda Azurdia. 2007. "Transitional Jobs for Ex-Prisoners: Early Impacts from a Random Assignment Evaluation of the Center for Employment Opportunities (CEO) Prisoner Reentry Program." MDRC Working Paper, MDRC, New York.

Bobonis, Gustavo J. 2009. "Is the Allocation of Resources within the Household Efficient? New Evidence from a Randomized Experiment." *Journal of Political Economy* 117 (3): 453–503.

Borraz, Fernando, and Ignacio Munyo. 2014. "Conditional Cash Transfers and Crime: Higher Income but Also Better Loot." Working paper, IEEM Business School, Universidad de Montevideo.

Bushway, Shawn. 2011. "Labor Markets and Crime." In *Crime and Public Policy*, edited by Joan Petersilia and James Q. Wilson, 183–209. New York: Oxford University Press.

Bushway, Shawn, and Peter Reuter. 2002. "Labor Markets and Crime Risk Factors." In *Evidence-Based Crime Prevention*, edited by Lawrence Sherman, David Farrington, Brandon Welsh, and Doris MacKenzie. New York: Rutledge Press.

Camacho, Adriana, and Daniel Mejía. 2013. "The Externalities of Conditional Cash Transfer Programs on Crime: The of Case Familias en Acción in Bogota." Working paper, Universidad de los Andes.

Card, David. 1999. "The Causal Effect of Education on Earnings." In *Handbook of Labor Economics*, Volume 3A, edited by Orley Ashenfelter and David Card. Amsterdam: Elsevier.

Card, David, Pablo Ibarraran, Ferdinando Regalia, David Rosas, and Yuri Soares. 2011. "The Labor Market Impacts of Youth Training in the Dominican Republic: Evidence from a Randomized Evaluation." *Journal of Labor Economics* 29 (2): 267–300.

Cave, George, Hans Bos, Fred Doolittle, and Cyril Toussaint. 1993. *JOBSTART—Final Report on a Program for School Dropouts*. New York: MDRC (Manpower Demonstration Research Corporation).

Cave, George, and Janet Quint. 1990. "Career Beginnings Impact Evaluation: Findings from a Program for Disadvantaged High Schools Students." Manpower Demonstration Research Corporation (MRDC), New York.

Chioda, Laura. 2014a. "Violence in Latin America: Dynamic Panel Data Analysis." Working paper.

———. 2014b. "The Determinants of Violent v. Property Crimes in Mexico: A Dynamic Panel Data Approach." Working paper.

———. 2014c. "Offending and Labor Force Participation over the Life Cycle in Mexico." Working paper.

Chioda, Laura, João M. P. De Mello, and Rodrigo R. Soares. 2016. "Spillovers from Conditional Cash Transfer Programs: Bolsa Família and Crime in Urban Brazil." *Economics of Education Review* 54 (October): 306–20.

Chioda, Laura, and Rojas-Alvarado 2014. "Violence across Brazilian Municipalities." Working paper.

Chiricos, T. 1987. "Rates of Crime and Unemployment: An Analysis of Aggregate Research Evidence." *Social Problems* 34 (3): 187–212.

Crane, Jon, and David Ellwood. 1984. "The Summer Youth Employment Program: Private Job Supplement or Substitute?" Harvard University.

Dahl, Gordon B., and Lance Lochner. 2012. "The Impact of Family Income on Child Achievement: Evidence from the Earned Income Tax Credit." *American Economic Review* 102 (5): 1927–56.

Di Tella, Rafael, Sebastian Galiani, and Ernesto Schargrodsky. 2010. "Crime Distribution and Victim Behavior during a Crime Wave." In *The Economics of Crime: Lessons for and from Latin America*, edited by Rafael Di Tella, Sebastian Edwards, and Ernesto Schargrodsky, 175–204. Chicago: University of Chicago Press.

Dix-Carneiro, Rafael, Rodrigo R. Soares, and Gabriel Ulyssea. 2016. "Local Labor Market Conditions and Crime: Evidence from the Brazilian Trade Liberalization." Working paper.

Dooley, Martin D., and Jennifer M. Stewart. 2004. "Family Income and Child Outcomes in Canada." *Canadian Journal of Economics* 37 (4): 898–917.

Drake, Elizabeth K., Steve Aos, and Marna G. Miller. 2009. "Evidence-Based Public Policy Options to Reduce Crime and Criminal Justice Costs: Implications in Washington State." *Victims and Offenders* 4 (2): 170–96.

Duncan, Greg J., Pamela A. Morris, and Chris Rodrigues. 2011. "Does Money Really Matter? Estimating Impacts of Family Income on Young Children's Achievement with Data from Random-Assignment Experiments." *Developmental Psychology* 47 (5): 1263–79.

Edmark, Karin. 2005. "Unemployment and Crime: Is There a Connection?" *Scandinavian Journal of Economics* 107 (2): 353–73.

Fagan, Jeffrey. 1992. "Drug Selling and Licit Income in Distressed Neighborhoods: The Economic Lives of Street-Level Drug Users and Dealers?" In *Drugs, Crime and Social Isolation: Barriers to Urban Opportunity*, edited by George E. Peterson and Adelle V. Harrell. Washington, DC: Urban Institute Press.

———. 1994. "The Political Economy of Drug Dealing among Urban Gangs." In *Drugs and Community*, edited by Robert Davis, Arthur Lurigio, and Dennis P. Rosenbaum. Springfield, IL: Charles Thomas.

Fagan, Jeffrey, and Richard B. Freeman. 1999. "Crime and Work." In *Crime and Justice: A Review of Research*, Vol. 25, edited by M. Tonry. Chicago: University of Chicago Press.

Farkas, George, D. Alton Smith, Ernst W. Stromsdorfer, and Robert Jerrett III. 1982. *Impacts from the Youth Incentive Entitlement Pilot Projects: Participation, Work, and Schooling over the Full Program Period*. New York: Manpower Demonstration Research Corp. (MDRC).

Farkas, G., R. Olsen, E. W. Stromsdorfer, L. C. Sharpe, F. Skidmore, D. A. Smith, and S. Merrill. 1984. *Post-Program Impacts of the Youth Incentive Entitlement Pilot Projects*. New York: Manpower Demonstration Research Corp. (MDRC).

Fiszbein, Ariel, and Norbert Schady. 2009. *Conditional Cash Transfers: Reducing Present and Future Poverty*. Washington, DC: World Bank.

Freeman, Richard B. 1983. "Crime and Unemployment." In *Crime and Public Policy*, edited by James Q. Wilson. San Francisco: Institute for Contemporary Studies Press.

———. 1996. "Why Do So Many Young American Men Commit Crimes and What Might We Do About It?" *Journal of Economic Perspectives* 10: 25–42.

———. 1999. "The Economics of Crime." In *Handbook of Labor Economics*, Vol. 3C, edited by Orley Ashenfelter and David Card, chapter 52. Amsterdam: North Holland Publishers.

Gelber, Alexander, Adam Isen, and Judd B. Kessler. 2014. "The Effects of Youth Employment: Evidence from New York City Summer Youth Employment Program Lotteries." NBER Working Paper 20810, National Bureau of Economic Research, Cambridge, MA.

Gennetian, L. A., G. Duncan, V. Knox, W. Vargas, E. Clark-Kauffman, and A. S. London. 2004. "How Welfare Policies Affect Adolescents' School Outcomes: A Synthesis of Evidence from Experimental Studies." *Journal of Research on Adolescence* 14: 399–423.

Gertler, Paul, James Heckman, Rodrigo Pinto, Arianna Zanolini, Christel Vermeersch, Susan Walker, Susan M. Chang, and Sally Grantham-McGregor. 2014. "Labor Market Returns to an Early Childhood Stimulation Intervention in Jamaica." *Science* 344 (6187): 998–1001.

Gould, Eric D., Bruce A. Weinberg, and David B. Mustard. 2002. "Crime Rates and Local Labor Market Opportunities in the United States: 1977–1997." *Review of Economics and Statistics* 84 (1): 45–61.

Gould Ellen, Ingrid, Michael C. Lens, and Katherine O'Regan. 2011. "Memphis Murder Revisited: Do Housing Vouchers Cause Crime?" Assisted Housing Cadre Research Report. Prepared for the Office of Policy Development and Research, U.S. Department of Housing and Urban Development, Washington, DC.

Greenberg, David, Victoria Deitch, and Gayle Hamilton. 2009. *Welfare-to-Work Program Benefits and Costs—A Synthesis of Research*. New York: Manpower Demonstration Research Corp. (MDRC).

Grogger, Jeffrey. 1998. "Market Wages and Youth Crime." *Journal of Labor Economics* 16 (4): 756–91.

Grossman, J. B., and C. L. Sipe. 1992. *Summer Training and Education Program (STEP): Report on Long-Term Impacts*. Philadelphia: Public/Private Ventures.

Heller, Sara. 2014. "Short-Term Results of the One Summer Plus 2012 Evaluation." Crime Lab Report, University of Chicago.

Heller, Sara, Brian A. Jacob, and Jens Ludwig. 2012. "Family Income, Neighborhood Poverty and Crime." In *Making Crime Control Pay: Cost-Effective Alternatives of Incarceration*, edited by Philip J. Cook, Jens Ludwig, and Justin McCrary. Cambridge, MA: National Bureau of Economic Research.

Henrichson, Christian, and Ruth Delaney. 2012. *The Price of Prisons: What Incarceration Costs Taxpayers*. New York: Vera Institute of Justice.

Hirschi, Travis. 1969. *Causes of Delinquency*. Berkeley: University of California Press.

Holzer, Harry, Diane Whitmore Schanzenbach, Greg Duncan, and Jens Ludwig. 2008. "The Economic Costs of Childhood Poverty in the United States." *Journal of Children and Poverty* 14 (1): 41–51.

Ibarraran, Pablo, Laura Ripani, Bibiana Taboada, Juan Miguel Villa, and Brigida Garcia. 2012. "Life Skills, Employability and Training for Disadvantaged Youth: Evidence from a Randomized Evaluation Design." IDB Working Paper IDB-WP-342, Inter-American Development Bank, Washington, DC.

IEG (Independent Evaluation Group). 2011. *Evidence and Lessons Learned from Impact Evaluations on Social Safety Nets*. Washington, DC: World Bank.

Jacob, Brian A., and Jens Ludwig. 2010. "The Effects of Housing Vouchers on Children's Outcomes." Working paper, University of Michigan, Ann Arbor.

Jencks, C., and L. Tach. 2006. "Would Equal Opportunity Mean More Mobility?" In *Mobility and Inequality*, edited by S. Morgan, D. Grusky, and G. Fields, chapter 2. Stanford, CA: Stanford University Press.

LaLonde, Robert J. 1986. "Evaluating the Econometric Evaluations of Training Programs with Experimental Data." *American Economic Review* 76 (4): 604–20.

———. 1995. "The Promise of Public Sector-Sponsored Training Programs." *Journal of Economic Perspectives* 9 (2): 149–68.

———. 2003. "Employment and Training Programs." In *Means-Tested Transfer Programs in the United States*, edited by Robert A. Moffitt, 517–86. Cambridge, MA: National Bureau of Economic Research.

Liberman, Akiva M. 2008. *The Long View of Crime: A Synthesis of Longitudinal Research.* New York: Springer.

Lin, Ming-Jen. 2008. "Does Unemployment Increase Crime? Evidence from U.S. Data 1974–2000." *Journal of Human Resources* 43: 413–36.

Lochner, Lance, and Enrico Moretti. 2004. "The Effect of Education on Crime: Evidence from Prison Inmates, Arrests, and Self-Reports." *American Economic Review* 94 (1): 155–89.

Ludwig, J. 2006. "The Costs of Crime." Testimony to the U.S. Senate Committee on the Judiciary, 109th Congress, September 19.

Lund, Crick, Alison Breen, Alan J. Flisher, Ritsuko Kakuma, Joanne Corrigall, John A. Joska, Leslie Swartz, and Vikram Patel. 2010. "Poverty and Common Mental Disorders in Low- and Middle-Income Countries: A Systematic Review." *Social Science and Medicine* 71 (3): 517–28.

Machin, Stephen, and Costas Meghir. 2004. "Crime and Economic Incentives." *Journal of Human Resources* 39 (4): 958–79.

Macours, K., N. Schady, and R. Vakis. 2012. "Cash Transfers, Behavioral Changes, and the Cognitive Development in Early Childhood: Evidence from a Randomized Experiment." *American Economic Journal Applied Economics* 4 (2): 247–73.

Mayer, Susan E. 1997. *What Money Can't Buy: Family Income and Children's Life Chances.* Cambridge, MA: Harvard University Press.

McConnell, S., and S. Glazerman. 2001. *The Benefits and Costs of Job Corps.* Washington, DC: Mathematica Policy Research.

Milligan, Kevin, and Mark Stabile. 2011. "Do Child Tax Benefits Affect the Well-Being of Children? Evidence from Canadian Child Benefit Expansions." *American Economic Journal: Economic Policy* 3 (3): 175–205.

MDRC (Manpower Demonstration Research Corporation). 1983. *Summary and Findings of the National Supported Work Demonstration.* Cambridge, MA: Ballinger.

Mullainathan, Sendhil, and Eldar Shafir. 2013. *Scarcity: Why Having Too Little Means So Much.* New York: Times Books.

Munyo, I. 2015. "The Juvenile Crime Dilemma." *Review of Economics Dynamics* 5 (18): 201–11.

Munyo, I., and M. Rossi. 2015. "First-Day Criminal Recidivism." *Journal of Public Economics* 5 (24): 81–90.

Mustard, David B. 2010. "How Do Labor Markets Affect Crime? New Evidence on an Old Puzzle." In *Handbook on the Economics of Crime*, edited by Bruce Benson and Paul Zimmerman, 342–58. Northampton, MA: Edward Elgar.

Neumark, David, and William Wascher. 2006. "Minimum Wages and Employment: A Review of Evidence from the New Minimum Wage Research." NBER Working Paper 12663, National Bureau of Economic Research, Cambridge, MA.

Oreopoulos, Philip, Marianne Page, and Ann Huff-Stevens. 2008. "The Intergenerational Effects of Worker Displacement." *Journal of Labor Economics* 26 (3): 455–83.

Ozer, Emily J., Lia C. H. Fernald, James G. Manley, and Paul J. Gertler. 2009. "Effects of a Conditional Cash Transfer Program on Children's Behavior Problems." *Pediatrics* 123 (4): e630–7.

Ozer, Emily J., Lia C. H. Fernald, Ann Weber, Emily P. Flynn, and Tyler J. VanderWeele. 2011. "Does Alleviating Poverty Affect Mothers' Depressive Symptoms? A Quasi-Experimental Investigation of Mexico's Oportunidades Programme." *International Journal of Epidemiology* 40: 1565–76.

Paxson, C., and N. Schady. 2007. *Does Money Matter? The Effects of Cash Transfers on Child Health and Development in Rural Ecuador.* Impact Evaluation Series. Washington, DC: World Bank.

Psacharopoulos, George, and Harry A. Patrinos. 2004. "Returns to Investment in Education: A Further Update." *Education Economics* 12 (2): 111–34.

Raphael, Steven. 2010. "The Causes and Labor Market Consequences of the Steep Increase in U.S. Incarceration Rates." In *Labor in the Era of Globalization*, edited by Clair Brown, Barry Eichengreen, and Michael Reich, 375–413. Cambridge: Cambridge University Press.

Raphael, Steven, and David F. Weiman. 2007. "The Impact of Local Labor-Market Conditions on the Likelihood that Parolees Are Returned to Custody." In *Barriers to Reentry? The Labor Market for Released Prisoners in Post-Industrial America*, edited by David Weiman, Michael A. Stoll, and Shawn D. Bushway. New York: Russell Sage Foundation.

Raphael, Steven, and Rudolf Winter-Ebmer. 2001. "Identifying the Effect of Unemployment on Crime." *Journal of Law and Economics* 44 (1): 259–84.

Rawlings, Laura B., and Gloria M. Rubio. 2005. "Evaluating the Impact of Conditional Cash Transfer Programs." *World Bank Research Observer* 20 (1): 29–55.

Reuter, Peter, Robert MacCoun, and Patrick Murphy. 1990. *Money from Crime: A Study of the Economics of Drug Dealing in Washington, DC.* Santa Monica, CA: RAND Corp.

Rosin, Hanna. 2008. "American Murder Mystery." *The Atlantic*, July/August. http://www .theatlantic.com/magazine/archive/2008/07/american-murder-mystery/6872/1.

Ruhm, Christopher J. 1995. "Economic Conditions and Alcohol Problems." *Journal of Health Economics* 14 (5): 583–603.

Saavedra, J. E., and S. Garcia. 2012. "Impact of Conditional Cash Transfer Programs on Educational Outcomes in Developing Countries: A Meta Analysis." Working Paper WR-921-1, Rand Corporation, Santa Monica, CA.

Sampson, R. J., and W. B. Groves. 1989. "Community Structure and Crime: Testing Social-Disorganization Theory." *American Journal of Sociology* 94 (4): 774–802.

Schochet, Peter, John Burghardt, and Sheena McConnell. 2006. *National Job Corps Study and Longer-Term Follow-Up Study: Impact and Benefit-Cost Findings Using Survey and Summary Earnings Records Data.* Princeton, NJ: Mathematica Policy Research, Inc.

———. 2008. "Does Job Corps Work? Impact Findings from the National Job Corps Study." *American Economic Review* 98 (5): 1864–86.

Schochet, Peter, Sheena McConnell, and John Burghardt. 2003. *National Job Corps Study: Findings Using Administrative Earnings Records.* Princeton, NJ: Mathematica Policy Research, Inc.

Shaw, C., and H. McKay. 1942. *Juvenile Delinquency and Urban Areas.* Chicago: University of Chicago Press.

Stanley, Marcus, Lawrence Katz, and Alan Krueger. 1998. "Developing Skills: What We Know about the Impact of American Employment and Training Programs on Employment, Earnings, and Educational Outcomes." Report to G8 Economic Summit, October.

Uggen, C. 2000. "Work as a Turning Point in the Life Course of Criminals: A Duration Model of Age, Employment, and Recidivism." *American Sociological Review* 65: 529–46.

Wadsworth, Tim. 2006. "The Meaning of Work: Conceptualizing the Deterrent Effect of Employment on Crime among Young Adults." *Sociological Perspectives* 49 (3): 343–68.

Yeung, W. Jean, Miriam Linver, and Jeanne Brooks-Gunn. 2002. "How Money Matters for Young Children's Development: Parental Investment and Family Processes." *Child Development* 73 (6): 1861–79.

# 6
# Neighborhoods and Urban Upgrading

This chapter reviews evidence on interventions that target the geographic unit surrounding the individual rather than the individual himself or herself. It focuses on two sets of interventions: those aimed at improving housing conditions, via relocation or via *in situ* upgrading; and those devised to alter the appearance of streets and neighborhoods.[1]

The premises behind these types of interventions are twofold and are interrelated. First, human decisions and behavior do not take place in a vacuum; they are the product of individuals taking their environment and context into account in their decision making. Social Interaction Theory provides explanations as to why decisions such as how much education to acquire, whether to engage in discrimination, whether to marry or divorce, and whether to participate in crime are not based exclusively (nor, for that matter, primarily) on individual considerations (Akerlof 1997). These decisions are social in nature; the social context (frequently determined by geographic proximity), networks of relationships, and communities can exercise social control on individual behavior.

The theoretical constructs that have emerged from the sociological and criminological literatures are social *control*, social *organization*, and social *efficacy*. The evidence presented here attempts to disentangle the effects on crime of neighborhood characteristics—particularly deprived neighborhoods—from those of the characteristics of people who populate them. Correlational estimates suggest that neighborhood effects might be economically important in magnitude. While there is a consensus on the importance of familial influence on behavior, there is a fundamental conceptual problem when interpreting both the neighborhood and family background effects as evidence of social interactions; this issue is discussed in detail below.

The second somewhat related notion is that the *appearance* of neighborhoods may encourage or deter criminal behavior. To the extent that this is the case, interventions designed to improve physical aspects of spaces may affect crime (for instance, by physical upgrading of the space or by increasing police presence to preserve an orderly appearance).

The theoretical underpinnings of this type of intervention can be traced back to an influential 1982 article in the *Atlantic Monthly*, in which James Q. Wilson and George L. Kelling posited that addressing minor disorder could help reduce more serious forms of crime. Their argument stipulated an important link between disorder and crime, whereby a "broken window" is a symbol of unaccountability. If one window in a building is broken and left unfixed, they argued, it is likely that the remaining windows would soon be broken, too.

Their idea was that potential criminals take cues from their environment and adjust their behavior based on what they see. If a neighborhood is litter-free and the grounds of its buildings well kept, potential criminals will be less likely to vandalize this area out of a sense that they will be held accountable; a neighborhood's characteristics, according to the theory, carry information about the zeal with which transgressions will be disciplined. The mechanisms underlying the "broken window" theory are related to social organization and efficacy.

Since Wilson and Kelling's (1982) influential article, numerous cities in Great Britain, Indonesia, the Netherlands, South Africa, and the United States—including its three largest cities, New York, Los Angeles, and Chicago—have embraced at least some element of the "broken window" theory, largely through more aggressive enforcement of minor misdemeanor laws. The scope of this metaphorical window has since expanded to include common, victimless crimes that occur every day in urban areas but are nuisances. As one article recently summed up the theory, "order begets accountability; disorder begets crime" (Kirchner 2014). Thus, the theory goes, enforcing the law for disorderly conduct and minor crimes could deter serious and violent crimes. Despite its broad adoption, only a surprisingly small consensus has emerged regarding the effectiveness of such policing strategies.

Empirical tests of the hypothesis typically proceed by relating the behavior of individuals to the characteristics of the neighborhoods in which they reside. Most research suggests that disadvantaged neighborhoods are "criminogenic" in the sense of having a higher incidence of crime (Sampson, Morenoff, and Gannon-Rowley 2002). Yet drawing causal inferences from such correlations is complicated by the possibility that the relationship is confounded by unmeasured individual- or family-level attributes that are related both to criminality and to the characteristics of the neighborhood in which they reside. Predicting the magnitude or even direction of this bias is difficult because it requires a complete accounting of all such unmeasured confounders.

These conceptual and methodological difficulties motivate some of the discussion in this chapter, which is organized as follows. The first section is dedicated to a review of research that quantifies the effects of neighborhood and social interactions either on crime itself or on factors understood to protect from it. It first provides a general review of evidence about the influence of neighborhoods on the life course of their residents, and then focuses more narrowly on the relationship between neighborhood characteristics and crime. Some recent research on dwelling upgrades and relocation in both Latin America and the Caribbean (LAC) and the United States is considered. These interventions (experimentally or quasi-experimentally) alter the characteristics of the neighborhoods in which poor people reside, thereby allowing credible measurement of the causal impact of the interventions on outcome of interests.

The second section of the chapter considers the impacts of cues from physical surroundings on antisocial behavior, as postulated by the broken window theory. In particular, broken window policing (aggressive enforcement of minor misdemeanor laws to curb disorder) and the recovery of public spaces aimed at reducing physical disorder (such as restoring public parks and improving street lighting) are considered. As in the previous chapters, the narrative highlights research from LAC, and complements it with evidence from the United States, which has led the way in rigorously testing some of the hypotheses in question.[2]

## Evidence on the effects of neighborhoods and social interactions on outcomes

That peers outside of the immediate family may influence decisions by individuals over such things as educational attainment, drug use, and employment is uncontroversial. A natural hypothesis is that role models and peer groups are drawn from one's residential environment, and that their behaviors may influence youth. Correlations have been documented between the economic conditions of neighborhoods and the outcomes of their residents at least since the seventeenth century. Numerous studies have since shown that people from distressed neighborhoods are more involved in criminal activity than those living in less distressed environments, complete fewer years of formal schooling, and lag behind them on a number of economic and health outcomes.[3]

Case and Katz (1991) were among the first economists to rigorously consider the influence of family and neighborhood peers on the behaviors and outcomes of youths. Focusing on disadvantaged neighborhoods in Boston, they document that the characteristics and behaviors of neighborhood peers[4] are meaningfully related to youth behaviors, consistent with contagion models of neighborhood effects.[5] Specifically, they show that the behaviors of an individual's neighbors are highly predictive of his own likelihood of participating in criminal activity, drug and alcohol use, church attendance, and idleness (staying out of school and being unemployed). No such neighborhood effects are present for out-of-wedlock parenting. Relatedly, Case and Katz (1991) also draw attention to the strength of family links; the participation of family members in these behaviors is highly predictive of the same behaviors among the youths within the household. This relationship is much stronger than that with neighborhood peers.

Both sets of results appear to be substantiated by Gibbons (2002), who asks whether the characteristics of the residential neighborhood influence the ultimate educational attainment of teenagers in subsidized housing (so-called social tenants) in Britain. He exploits the fact that there is considerable variation in the "quality" of neighborhoods in which social tenants reside. He finds that average neighborhood educational attainment is related to the attainment of young social tenants, independently from family resources. However, as with Case and Katz (1991), the magnitude of this effect is relatively small, consistent with the view that neighborhoods determine only a small proportion of the variation in individual outcomes, and that family background matters considerably more. Accordingly, Gibbons (2002) concludes that although there may be social benefits from improvements in neighborhood quality in disadvantaged locations, these are likely small.

The preceding results imply that two inner city youths with similar personal characteristics may have quite different socioeconomic experiences, depending on the family members and peer influences in their neighborhoods. From a policy perspective, these family and neighborhood effects are important because they suggest the existence of *social multipliers* in behavior: a policy that alters the behavior of one individual may have ripple effects onto others through the influence of his or her behavior on that of his or her peers. This alters the cost-benefit calculus of a hypothetical policy or intervention, because ignoring the (external) neighborhood and family effects could understate the benefits (or costs) associated with the policy.[6]

While the results of Case and Katz (1991) and Gibbons (2002) are consistent with neighborhoods exerting influence on youth (through "social interactions"), their evidence could also have a variety of other explanations (see Manski 1993). Neighborhood characteristics may be predictive of unobserved individual characteristics that affect outcomes and behavior but are omitted from the estimating equations. For instance, observed neighborhood characteristics that do not operate on outcomes through social interactions could be related to such neighborhood inputs as expenditures on schooling and school quality, which have more direct impacts on educational attainment. Alternatively, endogenous neighborhood choice (people sorting into neighborhoods based their characteristics) could account for the observed neighborhood effects without any effects from social interactions. Indeed, Gibbons (2002) acknowledges that families from the type of social housing that he considers may not locate randomly, and does not assess whether random assignment occurred. Analogous problems arise in the interpretation of coefficients on family characteristics when youth outcomes are regressed on characteristics of their environment, including their families.

These observations have led researchers to pay closer attention to the sources of variation in neighborhood characteristics, and to focus on natural experiments that (ideally) eliminate concerns such as confounding unobserved neighborhood characteristics and endogenous sorting across neighborhoods.

Gibbons, Silva, and Weinhardt (2013) provide one such attempt with detailed administrative data from the United Kingdom. They track four cohorts of more than 1.3 million students through the first three years of secondary schooling. In an effort to overcome the methodological problems mentioned earlier, their longitudinal research design is based on changes in neighborhood composition for *immobile* students, for whom the changes in community characteristics arise from in-migration and out-migration of other students in their data set. In their analysis, changes in community characteristics have no effects on test scores. However, they uncover evidence that neighborhood composition exerts small effects on students' behavioral outcomes, such as attitudes toward schooling and drug use (on their soft skills), and that these effects differ according to student gender. This is qualitatively consistent with a growing body of evidence that girls are more sensitive than boys to environmental and educational inputs[7]—a conclusion encountered later in this chapter.

While Gibbons, Silva, and Weinhardt (2013) provide more rigorous results than previously mentioned studies, it might be argued that the sample of students whose families do not relocate in response to changing neighborhood characteristics is similarly selected. Jacob (2004) overcomes this (and other) concerns regarding research design. He exploits the displacement of public housing tenants resulting from a series of closures of high-rise public housing in Chicago to study the effect of concentrated public housing on students' academic achievement. During the 1990s, the Chicago Housing Authority demolished over 7,400 public housing units in 12 developments. Families in the affected buildings—who had no option but to move—were offered vouchers to move to private housing elsewhere in the Chicago area. The academic achievements of affected students are compared to those of peers living in units in the same project that were not closed. Jacob (2004) finds that children in demolished housing do no better or worse than their peers on a wide variety of achievement measures. Given that most of affected households moved to neighborhoods and schools that closely resembled those they left (neighborhood characteristics were effectively not affected by the interventions), this null effect can be thought of as an estimate of the causal impact of living in public housing.

Jacob's (2004) (somewhat surprising) null results are buttressed by Oreopoulos (2003), who instead studies the effects on longer-term labor market outcomes—including market earnings, total income, unemployment participation, and welfare receipt—of neighborhoods in Toronto. In Jacob's context, families affected by public housing closures were required to move, while control group families remain in their original location, making the impact from relocation difficult to distinguish from that of a change in neighborhood environment. In the Toronto public housing program, families are assigned chiefly on the basis of household size to various neighborhoods throughout the city; there is virtually no discretion in choice of location. The neighborhoods and housing to which families are assigned vary widely in their characteristics and quality: some projects accommodate more than 10,000 individuals, while others no more than 100; some are located in the city center, while others are in middle-income suburbs.

As a first pass, Oreopoulos (2003) estimates models of long-term labor market outcomes on the characteristics of neighborhoods for an unrestricted sample of youth—whether they live in public housing or not. After controlling for a number of observable family characteristics, he finds sizable positive relationships between youths' labor market outcomes and living in wealthier residential areas. However, once he restricts attention to children in the housing program, the positive effects disappear, implying that the positive relationship that is estimated from the full sample is likely driven by residents sorting into neighborhoods whose characteristics they value. Removing this choice from the public housing residents reveals that neighborhoods in fact have little causal bearing on long-term labor market outcomes; unemployment, mean earnings, income, and welfare participation rates do not vary systematically between adolescents who live in different types of public housing.

While the correlations between neighborhood characteristics and individual outcomes are sizable in observational studies, more careful approaches reveal little impact of neighborhood-level interactions on educational and labor market outcomes, or on receipt of welfare. However, the research reviewed so far has been limited in the outcomes it considered. It is possible that other behaviors and outcomes—such as attitudes toward risk, aggression, and criminality—are more sensitive to the social interactions that are formed in neighborhoods and, by extension, to neighborhood quality. These behaviors and outcomes are explored in the following section.

## Neighborhoods and crime

This section considers the connections between neighborhood characteristics and crime. The organizing (ecological) framework of this study views the sphere of individuals' social interactions as expanding as they progress through childhood and adolescence: from their immediate families to neighbors, to the surrounding community, and ultimately to society at large. Through these interactions, which become increasingly important as individuals age, social ties are formed and peer groups are defined. These peers, in turn, help determine individuals' social norms, drawing lines between what is and what is not acceptable behavior within the peer group.

### Theory and channels

From a policy perspective, targeting children and youth in the home environment is difficult because as they age (and exit school, for instance), they are progressively less under parental control, whose influence therefore declines. Declining parental influence may be especially relevant for those youth who are at most risk of offending, and who are also ostensibly the least likely to take advantage of public programs to improve or remediate their outcomes. For policy makers, these individuals are difficult to target.[8] Instead, urban interventions that direct attention to neighborhoods and public spaces are more practical, particularly in the case of crime, since the incidence of crime in a community is generally observable to a policy maker.

For instance, if the idleness of one's (neighborhood) peers affects one's own idleness through a process akin to social contagion, then additional resources dedicated to combating idleness may pay off by inducing not only idle individuals to join the labor force or complete their schooling, but also their (idle) peers. By the same token, assuming that crime exhibits a form of contagion, then discouraging one youth from engaging in crime via an after-school program, for instance, may prevent his or her peers from adopting criminal habits.

Alternatively, neighborhoods may influence criminality, for instance, by raising the likelihood of being caught for committing a crime if the community is intolerant of crime and devotes substantial resources to policing. On the other hand, in communities in which law enforcement and the criminal justice system are not generally trusted, crime may be more tolerated.

In sum, individual decisions are rarely simple choices based exclusively on individual considerations; they are conditioned by social forces (Akerlof 1997). In the context of criminality, Glaeser, Sacerdote, and Scheinkman (1996) provide arguments why social interactions likely play an important role in the decision to participate in crime. Their starting point is the well-documented observation that crime rates vary widely across geographic areas and over time, as chapter 2 corroborated for LAC. This degree of variation, they argue, is difficult to rationalize on the basis of Beckerian benefits and costs. That is, the economic benefits and costs (that accrue to the individual) of committing crimes likely do not vary enough from place to place and over time to explain the wide dispersion in crime rates. Indeed, in their two samples, one of U.S. cities and the other of New York City precincts, observable costs and benefits explain at most 30 percent of the total variation in crime rates. Thus other explanations need to be invoked to reconcile patterns of extreme dispersion.[9]

As an illustration from LAC, map 2.5 in chapter 2 presents the distribution of homicide rates per 100,000 residents across municipalities in Colombia, Guatemala, and Mexico, which revealed a high variance in violence across municipalities. In the spirit of Glaeser, Sacerdote, and Scheinkman's (1996) arguments applied to the Mexican context, the high degree of cross-sectional variation in violence across municipalities would imply an implausible amount of variation in its costs and benefits to rationalize it on the basis of the Beckerian model. The spirit of this argument also holds over time, given the dramatic rise in violence observed over the last decade. Indeed, a regression of the homicide rate focused only on municipal fixed effects over the 2000–10 period reveals that the fixed effects account for roughly 37 percent of the total variation (that is, the cross-sectional plus time series variation) in homicides. This implies that a large proportion of the changes in municipal-level violence over the last decade is left unexplained by time-invariant locality characteristics. In Brazil, in turn, municipal fixed effects absorb closer to 75 percent to 80 percent of the total variation in homicides, suggesting that over the 1998–2008 period, there was little change in the location of violence in Brazil (see table 6.1).

TABLE 6.1: Residual variation in homicide rates after controlling for municipal fixed effects

| | (1) | (2) | (3) | (4) | (5) | (6) | (7) | (8) | (9) | (10) | (11) |
|---|---|---|---|---|---|---|---|---|---|---|---|
| | Mexico | | | Brazil | | | Colombia | | | | Guatemala |
| Rate | Mexy00-y10 | Mexy94-y10 | Mexy97-y10 | Bray98-y08 | Bray00-y08 | Bray03-y08 | Coly93-y09 | Coly00-y09 | Coly03-y09 | Coly05-y09 | Guay06-y11 |
| Constant | 12.20*** | 13.12*** | 12.47*** | 25.97*** | 26.18*** | 25.68*** | 60.66*** | 55.18*** | 46.51*** | 41.80*** | 43.82*** |
| | (7.125e-17) | (1.296e-16) | (1.278e-16) | (2.131e-16) | (1.819e-16) | (1.300e-16) | (4.901e-16) | (6.103e-16) | (1.243e-15) | (1.737e-15) | (1.098e-14) |
| Observations | 26,994 | 41,718 | 34,356 | 61,017 | 50,003 | 33,376 | 15,407 | 8,252 | 5,186 | 3,123 | 1,655 |
| R-squared | 0.370 | 0.384 | 0.371 | 0.724 | 0.749 | 0.804 | 0.473 | 0.550 | 0.678 | 0.846 | 0.894 |

*Source:* World Bank.

*Note:* OLS (ordinary least squares). Homicides rate per 100,000 inhabitants, weighted by population. Municipal fixed effects only and clusters at the municipal level.

*Significance level:* \* = 10 percent, \*\* = 5 percent, \*\*\* = 1 percent.

Glaeser, Sacerdote, and Scheinkman (1996) argue that in order to reconcile the excess variance of crime rates over the variance of local economic net benefits of crime, there needs to be positive correlation between agents' decisions to commit crimes within cities. These positive correlations are posited to arise from social interactions that occur at the local level, in such a way that an individual's decision to become criminally active is positively related to his or her neighbor's decision to commit crimes. If this is the case, from an empirical perspective, cities' crime rates may deviate substantially from the rates predicted by their characteristics, and will differ substantially across locations and over time. Glaeser, Sacerdote, and Scheinkman's (1996) results are consistent with the theory of social interactions in the commission of crime. They document a high degree of spillovers across individuals for more minor offenses such as larceny and auto theft; moderate (but still substantial) spillovers for assault, burglary, and robbery; and very low spillovers for more serious crimes such as arson, murder, and rape.

### Social disorganization: Theory and channels

Glaeser, Sacerdote, and Sheinkman (1996) provide a formal theory for what has been discussed in detail in the criminological and sociological literatures, where attention focuses more on the mechanisms through which social interactions operate. Empirically, there are a number of durable and stable neighborhood-level correlates of crime (Sampson 2011). First, there is a substantial inequality in socioeconomic resources across neighborhoods.[10] Second, a number of social ills tend to cluster at the neighborhood level—including adolescent delinquency, dropping out of school, child maltreatment, and ultimately crime—which are themselves highly correlated with the local concentration of poverty, broken families, and even home ownership and tenure in the current residence. Third, these neighborhood attributes tend to persist over time, with little variation from one period to the next (Sampson, Morenoff, and Gannon-Rowley 2002). With these basic facts in mind, what are the mechanisms and social processes that help explain why environmental and neighborhood factors are related to increased crime and violence? Figure 6.1 summarizes possible mechanisms and social processes.

The most renowned approach to mechanism-based theory can be traced back to the Chicago School's Social Disorganization Theory[11] (Shaw and MacKay 1942), defined as the inability of a community to structure itself to realize the common interest of its residents in maintaining social order and control (Sampson and Groves 1989). This approach views communities and neighborhoods as complex systems of interdependent relationships and networks. In this framework, social disorganization arises from a system of networks that fails to exercise social control.

**FIGURE 6.1:** Neighborhoods, social interactions, and crime: Theory and channels

| Social cohesion | Social contagion | "Correlated" effects |
|---|---|---|
| • Density of social networks and their connectivity are associated with increased control over deviant behavior.<br><br>• Social cohesion (collective efficacy) is a protective factor through maintenance of social order by individuals in the neighborhood. | • The tendency of others to engage in certain criminal behaviors in a particular area may alter an individual's likelihood of engaging in them.<br><br>• The mechanisms include lowering social stigma, changing beliefs about returns to crime, and likelihood of arrest. | • Specific neighborhood characteristics—such as intensify of policing, schools, or other local institutional characteristics—may shape criminal behavior, not social interaction per se. |

According to this theory, the density of social networks and their connectivity are associated with increased control over deviant behavior. However, density and connectivity are not sufficient characteristics to understand communities. Connected and dense networks may impede social organization if they are isolated or weakly tied to collective expectations of rules (Sampson 2012). For instance, the willingness of local residents to intervene in the name of public safety ultimately depends on conditions of mutual trust and expectations among residents. Linkages of mutual trust and common expectations are at the heart of what Sampson, Raudenbush, and Earls (1997) term "collective efficacy" and are what empower neighbors to take action to ensure social control (box 6.1). Collective efficacy is context- and task-specific, however. Its influence may be internalized by residents and have effects on loitering, for instance, while being weak with respect to more severe crimes and public disorder.[12]

In addition to social disorganization theory, a vast theoretical literature has developed to explain why social context matters for an individual's behavior in general, and their inclination to participate in crime, in particular. The main hypotheses are summarized in the discussion that follows.

First, criminal behavior may exhibit contagion—what Manski (1993) termed an "endogenous" effect. The prevalence of criminal acts in a particular area may alter an individual's likelihood of engaging in them himself by lowering its social stigma (operating on individuals' preferences), or by changing beliefs about the returns to the behavior (changing individuals' information), or even about the likelihood of arrest (altering constraints).[13]

An alternative possibility, as discussed, is that criminal behavior is subject to "contextual" effects: other characteristics of neighborhood residents affect criminality

Over the past 15 years, important infrastructure and transportation initiatives have been undertaken in Latin America and the Caribbean (LAC) to bridge the divide between the urban centers and their most isolated neighborhoods and informal settlements. The idea is to improve connectivity and collective efficacy, and mitigate marginalization in those areas too often plagued by violence and/or ruled by criminal organizations. LAC was first to consider using cable cars for urban transit. The most significant experiments took place in the 2000s in Medellín, Colombia, and Caracas, Venezuela. Medellín's achievements with Metrocable led other cities to replicate the urban cable car system, with Rio de Janeiro connecting some of the most violent *favelas* to the rest of the city in July 2011. In Honduras, the World Bank–funded urban upgrading and crime and violence prevention project, Barrio Ciudad, seeks to develop public works and prevention strategies that enhance community security and integration, particularly by mainstreaming prevention into the overall project through improved physical living conditions, community participation, and community support. While not a panacea for violence in the country, the urban crime and violence prevention component of the project aspires to reduce homicides and youth violence, and focuses on risk factors in the most vulnerable neighborhoods of participating municipalities. The project adopts an urban renewal approach that goes beyond traditional police responses, exploiting economies of scope between infrastructure, neighborhood upgrading, and situational prevention and community-based social prevention activities.

While these interventions have not been rigorously evaluated, an observational study of Medellín's Metrocable provides evidence consistent with the hypothesis that the infrastructure project may have accelerated the decline in crime (Cerdá and others 2012). While the government was building the Metrocable, they were simultaneously making other improvements to the gondola neighborhoods—including additional lighting for public spaces; new pedestrian bridges and street paths; "library parks"; school buildings; recreational centers; centers to promote microenterprises; additional police patrols; and a family police station next to a gondola station.

but are unobserved to the researcher, including some dimensions of socioeconomic status, or the degree to which residents are willing to become involved in the maintenance of local order (that is, the degree of collective efficacy).

A third possibility is the existence of "correlated" effects, such as intensity of policing, the quality of schools, and other institutional characteristics of neighborhoods to which all of its residents are exposed.[14] Determining which of these sources explain neighborhood variation in crime is important because policy interventions are magnified by social multipliers only with contagion (Glaeser, Sacerdote, and Scheinkman

1996, 2003). Furthermore, depending on the source of neighborhood effects, certain policies may be ineffective, while others may be highly effective.

## The evidence on social interactions and crime

Despite the extensive theoretical literature on the mechanisms and channels by which neighborhoods and social interactions may matter for antisocial behavior, the empirical evidence is limited or is not definitive.

As noted, variation in crime across geographical areas far exceeds what could be explained by standard determinants of the personal benefits and costs of crime, which are typically slow moving. Glaeser, Sacerdote, and Scheinkman (1996) take this to mean (and provide evidence) that there are positive correlations in behavior within geographical areas, though the question as to the source of this correlation is left open. It is unclear what types of effects generate the positive correlation (contextual, correlated, or endogenous) or if it is driven by residential sorting across areas based on local characteristics and amenities (security being one of them). This section discusses evidence of contextual and correlated effects on the behavior and organization of neighborhoods.

Sampson and coauthors argue that collective efficacy plays a role, with early evidence being provided by Sampson, Raudenbush, and Earls (1997). The authors undertook a longitudinal study of approximately 3,000 children ages zero to 18 in 1997, as part of the Project on Human Development in Chicago Neighborhoods. They carefully document that measures of collective efficacy are consistently associated with lower rates of violence. After controlling for demographic composition, they find that violent offending was especially high in communities with high levels of cynicism/distrust and where legal rule is perceived to be illegitimate. As acknowledged by the authors—and as discussed later in the section—however, these relationships may certainly be driven by residential sorting or by reverse causality; high levels of crime and violence are themselves detrimental to social efficacy as they lead to withdrawal from community life, to declines in economic activity, and to fear and dissatisfaction.

In line with this pioneering work, Sampson (2011) provides a review of the empirical evidence on collective efficacy, measures of which exhibit a significant correlation with crime and violence, supporting the hypothesis that social control of public spaces acts as a protective factor with respect to crime. Notably, numerous correlations persist even after controlling for income and socioeconomic status (which are themselves significant predictors of organizational participation). If the relationship between social efficacy and crime were causal, policy could be designed to target social efficacy in an effort to control crime, thereby again expanding the menu of available interventions intended to improve security. Indeed, recent research has begun to measure the effects of policies directed at collective efficacy and disorder. Box 6.2 summarizes the findings of two novel studies that link conditional cash transfer programs

**BOX 6.2:** Social cohesion and public policy: The case of cash transfers in Colombia and Indonesia

Poverty reduction and social assistance programs are often designed with only poverty alleviation in mind. Programs such as conditional cash transfers (CCTs) have accumulated an abundance of evidence as to their efficacy in reducing poverty. However, unintended consequences of such programs could result if recipients are stigmatized and social cohesion deteriorates (see Vigorito and others 2013). This box reports the results of an experiment conducted by Attanasio, Polania-Reyes, and Pellerano (2015) in Colombia, which tested the theory that social transfers erode social ties and increase social stigma, thereby undermining social cohesion.

In 2007, the authors conducted a public goods game in Cartagena, Colombia. They interpret the degree of cooperation in the game as a measure of "social capital." The game was played by residents in two similar and adjacent neighborhoods: El Pozón, which had been targeted for more than two years by a CCT program Familias en Acción; and the "control" neighborhood of Ciénaga de la Virgen, which had not. In 2008, when the CCT reached both neighborhoods, the public goods game was again played, so the authors were able to implement a difference-in-differences strategy to estimate the impact of the CCT on their measure of social capital.

At baseline in 2007, the treatment community exhibited significantly higher cooperation than the control neighborhood. In 2008, the degrees of cooperation in the two neighborhoods were statistically identical, and not dissimilar to the levels observed in El Pozón in 2007. Attanasio, Polania-Reyes, and Pellerano (2015) conclude that the CCT program enhanced social capital.

Alternatively, public policies run the risk of eroding social capital if they poorly targeted or poorly implemented. This hypothesis is explored by Cameron and Shah (2014), who consider the potential negative spillovers of a CCT in Indonesian villages. The authors provide suggestive evidence that the large-scale national antipoverty program contributed to the deterioration of social harmony. The program, Bantuan Langsung Tunai, was intended to compensate poor households for a sudden and large increase in fuel costs that resulted from the removal of fuel subsidies. Its rapid implementation resulted in poor targeting; nearly $500 million was disbursed to ineligible households. The social unrest that followed was widely reported in the media and escalated to the point that the offices of village heads were burned down and stoned (Widjaja 2009). Certain types of mistargeting appear to be more harmful than others. Leakage (the share of ineligible households that receive the funds) is a strong

*(continued on next page)*

to improvements in (or erosion) of social capital. In the case of Colombia's Familias en Acción, Attanasio, Polania-Reyes, and Pellerano (2015) document positive spillovers of the CCT on social cohesion. In the case of Indonesia, the poor targeting and implementation of the poverty alleviation program—in particular, the elevated share of ineligible households that received the funds—led to considerable deteriorations in social capital, which eventually culminated in violent crime and protests (Cameron and Shah 2014).

An alternate measure of the characteristics of a neighborhood is the presence of criminals residing in them. If crime were contagious, the concentration of criminals in a neighborhood would be predictive of the extent to which criminal behavior is adopted and replicated by others. In the LAC context, Medina, Tamayo, and Posso (2013) attempt to quantify the degree of contagion and investigate the likelihood that youth in a given locality will become criminally active as a function of whether an adult criminal is present in their neighborhood. They make use of a uniquely rich data set constructed by combining the census of arrested individuals between 2000 and 2010 in Medellín, Colombia.[15] After controlling for neighborhood characteristics, they find that the presence on the block in 2002 of someone who committed a homicide is associated with a greater likelihood of committing a subset of related crimes: namely, homicides, and carrying and trafficking weapons. These effects are consistent with the evidence presented in chapter 3 on the persistent and proximal nature of homicides and how they occur in very concentrated areas. These effects might represent endogenous or correlated effects. However, here again, the concern is that criminals may not locate randomly across the city but in fact sort into neighborhoods with certain unobserved characteristics (which may have varied over the 2002–10 period), such as "criminal capital" and weak supervision and/or tolerance for crime. Such a possibility weakens the interpretation of their estimates as evidence of endogenous/contagion effects.

Box 6.3 reviews two recent papers that test the hypothesis of contagion in criminal offending by exploiting policies that experimentally altered the characteristics of neighborhoods among at-risk families. They come to opposing conclusions, largely

## BOX 6.3: Is crime contagious?

If criminal behavior is "contagious," law enforcement and other public resources can be devoted to high-crime areas with the expectation that social multipliers will accelerate the rate of desistance. Conversely, if crime is not addressed early, contagion implies that it can be expected to propagate. Ludwig and Kling (2007) test the hypothesis that criminal behavior is contagious by using data from the Moving to Opportunity (MTO) program to evaluate whether lower local area crime rates in neighborhoods receiving MTO assistance decrease arrest rates among relocated households. Their analysis exploits the fact that random assignment to the treatment group produced different types of neighborhood changes across the five cities in which MTO operated. This enables the authors to use site-by-treatment interactions as instrumental variables for neighborhood characteristics in order to overcome the difficulty that individuals ordinarily sort into neighborhoods based on their attributes (including the incidence of crime). Ludwig and Kling (2007) find no evidence that MTO participants are arrested for violent crimes at higher rates in communities with more violent crimes. Their estimates allow them to rule out very large contagion effects, but not modest ones.

Damm and Dustmann (2014) tackle the same problem by exploiting a unique Danish policy between 1986 and 1998 that had the effect of quasi-randomly allocating immigrant refugees to neighborhoods with varying levels of crime. Their detailed administrative records permit them to construct more precise and more diverse measures of the criminal environment in receiving neighborhoods than was possible in previous research. Consistent with Ludwig and Kling (2007), they also find that the crime rate in the neighborhood in which an individual grows up is unrelated to subsequent offending. However, thanks to their detailed data, they document that the share of convicted criminals in the area to which an immigrant family was assigned raises later conviction probabilities and the number of crimes for which a young man is convicted. Damm and Dustmann (2014) thus argue that it is the share of criminals living in the area, and not the crime rate per se, that influences later criminal participation. This argument is consistent with the view of social interactions playing a role in linking neighborhood crime with later criminal behavior.

because of differences in the way exposure to crime is measured. Ludwig and Kling (2007) measure it as the crime rate that prevails in a youth's neighborhood and find that it is unrelated to subsequent criminal offending; that is, they do not find support for the contagion hypothesis. In turn, Damm and Dustmann (2014) document a relationship between the share of youth convicted for crimes, particularly violent ones, in the neighborhood and young men's subsequent probabilities of conviction, as well as with the number of crimes for which they are convicted.

Glaeser and Sacerdote (2000) were among the first to establish the relationship between housing structure and citizenship, social connectivity, and ultimately crime.[16] Compared to single family homes, large apartment buildings have two subtle mechanical effects on the interactions of their residents with the rest of the community: they reduce the distance between neighbors within the building, but tend to increase the distance between building residents and the streets. These features, they argue, explain why apartment buildings increase the social connections between neighbors, but reduce individual involvement in local politics, an indirect measure of collective efficacy. Big apartment buildings are also strongly associated with robberies and thefts. The relationship exhibits a gradient in building size; the larger (taller) the apartment building is, the higher the likelihood of victimization on neighboring streets. The authors hypothesize that this is likely due to the weaker connections between residents of apartment buildings and the streets that surround them. These results confirm that the structure of housing arrangements influences the extent of social connections between residents, their civic engagement, the strength of their ties to the community, and ultimately the likelihood of victimization.

The evidence reviewed so far provides support for the hypothesis that antisocial behavior responds to social context as well as the physical characteristics of housing, suggesting a role for social externalities in shaping individual behavior. Observations such as these have generated concern that disadvantaged neighborhoods might adversely affect residents' welfare. However, a great deal of uncertainty remains as to whether the degree to which variation across neighborhoods in residents' outcomes reflects the independent causal effect of neighborhood environment per se, rather than the propensity of different types of individuals to sort into different areas, with different attributes. Even the most detailed observational data may be unable to adequately measure the exhaustive set of family- and individual-level characteristics that influence both neighborhood selection and life outcomes. This type of selection bias can substantially distort nonexperimental estimates of neighborhood effects (see Ludwig and Kling 2007 and Damm and Dustmann 2013, discussed in box 6.3). Determining the relevance of neighborhood attributes to people's life-cycle outcomes is a central issue for these types of policies. If residential sorting on unobserved amenities drives the observed relationships, then redistributing individuals across geographical areas will have little effect on crime and would be welfare-reducing to the extent that it forces people out of their preferred locations. Knowing the source of the correlation is similarly paramount for the optimal allocation of policing resources. For instance, if neighborhood residents have thresholds beyond which they will not tolerate delinquency and will move once these thresholds are exceeded (as in the theory of "tipping points"), then the marginal benefit of spending on law enforcement could vary widely across areas.

# Can urban and in situ upgrading affect antisocial behavior? Evidence from the United States and Latin America and the Caribbean

As noted, a central issue in the estimation of causal neighborhood or peer effects is distinguishing endogenous (contagion) effects from contextual and correlated effects, and purging them of sorting effects. One appealing approach is to focus on natural or quasi-experiments that overcome one or more of these obstacles. In the United States, much of the evidence comes from a remarkable intervention called Moving to Opportunity.

In 1967, Chicago resident Dorothy Gautreaux led a group of plaintiffs to sue the Chicago Housing Authority (CHA), arguing that placing poor families in public housing in inferior neighborhoods was tantamount to discrimination. Settlement between the plaintiffs and the CHA was achieved with the creation of a housing program that effectively assigned one group of families to other parts of the city and another to suburban communities outside of Chicago. Rosenbaum and Popkin (1991) and Rosenbaum (1995) demonstrated that families living in suburbs experienced substantially better socioeconomic outcomes along a number of dimensions. These differences were particularly pronounced among children, for whom the likelihood of college attendance doubled if displaced to suburbs, compared to children who moved within Chicago. While Rosenbaum acknowledged that his data suffered from certain self-selection problems that would complicate giving his estimates causal interpretations, they were suggestive and have greatly stimulated research on neighborhood effects.

The importance of the Gautreaux findings lies in the fact that they were an early attempt to provide evidence of neighborhood effects based on an external intervention, which would ideally overcome the conflating effects of residential sorting, for instance. However, because the ultimate allocation of families across new neighborhoods in Chicago versus suburbs turned out to depend on unobserved characteristics of the families—thereby complicating policy inferences based on the program—the U.S. Department of Housing and Urban Development (HUD) devoted considerable resources to conducting experiments that altered neighborhood membership in a manner that is consistent with causal inferences. The resulting program, MTO, has been in place in five cities since 1994: Baltimore, Boston, Chicago, Los Angeles, and New York.[17]

The next section describes the results of a series of studies that exploit the experimental design of MTO to address questions about neighborhood effects up to 15 years after the intervention.

## Moving to Opportunity

Eligibility for MTO is restricted to low-income families with children in the five participating cities, living in public or quasi-public housing in selected high-poverty neighborhoods.[18] Among the 4,600 or so families that volunteered for the program between 1994 and 1997, roughly two-thirds were African-American, and most of the remainder were Hispanic. These families were randomly assigned to one of three groups labeled as experimental, Section 8, and control. Experimental group families were offered a voucher that gave them the opportunity to relocate only to a unit in census tracts with 1990 poverty rates below 10 percent. The Section 8 group was offered a voucher with no constraints on where it could be redeemed. Families in the control group were offered no services under MTO, but did not lose access to social services to which they were otherwise entitled.[19]

As a result of random assignment to groups, MTO delivered groups of families that were similar in terms of their observable and unobservable characteristics but lived in neighborhoods with very different characteristics during the period following the program.[20] Kling, Ludwig, and Katz (2005) show that parents of youth ages 15 to 25 assigned to the experimental group are more likely to report that their neighbors would react to truant youth or graffiti[21] than parents in the control group. Parents in the experimental group are also less likely to report that police do not come when called.

The authors exploit random assignment treatment arms to estimate the effect of changing neighborhoods: that is, the effects of treatment on the treated (TOT), where, in the current context, treatment is defined as *relocation* through the MTO program. They are able to estimate TOT precisely because random assignment to MTO groups generated substantial changes in neighborhood characteristics.[22]

Their main results are that moving to a lower-poverty, lower-crime neighborhood has differing effects on the criminal behavior of male youth versus the criminal behavior of female youth. In the first two years following random assignment, the MTO voucher offer had effects on youth delinquency that are consistent with theories of social interactions: both males and females in the experimental group experienced fewer violent crime arrests compared to those in the control group, and females' arrest rates were also lower for other types of crimes.

However, several years after random assignment, when most children in the household were adolescents, the treatment effects for male and female youth diverged: while the beneficial (protective) effects persisted for females, the incidence of property crime arrests among males in the experimental group increased relative to that of their counterparts in the control group. This pattern is difficult to reconcile with theories of endogenous neighborhood effects—that is, with the proposition of contagion in criminal offending. Interestingly, the effect on the total number of lifetime arrests was much larger than the effect on ever being arrested; the effect of offering vouchers is much larger along the intensive margin of criminality (number of arrests) than along the extensive margin (whether or not getting arrested). Much of the detrimental effect for males of relocation therefore appears to operate on the *volume* of arrests for those who are criminally involved, rather than on those who are at the margin of criminal offending.

Further buttressing these results, the experimental group of males also experienced more elevated rates of self-reported behavioral problems,[23] suggesting a mediating factor. The previously discussed effects on lifetime arrests result from behavioral problems developing among males in the experimental group, rather than from more intense policing by law enforcement in experimental areas, for instance, which might otherwise confound the effect on property crime arrests.

In a follow-up study on the medium-term labor market outcomes and health of MTO beneficiaries, Kling, Liebman, and Katz (2007) report that the offer of vouchers had no significant effects on adult economic self-sufficiency or physical health. However, it generated substantial mental health benefits among adults, who reported less psychological distress and greater calmness. Similarly, female youths in the experimental arm reported fewer symptoms of generalized anxiety, depression, and psychological distress; the reduction in distress was large in magnitude. Female youths also reported engaging in fewer risky behaviors, such as use of alcohol or marijuana, than their counterparts in the control group, as well as a higher likelihood of being enrolled in school. However, some of these benefits are offset by males adopting more risky behaviors. These qualitative results persist longer. Ludwig and others (2012, 2013) report on the long-term effects of MTO and confirm that 10 to 15 years after randomization, adult recipients of voucher offers experience improvements in mental and physical health, including large gains in subjective well-being, but show no consistent differences in economic self-sufficiency, and the previously discussed gender differences in outcomes among children persist.

These striking gender differences in the youth outcomes bear explaining. Kling, Ludwig, and Katz (2005) hypothesize that the gender differences in neighborhood effects may reflect differences in how males and females respond to similar circumstances, and acclimate to new neighborhoods. Why? Clampet-Lundquist and others (2011) endeavor to answer this question with survey data from MTO's Baltimore and Chicago sites. While their sample size is small, they conclude that six factors may contribute to the divergent experiences of young males and females: daily routines, fitting in with neighborhood norms, neighborhood navigation strategies, interactions with neighborhood peers, delinquency among friends, and involvement with father figures.

Regarding daily routines, experimental females were significantly more likely to spend time in the neighborhoods of school, work, friends, or relatives than any other program group. They spent their time there typically indoors with friends or family, whereas boys more frequently spent their time outside or on the street. While girls in all groups reported similar relationships with adult father figures, boys in the treatment arm were half as likely as control males to describe a meaningful relationship with a close, caring male other than a biological father or to report that they had such a presence in their lives.

A companion paper by Kessler and others (2014) is specifically concerned with the impact of MTO on the well-being and mental health of adolescents. At the time of the 10- to 15-year follow-up interviews, MTO children were between 13 and 19 years of age, with a median of 16. Strikingly, boys who relocated out of disadvantaged neighborhoods reported higher rates of major depression, post-traumatic stress disorder (PTSD), and conduct disorder than boys in the control group. The opposite was true for girls, who reported substantially better mental health than their counterparts who stayed in disadvantaged neighborhoods. The magnitudes of the mental health effects are staggering: for boys, rates of PTSD were comparable to those of veterans of war. In turn, the size of the improvement in girls' mental health is roughly equal to that of the depression that results from sexual assault among young women, only of opposite sign.

In an interview with the *New Republic*, Kessler suggested that girls profited more than boys from moving to better neighborhoods in part because they had better baseline interpersonal skills and could more readily acclimate to the new neighborhood, but also because of the perceptions of the receiving community: "We had an anthropologist working with us, and the anthropologist went and talked to and watched the kids in the old neighborhoods and the new neighborhoods, and their perception was that when the boys came into the new neighborhood they were coded as these juvenile delinquents. Whereas with the girls, it was exactly the opposite: they were embraced by the community: 'You poor little disadvantaged thing, let me help you'" (Sloat 2014).

From a policy perspective, the MTO experiment delivers conclusions that are of paramount importance. On one hand, it refutes the hypothesis that crime and other antisocial behaviors are contagious, implying that policy makers should not expect large social multipliers in criminality from urban policies that alter the characteristics of neighborhoods or the living conditions of their residents. On the other, MTO provides robust evidence that neighborhoods matter for the well-being of their residents in that their characteristics and amenities have statistically and economically meaningful effects on parents and children, with the sign of the effect on children depending on gender.

As acknowledged by Kling, Ludwig, and co-authors, these results represent something of a Catch-22 for policy makers: How does one trade off the substantial welfare gains for girls against the harm that results for boys? Are relocation efforts that aim to break up clusters of poverty ultimately detrimental? The answer likely lies in future research to better explain the interactions between the individual, family, and neighborhood to guide policy regarding public housing. In all likelihood, thoughtful strategies are required to prepare young boys for the transition to complement the physical relocation (such as providing case worker assistance or a mentor in the receiving community). Furthermore, if Kessler's interview comments hold true, some preparation may be necessary in the receiving communities as well, so as to avoid adverse reactions to relocated boys.

## Evidence of neighborhood effects from Latin America and the Caribbean

In the United States, MTO is a unique experiment that allows researchers to pose a variety of questions, both related and unrelated to crime, and to give causal interpretations to their estimates. One of its unique features is that it relocates families altogether, from disadvantaged neighborhoods to destination communities with better characteristics. Whether in the United States or elsewhere in the world, such disruptive interventions are difficult to implement. In LAC, in situ interventions are more common. Rather than displace individuals and families, these interventions provide improved amenities for recipient households and/or neighborhoods. Examples of on-site interventions include urban upgrading schemes, which enhance or alter the attributes of existing neighborhoods. Such programs provide fruitful opportunities to evaluate the relationship between housing characteristics and the outcomes of beneficiary families, as well as assess whether neighborhood-level improvements have external benefit on all its residents.

The background paper by Galiani and others (2013) provides some of the first rigorous evidence from LAC regarding the causal effect of housing upgrading on the living conditions and welfare of the extremely poor. In three countries that span the distribution of income and incidence of violence in the region—El Salvador, Mexico, and Uruguay—the authors estimate the impact of extremely inexpensive but sturdy houses constructed by TECHO,[24] a nongovernmental organization (NGO) that provides basic prefabricated houses to the extremely poor in LAC: namely, families who live in very substandard housing in the poorest of informal settlements.

TECHO houses are mainly made either of wood (Mexico and Uruguay) or aluminum (El Salvador). They are typically 18 square meters in size, and cost $1,000. While these dwellings represent substantial improvements over recipients' existing housing units in terms of their flooring, roofs, and walls, they do not have indoor sanitation facilities, running water, or kitchens. However, receipt of prefabricated houses has two effects: it represents a large wealth transfer to recipient households, as well as a large exogenous improvement in the characteristics of neighborhoods where the houses are put into place. As a result, the two potential channels through which the intervention may affect crime and violence may not be disentangled (nor can their respective signs); instead, the aggregate effect of both channels may be assessed.

Because there was excess demand for housing units resulting from limited staffing and resources at the NGO, only a limited number of housing units could be upgraded at once. Program administrators therefore decided to allocate dwellings by lottery. The lottery was designed in such a way that all eligible households in a given geographical location and in a given year had equal likelihood of receiving a prefabricated unit. The lottery implied that receipt of benefits was by construction unrelated to the preferences and neighborhood characteristics of beneficiaries, whether observed by the researchers or not. Galiani and others (2013) are therefore able to exploit this experimentally generated variation to assess the effects of upgraded housing on a number of measures of welfare and living conditions. The randomization enables them to overcome concerns about program participation being driven by self-selection or by systematic differences between those households that did and did not receive the upgrade, such as their motivations to improve their conditions.

The authors conducted baseline surveys approximately one month before the start of each the two program's phases,[25] and follow-up surveys between 17 and

| Country | Beneficiaries (intention-to-treat group) | Nonbeneficiaries (non-intention-to-treat group) |
|---------|------------------------------------------|--------------------------------------------------|
| El Salvador | 421 households (2,111 individuals) | 277 households (1,363 individuals) |
| Mexico | 457 households (2,239 individuals) | 439 households (2,152 individuals) |
| Uruguay | 478 households (2,067 individuals) | 301 households (1,259 individuals) |

*Source:* Galiani and others 2013.

27 months after each assignment to treatment groups. Table 6.2 summarizes the number of beneficiary and nonbeneficiary families and individuals in each country.

After verifying the balance in their survey measures at baseline between treatment and control groups, Galiani and others (2013) begin by showing that the intervention had the desired effect of raising housing quality. Treated households in all three countries reported increases in share of their dwellings' rooms with good-quality floors, walls, and roofs, and with a window. They next document that these improvements in housing translated into increases in self-assessed welfare: in all countries, families are happier with their houses and with their lives. Effects were particularly large in El Salvador, where the TECHO dwelling represented a much bigger improvement in housing than in Mexico and Uruguay. Furthermore, Galiani and others (2013) are able to assess improvements in child health through measures of the incidence of diarrhea and respiratory disease. They find suggestive evidence of sizable declines in the incidence of diarrhea in El Salvador and Mexico, but not in Uruguay, where housing and sanitation are much better at baseline than in the other two countries.

Among residents of slums, security is a foremost concern. In El Salvador, the baseline survey reveals that 49 percent of the heads of household often or always felt unsafe and 59 percent felt unsafe when leaving their homes alone. A natural question, which Galiani and others (2013) test, is therefore whether TECHO's improved dwellings provide tenants with a greater sense of security. Their survey data record information about whether residents feel safe inside the house, whether they feel that it is safe to leave the house alone, whether it seems safe to leave children alone in the house, and whether the house has been burglarized. All measures refer to the preceding 12 months.

First, in all countries, beneficiaries did not experience a rise in the incidence of burglaries. This is interesting in its own right because it implies that the housing upgrade had no impact on this type of crime. Recipients were not targeted at higher rates, nor were criminals deterred by any changes in the neighborhood characteristics that resulted from the upgrade. Given the unchanged rate of burglaries, one might expect that self-assessed safety would not change after the TECHO dwellings were constructed. This is confirmed in Mexico and Uruguay, where there is no evidence that the housing upgrade affected any measures of self-assessed safety. In El Salvador, however, beneficiaries experienced dramatic improvements in their sense of security; TECHO recipients were 18, 16, and 14 percentage points more likely than nonrecipients to report that they felt safe inside the house, safe leaving the house alone, and safe leaving children alone in the house, respectively. These represent 28 percent, 26 percent, and 58 percent improvements in self-assessments of safety relative to the control group's mean levels of safety, respectively. Given that there were no changes in the likelihood of burglary in any country, the substantial improvements in the sense of security in El Salvador might suggest that burglaries are not a great concern to Salvadoran residents, but perhaps that there are other threats to personal safety that the authors' survey was unable to capture.

Improvements in the sense of personal safety induced by the housing upgrade in El Salvador are interesting for the parallels they draw with MTO's effects on self-assessed well-being in the United States. The relationship between crime, sense of security, and well-being is not surprising. Indeed, chapter 2 documented that perceptions of neighborhood security are strongly related to measures of self-assessed well-being and, accordingly, that individuals in LAC sort into neighborhoods based on their safety (when their income allows it) as a strategy to reduce the likelihood of victimization (thereby raising their psychological well-being).

The relationship has also been documented by Medina and Tamayo (2012) in their analysis of violence in Medellín's neighborhoods, and its relationship with neighborhood security and subjective well-being. Specifically, they construct detailed, block-level homicide rates, which vary dramatically across the city, and link them to the 2008 Encuesta de Calidad de Vida de Medellín (Living Standards Measurement Study of Medellín), from which they obtain measures of self-assessed life satisfaction, perceptions of security in the neighborhood, and victimization. They then estimate associations between self-assessed life satisfaction, the homicide rate, perceptions of security in the neighborhood, and victimization. Controlling for a battery of socioeconomic variables at the household level, and fixed effects for the neighborhoods where the household currently lives and previously resided, they confirm a negative relationship between the homicide rate and well-being for the subsample of individuals living in their current location for at least five years. For the entire sample, they also estimate a positive association between perceptions of security in the households' neighborhood and subjective well-being.

Assessing whether these associations are causal is not straightforward, however, especially in a cross-sectional analysis such as that of Medina and Tamayo (2012). As mentioned, unobserved residential sorting of households across neighborhoods on the basis of preferences for their characteristics and amenities (including the level of current and expected violence) may generate the observed statistical relationship.

In sum, housing upgrades can take the form of in situ improvements in dwellings or relocate residents from distressed neighborhoods altogether to other neighborhoods with lower poverty and crime. Two surprisingly consistent results emerge from both types of interventions. First, neither one reduces the incidence of crime and violence. Second, although MTO and TECHO may have targeted poverty or other economic outcomes (such as self-sufficiency), they were more successful in changing cognitive and physical elements of individual well-being. The 10- to 15-year follow-up for MTO indicates that moving from a high-poverty to low-poverty neighborhood yields improvements in adult physical and mental health and subjective well-being, without affecting economic self-sufficiency (Ludwig and others 2012, 2013). As Sampson (2012) put it, "MTO thus impacted what the residents cared most about, rather than what policy makers deemed most important." As discussed in the context of Galiani and others (2013), Sampson's conclusion also holds true for TECHO, which induced sizable improvements in subjective well-being and, in El Salvador, feelings of physical safety. While it may have had desirable effects on the welfare of parents, it bears repeating that an invasive intervention such as MTO is costly, not only to the taxpayer, but as documented by Kling, Ludwig, and co-authors, also to young boys in the household, in terms of perverse unintended effects on their well-being.

There are numerous channels through which local crime and violence may operate to lower subjective well-being. Among them are the resources that must be devoted to securing one's safety, the elevated likelihood of victimization, and individuals' own sense of insecurity.

A further channel through which nearby crime may affect welfare is through property values; crime represents one of many amenities and characteristics of neighborhoods—or in this instance, a disamenity. High-crime neighborhoods are less desirable, a fact that is sure to get capitalized into housing prices as households sort themselves across neighborhoods. Vetter, Beltrão, and Massena (2013) document that this is the case in Brazil. They estimate a hedonic model of the residential housing market in Brazil's metropolitan areas, with housing prices expressed as a function of measures of security, among other factors. Their estimates imply that a 1 standard deviation increase in security would raise average housing values by the equivalent of $13.6 billion across the 18 million households in their data.

An alternative channel though which crime affects welfare is more subtle. Mexico's recent escalation of violence has contributed to a widespread sense of insecurity. Research has documented some of the explicit effects of the violence, such as increased victimization (extortion, kidnappings), loss of earnings and employment, and poor economic outcomes (see Robles, Calderón, and Magaloni 2013, and Dell 2012). In addition, recent research documents the toll that increased violence has on the biological development and well-being of the next generation.

For instance, Brown (2014) exploits the dramatic rise in violence related to drug wars in Mexico over the 2000s to estimate the effect of in utero exposure to violence (or the threat of violence) on the development of infants. He finds that the adverse effects of violence in terms of reduced infant birth weight (a common marker of new-born health) are equivalent in magnitude to the gains in the birth weight from mothers' receipt of Mexico's conditional cash transfer program, Oportunidades. It is hypothesized that the main mechanisms through which infant health is compromised is psychological cost of exposure to violence; the magnitude and scope of drug war violence in Mexico are such that exposure to it is unavoidable in the most affected areas. This in turn leads to high levels of stress among pregnant women, which is itself associated with the retardation of intrauterine growth and shortened gestation for infants whose mothers are exposed to high levels of violence (Beydoun and Saftlas 2008). Such intergenerational effects of violence, mediated by maternal stress, might imply that the benefits of in situ upgrades (such as TECHO) or relocation programs (such as MTO) are understated by Galiani and others (2013) and Kling, Ludwig, and co-authors, respectively, because they fail to take into account the health and developmental benefits that accrue to the next generation. That is, if relocation/upgrading lowers residents' stress levels, and high stress levels among pregnant women lead to higher levels of perinatal infant cortisol and deteriorations in infant health, which are in turn related to antisocial and violent behavior later in youth and adolescence, then programs such as these may carry long-term additional (unmeasured) benefits in the form of lower levels of violence in the next generation.

## Broken window theory: The evidence

Dwelling upgrades and relocations are fairly disruptive and produce substantial changes in the characteristics of individuals' surroundings and neighborhoods. Broken window theory postulates that much less intrusive interventions[26]—the strict enforcement of minor misdemeanor laws, strict policing, and/or improved neighborhood appearance (such as providing more and better street lighting and removing graffiti)—may remove disorderly cues that influence antisocial behavior. This section reviews the evidence for the broken window hypothesis (mostly from the United States). It first looks at evidence on the basis of changes in social and physical disorder of neighborhoods in which people reside (which is a key channel through which the theory is hypothesized to operate). Next it examines evidence on the basis of very localized variations in petty crimes. It then reviews suggestive results from community-wide interventions in Jamaica that altered the characteristics of neighborhoods, and concludes with a discussion of the efficacy of improvements in street lighting.

### Broken window policing: Enforcement of misdemeanor laws

Since Wilson and Kelling's (1982) original article formulating their theory, a number of cities across the United States—most prominently, New York City[27]—as well as in certain developed countries, have embraced some elements of Wilson and Kelling's so-called "broken window" theory—chiefly through aggressive enforcement of minor misdemeanor laws. One of the principal tenets of the theory is the proposition that curbing signs of disorder or impunity sends signals to potential offenders that their behavior is unambiguously not tolerated. The metaphorical window was expanded to include the minor (possibly victimless) crimes that occur every day in large urban areas, but are nuisances, as a means of deterring more serious crimes by signaling the heavy hand of the law. The theory also has its supporters in LAC, where analogous "zero tolerance" policing has been implemented (either in part or in whole) in municipalities in Argentina, Brazil, Chile, the Dominican Republic, Ecuador, El Salvador, Guatemala, Honduras, Mexico, and Venezuela (Swanson 2013), to name a few.

The proposition that broken window policing might reduce crime is plausible because many of the behavioral mechanisms underlying the strategy are in principle consistent with models of contagious criminality. However, in spite of its apparent popularity, the theory is also highly controversial for its lack of empirical support (Keizer, Lindenberg, and Steg 2008). Little is known about the effects of broken window policing on crime. Some critics argue that aggressive policing of low-level offenses (and low-level offenders) carries unjust side effects; others argue that there is little evidence that it lowers crime. Skogan and Frydl (2004), reporting on the conclusions of a blue ribbon panel commissioned by the United States National Research Council, concluded that, with the exception of one study of New York City (co-authored by one of the founders of the theory), existing observational research yielded little support for the broken window hypothesis.

Harcourt and Ludwig (2006) re-examined the (outlying) New York City study (Kelling and Sousa 2001), finding it lacking in a number of methodological dimensions, and providing a new analysis based (once again) on Moving to Opportunity. The reason the MTO experiment can be exploited in this context is that it randomly relocated people in troubled neighborhoods to communities with less social or physical disorder, which is the key mediating/deterring factor in the broken window theory. The authors can thus compare the outcomes of families from neighborhoods characterized by high amounts of social disorder to those of their observationally equivalent counterparts that were experimentally induced to relocate to more orderly communities. They document that relocation to less disorderly communities does not induce less offending.

From their review, Harcourt and Ludwig (2006) conclude that the evidence from the MTO experiment offers little support for the disorder-crime relationship hypothesized by Wilson and Kelling's (1982) theory. Since broken window policing is costly to implement in terms of the law enforcement resources that must be deployed, the authors also conduct a cost-benefit analysis of the effectiveness of different allocations of the scarce law enforcement resources under alternative regimes: zero tolerance of minor misdemeanors (consistent with broken window) versus narrowing focus on violent crimes. Here again, they reject the hypothesis of broken window policing as an optimal use of scarce law enforcement resources.

Caetano and Maheshri (2013) argue that crime statistics usually employed in the literature on broken windows are insufficiently detailed and disaggregated, both geographically and temporally, to adequately test the broken window theory. They exploit a finely detailed data set from Dallas that contains every police report filed with the Dallas Police Department from 2000 to 2007, recording precise times and locations of nearly 2 million police reports, including light crimes such as broken windows and graffiti, which are not typically observed in most criminal data sets, yet play a central role in the broken window theory.[28]

From these data, Caetano and Maheshri (2013) construct a panel data set containing weekly records of rape, robbery, burglary, motor vehicle theft, assault, and light crime in 32 neighborhoods. They then estimate vector autoregressions that represent the short-term dynamics in each category of crime as a function of lagged levels of all categories of crime, as well as measures of policing efficacy and responses. These models are intended to disentangle the dynamics of crime from the behavioral responses of law enforcement to crime. Based on the estimates from these models, they compute the long-term effects of a one period change in each type of crime on all future crimes.

Most relevant for the broken window theory, Caetano and Maheshri (2013) find no statistically significant cross-crime spillovers associated with reductions in light crime, implying that a broken window policy would have little success in reducing more severe types of crimes. To the contrary; their estimates imply that the dynamic spillover benefits associated with a policy that targets either robbery or auto theft dominate the dynamic spillover benefits of a policy that targets light crime by a wide margin. They thus conclude not only that zero tolerance policing fails to have the hypothesized effects on other crimes, but also that the policy is not cost-effective relative to other models of law enforcement.

All told, the most methodologically careful studies provide little support for the hypotheses that underpin the broken window theory, and the evidence suggests that alternative forms of law enforcement are more cost-effective. Indeed, Wilson conceded in a 2004 interview in *The New York Times* that the theory lacked substantive scientific evidence that it worked, adding: "I still to this day do not know if improving order will or will not reduce crime, people have not understood that this was a speculation."[29]

## *Broken windows and social cohesion: Upgrading public spaces and physical disorder*

While rigorous evaluations indicate little relation between strict enforcement of misdemeanor offending and the incidence of more serious crimes, Harcourt and Ludwig (2006) are careful not to conclude definitively that there is no relationship between disorder and crime. As discussed at the opening of this chapter, the original formulation of the broken window theory rested on the hypothesis that signs of disorderly and petty behavior trigger further disorderly and criminal behavior, thereby causing the behavior to spread. This broader hypothesis has not definitively been refuted.

Does the presence of physical disorder cue individuals as to its acceptability and encourage them to replicate "disorderly" behavior? Keizer, Lindenberg, and Steg (2008) conduct a series of small-scale situational experiments in Groningen, the Netherlands, in which they experimentally manipulate the orderliness of public spaces. They conclude the following: If people see one norm or rule being violated (such as graffiti or a vehicle parked illegally), they are more likely to violate others, such as littering, or even stealing a bill (the equivalent of five U.S. dollars) left unattended outside a mailbox covered in graffiti—consistent with the broken window theory of diffusing disorder. However, the stakes in their experiments are small, and it is unclear whether misconduct spreads when the pay-offs and consequences of getting caught are both higher. Moreover, the authors do not provide details as to whether the experimentally manipulated situation of "disorder" differentially attracted people with different demographic characteristics and inclinations toward offending, which could explain the higher incidence of disorder. Their results are at best suggestive of a link between physical environment and conforming behavior.

This section considers evidence emerging from larger-scale efforts to control antisocial behavior by modifying the appearance and organization of public spaces (box 6.4). The discussion first reviews an observational study by Guerra and others (2013) of a number of interventions in very-high-risk communities. Among them are

---

**BOX 6.4: Medellín: From one of the world's deadliest cities to a showcase for educational and architectural projects**

Medellín's urban development began with the management of mayors Sergio Fajardo (2003–07) and Alonso Salazar (2007–11). The administration of Mayor Fajardo was vital to the city's development. His aim was to recover the marginalized areas of the city through a process of "social urbanism." He sought to enhance awareness of the injustices of traditional urban development and municipal management and implemented projects that reflected his interest in improving the education system through new schools, libraries, and parks with high architectural value, in order to show that violence can be fought by means of cultural development and social inclusion. He called his model, "Medellín, the most educated," and it was based on culture, education, social urbanism, and inclusion.

In Fajardo's words, the idea was that "the beauty of the architecture is essential. Where before there was death, fear and dislocation, today there are the most impressive buildings, all of the highest quality—cultural and educational focal points around which we can all come together in peaceful coexistence. In this way we are sending out a political message

*(continued on next page)*

---

about the dignity of the space which is open, without exception, to all citizens, which means recognizing the value of everyone, reaffirming our self-esteem and creating a feeling of belonging. Our buildings, parks and pedestrian precincts are beautiful and modern. Just as they are in any other city in the world."

The city placed education, in the broadest sense of the term, at the heart of its policies, making it the driving force for social transformation in order to tackle three principal problems: social inequality, historically accumulated debt, and violence. City spending on education surged, bringing it to 40 percent of Medellín's annual budget of $900 million. Spending on public transportation and microlending projects for small businesses also grew. Five new libraries were at the center of Fajardo's social policies in Medellín, but he also built a sprawling public science center and dozens of schools, and expanded public transportation by building cable cars from the city center up to the slums on the city's hills. He contends that the poor will develop the skills they need to compete through these investments in education and new public spaces, reflecting a faith in architecture to help achieve this goal. The "Medellín, the most educated" model promoted programs developed around the concept of social urbanism as an instrument for social inclusion.

urban upgrading projects in neighborhoods of Kingston, Jamaica, where, in extremely poor communities, there are many signs of disorder and physical spaces where it is easy to commit crimes because they are hidden from view. Among other things, these interventions aimed to improve the physical environment and to restore public spaces. The section closes with a short review of the existing evidence on the deterrence effect of improved street lighting.

Interventions such as TECHO and MTO are relatively large scale and intrusive. Slum upgrading programs are less intrusive. Debris and barriers are removed and cleaned up, new infrastructure is put into place, and public spaces are restored, for instance. One of the background papers for this study, Guerra and others (2013), reports on a number of interventions in Jamaica, including the World Bank–funded Inner City Basic Services for the Poor (ICBSP) project. The program's objective is to "improve quality of life in 12 Jamaican inner-city areas and poor urban informal settlements" by:

- Increasing access and improving the quality of water, sanitation, solid waste collection systems, electricity, roads, drainage and related community infrastructure for over 60,000 residents of poor urban informal settlements through capital investments and innovative arrangements for operations and maintenance

- Facilitating access to microfinance for enterprise development and incremental home improvement for entrepreneurs and residents in project areas

- Increasing security of tenure for eligible households in project areas

- Enhancing public safety through mediation services, community capacity building, skills training, and related social services.[30]

The infrastructure component was explicitly intended to adhere to certain principles of the Crime Prevention through Environmental Design approach, which is a multidisciplinary approach to deterring criminal behavior through environmental design.

Although the program has not had a formal evaluation, Guerra and others (2013) build on a report and data from the United Nations Development Programme (UNDP 2009) to provide preliminary evidence about the effects of certain components of the intervention. However, they are hampered by the fact that they do not have detailed baseline and follow up-data that would have been necessary in a formal evaluation—which would have been further complicated by the simultaneous overlap of a number of other interventions that have similar objectives in the 12 communities in question. Instead, they provide suggestive evidence as to the effects of certain components of the interventions on the basis of survey data from the UNDP (2009) report and case studies of four communities, in which ICBSP was present in three (Flanker, Dunkirk, and Whitfield Town).

Very poor communities in Jamaica frequently have signs of disorder, such as lack of trash removal, and spaces where crimes are easily committed without consequence, such as poorly lit streets and high (zinc) fences (which trap victims and behind which criminals can hide). In response, a number of communities have undertaken to improve the built physical environment, including adding street lighting, removing zinc fencing, and increasing access to basic services.

Of a number of infrastructure interventions that the UNDP (2009) reviewed, the one that had greatest potential impact on crime and violence was the removal of zinc fences in Whitfield Town, where the decline in violence from 2006 to 2008 was particularly rapid. These fences line the streets and walkways of the community and many interviewees reported that their removal has reduced barriers between community members while increasing security. One child noted that "gunmen used to hide behind the fences but now they can't," while one of the community leaders commented that removing the fences "has given the community a moral lift." Nevertheless, while acknowledging that crime and violence had declined since removal of the zinc fences had started, interviewees in Whitfield Town expressed fear that violence might return as soon as the project ended and the work of laborers temporarily employed for this component (typically young men) dried up. That is, the community was keenly aware of the possibility that the presence of laborers during the intervention might simply displace crime temporarily, and that the economic incentives to offend might be restored once the temporary employment ended.

Guerra and others (2013) complement this narrative with a number of additional data sources, such as police records and hospital admissions data, which do not always coincide since the former rely on the citizenry's reports to police, while the latter tend to encode events of higher severity. While conceding that theirs is not an experimental study, they argue that these data tell a coherent story that crime declined over the relevant period. In the four communities for which they conduct case studies, rates of crime and violence declined steadily according to multiple sources, with different types of information providing a reliable picture of trends within each community. The fact that police reports mirror hospital-injury records suggests that residents actually report crimes to the police (which might in and of itself be considered an indicator of improved community safety, cohesion, and collective efficacy). The authors consider the fact that the independent data sources are consistent with one another as evidence that declines in crime and violence are real and not an artifact of a particular type of reporting.

Assuming that these declines in crime and violence are causally related to the interventions in question,[31] Guerra and others (2013) then study the possible mediators of the declines. How might improvements in communities' built physical environment affect crime and violence? Such interventions rest primarily on two assumptions: that making public spaces more visible eliminates opportunities for crime; and that disorder and urban decay signal a general disregard for social order and responsible behavior, consistent with the broken window theory. While they are unable to causally relate them to declines in crime and violence, the authors' re-analyses of the UNDP survey data suggest that certain aspects of the physical environment—such as street lighting and tall fences, which directly affect criminal opportunities—did have significant impacts on perceptions of safety. Better street lighting was associated with greater perceptions of safety in the community which, as noted in the context of MTO and TECHO, can be substantially welfare-enhancing. However, improved street lighting and removal of barriers in the line of sight arguably do not address the hypotheses of the broken window theory because these directly affect the visibility of crime, rather than potential offenders' perceptions of what is admissible in the community. Improvements in recreational spaces could provide a better assessment of the theory. Although the *quantity* of recreational spaces was not associated with perceptions of safety, improvements in *existing* recreational spaces were. Recreational spaces in disrepair may provide more opportunities for crime than better tended ones or, consistent with the broken window theory, criminals infer from well-tended spaces that the community does not tolerate crime. In the current context, it is unfortunately impossible to disentangle the two.

## Street lighting

Improved street lighting is intended to serve many purposes; one of them is the prevention of crime. While street lighting improvements may not often be implemented with the explicit aim of preventing crime, that may be seen as an important consequence. The relationship between visibility, social surveillance, and criminal opportunities is a recurring theme in this literature, and suggestive evidence of its importance was just discussed in the Jamaican context. A core assumption in both opportunity models and informal social control models of prevention is that criminal opportunities and risks are influenced by environmental conditions, which interact with the characteristics of residents and offenders. The degree of street lighting is a tangible element of the built environment, but does not constitute a physical barrier to crime, per se. However, it can act as a catalyst to stimulate crime reduction through a change in the perceptions, attitudes, and behavior of residents and potential offenders.

Why might improved street lighting induce reductions in crime? There are two principal theories. First, improved lighting implies greater visibility and thus leads to increased surveillance. In addition, through a behavioral response, as lighting improves, the number of people on the street rises, further increasing surveillance. Both these mechanisms act to deter potential offenders. The second theory rests on a principle from social control theory that better lighting signals a more involved and invested community, with a greater sense of pride and cohesiveness and, to a certain extent, signals more social control over what happens within the community. This last channel is highly related to the broken window theory, wherein physical aspects of the community are hypothesized to signal its tolerance for delinquency as well as more severe antisocial behavior.

As stated, the first theory predicts declines in crime during the hours of the day when lighting is needed: namely, at night. In turn, the second implies declines during both daytime and night-time, since the signal about community investment to poten-tial offenders is transmitted by the mere presence of lighting. However, improved street lighting could, in principle, have the perverse effect of increasing the incidence of crime because attracting more foot traffic means a larger number of criminal opportu-nities, all else constant. It may thus attract criminals. Increased numbers and visibility of potential victims could allow criminals to make better judgments about their vulner-abilities and attractiveness as targets (in terms of the valuables they carry). Similarly, increased social activity outside the home increases the number of unoccupied homes available for burglary. The sign and magnitude of the net effect of increased street light-ing on crime and violence are ultimately an empirical question, with existing studies focusing on developed countries.

Welsh and Farrington (2008) provide the most recent and comprehensive review of eight evaluations in the United States and five evaluations in the United Kingdom of street lighting interventions. In order to be included in the review, studies had to meet minimal standards regarding their experimental or quasi-experimental designs. In practice, all of them rely on a difference-in-differences approach, which in some instances was coupled with matching techniques to enhance comparability between treatment and control areas.[32]

Results for the United States were mixed. Half the studies concluded that improved street lighting had crime-reducing effects, while the other half did not. Across the eight studies, improved street lighting led to an aggregate 7 percent decline in crime, which was marginally statistically significant at standard levels. In turn, the evaluations of U.K. interventions provided consistently positive results. Improved lighting induced significant declines in crime on the order of 30 percent. In two of the studies, the social savings from reduced crimes far exceeded the financial burden of the improved street lighting.

Interestingly, the "effective" studies from the United States tended to measure both daytime and night-time crime, while "ineffective" studies tended to measure crime only during the night-time. None of the evaluations (across both U.S. and U.K. interventions) found that night-time crime decreased more than daytime crime. This suggests that deterrence does not appear to operate through greater visibility. Instead, this pattern is consistent with the theory that improved lighting carries information about the community in question. That is, it signals to offenders a greater degree of "community pride" in the form of community involvement, vigilance, and exercise of social control. An alternative explanation for the observed pattern of effects is that lighting did not in and of itself induce the declines in crime. Rather, residential sorting across neighborhoods led to a higher degree of community pride, which in turn led the community to implement improved lighting. In only two of the studies considered by Welsh and Farrington (2008) were the authors able to rule out the fact that increased community pride preceded the adoption of improved street lighting.

In sum, the authors suggest that improved lighting might be effective in deterring crime under certain circumstances. However, the exact confluence of circumstances for which this might hold remains unclear and needs to be the subject of future research. Given some of the methodological difficulties involved in assessing the effects of improved lighting (such as residential sorting on unobserved characteristics and preferences), they call for improvements in the design of evaluations to increase the reliability of the findings. In particular, they propose that future research should ideally include several experimental areas and several comparable adjacent/control areas. Adjacent areas are needed to test hypotheses about potential displacement of crimes as well as their diffusion. The comparability of experimental, adjacent, and control areas should be investigated.[33]

# Notes

[1] Interventions that directly target a community's collective efficacy are not reviewed. Rigorous evidence for Latin America is largely absent, while that for developed countries is in its infancy and still confronts "threats to internal validity" and concerns related to small sample sizes. See, for example, Hawkins, Van Horn, and Arthur (2004) and Feinberg and others (2009).

[2] Because policing is not the main focus of this chapter, but there is a version of broken window theory that focuses more narrowly on aggressive enforcement of minor misdemeanor laws, this chapter discusses some recent evidence about the effectiveness of this approach.

[3] See Sampson, Raudenbush, and Earls (1997); Sampson, Morenoff, and Gannon-Rowley (2002); and Macintyre and Ellaway (2003).

[4] Case and Katz (1991) define neighbors to be youths in the same one- to two-block area and in immediately adjacent areas.

[5] Early contagion models, such as those developed by Montgomery (1990) and Crane (1991), assume that an individual's likelihood of participating in an activity depends positively on the fraction of his or her neighborhood peers involved in the activity.

[6] See also Damm and Dustmann (2014), who study the implications of early exposure to neighborhood crime for the subsequent criminal behavior of youth.

[7] See Anderson (2008); Angrist and Lavy (2009); and Lavy and Schlosser (2011).

[8] That is, unless the intervention takes place the moment youth come into contact with the criminal justice system, in which case prevention is too late.

[9] This point is taken up in greater detail and with greater care by Glaeser and Sacerdote (1999), who confirm the puzzle of excess variation in crime rates and identify new ones (for instance, that high-crime cities have more female-headed households).

[10] In the United States, these inequalities are strongly related to racial and ethnic segregation.

[11] Shaw and McKay (1942) posited that deviant (or seemingly antisocial) behavior is not an individual trait or failing, but is a normal response by normal individuals to abnormal circumstances. Should a community be unable to police itself, certain individuals will exercise unrestricted freedom to express their predispositions, which often results in antisocial behavior.

[12] The theory of social organization and collective efficacy cannot abstract from wider social institutions and the political environment to which communities belong. Neighborhoods may exhibit narrow ties but still lack the institutional capacity to achieve effective social control (Hunter 1985). The role of institutions—and of policy to improve them—is beyond the scope of this study, however, and is therefore not discussed in this chapter.

[13] Manski (1993, 2000); Cook and Goss (1996); Becker and Murphy (2000).

[14] Jencks and Mayer (1990); Levitt (1997, 2002); Sherman (2002); Lochner and Moretti (2004).

[15] In addition to the census of arrested individuals, the authors also rely on national census data for 2005, which deliver measures of socioeconomic conditions at the block level, and the 2002 SISBEN (the Colombian census of the poor, used in the targeting of social programs to the poorest of households), which identifies the offenders' addresses in 2002.

[16] They employ data from the U.S. General Social Survey, which records a wide range of both economic and social variables, including living arrangements (apartment versus single family home) and such questions as whether the respondent voted in the previous election, knows the name of the head of the local school system, helps solve local problems, spends social evenings with someone from the neighborhood, or goes to a bar or tavern. They also complement their estimation with an analysis of the German Socio-Economic Panel, which although it relates to a different country, has the advantage of being longitudinal, allowing Glaeser and Sacerdote (2000) to control for unobserved but time-invariant characteristics of respondents.

[17] See Durlauf (2004) and the citations therein for the detailed genesis of MTO.

[18] Quasi-public housing, referred to as "Section 8" project-based housing, can be thought of as privately operated public housing: HUD contracts with private providers to manage housing reserved for low-income families.

[19] It is important to note that only families assigned to the experimental and Section 8 groups were offered the opportunity to relocate. Not all families in each treatment arm ultimately cashed in their vouchers; of the households with youth 15 to 25 at the end of 2001, 41 percent of those in the experimental group and 55 percent of those in the Section 8 group relocated through MTO.

[20] Some of these differences, however, ultimately narrowed over time because of the subsequent mobility of the treatment and control families.

[21] These are common measures of social organization and maintenance of order (see, for instance, Sampson, Raudenbush, and Earls 1997).

[22] See also Katz, Kling, and Liebman (2001) for early estimates of MTO's effects in Boston. They find no significant short-term effects on the employment, earnings, or welfare receipt of household heads. However, children in experimental households experienced fewer injuries, asthma attacks, and victimizations by crime.

[23] Kling, Ludwig, and Katz's (2005) behavioral problems index is the proportion of the following problems that youth self-report to experience "often" or "sometimes": has difficulty concentrating; cheats or lies; teases others; is disobedient at home; has difficulty getting along with other children; has trouble sitting still; has a hot temper; would rather be alone; hangs around other children who get into trouble; is disobedient at school; and has trouble getting along with teachers.

[24] TECHO is also known as Un Techo para mi País (UTPMP).

[25] Since TECHO lacked the capacity to work in all settlements simultaneously, the program was rolled out in two phases in all three countries. In El Salvador, Phase I occurred between August and December 2007, while Phase II was carried out between March and August 2008. In Mexico, Phase I took place between April and June 2010, while Phase II was conducted between September and December 2010. In Uruguay, Phase I was held between October and December 2007, while Phase II took place between July and September 2008.

[26] At least, in theory, they are much less intrusive. In practice, aggressive policing can prove fairly intrusive, for instance among minority populations in New York City and other "broken window" adopters.

[27] The theory provided the intellectual foundation for a crackdown on "quality of life" crimes in New York City under Mayor Rudy Giuliani (1994–2001).

[28] In addition, each police report contains information on police response times, which is also rarely observed.

[29] "Scientist at Work—Felton Earls; On Crime as Science (A Neighbor at a Time)," *New York Times*, January 6, 2004.

[30] UNDP 2009.

[31] Although the trends in crime and violence in the four communities are real, without information on "untreated" communities, it is difficult to assess whether these declines represent causal effects of the interventions or secular trends that were experienced country-wide. In addition, data were available only up to 2008, when the many of the infrastructure/upgrading interventions were still being carried out. Data for the periods following the completion of the projects might also provide more confidence that criminals did not "shy away" from the project communities for the duration of construction, with the intention of returning when the physical improvements were completed.

[32] Studies that were included in Welsh and Farrington's (2008) review had, at a minimum, an evaluation design that involved pre- and post-intervention measures of crime in experimental and (reasonably) comparable control areas.

[33] Welsh and Farrington (2008) emphasize the importance of data quality and availability. For instance, they call for long time series of crime data to investigate pre-existing crime trends for the purposes of comparability across treatment arms, as well as to assess how lasting the effects of street lighting are. Finally, they stress that improvements in lighting in different areas should be carefully measured, including vertical and horizontal levels of illumination.

# References

Akerlof, George A. 1997. "Social Distance and Social Decisions." *Econometrica* 65 (5):1005–27.

Anderson, Michael L. 2008. "Multiple Inference and Gender Differences in the Effects of Early Intervention: A Reevaluation of the Abecedarian, Perry Preschool, and Early Training Projects." *Journal of the American Statistical Association* 103 (484): 1481–95.

Angrist, Joshua D., and Victor Lavy. 2009. "The Effect of High-Stakes High School Achievement Awards: Evidence from a Randomized Trial." *American Economic Review* 99 (4): 1384–14.

Attanasio, Orazio, Sandra Polania-Reyes, and Luca Pellerano. 2015. "Building Social Capital: Conditional Cash Transfers and Cooperation." *Journal of Economic Behavior & Organization* 118 (C): 22–39.

Becker, G. S., and K. M. Murphy. 2000. *Social Economics: Market Behavior in a Social Environment.* Cambridge, MA: Harvard University Press.

Beydoun, H., and A. F. Saftlas. 2008. "Physical and Mental Health Outcomes of Prenatal Maternal Stress in Human and Animal Studies: A Review of Recent Evidence." *Paediatric and Perinatal Epidemiology* 22: 438–66.

Brown, Ryan. 2014. "The Mexican Drug War and Early-Life Health: The Impact of Violent Crime on Birth Outcomes." Working paper, Duke University.

Caetano, Gregorio, and Vikram Maheshri. 2013. "Do 'Broken Windows' Matter? Identifying Dynamic Spillovers in Criminal Behavior." Working Paper 2013-252-22, Department of Economics, University of Houston.

Cameron, Lisa, and Manisha Shah. 2014. "Can Mistargeting Destroy Social Capital and Stimulate Crime? Evidence from a Cash Transfer Program in Indonesia." *Economic Development and Cultural Change* 62 (2): 381–415.

Case, Anne, and Lawrence Katz. 1991. "The Company You Keep: The Effects of Family and Neighborhood on Disadvantaged Youths." NBER Working Paper 3705, National Bureau of Economic Research, Cambridge, MA.

Cerdá, Magdalena, Jeffrey D. Morenoff, Ben B. Hansen, Kimberly J. Tessari Hicks, Luis F. Duque, Alexandra Restrepo, and Ana V. Diez-Roux. 2012. "Reducing Violence by Transforming Neighborhoods: A Natural Experiment in Medellín, Colombia." *American Journal of Epidemiology* 175 (10): 1045–53.

Clampet-Lundquist, Susan, Kathryn Edin, Jeffrey R. Kling, and Greg J. Duncan. 2011. "Moving Teenagers Out of High-Risk Neighborhoods: How Girls Fare Better Than Boys." *American Journal of Sociology* 116 (4): 1154–89.

Cook, Philip J., and Kristin A. Goss. 1996. "A Selective Review of the Social-Contagion Literature." Working paper, Sanford Institute of Policy Studies, Duke University.

Crane, J. 1991. "The Epidemic Theory of Ghettos and Neighborhood Effects on Dropping Out and Teenage Childbearing." *American Journal of Sociology* 96: 1226–59.

Damm, Anna Piil, and Christian Dustmann. 2014. "Does Growing Up in a High-Crime Neighborhood Affect Youth Criminal Behavior?" *American Economic Review* 104 (6): 1806–32.

Dell, M. 2012. "Path Dependence in Development: Evidence from the Mexican Revolution." Working paper, Department of Economics, Harvard University.

Durlauf, S. 2004. "Neighborhood Effects." In *Handbook of Regional and Urban Economics*, Vol. 4, Cities and Geography, edited by J. V. Henderson and J.-F. Thisse, 2173–2242. Amsterdam: Elsevier Science B.V.

Feinberg, Mark E., Damon Jones. Mark T. Greenberg, and Wayne Osgood. 2009. "Effects of the Communities That Care Model in Pennsylvania on Change in Youth Risk and Problem Behaviors." Evaluation Report. Prevention Research Center, Pennsylvania State University.

Galiani, Sebastian, Paul Gertler, Ryan Cooper, Sebastian Martinez, Adam Ross, and Raimundo Undurraga. 2013. "Shelter from the Storm: Upgrading Housing Infrastructure in Latin American Slums." NBER Working Paper 19322, National Bureau of Economic Research, Cambridge, MA.

Gibbons, Stephen. 2002. "Neighbourhood Effects on Educational Achievement: Evidence from the Census and National Child Development Study." Centre for the Economics of Education Report, London School of Economics and Political Science.

Gibbons, Stephen, Olmo Silva, and Felix Weinhardt. 2013. "Everybody Needs Good Neighbours? Evidence from Students' Outcomes in England." *Economic Journal* 123 (571): 831–74.

Glaeser, Edward L., and Bruce Sacerdote. 1999. "Why Is There More Crime in Cities?" *Journal of Political Economy* 107 (S6): S225–S258.

———. 2000. "The Social Consequences of Housing." *Journal of Housing Economics* 9 (1/2): 1–23.

Glaeser, Edward L., Bruce Sacerdote, and José A. Scheinkman. 1996. "Crime and Social Interactions." *Quarterly Journal of Economics* 111 (May): 507–48.

———. 2003. "The Social Multiplier." *Journal of the European Economic Association* 1 (2–3): 345–53.

Guerra, Nancy, Kirk R. Williams, Ian Walker, and Julie Meeks-Gardner. 2013. "Building an Ecology of Peace in Jamaica: New Approaches to Understanding Youth Crime and Violence and Evaluating Prevention Strategies." Background paper for this study.

Harcourt, Bernard, and Jens Ludwig. 2006., "Broken Windows: New Evidence from New York City and a Five-City Social Experiment." *University of Chicago Law Review* 73: 271–320.

Hawkins, J. D., M. L. Van Horn, and M. W. Arthur. 2004. "Community Variation in Risk and Protective Factors and Substance Use Outcomes." *Prevention Science* 5 (4): 213–20.

Hunter, A. 1985. "Private, Parochial, and Public Social Orders: The Problem and of Crime and Incivility in Urban Communities." In *The Challenge of Social Control: Citizenship and Institution Building in Modern Society,* edited by G. Suttles and M. N. Zald, 230–42. Norwood, NJ: Ablex Publishing.

Jacob, Brian A. 2004. "Public Housing, Housing Vouchers, and Student Achievement: Evidence from Public Housing Demolitions in Chicago." *American Economic Review* 94 (1): 233–58.

Jencks, C., and S. E. Mayer. 1990. "The Social Consequences of Growing Up in a Poor Neighborhood." In *Inner City Poverty in the United States,* edited by L. E. Lynn, Jr. and M. G. H. McGeary. Washington, DC: National Academy Press.

Katz, Lawrence F., Jeffrey R. Kling, and Jeffrey B. Liebman. 2001. "Moving to Opportunity in Boston: Early Results of a Randomized Mobility Experiment." *Quarterly Journal of Economics* 116 (2): 607–54.

Keizer, K. S., S. Lindenberg, and L. Steg. 2008. "The Spreading of Disorder." *Science* 322 (5908): 1681–85.

Kelling, George L., and William H. Sousa, Jr. 2001. "Do Police Matter? An Analysis of the Impact of New York City's Police Reforms." Report 22, Center for Civic Innovation, Manhattan Institute for Policy Research, New York.

Kessler, Ronald C., Greg J. Duncan, Lisa A. Gennetian, Lawrence F. Katz, Jeffrey R. Kling, Nancy A. Sampson, Lisa Sanbonmatsu, Alan M. Zaslavsky, and Jens Ludwig. 2014. "Associations of Housing Mobility Interventions for Children in High-Poverty Neighborhoods with Subsequent Mental Disorders during Adolescence." *JAMA (Journal of the American Medical Association)* 311 (9): 937–47.

Kirchner, Lauren. 2014. "Breaking Down the Broken Windows Theory." *Pacific Standard,* January 7. https://psmag.com/breaking-down-the-broken-windows-theory-bbe9c06ae2a2#.9tdi67k52.

Kling, Jeffrey R., Jeffrey B. Liebman, and Lawrence F. Katz. 2007. "Experimental Analysis of Neighborhood Effects." *Econometrica* 75 (1): 83–119.

Kling, Jeffrey R., Jens Ludwig, and Lawrence F. Katz. 2005. "Neighborhood Effects on Crime for Female and Male Youth: Evidence from a Randomized Housing Voucher Experiment." *Quarterly Journal of Economics* 120 (1): 87–130.

Lavy, Victor, and Analia Schlosser. 2011. "Mechanisms and Impacts of Gender Peer Effects at School." *American Economic Journal: Applied Economics* 3(2): 1–33.

Levitt, Steven D. 1997. "Using Electoral Cycles in Police Hiring to Estimate the Effect of Police on Crime." *American Economic Review* 87 (3): 270–90.

———. 2002. "Using Electoral Cycles in Police Hiring to Estimate the Effects of Police on Crime: Reply." *American Economic Review* 92 (4): 1244–50.

Lochner, Lance, and Enrico Moretti. 2004. "The Effect of Education on Crime: Evidence from Prison Inmates, Arrests, and Self-Reports." *American Economic Review* 94 (1): 155–89.

Ludwig, Jens, Greg J. Duncan, Lisa A. Gennetian, Lawrence F. Katz, Ronald C. Kessler, Jeffrey R. Kling, and Lisa Sanbonmatsu. 2012. "Neighborhood Effects on the Long-Term Well-Being of Low-Income Adults." *Science* 337 (6101): 1505–10.

Ludwig, Jens, Greg J. Duncan, Lisa A. Gennetian, Lawrence F. Katz, Ronald C. Kessler, Jeffrey R. Kling, and Lisa Sanbonmatsu. 2013. "Long-Term Neighborhood Effects on Low-Income Families: Evidence from Moving to Opportunity." *American Economic Review Papers and Proceedings* 103 (3): 226–31.

Ludwig, Jens, and Jeffrey R. Kling. 2007. "Is Crime Contagious?" *Journal of Law and Economics* 50: 491–518.

Macintyre, S. A., and A. Ellaway. 2003. "Neighborhoods and Health: An Overview." In *Neighborhoods and Health*, edited by I. Kawachi and L. F. Berkman, 20–42. New York: Oxford University.

Manski, Charles F. 1993. "Identification of Endogenous Social Effects: The Reflection Problem." *Review of Economic Studies* 60: 531–42.

———. 2000. "Economic Analysis of Social Interactions." *Journal of Economic Perspectives* 14 (3): 115–36.

Medina, Carlos, and Jorge Andrés Tamayo. 2012. "An Assessment of How Urban Crime and Victimization Affects Life Satisfaction." Chapter 6 in *Subjective Well-Being and Security*, edited by D. Webb and E. Wills-Herrera, 91–147. New York: Springer.

Medina, Carlos, Jorge Andrés Tamayo, and Christian Posso. 2013. "The Effect of Adult Criminals' Spillovers on the Likelihood of Youths Becoming Criminals." *Borradores de Economía* 755, Banco de la Republica de Colombia.

Montgomery, James D. 1990. "Is Underclass Behavior Contagious? A Rational-Choice Analysis." Center for Urban Affairs and Policy Research, Northwestern University.

Oreopoulos, Philip. 2003. "The Long-Run Consequences of Living in a Poor Neighborhood." *Quarterly Journal of Economics* 118 (4): 1533–75.

Robles, Gustavo, Gabriela Calderón, and Beatriz Magaloni. 2013. "The Economic Consequences of Drug Trafficking Violence in Mexico." Poverty and Governance Working Paper, Stanford University.

Rosenbaum, J. 1995. "Changing the Geography of Opportunity by Expanding Residential Choice: Lessons from the Gautreaux Program." *Housing Policy Debate* 6 (1): 231–64.

Rosenbaum, James E., and Susan J. Popkin. 1991. "Employment and Earnings of Low-Income Blacks Who Move to Middle-Class Suburbs." In *The Urban Underclass*, edited by Christopher Jencks and Paul E. Peterson. Washington, DC: Brookings Institution Press.

Sampson, Robert J. 2011. "Neighborhood Effects, Causal Mechanisms, and the Social Structure of the City." In *Analytical Sociology and Social Mechanisms*, edited by Pierre Demeulenaere, 227–50. New York: Cambridge University Press.

———. 2012. "Moving and the Neighborhood Glass Ceiling." *Science* 337 (6101): 1464–65.

Sampson, R. J., and W. B. Groves. 1989. "Community Structure and Crime: Testing Social-Disorganization Theory." *American Journal of Sociology* 94 (4): 774–802.

Sampson, R. J., J. D. Morenoff, and T. Gannon-Rowley. 2002. "Assessing 'Neighborhood Effects': Social Processes and New Directions in Research." *Annual Review of Sociology* 28: 443–78.

Sampson, R. J., S. W. Raudenbush, and F. Earls. 1997. "Neighborhoods and Violent Crime: A Multilevel Study of Collective Efficacy." *Science* 277 (5328): 918–24.

Shaw, C., and H. McKay. 1942. *Juvenile Delinquency and Urban Areas*. Chicago: University of Chicago Press.

Sherman, Lawrence W. 2002. "Trust and Confidence in Criminal Justice." *National Institute of Justice Journal* 248: 23–31.

Skogan, Wesley, and Kathleen Frydl, eds. 2004. *Fairness and Effectiveness in Policing: The Evidence*. Washington, DC: National Research Council of the National Academies.

Sloat, Sara. 2014. "For Boys, Moving to a Wealthier Neighborhood Is as Traumatic as Going to War: Leaving Poverty Is More Complicated Than You Think." *The New Republic*, March 5. http://www.newrepublic.com/article/116886/boys-report-ptsd-when-they-move-richer-neighborhoods.

Swanson, K. 2013. "Zero Tolerance in Latin America: Punitive Paradox in Urban Policy Mobilities." *Urban Geography* 34 (7): 972–88.

UNDP (United Nations Development Programme). 2009. *Assessment of Community Security and Transformation Programmes in Jamaica*. Commissioned by the Government of Jamaica. http://www.undp.org/content/dam/jamaica/docs/researchpublications/governance/CommunitySecurityAssessmentReport.pdf.

Vetter, David M., Kaizô I. Beltrão, and Rosa M. R. Massena. 2013. "The Impact of the Sense of Security from Crime on Residential Property Values in Brazilian Metropolitan Areas." IDB Working Paper 415, Inter-American Development Bank, Washington, DC.

Vigorito, Andrea, Andrés Rius, Gustavo Pereira, Martín Leites, and Gonzalo Salas. 2013. "What Are the Effects of Direct Public Transfers on Social Solidarity? A Systematic Review." *Campbell Collaboration* May 2.

Welsh, B., and D. Farrington. 2008. "Effects of Improved Street Lighting on Crime." *Campbell Systematic Reviews* 2008: 13 (September 24).

Widjaja, M. 2009. "An Economic and Social Review on Indonesian Direct Cash Transfer Program to Poor Families Year 2005." Paper presented at the Association for Public Policy Analysis and Management International Conference, Singapore, January 7–9.

Wilson, J. Q., and G. L. Kelling. 1982. "The Police and Neighborhood Safety: Broken Windows." *Atlantic Monthly* 127: 29–38.

# 7

# General and Specific Deterrence

This chapter discusses the preventive role of deterrence. The study's organizing framework builds on the Beckerian model of the supply of criminal offenses, according to which individuals engage in crime based on whether the benefits outweigh the costs. The most likely salient cost of committing a crime is the expected "punishment" associated with it, which is in turn a function of two key institutional parameters over which policy makers have control: the likelihood of conviction, and the severity of sanctions conditional on conviction (figure 7.1). As a simple illustration, from the perspective of the offender, the benefits of committing a robbery are the immediate payoffs in terms of the value of the goods obtained (such as jewelry). The costs are related to the expectation of being apprehended and, conditional on apprehension, the severity of criminal sanctions (such as the length of prison sentence). In addition to the direct costs of incarceration, the offender would also forgo the wages he/she would have earned in the labor market for the duration of his/her sentence, as well as whatever penalty in wages he/she will incur upon exit from prison.[1] Since these costs accrue over potentially many years, the "weight" that is placed on them (and particularly on the expected severity of the sentence) by the potential offender is a function of an array of factors captured by the framework, such as risk aversion, preference for order, shortsightedness, socioeconomic background, developmental stages, cognitive abilities, peer network, and community context. Thus, the offender's personality traits and interactions within the spheres in which he/she circulates affect how he/she values each component of costs, as well as the likelihood of apprehension.

The proposition that criminal behavior may respond to the incentives presented by criminal sanctions (in the form of expected sentence length or expectations about conditions in prison) may be called into question. However, as mentioned in chapter 1, while the analytical framework builds on the neoclassical model, it can accommodate alternative theories from behavioral economics (such as bounded rationality, overconfidence, subjective probability, and impatience) that allow for crime to result

**FIGURE 7.1:** A model of the supply of criminal offenses, but also a model of crime and violence prevention

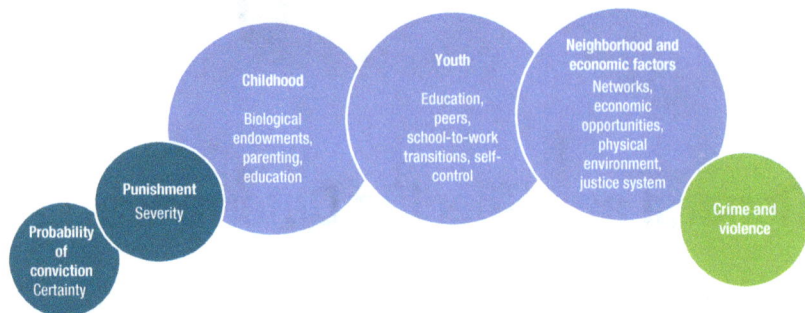

from less-than-purely rational decisions. Even if criminal behavior were less than fully rational (in the neoclassical sense), it could still be responsive to incentives, as is documented at length in this chapter.[2] Indeed, previous chapters have corroborated the hypothesis, with instances in which crime and violence are responsive to cues from the environment and/or to economic incentives (see, for instance chapter 5, which documents a robust association between the wages of low-skilled workers and the incidence of property crime; and chapter 4, which provides evidence of a causal relationship between education and criminality, one of the channels of which is higher expected future wages). Although the discussion finds it useful to refer to the organizing framework and to the Beckerian model, no assumptions are made about the underlying model that generates criminal behavior.[3]

By virtue of the focus on prevention, it is worth clarifying that the chapter concentrates only on the preventive role of expected punishment, as measured by certainty and length of the sentence. Attention is devoted to the instruments that are available to policy makers in the criminal justice system—which define particular aspects of the certainty of criminal sanctions and their severity—and, importantly, to how they influence criminal behavior.

As a final remark, the study abstracts from the mechanical reductions in crime that result from incapacitating offenders through sentencing.[4] Nevertheless, the research cited in this chapter discusses channels through which certainty and severity operate, which inevitably requires evaluating the relative magnitudes of deterrent and incapacitation effects, among others.

This chapter is organized into two parts. The first is dedicated *general deterrence*; that is, deterrence intended to discourage individuals other than the person who has already offended from committing a similar offence. It reviews the roles (and effectiveness) of certainty and severity of punishment in preventing crime, and places them in a much broader discussion about the efficiency of criminal justice systems. Initial attempts to evaluate deterrence effects estimated the relationship between the prison population (or incarceration rates) and the incidence of criminal offending, but delivered wildly varying discouragement effects, due in large part to a number of methodological flaws, including a failure to acknowledge that higher certainty of apprehension implies that more criminals are incapacitated. This generates a mechanical relationship between criminality and incarceration rates that reflects incapacitation rather than a behavioral response to the likelihood of punishment.

As a result, criminologists and economists have since turned their attention to quasi-experimental methods that are narrowly focused on the deterrent effects of specific policies that manipulate either certainty or severity. The main conclusions from the most rigorous studies indicate that crime is responsive to incentives, although the nature of the incentive matters.

The severity of sanctions has only a weak deterrent effect on criminal offending, but —to the extent that it does have an effect—it appears to exhibit diminishing marginal returns. For short sentences, there is evidence of a decline in offending, but this gradient soon flattens out at even moderate sentence lengths.

The certainty of punishment has more sizable effects on offending. Expansions in the police force are related to declines in criminal offending; there is some evidence that this effect is driven by deterrence rather by incapacitation (though this is not definitive). For a given size of the police force, strategically focused deployment of its resources can have large effects on the incidence of crime. Examples are "hot spots" and problem-oriented policing; there is strong evidence for their effectiveness. Hence, from a (general) deterrence perspective, the evidence points to short but certain prison sentences as a means of increasing the efficiency of the penal system.

The second part of the chapter turns attention to *specific deterrence*; that is, deterrence that relates to those who have already offended, to the experience of punishment, and how it affects recidivism. To the extent that imprisonment is painful, theory predicts that the desire to avoid it would generate reductions in recidivism. Incarceration may also have beneficial effects by distancing offenders from their criminal networks or raising human capital in the event that training programs are available in prison. However, the experience of conviction may also entail substantial costs, such as stigma, severing ties with family and the labor market, and exposing offenders to larger criminal networks in prison, within which they may acquire additional *"criminal" capital*; that is, skills learned and information gained while incarcerated that is specific to criminal acts. In turn, whatever productive human capital they had upon entry could decay during incarceration. These factors serve to render reentry into society more difficult.

The relative importance of these alternative channels can only be established empirically. The evidence is reviewed in the second part of this chapter. The treatment of specific deterrence distinguishes between the youth and adult populations. On the one hand, criminal justice systems typically treat youth differently. On the other hand, as documented in chapter 4, there are reasons to believe that adolescents respond differently to risks and rewards. Despite its paucity, the evidence suggests that, if anything, incarceration has a criminogenic effect on both adults and juveniles: sentencing criminals to prison (and to longer and harsher sentences) raises the likelihood of re-offending after they are released. This conclusion is inconsistent with the theory of specific deterrence. Incarceration is particularly harmful for juveniles, for whom the likelihood of completing secondary education declines substantially if incarcerated. Furthermore, post-release criminal behavior among juveniles seems particularly susceptible to peer effects; the social networks formed in custody have strong impacts on the likelihood of re-offending and on the types of crimes on which they recidivate.

## The prison population and general deterrence: Insights and limitations

When studying the relationship between sanctions and crime, it is natural first to examine the responsiveness of crime to changes in the size of the prison population, given the limited variation in sanctions encoded in the law. First-generation (cross-sectional) and second-generation (longitudinal) studies based on this approach concluded that crime was inversely related to imprisonment rates and to the size of the prison population.[5] However, the magnitudes of the elasticities that resulted from these studies varied wildly, in large part because of methodological limitations.

However, to the extent that policy is responsive to local conditions, higher crime rates are likely to induce policy makers to impose more severe criminal sanctions; thus the sanctioning regime and crime are simultaneously determined. Many of these studies ignored the endogeneity of criminal sanctions, and those that did not relied on implausible alternative identifying assumptions.[6]

Methodological concerns such as these have led researchers who are interested in the (causal) behavioral response of crime to criminal sanctions to pay close attention to the sources of variation in sanctions on which their estimates rely. To break the simultaneous determination of incarceration rates and crime, Levitt (1996) relies on the variation in imprisonment rates across U.S states from 1971 to 1993 induced by court-ordered reductions in prison populations that result from the court's concerns about prison overcrowding. Levitt finds that the declines in the prison population generated by court order lead to short-term increases in crime rates, with elasticities of −0.4 for violent crimes and −0.3 for property crimes.[7]

To the extent that there is heterogeneity across states in the severity of sanctions, in the size of the imprisoned population, and in the deterrent effect of incarcerations, Levitt's (1996) estimates provide an average across them. Indeed, Johnson and Raphael (2013) present evidence of nonlinearities in the deterrent effect with respect to the incarcerated population.[8] Over the 1978–90 period, they estimate an elasticity of crime with respect to the incarceration rate that is similar in magnitude to Levitt's (1996). However, for the subsequent period (1991–2004), when prison populations grew substantially, their estimate falls by almost 75 percent, suggesting that the responsiveness of crime to the incarceration rate declines with the incarceration rate. That is, basing policy in 2004 on estimates from a period of much more modest prison populations would have been misleading and cost-ineffective.

While these estimates are informative, from the point of view of this study, a limitation of studying the effect of the prison population as a marker for expected punishment is that it conflates the effects of certainty and severity; the two are not separately identifiable in this setting. Also, this approach fails to account for the mechanical relationship between incarceration rates and the incidence of crime (incapacitation). That is, the larger the prison population, the smaller the population of potential criminals, so that the observed reduction in crime could be attributable to incapacitation rather than deterrence. Policy makers require guidance as to the effectiveness of certainty versus severity because these are parameters that they can directly and independently manipulate. Instead, prison populations are more appropriately thought of as an outcome (Nagin 2013), and result from the interplay between the sanctioning instruments and the various determinants of criminality. As a result, parameters estimated on the basis of the prison population are not amenable to counterfactual analysis, which would require the assumption that the size of the incarcerated population could instantaneously be manipulated by policy makers. Given the implausibility of this assumption, the sections that follow review research on the effects of criminal sanctions that disentangles certainty from severity effects (based on the parameters available to policy makers), focusing on studies that deliver the most credible estimates by relying on experiments or quasi-experiments.

## Severity versus certainty and their relationship to general deterrence

In reaction to methodological concerns related to inferring deterrence effects from the relationship between crime and the size of the prison population, criminologists and economists have shifted their focus to the deterrent effects resulting from specific policies that manipulate the severity or certainty of punishment in experimental or quasi-experimental settings.

As motivation for a discussion of the existing evidence, it is worth stressing that, for a given level of expected punishment (defined as the product of the probability of punishment and its severity), different combinations of severity and certainty will give rise to different levels of efficiency of the criminal justice system (see box 7.1). As such, only empirical evidence can inform debates regarding the optimal combination of certainty and severity parameters that maximizes the overall deterrence effect of the criminal justice system.

In accordance with recent reviews on deterrence,[9] this section begins with a discussion of general deterrence, with regard first to severity and then to certainty. Do harsher, longer sentences deter crimes? The evidence suggests that the relationship between criminal behavior and severity of punishment is somewhat weak; the elasticity of crime with respect to severity (longer sentences, for instance) is small. Furthermore, certain forms of heavy-handed regimes (such as three strikes laws in the United States) may have the unintended consequence of inducing criminals to engage in more severe and more violent offenses.[10]

In turn, from the perspective of a potential offender, the expected cost of offending is also a function of the likelihood of apprehension; that is, of the certainty of detection. Is crime responsive to a higher probability of detection as measured by the size of the police force? Alternatively, holding constant the size of law enforcement, are there particular police deployment strategies that lead to greater reductions in crime? Empirically, the relationship between crime and certainty is more pronounced than for severity; the deterrent effect of certain punishment tends to be stronger than that of severity.[11]

## Severity and Deterrence

A fundamental question in the economics of crime is whether tougher criminal sanctions deter crime. The degree of severity of punishment can be proxied by the overall length of sentences or by how the sanctions depend on the gravity and/or frequency of criminal behavior (such as prison sentences that are conditioned on the individual's criminal history) or how they depend on the characteristics of offenders (such as age). The review of the evidence on the deterrent effect of severity that follows preserves this distinction, focusing first on changes in the severity of punishment that result from nonlinear or discontinuous dependencies of sanctions on the characteristics of the offender, such as the (legal) age of adulthood and sentence enhancements that depend on the offender's criminal history. The section then moves to research that focuses on exogenous changes in the length of the sentence, which may originate, among other factors, from collective pardons (Buonanno and Raphael 2013), random assignment to judges who systematically differ in their sentencing patterns (Abrams 2011), changes in parole guidelines (Kuziemko 2013), or across-the-board declines in the severity of punishment for juveniles in accordance with international treaties and agreements (Ibáñez, Rodríguez, and Zarruk 2013).

The evidence provided here points to nonlinearities in the response of criminal offenses to the severity of sanctions. In particular, large increases in sanctions do not result in correspondingly large declines in criminal offending; they are mild at best. Instead, the deterrent effect of sanctions appears to be strongest at low levels of sanctions.

## *Severity as measured by discontinuities in criminal sanctions*

Whereas there is considerable work on the effects of sentence enhancements, whereby the severity of sanctions depends on an offender's criminal history, research on the effects of length of sentence per se on offending is more scarce. This scarcity likely results from the observation that changes in the length of sentences that are unrelated to the prevailing criminal environment (that are not endogenous to current crime rates) are rare. One notable exception is the acute change in criminal sanctions that results from differences in the way many criminal justice systems treat juvenile offenders compared to adult offenders. Juveniles are often granted greater leniency relative to their adult counterparts for similar crimes. This section begins with a review of evidence as to whether the significant change in sanctions—and therefore incentives—that criminals face upon crossing the threshold of (legal) adulthood generates any discernible changes in offending near the age cutoff. It then turns to evidence on the deterrent effects of sentence enhancements.

### Age of adulthood

In many countries, the severity of criminal sanctions changes discontinuously at the legal age of adulthood, with criminal justice systems typically treating adults more severely than juveniles for similar crimes. For most types of offenses, when a minor reaches the age of majority, there is an immediate (and large) increase in the expected cost of offending; thus, certainty and severity both change discontinuously at the age of majority.[12] While other determinants of criminal offending may change rapidly with age, they do not change discontinuously at the age of majority. Lee and McCrary (2009) exploit this observation to attribute any discontinuous decline in offending at age 18 (the legal age of adulthood in the U.S. state of Florida) to the behavioral response to adult sanctions, relative to those faced by juveniles.[13,14] The richness of their data, which consists of individual-level crime histories for the state of Florida, allows them to measure the exact age of offenders at arrest and to isolate short-term effects of the discontinuity on criminal behavior. Their analysis yields consistently small estimates across all crime categories, none of which are statistically significant, casting doubts on larger magnitudes reported in the literature—a point to which this chapter returns later.[15]

Furthermore, thanks to the high-frequency nature of their data, Lee and McCrary (2009) are able to disentangle the deterrence and incapacitation effects. They show that the potential for conflating the two can be large in annual data when differences between adult and juvenile incarceration rates appear within a year of the 18th birthday. The authors show empirically that differences in incapacitation rates emerge rapidly and are perceptible even within 30 days of offenders' 18th birthdays, with those arrested at age 18.02 being 10 percent less likely to re-offend than those arrested at age 17.98. Their ability to shed light on how quickly the incapacitation effect can confound the estimate of deterrence helps reconcile the variability in estimated elasticities in other studies (such as Levitt 1999; and Drago, Galbiati, and Vertova 2009). While these may have relied on valid regime changes as sources of identification, by not benefiting from high-frequency data, they could not isolate the deterrence effect from the incapacitation effect.

Interestingly, Lee and McCrary's (2009) conclusion that there is little evidence of a deterrent effect upon crossing the threshold of adulthood is not limited to the United States, but is replicated in the context of Medellín, Colombia, by Guarín, Medina, and Tamayo (2013), who adopt a similar approach. They conduct an analysis based on information on all individuals arrested in the Medellín metropolitan area between January 2002 and October 2012 by type of crime, including homicide, theft, and possession of weapons and drugs. Over the 10-year period covered by their sample, minimum and maximum sentences for adults underwent numerous legislative changes. To illustrate the change in severity of sanctions at age 18, the minimum sentence for adults across all types of crimes is on average 400 percent larger than that for juveniles. For instance, whereas the minimum sentence for extortion was 2 years for juveniles, it was 12 years for adults until 2005, when it rose to 16 years. Despite these very large increases in the severity of punishment, Guarín, Medina, and Tamayo (2013) test for a discontinuity in the probability of offending at age 18, and likewise fail to find an effect that is statistically distinguishable from zero, consistent with Lee and McCrary (2009).[16]

In short, estimates of deterrence based on discontinuities in sanctions at the legal definition of adulthood are small—with an estimated elasticity of 0.007,[17] and which can be bounded statistically as no greater than 0.047 in magnitude —but still suggest a negative causal relationship running from severity to crime. In this sense, offenders' behavior in the face of changing incentives appears to be consistent with some degree of rationality. Arguably, however, the magnitudes of the effects are more consistent with high degrees of impatience and/or myopia. Lee and McCrary's (2009) results (and those of the evaluation of California's "three strikes" law, discussed in the next subsection) can both be interpreted as resulting from highly impatient individuals who place low weight on future punishments.

An alternative explanation for the very mild behavioral response to the large increase in the actual incarceration length is provided by Hjalmarsson (2009). Although she studies perceptions of the likelihood of incarceration conditional on offending, her results are qualitatively informative for interpreting the low estimates of Lee and McCrary (2009). She hypothesizes that youth underestimate the actual change in the severity of sanctions at majority, which she confirms with data from the 1997 National Longitudinal Survey of Youth, finding that the magnitude of the subjective change in the likelihood of incarceration at the age of majority substantially understates the objective probability. It is therefore not surprising that behavior is less responsive than would be expected if youth were aware of the objective (actual) risks of apprehension.

### Sentence enhancements as a function of the offender's criminal history

In the United States, a number of jurisdictions have statutes that increase the severity of punishment for those previously convicted of a crime, frequently in the form of longer sentences—so-called "sentence enhancements." Among these, the best known—and most widely studied—is California's repeat-offender reform, which took effect in 1994: the "three strikes" law, which Zimring, Hawkins, and Kamin (2001) labeled "the largest penal experiment in American history." In this context, a "strike" is a conviction for a serious or violent offense, as defined by California law.[18] Despite the name, the law incorporates significant escalations of penalties for both second and third strikes; an individual with one strike who is convicted of a subsequent felony faces an automatic doubling of the sentence length on that conviction and cannot be released before serving at least 80 percent of the sentence length, while a criminal with two strikes who is convicted of a subsequent felony faces a prison sentence of 25 years to life and cannot be released before serving at least 80 percent of the term. Among states with sentence enhancements, California's is by far the most severe and the one that is enforced with greatest regularity (Zimring, Hawkins, and Kamin 2001; Shepherd 2002).[19]

In their evaluation of the law's deterrent effects, Zimring, Hawkins, and Kamin (2001) adopt a regime-change approach and conclude that it reduced total felony crime by a very small amount—at most 2 percent— despite its sharp escalation of sanctions, and only repeat offenders with two "strikes" reduced their rate of offending.[20]

Helland and Tabarrok (2007) are similarly interested in the effects of the three strikes law. Rather than relying on an identification strategy based on regime change, they propose to compare the future criminal behavior of individuals with two strikable offenses with that of individuals who were tried in court for a second strikable offense but were ultimately convicted of a nonstrikable offense. They find that arrests were roughly 20 percent lower for the members of the former group, who faced much more severe sanctions for their next strikable offense. While Helland and Tabarrok's (2007) strategy is novel, it could be argued that their control group (those who were tried but not convicted of a second strikable offense) are positively selected relative to the treatment group, in the sense that they might represent lower criminal risk at baseline, or have had access to better resources in their legal representation. In this event, their results might be interpreted as a lower bound on the deterrence effect associated with the law. While these are not negligible responses to the severe sanctions, the total effect on crime in California was likely small, given that most crime is committed by individuals with no strikes. As Helland and Tabarrok (2007) point out, in a sample of three large cities in the state, 6 percent of felony arrestees have one strike and just 4.3 percent have two or more strikes.

While the evidence of behavioral responses for this class of violent offending may seem reassuring because the change in sentencing is so large, the implied elasticity of crime with respect to sentence length is in fact relatively low: only −0.06. A low responsiveness to sentence enhancements is also estimated by Raphael and Ludwig (2003), who examine the deterrent effect of enhancements for gun crimes in Richmond, Virginia's Project Exile. Crimes that had historically been prosecuted under state law were shifted to the federal system, where sanctions for weapons violations were more severe than under Virginia law. Their analysis is based on comparisons of adult homicide arrest rates with those of juveniles within Richmond and on comparisons of Richmond's gun homicide rate with the rates of other comparable cities (based on pre-intervention characteristics and trends). They conclude that, contrary to claims in the media and political proclamations, enhanced sentences had no discernible deterrent effect.

A related study by Abrams (2012) examines the effects of sentence enhancements related to gun violations, this time generated by add-on gun laws. Add-on gun laws have sentence enhancement provisions for perpetrators who are convicted of possessing a firearm while committing a crime. These laws' key feature for the purposes of studying deterrence is that they apply only to offenders who would otherwise receive a sentence of incarceration and therefore allow the researcher to distinguish between the deterrent and incapacitation effects of incarceration; the short-term effects of add-on gun laws should be purely deterrent. Abrams (2012) exploits the staggered introduction of these laws across U.S. states to estimate that the average add-on gun law results in a roughly 5 percent decline in gun robberies within the first three years. This implies an elasticity of gun robberies with respect to sanctions of approximately −0.10, a relatively mild effect, consistent with other estimates discussed in this chapter.

One concern with sentence enhancements, first articulated and analyzed by Iyengar (2010a), is that they take effect independently of the severity of the strike. In the context of California's three strikes law, Iyengar is able to separately identify the extensive margin (whether to offend) and the intensive margin (the severity of offenses) along which criminals adapt to sentence enhancements, thereby providing a good measure of their overall deterrence effect. In particular, her analyses document the general responsiveness of criminals to cost-based incentives and the relative magnitudes of their responsiveness across different margins of adjustment.

Iyengar (2010a) confirms a roughly 20 percent decline in participation in criminal activity for second-strike-eligible offenders and estimates a 28 percent decline for third-strike-eligible offenders.

However, she also documents two important unintended consequences of the law. First, three strikes eliminated the penalty gradient with respect to severity such that, conditional on offending for the third time, the marginal cost of the severity of the crime was effectively zero. As a result, criminals who would offend for the third time were more likely to commit more violent strikable offenses. For third-strike-eligible offenders who would ultimately commit their third crime, the likelihood of the crime being violent rose by 9 percentage points. While smaller than the effect on the participation margin, this effect is neither a negligible nor socially costless consequence of sentencing policies for which there is no incremental penalty for the severity of a crime.

The second unintended consequence of the law is that part of the reduction in criminal participation in California was achieved by a migratory response among repeat offenders, who opted to move to lower-sanctioning states. The law therefore appears to have generated a "beggar thy neighbor" spillover effect that pushed potential criminals out of the state. All told, the high cost of incarceration in combination with the high cost of violent crime suggests that California's three strikes law may not be a cost-effective means of deterring crime.

Evidence on the effects of enhancements to criminal sanctions is also provided by Drago, Galbiati, and Vertova (2009). They consider the impact of a 2006 Italian clemency act, which led to the release of prisoners who committed crimes before May 2006. The act also contained a sentence enhancement provision whereby if released prisoners were re-arrested within five years of release and subsequently sentenced to more than two years, their sentence would be raised by the duration that remained on their first sentence at the time of clemency. This is equivalent to a policy that manipulates incentives to offend since it commutes one month of time from the original sentence to be served as an additional month served in expectation for future offenses.

Since prisoners incarcerated after May 2006 were ineligible for the clemency, the intervention created a situation in which individuals who were convicted for the same crime faced dramatically different sanction regimes, with the sanctions of those who were eligible for clemency depending on the date of an inmate's entry into prison—which is plausibly as good as random. Drago, Galbiati, and Vertova (2009) thus study the relationship between re-arrest within seven months of release and the time remaining on the sentence length at time of clemency, controlling for other observables, including the original sentence length. Because the variation is based on sentence enhancements, their estimates primarily represent deterrence effects. Their results indicate that a marginal increase in the remaining sentence reduces the probability of recidivism by 0.16 percentage point, implying an elasticity of offending with respect to sentence length of approximately −0.5 at the one-year follow-up

(Chalfin and McCrary 2014). Interestingly, their effects are fairly homogeneous across ex-offenders; for instance, the behavioral responses of younger individuals are similar to those of adults. Only individuals originally convicted with relatively longer sentences (whose original sentence exceeded 69 months) seem undeterred; those offenders correspond to the upper 12.5 percent of the sentencing distribution. This would conform to the hypothesis that the most serious offenders are least responsive to incentives. Indeed, the −0.5 elasticity estimated by Drago, Galbiati, and Vertova (2009) is relatively high by the standards of other estimates reviewed in this section. One way to reconcile these magnitudes is to note that typical sentences in Italy are considerably shorter than in the United States, which has a relatively punitive regime. To the extent that there is heterogeneity in the response to sanctions that is tied to the level of sanctions, so that crime is more responsive at low levels of severity than at high levels, larger elasticities might be expected in the Italian context.

In sum, while there is evidence of a criminal response to sanctions, deterrence effects that can be ascribed to enhancements in existing sentences are mostly small in magnitude. Furthermore, in combination, the evidence from Italy's clemency and California's three strikes law is consistent with diminishing marginal returns (in terms of deterrence) to length of sentence. In the case of the three strikes law, which untethered the severity of the penalty from the severity and violence of the crime, unintended consequences resulted, whereby the severity of offenses escalated for those committing their third offense.

### Severity as measured by variation in the length of the sentence

The severity of sanctions, as proxied by their length, may affect the likelihood of engaging in criminal behavior of the general population (general deterrence) as well as the likelihood of re-offending (recidivism). In particular, if the focus is narrowed to the set of individuals who have already committed an offense and are at risk of recidivating once released, one of the main conditions for the length of sentence to have any deterrence effect is that, all else equal, the probability of recidivism declines with time in prison. Testing this assumption requires addressing the fact that time served and risk of recidivism are jointly determined; that is, it requires overcoming the endogeneity of time served.

Recent work has attempted to solve the endogeneity problem by exploiting natural experiments, providing quasi-experimental evidence for the effect of incarceration spells on recidivism and other outcomes. Maurin and Ouss (2009) and Buonanno and Raphael (2013) both exploit variation in sentence length arising from unexpected releases from prison. Maurin and Ouss (2009) find that individuals who were released early due to a mass clemency in France on Bastille Day in 1996 recidivated at higher rates than those who were not, suggesting that longer incarceration spells lower recidivism risk. Buonanno and Raphael (2013) exploit a similar type of clemency in Italy in August 2006, whereby one-third of the country's inmates were pardoned, and also document substantial increases in crime following the pardon. In turn, Bell, Jaitman, and Machin (2014) exploit a rapid escalation of sanctions that followed the August 2011 riots in London, whereby sentences for rioters were made much more severe. They document a large decline in riot crimes across London in the six months that followed. In all three of these instances, however, the effects identified are a combination of incapacitation and deterrence. It is therefore not surprising that each of these studies identifies reasonably large effects on crime.

Instead, Abrams (2011) provides estimates of deterrence that are not conflated by incapacitation by adopting a strategy similar in spirit to that of Kling (2006), who was interested in the effects of increases in incarceration length on the employment and earnings prospects of incarcerated individuals following their release from prison. Abrams (2011) exploits the random assignment of cases in the public defender's office in Clark County, Nevada, to attorneys who differ substantially in their abilities to defend their clients. Specifically, to break the link between risk of recidivism and sentence length, he instruments for sentence length using the ability of the randomly assigned public defender. When he ignores the endogeneity of sentence length, he finds a strong negative correlation between recidivism and sentence length. However, when addressing the endogeneity problem by instrumenting with public defender ability, the relationship vanishes. However, his analysis reveals substantial nonlinearities in the relationship; for short sentences, the relationship between recidivism and sentence length is negative, but longer sentences tend to lead to more severe crimes once the offender is released. One interpretation is that criminals who commit minor offenses (and therefore get lighter prison sentences) are most affected by the experience and are thus less likely to recidivate.

In turn, Kuziemko (2013) is able to overcome endogeneity by exploiting a number of natural experiments in the U.S. state of Georgia, as well as discontinuities in its criminal justice process. In particular, she explores whether time in prison actually reduces the risk of recidivism upon release and takes advantage of sharp discontinuities in Georgia's parole board guidelines between 1995 and 2006. Kuziemko estimates that an extra month in prison reduces the probability that an inmate recidivates within three years of his release by 1.3 percentage points. The richness of the analysis allows her to compare fixed sentences to parole regimes, whereby parole boards have discretion to reduce certain prisoners' sentences in the event that the board deems the prisoner to have a low risk of re-offending. Interestingly, she finds that prisoners appear to respond to the incentives set by the elimination of the possibility of parole; after a reform eliminated parole for certain offenders, these offenders accumulated a greater number of disciplinary infractions, completed fewer prison rehabilitative programs, and recidivated at higher rates than inmates unaffected by the reform. That is, the possibility that parole boards may exercise their discretion in reducing an inmate's sentence induces the inmate to engage in more pro-social behavior and invest more in rehabilitative programs.

Finally, evidence from LAC on the deterrence effect of severity is scarce. One exception, however, is Ibáñez, Rodríguez, and Zarruk (2013), who study the effects of a weakening of sanctions imposed on Colombian adolescents in 2006 with the enactment of Law 1098, which brought Colombia in line with international treaties and agreements in order to implement a system of restorative justice for juvenile offenders. Rather than placing juveniles in custody, the law developed other mechanisms, such as community service and partial confinement, as the main forms of rehabilitation. It increased the age of imprisonment from 12 to 14 and reduced the severity of sentences for all teenagers under 18. Moreover, offenders ages 14 to 16 could be sent to jail only for homicide, kidnapping, and extortion. Unlike the studies from developed countries reviewed above, the focus here is explicitly general deterrence. That is, it tackles the questions of how changes in the expected length of sentence affect criminal behavior among youth (without distinguishing between first-time offending and reoffending).

To evaluate the effects of the legislation, Ibáñez, Rodríguez, and Zarruk (2013) adopt a difference-in-differences strategy that exploits the staggered implementation of the law across the country, whereby certain judicial districts transitioned to the new regime before others. The staggered implementation, paired with detailed municipal-level data on crime and demographics, permit the authors to estimate the reduced form effects of the law on the crime rate. Their results indicate that theft increased in urban areas after implementation of the law, with larger effects in municipalities with higher proportions of adolescents, but that homicide rates were unaffected by the new legislation. Moreover, their results suggest a change in the age composition of offenders, with increased thefts in municipalities with a higher proportion of teens under 14 and declines in municipalities with a higher proportion of teenagers between 14 and 17, presumably because of the milder sanctions for those under 14.

However, the interpretation of their estimates as resulting purely from a deterrent effect from changes in the severity of sanctions is complicated by a simultaneous (and unintended) change in policing behavior. Following the implementation of the law, the juvenile arrest rate also declined substantially among the affected age groups, perhaps as a result of confusion among law enforcement as to how to implement the new law. Nevertheless, whether in reaction to certainty or severity of punishment, their results suggest that juvenile offending was responsive to the overall change in the expected costs of crime.

Taken together, the evidence on the deterrent effect of increases in sentence duration is that recidivism is mildly responsive to criminal sanctions. However, there is evidence of nonlinearities in the tendency to recidivate with respect to severity of sentence, with recidivism being more sensitive at low levels of sanctions and becoming less sensitive soon thereafter, consistent with a view that more "hardened" criminals (whose offenses are particularly severe) are less responsive to the risk of harsher sentences.

Qualitatively, these results conform to theory (and intuition) that the deterrent effect with respect to a unit increase in severity (the intensive margin of punishment) would decline as severity increases; that is, in terms of deterrence, there are diminishing marginal returns to severity. This relationship does not hold with respect to the probability of punishment (the extensive margin). In the event that offenders incur fixed costs from being arrested and/or convicted (in the form of pre-trial time in custody, bail, harm to reputation, or the like), the sentence is merely one component of the total cost of committing a crime. In this event, a deterrent effect of arrests would be expected even in the absence of a formal punishment (that is, where the length of the sentence is zero). The section that follows changes the focus to the effects of certainty on criminal behavior.

## Certainty and deterrence

Certainty of punishment in a criminal justice system is the product of law enforcement's ability to apprehend offenders and the subsequent success in prosecuting and sentencing them in the courts. For the purposes of research into its deterrent effects, however, certainty of punishment is de facto embodied by the ability of police to identify and apprehend offenders.

The reasons are as follows. On one hand, police are the most important actors in ensuring apprehension, which is the necessary first step in enforcing sanctions. From the perspective of a potential offender, it is also the most visible part of the justice system, and therefore the one that is most likely to have an effect on their criminal behavior. In addition, as mentioned, apprehension alone and detention in a local jail, for instance, may not be costless to potential offenders and may have deterrent properties themselves. On the other hand, more practically, there has been very little research on deterrence related to certainty of prosecution or sentencing, either because there is little variation in the certainty of prosecution and sentencing conditional on apprehension or because of the difficulties associated with breaking the endogenous link between the intensity/success of prosecution and crime.

There are a number of ways in which police may prevent crime (Durlauf and Nagin 2011; Wilson and Petersilia 2011). Apprehension of criminals is the necessary first step for punishment. The apprehension of active offenders may also have a deterrent effect for potential criminals by raising their perception that the risk of apprehension is substantial and the risk of punishment is more certain. Police may also deter without actually apprehending anyone, but by virtue of their very presence, which projects the threat of apprehension in the event of a crime (Wilson and Petersilia 2011).

Research on the deterrent effect of police has two main strands. One focuses on the deterrent effect of the aggregate police force, as measured by police per capita; for instance, based on an abrupt change in police presence in response to some event or threat. The second strand focuses on the prevention of crime through different police deployment strategies. In accordance with recent literature reviews (Durlauf and Nagin 2011; Nagin 2013), both strands are reviewed next, following this categorization.

## Police presence

Sound evidence on the link between law enforcement resources and crime is growing. A number of surveys of the effect of police on crime report that the majority of studies fail to find a relationship between the two.[21] The null result is perhaps not surprising, given the challenges related to causal inference in this context. Among these are differences in crime reporting across jurisdictions; feedback effects from crime rates to police hiring, whereby spikes in crime induce policy makers to increase the size of the police force; the confounding of deterrence and incapacitation effects; and aggregation of law enforcement staff across heterogeneous units (see Nagin 1998). Of these, the challenge that has received the most attention in empirical applications is the endogeneity problem: namely, the feedback from crime rates to police hiring.

The endogeneity problem was best articulated by Levitt (1997), who observed that higher crime rates may increase the marginal productivity of police. For example, cities with high crime rates are likely address the problem by expanding their police forces. The problem may be so severe as to find a *positive* correlation between the size of the police force and the incidence of crime.

Studies by Marvell and Moody (1996) and Levitt (1997) are notable for their acknowledgment of the identification problem and for their attempts to overcome it, as well as for renewing interest in the question. Marvell and Moody (1996) base their analysis on two panel data sets, one composed of 49 U.S. states from 1968 to 1993 and the other of 56 large U.S. cities from 1971 to 1992. To attempt to overcome the problem of joint determination of crime and the police force, they adopt a time-series–based Granger causality-type approach and regress the current crime rate on lags of both the crime rate and the size of the police force.[22] In their city-level analysis, they provide evidence of an impact of police hiring on total crime rates, with fairly small estimated elasticities of −0.3 and −0.15 for vehicle theft and burglary, respectively. They also find weak evidence of feedbacks from criminal history to policing, suggesting that causality runs both from policing to crime and vice versa, though the magnitude of the latter is small.

Levitt (1997) relies on the same data as Marvell and Moody (1996), but tackles the endogeneity problem by arguing that exogenous variation in police manpower is generated by local political cycles. Specifically, local political incumbents have incentives to devote more resources to law enforcement and expand the police force in anticipation of upcoming elections. He exploits this timing and finds large preventive effects of police on violent crimes (elasticities of −3.0 and −1.3 for murder and robberies, respectively) and smaller but still significant effects on property crime (−0.55). However, many of these results were eliminated when a technical problem was identified in Levitt's (1997) analysis. Levitt (2002) then uses an alternative identification strategy based on the number of firefighters and civil servants and obtains elasticity estimates similar to those of his original analysis.

Evans and Owens (2007) examine the crime prevention effects of police by adopting an alternative approach. They exploit federal subsidies to municipalities through the Community Oriented Policing Services (COPS) program for the hiring of new police officers. With annual data from 1990 to 2001 on roughly 2,000 cities with populations exceeding 10,000, they show that for each officer hired with grant funds, the size of the force expanded by 0.70 officer, so that the grants had the desired effect. Their resulting estimates of the elasticity of the crime rate with respect to police expenditures per capita are −0.99 for violent crime (robbery, murder, rape, assault) and −0.26 for property crime (burglary, auto theft, larceny).[23]

Other approaches have involved considering the impact on crime rates of reductions in the police's presence and productivity as a result of large-scale budget cuts or lawsuits in the United States following racial profiling scandals. Such studies have examined the Cincinnati Police Department (Shi 2009), the New Jersey State Police (Heaton 2010), and the Oregon State Police (DeAngelo and Hansen 2014). Each of these concluded that declines in police presence substantially increase crime, confirming the responsiveness of crime to the size of the police force and, importantly, to the likelihood of apprehension (that is, to certainty).

In this strand of the literature, even when concerns about endogeneity are carefully addressed, the elasticity of crime with respect to the police force spans a wide range, although a consistent pattern emerges: violent crime appears to be systematically more responsive to the police force than property crime. Chalfin and McCrary (2014) confirm this result and argue that the main obstacle in accurately establishing the effect of the police force on crime is not necessarily simultaneity bias, but bias that results from mismeasurement of the police force. They then construct a new panel data set on crime in medium-sized to large U.S. cities from 1960 to 2010, and obtain estimates of the crime elasticity with respect to the police force of roughly −0.5.

### Police deployment in response to threat levels

Recently, a number of studies have endeavored to break the simultaneity of crime and police by exploiting escalations in police alertness in response to terrorist threats. These induce variations in policing that are plausibly unrelated to crime levels. Examples of such escalations include Buenos Aires (Di Tella and Schargrodsky 2004); Washington, DC (Klick and Tabarrok 2005); Stockholm (Poutvaara and Priks 2006); and London (Draca, Machin, and Witt 2011). This group of studies is addressed separately since the interpretation of their estimates differs slightly from that of permanent changes in the police force; they should be interpreted as short-term deterrent effects, with possible temporal (or spatial) displacement of crime to the extent that criminals "wait it out" until the terror threat has subsided (or move where police are less concentrated). In other words, offenders may consider delaying (relocating) their crimes until the elevated threat of detection subsides.

One limitation of these approaches thus relates to general equilibrium effects. The evidence of lower crime during periods of heightened police presence cannot be extended to claims about the effects of a permanent increase in the police presence because it is difficult to establish definitively the extent to which criminals are merely adjusting the timing of activity.

The results of Draca, Machin, and Witt (2011) are consistent with the theory of short-term temporal displacement. The authors document substantial declines in crimes resulting from the temporary 30 percent increase in London's police force that followed a July 2005 bombing, with an implied elasticity of crime with respect to police of approximately −0.3 to −0.4. When police deployments reverted to pre-attack levels roughly six weeks later, the crime rate rapidly returned to its pre-attack level. Interestingly, while there is evidence of temporal displacement of crime, their estimates do not appear to result from *contemporaneous* spatial displacement to less policed areas.

Di Tella and Schargrodsky (2004) were among the first to employ a strategy that relied on alertness to terror threats. They study the reaction to a terrorist attack on the main Jewish community center in Buenos Aires (the AMIA) in July 1994, in which 85 people died and more than 300 were wounded. One week after the attack, all Jewish and Muslim institutions in the country were assigned police protection by the federal government. Because the geographical distribution of these institutions is unrelated to the distribution of criminal opportunities, the attack constitutes a natural experiment whereby crime and police presence are not simultaneously determined; that is, there is no feedback from crime to law enforcement resources. The authors collected information on the number of motor vehicle thefts per block in three Buenos Aires neighborhoods before and after the terrorist attack, as well as information on the location of each Jewish institution in these neighborhoods. Their information covers a nine-month window surrounding the date of the attack. They then estimated the effect of police presence on car thefts, adopting a difference-in-differences strategy, and showed that blocks that received police protection in a given neighborhood experienced significantly fewer car thefts than the remaining neighborhood. Relative to the control group, car thefts fell by 75 percent on blocks in which the protected institutions were situated. However, this large effect was extremely local; they found no evidence that police presence on a given block reduces car theft one or two blocks away.[24]

### Police deployment: Mandatory arrest, hot spots, and problem-oriented policing

The last strand of research related to the deterrent effect of police focuses on the effectiveness of different deployment strategies, which are designed with the hope that they will raise the certainty of punishment through their impact on the probability of apprehension. Certain strategies that deploy law enforcement resources after an offense has been committed can be particularly ineffective, whereas targeted deployment of the police force to especially high-crime areas ("hot spots") and more flexible and diverse approaches to policing that are tailored to the particular problems that municipalities face have proven more effective.

*Rapid response and mandatory arrest.* One deployment strategy—rapid response—is to mobilize police quickly following a crime is committed so as to increase the likelihood that an offender will be arrested *after* committing a crime. Unfortunately, strong evidence of a deterrent effect of such deployment is lacking; Spelman and Brown (1981) find no evidence of a crime prevention effect, for instance. However, there is little scope for an effect if most calls for service occur well after the criminal act, so the offender has had ample time to flee the scene; this delay is the case empirically. Thus it is doubtful that rapid response of this form will materially affect the risk of apprehension. By extension, because most arrests result from the presence of witnesses or physical evidence, improved investigations are not likely to yield a great deal of deterrence because, here again, apprehension risk is unlikely to be affected (Nagin 2013).

In the context of domestic violence, starting with an early trial in the U.S. city of Minneapolis conducted by Sherman and Berk (1984), a set of experiments across a number of U.S. cities funded by the National Institute of Justice tested the effect of raising the likelihood of arrest on future incidences of spousal abuse through the Spousal Assault Replication Program. The initial experiment provided some support for the proposition that mandatory arrest could be effective in reducing repeated domestic violence offenses, showing reductions in future violence of more than 50 percent.[25] However, follow-up replications delivered inconsistent results, with experiments in two other cities indicating deterrence, but no effects in three others (Maxwell, Garner, and Fagan 2002). Interestingly, Berk and others (1992) observed that the response to mandatory arrest was conditioned on background characteristics, with individuals of a higher socioeconomic status behaving in accordance with a deterrence effect, while those of a lower socioeconomic status became more violent. Heterogeneity in the response to this and other interventions is important because it illustrates the point that the response to the risk of punishment or sanction need not be uniform across the population and that individuals need not adhere to one model of behavior.

While uncertainty remains as to the experiments' true effects, Iyengar (2010b) cautions against the possibility that the policy had perverse effects. Since the Minnesota experiment, many states have passed mandatory arrest laws requiring the police to arrest abusers whenever a domestic violence incident is reported. Making use of the FBI Supplementary Homicide Reports, she finds that mandatory arrest laws decreased arrests and *increased* the incidence of intimate partner *homicides*. She hypothesizes that this increase in homicides—in conjunction with the decline in arrests—is driven by a decreased incidence of reporting of intimate partner violence. She tests the hypothesis by examining the effect of mandatory arrest laws on family homicides, where victims are less frequently responsible for reporting. For family homicides, mandatory arrest laws appear effective in reducing the number of homicides, thereby buttressing the theory that the rise in intimate partner homicide is due to the decline in reporting intimate partner abuse. This draws dramatic attention to the unintended effects of mandatory arrest, which ended up harming the very people the strategy was designed to help and protect.

Both rapid response and mandatory arrest can be thought of as ex post strategies that organize police action after an offense has been committed. An alternative method of police deployment involves trying to avert crime altogether. In this case, there is no apprehension because the offense is averted. In all likelihood, this is the primary source of deterrence from the presence of police. If an occupied police vehicle is stationed outside a corner store, potential robbers will likely avoid it since apprehension is a virtual certainty. This has implications for measures of apprehension risk that are based only on enforcement and crimes that actually occur, such as arrests per reported crime, which are incomplete, given that they miss those instances of crime that were not acted upon by potential offenders for fear of apprehension. These observations are important because they highlight the different functions of law enforcement—apprehension conditional on a crime occurring, and deterrence of criminal acts altogether—as well as the possibility that police may be effective in one dimension but less so in the other.

Two examples of police deployment strategies have been shown to be particularly effective in averting crimes in the first place: "hot spots" policing, and problem-oriented policing. Both deploy police resources in narrow geographic areas where criminal activity is particularly elevated; that is, crime "hot spots." Weisburd and Eck (2004) favor these strategies in their review of the effectiveness of police in reducing crime.

*Hot spots policing.* An alternative deployment strategy relies on the observation that crime tends to be very geographically and spatially concentrated. This principle was discussed in chapter 2 and documented for Guatemala City, Colombia, and Mexico (for more on Colombia, see box 7.2). The genesis of hot spots policing lies in the striking observation that only 3 percent of addresses and intersections in Minneapolis produced 50 percent of all calls to the police (initially documented by Sherman, Buerger, and Gartin 1989). This pattern of extreme concentration has since been replicated elsewhere. Weisburd and Green (1995) show that 20 percent of all disorder crimes and 14 percent of crimes against persons in Jersey City, New Jersey, took place in 56 drug crime hot spots. In Seattle, between 4.7 and 6.1 percent of street segments account for 50 percent of the crimes, and 50 percent of criminal incidents in Tel Aviv were concentrated in 5 percent of the streets segments (Weisburd, Groff, and Yang 2012). Crime is similarly concentrated in Medellín, Colombia, where 13 and 30 percent of its 317 neighborhoods accounted for approximately 50 and 75 percent of its intentional homicides in 2013, respectively. In the same year, four of Antioquia's municipalities accounted for close to half of the province's homicides. As in the corner store example, the rationale for concentrating police in crime hot spots is to create a prohibitively high risk of apprehension and thereby deter crime at the hot spot in the first place.

**BOX 7.2:** Police reform, training, and crime: Experimental evidence from Colombia's Plan Cuadrantes

In 2010, the Colombian National Police launched its new police patrolling program, the Plan Nacional de Vigilancia Comunitaria por Cuadrantes (PNVCC), in the eight major cities. The plan consisted of dividing the cities into small geographical areas (*cuadrantes*), to which six policemen would be assigned, and established new patrolling protocols, which involve greater community involvement and greater accountability for its officers, who were held liable for crimes committed in their assigned *cuadrante*. This required training over 9,000 police officers to improve their interpersonal skills and learn the new patrolling protocols. García, Mejía, and Ortega (2013) were able to study the effects of the reform, taking advantage of a staggered the training schedule among three randomly chosen cohorts of police stations, such that the exposure to training and to the effective implementation of the new police protocols was as if experimental. The authors attribute statistically (and economically) significant declines in a number of crimes to the training program, ranging from 0.13 to 0.18 standard deviations for homicides and fights, respectively. Most of the declines were concentrated in high-crime areas, with minimal effects in low-crime areas. Their estimates imply that the PNVCC generated roughly a 22 percent reduction in homicides. The authors argue that the large effects were achieved by raising policemen's sense of accountability to the population and ownership of incidents in the community.

*Source:* García, Mejía, and Ortega (2013).

Braga's (2008) review of hot spots policing summarizes the findings from nine experimental or quasi-experimental evaluations. The studies were conducted in five large U.S. cities and in one suburb of Brisbane, Australia. All but two of them found evidence of significant declines in crime. Further, no evidence was found of meaningful crime displacement to immediately surrounding locations. In fact, some found evidence of positive spillover effects, with crime falling in adjacent areas.

Weisburd and others (2006) provide a more nuanced view of displacement effects from hot spots policing. They provide a detailed account of the experience of Jersey City, New Jersey and document that, at least for drug possession and prostitution, crime markets do not simply relocate around the corner, precisely because these two activities require a confluence of very particular geographic conditions. Accordingly, not only does hot spots policing yield declines in these two types of crime, but it also diffuses crime control benefits to nearby areas. However, the authors also urge caution against the view that hot spots policing represents a panacea and will indiscriminately lead to declines in crime without displacing it. Indeed, they suggest that while some offenders desist from criminality as a result of hot spots targeting, others seek out adaptations that allow them to continue offending, which may lead to a temporary decline in crime followed by displacement elsewhere (that is, both geographical and temporal displacement).

The hot spots literature thus concludes that strategically concentrating police resources on well-identified "hot spots" can be very effective in reducing crime, as had been documented (to a degree) in the case of increased police presence following terror threats. The scope for displacement or positive spillover (diffusion) effects will ultimately depend on the types of crime and the ability of offenders to adapt. The channel through which hot spots policing operates has not been formally established; whether it is incapacitation of frequent offenders at hot spots or deterrence is as yet unknown. However, the stark contrast in the effectiveness of hot spots policing relative to that of rapid response policing, which delivers no crime reduction at all, is instructive, and suggests that the mechanism at play is deterrence rather than incapacitation. Indeed, as Chalfin and McCrary (2014) argue, offenders are likely to be very aware of a greater police presence in small, local areas.

*Problem-oriented policing.* Finally, Weisburd and Eck (2004) highlight an alternative dimension of policing: namely, the diversity of approaches that law enforcement agencies employ to strengthen public safety. For instance, low diversity typically implies reliance on traditional law enforcement tactics to raise the threat of apprehension, such as by increasing police presence. Greater diversity involves a broader scope of practices that go beyond conventional practices. One such example is problem-oriented policing (POP). This approach works to identify the determinants of crime and disorder that are specific to a community and to generate responses using a wide array of (often nonstandard) approaches (Goldstein 1979). Using iterative approaches to identify, analyze, respond to, and evaluate problems, and then readjust the response, POP has been shown to be effective against a wide array of crimes (Eck and Spelman 1987; Goldstein 1990; Braga and others 1999). The principle underlying POP is to devise strategies to increase the likelihood of apprehension (which, as discussed earlier in this chapter, is a powerful deterrent) or reduce criminal opportunities that are tailored to the specific crime problems of a particular location or involve a specific type of activity (such as adolescents fighting in schools) (see box 7.3).

Braga and others (2001) provide a detailed evaluation of Boston's famous Operation Ceasefire, which sought to reduce gun violence among Boston's youth. The intervention was multifaceted, and included police communicating directly with gang members that authorities would use every available "lever" at their disposal to punish gangs collectively for violent acts committed by individual gang members. For instance, police indicated that the aggressiveness of drug enforcement would depend on the degree to which gangs used violence to settle their disputes. As a result of the intervention, youth violence fell considerably in Boston relative to other U.S. cities.

**BOX 7.3:** The Cure Violence (cease-fire) model: A disease control method for reducing violence

The contagious nature of crime is one of its defining characteristics in both developed and developing countries (see chapter 2). Slutkin (2013), an epidemiologist by training, noticed how maps of gun violence in Chicago exhibited patterns similar to those that track infectious diseases. This similarity informed Slutkin's "Cease Fire" prevention program, recently renamed "Cure Violence." Cure Violence aims to stop the spread of violence in communities by using the methods and strategies associated with disease control: detecting and interrupting conflicts, identifying and treating the highest-risk individuals, and changing social norms. The program includes community mobilization and public education campaigns, outreach workers and community partners that provide employment and educational services, and "violence interrupters" who intervene in gang-related conflicts to inhibit the escalation of violence and retaliation. The initial results of the program, which was pioneered in Chicago, have suggested declines in shootings and in their intensity in five of the eight neighborhoods in which the program was implemented. The Cure Violence prevention model has since been adopted by several other cities, including Baltimore and New York, and shows analogously promising results in these cities. While encouraging, the results may not be conclusive because of the small sample of sites considered in each study. The model has been replicated dozens of times around the world, including in Basra, Iraq; Cape Town, South Africa; and London, England.

The promise of the initiative has also attracted the interest of cities in developing countries, including (but not limited to) two in LAC: Loiza, Puerto Rico, and San Pedro Sula, Honduras. In Honduras, the local partner, Cristo de la Roca, supports eight violence interrupters. As of April 2014, there were 504 high-risk mediations, which are estimated to have prevented hundreds of shootings. A formal evaluation of the program is under way. Cure Violence is currently in the planning stages of implementation in Barranquilla, Colombia; Recife, Brazil; and Port of Spain, Trinidad and Tobago, and the possibility of programming is being considered in Colombia, El Salvador, Guatemala, and Jamaica.

Operation Ceasefire has been deemed so successful that a number of similarly motivated strategies have been adopted in other cities, under the collective heading of "pulling levers."

In their review of POP evaluations, Weisburd and others (2010) report overwhelming support for the effectiveness of POP. Eight of the 10 studies whose designs are reliable enough to review (for the purposes of the *Campbell Reviews*) report statistically significant reductions in crime. Their findings are noteworthy for a number of reasons. First, effect sizes vary considerably across interventions—a fact that reinforces the argument that police-related deterrent effects are heterogeneous as a result of how police deploy their resources and the circumstances in which those resources are used. A second point relates to the scope of interventions; 2 of the 10 involved monitoring probationers to avert recidivism and/or violations of conditions of parole that would lead to revocation of probation. This illustrates the point that police can effectively be deployed to deter a variety of crimes, including among high-risk individuals. The heterogeneity in POP's effects is further illustrated by Groff and others (2015), who compare three different POP approaches in Philadelphia. They find that "offender-focused" policing, which recognizes that a small percentage of offenders is responsible for a large proportion of crime and therefore focuses police monitoring on them, has large effects on crime, whereas foot patrols and alternative POP approaches in hot spots show little effect.

### Does certainty, proxied by police manpower and strategy, prevent crime?

In sum, the literature on the preventive potential of policing provides a compelling case that the size of law enforcement resources prevents crime. It also makes clear that the effects of police on crime are heterogeneous; not all methods of deployment are effective in reducing crime (including some that seem completely ineffective, such as rapid response and broken window policing),[26] whereas others exhibit sizable effects, such as hot spots and POP. From a policy perspective, the implication is that recommendations to increase law enforcement resources for crime prevention are incomplete without details as to how the resources will be employed.

Furthermore, establishing whether these effective policing strategies operate through deterrence or incapacitation is critical for policy and to understand their implied social costs. If law enforcement is able to deter potential criminals, then police-induced crime reductions come at relatively low social cost. If, instead, the effect of increased police presence is simply to increase the number of arrests and subsequent incarcerations, then resources devoted to law enforcement may be socially wasteful (to the extent that there are other outlets that generate deterrence) since they require resources both for law enforcement and for the additional incarcerations that result (Owens 2013).

As argued earlier in the context of deployment strategies (hot spots and POP), the deterrence channel appears to be more plausible. Individuals are more likely to be aware of police presence in small, targeted areas. Furthermore, the crime reduction related to effective deployment is not achieved through increases in arrests and convictions, and the number of incidents of robberies and violent crimes also appears to decline in treatment areas, thereby corroborating the deterrence hypothesis. However, whether deterrence or incapacitation operates and the relative importance of their effects remain open questions, which have yet to be fully addressed by studies relating the size of the police force to crime reduction. For instance, in the context of the COPS hiring program referenced earlier in this chapter, Owens (2013) shows that while the program led to declines in crime, it had no effect on arrests, consistent with the view that expansions of law enforcement operate by deterring crime. However, this pattern is also consistent with the hypothesis that the productivity of police declines when there are fewer crimes to investigate; thus it is difficult to definitively disentangle deterrence from incapacitation (Chalfin and McCrary 2014). Further complicating the deterrence argument is the fact that studies have yet to document the extent to which potential offenders are aware of increases in police manpower (Nagin 1998).[27]

While promising, the effect of certainty on crime—in particular, the police-crime relationship—has been found largely in the context of developed countries. Should similar effects be expected for LAC? The crime-reducing effects of police are plausibly heavily dependent on the quality of and trust in local institutions. Indeed, as discussed in chapter 2, victimization rates are significantly related to the degree of corruption and corruptibility of law enforcement in LAC; whether police ask for bribes is associated with a 40 percent increase in the likelihood of self-reported victimization (see figure 2.26).

The evidence provided here suggests that sanctions in the form of short but certain sentences are quite effective deterrents to criminal offending. The relationship between severity of sanctions and deterrence is nonlinear; small (but positive) sanctions have non-negligible deterrent effects.

This observation has led some commentators and policy analysts to espouse strategies of certain but nondraconian punishments. Two programs exemplify the application of this principle. The first is Project HOPE (Hawaii's Opportunity Probation with Enforcement), a program for Hawaii's probationers. The cornerstone of HOPE is regular but random drug testing, coupled with certain but short punishments (one or two days) for positive drug tests or other violations of their conditions of probation. In a randomized experiment, probationers assigned to this structure of sanctions had much lower rates of positive drug tests, missed fewer appointments, and, most important, were significantly less likely to be arrested and imprisoned (Hawken and Kleiman 2009).

The second example comes from Weisburd, Einat, and Kowalski (2008), who report on a randomized experiment of alternative strategies to incentivize the payment of court-ordered fines. They document that the threat of incarceration provides a powerful incentive to pay delinquent fines, even when the period of custody is short. They refer to this effect as "the miracle of the cells," which provides valuable evidence that certainty is a more powerful deterrent than severity.

## Specific deterrence and recidivism: Is prison always best to prevent future crime?

Other than incapacitating criminal offenders, one other justification for incarceration and punishment is its potential to reduce recidivism by teaching offenders that "crime does not pay." This argument is based on choice theory and is premised on the view that incarceration is painful and thus exacts a higher cost than alternatives. As such, potential offenders will tend to commit fewer crimes as the costs associated with them increase.

However, most criminologists reject the idea that the extended experience of imprisonment can adequately be expressed in terms of a simple price tag or a psychic cost; this provides only a partial view of the incarceration experience. Instead, "social experience" theory argues that imprisonment increases exposure to criminogenic factors, thereby raising criminal tendencies and recidivism. These include associations with offenders in a "school of crime," stress, severing conventional social and family bonds, and facing stigma following release. Even if exiting inmates wished to avoid prisons in the future, they reenter society harboring a more intense propensity to offend.

As an illustration of the potential effects of stigma on ex-offenders, Chiricos and others (2007) examined a Florida law that allowed judges who sentenced felons to probation to withhold a formal adjudication of guilt, with the record of arrest vanishing if felons successfully completed probation. Some offenders therefore received a felony label whereas others did not, allowing the authors to test a theory of "labeling," whereby the receipt of a felony label could increase the likelihood of recidivism through a labelling mechanism (contrary to the theory of specific deterrence).[28] The authors find that those who received a formal label were more likely to recidivate within two years than those who did not.

Ultimately, which of these countervailing effects dominates and whether the net effect of incarceration on recidivism is positive or negative is an empirical question. This section discusses recent research on the impact of prisons (or alternative forms of punishment and rehabilitation) on recidivism, placing a premium on studies that credibly measure the causal effects. Research on specific deterrence is presented separately for adult and youth populations. Youth are especially important to study, given the life-cycle trajectory of human and social capital formation. Juvenile incarceration risks interrupting this trajectory, thus altering the path of their future earnings in the legal sector and raising the likelihood of future criminality.

## Specific deterrence in adult populations

One of the central studies of specific deterrence in the adult population is by Sampson and Laub (1993). This longitudinal study examines how the length of incarceration as a juvenile and as an adult influences subsequent offending. It finds no direct effects, leading the authors to note that "these results would seem to suggest that incarceration is unimportant in explaining crime over the life course" (page 165). Such a conclusion, however, would be misleading; after controlling for criminal propensity, time incarcerated substantially lessened job stability, which in turn affected recidivism. In other words, imprisonment had strong indirect effects on criminality. The authors are especially troubled by the life-cycle consequences of incarcerations: "Many of the ... men were simply cut off from the most promising avenues of desistance from crime" (page 57).

However, such an approach fails to account for the influence of individual characteristics (such as cognitive ability and self-control) that may jointly affect sentence length and the future likelihood of recidivism, as well as other outcomes. In turn, the modern labor economics literature—for instance, on the impact of male adult incarceration on labor market outcomes—generally goes to great lengths to overcome the potential endogeneity of incarceration or sentence length. In the context of studying the relationship between sentence length and the subsequent labor market outcomes of criminal offenders in California and Florida, Kling (2006) adopted a very innovative approach (which has subsequently been mimicked in other contexts) by using criminals' random assignment to judges, who differ systematically in their sentencing propensities, as an instrument for sentence length. He finds no adverse effects of longer spells of incarceration on future labor market outcomes.

Adopting a similar approach to Kling (2006), Nagin and Snodgrass (2013) likewise take advantage of offenders' random assignment to judges in Pennsylvania to overcome the biases that result from the likelihood that incarcerated offenders differ systematically from offenders who were not imprisoned, even after controlling for extensive background characteristics. If incarceration is a deterrent, then the recidivism rates of caseloads assigned to harsh judges should be lower than those assigned to more lenient judges. However, Nagin and Snodgrass (2013) fail to confirm this relationship. Their analysis revealed no differences in the recidivism of caseloads across judges; incarceration had no deterrent effect for this group.

There are numerous reviews of the literature on the criminogenic effects of incarceration. One of the most comprehensive, by Jonson (2010), undertakes a meta-analysis of 57 studies. Across all studies, incarceration was found to be slightly criminogenic, increasing recidivism by 14 percent. When Jonson limited her attention to the most methodologically sound studies, the effect of custodial sanctions fell, but still suggested that they raised re-offending by 5 percent. She also examined a limited number of studies that explored whether harsher prison conditions were associated with greater recidivism (such as Chen and Shapiro 2007, who consider the effects of harsh conditions in U.S. federal prisons). She finds that harsher conditions are associated with increased recidivism, which is inconsistent with deterrence theory.

Qualitatively similar results are provided by Drago, Galbiati, and Vertova (2011), who use variation in prison assignment to identify the effects of prison overcrowding, deaths in prison, and isolation on the likelihood of recidivating. Their estimates imply that harsh prison conditions raise re-offending rates following release from prison, though the increase is not always precisely estimated. Abrams (2011), discussed earlier, also documented that, despite observing a deterrent effect of sentence length on recidivism *at low sentence durations*, the relationship was reversed for longer sentences; offenders convicted to long sentences are more likely to re-offend.

### Criminal recidivism after electronic monitoring versus prison

One of the more intriguing and creative experiments in this area is the substitution of electronic monitoring (EM) or electronic tagging, which involves fitting offenders with an electronic device on the ankle or wrist, instead of incarceration. The device can be monitored remotely by employees of a correctional facility, who can then verify whether the individual is violating a set of pre-established conditions. One common condition is a requirement to stay at home, although in many cases, a provision for attending work or school is included. One of the background papers for this study (Di Tella and Schargrodsky 2013) considers just such an intervention in Argentina, and provides a context in which to test the theory that recidivism is lower among offenders who experience incarceration than among those who experience EM.

Theoretically, the magnitude of the effect on recidivism of EM relative to incarceration is ambiguous. On the one hand, EM represents an a priori less unpleasant experience than incarceration; the theory of specific deterrence would therefore predict more elevated recidivism under an EM regime. On the other hand, EM eliminates harsh prison conditions and potentially criminogenic peer effects that result from contact and fraternization with a large number of criminals. Importantly, EM could have less harmful effects than prison on offenders' future labor market prospects and social integration, for instance, through weaker stigmatization or by being less disruptive to the offender's accumulation of human capital and schooling.[29]

An evaluation of the merits of EM over incarceration, as measured by lower recidivism, cannot be achieved by a simple comparison of outcomes under the two regimes. It is complicated by at least two concerns. First, the population of offenders who are eligible for EM is likely to be lower risk than the overall prison population. Failing to observe a decline in recidivism among offenders receiving EM relative to those who are sent to prison may simply reflect their low baseline risk of recidivism. Second, an offender may be sentenced to EM based on the judge's perception of recidivism risk; she may assign EM to those offenders in whom she foresees the least risk of re-offending. Thus, a low recidivism rate among those offenders who were sentenced to EM could be taken as an indication that the legal system is relatively successful at identifying low-risk offenders and selecting them for less harsh sentences.

### Criminal recidivism in Argentina: Prison versus electronic monitoring

In one of the background papers for this study, Di Tella and Schargrodsky (2013) consider EM as an alternative to incarceration in the Province of Buenos Aires, Argentina, where it has been an option for judges since the late 1990s. They compare the recidivism (as measured by re-arrest rates) of offenders sentenced to EM to that of a control group of former prisoners with similar observable (baseline) characteristics who were instead sentenced to prison. They find a sizable negative and significant correlation between EM and re-arrest rates.

Two institutional features of the setting, which are similar in spirit to those exploited by Kling (2006) in his study of the effect of incarceration length on subsequent labor market outcomes, suggest that it is reasonable to interpret their estimate as the causal effect of treating an apprehended offender with EM instead of prison. The first feature is that court cases are randomly matched to judges. The second is that, for a given set of case characteristics, judges differ substantially in their propensities to sentence offenders to EM instead of prison. This second feature results from common ideological differences across judges, which Di Tella and Schargrodsky (2013) argue are particularly polarized in Argentina.

Human rights organizations have repeatedly decried the cruelty of Argentine correctional facilities. *Garantista* (lenient) judges therefore tend to assign offenders to EM, for their emphasis on "individual guarantees." By contrast, *mano dura* (harsh) judges rarely do so. Since detainees are assigned to whichever judge is on duty on the day of their arrest, and duty days are randomly assigned across judges, prisoners' characteristics will be unrelated to judges' ideological inclinations. Importantly, this implies that the judge's propensity to assign EM is exogenous to the offenders' ex ante risk of recidivating. These features imply that an offender's assignment to EM versus prison can be instrumented with a proxy for his/her judge's ideological tendency.

Interestingly, in Argentina, the application of EM is not reserved to low-risk individuals but is available even to offenders who have committed relatively serious crimes. The vast majority of alleged offenders are under pre-trial detention which, because of the slow pace of the Argentine judicial system, can be quite lengthy and costly to finance. The use of EM is thus intended to reduce the costs of the pre-trial period. As a result, the assignment of EM to offenders is unrelated to the severity of their crimes. Indeed, the authors document that 7.8 percent and 58 percent of the sample of detainees assigned to EM are accused of homicide and aggravated robbery, respectively, whereas the corresponding proportions in the prison sample are 5.8 percent and 49 percent, respectively. Thus, the approach that exploits judges' ideology as an instrument delivers estimates that are representative of the effects across the spectrum of severity of crime. That is, they are not limited to the narrow subpopulation that has committed minor offenses.

One final concern in the interpretation of the estimates delivered by Di Tella and Schargrodsky's (2013) instrumenting approach is that EM might be complemented by some other rehabilitative services, such as apprenticeships or substance abuse programs. However, this is not the case in Argentina; EM is a stand-alone sentence that is not tied to additional services. As such, instrumenting assignment to EM with a judge's ideological tendencies delivers estimates of the effects on recidivism of being assigned to EM *alone*.

Given that judges' pretrial detainment decisions are based on relatively little information, judges do not have much more information than is available to Di Tella and Schargrodsky (2013) for their regressions. Thus, one could argue that their ordinary least squares (OLS) estimates have a causal interpretation. Indeed, the authors confirm that, with the exception of prisoner age and the number of previous offenses on the prisoner's record, assignment to EM is virtually unrelated to any specific case characteristics once the judge's historical propensity for assigning EM is controlled for. That is, almost no characteristics other than the judge's "ideology" are predictive of EM assignment.

Adopting the approach that instruments assignment to EM with judge ideology reveals a large negative (and significant) effect of EM on subsequent re-arrest rates of between 11 and 16 percentage points. To place these estimates into context, the recidivism rates among offenders in the prison and EM samples are 22 and 13 percent, respectively, implying that the instrumental variables estimates are slightly superior in magnitude to the raw differences in recidivism rates between the two groups of offenders. This represents roughly a 50 percent decline in recidivism and is inconsistent with the theory of specific deterrence, which holds that a painful prison experience acts as a strong disincentive to re-offend.[30]

Finally, armed with their estimate of the benefits of EM relative to incarceration, the authors provide a back-of-the-envelope assessment of the short-term welfare implications of transitioning to EM. They conservatively estimate that the total benefit of sending an alleged offender to EM instead of prison over the 4.66 years is $18,460, or 2.4 times Argentina's GDP per capita in 2009.

It is interesting to observe that the magnitudes of the recidivism effects documented by Di Tella and Schargrodsky (2013) are not specific to the Argentine setting, but have some degree of generalizability. Marie (2013) studies a similar program in England and Wales, exploiting two administrative rules related to offender age and sentence length that make certain prisoners ineligible for early release with EM and result in discontinuities in EM assignment. He then estimates the impact of early release with EM on recidivism, adopting a regression-discontinuity approach using detailed data on all prisoners released between 2000 and 2006, including information on their criminal history and subsequent offending. He finds early release with EM reduces the likelihood of offender re-arrest by between 20 and 40 percent within two years, confirming that it is highly cost-effective in reducing recidivism, since EM is much less onerous than time spent in jail.

## Specific deterrence in juvenile populations

Most research on the deterrent effect of incarceration focuses on adult offenders. However, these estimates may not apply to juveniles. To the extent that incarceration among juveniles makes the cost of later incarceration more salient, all else equal, such detention may reduce the likelihood of future criminal activity. However, the standard model of crime treats human capital as fixed. This is a reasonable assumption in adult populations, for whom years of schooling and other measures of human capital are largely predetermined.[31]

In contrast, for juveniles, incarceration can have a negative impact on the accumulation of human capital by interrupting schooling, by making it more difficult to subsequently resume schooling, and by increasing the likelihood of future criminal activity through two potential channels. The first is by facilitating the accumulation of "criminal capital" in custody (see Bayer, Hjalmarsson, and Pozen 2009) and by hindering the accumulation of social capital that can aid in job search, thereby lowering the probability of employment after release (Granovetter 1995). The effect of acquiring criminal capital is to raise the expected benefit of re-offending.[32] The second way in which juvenile incarceration can have a negative impact on human capital is by interrupting schooling and lowering the likelihood of completing high school, thereby greatly reducing future labor market wages—and thus lowering the opportunity cost of offending—and ultimately increasing future criminality (as suggested by Samson and Laub 1993, 1997).

Ultimately, whether deterrence outweighs the effects of incarceration on human and criminal capital is an empirical question. The discussion that follows reviews the evidence on how the experience of incarceration affects youth outcomes and the likelihood of re-offending.

Nieuwbeerta, Nagin, and Blokland (2009) used data from the Criminal Career and Life-Course Study, which follows the conviction histories through 2002 of a sample of individuals convicted in the Dutch courts in 1977. They studied 1,475 men who were imprisoned for the first time between the ages of 18 and 38. Their focus on first-time imprisonment was innovative because it avoided the problem of distinguishing the effects of current incarceration experiences from past ones. The comparison group included 1,315 offenders who were convicted but not imprisoned. To address concerns that the convicted group is negatively selected relative to its nonconvicted counterpart (that is, selection bias), Nieuwbeerta, Nagin, and Blokland (2009) employ group-based trajectory modeling combined with propensity score matching. With this method, those imprisoned at age $t$ are matched with those not imprisoned based on pre-imprisonment trajectories of offending, as well as a time-varying imprisonment propensity score. This combined matching method allows the authors to show that the imprisoned and their non-imprisoned controls are comparable on a wide range of factors, including prior record and seriousness of the conviction offense, that might otherwise bias estimates of the effect of imprisonment on criminal career development.

Over a three-year follow-up period, they report that first-time imprisonment is associated with an increase in criminal activity, a conclusion that holds across a number of types of offenses. These results are interesting because they were recorded in the Netherlands, where the conditions of confinement are less harsh than in the United States, for instance, and for a sample where the mean stay in prison was only 14 weeks. It is possible that the effects of imprisonment might be stronger where the conditions of confinement are worse, but also that any form of imprisonment is so disruptive as to have such unintended consequences for recidivism.

As previously mentioned, the experience of incarceration may act to raise the likelihood of subsequent re-offending among juveniles, either by interrupting their education or by facilitating the accumulation of criminal capital by exposing them to wider networks of criminals, or both. The next subsection reviews research on the two channels that suggests that both may contribute to recidivism. Although sanctions may serve a short-term incapacitating function for juveniles, the conclusions here cast doubt on the ability of criminal penalties to function as a cost that, when imposed, dissuades offenders from recidivating.

### Juvenile incarceration, education, and recidivism

Estimating the causal effect of juvenile incarceration on human capital accumulation and recidivism as an adult is complicated by the fact that juveniles who are incarcerated differ in systematic ways from those who are not. They have likely committed more serious crimes, and their underlying propensity to drop out of school and commit crimes in the future may be higher than that of juveniles who were not incarcerated. Failing to account for these differences would bias estimates of the relationship between juvenile incarceration and both subsequent high school completion and adult incarceration. This problem is similar to the one that plagues estimates of the effect of severity of punishment on recidivism: severity is not random.

A second complicating factor is that the effects for youth on the margin of incarceration may differ from those for the average juvenile, but it is juveniles on the margin who are most likely to be affected by any changes in incarceration policy.

To overcome these obstacles, Aizer and Doyle (2013) exploit plausibly exogenous variation in juvenile detention stemming from the random assignment of cases to judges who vary systematically in their tendency to sentence, even after controlling for case characteristics. This strategy addresses the issue of negative selection into juvenile incarceration (because it relies on factors unrelated to the case to assign custody) and estimates effects for those at the margin of incarceration, where the judge's assignment matters for the incarceration decision. This strategy is similar to that used by Kling (2006) and Di Tella and Schargrodsky (2013) to estimate the impact of length of sentence on labor market outcomes and recidivism, respectively, among adults. But unlike previous work, Aizer and Doyle (2013) focus on a context in which human capital and educational attainment are not yet fixed, so that the long-term effects may well exceed those for adults.

Their data are based on administrative records of over 35,000 juveniles over 10 years who came before a juvenile court in Chicago, Illinois.[33] The data are linked to both public school data for the same city and adult incarceration data for the same state to investigate effects of juvenile incarceration on high school completion and subsequent adult imprisonment.

Aizer and Doyle (2013) find that juvenile incarceration reduces the probability of completing high school and increases the probability of incarceration later in life. While some of this relationship reflects unobserved factors, even when potential omitted variables are accounted for using the instrumental variables (IV) techniques that exploit random assignment to judges, the relationships remain strong. In their most complete models, Aizer and Doyle find that juvenile incarceration is estimated to decrease high school graduation by 13 percentage points and to increase adult incarceration by 22 percentage points. While smaller in magnitude than the initial OLS estimates, these IV results remain large and suggest substantial harmful effects of juvenile incarceration on long-term outcomes.

A closer subgroup analysis reveals that marginal cases are at particularly high risk of failing to complete high school and of adult incarceration as a result of juvenile custody. These results are also consistent with the idea that the timing of incarceration matters; the strongest effects are for juveniles ages 15 and 16—a critical period of adolescence when incarceration is most likely to end one's high school education.

The finding of a strong negative impact of juvenile incarceration on high school completion suggests that there may be a negative effect on recidivism when these juveniles become adults as well, which Aizer and Doyle (2013) then explore by defining adult incarceration according to whether an individual was present in an adult correctional facility anywhere in the state at any point by the age of 25. Ignoring selection, their analysis indicates a strong relationship between juvenile incarceration and adult incarceration; after controlling for a number of individual characteristics and the type of crime, and limiting the control group to those who came before the court but were not committed, they find that those who were in juvenile detention are 15 percentage points more likely than other juveniles residing in the same community to be found in an adult correctional facility by age 25. In turn, after accounting for the endogeneity of juvenile incarceration, the instrumental variable estimate of 0.22 is similar in magnitude but slightly larger than the most restrictive OLS estimates for adult recidivism. This estimate is somewhat imprecisely calculated, however; thus it is not statistically significantly distinguishable from the OLS estimate, and both can be characterized as large—incarceration as a juvenile raises the likelihood of recidivism as an adult by 22 percentage points.

These estimates represent very large effects and suggest that of the two potential effects of juvenile incarceration on future criminal activity—deterrence versus reductions in human capital accumulation, social capital, and positive social networks—the latter dominates. When Aizer and Doyle (2013) conduct an analysis by type of crime, they find that people incarcerated as juveniles are not only more likely to recidivate as adults, but also that the types of crime on which they recidivate are both serious and costly, such as homicide, violent crime, and property crime. The next section explores a particular mechanism by which incarcerated juveniles may end up recidivating: peer effects and the accumulation of criminal capital while in custody.

### Juvenile incarceration, peer effects, and re-offending

Social networks and peer interactions are likely to play an important role in the proliferation of criminal activity. Understanding the nature of these interactions is important from a policy perspective; it can inform decisions about how to group individuals optimally within correctional facilities, and can provide a basis for assessing the dynamic benefits and costs of a wide range of policy decisions.

Prior empirical research has documented evidence consistent with the possibility that social interactions are of first-order importance, as reviewed in chapter 6. Glaeser, Sacerdote, and Scheinkman (1996), for example, show that crime exhibits extremely high variance across time and space, and that only a small portion of this variability can be explained by detailed measures of fundamental economic and social conditions. A long-standing criminology literature dating to Glueck and Glueck (1950) documents a strong positive correlation between individual and peer criminal (delinquent) behavior. Few papers convincingly document the causal effects of peers on one another. One such paper is by Jacob and Lefgren (2003), who find that school attendance increases violent crimes but decreases property crimes in the very short run, underscoring the role played by social interactions in explaining violent crimes. As discussed in detail in chapter 6, other research centers on the role of neighborhoods in determining criminal behavior.[34]

Bayer, Hjalmarsson, and Pozen (2009) study whether the behavior of a juvenile offender after release from a correctional facility is influenced by the characteristics of individuals with whom he or she served time. Their analysis is based on information on over 8,000 individuals who served in 169 juvenile correctional facilities during a two-year period in Florida. These data provide a complete record of past crimes, facility assignments, and arrests and adjudications in the year following the release of each individual.

Their empirical analysis consists of a series of regressions of recidivism in each of 10 crime categories on individual demographic characteristics and own criminal history, demographic characteristics and criminal histories of peers, and interactions between individual and peer characteristics. To control for the nonrandom assignment of juveniles to facilities, Bayer, Hjalmarsson, and Pozen (2009) control for facility and facility-by-prior-offense fixed effects, ensuring that the impact of peers on recidivism is identified using only the variation in the length of time that any two individuals who are committed to the same facility happen to overlap.

Relative to other settings where the estimation of social interactions is more difficult (see chapter 6), their empirical strategy exploits a unique feature of correctional facilities: namely, that the peer group is constantly evolving over time with the admittance and release of individuals as their sentences begin and expire. As long as the date at which a given individual is assigned to a facility within the two-year sample period is random with respect to the composition of peers in the facility at that time, this empirical strategy properly accounts for the nonrandom assignment of individuals to facilities.

Their results provide strong evidence of the existence of peer effects in juvenile correctional facilities. In almost all instances that they consider, these peer effects are reinforcing in nature; exposure to peers with a history of committing a particular type of crime increases the probability that an individual who has already committed the same type of crime recidivates in that crime. This form of reinforcing peer effect is positive and significant for burglary, petty larceny, felony drug offenses, misdemeanor drug offenses, aggravated assault, and felony sex offenses. In contrast, they find no evidence that exposure to peers with particular criminal histories significantly increases an individual's propensity to recidivate in a crime category in which the individual had no prior experience. Thus exposure to a greater percentage of peers with a history of having committed burglaries increases the likelihood that an individual with a prior record of burglary will commit another burglary upon release; but no such effect exists for those without a prior history of burglary. In addition, there are large reinforcing peer effects for auto thefts and felony drug offenses in nonresidential facilities. The authors speculate that the grouping of juveniles from nearby neighborhoods may inadvertently foster the formation and expansion of criminal networks.

### Mechanisms of specific deterrence

What explains the strong reinforcing peer effects and limited effects on those without prior experience in a crime category? A number of mechanisms have been hypothesized.

*Addictive behavior.* One explanation is that peers reinforce addictive behavior. This may explain part of the large reinforcing peer effect for misdemeanor drug crimes.[35]

*Sorting and comparative advantage.* An alternative explanation is that individuals experience different returns from participation in different types of crimes resulting from their natural abilities, opportunities, human capital, involvement in crime networks, or other factors. In short, individuals have already sorted into crimes that fit their comparative advantages and maximize returns. In this case, individuals with a history in a given crime category have already revealed themselves to have high returns—and probably have substantial human capital—in this category. Access to peers who increase the individual's returns to this type of crime through social learning, for example, may lead to increased activity in this category.

*The creation and expansion of criminal networks.* Bayer, Hjalmarsson, and Pozen (2009) assess whether the estimated peer effects are heterogeneous across facility characteristics; for instance, by estimating models separately for individuals in residential facilities and then for individuals in nonresidential facilities. The reinforcing peer coefficient for the sample in residential facilities is very similar to that of the entire sample, while the coefficient is 70 percent larger for nonresidential facilities; the reinforcing peer effects are considerably larger in nonresidential facilities. However, this conclusion is driven by especially large coefficients for the crimes of auto theft, robbery, felony drug offenses, and aggravated assault. A potential explanation for these effects is that auto theft and felony drugs are largely dependent on access to criminal networks. Nonresidential facilities may inadvertently increase the formation and expansion of criminal networks by bringing together young offenders from surrounding neighborhoods. This points to a difficult issue for policy makers as to how best to deal with first-time and other young juvenile offenders. The evidence provided by Bayer, Hjalmarsson, and Pozen (2009) implies that grouping them together in nonresidential facilities may lead to the rapid expansion of criminal networks.

In sum, juveniles appear to be not very sensitive to the changes in criminal sanctions (in the deterrence sense), as documented by Lee and McCrary (2009), while their behavior is instead quite sensitive to the composition of their peers, and in particular to peers who have committed crimes similar to their own. According to Bayer, Hjalmarsson, and Pozen (2009), while a policy of grouping offenders with others who have committed similar crimes may seem prudent to prevent the exposure of young offenders to peers with experience in other criminal activities, such a policy may inadvertently increase exposure to peers with experience precisely in those crime categories where it is likely to be of greatest use.

Second, and more broadly, the existence of peer effects in juvenile criminal behavior suggests that any reduction in crime may lead to future reductions in crime through reductions in the criminal histories of peers. As discussed in chapter 6, there is potential for double dividends in crime reduction policies: the direct effect that operates on the individual, and the indirect effect of reduced criminal activity that operates on his or her peers. It is important to account for these dynamic benefits when considering the overall benefits of reducing crime.

## Notes

[1] In actuality, there are many more benefits and costs associated with criminal acts. For instance, the benefits might include the excitement (or rush) at the time of the act, and the costs might include ostracism from one's family and friends and the psychic costs of being labeled an offender.

[2] See also Cook and Ludwig (2012) and their discussion of the value added of the economic approach to crime.

[3] Nevertheless, the literature review occasionally comments on the degree to which the conclusions are consistent with rational versus irrational models of behavior, to the extent that this commentary informs policy.

[4] For discussions and reviews of incapacitation effects of imprisonment, see Spelman (1994); Owens (2009); Cullen and Jonson (2011); and Barbarino and Mastrobuoni (2014). Addressing crime only by incapacitation necessarily requires higher imprisonment rates and many more public resources. If a crime can be averted by deterrence, however, there is no one to punish; accordingly, deterrence does not imply a trade-off between crime rates and incarceration rates (see Durlauf and Nagin 2011).

[5] First-generation studies include Ehrlich (1973), Sjoquist (1973), and Forst (1976). Second-generation studies include Marvell and Moody (1994) and Spelman (2008).

[6] As a result of these shortcomings, Durlauf and Nagin (2011) are skeptical of estimates based on these approaches.

[7] That is, a 1 percent decline in the prison population yields a 0.3 percent increase in property crime, for example.

[8] Like Levitt (1996), they also adopt an instrumental variable approach to account for the endogeneity of criminal sanctions with respect to imprisonment rates. Their instrument is based on

predictions of incarceration rates from a dynamic model that describes the response of incarceration rates to a given shock to the probabilities of prison entry and exit. Since this model has no behavioral component but is rather a mechanical description of how imprisonment rates might change for a given change to entry and exit probabilities, it is plausibly a valid instrument.

[9] See Durlauf and Nagin (2011); Nagin (2013); and Chalfin and McCrary (2014).

[10] Three strikes laws dramatically increase prison sentences for persons convicted of two or more violent crimes or serious felonies. Thus, for criminals who have at least two convictions, the marginal cost of severity of crime (in terms of sentence length) is zero, conditional on committing the third offense—a form of moral hazard.

[11] Theoretically, it could be argued that increases in the certainty or severity of punishment can induce changes in behavior among potential victims that might weaken the incentives faced by potential offenders not to offend. For instance, suppose a law is passed imposing harsher sentences on property crime. If potential victims expect offenders to be deterred by the law, they may reduce their own investments in security and safety, such as by not purchasing an alarm system. The countervailing effects of harsher sentences and weaker investments in personal protection could thus yield no net change in potential offenders' expectations of punishment. Throughout this section, however, the emphasis is on natural experiments (such as unannounced prisoner releases and random assignment within criminal courts to judges who differ systematically in their leniency) that eliminate (or minimize) potential victims' abilities to unwind the incentives faced by criminals.

[12] Munyo (2015) corresponds to the structural analog of the reduced form channels summarized in the chapter.

[13] Lee and McCrary (2009) provide evidence that, on the day of a youth's 18th birthday, there is no discontinuous change in the ability of law enforcement to apprehend an offender, no discontinuous change in wages or in the distribution of criminal opportunities, and so on. There are a few exceptions (the right to vote and the right to gamble change discontinuously on the 18th birthday), but these may reasonably be considered negligible factors in an individual's decision to offend.

[14] Lee and McCrary's (2009) framework differs conceptually from the standard regression discontinuity (RD) design, which rests on the assumption that individuals do not manipulate the forcing variable around the relevant cutoff. McCrary (2008) shows that in a standard RD context, a discontinuity in the density of the forcing variable at the threshold represents evidence against the validity of the RD's assumptions. However, in the current context, the discontinuity in the density of age (measured by the number of days away from the offenders' 18th birthday) at the time of offense provides a measure of deterrence and is precisely the object of interest.

[15] An alternative interpretation of Lee and McCrary's (2009) relatively small effects is that the juveniles who commit offenses in their data have already had contact with adult criminals and/or with the juvenile justice system. They may have already adopted "adult" behaviors in terms of offending, complicating the interpretation of their specific test as implying that increased severity has no effect on offending.

[16] Only their results conditional on arrest at age 17 are relevant and appropriate for the analysis, and the comments herein pertain only to that subset of results. Furthermore, because drug consumption becomes legal at the age of 18, their analysis of the drug consumption outcome should be disregarded because turning 18 should mechanically be associated with a decline in arrests for behavior that is sanctioned for those below 18.

[17] Their estimate of the decline in criminal offending at age 18 is 2 percent, which is induced by a roughly 230 percent increase in the expected incarceration length if arrested.

[18] Under California law, qualifying convictions include murder, rape, robbery, attempted murder, assault with intent to rape or rob, any felony resulting in bodily harm, arson, kidnapping, mayhem,

burglary of an occupied dwelling, grand theft with a firearm, drug sales to minors, or any felony with a deadly weapon (Zimring, Hawkins, and Kamin 2001).

[19] For greater institutional detail on California's three strikes law, see Helland and Tabarrok (2007) and Zimring, Hawkins, and Kamin (2001).

[20] These qualitative results are also corroborated by Greenwood and Hawken (2002).

[21] See, for example, Cameron (1988); Marvell and Moody (1996); and Eck and Maguire (2000).

[22] By relying on this time series approach, Marvell and Moody (1996) do not necessarily break the relationship that runs from crime to policing. If hiring of police occurs with a lag relative to the crime rate, for instance, the endogeneity problem will persist.

[23] Machin and Marie (2011) study the relationship between police resources (not the size of the police force) and crime by considering a large-scale program—the Street Crime Initiative (SCI)—that was introduced in England and Wales in 2002. The program allocated additional resources to certain police forces specifically to tackle street crime, whereas other police forces received no additional funding. Their estimates indicate that robberies fell significantly in areas served by SCI police forces relative to non-SCI forces after the initiative was introduced. Moreover, the program seems to have been cost-effective and did not result in displacement or diffusion effects onto other crimes or into adjacent areas.

[24] That the additional police resources induced no spatial displacement has been called into question by Ho, Donohue, and Leahy (2013). They reexamined Di Tella and Schargrodsky's (2004) original data and argue that the evidence is more consistent with spatial displacement of crime rather than crime reduction.

[25] See Iyengar (2010b) for a detailed discussion of the experiment and its follow-up studies.

[26] Evidence on broken window theory and policing (along with relevant references) is discussed in chapter 6.

[27] In his analysis of the perceptions of potential offenders, Lochner (2007) shows that beliefs about the probability of arrest significantly deter crime; that is, crime is responsive to what individuals *perceive* is the likelihood of apprehension. However, he also documents that individuals' perceptions are not well correlated with true probabilities of arrest and, furthermore, that they do not update their beliefs when information about the actual likelihood of apprehension is provided. These patterns are consistent with Nagin's (1998) concern that potential offenders may be unaware (or only partially aware) of changes in certainty when the police force expands.

[28] In Chiricos and others (2007), the outcome of interest is whether someone on probation re-offends within two years of sentencing. The authors control for assigned length of probation (the assignment rule) rather than actual probation time, as it is less endogenous. In this model, the completion of probation is not a threat to validity. However, the judge's decision to adjudicate the offender may be endogenous and related to unobserved factors that would explain recidivism. The authors therefore proceed to model the selection process of adjudication and use whether the offender went to trial as an exclusion restriction to predict adjudication but not recidivism

[29] See, for instance, Aizer and Doyle (2013).

[30] Some offenders assigned to EM ultimately escape by breaking their monitoring devices. The authors consider the possibility that these perpetrators re-offend with more severe crimes by examining the seriousness of the crimes committed by escapees relative to their original crime or relative to other groups, such as offenders who were previously assigned EM or were formerly incarcerated. However, Di Tella and Schargrodsky find no statistically significant difference in the severity of their re-offenses.

[31] Incarceration may have the effect of increasing the probability that high school dropouts earn a high school equivalency diploma (general equivalent development, or GED) while in prison. However,

having a GED is associated with much lower earnings than a high school diploma (Cameron and Heckman 1993). Moreover, existing studies suggest that once one controls for potential selection into GED programs, earning a GED in prison is not associated with lower recidivism or higher earnings (Wilson, Gallagher, and MacKenzie 2000; Tyler and Kling 2007).

[32] While these mechanisms are likely more acute for juveniles, they are also relevant for adults.

[33] In Chicago, juvenile offenders of minor crimes are often dealt with directly by police. Only after a number of smaller infractions or a major infraction will a child enter the juvenile court system. Every juvenile arrest is reviewed twice before proceeding to juvenile court: first by the police, and a second time by the prosecutor's office. At each review, the juvenile's case can be dismissed. Only those cases that are not dismissed by the police or the prosecutor proceed to juvenile court.

[34] See, for example, Case and Katz (1991); Ludwig, Duncan, and Hirschfield (2001); and Kling, Ludwig, and Katz (2005).

[35] Becker and Mulligan (1997) develop a theoretical model in which drug addiction causes a rational increase in future discounting. Experimental studies show that drug consumption substantially increases discount rates. See Bretteville-Jensen (1999); Petry (2003); Coffey and others (2003); and Kirby and Petry (2004).

# References

Abrams, David S. 2011. "Building Criminal Capital vs. Specific Deterrence: The Effect of Incarceration Length on Recidivism." Working Paper, Wharton School, University of Pennsylvania.
———. 2012. "Estimating the Deterrent Effect of Incarceration Using Sentencing Enhancements." *American Economic Journal: Applied Economics* 4 (4):32–56.
Aizer, Anna, and Joseph J. Doyle Jr. 2013. "Juvenile Incarceration, Human Capital and Future Crime: Evidence from Randomly-Assigned Judges." NBER Working Paper 19102, National Bureau of Economic Research, Cambridge, MA.
Barbarino, Alessandro, and Giovanni Mastrobuoni. 2014. "The Incapacitation Effect of Incarceration: Evidence from Several Italian Collective Pardons." *American Economic Journal: Economic Policy* 6 (1): 1–37.
Bayer, Patrick, Randi Hjalmarsson, and David Pozen. 2009. "Building Criminal Capital behind Bars: Peer Effects in Juvenile Corrections." *Quarterly Journal of Economics* 124 (1): 105–47.
Becker, Gary S., and Casey B. Mulligan. 1997. "The Endogenous Determination of Time Preference." *Quarterly Journal of Economics* 112 (3): 729–58.
Bell, B., L. Jaitman, and S. Machin. 2014. "Crime Deterrence: Evidence from the London 2011 Riots." *Economic Journal* 124 (576): 480–506.
Berk, R., A. Campbell, R. Klap, and B. Western. 1992. "The Deterrent Effect of Arrest in Incidents of Domestic Violence: A Bayesian Analysis of Four Field Experiments." *American Sociological Review* 57 (5): 698–708.
Braga, Anthony A. 2008. "Crime Prevention Research Review No. 2: Police Enforcement Strategies to Prevent Crime in Hot Spot Areas." Office of Community Oriented Policing Services, U.S. Department of Justice, Washington, DC.
Braga, Anthony A., David M. Kennedy, Elin J. Waring, and Anne Morrison Piehl. 2001. "Problem-Oriented Policing, Deterrence, and Youth Violence: An Evaluation of Boston's Operation Ceasefire." *Journal of Research in Crime and Delinquency* 38 (3): 195–225.
Braga, Anthony A., David L. Weisburd, Elin J. Waring, Lorraine Green Mazerolle, William Spelman, and Francis Gajewski. 1999. "Problem-Oriented Policing in Violent Crime Places: A Randomized Controlled Experiment." *Criminology* 37: 541–80.
Bretteville-Jensen, A. L. 1999. "Addiction and Discounting." *Journal of Health Economics* 18 (4): 393–407.

Buonanno, Paolo, and Steven Raphael. 2013. "Incarceration and Incapacitation: Evidence from the 2006 Italian Collective Pardon." *American Economic Review* 103 (6): 2437–65.

Cameron, Samuel. 1998. "The Economics of Crime Deterrence: A Survey of Theory and Evidence." *Kyklos* 41 (2): 301–23.

Cameron, Stephen V., and James J. Heckman. 1993. "The Nonequivalence of High School Equivalents." *Journal of Labor Economics*, Part 1: Essays in Honor of Jacob Mincer 11 (1): 1–47.

Case, Anne, and Lawrence Katz. 1991. "The Company You Keep: The Effects of Family and Neighborhood on Disadvantaged Youths." NBER Working Paper 3705. National Bureau of Economic Research, Cambridge, MA.

Chalfin, Aaron, and Justin McCrary. 2014. "Criminal Deterrence: A Review of the Literature." Working paper.

Chen, M. Keith, and Jesse M. Shapiro. 2007. "Do Harsher Prison Conditions Reduce Recidivism? A Discontinuity-Based Approach." *American Law and Economics Review* 9 (1): 1–29.

Chiricos, Ted, Kelle Barrick, William Bales, and Stephanie Bontrager. 2007. "The Labeling of Convicted Felons and Its Consequence for Recidivism." *Criminology* 45 (3): 547–81.

Coffey, S., G. Gudleski, M. Saladin, and K. Brady. 2003. "Impulsivity and Rapid Discounting of Delayed Hypothetical Rewards in Cocaine-Dependent Individuals." *Experimental and Clinical Psychopharmacology* 11 (1): 18–25.

Cook, Philip J., and Jens Ludwig. 2012. "Economical Crime Control." In *Making Crime Control Pay: Cost-Effective Alternatives of Incarceration,* edited by Philip J. Cook, Jens Ludwig, and Justin McCrary. Cambridge, MA: National Bureau of Economic Research.

Cullen, Francis T., and Cheryl Lero Jonson. 2011. *Correctional Theory: Context and Consequences.* Thousand Oaks, CA: SAGE Publications.

DeAngelo, G., and B. Hansen. 2014. "Life and Death in the Fast Lane: Police Enforcement and Traffic Fatalities. *American Economic Journal: Economic Policy* 6 (2): 231–57.

Di Tella, Rafael, and Ernesto Schargrodsky. 2004. "Do Police Reduce Crime? Estimates Using the Allocation of Police Forces after a Terrorist Attack," *American Economic Review* 94 (1): 115–33.

———. 2013. "Criminal Recidivism after Prison and Electronic Monitoring." *Journal of Political Economy* 121 (1): 28–73.

Draca, Mirko, Stephen Machin, and Robert Witt. 2011. "Panic on the Streets of London: Police, Crime, and the July 2005 Terror Attacks." *American Economic Review* 101(5): 2157–81.

Drago, Francesco, Roberto Galbiati, and Pietro Vertova. 2009. "The Deterrent Effects of Prison: Evidence from a Natural Experiment," *Journal of Political Economy* 117 (2): 257–80.

———. 2011. "Prison Conditions and Recidivism." *American Law and Economics Review* 13 (1): 103–30.

Durlauf, Steven N., and Daniel S. Nagin. 2011. "Imprisonment and Crime." *Criminology & Public Policy* 10 (1): 13–54.

Eck, J., and E. Maguire. 2000. "Have Changes in Policing Reduced Violent Crime? An Assessment of the Evidence." In *The Crime Drop in America*, edited by A. Blumstein and J. Wallman. New York: Cambridge University Press.

Eck, J., and W. Spelman. 1987. *Problem-Solving: Problem-Oriented Policing in Newport News.* Washington, DC: National Institute of Justice.

Ehrlich, Isaac. 1973. "Participation in Illegitimate Activities: A Theoretical and Empirical Investigation." *Journal of Political Economy* 81 (3): 521–65.

Evans, William, and Emily Owens. 2007. "COPS and Crime." *Journal of Public Economics* 91 (1–2): 181–201.

Forst, B. E. 1976. "The Deterrent Effect of Capital Punishment: A Cross-State Analysis of the 1960s." *Minnesota Law Review* 61: 743–68.

García, Juan Felipe, Daniel Mejia, and Daniel Ortega. 2013. "Police Reform, Training and Crime: Experimental Evidence from Colombia's Plan Cuadrantes." CAF Working Paper 2013/01, CAF (Development Bank of Latin America).

Glaeser, Edward L., Bruce Sacerdote, and José A. Scheinkman. 1996. "Crime and Social Interactions." *Quarterly Journal of Economics* 111 (May): 507–48.

Glueck, Sheldon, and Eleanor Glueck. 1950. *Unraveling Juvenile Delinquency.* New York: Commonwealth Fund.

Goldstein, Herman. 1979. "Improving Policing: A Problem-Oriented Approach." *Crime & Delinquency* 25 (2): 236–43.

———. 1990. *Problem-Oriented Policing.* Philadelphia: Temple University Press.

Granovetter, Mark S. 1995. *Getting A Job: A Study of Contacts and Careers,* 2nd edition. Chicago: University of Chicago Press.

Greenwood, P. W., and A. Hawken. 2002. "An Assessment of the Effects of California's Three Strikes Law." Working Paper, Greenwood and Associates.

Groff, E. R., J. H. Ratcliffe, C. P. Haberman, E. T. Sorg, N. M. Joyce, and R. B. Taylor. 2015. "Does What Police Do at Hot Spots Matter? The Philadelphia Policing Tactics Experiment." *Criminology* 53 (1): 23–53.

Guarín, Arlen, Carlos Medina, and Jorge Tamayo. 2013. "The Effects of Punishment of Crime in Colombia on Deterrence, Incapacitation, and Human Capital Formation." IDB Working Paper IDB-WP 420, Inter-American Development Bank, Washington, DC.

Hawken, Angela, and Mark Kleiman. 2009. "Managing Drug Involved Probationers with Swift and Certain Sanctions: Evaluating Hawaii's HOPE." National Institute of Justice, Office of Justice Programs, U.S. Department of Justice, Washington, DC.

Heaton, P. 2010. "Understanding the Effects of Antiprofiling Policies." *Journal of Law and Economics* 53 (1): 29–64

Helland, E., and A. Tabarrok. 2007. "Does Three Strikes Deter? A Nonparametric Estimation." *Journal of Human Resources* 42 (2): 309–30.

Hjalmarsson, Randi. 2009. "Crime and Expected Punishment: Changes in Perceptions at the Age of Criminal Majority." *American Law and Economics Review* 11 (1): 209–48.

Ho, Daniel E., John J. Donohue III, and Patrick Leahy. 2014. "Do Police Reduce Crime? A Reexamination of a Natural Experiment." In *Empirical Legal Analysis: Assessing the Performance of Legal Institutions,* edited by Yun-Chien Chang. London: Routledge.

Ibáñez, Ana María, Catherine Rodríguez, and David Zarruk. 2013. "Crime, Punishment, and Schooling Decisions: Evidence from Colombian Adolescents." IDB Working Paper IDB-WP-413, Inter-American Development Bank, Washington, DC.

Iyengar, Radha. 2010a. "I'd Rather be Hanged for a Sheep Than a Lamb: The Unintended Consequences of 'Three-Strikes' Laws." CEP Discussion Paper 1017, Centre for Economic Performance, London School of Economics and Political Science, London.

———. 2010b. "Does Arrest Deter Violence? Comparing Experimental and Nonexperimental Evidence on Mandatory Arrest Laws." Chapter 12 in *The Economics of Crime,* edited by Rafael Di Tella, Sebastian Edwards, and Ernesto Schargrodsky, 421–53. Chicago: University of Chicago Press.

Jacob, Brian A., and Lars Lefgren. 2003. "Are Idle Hands the Devil's Workshop? Incapacitation, Concentration, and Juvenile Crime." *American Economic Review* 93 (5): 1560–77.

Johnson, R., and S. Raphael. 2013. "How Much Crime Reduction Does the Marginal Prisoner Buy?" *Journal of Law and Economics* 55 (2): 275–310.

Jonson, C. L. 2010. "The Impact of Imprisonment on Reoffending: A Meta-Analysis." PhD thesis, University of Cincinnati.

Kirby, K., and N. Petry. 2004. "Heroin and Cocaine Abusers Have Higher Discount Rates for Delayed Rewards Than Alcoholics or Non-Drug-Using Controls." *Addiction* 99 (4): 461–71.

Klick, J., and A. Tabarrok. 2005. "Using Terror Alert Levels to Estimate the Effect of Police on Crime." *Journal of Law and Economics* 48 (1): 267–80.

Kling, Jeffrey. 2006. "Incarceration Length, Employment, and Earnings." *American Economic Review* 96 (3): 863–76.

Kling, Jeffrey R., Jens Ludwig, and Lawrence F. Katz. 2005. "Neighborhood Effects on Crime for Female and Male Youth: Evidence from a Randomized Housing Voucher Experiment." *Quarterly Journal of Economics* 120 (1): 87–130.

Kuziemko, Ilyana. 2013. "How Should Inmates Be Released from Prison? An Assessment of Parole versus Fixed Sentence Regimes." *Quarterly Journal of Economics* 128 (1): 371–424.

Lee, D. S., and J. McCrary. 2009. "The Deterrence Effect of Prison: Dynamic Theory and Evidence." Working Paper 189, Center for Economic Policy Studies, Princeton University; Working Paper 550, Industrial Relations Section, Princeton University.

Levitt, Steven. 1996. "The Effect of Prison Population Size on Crime Rates: Evidence from Prison Overcrowding Litigation." *Quarterly Journal of Economics* 111 (2): 319–51.

———. 1997. "Using Electoral Cycles in Police Hiring to Estimate the Effect of Police on Crime." *American Economic Review* 87 (3): 270–90.

———. 1999. "The Changing Relationship between Income and Crime Victimization." *Economic Policy Review* 5 (3): 87–98.

———. 2002. "Using Electoral Cycles in Police Hiring to Estimate the Effects of Police on Crime: Reply." *American Economic Review* 92 (4): 1244–50.

Lochner L. 2007. "Individual Perceptions of the Criminal Justice System." *American Economic Review* 97: 444–60.

Ludwig, Jens, Greg J. Duncan, and Paul Hirschfield. 2001. "Urban Poverty and Juvenile Crime: Evidence from a Randomized Housing-Mobility Experiment." *Quarterly Journal of Economics* 116 (2001): 655–80.

Machin, Stephen, and Olivier Marie. 2011. "Crime and Police Resources: The Street Crime Initiative." *Journal of the European Economic Association* 9 (4): 678–701.

Marie, Olivier. 2013. "Early Release from Prison on Electronic Monitoring and Recidivism: A Tale of Two Discontinuities." Working paper.

Marvell, T., and C. Moody. 1994. "Prison Population Growth and Crime Reduction." *Journal of Quantitative Criminology* 10 (2): 109–40.

———. 1996. "Specification Problems, Police Levels, and Crime Rates." *Criminology* 34 (4): 609–46.

Maurin, Eric, and Aurelie Ouss. 2009. "Sentence Reductions and Recidivism: Lessons from the Bastille Day Quasi-Experiment." IZA Discussion Paper 3990, Institute for the Study of Labor, Bonn.

Maxwell, C. D., J. H. Garner, and J. A. Fagan. 2002. "Research, Policy and Theory: The Preventive Effects of Arrest on Intimate Partner Violence." *Criminology and Public Policy* 2 (1): 51–80.

McCrary, J. 2008 "Manipulation of the Running Variable in the Regression Discontinuity Design: A Density Test." *Journal of Econometrics* 142 (2): 698–714.

Munyo, I. 2015. "The Juvenile Crime Dilemma." *Review of Economics Dynamics* 5 (18): 201–11.

Nagin, Daniel S. 1998. "Criminal Deterrence Research at the Outset of the Twenty-First Century." *Crime and Justice* 23: 1–42.

———. 2013. "Deterrence: A Review of the Evidence by a Criminologist for Economists." *Annual Reviews of Economics* 5 (August): 83–105.

Nagin, D. S., and G. M. Snodgrass. 2013. "The Effect of Incarceration on Re-Offending: Evidence from a Natural Experiment in Pennsylvania." *Journal of Quantitative Criminology* 29 (4): 601–42.

Nieuwbeerta, Paul, Daniel S. Nagin, and Arjan A. J. Blokland. 2009. "Assessing the Impact of First-Time Imprisonment on Offenders' Subsequent Criminal Career Development: A Matched Samples Comparison." *Journal of Quantitative Criminology* 25 (3): 227–57.

Owens, Emily G. 2009. "More Time, Less Crime? Estimating the Incapacitative Effect of Sentence Enhancements." *Journal of Law and Economics* 52 (3): 551–79.

———. 2013. "COPS and Cuffs." In *Lessons from the Economics of Crime: What Works in Reducing Offending?* edited by Philip J. Cook, Stephen Machin, Olivier Marie, and Giovanni Mastrobuoni, 17–44. Cambridge, MA: MIT Press.

Petry, N. 2003. "Discounting of Money, Health, and Freedom in Substance Abusers and Controls." *Drug and Alcohol Dependence* 71 (2): 133–41.

Poutvaara, Panu, and Mikael Priks. 2006. "Hooliganism in the Shadow of the 9/11 Terrorist Attack and the Tsunami: Do Police Reduce Group Violence?" CESifo Working Paper 1882, CESifo, Center for Economic Studies & Ifo Institute for Economic Research, Munich.

Raphael, Steven, and Jens Ludwig. 2003. "Prison Sentence Enhancements: The Case of Project Exile." In *Evaluating Gun Policy: Effects on Crime and Violence*, edited by Philip J. Cook and Jens Ludwig, 251–86. Washington, DC: Brookings Institution Press.

Sampson, Robert J., and John H. Laub. 1993. *Crime in the Making: Pathways and Turning Points through Life*. Cambridge, MA: Harvard University Press.

———. 1997. "A Life-Course Theory of Cumulative Disadvantage and the Stability of Delinquency." In *Developmental Theories of Crime and Delinquency*, edited by Terence P. Thornberry. New Brunswick, NJ: Transaction.

Shepherd, J. M. 2002. "Fear of the First Strike: The Full Deterrent Effect of California's Two and Three-Strikes Legislation." *Journal of Legal Studies* 31: 159–201.

Shi, Lan. 2009. "The Limits of Oversight in Policing: Evidence from the 2001 Cincinnati Riot." *Journal of Public Economics* 93 (1–2): 99–113.

Sherman, Lawrence W., and Richard A. Berk. 1984. "The Specific Deterrent Effects of Arrest for Domestic Assault." *American Sociological Review* 49 (1): 261–72.

Sherman, L. W., M. E. Buerger, and P. R. Gartin. 1989. *Repeat Call Address Policing: The Minneapolis RECAP Experiment*. Final Report to the National Institute of Justice, U.S. Department of Justice. Washington, DC: Crime Control Institute.

Sjoquist, D. 1973. "Property Crime and Economic Behavior: Some Empirical Results." *American Economic Review* 53: 439–46.

Slutkin, G. 2013. "Let's Treat Violence like a Contagious Disease." TEDMED 2013. https://www.youtube.com/watch?v=CZNrOzgNWf4.

Spelman, W. 1994. *Criminal Incapacitation*. New York: Plenum.

———. 2008. "Specifying the Relationship between Crime and Prisons." *Journal of Quantitative Criminology* 24 (2): 149–78.

Spelman, William, and Dale K. Brown. 1981. *Calling the Police: A Replication of the Citizen Reporting Component of the Kansas City Response Time Analysis*. Washington, DC: Police Executive Research Forum.

Tyler, John H., and Jeffrey R. Kling. 2007. "Prison-Based Education and Re-Entry into the Mainstream Labor Market." In *Barriers to Reentry? The Labor Market for Released Prisoners in Post-Industrial America*, edited by Shawn Bushway, Michael Stoll, and David Michael. New York: Russell Sage Foundation Press.

Weisburd, D., and J. Eck. 2004. "What Can Police Do to Reduce Crime, Disorder, and Fear?" *Annals of the American Academy of Political and Social Science* 593 (May): 42–65.

Weisburd D., T. Einat, and M. Kowalski. 2008. "The Miracle of the Cells: An Experimental Study of Interventions to Increase Payment of Court-Ordered Financial Obligations." *Criminology and Public Policy* 7 (1): 9–36.

Weisburd, David, and Lorraine Green. 1995. "Policing Drug Hot Spots: The Jersey City Drug Market Analysis Experiment." *Justice Quarterly* 12: 711–35.

Weisburd, D., E. Groff, and S. Yang. 2012. *The Criminology of Place: Street Segments and Our Understanding of the Crime Problem*. Oxford: Oxford University Press.

Weisburd, David, Cody W. Telep, Joshua C. Hinkle, and John E. Eck. 2010. "Is Problem-Oriented Policing Effective in Reducing Crime and Disorder?" *Criminology & Public Policy* 9 (1): 139–72.

Weisburd, D., L. A. Wyckoff, J. Ready, J. E. Eck, J. C. Hinkle, and F. Gajewski. 2006. "Does Crime Just Move Around the Corner? A Controlled Study of Spatial Displacement and Diffusion of Crime Control Benefits." *Criminology* 44 (3): 549–92.

Wilson, David B., Catherine A. Gallagher, and Doris L. MacKenzie. 2000. "A Meta-Analysis of Corrections-Based Education, Vocation, and Work Programs for Adult Offenders." *Journal of Research in Crime and Delinquency* 37 (4): 347–68.

Wilson, James Q., and Joan Petersilia, eds. 2011. *Crime and Public Policy.* New York: Oxford University Press.

Zimring, F., G. Hawkins, and S. Kamin. 2001. *Punishment and Democracy: Three Strikes and You're Out in California.* New York: Oxford University Press.

# Appendix: World Bank Citizen Security Program in Latin America and the Caribbean

The World Bank has been supporting citizen security initiatives in Latin America and the Caribbean (LAC) since 2004. In recent years, responding to growing demand from governments, the Bank has increased its efforts in this area substantially. The Social, Urban, Rural, and Resilience Global Practice (GP SUR) hosts the Citizen Security Team, which works closely with a broad range of units (including Transport, Education, Health, Social Protection, Public Sector, Poverty and Gender, and the LAC Chief Economist Office). These efforts have led to a growing suite of knowledge, advisory, convening, and financial services.[1]

The World Bank's approach to citizen security is grounded in the recognized principle that prevention is the most effective way to respond to crime and violence. It focuses on the prevention of conventional crime and interpersonal violence and involves activities that span four key areas: knowledge services, project financing, strategic partnerships, and capacity building.

1. *Knowledge services.* Studies combine quantitative and qualitative methods and geospatial analysis, and seek to inform both government policies and World Bank operations. The research agenda aims at deepening the understanding of the dynamics of violence and analyzing policy responses made by governments in the region. Examples of this work include several reports: *Trends, Costs, and Policy Options on Crime and Violence in the Caribbean* (UNODC and World Bank 2007); *Crime and Violence in Central America: A Challenge for Development* (World Bank 2011); and *Making Brazilians Safer: Analyzing the Dynamics of Violent Crime* (World Bank 2013). In March 2014, a new impact evaluation program, Impact Evaluation 4 Peace—focusing on fragility, conflict, crime, and violence—was launched with the support of the World Bank research unit on impact evaluation (DIME). See Box A.1.

More than 1.5 billion people live in countries affected by violent conflict; poverty rates are 20 percent higher in countries affected by repeated cycles of violence. By 2015, an estimated 52 percent of the world's poor will live in areas characterized as fragile or conflict-affected. Developmental challenges in such settings transcend national boundaries through the displacement of populations, spread of disease, reduced trade, and spread of organized crime and terrorism. Furthermore, high levels of fragility and violence exist in countries normally considered relatively stable. Many countries in Latin America and the Caribbean, for example, suffer levels of violence comparable to those in the most conflict-ravaged states. Despite the development imperative, we know very little about *what* works, and *how* to foster development in settings characterized by fragility, conflict, and violence. This knowledge vacuum impedes our ability to design effective interventions to promote poverty reduction and welfare improvement.

The program Impact Evaluation 4 Peace was launched by the World Bank Development Impact Evaluation (DIME) and partners in March 2014 to work toward addressing this gap. This cross-institutional program focuses on four key challenges: (1) jobs for the poor and at-risk youth as a tool for resilience; (2) public sector governance; (3) gender-based violence; and (4) urban crime and violence. In addition to these four areas that are tightly related to World Bank operations, we have ongoing work in the political economy of post-conflict reconstruction—often carried out in partnership with other development organizations.

**Urban crime and violence**

Countries affected by high-levels of urban crime suffer from levels of violence comparable to those in conflict-ravaged states. Seven of the ten most violent countries are in Latin America and the Caribbean, making it the world's most violent region. DIME-led work on urban crime and violence prevention is ongoing in countries such as Brazil, Honduras, and Mexico. In Mexico, DIME will work with the Ministry of the Interior to evaluate whether behavioral therapy, intensive mentoring, and jobs can reduce the recidivism of youth incarcerated for serious crimes.

**Partners**

The Impact Evaluation 4 Peace program is a collaborative effort between the World Bank's DIME unit, the Fragility, Conflict, and Violence Group, Cross Cutting Solutions, the State- and Peacebuilding Fund, the Center for Conflict, Security, and the International Initiative for Impact Evaluation, and Innovations for Poverty Action. Some of the program work is being carried out

*(continued on next page)*

2. *Project financing.* At the request of governments, the World Bank provides
funding for the implementation of multisectoral interventions to prevent
violence. Project financing is provided through three main types of lending
instruments:

*Investment loans* include integrated security projects at the municipal
and community levels, such as the Safer Municipalities Project in Honduras
(see box A.2); projects aimed at the integration of crime and violence
prevention in slum upgrading plans (such as the Basic Services Project
in Marginal Urban Areas, in Jamaica); and projects to strengthen citizen
security information systems (such as the Rio Grande do Norte Regional
Development and Governance Project in Brazil).

*Loans to support development policies* include support for innovative
institutional reforms, such as territorial coordination of social policy and
infrastructure in the pacified *favelas* of Rio de Janeiro, or violence prevention programs associated with drug addiction in Pernambuco, Brazil.
This type of instrument can also support the creation/design of institutional arrangements within countries to help implement integrated and
multisectoral policies, laws, and projects, and assist in the drafting and/
or passing of legislation/policies to restrict the use/availability of firearms,
or on crime and violence prevention. The Honduras First Programmatic
Reducing Vulnerabilities for Growth Development Policy Credit, for
example, provided support for citizen security reform by strengthening
institutional coordination mechanisms and programs needed for an
integrated violence prevention strategy.

*Nonreimbursable funds* support and test innovative programs that can then
be scaled up, such as the Regional Program for Municipal Citizen Security

**BOX A.2:** Honduras Safer Municipalities: The World Bank's first stand-alone citizen security project

The Honduras Safer Municipalities Project, launched in 2012, invests in integrated approaches to prevent interpersonal violence at the municipal level, with a focus on those subpopulations most at risk for perpetrating violence or becoming victims: youth, women, and children in hot spot communities. The project aims to address the most prominent and malleable risk factors that increase the likelihood of a person becoming either a victim or perpetrator of violence; it works through multiple, coordinated interventions and activities, at the individual, family, peer, school, community, and societal levels. The project also includes an institutional strengthening component to support government bodies in charge of coordinating and planning violence prevention initiatives at the national and municipal levels, as well as their capacity to collect, analyze, and use crime-related data for policy-making purposes.

in Central America's Northern Triangle, which supports innovative experiments in community policing, and the generation of employment opportunities for young people involved in gangs or at risk of engaging in violence. Another example is the strategic initiative, Sustainable Peace and Victims Reparation in Colombia. It seeks to support the government of Colombia at a critical point in the peace process and its aftermath through the implementation of a programmatic approach that combines a package of knowledge services, demand-driven technical assistance, and innovative community/municipal-based interventions to address victims' reparations and promote reconciliation and peace.

3. *Strategic partnerships.* Such partnerships optimize initiatives to prevent crime and violence and enhance coordination among donors. The main World Bank external partnerships include:

- The Inter-American Coalition for the Prevention of Violence, a group of eight agencies coordinated by the World Bank from 2013 to 2015, bringing together the U.S. Centers for Disease Control and Prevention (CDC); the Inter-American Development Bank (IDB); the Organization of American States (OAS); the Pan American Health Organization (PAHO); the United Nations Educational, Scientific, and Cultural Organization (UNESCO); the United Nations Human Settlements Program (UN-HABITAT); and the United States Agency for International Development (USAID).

- The Regional System of Standardized Indicators in Peaceful Coexistence and Citizen Security (RIC), coordinated by the IDB, which brings together more than 15 countries in the region to share and improve their crime statistics.

- The Friends of Central America, a group created in 2011 to increase donor coordination working to support citizen security strategy in Central America.

4. *Capacity building.* To generate appropriate and sustainable solutions for crime and violence, strengthening the capacities of local governments and communities is crucial because these are the players that are closer to the problem, have the power to convene various sectors and departments necessary for the required multisectoral responses, and often have greater incentives to find a solution. This type of capacity building can include topics such as the production and management of statistical information applied to decision making; comprehensive and targeted citizen security municipal planning; community mobilization and building local alliances; access to best practices in prevention; and monitoring and evaluation. The World Bank's efforts can be organized according to the following three pillars:

First, *toolkits* systematize and disseminate good practices. Examples include the "Municipal Capacity Building Course on Crime and Violence Prevention," which contains eight modules ranging from diagnosis and municipal security planning to the implementation of community policing models, youth violence, gender-based violence, and situational prevention; the "School-Based Violence Prevention Toolkit," which consists of a manual with six modules on how to plan, develop, implement, and evaluate projects to prevent violence in schools and communities; the "Local Public Private Partnerships to Community Safety: A Guide for Action"; and the "Urban Crime and Violence Prevention e-course." A companion toolkit to facilitate community action in violence prevention is forthcoming.

Second, *technical assistance* to governments supports the design and implementation of citizen security initiatives. This includes support for the design and implementation of regional, national, or municipal public security strategies (such as the Mexican government's 2012 national policy guidelines for youth violence prevention and the Jamaican government's national strategy for crime prevention and community safety); policy dialogue focused on specific areas; development of integrated urban and social development programs with a focus on public safety; and the development of reliable crime and violence information systems that are accessible and linked to public policies management, such as violence observatories at the regional, national, and local levels, including the Central America Regional Violence Observatory (Observatorio e Índice de Seguridad Democrática del sistema de integración centro-americano, OBSICA), and the National Violence Observatory in Jamaica.

Third, *knowledge management services* include knowledge-sharing and dissemination events, South-South exchanges, workshops, and study tours. For instance, an evidence-based crime and violence workshop, modeled on the U.S. Institute of Medicine / National Academy of Science Global Youth Violence Forum Workshop, was held in Cali, Colombia, in June 2013, with over 500 attendees and over 50 municipal teams from the region. An event in Jamaica brought international experts to a state-of-the-art conference on community safety to launch the Jamaican Forum on Violence Prevention in January 2014, with over 1,000 attendees. A Conference on Youth Violence Prevention was held in Guatemala in 2014, and co-sponsored with USAID and the U.S. National Forum on Youth Violence Prevention.

To facilitate clients' access to a global network of experts knowledgeable about the various aspects of violence prevention, a network, Solutions to Violence (RESOL-V), was established. It aims to support the implementation of evidence-based policies and programs (see box A.3).

---

**BOX A.3: RESOL-V, Solutions to Violence network: Connecting knowledge and decision making**

As part of its efforts to promote knowledge generation and exchange, in 2013 the World Bank Citizen Security Team launched the RESOL-V Network (Red de Soluciones a la Violencia / Solutions to Violence Network), an initiative to produce policy-relevant knowledge and strengthen the links between researchers, policy makers, and practitioners working in this field.

The core function of RESOL-V is to find the best available evidence on what works to prevent and reduce violence, and to make this knowledge available to relevant decision makers. The network aims to address key bottlenecks and thematic priorities for municipal citizen security efforts in the Americas, with a focus on promoting the integration of the best available evidence into policy and practice-related decisions in municipal efforts to reduce or prevent crime and violence; and to connect and nurture centers/nodes of expertise that exist throughout the Americas and link them to decision makers and practitioners to strengthen the generation, translation, use, and assessment of evidence-based approaches to citizen security in the region.

RESOL-V will facilitate the generation, translation, assessment, and use of evidence for crime prevention policy and programming, and build the capacity of institutions to carry out more effective programming. By connecting and strengthening centers of expertise in the Americas and linking them to decision makers and practitioners, it will promote the use of evidence-based approaches to citizen security in the region. The primary clientele for RESOL-V includes mayors and their technical teams, officials of line ministries, the private sector, and academics and professionals involved in violence prevention.

# Note

[1] A stocktaking of World Bank projects on citizen security and violence prevention, which looked at 44 projects approved by the Bank since 1996, shows that the World Bank has spent $1.66 billion on studies, technical assistance, and lending interventions that focus on security outcomes and feature interactions with the security sector. Of this, $1.2 billion has centered on Latin America and the Caribbean—with the caveat that this figure includes development policy loans, which include other sectors beyond citizen security (Harborne and Bisca 2013).

# References

Harborne, Bernard, and Paul Bisca. 2013. "Capturing the Security-Development Nexus in the World Bank's Security Sector Portfolio." Social Development Department, World Bank, Washington, DC.

UNODC (United Nations Office on Drugs and Crime) and World Bank. 2007. *Trends, Costs, and Policy Options on Crime and Violence in the Caribbean.* Report 37820. Joint Report by the United Nations Office on Drugs and Crime and the Latin America and the Caribbean Region of the World Bank.

World Bank. 2011. *Crime and Violence in Central America: A Challenge for Development.* Washington, DC: Sustainable Development Department and Poverty Reduction and Economic Management Unit, Latin America and the Caribbean Region, World Bank.

———. 2013. *Making Brazilians Safer: Analyzing the Dynamics of Violent Crime.* Report 70764. Washington, DC: Sustainable Development Sector Management Unit, Latin America and the Caribbean Region, World Bank.

www.ingramcontent.com/pod-product-compliance
Lightning Source LLC
Chambersburg PA
CBHW060958280326
41935CB00009B/753